Uniting Europe

Europe Today
Series Editor: Ronald Tiersky

Uniting Europe

An Introduction to the European Union, Second Edition

JOHN VAN OUDENAREN

ROWMAN & LITTLEFIELD PUBLISHERS, INC.
Lanham • Boulder • New York • Toronto • Oxford

ROWMAN & LITTLEFIELD PUBLISHERS, INC.

Published in the United States of America
by Rowman & Littlefield Publishers, Inc.
A wholly owned subsidary of The Rowman & Littlefield Publishing Group, Inc.
4501 Forbes Boulevard, Suite 200, Lanham, MD 20706
www.rowmanlittlefield.com

P.O. Box 317, Oxford OX2 9RU, UK

British Library Cataloguing in Publication Information Available

Library of Congress Cataloging-in-Publication Data

Van Oudenaren, John.
    Uniting Europe : an introduction to the European Union / John Van Oudenaren.—
2nd ed.
        p.   cm. — (Europe today)
    Includes bibliographical references and index.
        ISBN 0-7425-3660-2 (cloth : alk. paper) — ISBN 0-7425-3661-0 (pbk. : alk. paper)
        1. Europe—Economic integration.   2. Europe—Politics and government.   3. Post-
communism.   I. Title.   II. Series: Europe today (Rowman and Littlefield, Inc.)
    HC241 .V352   2004
    341.242'2—dc22   2004008118

Printed in the United States of America

∞ ™ The paper used in this publication meets the minimum requirements of American
National Standard for Information Sciences—Permanence of Paper for Printed Library
Materials, ANSI/NISO Z39.48-1992.

Contents

Tables

Boxes

Abbreviations

ACP	African, Caribbean, and Pacific
APEC	Asia Pacific Economic Cooperation
CAP	Common Agricultural Policy
CARDS	Community Assistance for Reconstruction, Development and Stabilisation
CENELEC	European Committee for Electrotechnical Standardization
CFSP	Common Foreign and Security Policy
CIS	Commonwealth of Independent States
CMEA	Council for Mutual Economic Assistance
CSCE	Conference on Security and Cooperation in Europe
EAGGF	European Agricultural Guidance and Guarantee Fund
EBRD	European Bank for Reconstruction and Development
EC	European Community
ECB	European Central Bank
ECJ	European Court of Justice
ECOFIN	Council of Ministers (Economics and Finance Ministers)
ECSC	European Coal and Steel Community
ECU	European Currency Unit
EDC	European Defense Community
EDF	European Development Fund
EEA	European Economic Area
EEC	European Economic Community
EFTA	European Free Trade Association
EIB	European Investment Bank
EMS	European Monetary System
EMU	Economic and Monetary Union
EP	European Parliament
EPC	European Political Cooperation
EPU	European Payments Union
ERDF	European Regional Development Fund
ERM	Exchange Rate Mechanism
ERT	European Roundtable of Industrialists
ESC	Economic and Social Committee
ESCB	European System of Central Banks
ESDI	European Security and Defense Identity
ESPRIT	European Strategic Program for Research and Development in Information Technology
EU	European Union
FRG	Federal Republic of Germany
FYROM	Former Yugoslav Republic of Macedonia
GATS	General Agreement on Trade in Services
GATT	General Agreement on Tariffs and Trade
GDR	German Democratic Republic
HST	High Speed Train
ICAO	International Civil Aviation Organization

IFOR	Implementation Force
IGC	Intergovernmental Conference
ILO	International Labor Organization
ILSA	Iran-Libya Sanctions Act
IMF	International Monetary Fund
ISAF	International Security Assistance Force
JHA	Justice and Home Affairs
KLA	Kosovo Liberation Army
MEP	Member of the European Parliament
MFN	Most-favored nation
MRA	Mutual Recognition Agreement
NAFTA	North American Free Trade Agreement
NATO	North Atlantic Treaty Organization
NIS	Newly Independent States
NTA	New Transatlantic Agenda
NTB	Non-Tariff Barrier
OECD	Organization for Economic Cooperation and Development
OEEC	Organization for European Economic Cooperation
ONP	Open Network Provision
OSCE	Organization for Security and Cooperation in Europe
PCA	Partnership and Cooperation Agreement
PHARE	*Pologne et Hongrie: Actions pour la Reconversion Économique*
PTT	Post, Telephone and Telegraph
QMV	Qualified majority voting
SAA	Stabilization and Association Agreement
SEA	Single European Act
SGP	Stability and Growth Pact
SIS	Schengen Information System
TABD	Transatlantic Business Dialogue
TAC	Total Allowable Catch
TACIS	Technical Assistance to the Commonwealth of Independent States
TAFTA	Transatlantic Free Trade Agreement
TEN	Trans-European Network
TEP	Transatlantic Economic Partnership
TRIMS	Trade-Related Investment Measures
TRNC	Turkish Republic of Northern Cyprus
UK	United Kingdom of Great Britain and Northern Ireland
UNFCCC	United Nations Framework Convention on Climate Change
UNPROFOR	United Nations Protection Force
USSR	Union of Soviet Socialist Republics
VAT	Value-Added Tax
VER	Voluntary Export Restraint
WEU	Western European Union
WTO	World Trade Organization

Chronology

World Events	European Integration

August 1945
U.S. drops atomic bombs on Japan; war in Pacific ends

October 1945
United Nations established

December 1945
29 countries sign Articles of Agreement establishing the IMF

June 1947
Marshall Plan announced

August 1947
British rule in India ends; India and Pakistan gain independence

January 1948
GATT comes into force

February 1948
Communist coup in Czechoslovakia; Soviet hegemony in Eastern Europe fully established

March 1948
Brussels Treaty establishing Western European Union enters into force

April 1948
OEEC established to coordinate Marshall aid

May 1948
State of Israel established

April 1949
North Atlantic Treaty signed

May 1949
Council of Europe established

World Events	*European Integration*
October 1949 Communists triumph in China; People's Republic established	
	May 1950 Schuman announces plan for coal and steel pool
June 1950 Korean War begins	
	April 1951 ECSC treaty signed
	May 1952 European Defense Community (EDC) treaty signed
	July 1952 ECSC established
March 1953 Stalin dies, leading to "thaw" in East-West relations	
May 1954 French suffer defeat at Dien Bien Phu, leading to independence for North and South Vietnam	
	August 1954 French National Assembly defeats EDC treaty
November 1954 Algerian war of independence against France begins	
May 1955 Warsaw Treaty Organization formed	
	June 1955 Six convene Messina conference to consider next stage of integration
July 1956 Egypt seizes Suez Canal; followed by October war between Egypt and Israel, France, Britain	
	March 1957 Treaties of Rome establishing EEC and Euratom signed
October 1957 USSR launches *Sputnik I*	

World Events	European Integration
	January 1958 EEC and ECSC established
	July 1958 Basic principles of the CAP agreed
January 1959 Fidel Castro takes power in Cuba	**January 1959** First tariff reductions and lowering of quotas toward the establishment of the customs union
	May 1960 EFTA established
June 1960 Belgian Congo becomes independent	
October 1960 Nigeria gains independence from Britain	
	December 1960 OECD established, replacing the OEEC
	July–August 1961 UK, Ireland, and Denmark apply for membership in the Community
November 1961 President Kennedy steps up U.S. military involvement in Vietnam	
	January 1962 CAP established
July 1962 Algeria becomes independent	
October 1962 Cuban missile crisis; India-China war	
	January 1963 De Gaulle vetoes British application for membership
	July 1963 EC signs Yaoundé Convention with 17 African countries
August 1964 U.S. Congress passes Gulf of Tonkin resolution, paving way for escalation of the Vietnam War	
	July 1965 France precipitates "empty chair" crisis to protest supranational tendencies in the Community

World Events   *European Integration*

September 1965
China calls for a "people's war" in Africa,
Asia, and Latin America

July 1966
Luxembourg Compromise agreed

January 1967
Cultural Revolution rages in China

June 1967
Israel wins Six Day War against Egypt,
Jordan, Syria, and Iraq

July 1967
Merger Treaty comes into effect

July 1968
Customs union achieved

August 1968
Warsaw Pact troops invade Czechoslovakia to reverse the liberalization of communism

March 1969
Sino-Soviet clashes on the Manchurian
border

July 1969
U.S. astronaut Neil Armstrong lands on
moon

December 1969
Hague summit sets ambitious goals for
the Community in the 1970s, including
the start of EPC

April 1970
Council agrees on introduction of the
own-resources system

August 1971
Nixon suspends the convertibility of the
dollar into gold

December 1971
India defeats Pakistan in war that results
in creation of an independent Bangladesh

April 1972
Agreement to establish the "snake," a
form of currency cooperation

May 1972
Nixon becomes first U.S. president to
visit Russia; signs arms control agreement

World Events

August 1972
Arab terrorists kill Israeli athletes at Munich Olympics; international terrorism emerges as a serious challenge to governments worldwide

January 1973
United States, North Vietnam, South Vietnam, Viet Cong sign Paris agreements ending war in Vietnam

March 1973
Group of Ten finance ministers agree to float currencies, ending Bretton Woods system of pegged exchange rates

October 1973
Fourth Arab-Israeli war, followed by Arab ban on oil exports to the United States and huge increases in the price of oil

July 1974
Turkey invades Cyprus

April 1975
South Vietnam collapses, after North, violating Paris agreements, invades

January 1979
Shah of Iran overthrown by Islamic revolution

European Integration

January 1973
UK, Ireland, and Denmark become members of the Community

December 1974
Paris summit establishes European Council

February 1975
Lomé Convention signed with African, Caribbean, and Pacific countries

March 1975
European Regional Development Fund established

July 1978
Bremen European Council agrees plans to establish European Monetary System (EMS)

March 1979
EMS begins to operate

June 1979
First direct elections to the European Parliament

World Events

European Integration

December 1979
NATO decision to install medium-range nuclear missiles in Europe; USSR invades Afghanistan

August 1980
Solidarity established in Poland as an opposition trade union

January 1981
Greece becomes a member of the Community

November 1981
Germany and Italy present Genscher-Colombo plan for institutional improvements

December 1981
Communists impose martial law in Poland, crushing Solidarity

April 1982
Falklands war between Britain and Argentina

June 1983
Leaders sign Solemn Declaration on European Union at the Stuttgart European Council

July 1983
Council adopts resolution on an EC framework program for research

December 1983
Council agrees to Common Fisheries Policy

June 1984
Member states reach agreement on British rebate at the Fontainebleau European Council

January 1985
Jacques Delors becomes Commission president

June 1985
Commission submits white paper on the completion of the internal market by 1992; five member states sign Schengen Agreement on elimination of border controls

World Events

European Integration

July 1985
Member states decide to convene inter-governmental conference (IGC) to amend the treaties

January 1986
Portugal and Spain become members of the Community

February 1986
Single European Act establishing single market goal for 1992 signed; also strengthens power of the European Parliament (EP) and provides a treaty basis for EPC

April 1986
Chernobyl nuclear accident in Ukraine

September 1986
GATT signatories launch Uruguay Round of trade talks

July 1987
Single European Act (SEA) enters into force after ratification by the member states

June 1988
Hanover European Council establishes committee to examine prospects for economic and monetary union; EC and Council for Mutual Economic Assistance (CMEA) establish relations

October 1988
Council adopts decision establishing the Court of First Instance

February 1989
Roundtable talks begin between Solidarity and the government begin in Poland, after economy languishes through the 1980s

June 1989
Partially free elections in Poland

July 1989
G-7 agrees to provide economic restructuring aid to Hungary and Poland

November 1989
Berlin Wall opened; communism collapses in central and eastern Europe

World Events

European Integration

December 1989
Strasbourg European Council agrees to
convene IGC on EMU

June 1990
Dublin European Council decides to
convene an IGC on political union, to
run in parallel with the IGC on EMU

July 1990
Stage 1 of EMU begins

August 1990
Iraq invades Kuwait

December 1990
IGCs agreed at Strasbourg and Dublin
are launched

January 1991
U.S.-led coalition begins war to liberate
Kuwait

December 1991
Soviet Union dissolved

December 1991
Maastricht European Council reaches
agreement on draft of the Maastricht
Treaty on European Union; Europe
Agreements signed with Poland, Hun-
gary, and Czechoslovakia

February 1992
Maastricht Treaty signed

May 1992
Agreement on European Economic Area
(EEA) signed

June 1992
Voters in Denmark disapprove ratification of the Maastricht Treaty

August 1992
Crisis in the EMS

December 1992
Edinburgh European Council paves way
to a second Maastricht ratification referendum in Denmark

January 1993
Single European market enters into effect

November 1993
Maastricht Treaty enters into force, formally establishing the EU and creating
the legal basis for the achievement of a
single currency by 2002

World Events

January 1994
North American Free Trade Agreement (NAFTA) comes into effect

January 1995
World Trade Organization (WTO) established

European Integration

January 1994
Stage 2 of EMU begins; (EEA) agreement enters into force

November 1994
Norwegian voters reject EU accession

January 1995
Austria, Finland, and Sweden become members of the Union

March 1995
Schengen Agreement enters into force among seven EU member states

July 1995
Member states sign Europol Convention

November 1995
Euro-Mediterranean Conference in Barcelona establishes a comprehensive partnership with countries of North Africa and the Middle East

December 1995
U.S.-EU Transatlantic Declaration signed

March 1996
IGC to revise the Maastricht Treaty opens in Turin

June 1997
IGC concludes with agreement on a draft Treaty of Amsterdam

July 1997
Commission issues *Agenda 2000* containing evaluations of the candidate countries' membership applications and proposals for reform of the EU

October 1997
Treaty of Amsterdam signed

December 1997
European Council meets in Luxembourg and approves start of enlargement negotiations with six candidate countries

March 1998
Conference in London kicks off enlargement negotiations

World Events	*European Integration*
May 1998 India and Pakistan test nuclear weapons	**May 1998** Special session of the European Council decides that eleven countries have qualified to adopt the euro; Wim Duisenberg selected to head European Central Bank (ECB)
	January 1999 Stage 3 of EMU begins; euro officially launched
March 1999 NATO begins war against Yugoslavia over Kosovo	**March 1999** Collective resignation of the Santer Commission following charges of mismanagement; special summit in Berlin establishes budget for 2000–2006
	May 1999 Treaty of Amsterdam enters into force
	June 1999 Cologne European Council endorses a post-Amsterdam IGC focused on institutional reform
December 1999 Seattle WTO ministerial fails to launch Millennium Round of trade talks	**December 1999** Helsinki European Council agrees to establish European military force for peacekeeping, endorses start of enlargement negotiations with six more countries
	February 2000 Enlargement negotiations begin with second wave of applicants; IGC on institutional reform convenes
	March 2000 Lisbon European Council adopts new economic strategy and goal for 2000–2010
	June 2000 EU signs Cotonou [Benin] convention with ACP countries to replace the Lomé agreements
	September 2000 Voters in Denmark reject adoption of the euro
	December 2000 Nice European Council concludes IGC with political agreement on the Treaty of Nice and formally proclaims the Charter of Fundamental Rights of the European Union

World Events

European Integration

January 2001
Greece joins the eurozone

June 2001
Irish voters reject the Treaty of Nice

September 2001
Terrorist attacks on New York and
Washington

September 2001
Special session of the European Council
declares support for the United States
and formulates the EU policy response to
the terrorist attacks on New York and
Washington

October 2001
United States begins Operation Enduring
Freedom to overthrow the Taliban in
Afghanistan

November 2001
WTO ministerial in Qatar launches the
Doha round of trade negotiations

January 2002
Euro notes and coins enter circulation in
twelve participating member states

February 2002
Convention on the Future of Europe
opens in Brussels and begins work on a
draft constitution for the Union

July 2002
Fifty-year treaty establishing the ECSC
expires; functions of the ECSC absorbed
by the EC

December 2002
European Council finalizes terms of
accession with Cyprus, Malta, and eight
central and east European countries

March 2003
United States launches Operation Iraqi
Freedom to topple Saddam Hussein

April 2003
Treaty of Accession signed in Athens
between the EU and ten accession
countries

June 2003
European Convention president Giscard
d'Estaing presents draft EU constitution
to the European Council

World Events

September 2003
Cancun WTO ministerial breaks down after failing to achieve progress toward completion of the Doha Development Round

March 2004
Vladimir Putin re-elected president of Russia in a landslide

April 2004
United States loses more than one hundred soldiers in Iraq, highlighting continued instability in the country in advance of the June 30, 2004, restoration of sovereignty

European Integration

September 2003
Voters in Sweden reject adoption of the euro

October 2003
IGC convenes in Rome to discuss the draft European Constitution

December 2003
European Council fails to approve the draft Constitution

March 2004
Islamic terrorists kill more than 190 people in Madrid bombings; Aznar government defeated in elections four days later

April 2004
Greek Cypriot voters reject UN plan to reunite the island in advance of EU accession

May 2004
Ten new member states admitted to the EU, bringing membership to 25

June 2004
Voters elect the EP for the 2004–2009 term; turnout is a record-low 45 percent; Euroskeptic parties make gains in many countries

European Council reaches political agreement on the EU Constitution by modifying elements of the European Convention draft. Key elements of the compromise include:
  —reform of the Commission is postponed to 2014. From 2014 onward, the size of the Commission will be two-thirds the number of member states; commissioners to be selected on the basis of a system of equal rotation among the member states
  —QMV is defined as at least 55 percent of the member states comprising at least 65 percent of the total EU population; blocking minorities to include at least four member states

World Events   *European Integration*

—size of the EP to increase to 750;
each member state to have at least six
representatives; no member state to
have more than 96 representatives.

UK ratification referendum expected to
take place at the earliest in the spring of
2006

Current EU Members
Candidate Countries
Likely Future Members

ICELAND
Reykjavik

NORWAY
Oslo
SWEDEN
Stockholm
FINLAND
Helsinki

ESTONIA
Tallinn
RUSSIA
LATVIA
Riga
LITHUANIA
Vilnius
BELARUS

North Sea
Baltic Sea

NORTHERN IRELAND
DEN.
Copenhagen
Dublin
IRELAND
GREAT BRITAIN
London
Amsterdam
NETH.
Berlin
Warsaw
POLAND
UKRAINE

Brussels
BELG
LUX.
GERMANY
Prague
CZECH REP.
SLOVAKIA
Bratislava
MOLDOVA

Paris
Vienna
Budapest
HUNGARY
ROMANIA
Bucharest

Bay of Biscay
FRANCE
Bern
SWITZ.
AUSTRIA
SLOVENIA
CROATIA
BOSNIA & HERZEGOVINA
SERBIA & MONTENEGRO
BULGARIA
Sofia
Black Sea

Atlantic Ocean

PORTUGAL
Madrid
SPAIN
Lisbon
ITALY
Rome
MACE.
ALB.
GREECE
Athens
TURKEY

Mediterranean Sea
MALTA

CHAPTER 1

Introduction
PEACE, PROSPERITY, AND THE CHALLENGES OF EUROPEAN INTEGRATION

Beginnings: 1945–1949

European economic and political integration began in part as an attempt by European leaders, strongly supported by the United States, to overcome the national rivalries that had led to two world wars in the first half of the twentieth century. The main victors on the Western side, the United States and Great Britain, ended the war committed to promoting democracy and political reform in the defeated Axis powers, Germany and Italy. They also sought to establish a more open international economic system to replace the prewar order, which had been characterized by protectionism, competitive currency devaluations, and other policies by which the major powers sought to gain economic and political advantage at the expense of their rivals.

At a series of diplomatic conferences in 1944 and 1945, the United States and Britain agreed to establish a new monetary system based on stable currencies pegged to the value of gold, an international bank to promote reconstruction and development in poor and war-torn countries, and an international organization for negotiating lower tariffs and eliminating other barriers to international trade. These understandings led to the establishment, in 1946, of the International Monetary Fund (IMF) and the World Bank, informally known as the Bretton Woods institutions after the small New Hampshire town in which the most important of these economic conferences took place. The following year twenty-three countries concluded the General Agreement on Tariffs and Trade (GATT), under which the signatories pledged to lower barriers to trade through negotiations conducted in accordance with the "most favored nation" (MFN) principle.

The design of the postwar international economic order reflected what has been called the "universalist" tendency in the American approach to foreign policy—the idea that a single set of rules should apply to all countries and that discriminatory economic behavior and zones of preference be abolished.[1] In the monetary sphere, universalism meant the convertibility of all currencies into each other and, indirectly, into gold. In trade, it meant application of the MFN principle, under which each country agreed to grant trade conditions to every other country no worse than those granted to the most favored nation. In both areas, the postwar approach was intended as a break with the 1930s, when Germany and

other dictatorships created special economic zones based on exclusive trading relationships and government manipulation of currency values, and when even traditionally free-trade-oriented Britain resorted to Imperial Preference—a system of
special trade relationships that encouraged trade within the British Empire at the
expense of the rest of the world—to combat unemployment at home.

Whatever its merits in principle, the universalist approach proved difficult to
apply in economically crippled postwar Europe. The war had resulted in widespread dislocation of peoples and destruction of factories and infrastructure. Germany was divided, with its western part cut off from traditional supplies of grain
in the east. As they attempted to rebuild their economies, the countries of Western
Europe mainly needed to obtain new machinery and goods from the United
States, which they lacked the dollars to buy. They were less interested in trading
with neighbors who were struggling with the same shortages and reconstruction
problems.

Under these conditions, it was all but impossible for European countries to
apply the universalist principles espoused by the United States and by some Europeans at the end of the war. They were simply too weak to participate in a new
international economic order. Britain announced in July 1947 that it was prepared
to convert sterling into dollars and other currencies, but it was forced to abandon
this policy after a mere six weeks, as demand for dollars led to the collapse of its
currency. Throughout Europe, governments maintained tight controls on currency flows and strictly regulated foreign trade. Businesses had to secure licenses
to obtain foreign currency to buy goods from or invest in other countries, and
trade took place in the context of bilateral agreements in which, for example, one
country would agree to sell a certain number of tons of coal to another country
which in turn would commit to selling so many bushels of wheat. Moreover, in
all European countries there were powerful groups—ranging from Communist-
controlled trade unions to private corporations shielded from international competition by cartels and protectionism—that did not accept the philosophy of
openness and wanted to retain or even strengthen the autarkic features of the wartime and prewar economic orders. Shortages and difficult economic conditions
tended to strengthen the hand of these forces, and to weaken the case for freer
trade and economic liberalization.[2]

For its part, the Soviet Union declined altogether to participate in the IMF,
the World Bank, or the GATT, choosing instead to pursue the same policies of
economic isolation that it had followed in the 1930s. Instead of building "socialism
in one country," Stalin's prewar slogan, the Soviets in effect were building "socialism in one empire," as they established exclusive trading links with countries of
central and eastern Europe that they had overrun in the last year of the war. At
least initially, these links were highly exploitative, as the Soviet Union imposed
one-sided economic deals on its partners in order to obtain raw materials and
equipment badly needed for the reconstruction of the Soviet economy.

THE MARSHALL PLAN

By early 1947 the Truman administration had concluded that the United States
needed to take decisive action to stabilize the economic and political situation in

Europe. In a speech at Harvard University in June 1947, U.S. Secretary of State George C. Marshall proposed a program of aid designed to pull Europe to its feet. The United States offered to provide Europe with money and goods, but only if the Europeans themselves came up with a plan for using the aid, and only if the plan was designed as a joint effort rather than a hodgepodge of national requests.

After a series of preliminary meetings, in April 1948 sixteen European states founded the Organization for European Economic Cooperation (OEEC). Based in Paris, this organization helped to administer Marshall aid and provided a forum in which the member states negotiated arrangements to lower intra-European trade and currency barriers. The European Recovery Program (ERP), as the Marshall Plan formally was known, provided a powerful external stimulus to intra-European trade. Under OEEC auspices, in 1948 the member countries began to remove quotas and restrictions on the imports of manufactures and foodstuffs.

The ERP also financed the European Payments Union (EPU), which was established in mid-1950 under OEEC auspices. The EPU was intended as a temporary solution to the problem of currency convertibility in Europe—a halfway house between the full dollar convertibility mandated in the Bretton Woods system and the rigid bilateralism that characterized trade and exchange in the late 1940s. The EPU was based on an elaborate system that summed up a country's surpluses and deficits with all of the other countries of the union and converted them into a single surplus or deficit position that could be settled by dollars, gold, or limited credits. The EPU restored a large measure of currency convertibility within Europe, although it did not entail convertibility of the European currencies into the dollar. In monetary affairs as in trade, Western Europe, with support from the United States, was finding regional solutions to its economic problems. These solutions were a far cry from fulfillment of the universalist aspirations of 1945, but they represented a step toward integration on the regional level and played an important role in reviving the European economies.

Between 1948 and 1951 the United States provided $12.4 billion in grant aid to the European Marshall Plan recipients, the equivalent of over $70 billion in 1999 prices. This aid was important not only for its direct assistance to the economies of Europe, but also for its indirect effects—within and among countries—in promoting a postwar order in which economic growth could be revived and sustained. As Barry Eichengreen has remarked, "The Marshall Plan was a source of US leverage to prompt liberalization and stabilization on the part of European governments and to encourage their adherence to the norms and standards of what might be called the Bretton Woods regime. It strengthened the hand of European leaders seeking to control the levers of economic policy and rebuff the opponents of the market economy."[3] In this sense, the Marshall Plan played an enormous role in placing Europe on the path toward integration along market-oriented principles that was to culminate in the establishment of the European Union.

The Soviet Union at first showed interest in receiving reconstruction aid from the United States, but it was unwilling to participate in a cooperative plan that would have required it to give information about its economy and to yield influence over economic policy-making to outsiders. It thus declined to participate in the plan, as well as blocked participation by its east European satellites. Instead, it established, in January 1949, the Council for Mutual Economic Assistance (CMEA, also known as Comecon) to organize trade in the Soviet sphere of influence and to serve as a political and propaganda counterweight to the integration efforts of the West.

As the Cold War deepened, the Marshall Plan became the linchpin of an increasingly determined American strategy to block the expansion of Soviet power. This in part helped to explain the strong political support for the plan in the United States. As Secretary of State Dean Acheson later wrote in his memoirs, "what citizens and representatives in Congress alike always wanted to learn in the last analysis was how Marshall aid operated to block the extension of Soviet power and the acceptance of Communist economic and political organization and alignment."[4]

THE BRUSSELS TREATY AND THE COUNCIL OF EUROPE

In addition to the Marshall Plan, there were several specifically European attempts at closer economic, political, and security cooperation in the late 1940s. In 1947 Belgium, the Netherlands, and Luxembourg formed a common customs union, known as the Benelux. In the same year, France and Britain signed the Treaty of Dunkirk, in which they pledged to come to each other's assistance if either was attacked in Europe. This was followed, in March 1948, by the signing by France, Britain, and the three Benelux countries of the fifty-year Brussels treaty "for collaboration in economic, social and cultural matters and for collective self-defense."[5] The treaty established the Brussels Treaty Organization, which later became the Western European Union (WEU)

For some in Europe, these initial steps toward economic and political cooperation did not go far enough. They wanted to leapfrog the cautious process of intergovernmental negotiation and to create a fully fledged United States of Europe directly based on the popular will of the European electorates. Known after the American example as federalists, they included academics, journalists, trade union leaders, and prominent veterans of the resistance to Nazi and Fascist regimes in World War II. At a Congress of Europe in The Hague in 1948, nearly one thousand delegates from twenty-six countries discussed the federalist project and issued a concluding call to convene a European Assembly that would serve as the constituent body for a united Europe.

In response to these demands, the ministerial council of the Brussels Treaty Organization convened a special intergovernmental conference in London in early 1949 to discuss the various proposals for a federal Europe. In addition to the five Brussels powers, five other countries—Denmark, Norway, Sweden, Ireland, and Italy—participated in this meeting. The London deliberations soon revealed a wide difference of views between Britain and the Scandinavian countries on the one side and the continental countries on the other over the key question of whether integration should be a matter of agreement among sovereign states represented by their governments or whether, as the name European Assembly suggested, it was to be based directly on a movement of peoples with their own representation at the European level. The British Labour government of Prime Minister Clement Attlee took a rather skeptical view of integration and preferred an intergovernmental committee of ministers. The continental countries endorsed the call for establishment of a European Assembly comprised of members not controlled by the member state governments.

In the end, the conference participants compromised by concluding, in May 1949, the Statute of the Council of Europe. This agreement established a bicameral organization that consisted of both a ministerial committee and a Consultative Assembly of parliamentarians. It stipulated that every member "must accept the principles of the rule of law and of the enjoyment by all persons within its jurisdiction of human rights and fundamental freedoms."[6] The objective of the Council of Europe, as stated in the 1949 agreement, was "to achieve a greater unity between its Members for the purpose of safeguarding and realizing the ideals and principles which are their common heritage and facilitating their economic and social progress."[7] The main areas of cooperation specified in the organization's statute were economic, social, cultural, scientific, legal, and administrative matters, and "the maintenance and further realization of human rights and fundamental freedoms."[8]

The gap between these sweeping aims and the limited means established to carry them out soon became apparent. The Council of Europe developed mainly as a body in which ministers met to discuss and to conclude agreements for common action on an intergovernmental basis. The Consultative Assembly laid the groundwork for future cooperation among parliamentarians and governments, but the continental federalists never were able to overcome British and Scandinavian resistance to expanding its power at the expense of the ministerial committee.

Although the Council of Europe was a disappointment to the federalist movement that had pressed for its creation, it nonetheless was important as the first permanent, Europe-specific nondefense institution created after World War II. Located in Strasbourg, France, the committee of ministers and the parliamentary assembly contributed to the harmonization of national laws affecting the welfare of Europeans as citizens, with a strong leveling bias in the areas of social welfare, health, migration, and other areas. The parliamentary assembly had limited powers, but its members were selected directly by national parliaments and not subject to control by national governments. Periodic visits to Strasbourg convinced many parliamentarians of the value of closer ties with their counterparts from other European countries and helped to lay the basis for more ambitious attempts at integration later in the postwar period.[9]

THE ATLANTIC ALLIANCE

The other major institutional development of the late 1940s was the creation of the Atlantic alliance linking Europe and North America. The United States had emerged from World War II committed to promoting economic and political stability in Europe, but it did not intend to conclude a military alliance with West European states. To do so would go against the American tradition of "no entangling alliances" and was opposed by powerful isolationist forces in the U.S. Congress. However, the communist takeovers in eastern Europe and the onset of the Cold War led to a shift in American attitudes. In April 1949 the United States, Canada, the five Brussels powers, and four other European states signed the North Atlantic Treaty, in which they pledged to come to each other's assistance in the event of external attack. The signing of the treaty was followed by the creation of the North Atlantic Treaty Organization (NATO) and the establishment of an integrated military command.

Like the Marshall Plan, NATO was an important American contribution to the postwar revival of Europe and to the fledgling process of building a united Europe. It allowed the European countries to concentrate on economic cooperation, leaving sensitive and contentious matters of defense to the transatlantic organization. The early Cold War was a time of great tension in Europe, marked by crises over Berlin in 1948–1949 and again in 1960–1961, violent anticommunist uprisings in East Germany in 1953 and in Hungary in 1956, and fear that World War III might break out at any time. The American connection and the guarantee contained in the Washington Treaty combined with strong and decisive leadership by American presidents such as Truman and Eisenhower helped to give Europe the confidence to build, invest, and consolidate the economic and political recovery that began in 1945.

TWO GERMAN STATES

Germany, after the USSR the most populous country in Europe and by far the largest in Western Europe, at first played no direct role in the early postwar steps toward European integration. Indeed, these steps, and in particular the Dunkirk and Brussels treaties, were directed partly against a possible revival of an aggressive German power.

Following the unconditional surrender of the German armed forces in May 1945, Germany had no government. Britain, France, the United States, and the Soviet Union each took responsibility for an occupation zone. Greater Berlin, located deep within the Soviet zone, was divided by agreement among the victors, while large parts of formerly German territory in the east were incorporated into Poland and the USSR.

At the wartime conferences among the allied powers, Churchill, Stalin, and Roosevelt agreed to settle most questions relating to Germany at a postwar peace conference. However, after the war it gradually became apparent that the victors would not be able to reach an agreement on Germany. The Western powers suspected the Soviets of trying to hinder economic recovery in Germany and delaying a political settlement in hopes of facilitating an eventual communist takeover. Much of central and eastern Europe already had slipped into the communist camp, and there was fear that Germany was another target. For its part, the USSR was unwilling to withdraw Soviet forces from the eastern zone of occupation and conclude a peace treaty with a united Germany if this meant the establishment of a westward-oriented state under U.S. and British influence.

In addition to these strategic considerations, the Western powers were increasingly concerned about the economic burdens of occupation. With the German economy languishing, the victor powers were legally and morally obligated to provide food and fuel to the destitute German civilian population. Britain, which was recovering from its own war effort and straining to meet its worldwide military commitments, was especially concerned about the occupation burden. The United States was better placed to help the Germans, but it was unclear how long the Congress and the American taxpayer would sustain subsidies for a defeated power. Western governments thus wanted to promote economic recovery in Germany, although they also were wary of a too-rapid resurgence of German power.

One way to revive German economic life was to encourage trade among the occupation zones and to restore the internal German market that had existed before 1945. In January 1947 the United States and Britain combined their zones under a single economic administration; they later were joined by the French. The Soviets, however, refused to participate in these efforts and accused the Western powers of unilaterally deciding the fate of Germany in contravention of the wartime agreement to seek collective solutions. The Soviets tightened their grip on the eastern zone, expropriating private property and shipping massive amounts of goods and machinery back to Russia as reparations for the war.

With prospects for a diplomatic solution for the whole of Germany waning, the Western powers and the Soviet Union each began establishing separate German states. In June 1948 Britain, France, and the United States agreed on a central government for the western zones, and in September 1949 they altered the Occupation Statute to permit the establishment of a new West German state, the Federal Republic of Germany. West Germany was not yet fully sovereign, however, and the Western powers retained certain legal rights over German foreign and domestic policy, including the right to enforce restrictions on German rearmament and the ultimate decision-making power with regard to a future peace treaty with a united Germany. The West Germans themselves took the view that the new state was provisional and that it might be replaced in the future by a united German state.

The Soviet Union reacted to these developments by working through the German communists to establish a separate East German state. Officially called the German Democratic Republic (GDR), it was proclaimed in October 1949. Henceforth Germany was divided into two countries, each of which became the linchpin of its respective economic and political grouping. West Germany, having participated in the Marshall Plan under the occupation, assumed its place in the OEEC and the EPU alongside the other Marshall aid recipients. Despite misgivings in other countries about German rearmament, it signed the European Defense Treaty of 1952 and became a member of the WEU and NATO in 1955. For its part, the GDR joined the Council for Mutual Economic Assistance (CMEA) in 1949 and became a founding member of the Warsaw Pact in 1955. Not until 1990, following the collapse of the Berlin wall and sweeping political changes in the Soviet Union, were the two German states united in a single Federal Republic of Germany.

The Community and the Union

ESTABLISHMENT

By the end of the 1940s many of the basic outlines of the post–World War II European order had been established. Germany and Berlin were divided. The key West European countries were (or, in the case of West Germany, were soon to be) linked to the United States through the North Atlantic Treaty and cooperating among each other in the OEEC and the Council of Europe. The east European countries were tied to the Soviet Union by bilateral treaties and the CMEA. In both parts of Europe economic recovery was underway, but prosperity still lagged U.S. levels.

As will be seen in the next chapter, however, the perceived shortcomings of the OEEC and the Council of Europe led to the decision, in the early 1950s, by a group of just six countries to found a new set of organizations and to begin a process of deeper integration involving the transfer of sovereignty to new "supranational" institutions (see box 1.1). This began with the founding, in 1952, of the

---

Box 1.1   Supranationalism and Intergovernmentalism

Supranationalism is an approach to international integration under which national governments cede sovereignty over certain matters to transnational institutions. These institutions then can make laws and policies that are binding upon those governments. Key features of supranationalist (often also known as federalist) integration include an executive authority independent of national government control, decision-making procedures in which national governments can be outvoted, a court empowered to impose decisions on national governments, and a parliamentary body whose members directly represent the voters rather than national governments.

There are several explanations for the willingness of governments to sometimes cede powers to supranational institutions. They include ideological commitment to the cause of integration, the desire to create effective institutions able to cope with problems no longer solvable in a national framework, and a perceived need to establish binding rules that govern the behavior of *other* countries, even if it means limiting their own freedom of action.

Intergovernmentalism is an approach to integration in which national governments establish institutions and procedures to pursue common interests, but in which those governments retain the ultimate authority to pursue an independent policy if they desire. Key features of intergovernmental integration include the retention of the national veto over decision making (unanimity rather than majority voting) and the absence of a supranational court and executive with binding powers over national governments. Countries tend to pursue intergovernmental integration when they want to reap the benefits of stable international cooperation without surrendering their independence.

The EU is a hybrid of supranational and intergovernmental integration. Compared with other international institutions, however, its distinguishing feature is its high degree of supranationalism, as reflected in the European Court of Justice, the directly elected European Parliament, majority voting in the Council of Ministers, and the European Commission as an independent executive.

European Coal and Steel Community (ECSC), an enterprise that was more limited in geographic and functional scope than the OEEC or the Council of Europe but more ambitious in its long-term economic and political objectives. The new organization was largely the idea of two Frenchmen, Jean Monnet and Robert Schuman, who championed a new approach to integration—one that focused on practical steps in the economic field, the building of permanent institutions, and the harnessing of day-to-day economic cooperation to a long-term political vision.

ASCENDANCY

The other European organizations established in the late 1940s—the OEEC, the Council of Europe, and the WEU—continued to exist, but over time they were transformed in one way or another by interaction with what gradually became the mainstream process of integration flowing out of the three European Communities. With the ending of U.S. aid and the return of economic health to Western Europe, the OEEC and its offshoot, the EPU, lost much of their original rationale. By the end of 1958 the ten European OEEC countries had restored full convertibility with the dollar. The EPU was abolished, its mission having been accomplished. In 1961 the OEEC was transformed into a new body, the Organization for Economic Cooperation and Development (OECD), with the United States and Canada as founding members. Japan, New Zealand, and Australia later joined. Located in Paris, the OECD took on a new mission of promoting economic and social welfare in all developed countries through analysis of policy problems and coordination of economic policies.

The Council of Europe continued its work of harmonizing legislation and promoting human rights, as well as expanding its membership. Greece and Turkey joined in 1949, followed by Iceland in 1950, the Federal Republic of Germany in 1951, Austria in 1956, and most of the remaining West European countries in the 1960s and 1970s. In the 1990s the Council of Europe opened its doors to the ex-communist countries of central and eastern Europe and played a role in helping these countries to harmonize their laws with those of Western Europe and to establish protections against political and human rights abuses.

The WEU played an important part in 1955 in bringing West Germany into NATO on terms that satisfied both the demands of the Germans for equality of status and of the other European states that a rearmed Germany still be subject to some international controls. The Federal Republic became a member of both the WEU and NATO, and the former was used as a mechanism to ban or regulate German production of missiles, certain types of ships and aircraft, and chemical and nuclear weapons. In the main, however, the WEU was rendered superfluous by NATO. It ceased to be an important European security institution and was all but moribund by the early 1980s. Only in the mid-1980s was it revitalized by a French initiative designed to give the European Community countries greater potential to deal with security issues outside the NATO system. In the 1992 Maastricht treaty it was made "an integral part of the development of the [European]

Union,"[10] and by the end of the decade its members had agreed in principle to abolish the organization by merging it with the EU.

THE NATO EXCEPTION

In contrast to these other organizations, NATO played an important role in Europe throughout the Cold War period and continues to be a key element in the post–Cold War European order. As long as the Soviet military threat existed, the West European countries and especially West Germany were unwilling to entrust their security to any organization that did not include the United States. With the end of the Cold War, however, even NATO was forced to redefine itself in relation to the EU. Having rendered superfluous attempts by the European powers in 1947–1955 to develop an autonomous defense capability, in the early 1990s NATO itself faced questions about its future role following the collapse of the communist threat that had led to its creation.

At the 1991 Intergovernmental Conference that led to the adoption of the Maastricht treaty, the major West European countries agreed to develop their own security identity in the new political union. This identity was to exist alongside and complement rather than replace NATO, but many in the United States feared that a newly confident Western Europe was in fact turning away from the Atlantic alliance. Accomplishing the Maastricht objectives proved far more difficult than was at first assumed, however, and in the course of the 1990s NATO reasserted its centrality for European security. Under U.S. leadership, it organized the peace-keeping force that was sent to Bosnia-Herzegovina in late 1995, conducted the 1999 war against Serbia over Kosovo, and reached out to central and eastern Europe, providing the countries of this region with an early and important link to the West that helped to underpin the process of economic transformation by providing long-term security against external threats. Poland, Hungary, and the Czech Republic were admitted to NATO in 1999, several years before they were expected to complete the more complicated and politically difficult process of joining the EU. Other central and east European countries continued to press for membership in both organizations, which they saw as providing different but complementary kinds of support for the transition process. In March 2003, seven other formerly communist countries—Bulgaria, Estonia, Latvia, Lithuania, Romania, Slovakia, and Slovenia—were invited to sign accession protocols with the expectation that they would become members of the alliance in 2004.

NATO thus continues to play an important role in Europe. Nonetheless, the EU is clearly the more important of the two organizations, with a much deeper and more pervasive effect on the lives of ordinary citizens in all parts of Europe. As will be seen in chapter 9, even in the defense area NATO's future role will be linked increasingly to the efforts by the EU to establish under its own auspices a European pillar of the Atlantic alliance.

Deepening and Widening

As the OEEC, Council of Europe, WEU, and even NATO were transformed or declined in importance, the integration process that began with the signing of the ECSC Treaty has taken on ever greater significance. By the 1990s, the EU had clearly emerged as the most important economic and political (although as yet not security) organization in Europe.

This emergence was the result of more than four decades of development along two dimensions. The first was an increase in the level and scope of integration. Starting with a relatively simple scheme to pool their coal and steel production, the original members of the ECSC went on to create a common market for trade in all goods and common policies for external trade, agriculture, and transport. They later added the single market program, policies in the environmental, social, regional, and other areas, a single currency, shared policies on immigration and related matters, and at least the rudiments of a common foreign and security policy. This process of increasing the range and intensity of integration often is called *deepening*. It is reflected in the institutional and legal evolution from the original "community" to the "union" established by the Maastricht treaty.

The other dimension has been the expansion of the original six to other European countries, a process often referred to as *widening* (see table 1.1). The first enlargement took place in 1973 with the accession of Britain, Denmark, and Ireland, effectively ending an attempt by the UK to establish the European Free Trade Association (EFTA) as a rival to the Community. Greece, an important NATO member, was admitted in 1981. Spain and Portugal joined in 1986, following the establishment of democracy in those countries in the 1970s. The first post–Cold War enlargement took place in 1995, as three neutral countries, Austria, Finland, and Sweden, joined what by then had become the EU, bringing the total membership to fifteen. Cyprus, Malta, and eight formerly communist countries of central and eastern Europe joined the Union in 2004.

As shown in table 1.2, as many as a dozen other European countries are actual or potential candidates for membership. At the time of the 2004 enlargement, Bulgaria and Romania were in the process of completing negotiations aimed at becoming members in 2007. Turkey had been accorded formal candidate status but had

Table 1.1   Enlargement of the EC/EU, 1958–2004

Founding members, 1958	Belgium, Federal Republic of Germany, France, Italy, Luxembourg, the Netherlands
January 1, 1973	Denmark, Ireland, United Kingdom
January 1, 1981	Greece
January 1, 1986	Portugal, Spain
January 1, 1995	Austria, Finland, Sweden
May 1, 2004	Cyprus, Czech Republic, Estonia, Hungary, Latvia, Lithuania, Malta, Poland, Slovakia, Slovenia

Table 1.2   Candidate and Potential Member States of the Union

Country	Applied	Started negotiations
Bulgaria	December 1995	February 2000
Romania	June 1995	February 2000
Turkey	April 1987	
Switzerland	May 1992	(Negotiations suspended in 1994 following defeat of the European Economic Area agreement by referendum)
Norway	July 1967	January 1972
	November 1992	June 1994
		(Negotiations completed both times but in each case rejected by popular referendum in Norway)
Croatia	February 2003	
Macedonia	February 2004	
Bosnia		
Serbia		
Albania		
Ukraine		
Moldova		

not yet been asked to begin accession negotiations. A number of other European countries either had applied or declared their intention to seek membership, but had not yet been formally accorded candidate status. If all of the countries that wish to join were to complete the accession process, the EU of 2010–2020 could have more than thirty members.

The magnitude of the widening that has occurred or is underway must be seen in a broad historical context. In the years just after the EC was established, Europe was divided into four groups of countries with very different approaches to integration. The six countries of the original ECSC were taking a highly integrationist approach, forging ahead with explicit political goals and plans to merge many areas of economic activity. Led by Britain, the seven-member EFTA was committed to a much looser form of integration that focused mainly on free trade in industrial goods. In southern Europe, Spain, Portugal, and Greece still were largely cut off from economic and political trends in northern Europe and were participating only marginally in the integration process. The countries of central and eastern Europe had been coerced by the Soviet Union into a separate trading bloc organized in accordance with the principles of state ownership and central planning and had even less contact with Europe's core.

Since 1973, however, these separate zones of economic integration have merged into one—a single zone formed around the core six members of the original coal and steel community. In effect, the pattern of integration championed by Monnet and Schuman in the early 1950s has triumphed, albeit with modifications and for reasons that they did not entirely foresee. The result has been a rewidening of the integration process from the original six to all of those countries that were involved in the founding of the OEEC and the Council of Europe and, with the enlargement to central and eastern Europe, even to countries that never participated in the Marshall Plan, the OEEC, or, until the 1990s, the Council of Europe.

In looking to the future of the EU, a key question is whether the expansion of the Union can go forward without undermining the progress that has been made toward a deeper and more cohesive Union—whether, in effect, deepening and widening can proceed together. There are many aspects to this question, but four are especially important: (1) governance in a larger Union; (2) identity in a more diverse Union; (3) the relationship between European integration and the broader process of globalization; and (4) the goals and endpoints of the integration process and how they may change as a consequence of enlargement.

SIZE AND GOVERNANCE

On the eve of the 2004 enlargement, the EU had fifteen member states and a population of approximately 381 million. With the May 2004 accessions, it had twenty-five member states and approximately 455 million people (table 1.3). If the EU is considered as a political entity—a political union with many state-like characteristics although not itself a state—then only China and India outrank it in size. Enlargement to Bulgaria and Romania will increase membership to twenty-seven countries and population to nearly 500 million. Admission of countries in the Balkans, Turkey, and possibly Ukraine could push the total to more than thirty members and 600 million citizens.

Widening on this scale raises questions about cohesion and the governance. Even in the United States, which is smaller in population and more homogeneous than the EU, there has been a tendency in recent years for power to devolve from the federal to the state and local levels, as voters have lost faith in the efficacy of decisions taken in Washington, D.C. Since the early 1990s the EU has had analogous discussions about the drawbacks of centralization. Consistent with the principle of "subsidiarity" enshrined in the Maastricht treaty, the EU is supposed to take decisions at the Union level only when there are compelling reasons not to leave decisions at the national or local level. But there is no universal agreement on how to interpret or apply subsidiarity.

As the EU expands and becomes more diverse, centralization of decision making and regulation will become more difficult to achieve and could command less political support from the voters. But leaving decisions at (or devolving them to) the national level also will be risky. If carried too far it would call into question the Union's core achievement of a single internal market. As will be seen in later chapters, one of the reasons why the EU member states have tried to establish EU-wide rules and standards for the environment, competition policy, social policy, and other areas is not to pursue standardization for its own sake, but because fail-

Table 1.3   EU Member States—Basic Data

Country	Population (millions, 2004)	Area (1,000 km²)	GDP (billion U.S.$, 2002)	Per capita gross national income (U.S.$, 2002)
The Fifteen				
Austria	8.092	84	203.0	23,390
Belgium	10.397	31	247.6	23,250
Denmark	5.398	43	174.8	30,290
Finland	5.220	305	130.8	23,510
France	59.896	544	1,300	22,010
Germany	82.585	357	2,000	22,670
Greece	11.047	132	132.8	11,660
Ireland	4.025	70	119.9	23,870
Italy	57.482	301	1,100	18,960
Luxembourg	.451	3	20.1	38,830
Netherlands	16.258	34	413.7	23,960
Portugal	10.480	92	121.3	10,840
Spain	40.978	505	649.8	14,430
Sweden	8.975	411	29.8	24,820
UK	59.518	244	1,600	25,250
New Member States (2004)				
Cyprus	.728	9	9.1	12,320
Czech Republic	10.221	79	69.6	5,560
Estonia	1.351	45	6.4	4,130
Hungary	10.115	93	65.8	5,280
Latvia	2.319	65	8.4	3,480
Lithuania	3.447	65	13.8	3,660
Malta	.400	.3	3.6	9,200
Poland	38.194	313	187.7	4,570
Slovak Republic	5.381	49	23.7	3,950
Slovenia	1.997	20	21.1	9,810
Total EU-15	380.759	3,048	8,243	—
Total EU-25	454.900	3,786	8,652	—

Sources: Eurostat; World Bank Development Indicators Database, August 2003

ing to have common minimum standards would allow markedly different competitive conditions in different parts of the Union to disrupt the functioning of the single market. The EU thus will have to wrestle with the choice between risking resentment of more and more vigorously enforced EU-level legislation in a large and disparate Union and scaling back its legislative ambitions in a way that could threaten the coherence of the Union. It also will have to deal with suggestions that frequently arise about a pioneer or vanguard group of countries, probably led by France and Germany, that could push ahead with integration where others are not prepared to go, for example by establishing a European defense force separate from NATO. But such ideas are difficult to implement in practice and in any case raise concerns about re-creating the very divisions in Europe that integration was meant to overcome.

IDENTITY

How effective and cohesive the EU proves to be also relates to the question of identity. The original Community had just six members speaking four languages, with a total population of about 170 million. The member countries were all (except for Italy) located in a compact region of northwestern Europe. They were predominantly Roman Catholic (although West Germany and the Netherlands had large Protestant populations) and all occupied territories that had been part of Charlemagne's empire (and for this reason were sometimes referred to as "Carolingian Europe"). They also had a certain economic coherence. Their coal and steel industries were concentrated in a belt stretching a few hundred kilometers from the Ruhr in Germany's northwest to the industrial regions of France's northeast.

In contrast, the EU of today has twenty-five members and twenty official languages (using two alphabets, the Greek and Roman). Economically, culturally, and socially it is far more diverse than the Carolingian Europe of 1957. The future Union will have at least twenty-seven members, speak more than twenty-five languages, and use three alphabets (with the addition of Cyrillic for Bulgaria). Accession of Turkey would add a large Islamic population to the already substantial Muslim minorities that live in the countries of Western Europe. Some academics and policymakers question whether a political and economic entity of this complexity can function effectively and command the support of its citizens.

For years officials in Brussels referred to the EC and later the EU as "Europe," a practice that irritated politicians in nonmember countries and in some member countries such as Britain. As the EU expanded to include nearly all of what traditionally has been called Western Europe, the countries of central and eastern Europe (and Turkey) came to see membership in the Union as the most important sign of their acceptance into "Europe." Such acceptance is important for practical reasons (access to trade, as a bulwark against external pressures, and as an external "pacifier" of internal conflicts), but it also has symbolic significance. For member states and aspirants alike, Europe has come to be seen not as a geographical expression but as a community of values.

It is not self-evident, however, why accepting these values should require having the same agriculture and transport policies or, conversely, why being in a Union formed around such policies necessarily means that member states share the same interpretation of those values. "Europe" is a political construction, a myth created to overcome the divisions and conflicts of the twentieth century. The real Europe has enormous cultural, linguistic, and religious diversity. It has never been united on the scale planned for the twenty-first century—from Finland to Portugal and from Ireland to the Balkans.

Diversity on this scale could set limits to the development of a European identity. Opinion polls show that many people in Europe—particularly younger people—increasingly identify with Europe as well as with their own country. But the depth of this identification is open to question and varies greatly from country to country.[11] And without a strong sense of European identity, it may be difficult to sustain the sense of shared destiny and purpose that underpins support for common policies. A common European defense, for example, will be difficult to achieve if Europeans do not feel enough of a sense of solidarity to come to each other's assistance if attacked (however remote such a possibility may seem at present). The same is true on a less dramatic scale with regard to taxation, expenditure, and the redistribution of wealth that occurs as a consequence of government involvement in the economy. In their own countries, most citizens support some redistribution from the young to the old, the employed to the unemployed, the healthy to the sick, and from wealthy to poorer regions (although even this support has declined as enthusiasm for the welfare state has waned). They are less willing to do so on a European scale—precisely because the citizens of the individual member states do not yet (and may never) feel the same sense of community with citizens of other European countries. The extent to which a European identity emerges and whether there are geographical and cultural limits to how far such an identity can be stretched thus will be key questions for the future, the answers to which will determine in part how successful the EU is in managing the conflicting demands of widening and deepening.

THE EU AND GLOBALIZATION

A third issue that will affect the future of the Union concerns how it relates to an international system characterized by globalization and in which the very nature of the nation-state is changing in response to global trends. Globalization is the process by which markets for goods, technology, and capital are spreading worldwide, driven by the lowering of tariff barriers, the activities of multinational corporations, and the declining cost of moving goods, information, money, and people. It means that workers and firms must compete not just with rivals in their own country or region, but on a worldwide basis.

Globalization creates both economic "winners" and "losers." The former tend to be skilled, high-technology workers who are well positioned to compete in the expanded global marketplace; the latter are unskilled or semi-skilled workers in industries such as textiles and steel that are exposed to low-cost competition from the developing and other developed countries.[12] Globalization also has a cultural dimension. It is often associated with cultural homogenization and Americanization, since it involves expansion by companies in the service and entertainment industries, most of them American (e.g., MacDonald's, Microsoft, CNN), that are seen by some as imposing American norms on local culture and language.

Globalization impinges upon the traditional power and prerogatives of the nation-state. Since countries must compete for investment (not only foreign investment, but investment by their own firms and citizens, who are free to seek higher returns elsewhere), they are under pressure to attract companies by lowering taxes and offering incentives. This in turn weakens their ability to pay for benefits and sustain the welfare state. Given these factors, it is not surprising that in recent years there has been a backlash against globalization.

The relationship between the EU and globalization is complex. On the one hand, the EU is in the same position relative to global trends as the individual nation-states. Working with the member states, it must compete harder to attract capital in ways that impinge on its freedom to pursue social, environmental, and other policy objectives. As will be seen in subsequent chapters, the EU's proposals in the 1990s to levy "eco-taxes" to combat global warming and its ambitious plans for expanded social legislation both had to be scaled down in response to concerns about competitiveness. On the other hand, because the EU is so big, it can present itself as a unified European response to the forces of globalization—one that can equalize the balance of power between international economic forces and the rights and interests of the European citizen. The global economy operates according to rules and standards, and the EU helps to set those rules and standards in forums such as the World Trade Organization (WTO). It cannot always get its way—it must negotiate with other countries and there are market forces which no government or combination of governments can control—but in the main the EU is better positioned than any of its member states to help shape the international system in directions favorable to Europe (provided those directions can be defined and command consensus).

Increasingly, the EU presents itself as a necessary response to globalization— one that can help the citizens reap more of its benefits while suffering fewer of its negative effects. Not everyone sees the EU in this light, however. For ordinary workers and citizens, the EU can seem as much a vehicle of as a buffer against globalization. For a worker in France who loses his or her job to "foreign" competition, it probably matters little whether the competition came from Asia or from one of the new EU member countries in central and eastern Europe. Similarly, while the EU presents itself as a necessary response to global challenges such as increased immigration or drug-trafficking, citizens may just as easily regard it, with its focus on free movement of goods, services, capital, and people, as a cause of rather than a response to problems emanating from beyond the familiar borders of the nation. For regions or countries confronted with the implications of globalization, the EU may be too much of a globalizing and liberalizing force. They may be tempted to reassert the primacy of national and regional solutions rather than to work to strengthen the Union.

At the same time, there are those who see the EU and its policies as barriers to the positive effects of globalization. Many business leaders, for example, have warned that too much rule-making and regulation is damaging the EU's position in the global economy, causing it to miss out on the benefits of e-commerce, financial market innovation, and other aspects of the twenty-first-century economy.

How the relationship between the EU and globalization unfolds in the coming years will have a major influence on the development of the Union. Whether the

EU will be seen as a necessary response to globalization and its negative effects that therefore should be strengthened, as a bearer of unwelcome trends from in and outside Europe that should be weakened, or as an obstacle to some of the potential benefits of globalization that needs to be changed to realize those benefits, is a key question.

OBJECTIVES AND ENDPOINTS

A final issue that relates to the prospects for uniting Europe concerns the desired endpoint—the ultimate objective—of the European integration process. It is difficult to assess the progress of European integration or to evaluate its successes without having at least a general idea of what the desired final outcome is or should be. While it is easy to say that the EC/EU has continued to develop new policies and to strengthen its internal and external identity even as it has added new members—and that this process can be extended into the future—it can be argued that the most ambitious schemes for political integration have already been abandoned and that, to the extent that integration is a success, it is one that has been purchased at the price of scaling down goals that were once far more ambitious.

There is no talk in today's EU about the creation of a "United States of Europe," such as was discussed with enthusiasm in the early postwar period. There are many reasons why the ambitious federalist visions of the 1940s and early 1950s lost their appeal. The idealism of the generations that suffered under Hitler has faded, giving way to more pragmatic concerns about economic competitiveness. Voters have grown more suspicious about distant governments and bureaucracies and the assumption that "bigger is better." National loyalties and identities have proven more resilient than many expected, while the end of the Soviet threat removed an external motive for the creation of a strong federal Europe.

But progressive enlargements also have contributed to the demise of the most far-reaching schemes for political union, as an earlier sense of purpose has been lost by the growing complexity of decision making, squabbles over budgets, and the accession of new member states that never signed on to the vision of the 1950s. If a future generation of political leaders were to try to revive the visions of the 1940s and to establish something like a "United States of Europe," it would find the task enormously complicated by the size and diversity of the EU wrought by successive enlargements.

The pressures of enlargement and institutional reform linked to enlargement have given rise to debate in Europe about the ultimate objectives and limitations of the integration process. Some participants in this debate see little choice for the EU but to press forward to build a stronger and more cohesive order. Others believe that such talk is unrealistic and that Europe will continue along its current trajectory, perhaps even evolving toward a looser organization with more diverse patterns of cooperation. The European Convention that convened in 2002 to draft a formal constitution for the Union in some sense grew out of this debate but by no means resolved it, as the draft European Constitution has remained a controversial and in any case ambiguous document, arguably able to lead the EU to a number of alternative futures.

Key Challenges

This book provides an introduction to the European Union and a framework for analyzing how it will address the challenges outlined in the previous section. Following a brief historical overview in chapter 2, succeeding chapters examine seven major topics: institutions (chapter 3), market integration (chapter 4), policy integration (chapters 5–7), external identity (chapters 8–9), enlargement (chapter 10), relations between the EU and the United States (chapter 11), and, by way of conclusion, the future of Europe as it relates to the citizen (chapter 12).

INSTITUTIONS

The aspect of the EU that most distinguishes it from the other postwar organizations in Europe is its institutions. Whereas other European and international organizations were little more than forums where member states met to pursue agreed goals, from its founding the Community had its own executive, a parliamentary arm, and a court to enforce the founding treaties and Community legislation. The member states were still the key actors in the development and implementation of Community policy, but they no longer enjoyed absolute veto powers over decisions taken in and by the new Community.

The institutional structures established in the 1950s have undergone constant adaptation over time, especially with the transformation of the original Community into the Union. Despite these changes, there is almost universal agreement in the EU that fundamental institutional reform is needed to ensure that an enlarged Union can function effectively—that it is able to take decisions, see these decisions implemented down to the level of individual citizens and firms, and convince the voters that such decisions should be accepted as fair and democratic. The Amsterdam (1999) and Nice (2002) treaties were attempts by the member states to reform the institutions in advance of enlargement. But European political leaders generally concluded that the changes wrought by these agreements were inadequate. The proposed European Constitution represented yet another attempt at reform, intended by its drafters to settle "once and for all" the institutional makeup of the Union. But the Constitution subsequently became mired in political disagreements among the member states, leaving important details of the EU's institutional setup unresolved past the May 1, 2004, enlargement.

MARKET INTEGRATION

The single market remains the core achievement of European integration—the cement that holds the EU together. Building upon the initial trade liberalization that took place in the GATT and the OEEC shortly after World War II, this market developed in two concentrated phases: in 1958–1968 with the completion of the common market and customs union, and in 1986–1992 with the single market program.

Maintaining and expanding the single market is a continuing effort, however, one that presents ongoing challenges to the Union. It entails curbing the use by member states and firms of subsidies, hidden protectionism, and cartels that disrupt the functioning of the market. It also means extending the market to sectors such as energy that are still divided along national lines, broadening market integration to the new member states and to new industries and technologies, and, not least, dealing with the complex and politically sensitive issue of how market integration within Europe relates to the broader processes of globalization and the integration of world markets that have accelerated in recent years.

POLICY INTEGRATION

Since the 1950s, the EU has acquired a wide range of policy responsibilities. Market integration thus has been complemented by extensive policy integration. There are two reasons why this is so. The first concerns the single market. Given the heavy involvement of the member states in their national economies, policy integration has been an essential component to establishing the open and level playing field on which the single market rests. A Europe-wide market based on the free movement of goods, services, capital, and people requires some degree of convergence among the member states with regard to policies for agriculture, transportation, and competition and even social policy.

The second reason concerns the scale of integration. Many policy problems— missing transportation links, cross-border environmental pollution, international drug trafficking—can only be tackled on an international scale. When the EC comprised only a small portion of the European continent, many of these issues were addressed in broader European forums such as the OEEC/OECD, the United Nations Economic Commission for Europe, or the Council of Europe. As the EC/EU has enlarged, however, it increasingly has become the logical venue for such Europe-wide cooperation.

But policy integration in the EU is uneven, and there is no definitive consensus within and among the member states about the right mix of EU versus national policy approaches. Implementation and enforcement also are problematic. As an enlarged Union grapples with increasingly complex economic and social problems, it will be under pressure to improve policy performance in all areas. It also will need to decide when policy problems should *not* be brought within the purview of the Union but left to the member states or lower levels of government.

EXTERNAL IDENTITY

The EU is the world's largest trading power. Along with the United States, it plays the dominant role in the WTO and has special bilateral and multilateral trade and cooperation arrangements with many countries and regions. Since 1999, the EU has had its own currency, the euro. Since the 1970s, it has tried to be a more important political actor, influencing, for example, the Middle East peace process and the human rights situation in countries around the world. Since the 1990s, the EU has been trying to develop a security and defense identity. A "European army" is still a long way off, but it cannot be ruled out as a possibility.

But how cohesive the EU will become as an international actor and the purposes to which it will put its economic and political power are still unanswered questions. Since the establishment of the Common Foreign and Security Policy (CFSP) in the Maastricht treaty, the EU has made enormous strides in getting its members to coordinate policy toward other regions and in making Europe a more assertive force on the international scene. At the same time, however, the bitter splits within the Union over the 2003 Iraq war—with some member states strongly supporting the United States while others, notably France and Germany, actually outdoing such traditional U.S. rivals as Russia and China in seeking to frustrate U.S. objectives—revealed that much of the past decade's convergence on foreign policy issues was superficial. Member states still could differ over key international issues, and above all their relations with the United States. Even worse, they could deliberately accentuate their differences over international issues in battles for influence *within* the Union.

In the future, increasing size and diversity and the pressures of globalization could make for a blurring of the EU's external identity. Alternatively, these trends could encourage European leaders to accentuate foreign policy (and especially differences with the United States) as a way of managing diversity and creating a greater sense of European solidarity vis-à-vis the outside world. Either way, the EU's external policies will have influence far beyond the EU itself and will have implications for the international system as a whole.

ENLARGEMENT

Enlargement cuts across all issues and policy areas in the EU, including the reform of the institutions, the operation of the single market, and the various policies. It is also a process that needs to be examined in its own right—one that is governed by legal provisions in the EU's founding treaties, that draws upon the experience of past enlargements, and that above all is shaped by the particular character of the candidate countries. Managing enlargement requires deciding when countries are ready to become members of the Union, successfully integrating these countries and, not least, deciding where enlargement should stop and which countries by what criteria should *not* be considered as potential members.

With the 2004 enlargement to ten countries, the EU passed a huge milestone. But enlargement is likely to remain a subject of enduring academic and policy interest. For one thing, the experience of the pre-accession process will shape how these countries perform as full members of the Union: how successful they are in adapting to existing structures, but also how their presence as members might

Box 1.2   What's in a Name: ECSC, EEC, EC, and EU

The terminology of the European Union (EU) is confusing, and reflects the history of the integration process and the complexities of the EU's constitutional and legal order. The European Coal and Steel Community (ECSC) was established in 1952; the European Economic Community (EEC) and the European Atomic Energy Community (Euratom) in 1958. These organizations were referred to collectively as the European Communities. The EEC was by far the most important of these organizations and before 1993 often was referred to simply as the European Community (EC). The EEC and Euratom treaties were of indefinite duration, but the ECSC treaty was concluded for a period of fifty years from its entry into force. Accordingly, the treaty expired on July 23, 2002. The ECSC ceased to exist, and its functions and assets and liabilities were transferred to the EC.

The Treaty of Maastricht, which was signed in February 1992 and went into effect on November 1, 1993, formally renamed the EEC the European Community. It also established the EU, which consisted of the EC as the EU's first pillar, the Common Foreign and Security Policy as the EU's second pillar, and cooperation in Justice and Home Affairs as the third pillar of the Union. The three pillars have distinct identities and decision-making processes, but they are tied together by a single institutional framework.

The European Constitution, drafted in 2002–2003 by a special convention but not yet in effect, proposes to eliminate the pillar structure altogether and to create a single entity: the European Union.

In this book, EC generally is used to refer to the historical development of the Community up to 1993; EU generally is used to refer to these organizations after 1993. In some cases, however, it is necessary for the sake of clarity to refer to component parts of the Union.

change the EU. For another, enlargement remains an ongoing process, with Bulgaria, Romania, Turkey, and several Balkan countries all at different stages of preparation for EU membership.

EU-U.S. RELATIONS

The EU and the United States are hugely important for each other. Economically, they are intertwined by trade and investment. In the security field, they are linked by the NATO alliance, which is responsible not only for security in Europe but increasingly has taken on missions outside Europe, for example in Afghanistan. The two sides work together or at least in parallel in addressing many of the world's most pressing problems, including poverty and disease in the developing world, the threat of terrorism, and the proliferation of weapons of mass destruction. And Europe and the United States share common histories and values based on cultural, religious, and ethnic ties.

In the 1990s, there was widespread hope on both sides of the Atlantic that these shared bonds, coupled with the demise of communism and the EU's own post-Maastricht development as a political as well as an economic actor would lead to a new U.S.-European relationship built around a U.S.-EU partnership. In recent years, however, the transatlantic relationship has soured. Relations increasingly are marred by economic disputes, differences over approaches to problems such as Iraq and conflict in the Middle East, and even by what some see as a growing divergence in values. A key question for the future of both Europe and the United States is whether these negative trends will deepen or whether the two sides will find ways to build on the many positive aspects of their relations to create the kind of partnership that was discussed in the 1990s but that failed to develop.

EUROPE AND THE CITIZEN

EU and national political leaders in Europe frequently talk about the need to bring the Union "closer to its citizens." This is a slogan intended to generate political support for integration among a public that has grown skeptical about what it perceives as a remote bureaucracy based in Brussels. It is, nonetheless, a slogan that expresses an important truth. The public is not very interested in abstract debate about widening, deepening, identity, or the reform of institutions. It does care about concrete issues such as unemployment, the environment, old-age security, food safety, crime, and matters of war and peace.

The ultimate success of the EU and of the European integration project thus is likely to be determined by how relevant the EU is in addressing these concrete problems and issues. Future prospects for the Union as they relate to these problems are discussed throughout the book, but especially in the concluding chapter, which addresses the challenges of the future and how they relate to the everyday concerns of the citizen.

Theoretical Frameworks

The EU affects the interests of people and businesses not only in Europe but around the world—through its role in trade, the environment, international finance, aid to the developing countries, and many other areas. It is not surprising, therefore, that sources of information about the EU have proliferated in recent years. Some information can be found in the general and business sections of American newspapers and magazines. More is available in international publications such as the *Financial Times* and *The Economist* (not to mention publications in French, German, and other European languages) and on the Internet. The EU's own web server—http://europa.eu.int—is a vast store of explanatory material, texts of treaties, proposals, laws, green papers, white papers, statistics, records of parliamentary debates, minutes of meetings, and more.

But information alone is not sufficient to provide an understanding of the EU. It needs to be related to a conceptual framework in which it can be interpreted. Ever since the founding and initial successes of the three European Communities in the 1950s, scholars have developed theories to try to explain the integration process and relate it to other trends in domestic and international politics.[13] Among the earliest and most influential theories was neofunctionalism, developed mainly by U.S. academics such as Ernst B. Haas and Leon N. Lindberg.[14] Neofunctionalism took seriously the "Monnet method," and was based heavily on the concept of spillover. The neofunctionalists argued that two types of spillover operated to propel the integration process forward.

The first was economic spillover. Successful integration in one economic sector would produce pressures for integration in other sectors of the economy. The second was political spillover. The accumulation of integration in economic fields would lead to political integration, as elites would become increasingly disposed toward working politically with their economic partners, and as the accumulation of economic integration increased the demand for common decision making by the political authorities.

As will be seen throughout this book, the experience of fifty years seems to have confirmed some aspects of the spillover concept, especially in the economic field. Establishment of a common market for goods created pressures to harmonize standards and regulations; pursuit of the single market spilled over into calls for a common currency which, once achieved, resulted in further pressures for the harmonization of tax policy and company law. The argument for political spillover has found less support, as national governments and political elites have proven more reluctant than expected to transfer power to joint or supranational institutions in order to manage economic spillover. Rather, the scope of economic integration at times has seemed to foster intense bargaining among national governments as they seek to maximize the gains from the integration process. Neofunctionalism had its heyday in the 1960s. It declined in the 1970s and 1980s, as the integration process seemed to lose momentum, but it has found new adherents (in revised form) in recent years, particularly as economic spillover seems to have accelerated.

Another influential theoretical approach, directly opposed to neofunctionalism, is intergovernmentalism. The intergovernmentalists argued that despite the limited steps toward supranational integration and institutions such as the Commission and the Court of Justice, the member states remained firmly in control of the integration process, which could best be explained as a game of intergovernmental bargaining in which national governments sought to cut the most advantageous deals possible with their partners, based on traditional concepts of national political and especially economic interest.

Intergovernmentalism always has been present in discussions of European integration, and seems to have found its confirmation in the behavior of national leaders such as French President Charles de Gaulle and British Prime Minister Margaret Thatcher, both of whom saw the Community as primarily an arena for the pursuit of national interests. The most prominent intergovernmentalist theoretician in recent years has been Andrew Moravscik, who has argued that all of the most important turning points in the history of European integration can be seen as negotiated bargains among the largest member states, acting overwhelmingly in pursuit of traditional national interests.[15] Critics argue that the intergovernmental-ists go too far in exaggerating the acknowledged importance of member state in-terests and concentrate too much on high-profile events such as summits, with not enough attention paid to the agenda-shaping and the accretion of rules and pat-terns of behavior that goes on in the bureaucracy and lower levels of government, unnoticed by headline news.

In addition to such grand theories as neofunctionalism and intergovernmen-talism, scholars have developed theories that seek to make sense of particular as-pects of European integration. The new institutionalists argue that institutions (and not just national governments articulating national interests) matter in the shaping of decisions. They concentrate on the role that institutions play in shaping policy outcomes in particular areas. They look not only at the formal powers and structures of policy-making institutions (the Commission, Council of Ministers, and so forth), but also at informal practices and patterns of interaction that are harder to observe but that go on behind the scenes as policymakers set agendas and cut deals.

Another theoretical approach focuses on policy networks. Such networks form in particular policy areas and comprise all of the institutions and actors inter-ested in a policy outcome. In telecommunications policy, for example, a policy network would include the national telephone authorities, industries that manu-facture telephone equipment, user groups, the parts of the European Commission responsible for telecommunications and industrial policy, and relevant ministries in member state governments.[16] These actors sometimes combine with each other to produce a policy outcome. For example, user groups in several countries might join together to promote lower telecommunications costs, in opposition to the telephone companies in several countries that might favor less competition and higher prices. National interests come into play up to a point, but the very concept of "national" is relativized by the role of transnational actors, such as companies working in several countries or Brussels-based lobbying associations representing interests from throughout Europe, and by the formation of cross-national coali-tions that are pitted against other cross-national alliances.

In recent years, adherents of the "constructivist" school of international rela-tions have begun to contribute to the debate over European integration. Construc-tivists argue that social realities are not, unlike forces of nature, immutable phe-nomena; they are in fact constructed by people. Categories such as "state," "nation," and indeed "Europe" can mean different things to different people and can change over time. In this sense, the constructivists argue that ideas matter as much as "objective" national interests or neofunctional spillover in shaping the integration process. Indeed, with constructivism the discussion of European inte-gration comes full circle, back to an appreciation of the idealist impulses that moti-vated the founders of the original Community.[17]

Many scholars of the EU would argue that there is no one theoretical ap-proach that can organize and lend coherence to the European integration process. Different theories can be applied, alone or in combination, to understand different aspects of a complex reality. Neofunctionalism may help to explain the accretion of responsibilities by the European Central Bank or the growth of environmental legislation; intergovernmental bargaining may be more appropriate to the study of major institutional and constitutional turning points, such as decisions to admit new members or to reform political decision-making structures; while constructivism is perhaps most relevant to changing European attitudes toward the international system and policies toward the United States.

As an introduction to the EU, this book does not focus heavily on the theoretical underpinnings of current research and writing on the Union. To the extent that theory is relevant, however, the book uses an eclectic approach. Neofunctionalism is given its due, as instances of spillover are highlighted, but the analysis also points to many instances of intergovernmental bargaining among the member states. Other theoretical approaches relating to specific policy decisions are cited in the notes and in the suggestions for further reading.

Notes

1. Richard N. Gardner, *Sterling-Dollar Diplomacy* (New York, McGraw-Hill, 1969).

2. See Lucrezia Reichlin, "The Marshall Plan Reconsidered," in Barry Eichengreen, ed., *Europe's Post-war Recovery* (Cambridge, UK: Cambridge University Press, 1995), 42–47.

3. Barry Eichengreen, "Mainsprings of Economic Recovery in Post-war Europe," in Eichengreen, ed., *Europe's Post-war Recovery*, 6–7.

4. Dean Acheson, *Present at the Creation: My Years in the State Department* (New York: Norton, 1969), 233.

5. *Treaty of Economic, Social and Cultural Collaboration and Collective Self-Defence*, Brussels, May 7, 1948, *Treaty Series No. 1*, Cmd. 7599 (London: HMSO, 1949), 2.

6. *Statute of the Council of Europe*, London, May 5, 1949, *Treaty Series No. 51*, 1949, Cmd. 7778 (London: HMSO, 1949), 2 [Article 3]. The current statute now in force, with all subsequent amendments and protocols, can be found at www.coe.int (accessed June 11, 2004).

7. *Statute*, 2 [Art. 1].

8. Ibid. [Art. 1].

9. For reminiscences by a British participant in early parliamentary sessions, see Julian Critchley, "The Great Betrayal—Tory Policy towards Europe from 1945 to 1955," in Martyn Bond et al., eds., *Eminent Europeans* (London: Greycoat Press, 1996), 85–96.

10. *Treaty on European Union* [Maastricht], in *European Union: Selected Instruments Taken from the Treaties* (Luxembourg: Office for Office Publications of the European Communities [hereinafter, OOPEC], 1995), 38 (Article J4).

11. European Commission, *Eurobarometer: Public Opinion in the European Union*, Report no. 50, March 1999, 59-60, available on the Eurobarometer website: http://europa.eu .int/en/comm/dg10/infcom/epo/polls.html.

12. Dani Rodrik, *Has Globalization Gone Too Far?* (Washington, D.C.: Institute for International Economics, 1997).

13. For a review of current theories, see Neill Nugent, *The Government and Politics of the European Union*, 4th ed. (Durham, N.C.: Duke University Press, 1999), 491–519, on which this section draws.

14. Ernst B. Haas, *The Uniting of Europe: Political, Social and Economic Forces 1950–57*

(Stanford, Calif.: Stanford University Press, 1958); Leon N. Lindberg, *The Political Dynamics of European Economic Integration* (Oxford, UK: Oxford University Press, 1963).

15. *The Choice for Europe: Social Purpose and State Power from Messina to Maastricht* (Ithaca, NY: Cornell University Press, 1998).

16. Volker Schneider, Godefroy Dang-Nguyen, and Raymund Werle, "Corporate Actor Networks in European Policy-Making: Harmonizing Telecommunications Policy," *Journal of Common Market Studies* 32, no. 4 (December 1994): 473–98.

17. Craig Parsons, "Showing Ideas as Causes: The Origins of the European Union," *International Organization* 56, no. 1 (Winter 2002): 47–84.

Suggestions for Further Reading

Gori, Francesca, and Silvio Pons, eds. *The Soviet Union and Europe in the Cold War, 1943–53.* New York: Macmillan, 1996.

Hogan, Michael J. *The Marshall Plan: America, Britain and the Reconstruction of Western Europe 1947–1952.* Cambridge, UK: Cambridge University Press, 1987.

Kaplan, Jacob J., and Guenther Schleiminger. *The European Payments Union: Financial Diplomacy in the 1950s.* Oxford, UK: Clarendon Press, 1989.

Milward, Alan S. *The European Rescue of the Nation-state.* Berkeley: University of California Press, 1992.

Osgood, Robert E. *NATO: The Entangling Alliance.* Chicago: University of Chicago Press, 1962.

Zurcher, Arnold J. *The Struggle to Unite Europe: 1940–1958.* New York: New York University Press, 1958.

The organizations discussed in this chapter have websites that provide information about their histories and current activities:

Council of Europe
www.coe.int

European Union
http://europa.eu.int

NATO
www.nato.int

OECD
www.oecd.org

CHAPTER 2

Development
FROM COMMON MARKET
TO CONSTITUTION

The European Union (EU) of today is the result of a process of political and institutional development stretching back to the early 1950s. The most important milestones in this process have been the conclusion of seven or eight major treaties among the member states. As summarized in table 2.1, these treaties generally have included both an institutional and a policy dimension. In them, the member states have agreed to pursue certain policy goals and have set up institutional mechanisms through which these goals are to be achieved. As will be seen in this chapter, the first stage in this process of institutional and political development was the conclusion of the European Coal and Steel Community (ECSC) Treaty in 1951; the most recent was the issuing of a draft constitution by the European Convention in June 2003 and the ensuing intergovernmental conference of the member states convened in the fall of that year to formally adopt the constitution.

The European Coal and Steel Community

The ECSC was the inspiration of Jean Monnet, a French businessman and government official who had spent the war years in the United States and who had devoted much thought to the problem of bringing about a European union. Monnet believed that the key to peace and prosperity in Europe was reconciliation between France and Germany, which had fought three wars with each other in the span of a single lifetime—from 1870 to 1940. To achieve this reconciliation, Monnet believed it was necessary to create permanent political institutions whose purpose was to advance collective European interests, rather than simply to reflect the national interests of the individual member countries. He also believed that it was more important to achieve concrete results in a few industrial sectors than to formulate grand plans for economic, social, and cultural union that had little chance of being realized. Because of their economic and political importance at the time and their link to the warmaking capacities of the modern state, coal and steel were the obvious sectoral choices.

Monnet managed to convince French Foreign Minister Robert Schuman and other influential political leaders that his plan was workable and that it offered a way for Europe to move beyond the limited intergovernmental cooperation that took place in the Organization for European Economic Cooperation (OEEC). On May 9, 1950, Schuman formally proposed to the French cabinet Monnet's plan

Table 2.1   The Founding Treaties and Treaty Revisions

Treaty signed Entry in force	Main institutional provisions	Main policy provisions
ECSC (Treaty of Paris) April 18, 1951 July 27, 1952	High Authority Parliamentary Assembly Council of Ministers European Court of Justice (ECJ)	Coal and steel pool

EEC (Treaty of Rome)
March 25, 1957
January 1, 1958
	EEC Commission
	EEC Council of Ministers
	Parliamentary Assembly and ECJ
	  shared with ECSC and Eur-
	  atom
	Economic and Social Committee
	European Investment Bank
		Customs union and common
		  external tariff
		Common Agricultural Policy
		  (CAP)

Euratom March 25, 1957 January 1, 1958	Euratom Commission Euratom Council of Ministers Parliamentary Assembly and ECJ shared with EEC and Euratom	Cooperation in atomic energy
Merger Treaty April 8, 1965 July 1, 1967	Merges commissions and councils of the three Communities	

Single European Act
January 17-18, 1986
July 1, 1987
	Increased powers for European
	  Parliament (EP)
	Greater use of qualified majority
	  voting (QMV)
		Completion of the single mar-
		  ket by 1993
		Legal basis for European Po-
		  litical Cooperation (EPC)
		Environmental, regional, and
		  R&D policy

European Union
  (Maastricht)
February 7, 1992
November 1, 1993
	Pillar structure
	Increased powers for EP
	More QMV
	European Central Bank
	Committee of the Regions
	Links EU with WEU
		Justice and Home Affairs
		  (JHA)
		Common Foreign and Secur-
		  ity Policy (CFSP)
		European citizenship
		Economic and Monetary
		  Union (EMU)

Amsterdam
October 2, 1997
May 1, 1999
	Increased powers for EP
	More QMV
	High Representative for CFSP
	Shift of some JHA matters to first
	  pillar
	Mechanism for enhanced cooper-
	  ation
		Employment chapter

Nice
February 26, 2001
February 1, 2003
	Reweighting of votes in Council
	  of Ministers
	Summit adopts EU Charter of
	  Fundamental Rights	

Constitutional Treaty	Eliminates pillar structure
	Elected European Council Presi-
	  dent
	Revamped QMV system
	Creates post of EU Foreign Min-
	  ister
	Reduces size of Commission
	EU Charter of Fundamental
	  Rights part of constitution	

for France and Germany to combine their coal and steel industries under a joint authority. The joint authority was to be independent of the governments of the two countries and would guarantee each country full and equal access to a common pool of resources. The long-term objective of the plan was as much political as economic, as Schuman made clear in his declaration:

> The pooling of coal and steel production should immediately provide for the setting up of common foundations for economic development as a first step in the federation of Europe, and will change the destinies of those regions which have long been devoted to the manufacture of munitions of war, of which they have been the most constant victims.
>
> The solidarity in production thus established will make it plain that any war between France and Germany becomes not merely unthinkable, but materially impossible.[1]

The Schuman Declaration was enthusiastically welcomed by the West German chancellor, Konrad Adenauer. Belgium, Luxembourg, the Netherlands, and Italy also expressed interest in joining the new community. The Benelux countries had already established an economic union among themselves, and were eager to cooperate on a new basis with their larger neighbors. For Italy, joining the ECSC reflected a decision by its postwar leaders to "scale the Alps"—to turn Italy's energies toward northern Europe and away from the disastrous African and Balkan ambitions of the former dictator, Benito Mussolini.

Britain did not become a member of the ECSC. Like the federalists at the 1948 Hague congress, Monnet hoped that Britain would play a leading role in the integration of Europe. But unlike the founders of the OEEC or the Council of Europe, he was not prepared to hold back the ECSC or dilute its supranationalist essence in order to win British participation. The British government participated in exploratory talks concerning the Schuman Plan, but in the end London declined to join the new organization for reasons that were both political and economic. An island nation with a long tradition of parliamentary democracy that had not been occupied or defeated in either of the world wars, Britain still played an important global role through its special relationship with the United States and by leading the Commonwealth of dominions and former colonies. It did not share the political aims of the founding members, who made clear their intention to form a new political entity by pooling and delegating some of their sovereign powers. As British Foreign Secretary Anthony Eden remarked to an American audience, to join a federation on the continent of Europe "is something which we know, in our bones, we cannot do."[2]

In the months following Schuman's dramatic declaration, the six negotiated the fifty-year treaty establishing the ECSC. It was signed in Paris in April 1951, and the ECSC became operational in July 1952. For the commodities covered—coal, coke, iron ore, steel, and scrap—the ECSC created a common market in which all tariff barriers and restrictions on trade among the six member countries were banned. To ensure the operation of this common market, the ECSC treaty provided for the establishment of four institutions—the High Authority, the

Council of Ministers, the Common Assembly, and a Court of Justice—roughly corresponding to the executive, legislative, and judicial branches of government, with extensive legal and administrative powers in the coal and steel sectors. The High Authority was empowered to issue decisions, recommendations, and opinions prohibiting subsidies and aids to industry that distorted trade, to block mergers and acquisitions and other types of agreements among firms, and under certain circumstances to control prices. It could impose fines to ensure compliance with its decisions. Monnet himself became the first head of the High Authority.

The coal and steel pool never functioned as well in practice as outlined in the Treaty of Paris. National governments and producers' cartels continued to intervene in the market, often clashing with the High Authority.[3] But the ECSC contributed to the rapid expansion of steel production in its member states and fostered even more dramatic increases in trade in coal and steel products. The effects of the elimination of national tariffs and quotas were especially marked for border regions. For example, in 1952 the Aachen region of Germany sold 56.7 percent of its coal to other parts of Germany, and only 15 percent to customers in nearby Belgium, the Netherlands, and Luxembourg. By 1959, its sales to other parts of Germany accounted for only 35.5 percent of the total, whereas shipments to the Benelux countries had risen to 34.9 percent of total sales.[4] Similar shifts were seen in steel, iron ore, and scrap, not only for Germany but for all ECSC members. The result was more efficient patterns of production, lower costs, and increased competition among producers that encouraged innovation and investment in new plants and equipment.

While these economic contributions were important, the greatest significance of the ECSC was political. It began the process of reconciliation between France and West Germany. Leaders such as Schuman, Monnet, and Adenauer were idealists who believed in European integration and Franco-German reconciliation, but they were also hard-nosed pragmatists determined to do what was best for their respective countries (see box 2.1 for biographies of Europe's "founding fathers."). Germany still was trying to overcome the shame and isolation that it had brought upon itself with World War II. It was a divided country, vulnerable to Soviet political and military pressure, dependent on the United States, and badly in need of allies and partners that could anchor its relatively young democracy in the West. Adenauer saw a close relationship with France as the key to embedding the Federal Republic in a broader framework that would allow Germany to regain an equal economic and political status, revive its industry, and, in his view, ultimately achieve reunification.

The French, in contrast, were wary of a revival of German power, which in their view would leave them exposed to the same threat they had faced in 1870, 1914, and 1940. But they had come to realize that Germany could not be held down indefinitely, especially since the Americans, as the leaders of the West and the key victor power, were interested in building up Germany (including a German army) as a bulwark against the Soviet Union. The French thus saw that their best possible course was to embed Germany in a broader European and international framework—one that allowed for a partial revival of German power but that gave France and other countries permanent levers of influence over Germany. The ECSC was the European core of that framework, soon to grow into the European Community (EC). There was also a transatlantic component to the framework, namely the North Atlantic Treaty Organization (NATO), which the United States and its allies began building with the 1949 Washington Treaty and which was completed with Germany's admission to NATO in 1955. Together these institutions provided a stable setting in which France and Germany gradually overcame their resentments and suspicions by working toward shared or at least mutually compatible objectives.

Over time, reconciliation came to be based as much on changed attitudes as on the external framework, as leaders such as Adenauer and French President Charles de Gaulle and later Helmut Schmidt and Valery Giscard d'Estaing developed close personal relationships and as new generations grew up without the wartime memories. As could be seen in the major turning points in the history of European integration, this combination of pro-European idealism and the pragmatic pursuit of national interest has been a key feature of the integration process, one that helps to explain and in turn itself reflects the Franco-German reconciliation that began with the founding of the ECSC.

The institutions of the ECSC also became the first genuinely supranational bodies in Europe, able to act in their areas of competence with a degree of independence from the national governments of the member states. For the first time European states had transferred sovereignty from the national level to central institutions. This supranationality was to become the decisive feature of European integration after 1950, and remains the aspect that most differentiates today's EU from other regional groupings such as the Association of Southeast Asian Nations (ASEAN) or the North American Free Trade Agreement (NAFTA).

Until the expiration of the Treaty of Paris in July 2002, the ECSC was one of the three European Communities that was folded into the EU established under the Maastricht treaty, exercising authority over the coal and steel industries of the Union. By the 1970s, its importance had declined with the relative decline of these industries. Indeed, it was ironic that an organization that was founded to manage a pool of what in the early 1950s were very scarce resources, by the 1970s had found a new role in managing the decline of parts of Europe's coal and steel industries—by, for example, monitoring state subsidies to loss-making plants and helping unemployed miners and steelworkers with retraining. The historical importance of the ECSC remains, however, and is reflected in the fact that the EU's institutions celebrate May 9 as Schuman Day, in effect the national holiday of united Europe.

The European Economic Community (EEC) and Euratom

The ECSC's scope of activity was by definition quite limited. It dealt with a single economic sector, and it could not negotiate tariffs with foreign countries. It thus was understandable that the members should try to build upon their initial success

Box 2.1   The Founding Fathers

Konrad Adenauer (1876–1967). As the first chancellor (1949–1963) of the Federal Republic of Germany, Adenauer was responsible for making West Germany a founding member of the EC. A lawyer by training, he was a member of the prewar Roman Catholic Center party and served as the mayor of Cologne from 1917 to 1933. An opponent of the Nazis, he was removed from his post when Hitler came to power. After World War II, he helped to draft the West German constitution and to found a new political party, the Christian Democratic Union. Adenauer believed that the key to restoring Germany's place in the world after its defeat and disgrace under Hitler was reconciliation with France and integration with the other West European democracies. He therefore embraced Schuman's ECSC proposal and later overcame domestic German opposition to the formation of the EEC and Euratom. Adenauer also won the trust of the United States and oversaw West Germany's integration into NATO.

Alcide de Gasperi (1881–1954). Born in what before World War I was still an Italian-speaking part of Austria-Hungary, de Gasperi was educated in Vienna and served for a time in the Austrian parliament. In 1925, he became a founder of the forerunner party to the postwar Italian Christian Democratic party. Persecuted by Mussolini for his political activities, he was imprisoned and later exiled to the Vatican, where he lived for fourteen years. He served as prime minister from December 1945 to July 1953 and was responsible for bringing Italy into the ECSC, thereby establishing Italy as a founding member of the Communities, a status that Italy continues to emphasize in today's enlarged EU.

Jean Monnet (1888–1979). Monnet is known as the "father of Europe." Born in Cognac, France, he entered the family brandy business at a young age and traveled widely on behalf of the firm. During World War I he gained experience in international cooperation by serving as a French official on a French-British committee that jointly managed shipping in the war against Germany. He worked in private business in the interwar years, but in World War II was again involved in supply matters, serving the British government as a senior official responsible for purchasing war material from the United States. After the war he headed the French planning agency responsible for modernizing French industry. In 1950 he hit upon the plan for a coal and

and look for ways to broaden the scope of economic integration. After an abortive attempt in 1952–1954 to form a European Defense Community, the foreign ministers of the six ECSC states met in Messina, Italy, in June 1955 to consider ways to carry forward the integration process. At the time, two potential courses of action were widely discussed: a further stage of *sectoral* integration based on a proposed atomic energy community, and a plan for *market* integration through the elimination of barriers to trade and the eventual creation of a common market. Those in Europe who saw integration primarily as a process of building up shared institutions and accomplishing common projects tended to stress the importance of the atomic energy community. They included Monnet himself and many of his compatriots. Others, especially in West Germany and the Netherlands, saw European integration more as a process of tearing down intra-European barriers and emphasized the common market. These two approaches came to be known as "positive" and "negative" integration, and both have played a role in the development of Europe.

steel community and managed to sell this idea to Schuman and other leading politicians. When the ECSC was established in 1952, he became the first president of its High Authority. In 1955 Monnet resigned this post to head the Action Committee for the United States of Europe, a group of politicians and trade union leaders that lobbied for further steps toward integration. He is associated with the "Monnet method" of taking practical steps in the economic field to advance the grand vision of a European political union.

Robert Schuman (1886–1963). Best known for proposing that France and Germany place their coal and steel industries under joint management, Schuman was ideally suited to the task of bringing about a reconciliation between these two former enemies. Born in Luxembourg of French parents, he grew up in his father's native province of Lorraine, which Germany had annexed from France in 1871 after the Franco-Prussian War. A devout Catholic, he spoke French at home but attended German universities. When Lorraine was restored to France after World War I, Schuman became active in French politics. He was elected to the French parliament in 1919, where he served for forty years. In World War II he was a member of the French resistance. After the war, he served as prime minister, foreign minister, and defense minister in various governments. As foreign minister, on May 9, 1950, he issued the famous Schuman Declaration, proposing what was to become the ECSC. A passionate advocate of European integration, Schuman later served as the first president of the ECSC-EEC-Euratom joint parliamentary assembly.

   Paul-Henri Spaak (1899–1972). Spaak was a prominent Belgian politician who served as prime minister in 1938–1939. After Belgium was occupied by Nazi Germany in May 1940, he fled to London, where he spent four years and was active in resistance circles. He emerged from the war committed to European integration and strong international alliances, which he saw as the best way to prevent yet another world war from breaking out on European soil. He served as prime minister and foreign minister in various postwar governments and was involved in many of the early steps toward building a new Europe: as the first chairman of the OEEC, as president of the Consultative Assembly of the Council of Europe, and as a supporter of the proposed ECSC. His most important contribution to European integration was to chair the Intergovernmental Conference (IGC) that negotiated the treaties establishing the EEC and Euratom.

At Messina, the ministers agreed to establish a committee charged with studying these options and formulating concrete proposals. The Spaak Committee (named for its chairman, Belgian Foreign Minister Paul-Henri Spaak) presented its report to the May 1956 Venice meeting of foreign ministers. It struck a balance between the two approaches to integration and proposed that the ECSC member states create both a European Atomic Energy Community (EAEC, also known as Euratom) and a European Economic Community (EEC). Following detailed and arduous negotiations, in Rome on March 25, 1957, the six signed two treaties creating these new entities.

Like the ECSC, Euratom subsequently came to play an important role in a single sector of the economy. It promoted the development of nuclear power and a common pool of radioactive fuels for Western Europe's growing stock of nuclear reactors. Of the two institutions created in 1957, however, the EEC proved to be by far the more important. The agreement establishing the EEC became known as the Treaty of Rome, and remains in many ways the core constitutional document of today's EU.

The central feature of the EEC was the establishment of a common market among its member states. (For many years the EEC was referred to in the American press simply as the common market, even though this was not its official designation.) The Treaty of Rome called for "the elimination, as between Member States, of customs duties and quantitative restrictions on the import and export of goods, and of all other measures having equivalent effect."[5] It provided for the creation of a customs union through the phasing out, in stages, of all tariffs and quantitative restrictions on trade among the member states. This was to be accomplished over a period of twelve years, from 1958 to 1970.

The treaty also called for the "abolition, as between Member States, of obstacles to the free movement of persons, services and capital."[6] The common market thus was not limited to trade in goods, but was to be built around what became known as the "four freedoms." The treaty further specified that the common market "shall extend to agriculture and trade in agricultural products."[7] However, the founders of the Community recognized that agricultural production and the problems faced by farmers required a separate set of policies from those that applied to the market for industrial goods. A common market in agricultural goods thus was introduced not through the removal of national barriers, but by the establishment of the Common Agricultural Policy (CAP), the general outlines of which were specified in the treaty.

The external counterpart to the customs union was the establishment of a common customs tariff and a common commercial policy toward third countries. The ECSC did not have a common external tariff for coal and steel products, which meant that it relied on a complicated system of rules of origin enforced by intra-ECSC border checks to ensure that steel imported from outside the ECSC and destined for a high tariff country could not be imported through a low tariff country and transshipped to its ultimate destination. In contrast, the common external tariff was intended to facilitate the free circulation of goods, both domestic and imported, throughout the Community. Products imported from the United States to, for example, the Netherlands could be shipped to Germany or another member state as if they were Dutch domestic products. The importer would pay the tariff only once, at the port of entry.

Like the customs union, the common external tariff was introduced progressively, with the first stage of harmonization completed by the end of 1962. The level of the common tariff was set by means of a simple arithmetic average. Relatively high French and Italian tariffs were averaged with the lower tariffs of Germany and the Benelux customs union to produce a common external tariff. The level of the tariff varied according to type of goods (industrial countries traditionally place low or even zero tariffs on fuel and raw materials needed by their domestic industries, and much higher tariffs on manufactured goods), but the average was around 15 percent at the end of the first stage. In addition to the common external tariff, the common commercial policy called for the adoption by the member states of uniform practices with regard to such trade-related matters as aid for exports to third countries, nontariff restrictions on imports from third countries, and measures against dumping and unfair trade practices by non-Community members.

The Treaty of Rome used the basic institutional framework established for the ECSC. The High Authority for the EEC was called the Commission. It was granted broad executive powers, including the sole right to initiate Community legislation. The original Commission had nine members, two from each of the large member states (France, Germany, and Italy) and one from each of the three smaller countries. A Council of Ministers was to be the main decision-making body of the EEC, in which representatives of the member states would vote on proposals put forward by the Commission. The chairmanship of the Council rotated, with each member state serving as Council president for a six-month period. As in the ECSC, votes in the Council could be made on the basis of unanimity or majority voting. Euratom had its own commission and council of ministers. The Treaty of Rome also introduced qualified majority voting (QMV)—a weighted system that assigns votes in rough proportion to the population sizes of the member states and that requires a certain critical mass of votes to pass a measure. In practice, qualified majority voting was disliked by some member state political leaders, notably de Gaulle of France, as too supranational and was little used until the 1980s.

The member states agreed that the three communities—the ECSC, Euratom, and the EEC—would share the same Common Assembly and Court of Justice. The ECSC High Authority remained in Luxembourg, but the new European Commission was established in Brussels, which became the de facto capital of uniting Europe. The Common Assembly was situated in Strasbourg, France, already the venue of the Parliamentary Assembly of the Council of Europe. The treaty also provided for the establishment of two other institutions, the Economic and Social Committee (ESC) and the European Investment Bank (EIB), that were to play much lesser roles in Community policy making.

BRITAIN AND THE FOUNDING OF EFTA

Like its predecessor, the ECSC, the EC was founded on a much narrower membership base than the institutions established in the late 1940s. Monnet and his colleagues were not opposed to participation by Britain and the Scandinavian countries, but they were unwilling to dilute or slow the pace of their ambitious plans to suit British preferences. At Messina, Britain was asked by the six to join the negotiations, but again it declined—for both political and what its leaders thought were valid economic reasons. Although much weakened by World War II and internal problems, Britain still was the largest and most productive economy in Europe. In areas such as banking and finance, aviation, and nuclear and defense technology, the British were accustomed to viewing themselves as competitors and partners of the United States rather than as one of the medium powers of Europe.

Britain also had special ties with the Commonwealth that were hard to reconcile with the Community's customs union and the exclusionary CAP. It obtained much of its food from traditional suppliers in Canada, Australia, and New Zealand, who would have been displaced by the Community agriculture policy, which was to be based on the principle of preference for other Community suppliers. Britain also was concerned about the pound sterling, which like the dollar was a reserve currency held by central banks and used by some countries in international transactions not necessarily involving British trade or business. By entering a European customs union, London might have lost the policy flexibility to take measures needed to protect sterling's role in the world.

Declining to participate in the Community but not wishing to lose out on the economic benefits of increased trade in Europe, Britain took the lead in organizing an alternative organization, the European Free Trade Association (EFTA). Proposed in 1959 and formally established the following year, EFTA included Britain, Portugal, the Scandinavian countries, Austria, and Switzerland. Finland became an associate member in 1961. All of these countries had close economic and cultural ties with Britain or were politically neutral and thus unwilling to join a European Community with supranational aspirations and whose members were also all members of NATO. EFTA established a free trade area for industrial goods among its members, but it did not erect a common external tariff or launch common agricultural, transport, or other policies. Above all, it had none of the supranational political institutions that were being established in Brussels, Luxembourg, and Strasbourg.

DEVELOPMENT OF THE COMMUNITY IN THE 1960s

The basic legal and institutional framework of the Community was set in the Treaty of Rome, and there were no major treaty revisions for nearly thirty years. This did not mean, however, that the legal and institutional situation was static. There was ongoing debate within and among the member states about how strong the central institutions of the Community should be, relative to the national governments. A series of judgments from the European Court of Justice (ECJ) tended to strengthen the integration process by ruling against national laws and policies that ran counter to the letter or the spirit of the founding treaties.

From 1958 to the mid-1960s, the Community was preoccupied with phasing in the policies outlined, mostly in framework form, in the Treaty of Rome. The Council of Ministers approved the basic principles for the CAP in December 1960. Tariffs and quotas on trade between member states were dismantled in accordance with the treaty. In part because economic growth was strong and incomes were rising, the member states refrained from invoking the various safeguard clauses contained in the treaty, and actually agreed to accelerate the timetable for completion of the common market. In other areas, development of the Community fell short of federalist aspirations. For example, the six did little to implement provisions in the treaty calling for a Common Transport Policy, and they largely ignored the area of social policy—in both cases as a result of member state opposition to strong action.

As the Community developed and proved its economic value, it somewhat paradoxically faced a growing political challenge from within its own ranks. The source of this challenge was de Gaulle, a leader of the French resistance in World War II who had retired from an active role in politics in 1946, but who returned to power in 1958 amid the crisis caused by France's colonial war in Algeria. De Gaulle had pushed through a series of constitutional changes that created a strong presidency, a post he himself occupied for the next decade. The French leader broke with his European partners on the issue of the powers and responsibilities of the Community's institutions. De Gaulle believed that France needed to be strong and independent—to recover the national greatness that she had lost in World War II. He thus was extremely wary of surrendering French sovereignty to the newly created supranational bodies in Brussels. He wanted a strong Europe, able to assert itself against the United States and the Soviet Union, but he wanted it to be a Europe of cooperating states, not a federal Europe in which historic nation-states such as France would lose their political freedom of action and ultimately their identity.

The issue of supranationalism came to a head in mid-1965 over the question of CAP financing. With the phasing in of the common market running ahead of schedule, in the spring of 1965 Commission president Walter Hallstein proposed that the EC acquire its "own resources" (i.e., revenue raised directly by the EC, rather than contributed to the EC budget by the member states) in July 1967, some three years ahead of schedule. Hallstein further proposed a new budgetary mechanism in which the Commission and the European Parliament would have enhanced powers, and the powers of the member states in the Council of Ministers would diminish through the use of qualified majority voting in place of unanimity for certain issues. De Gaulle saw these proposals as a grab for power by a nascent superstate in Brussels and an attack on French sovereignty. He responded by announcing the policy of the "empty chair." Throughout the second half of 1965 France boycotted all meetings of the Council of Ministers. The Commission and the other member states deplored this tactic, but for six months Community business all but ground to a halt.[8]

The crisis was resolved in January 1966 with the adoption by the six of what became known, after the site of the meeting, as the Luxembourg Compromise.[9] The "compromise" was little more than an agreement to disagree. The six pledged that when issues very important to one or more states were to be decided, the Council of Ministers would try to reach decisions by unanimity. France registered its view—not endorsed by others—that when important issues were at stake unanimity *had* to be reached to take a decision. While noting the disagreement on this constitutional point, the six concluded that there was no need to prolong the impasse in Community decision making. Hallstein retreated from his proposals, France took her place in the Council, and normal business resumed. The effect of the 1965 crisis on the Community was profound. While the other five members would not yield to de Gaulle's attempt to reinterpret the Treaty of Rome by imposing the unanimity requirement, they had no wish to provoke another crisis. They thus tended to make decisions by consensus—a practice that lasted until well into the 1980s. The powers of the Commission were cut back, as it was widely blamed for provoking the crisis by reaching prematurely for more authority. These developments all tended to slow decision making in the EC and helped to reverse the momentum toward a federal Europe that had built up in the late 1950s and early 1960s.

The second major issue over which France broke with its partners was that of British membership. It took only four years from the signing of the Treaty of Rome for the British government to conclude that it had underestimated the importance and the staying power of the EC and that Britain risked economic isolation by not becoming a member. The composition of British trade gradually was shifting from the Commonwealth to Europe, thereby reducing the importance of the CAP as an obstacle to membership and bolstering pro-European sentiment in British industry. Impressed by early successes in tariff reductions and the continued rapid economic growth in the Community, Britain formally applied for membership in August 1961. It was joined by Ireland, Denmark, and Norway, all of which conducted much of their trade with Britain and had little choice but to follow its lead on integration issues.

While the other member state governments generally were pleased by Britain's change of heart, de Gaulle had reasons for opposing London's application. He was suspicious of Britain's close ties with the United States and committed to a vision of the Community as primarily a Franco-German enterprise, with France playing the leading role in tandem with a politically docile Germany. He and other French officials were concerned that premature entry for Britain would hinder development of the CAP, important for French agriculture, and turn the Community into a loose free trade area rather than a cohesive customs union with emerging common policies and long-term ambitions to play a more assertive role on the world scene. In January 1963 de Gaulle publicly voiced his doubts about Britain's suitability for membership—a move that led to the suspension of accession negotiations with the four applicant countries shortly thereafter. Britain again applied to join in May 1967, accompanied by the same trio of countries. But it was not until de Gaulle's passing from the political stage in 1969 that negotiations could resume, and not until 1973 that Britain finally achieved what it might have had in the 1950s had it chosen to become a founding member.

THE HAGUE SUMMIT

Completion on July 1, 1968, of the transition period of the EC—the customs union and the common external tariff—and the retirement of de Gaulle from French politics in 1969 set the stage for a further phase of integration. The new French president, Georges Pompidou, was less suspicious than his predecessor of the UK and more interested in bringing it into the EC as a counterweight to the rising power of West Germany. Pompidou got off to a fresh start with Europe by proposing to convene a special meeting of heads of state and government to review developments in the Community and to launch new integration initiatives. Only the fourth such summit in EC history, this meeting took place in The Hague in December 1969.

The Hague summit was the starting point for several ambitious, long-term initiatives that were to preoccupy the Community over the next several decades and that even today are central to the EU's agenda. France lifted its opposition to enlargement, clearing the way for the start of accession negotiations with the four prospective member states in June 1970. At the same time, the leaders of the six adopted several proposals aimed at deepening the Community in parallel with the expected process of widening. They agreed in principle to the gradual formation of an economic and monetary union (EMU) and appointed Pierre Werner, prime minister of Luxembourg, to chair a committee of experts to develop a plan for such a union. They also asked their foreign ministers to prepare a report on progress toward political union, meaning primarily cooperation in foreign policy matters. In addition to these specific initiatives, the summit generated a new atmosphere—the "spirit of the Hague"—and a widespread feeling that the Community again was on the move after the setbacks of 1965–1969.

These decisions to both widen and deepen took place against the backdrop of a changing international situation that heightened the importance of the Community for its member states. The United States had been bogged down in Vietnam since the mid-1960s, turning somewhat away from the primary focus on Europe of the Cold War period. In Germany, Willy Brandt, a social democrat and the former mayor of West Berlin, had been elected chancellor in October 1969, and was beginning to pursue his Ostpolitik with the communist countries of central and eastern Europe, based on political agreements and expanded trade and cultural contacts.[10] As West Germany looked east, Brandt saw a need to anchor the country more firmly in the EC, both to dispel concerns among his allies about a more independent and assertive German policy and to bolster his negotiating leverage with the communist regimes. Along with continued turbulence in world financial markets—downward pressure on the dollar linked to inflation and the economic problems associated with the Vietnam War—these factors all argued in favor of a stronger and wider EC.

Negotiations between the six and all four prospective member states were completed in January 1972 with the signature of individual treaties of accession. The negotiations with Denmark and Ireland were relatively straightforward, although Ireland's neutral status and its desire to protect its right to set national laws on sensitive social and religious issues such as divorce and abortion presented some complications. The talks with Britain were more difficult and revolved around the import of butter and sugar from the Commonwealth, fishing rights for EC vessels in British waters, and Britain's contributions to the Community budget. With all sides committed to accession, these issues were resolved, but at the cost of storing up trouble for the next generation of British and EC leaders, as Britain's net contribution to the EC budget became a major point of contention in the late 1970s and early 1980s.

Following ratification in the parliaments of the candidate countries and of the six member states (and a March 1972 referendum in France called by Pompidou), Britain, Denmark, and Ireland became full members of all three communities on January 1, 1973. This was to be the first of five Community enlargements—one that set a pattern for subsequent negotiations between existing and aspiring member countries. Britain was admitted as a de facto large member state, with the same number of votes in the Council of Ministers and seats in the European Parliament as the big three, as well as the right to nominate two commissioners.

Despite its having signed a treaty of accession, Norway did not complete the accession process. In a national referendum held in September 1972, 53.3 percent of the Norwegian electorate voted against membership. In the debate leading up to the vote, farmers, fishermen, and nationalists concerned about preserving Norway's identity led the fight against membership, managing to prevail over the political and business establishment that generally favored joining the Community. The first country to reject membership, Norway was to some extent a special case, owing to its small size and geographic isolation, but in other respects the Norwegian vote presaged localist and nationalist reaction to European integration that was to become more pronounced in many countries in the 1990s.

Although enlargement was a major achievement, the post-Hague optimism about breakthroughs in other policy areas proved short-lived as Europe fell victim in the 1970s to unfavorable external economic and political conditions: monetary turbulence, the 1973 oil crisis, the 1974–1975 economic recession, and the rise of tensions with the Soviet Union. As a consequence, major policy initiatives were watered down or postponed. In October 1970 the Werner committee delivered its report on EMU, in which it proposed a three-stage plan leading to the completion of economic and monetary union by 1980. The Council of Ministers endorsed the report in March 1971 and the Community took initial steps toward implementation. However, in August of that year U.S. President Richard M. Nixon announced the suspension of the convertibility of the dollar into gold, effectively ending the Bretton Woods par value system and ushering in a new period of global monetary instability. The EC member countries persisted with plans to align their currencies more closely, but diverging inflation rates and different domestic responses to recession led to growing monetary divergences between Germany on the one hand and France, the UK, and Italy on the other. The Community tacitly abandoned the ambitious goals of the Werner report, and it was not until the end of the 1970s that it was able to resume progress toward monetary cooperation.

In accordance with recommendations of the Community foreign ministers solicited by the Hague summit, European Political Cooperation (EPC) was launched in November 1970. Member states agreed to consult on all questions of foreign policy and where possible to undertake common actions on international problems. EPC was to take place on an intergovernmental basis, outside the structures and institutions of the Community. It was based on a political commitment to work together on foreign policy matters, not a transfer of sovereignty to central institutions. But like monetary union, EPC fell short of initial intentions. It laid the groundwork for foreign policy cooperation among the Community member states and was useful in helping to coordinate the European response to changes in east-west relations in the 1970s. For the most part, however, EPC resulted in verbal statements with no real capability for enforcement, nor did it prevent the member states from responding very differently to such events as the 1973 Arab-Israeli war or the 1979 Soviet invasion of Afghanistan.

INSTITUTIONAL DEVELOPMENTS IN THE 1970s

There were two important institutional developments in the 1970s: the establishment of the European Council in 1974 and the first direct elections to the European Parliament (EP) in 1979. The success of the Hague summit and subsequent top-level meetings in 1972, 1973, and 1974 convinced European leaders of the value of periodic, informal summits. Such meetings were the best way to resolve complex issues through bargaining and compromises among the member states that cut across issue areas. They also provided a platform for launching new Community initiatives in a way that ensured political momentum. French President Valery Giscard d'Estaing, who assumed office after Pompidou's death in 1974, and German Chancellor Helmut Schmidt, who took power in the same year, were both former finance ministers used to dealing on a personal basis with their counterparts in other capitals, and both were strong proponents of the Franco-German relationship built upon the tradition of regular meetings between the leaders of the two countries. At the December 1974 Paris summit, the governments of the EC member states agreed to a proposal by Giscard that they meet at least three times each year. These regular gatherings (later changed to twice per year) came to constitute a new institution, the European Council, albeit one that was not given a formal legal base until the entering into effect of the Single European Act (SEA) some twelve years later.

While establishment of the European Council tended to push the Community in an intergovernmental direction—highlighting member state leaders as the driving force in the integration process—direct elections (replacing the existing system in which members of the European Parliament were appointed by national legislatures from among their members) counterbalanced this tendency by strengthening and giving enhanced legitimacy to one of the central institutions of the Community. Following agreement in the European Council in December 1975, the first such elections took place in June 1979. They brought to Strasbourg for the first time a popularly elected body of men and women who could claim to speak for Europe on behalf of the electorate. The powers of the Parliament were still strictly limited, but its members could claim to represent the wishes of the voters at the European level. On this basis they were able to press for increased powers in the following decade.

The 1970s also saw the completion of a remarkable set of political transitions in southern Europe that paved the way for the Community's second and third enlargements. Greece had concluded an association agreement with the Community in 1961 that was intended to lead to eventual membership. However, in April

1967 the Greek military seized control of the government and suspended the constitution, causing the Community to halt further development of ties with Greece.
Military rule collapsed in July 1974, following Greece's disastrous war with Turkey over Cyprus. The new civilian government applied for full EC membership
in June 1975. Although there were grave doubts in Western Europe about whether
this relatively backward country was ready to assume the responsibilities of membership and to compete with the other member states in a fully liberalized market,
European political leaders were keen to bolster the fragile Greek democracy by
welcoming it into the European fold. The Community thus initiated accession negotiations with Greece in July 1976.

Political change also took place on the Iberian peninsula. Since the 1940s,
Spain had enjoyed rather frosty relations with the rest of Western Europe, owing
to lingering resentment about General Francisco Franco's seizure of power during
the 1936–1939 Spanish Civil War and his closeness to the Axis powers during
World War II. When Franco died in November 1975, Spain was ripe for change.
Under Juan Carlos I, the grandson of the last Spanish king, it returned to democracy, becoming a constitutional monarchy, although not without a strong challenge from the newly legalized Spanish Communist Party.

Like Spain, Portugal was ruled by a right-wing dictator, Antonio Salazar. It
had traditionally close relations with Britain, but its position in Europe was marginal owing to its poverty and its determination to retain its African colonies long
after the French, British, and Belgians had relinquished their empires. In April
1974 a group of left-wing officers seized power with a program to stop the colonial
war in Angola and to erect a socialist order. After a political struggle in which
moderate socialist and social democratic forces, with financial and organizational
support from the German Social Democratic Party, rallied to defeat a communist
takeover, constitutional government was resumed in April 1976.

As was the case with regard to Greece, the EC countries wanted to bolster the
new Iberian democracies against threats from the right and the left by offering
economic and political support. Both countries applied for EC membership in
1977, and accession negotiations began with Portugal in October 1978 and with
Spain in February of the following year. Meanwhile, Greece signed an accession
treaty in May 1979 and became the tenth Community member on January 1, 1981.

It was not until well into the 1980s that negotiations were completed with
Spain and Portugal. With a population of over 35 million and a large agricultural
sector that competed directly with the farms of southern France, Italy, and Greece
in such products as wine and olive oil, Spain presented particular challenges that
took time and political will to resolve. Given its smaller size, Portugal posed fewer
difficulties, but its relative poverty and the backwardness of its industry also
dragged out the negotiations and argued for long transition periods in the phasing
in of many EC rules and regulations. Nonetheless, the groundwork for membership had been laid, and Iberian democracy was very much strengthened by its
prospect and the rapid development of business and other ties with the Community.

THE EUROPEAN MONETARY SYSTEM

As the 1970s ended, the Community returned to monetary affairs, establishing the European Monetary System (EMS) as the last major achievement of the decade and a building block of the Community's relaunch in the 1980s. At the time, the dollar was falling on world currency markets, largely in response to high inflation and rising oil imports in the United States. This tended to increase monetary instability in Europe (as investors and speculators sold dollars and bought German marks, thereby driving down the franc and lira against the mark), and damaged European exports on world markets. Irritated by what they saw as the "malign neglect" of the dollar in Washington and concerned about Europe's own weakness in the monetary sphere, the EC countries began to look anew at the problem of restoring monetary coherence in the Community.

While there was no question at the time of reviving the overly ambitious scheme for EMU put forward in the Werner report, in October 1977 Commission president Roy Jenkins put forward a proposal for enhanced monetary cooperation. Giscard and Schmidt expressed support for Jenkins's ideas and became the main political backers of a renewed push toward monetary cooperation. Their efforts led to the founding, in March 1979, of the EMS, a system of fixed but adjustable currency rates built around a central unit of account, the European Currency Unit (ECU). The main purpose of the EMS, which operated within the framework of the EC, was to limit and to smooth out divergences among the EC country currencies that had a disruptive effect on the functioning of the internal market. As will be seen in chapter 6, the relative success of EMS in the 1980s laid the basis for a renewed and ultimately successful effort to reach EMU in the 1990s.

Relaunch in the 1980s

The early 1980s was a difficult period for European integration. With economic recession and stagflation caused by the second oil crisis (precipitated by the 1979 revolution in Iran), governments were in no mood for bold new initiatives. European industry was threatened by intensified competition from Japan and other Asian countries, as Europe lost competitiveness in traditional industries such as cars, steel, shipbuilding, and textiles but failed to establish sufficiently strong positions in newer industries such as computers, electronics, and aviation.

Tensions between the United States and the Soviet Union were on the rise, which also led to increased strains across the Atlantic. Ronald Reagan, inaugurated U.S. president in January 1981, toughened the U.S. position toward the Soviet Union. He increased defense spending, was skeptical about arms control agreements, and in March 1983 called for the development of a space-based defense system against Soviet missiles. West European governments, committed to detente with the East and not eager to boost defense spending or cut back economic ties with the communist countries, resisted Reagan's policies. The high point of transatlantic tensions came in August 1982, when the United States imposed sanctions on French and British firms that were supplying equipment to the Soviet Union for the construction of a pipeline to carry natural gas from Siberia to Western Europe. The United States had tried to block the building of the pipeline, arguing that it would give the Soviet Union economic leverage over Western Europe. The EC strongly protested what it regarded as an "extra-territorial" exercise of U.S. law, and even enacted legislation forbidding European companies to comply with the sanctions.

While many of Europe's difficulties could be blamed on external factors over which it had little or no control, there also was a new questioning about the viability of the European welfare state model that in its different national forms had seemed to work so effectively in the 1950s and 1960s, reconciling high economic growth with concern for social justice, but that appeared to be breaking down since the 1970s. Britain had been experiencing economic decline (relative to other industrialized countries) since the 1940s, which usually was attributed to a variety of factors including low investment, strikes and trade union militancy, and stop-and-go government policies that resulted in a cycle of growth followed by inflation leading to recession. Prime Minister Margaret Thatcher was elected in May 1979 on a platform committed to reducing the government's role in the economy, privatizing nationalized industries, and breaking the power of the unions. Thatcher also was rather skeptical of European integration.

On the continent, the major economies fared somewhat better, but they too were under strain. After rapid wage increases associated with trade union militancy in the late 1960s, Italy suffered large trade and budget deficits, high inflation, and a weak lira in the 1970s. Italian governments sought to restructure the economy, but encountered strong resistance from the unions and the Italian Communist party. France and West Germany also struggled to adjust to more difficult economic circumstances by reining in the growth of wages and slowing the growth of the welfare state.

The EC of the 1970s and early 1980s had limited relevance for national governments as they struggled to cope with economic problems at home. To some extent Thatcher even assumed the role once played by de Gaulle—that of a nationalist opponent to Brussels-based integration. Thatcher's only important interest in the EC seemed to be to obtain a rebate of the large sums that Britain was paying into the Community budget, mainly as a consequence of the CAP. In this period, terms like "Europessimism" and "Eurosclerosis" took hold and were widely popularized.

The difficult economic and political circumstances of the early 1980s eventually led, by mid-decade, to a relaunch of the Community, the centerpiece of which was the SEA, the first major revision of the founding treaties since the conclusion of the Treaty of Rome in 1957. The product of an intergovernmental conference in 1985–1986, the first important IGC since the decisive Messina conference of 1955, the SEA had two aspects, one institutional and the other substantive. It reformed and strengthened the EC's institutions, and it set a new list of policy tasks for these institutions to pursue, notably the "1992" single market program.

Reform of decision making had been under discussion in the Community for some time. In November 1981 foreign ministers Hans-Dietrich Genscher of Germany and Emilio Colombo of Italy presented to the European Parliament a joint proposal for a European act designed to strengthen the external profile of the Community. The key elements of the Genscher-Colombo plan were a proposal to bring the existing structures of the three European Communities and EPC together in a single framework subject to the political guidance of the European Council, a strengthening of the powers of the EP, and a reform of the Community decision-making process by lessening the role of the national veto.[11] This German-Italian proposal was not embraced by all of the member states, but it was an early indicator of the pressures for reform building in at least some national capitals and in the EP.

The directly elected members of the Parliament tended to be strong supporters of European integration, and many of them were unhappy with the bogging down of the integration process that had taken place with the worsening economic conditions in the 1970s. Declaring that revision of the Treaty of Rome was the key to a successful relaunch of the Community, in February 1984 the European Parliament approved a "Draft Treaty establishing the European Union."[12] This was a purely political gesture—the conclusion or amendment of treaties was the prerogative of the member states—but one that reflected the growing sentiment in favor of a new treaty. As indicated in the title of the draft, much of the reform focus was on a "European Union," a somewhat vague term that meant not only a closer drawing together of the member states within the Community, but a fusion of the economic side of integration with aspects of cooperation, notably EPC, that took place outside the Community structures. In the view of the proponents of a union, the whole process of integration needed streamlining and rationalization.

Responding to these pressures, at the 1984 Fontainebleau summit the leaders agreed to a proposal by French President François Mitterrand to establish a committee to explore ways to improve the functioning of the Community and of EPC. Known as the Dooge Committee after its chairman, former Irish foreign minister James Dooge, this grouping consisted of one high-level representative from each member state. At the same meeting, the European leaders finally resolved the long-standing problem of British overpayments to the Community budget, thus at least neutralizing Thatcher's opposition to new Community initiatives.

THE SINGLE MARKET

Calls for institutional reform were accompanied by a growing interest in the relaunch of the Community through a single market program—a concerted effort to eliminate the barriers to trade in goods that had remained in place after the completion of the common market in 1968 and to liberalize trade in services and the flow of capital. The parallel development of these two themes—institutional reform and completion of the single market—was important in winning broad support for changes in the founding treaties. Thatcher was wary of surrendering sovereignty to Brussels and suspicious of proposals to strengthen the Community for its own sake, but she was open to institutional reform that might be needed to promote freer trade. The European business community, concerned about lagging economic growth and high costs, also generated ideas for and became a strong supporter of a program to complete the single market. Upon assuming the presidency of the European Commission in January 1985, Jacques Delors proposed an ambitious single market plan, choosing the end of 1992 as a target date for implementation. Under the leadership of Arthur Cockfield, the British commissioner responsible for the internal market, the Commission produced a white paper outlining three hundred measures that would need to be passed at the Community level to eliminate intra-EC barriers. Many of these proposals had been on the table for years, and completing the single market was not in itself a radically new idea. What was new was the sense of urgency, the existence of a comprehensive plan, and a willingness on the part of the member states to contemplate changes in Community decision making to ensure that plans were transformed into action.

THE INTERGOVERNMENTAL CONFERENCE

Dooge's Ad Hoc Committee on Institutional Reform presented its final report to the March 1985 Brussels summit.[13] It called for both a broadening of the EC's objectives and areas of responsibility and for selected institutional reforms that would strengthen the Community and speed decision making, particularly in regard to single market matters. To achieve these objectives, it recommended convening an IGC among the member states that would draw up a new Treaty of European Union. The report did not command universal support for all of its points. The British, Danish, and Greek members of the committee declined to endorse its central recommendation for an IGC, and other members dissented on lesser points. But the general thrust of the report was toward significant changes in the Treaty of Rome as a way of restarting the integration process and ensuring that a single market program could be implemented.

The European Council took up the Dooge Report at its June 1985 session in Milan, the same meeting at which it endorsed Delors's plan for the single market. Italy, a founding member and traditionally a strong proponent of closer integration, occupied the Council presidency, and Prime Minister Bettino Craxi was determined to achieve an outcome that would move the Community forward. Under Article 236 of the Treaty of Rome, the member states were empowered to call at any time, by simple majority vote, an IGC to negotiate treaty revisions.[14] This provision had never been invoked, however, in part because there was limited interest in such revisions but also because, following the Luxembourg Compromise, governments invariably took major decisions by consensus, even when the treaties allowed for majority or qualified majority voting. After hours of discussion in which Thatcher argued against convening an IGC, Craxi forced a vote on whether to call a conference. The result was 7 to 3, with Britain, Denmark, and Greece opposed. Thatcher was furious at what she saw as an unprecedented disregard of the rule of consensus within the European Council and concerned that the more integration-minded states would use the IGC to push forward a strengthening of the EC's supranational powers. But Britain also supported the single market program, the substance of which by then was closely intertwined with the perceived need for procedural reform. Thus Britain as well as the other dissenters approached the IGC ready to play a constructive role, although determined to block the most ambitious reform proposals.

The IGC began during the Luxembourg presidency in September 1985, and over the next six months entailed seven meetings of the Community foreign ministers, numerous other meetings of two high-level working groups, written submissions on the part of national governments, and intense bargaining among the Community leaders at the December 1985 Luxembourg summit. The result was a new treaty that was formally signed in Luxembourg on February 17, 1986.[15] The original proposal to conclude a Treaty on European Union had fallen away during the negotiations. It was Delors who suggested that the treaty be called *L'Acte Unique*—the Single Act or, as it came to be called, the Single European Act (SEA).[16] "Single" was used because the treaty unified the economic aspects of the Community, which had always been governed by the Treaty of Rome (and the founding treaties of Euratom and the ECSC), and European Political Cooperation, which hitherto had been carried out among the member governments outside the Community legal framework. The treaty came into effect on July 1, 1987, after all member states had ratified. Ten of the member states were able to do so following favorable votes in their national parliaments, but two—Denmark and Ireland—held national referendums in which the treaty was approved directly by the voters.

INSTITUTIONAL REFORM

The SEA both broadened the Community's areas of responsibility and, as had long been suggested by proponents of institutional reform, made important changes in decision-making processes. New policy areas not mentioned in the Treaty of Rome but added to EC competence included environment, research and technology, and "economic and social cohesion" (meaning regional policy aimed at narrowing income disparities between different parts of the Community). The SEA also inserted a new article in the Treaty of Rome that specified completion of the internal market by 1992.

Changes in decision-making procedures dealt with the Council of Ministers, the EP, and the ECJ. The SEA specified that for certain policy areas the Council was empowered to take decisions by qualified majority vote. These areas included some social policy matters, implementation of decisions relating to regional funds and Community research and development programs, and, most important, most measures "which have as their object the establishment and functioning of the internal market." This last amendment, expressed in a new article inserted in the Treaty of Rome, was the crucial change that Delors and others saw as essential to allowing the completion of the single market program by the 1992 deadline.[17]

The SEA also increased the power of the European Parliament. Whereas the Treaty of Rome required only that it be consulted on legislation proposed by the Commission before its adoption or rejection by the Council of Ministers, the SEA introduced a cooperation procedure under which the Parliament could demand from the Council of Ministers an explanation as to why its proposed amendments had not been adopted. The treaty also introduced an assent procedure under which the Parliament was required to approve, by simple majority vote, certain key legislative actions, including the Community budget and association agreements with other countries and international organizations. These changes expanded the power of the European Parliament and marked a further stage in its transition from a consultative to a genuinely legislative body.

In the judicial sphere, the SEA made one important change, by providing for the establishment of a new Court of First Instance. In the decades since the establishment of the ECSC, the importance of the ECJ had steadily increased, as the Court was called upon to interpret Community law and to adjudicate legal disputes between the Community and its member states, among institutions of the Community, and between private firms and citizens and member state governments. One effect of the growing importance of the Court was a rising workload. To address this problem, the SEA empowered the Council to establish a new Court of First Instance to hear cases of less than constitutional importance.

Finally, the SEA introduced an important change in the foreign policy sphere by creating a legal basis for EPC. Under the terms of the act, the signatories henceforth were bound by legal agreement, rather than just a political commitment, to consult and cooperate with each other in the foreign policy sphere. However, the EPC itself was not (unlike, for example, such new policy areas as environment or regional policy) incorporated into the Treaty of Rome. There thus was no such thing as a Community foreign policy, but only an agreement among the member states of the Community that they would forge a common foreign policy. This meant that foreign policy would remain a matter for intergovernmental cooperation rather than supranational coordination. Community institutions such as the Commission would not have a role in EPC, and foreign policy decisions would not be subject to the jurisdiction of the ECJ. To facilitate foreign policy cooperation, the SEA established an EPC secretariat that was charged with preparing meetings and assisting with policy coordination between meetings of the Council.

The SEA was an uneasy compromise between those in Europe who wanted a major push forward to political union and those, like the British and the Danes, who would have preferred not to convene an IGC at all. It introduced important reforms in the Community's founding treaty and demonstrated that the member states could use the mechanism of an intergovernmental conference to push the integration process forward. Above all, it elevated to the level of a legal principle the key goal—a single market by the end of 1992—that was to preoccupy the Community in the late 1980s and become all but synonymous with the relaunch that Delors had sought to achieve. It also provided added means to achieve that goal through expanded use of qualified majority voting and created the basis for a stronger Community external profile on the eve of what was to become an extraordinary period of international change.

THE IBERIAN ENLARGEMENT

The June 1985 decision to convene an IGC coincided with the conclusion, after many years of negotiation, of accession treaties with Portugal and Spain. The long period of negotiation reflected the many complex issues that needed to be resolved owing to the relative poverty of both countries and to the special characteristics of their economies. Both countries were formally admitted on January 1, 1986, raising the total membership to twelve. Spain was treated as a large member state with a right to nominate two members of the Commission but, given its smaller population, it was not accorded the same number of votes in the Council of Ministers or seats in the European Parliament as the four largest member states.

Following accession, the CAP had to adjust to the problems of expanded production of wine, olive oil, and other Mediterranean products. Enlargement also increased the importance of Community-funded development aid. The Community had long provided such aid to southern Italy, but it now was faced with the much more daunting task of trying to raise the two new members as well as Greece and Ireland to the average income level of the rest of the Community. On balance, however, the Iberian enlargement proceeded more smoothly than many experts had predicted, and membership enjoyed strong public support in both countries.

Maastricht and the European Union

By the end of the 1980s the situation in the EC was characterized by a mix of enthusiasm generated by the successes of the single market program and the Iberian enlargement and dissatisfaction in many quarters with what was seen as unfinished business on the Community agenda. The EMS had been functioning quite well for nearly a decade, but the plans for economic and monetary union outlined in the 1970 Werner report had been abandoned. Similarly, the modest institutional reforms of the SEA were a far cry from realization of the ambitious calls for political union discussed in the early 1980s.

For practical reasons, Delors in his first term had focused on the single market program, but he remained a keen supporter of EMU, ready to return to it when political conditions were more favorable. The French and several other member states also were interested in EMU, which was seen as a way of replacing the de facto German dominance over monetary policy in the EMS with a more symmetrical system in which all member states would make decisions in a European system of central banks. German Chancellor Helmut Kohl and Foreign Minister Genscher also were favorable toward EMU, although they had to tread warily in the face of domestic opposition from those afraid of losing the mark, a symbol of German postwar economic stability. Political reform was less prominent in discussions of the Community's future, but it played a certain role, especially since Germany had stated that moves toward economic and monetary union should be accompanied by a strengthening of political union, lest the "democratic deficit" in the Community increase and lead to political alienation on the part of the voters.

Prime Minister Thatcher continued to voice skepticism about both further economic and political integration but, as will be seen, she was unable to block progress in either of these areas.

In June 1988 the European Council appointed a committee, comprised mainly of central bankers and chaired by Delors, to propose specific steps that might lead to EMU. The Delors Committee unveiled its report in April 1989.[18] It followed the basic outlines of the earlier Werner Plan, proposing a three-stage process for reaching EMU and stressing the importance of creating favorable economic conditions before a single currency could be launched. While many in Europe remained skeptical about monetary union, new and more favorable conditions gave reason to believe that the Delors recommendations might succeed where Werner's had failed. EMS had created relative currency stability in Europe and the single market program—particularly those elements dealing with free movement of capital and financial services liberalization—included measures that would make EMU both more necessary and more easy to achieve.

Before the member states could proceed with the recommendations contained in the Delors Report, however, the entire project was unexpectedly caught up in the wider political upheavals rocking the continent. These upheavals helped to pave the way to EMU and ensured that it would be achieved in parallel with a revived project for political union.

THE COLLAPSE OF COMMUNISM

The fall of communism in 1989–1991 came as a surprise to most political leaders and experts in the West. The unraveling of the system began after the coming to power in March 1985 of Mikhail Gorbachev, a would-be reformer who turned out to be the last leader of the Soviet Union. Gorbachev hoped to modernize and strengthen the communist system, not destroy it, but he was unable to control the forces of change that he unleashed. The Soviet economy fell into crisis, some of the non-Russian peoples in the Soviet Union demanded independence, and the Soviet satellites grew restive. By early 1990 Moscow had lost its empire in central and eastern Europe, and by the end of 1991 the Soviet Union itself had fragmented into fifteen newly independent states.[19]

Change in central and eastern Europe began with popular movements for democracy in Poland and Hungary and soon spilled over into the hardline communist dictatorship of East Germany. In the summer and fall of 1989 the East German communist state began to weaken, as thousands of East German citizens emigrated to the West via Hungary, which had opened its border with Austria. On November 9 the East German authorities effectively lost control of their borders, as the Berlin Wall was thrown open. Germans from both sides of the Wall began to plan a common future. In March 1990 the East German regime was forced to stage free elections in which the voters opted overwhelmingly for the pro-unification Christian Democratic party. Following a set of fast-moving negotiations involving the governments of the two German states and the four World

War II victor powers—the Soviet Union, Britain, France, and the United States—
Germany was reunited in October 1990. The five states of the former German
Democratic Republic (GDR), with some 16 million inhabitants, automatically became part of the Community, making Germany by far the biggest member state
but one whose per capita GNP was substantially lower than before unification.

The end of the Cold War and the unification of Germany had enormous implications for the Community, both complicating and making more necessary reforms that had long been on the agenda. The EC had developed primarily as an
economic institution, but it also had been shaped by the political and ideological
conflict on the continent. Strengthening Western Europe against Soviet pressures
always had been an important motivation for supporters of the Community, and
the division of Germany had helped to facilitate integration by making France and
West Germany approximately equal in size and ensuring that the latter looked to
its western neighbors for economic and political partnership, rather than to the
east and southeast of Europe, traditional spheres of German influence. The collapse of communism thus negated two of the underlying preconditions for European integration—the presence of an external enemy and rough equality between
France and Germany—and inevitably raised questions about its future.

Leaders such as Thatcher, Mitterrand, and Dutch prime minister Ruud Lubbers had been skeptical about unification and sought by various diplomatic means
to block or delay it. Once unification became inevitable, however, Mitterrand in
particular was convinced of the need to push ahead with plans to deepen the Community so as to ensure that the new Germany remained firmly anchored in the
West and subject to French influence. He was supported in this by the Germans
themselves, notably Kohl, and by Delors, who saw in the collapse of communism
new and urgent reasons to strengthen the Community.

EMU, already on the political agenda, was a logical vehicle by which to pursue
deepening. The European Council received the Delors Report in June 1989, and at
the same meeting decided that stage one of EMU would begin in July 1990. Progress toward stages two and three would require an IGC and treaty amendments.
At the December 1989 Strasbourg summit the European Council agreed to convene an IGC on EMU by the end of 1990. The leaders also agreed to adopt a social
charter—a Community-wide agreement on labor standards that the trade unions,
strongly backed by Delors, had pressed for as a concomitant to the single European market. Britain did not sign the social charter and it opposed the IGC, but
on both issues it was unable to dissuade the other member states from moving
forward.

The changing international situation also gave new momentum to the old
project for political union. In a strong signal that France and Germany intended
to lead on this issue, in April 1990 Kohl and Mitterrand issued a joint letter in
which they called for new and concrete steps to realize the aspirations to European Political Union already expressed in the SEA. They argued that progress
toward EMU called for strengthening the Community's political side. European
voters could not be expected to accept the surrender of national authority over
economic policy to European institutions that were less subject to democratic con-

trol than national governments. Moreover, only by developing a strong external identity and an effective foreign policy could the Community expect to influence the changes occurring on its eastern borders.

The Kohl-Mitterrand letter set the agenda for an extraordinary session of the European Council in Dublin in April 1990, at which the twelve leaders reaffirmed their commitment to political union. Meeting in the same city two months later, the European Council agreed to convene an IGC on political union to begin at the same time as the IGC on EMU and to run in parallel with it. Both IGCs formally opened at the Rome summit in December 1990. Thus after not holding a single such conference in the three decades after 1955, the Community was to have three IGCs in five years, two of which would run concurrently. This extraordinary situation reflected the extent to which, as Delors had phrased it, history was "accelerating," forcing the Community to respond.

THE NEGOTIATIONS

Conducted as formal diplomatic conferences involving regular meetings at the ministerial and working levels, the IGCs focused on strengthening the decision-making process in areas in which the EC already had competence and on extending the range of issues subject to common policy making. If these were the general goals, there was little agreement among the twelve about how and how quickly they were to be accomplished. Italy and the Benelux countries were the strongest supporters of European integration and pressed for the most sweeping revisions. Britain and Denmark were leery of change, and sought to block many of the most extensive reforms. France wanted a strong Europe, but tended to be skeptical of the transfer of supranational powers to Brussels. It thus favored expanded use of intergovernmental cooperation, along the lines already established in EPC. Germany tended to align its positions with those of France, but on foreign policy and defense matters it was wary of endangering NATO and transatlantic cooperation by building up a European defense alternative. With regard to EMU, only Britain among the major member states was wholly opposed to the project, but the other member states differed widely about how and within what time frame to create a common currency. The presidency countries—Luxembourg in the first half of 1991, the Netherlands in the second—played important roles in putting forward draft treaties and in searching for compromises among these national perspectives.

The negotiations lasted a year, and concluded at the December 1991 Maastricht European Council with agreement on the Treaty on European Union (TEU), more commonly known as the Maastricht treaty. Agreement was achieved only after last-minute negotiations in which Britain and Denmark secured the right to opt out of certain treaty provisions. Neither country was required to adopt the common currency, and Britain refused to go along with a Social Charter, which as a consequence was adopted by the other eleven member states as a legally binding protocol to the treaty. In effect, agreement to disagree was in these cases the most that could be achieved.

Formally signed in Maastricht in February 1992, the treaty nonetheless was by far the most extensive revision of the founding treaties ever attempted. It had three main elements. First, it contained (in the form of amendments to the Treaty of Rome that were inserted by the Maastricht treaty) a detailed blueprint for the establishment of EMU by the end of the decade. This aspect of Maastricht is discussed in chapter 6. Second, it formally established the political union through a complicated structure that differentiated between economic matters on the one hand and foreign policy and internal security matters on the other. Third, it included other innovations, such as the Social Charter, EU citizenship, the strengthening of the Parliament, subsidiarity, and other reforms that in themselves were not so important but that in combination with EMU and political union increased the overall significance of the Maastricht achievement.

THE PILLAR STRUCTURE

As its formal name indicated, the treaty brought into being a new entity called the European Union, defined as "mark[ing] a new stage in the process of creating an ever closer union among the peoples of Europe."[20] The EU was established as a structure of three "pillars," each of which was to deal with different and partially overlapping policy areas using different decision-making processes. The first pillar was to consist of the three existing Communities—the EEC (renamed the European Community to reflect its broadened and no longer strictly economic areas of responsibility), the ECSC, and Euratom—in which the member states pooled sovereignty and transferred decision-making powers to the Commission, the Council of Ministers, the EP, and the ECJ, with a powerful guiding role also assigned to the European Council. EMU was to reside in the first pillar, but use a modified decision-making process involving, in addition to these institutions, the European Central Bank (ECB) and the national central banks of the member states.

The second pillar, Common Foreign and Security Policy (CFSP), replaced and was based upon EPC. Decisions would remain largely intergovernmental, with only a limited role for Community institutions. CFSP was not made subject to the jurisdiction of the Court of Justice or to decision making by qualified majority voting. The third pillar was to consist of cooperation in the fields of justice and home affairs, including asylum policy, control of external borders and immigration from outside the Union, and combating drug addiction and international crime. Decision making also would be intergovernmental, conducted more or less along the same lines as CFSP.

The security aspect of CFSP was among the most controversial issues negotiated in the 1991 IGC on political union. A Europeanist camp led by France supported the creation of a European defense identity and the merging of the EU and the Western European Union (WEU). Adherents of this position argued that Europe had to be prepared to take over responsibility for its own defense from the United States and that a Europe that relied on Washington for its security could never be an independent power exercising influence in the world commensurate with its economic weight and interests. In contrast, an Atlanticist camp led by the UK opposed a defense role for the EU and upheld the primacy of NATO. Mindful of its relations with the United States and France, Germany straddled both camps, but leaned more toward France.

The result was an especially ambiguous compromise. According to a key provision of the articles establishing the second pillar, "the common foreign and security policy shall include all questions related to the security of the Union, including the eventual framing of a common defense policy, which might in time lead to a common defense."[21] In contrast to the provisions on EMU, which specified a detailed timetable and guidelines for realizing monetary union, the treaty left undefined the meaning of such terms as "eventual" and "might in time." NATO's role in European defense was not overtly questioned, but the way was left open to a future EU role. The treaty declared that the WEU, which previously had not been linked to the structures of the EC, was an "integral part of the development of the European Union."[22] It requested the WEU to "elaborate and implement decisions and actions of the Union which have defense implications."[23]

The third pillar was also an area of political sensitivity, marked by sharp differences among the member states. The completion of the single market and the abolition of controls on the movement of people created strong arguments for European-level cooperation in this area. Proponents of cooperation stressed that international crime syndicates had adjusted to the single market, while the police and judges were still very national in their outlook. At the same time, the member states had very different legal traditions that made them reluctant to surrender sovereignty in this area. There were also genuine differences of interest. Germany, located in the center of Europe and the destination of most refugees and immigrants, had an interest in "Europeanizing" immigration policy so as to spread the burden of newcomers to its territory. The UK, an island nation with relatively secure borders, was better served by a national approach.

In the end the twelve compromised by establishing the third pillar on a loose intergovernmental basis. The members committed themselves to collaboration and agreed to certain provisions under which this collaboration could be strengthened over time. They also agreed to establish a new body, the European Police Office (Europol). The overall approach was cautious, however, and on balance disappointing to those who would have preferred stronger collective action with regard to the "people" side of European integration.

OTHER REFORMS

In addition to the three-pillar structure, the Maastricht treaty codified in the treaties the principle of "subsidiarity," a concept that attempts to define what decisions are to be taken at which levels. Subsidiarity was introduced in part as a response to fears of excessive centralization of power in Brussels. Under the terms of the treaty, the EU was to take action "only if and in so far as the objectives of the proposed action cannot be sufficiently achieved by the Member States."[24]

While there was no universally agreed definition of subsidiarity, its incorporation in the Maastricht treaty meant that the Commission and other EU bodies had to be mindful of the distribution of powers between the Union and the member states.

The treaty established a European citizenship to exist alongside and in addition to national citizenship. The provisions on citizenship strengthened the rights of EU citizens to move and reside freely on the territory of other EU member states and conferred certain other advantages, such as the right of an EU citizen to be represented by the consulate of any member state while overseas and the right to vote and run in municipal elections in an EU country of residence, irrespective of citizenship. The treaty also established the post of parliamentary ombudsman, through which citizens could file complaints about the actions of EU institutions.

Perhaps most significantly, the Maastricht treaty continued the pattern established in the SEA by strengthening the powers of the Parliament in first-pillar matters. It added a new procedure, called *co-decision*, under which the Parliament for the first time gained the power to block legislation introduced by the Commission and passed by the Council of Ministers. Co-decision was prescribed only for a limited number of policy areas, although one of these—the internal market—was quite important. In another change that strengthened its powers, the Parliament was given a say in the appointment of the Commission and the Commission president, hitherto a matter of exclusive concern for the Council of Ministers. Finally, the Maastricht treaty established a new institution, the Committee of the Regions, to provide a means by which regional entities in Europe could give direct input to policy making in Brussels.

The Maastricht treaty contained a final provision requiring the member states to convene another intergovernmental conference in 1996 to review the treaty. By inserting this requirement into Maastricht, the member states were acknowledging the treaty's inadequacies. In many areas it contained vague compromises and statements of intent that reflected underlying disagreements among the signatories. The 1996 IGC would review the workings of the treaty in the light of several years' experience and, it was expected, clarify and sharpen some of its provisions, particularly as they related to CFSP.

RATIFICATION AND BEYOND

Ratifying the Maastricht treaty proved to be unexpectedly difficult. After nearly a decade of rapid change in Europe, it was perhaps inevitable that reaction to further integration would set in. With Western Europe racing toward union and the old order in eastern Europe rapidly disintegrating, people needed time to digest the changes. After a short-lived economic boom, the costs of German reunification helped to precipitate an economic recession in Europe, bringing to an end the job growth of the late 1980s. The war in the Persian Gulf and the outbreak of civil war in the former Yugoslavia caused added uncertainty. After 1991 the mood in Europe became introspective, more focused on local and national concerns such as crime, immigration, and unemployment and more skeptical of the headlong rush to union.

The first highly visible sign that sentiments had changed occurred in June 1992, when voters in Denmark narrowly rejected the Maastricht treaty in the national referendum that was required under the Danish constitution. Since all twelve signatories had to ratify the treaty for it to go into effect, the Community was thrown into crisis. By late summer the political crisis had spilled over into the financial markets, threatening the integrity of the EMS, one of the key building blocks of the planned EMU. In Germany, the treaty was challenged in the supreme court, where opponents argued that it contravened the German constitution by transferring powers of the German states to Brussels.

In September 1992 the French electorate approved the Maastricht treaty, but only by the narrow margin of 51 to 49 percent. The European Council negotiated additional opt-outs for Denmark, and in May 1993 the Danish voters approved the treaty by a healthy margin in a second referendum. Legislatures in the other countries approved the treaty, as did the German federal court. Thus in the end the treaty was ratified. It went into effect on November 1, 1993, some ten months later than originally planned. The European Union was born, even though many voters were confused about the new name and uncertain of what it meant for them.

ENLARGEMENT AGAIN

Just as the collapse of communism intensified pressures to deepen the EC, it contributed, if only indirectly, to a further widening. Before the late 1980s, political leaders had come to accept the division of Europe as a more or less permanent feature of international politics. Many believed that some day communism would end, but this was seen as happening in the distant future, without immediate implications for policy.

The sudden collapse of the system in central and eastern Europe dramatically changed the geopolitical landscape, opening possibilities for enlargement that would have been hard to imagine even five years earlier. As a first step, the end of the Cold War encouraged the EFTA countries to reevaluate their stances on membership. Austria, Finland, Norway, Sweden, and Switzerland all were affluent, highly industrialized democracies with close economic and political ties to the EC. For political reasons, both international and domestic, these countries had chosen not to follow Britain and Denmark in leaving EFTA for the Community in 1973. All but Norway were neutral states, whose governments were concerned about domestic and Soviet reaction to any moves toward integration with NATO member countries. The success of the Community's single market program and the thawing of the Cold War under Gorbachev led to changes in policy. Beginning with Austria in July 1989 and concluding with Norway in November 1992, all five of these countries applied for membership, as did two small Mediterranean states, Cyprus and Malta.

The Community initially was not enthusiastic about taking in new members, and proposed a looser form of cooperation. Building upon earlier economic agreements, in early 1989 EFTA and the EC began to negotiate a European Economic Area (EEA) that would extend the single market to the EFTA countries but hold off on integrating them into the political and decision-making structures of what soon was to become the EU. The member states of the two groupings signed a treaty establishing the EEA in May 1992, to come into effect on January 1, 1994. The agreement extended the four freedoms of the single market to the EFTA countries, which also were required to adjust their domestic legislation to comply with EU single market directives and other important economic laws. The EFTA countries also gained the right to participate in certain EU programs.

The EEA was always an unsatisfactory arrangement, however, containing a mix of obligations and responsibilities that posed problems for both sides. It meant that the EFTA countries, as the weaker parties to the deal, had to comply with rules that they had no say in drafting. It also posed certain constitutional difficulties for the EU, since it established an EEA court for adjudicating disputes that the ECJ later ruled was incompatible with the EU's founding treaties.[25] Swiss voters rejected the agreement in a December 1992 referendum. Switzerland thus did not become part of the EEA and was forced to suspend its application for full EU membership. Austria, Finland, Sweden, and Norway ratified the agreement and entered the EEA as scheduled in January 1994, but they also decided to press ahead with their membership applications.

Accession negotiations with these countries opened in early 1993, and were concluded in June 1994. Voters in Norway rejected accession in a November 1994 referendum, reaffirming their 1972 verdict, but Austria, Finland, and Sweden ratified their accession treaties without major difficulty, becoming full EU members on January 1, 1995. The EEA thus operated as a substantial economic grouping for only one year. It continues to exist, but its only non-EU members are Norway, Iceland, and tiny Liechtenstein. (These countries, along with Switzerland, also constitute what remains of EFTA.)

Meanwhile, the former communist countries of central and eastern Europe also began to press the case for membership. For a time after the fall of communism it was unclear whether these countries would become full EU members or whether they would opt for a looser form of association based on free trade and cooperation in other spheres. Increasingly, however, the leaders of these countries ruled out the alternative possibilities that had been discussed, such as a Europe of concentric circles or an expanded EEA, and demanded full EU and NATO membership. In doing so, they were motivated by a strong desire to be fully integrated into the West, to buffer themselves against instability in the former Soviet Union and a possible resurgence of Russian power, and a desire to have influence over the institutions shaping the development of Europe.

Many of the EU countries were unenthusiastic about absorbing a relatively poor region with over 100 million inhabitants, but after a period of debate they concluded that the EU had little choice but to embrace the region. At the June 1993 Copenhagen summit the European Council agreed in principle that these countries could become members after a period of transition in which they prepared their economies and established working democracies. To do so, they would have to meet a set of economic and political conditions that became known as the Copenhagen criteria. The member states also agreed, at Copenhagen and again at the 1995 Madrid European Council, that the EU would need to reform its own institutions and policies to prepare itself for enlargement.

The applicant countries were not happy with what they saw as delaying tactics on the part of the existing member states, but it was clear that they needed a period of transition to modernize their economies and to adapt their domestic institutions and regulatory structures to EU norms. To assist in this process, the EU provided grants, loans, and technical assistance to the candidates under various programs.

Reform after Maastricht
THE TREATY OF AMSTERDAM

The prospect of adding ten or more member states lent new urgency to calls for the reform of EU institutions, the issue that was in any case expected to dominate the IGC. At fifteen, the Union was already too large to function with essentially the same set of institutions that had been devised in the 1950s for a community of six. With twenty members, the Commission had lost its collegial character. The EP, with 626 members, was already larger than most national parliaments. Under the rotating system of presidencies, member states could expect to chair the European Council and the Council of Ministers only once every seven-and-one-half years. And the large member states led by France were concerned that the accession of many new member states, most of them small, would dilute their influence in the Council of Ministers. Thus as 1996 approached, the impending IGC became ever more closely associated with a need to adjust the institutions to the needs of enlargement.

To prepare for the IGC, the European Council appointed a "reflection group" of high-ranking officials from the member states. In addition to proposing institutional reforms and a strengthening of the Union's much-maligned CFSP, the reflection group called upon the Union to win greater popular support by taking action on issues of direct concern to the citizen, for example, unemployment, immigration, and crime. It concluded that the second and third pillars were both ineffective and excessively complex, unable to meet the real situations that Europe had confronted in the 1990s: the civil war in the former Yugoslavia, the flows of refugees associated with that conflict, and rising international crime and drug trafficking.[26]

While they recognized the need for institutional reform, the member states were wary of yet another major revision of the treaties that would have to be explained to the voters and that might be difficult to ratify. Skepticism about European integration had grown in most countries since Maastricht. Moreover, the EU countries all were struggling to meet the convergence criteria for EMU that were stipulated in the Maastricht treaty. Governments were cutting spending to meet the debt and deficit criteria in a way that was unpopular with the voters. Member-state governments thus approached the post-Maastricht IGC with mixed attitudes. They recognized the importance of change but they also saw a need for caution in the face of increased voter skepticism.

The IGC convened in Turin in March 1996 and concluded in Amsterdam in June 1997 with agreement on yet another treaty. Formally signed in October of that year, the Treaty of Amsterdam amended the Maastricht treaty and the Treaty of Rome, albeit only modestly. It provided for some strengthening of the Union's CFSP and for closer cooperation in third-pillar matters such as immigration. It moved much of the third pillar to the first pillar, thereby transferring responsibilities in this area from the member-state governments to the Commission and the European Parliament. The treaty also formally incorporated the Schengen system, an agreement among the EU member states (Britain and Ireland excepted) to eliminate controls on the cross-border movement of citizens inside the EU while tightening controls at the external borders, into the structure of the EU.

But the IGC made only limited progress on the reforms regarded as essential for effective decision making in an enlarged Union. The treaty capped the future size of the European Parliament, strengthened the powers of the president of the Commission, and extended the co-decision powers of the Parliament to new policy areas. The treaty also inserted a flexibility clause into the Treaty of Rome establishing a legal procedure under which subgroups of member states could pursue closer cooperation among themselves within the Union. However, the member states did not make major changes in the composition or functioning of the EU institutions. Instead, they adopted a legally binding protocol to the treaty that stipulated that at least one year before membership reached twenty, a new IGC would be convened to carry out a review of the institutions and to examine in particular three factors: the size and composition of the Commission, the weighting of votes in the Council of Ministers, and the possible extension of QMV in the Council. The protocol stated that as of the first enlargement, the Commission would comprise one national of each member state, provided that by that time the weighting of votes in the Council had been modified, "whether by the reweighting of the votes or by dual majority."[27] In other words, the five large member countries agreed to give up the right to nominate two commissioners in exchange for added weight in the Council.

Eliminating the second commissioner for France, Germany, Italy, Spain, and the UK in exchange for a reweighting of votes in the Council could be a temporary measure geared toward an initial enlargement involving a few countries, but it would not be a permanent solution for a Union of twenty-eight or more countries. The protocol thus went on to state that at least one year before the membership of the EU exceeded twenty, a new IGC would be convened to carry out "a comprehensive review of the provisions of the Treaties on the composition and functioning of the institutions." It thus held out the theoretical possibility that accession of the first five candidate countries could take place without the convening of another IGC, provided the member states could reach agreement on the reweighting of votes in the Council. From the outset, however, some member states made clear that they would force the issue of institutional reform long before membership reached twenty. Belgium, France, and Italy issued a separate declaration stipulating their view that "the Treaty of Amsterdam does not meet the need, reaffirmed at the Madrid European Council, for substantial progress towards reinforcing the institutions. . . . Those countries consider that such reinforcement is an indispensable condition for the conclusion of the *first* accession negotiations."[28]

THE ENLARGEMENT NEGOTIATIONS

For all its shortcomings, the Amsterdam treaty was important in one respect: under the timetable adopted by the European Council earlier in the decade linking the accession of new members to the successful completion of a post-Maastricht IGC, it cleared the way for the start of enlargement negotiations with Cyprus, Malta, and the candidate countries of central and east Europe. In July 1997 the Commission issued a report entitled *Agenda 2000* that contained detailed opinions on the suitability of the candidate countries for membership along with proposals about how key EU policies such as the CAP would have to change to accommodate the newcomers.[29] Based on the Commission's recommendations, in December 1997 the Council decided that formal negotiations with Cyprus and five central and east European states—the Czech Republic, Estonia, Hungary, Poland, and Slovenia—could begin in March 1998. The five other candidate countries—Bulgaria, Latvia, Lithuania, Slovakia, and Romania—were judged to be not ready, but were promised additional aid and urged to redouble their pre-accession efforts with an eye toward beginning negotiations as soon as possible.

The negotiations began with an elaborate screening process intended to determine those areas in which each candidate country had achieved or was approaching EU norms and standards, and those in which further convergence was required. This was followed by the start of actual negotiations regarding the terms and conditions on which each of the six new candidates would enter the Union and in particular on whether they would be granted transitional periods for phasing in the more expensive and demanding EU policies, for example in the fields of environment and social policy. The member states tasked the Commission with issuing an annual report on the progress of the candidate countries, both those that were actively engaged in negotiations and those that had been put on hold by the Luxembourg summit.

At the December 1999 Helsinki summit, the European Council, acting upon the recommendation contained in the Commission's 1999 report, concluded that the second tier countries (which by then included Malta, which had joined the list of applicants) had made sufficient progress toward EU political and economic norms to begin accession negotiations. Negotiations with the six other candidates began in February 2000. In the addition, the European Council decided at Helsinki that Turkey could be considered a formal candidate for membership, although it put off any decision on the actual start of negotiations, which was made conditional upon Turkey's making progress in the areas of human rights and political stability, as well as continued economic progress.

POLICY ISSUES

While heavily preoccupied with the challenges of institutional reform and enlargement, the member states and the EU institutions could not ignore policy issues arising from the press of events. The latter included continued instability in the Balkans that culminated in the 1999 war in Kosovo by NATO against Serbia, the continued problems of cross-border crime, illegal immigration, drug trafficking, and other third-pillar issues (many of them exacerbated by the situation in the Balkans), and, not least, the problems of unemployment and economic competitiveness.

As will be seen in chapter 9, after the Kosovo crisis the Union moved to strengthen CFSP and to add to it a defense dimension that could cooperate with NATO but that also could act autonomously if necessary. At the December 1999 Helsinki summit the EU adopted a decision to establish a 50,000–60,000-person military force that would be capable of taking on the full range of peacekeeping and peace enforcement tasks, either in cooperation with NATO and the United States or, if need be, acting alone. Member states were slow to approve the added defense spending that was needed to turn these plans into reality, but the EU clearly was intent on building a defense identity apart from NATO.

At Tampere, Finland, in October 1999, the European Council held its first special session dedicated to justice and home affairs. Cooperation in these matters had been enshrined in provisions of the Maastricht treaty establishing the third pillar, but the actual progress achieved in the 1990s was modest. The member states continued to pursue separate policies on immigration, citizenship, combating terrorism, and other justice-related issues, and to resist the transfer of sovereignty to Brussels in these politically sensitive areas. Building upon the changes instituted in the Treaty of Amsterdam, Tampere called for the establishment of a common EU asylum and migration policy and the creation of a "genuine European area of justice" by means of steps such as mutual recognition of judicial systems and greater convergence in civil law, Union-wide efforts against crime, and stronger external action in the Justice and Home Affairs (JHA) area, for example in connection with EU policy toward the Balkans. The European Council also convened a special group of representatives to draft a Charter of Fundamental Rights of the European Union.

In the economic realm, the major preoccupation of the 1990s had been the Maastricht convergence criteria leading to the launch of the euro. The transition by eleven member states to the new currency occurred without major problems on January 1, 1999, marking a major milestone in the European integration process. With the euro successfully launched, attention shifted to structural reform at the microeconomic level and the need to address the problems of high unemployment, lagging economic growth, and what many saw as a lack of technological dynamism. In a symbolically important move, the first session of the European Council in the new century was a special summit in Lisbon, convened at the initiative of the Portuguese presidency, to adopt a new economic strategy for the Union for the period 2000–2010. The declared goal of the new strategy was for the Union "to become the most competitive and dynamic knowledge-based economy in the world capable of sustainable economic growth with more and better jobs and greater social cohesion."[30] To achieve the new strategic goal, Lisbon mandated action in six areas: creating an information society for all, establishing a European area of research and innovation, creating a better environment for starting and developing innovative businesses, furthering economic reforms to complete the internal market, building efficient and integrated financial markets, and coordinating macroeconomic policies of fiscal consolidation. Along with the policy initiatives agreed in Lisbon, the assembled heads of state and government agreed that the European Council would hold a special meeting every spring devoted to economic and social issues and to monitoring implementation, by the member states and the institutions of the Union, of the new economic strategy.

THE TREATY OF NICE

The Amsterdam treaty went into effect on May 1, 1999, following an uneventful ratification process in the fifteen member states. As noted, the closest Amsterdam came to fundamental reform was to adopt a protocol that dealt with the size of the Commission, weighting of votes in the Council of Ministers, and the possible extension of qualified majority voting in the Council. Because these issues were singled out by but not resolved at the 1996–1997 IGC, they became known as the Amsterdam "leftovers." By early 1999 there was general support among the member states for what had been the Belgian-French-Italian position at Amsterdam—namely that the institutional issues left over from Amsterdam be tackled before any further enlargement took place. At Cologne in June of that year the European Council formally decided to convene the IGC in early 2000 and set the end of the French presidency, or December 2000, as the target date for its conclusion.

For the remainder of 1999, there was a lively debate within the Union about the agenda of the forthcoming conference. Newly installed Commission president Romano Prodi appointed a committee of "wise men" to prepare a report on the institutional implications of enlargement. Chaired by former Belgian prime minister Jean-Luc Dehaene, the wise men presented their report in October 1999.[31] They argued for radical measures focused on avoiding institutional gridlock and on regaining public support for a decision-making process that they saw as remote from and not understood by the citizens. One of the reasons for public confusion, they argued, was that the treaties were undergoing constant revision. In their view it was important to break the cycle of revision—negotiation followed by ratification followed by new negotiations—that had been underway on an almost continuous basis since the mid-1980s. They therefore proposed a new approach to treaty change. They called for splitting the main treaty texts into two parts. The first would contain constitutional elements, or all provisions relating to basic aims, principles and general policy orientations, citizens' rights, and the institutional framework. These provisions could be amended only by unanimous agreement of the member states, acting in accordance with their requisite constitutional procedures. The second part of the treaties would contain all provisions relating to specific policy matters, for example CAP, EMU, social policy, and so forth. These provisions could be amended by a less demanding procedure, such as a decision of the Council of Ministers and the assent of the Parliament.

The IGC—the fourth to take place in less than a decade—formally convened in March 2000. For the next nine months, the member states engaged in tough bargaining over the future of the Union and the composition and functioning of its institutions. In the end the fifteen approved, at the December 2000 European Council, a new agreement that became known as the Treaty of Nice, the institutional provisions of which were to go into effect in November 2004, after the election of a new European Parliament and the installation of a new Commission. In one way or another all of the Amsterdam leftovers were resolved, on the basis of compromises that are discussed in chapter 3. The Nice summit also adopted an EU Charter of Fundamental Rights, although it left unresolved the legal status of this document—whether it would be incorporated into the treaties or a future constitution at some point and become binding under EU law or whether it would stand as a political declaration without direct legal applicability to the member states.

Although Nice technically cleared the way to enlargement by deciding the distribution of decision-making power in an enlarged Union, the treaty was hardly the simplification and streamlining of decision making that many European commentators thought was essential. Its provisions were more complicated than ever, leaving plenty of scope for determined minorities to block legislation. At the insistence of the member states, policy decisions in such key areas as taxation, social policy, cohesion policy, policy on asylum and immigration, and, above all, such constitutional issues as reform of the treaties remained subject to unanimity rather than qualified majority voting. The wise men's suggestion to split the treaties and to simplify the procedures for amending the "non-constitutional" parts of the treaties was not adopted. Perhaps most tellingly, the treaty was long, complicated, and difficult for the average citizen to understand and support, a circumstance that was underscored dramatically in June 2001 when the traditionally pro-Europe Irish electorate voted down the treaty. Nice finally went into effect after the Irish voters approved the treaty in a second referendum in October 2002. By this time it was clear, however, that Nice would only be an interim arrangement—an updating of the existing treaties that would allow enlargement to proceed—that would be superseded by a new and more ambitious effort at reform.

Toward a European Constitution

As the new millennium began, the EU could point to notable successes achieved since the end of the Cold War. The long pre-accession process for the candidate countries was moving toward conclusion. Negotiation with six new candidate countries began in early 2000, and most of the twelve candidate countries continued to make progress "on the ground" in adapting their legislation to EU norms and integrating their economies with that of the EU. At the December 2002 Copenhagen summit, final agreement was reached on admitting ten new member states on May 1, 2004. Two countries, Bulgaria and Romania, were making slower progress, but were expected to be ready for membership by 2007.

In January 2001, Greece became the twelfth country to adopt the euro, and in January 2002 euro notes and coins came into circulation in what had come to be called the eurozone, completing the transition to EMU and giving the Union tangible proof of its cohesion and its ability to accomplish ambitious, long-term goals. With CFSP, the EU was carving out a more distinct role for the Union in global politics. European politicians spoke about building a new European identity by distinguishing Europe from the United States over such issues as the death penalty and the role of the welfare state. CFSP became even more important after September 11, 2001, terrorist attacks on New York and Washington, D.C., as the EU saw an increased need to deal with increased security threats in its own environs, as well as to cooperate more closely with the United States in some areas. The same logic applied to cooperation in justice and home affairs, where the new threat environment prompted the EU to accelerate progress on the Tampere agenda and such longstanding projects as a common European arrest warrant and the strengthening of police and intelligence cooperation.

Notwithstanding the progress on these various fronts, there was still concern in the Union with the failure to achieve thorough-going institutional reform and doubts as to whether the EU really was ready for the 2004 enlargement. The perceived shortcomings of the Nice treaty thus led to renewed efforts at institutional reform and in particular to attempts to involve a wider circle of citizens and interest groups in the reform process. Even before the Nice treaty had been concluded, political leaders such as German Foreign Minister Joschka Fischer, British Prime Minister Tony Blair, and French President Jacques Chirac had given speeches calling for more vigorous and imaginative debate about the envisioned endpoint of the integration process ("finality") and the need for radical reforms going beyond institutional tinkering. Among the ideas suggested in the debate were creating an elected post of EU president, scrapping the Commission altogether to create an executive body of member-state government representatives, and setting up an additional legislative chamber parallel to the European Parliament that would be composed of members of national legislatures.

To thrash out these ideas, the European Council agreed, at the December 2001 Laeken summit, to launch a European Convention composed of representatives of member-state governments, members of national parliaments, Commission representatives, and representatives of the European Parliament. Even though they were not yet members of the Union, the candidate countries were invited to participate. Chaired by former French President Valery Giscard d'Estaing, the Convention was charged with drawing up proposals for a European Constitution. These proposals then could be presented to the member states for discussion at an IGC to be convened in late 2003 or early 2004. This approach reflected the emerging sense in Europe that after more than fifty years of integration, the EU needed a basic set of rules that would not be subject to change at frequent IGCs and that could be understood by and serve as a rallying point for the European citizenry. Whether a written constitution could resolve all of the internal disagreements and uncertainties about power-sharing and Europe's "finality" remained unclear. Nonetheless, the Convention began work in March 2002 with great enthusiasm, its members conscious that they were embarking on a constitution-building exercise that in some ways paralleled (although in others was very different from) the one that had taken place in the United States in the 1780s.

After sixteen months of intense work and deliberation, in June 2003 the Convention adopted a draft constitutional treaty and forwarded it to the European Council for further consideration by the member states. If adopted by the member states, the treaty would effect the most sweeping and radical changes in the history of the European integration project. The 1957 Treaty of Rome and all subsequent amendments and additions (the Single European Act, Maastricht, Amsterdam, and Nice) would be repealed and replaced by the new agreement. The three-pillar structure was to be abolished and replaced by a single European Union that would have legal personality and the ability to conclude binding agreements with other countries and international organizations. As discussed in detail in chapter 3, the draft Constitution also simplified and streamlined the institutions. Its design was by no means perfect, but in many areas it improved on the botched compromises of Nice.

The authors of the Constitution and most of the member states hoped that the document could be approved at an IGC to be convened under the Italian presidency in October 2003. The ratification process in twenty-five countries would mean that the Constitution almost certainly would not be in effect for the May 1, 2004, enlargement, but many of its key provisions were in any case scheduled to take effect only in late 2009. As will be seen, however, the IGC soon became bogged down in bitter debates between those member states who feared that they would lose power under the new institutional arrangements and those who stood to gain (or at least not to lose) by it. The December 2003 Brussels European Council failed the break the impasse, with Poland and Spain chiefly pitted against France and Germany. Negotiations continued into 2004 on resolving these issues, but as the EU's fifth and largest enlargement approached, there were still major uncertainties about how an enlarged Union would function and whether it would have a Constitution or would be forced to fall back on the unloved Treaty of Nice.

Notes

1. Text in European Parliament, *Selection of Texts Concerning Institutional Matters of the Community for 1950–1982* (Luxembourg: Office of Official Publications of the EC, 1982), 47.

2. Speech at Columbia University, January 11, 1952, quoted in Richard Mayne, *The*

Recovery of Europe: From Devastation to Unity (New York: Harper and Row, 1970), 204. Eden was referring both to the ECSC and to the even more ambitious plan to develop the European Defense Community.

3. John Gillingham, *Coal, Steel, and the Rebirth of Europe* (Cambridge, U.K.: Cambridge University Press, 1991).

4. Richard Mayne, "Economic Integration in the New Europe: A Statistical Approach," in Stephen R. Graubard, ed., *A New Europe?* (Boston: Beacon Press, 1964), 187, citing Statistical Office of the European Communities data.

5. For the original treaty text, see Intergovernmental Conference on the Common Market and Euratom, *Treaty Establishing the European Economic Community and Connected Documents*, Rome, March 25, 1957, Article 3a. The English version quoted here follows the official English text in *European Union: Selected Instruments.* Amended version substitutes "prohibition" for "elimination."

6. Article 3.1.c TOR (ex Article 3c). The Treaty of Amsterdam renumbered the articles of the Rome and Maastricht treaties to account for the many amendments, insertions, and deletions that had been made over the years. The numbered treaty articles in the notes refer to the renumbered versions; the original numbering ("ex") is given in parentheses.

7. Article 32 TOR (ex Article 38).

8. John Newhouse, *Collision in Brussels: The Common Market Crisis of 30 June 1965* (London: Faber & Faber, 1967).

9. *Bulletin of the European Communities* [hereinafter, Bull. EC], 3-1966, 9.

10. Timothy Garton Ash, *In Europe's Name: Germany and the Divided Continent* (New York: Vintage, 1993), 58–83.

11. Bull. EC 11-1981, 87–91.

12. Bull. EC 2-1984, 7–28.

13. "Report from the Ad Hoc Committee on Institutional Affairs to the European Council, Brussels, 29 and 30 March 1985," Bull. EC 3-1985, 102–11.

14. See Margaret Thatcher, *The Downing Street Years* (New York: HarperCollins, 1993), 548–51. Article 236 was deleted from the TOR and is now Article 48 TEU.

15. *Single European Act*, in *Official Journal of the European Communities* [hereinafter, O.J.], L169 (1987).

16. Charles Grant, *Delors: Inside the House that Jacques Built* (London: Nicholas Brealey, 1994), 74.

17. Article 18 of the SEA, inserting Article 100a.

18. "Report of the Committee for the Study of Economic and Monetary Union," Bull. EC 4-1989, 8–9.

19. J. F. Brown, *Surge to Freedom: The End of Communist Rule in Eastern Europe* (Durham, N.C.: Duke University Press, 1991); Jack F. Matlock Jr., *Autopsy on an Empire* (New York: Random House, 1995).

20. Article 1 TEU, ex Article A.

21. Ex Article J.4.1 TEU, subsequently amended as Article 17 TEU.

22. Ex Article J.4.2 TEU, subsequently amended as Article 17 TEU.

23. Ibid.

24. Article 5 TOR, ex Article 3b.

25. ECJ Opinion 1/91, December 14, 1991, *Re a Draft Treaty on a European Economic Area*, in *Court of Justice of the European Communities: Reports of Cases before the Court* (European Court Reports) [hereinafter, ECR], I-6079 (1992).

26. *Final Report from the Chairman of the Reflection Group on the 1996 Intergovern-*

mental Conference (Brussels: Commission of the European Communities [hereinafter, CEC], 1995).

27. "Protocol on the Institutions with the Prospect of Enlargement of the European Union," *Treaty of Amsterdam*, 111.

28. "Declaration by Belgium, France and Italy on the Protocol on the Institutions with the Prospect of Enlargement of the European Union," ibid., 144 (emphasis supplied).

29. *Agenda 2000: For a Stronger and Wider Union*, Bull. EC Supplement 5/97; country opinions in Supplements 6-15/97.

30. *Presidency Conclusions: Lisbon European Council, 23 and 24 March 2000*, SN 100/00, March 24, 2000, 4.

31. Richard von Weizsäcker, Jean-Luc Dehaene, and David Simon, *The Institutional Implications of Enlargement: Report to the Commission*, Brussels, October 18, 1999, 4.

Suggestions for Further Reading

Bond, Martyn, et al., eds. *Eminent Europeans: Personalities Who Shaped Contemporary Europe*. London: Greycoat, 1996.

Dinan, Desmond. *Europe Recast: A History of European Union*. Boulder, Colo.: Lynne Rienner, 2004.

Gillingham, John. *European Integration, 1950–2003: Superstate or New Market Economy?* Cambridge: Cambridge University Press, 2003.

Grant, Charles. *Delors: Inside the House that Jacques Built*. London: Nicholas Brealey, 1994.

Mayne, Richard. *The Recovery of Europe: From Devastation to Unity*. New York: Harper & Row, 1970.

Monnet, Jean. *Memoirs*. Garden City, N.Y.: Doubleday, 1978.

Moravcsik, Andrew. *The Choice for Europe: Social Purpose and State Power from Messina to Maastricht*. Ithaca, N.Y.: Cornell University Press, 1998.

Thatcher, Margaret. *Downing Street Years*. New York: HarperCollins, 1993.

CHAPTER 3

The Institutions and Laws of the European Union

As was seen in the previous chapter, the European Union (EU) treaties perform two main functions: they define the purposes and objectives of the Union, and they establish institutions and decision-making processes by which these objectives are translated into policy and law. This chapter deals with the institutions of the Union and the main characteristics of EU law.

Five major institutions set policy and make or interpret EU law: the Commission, the Council of Ministers, the European Council, the European Parliament (EP), and the European Court of Justice (ECJ). The Economic and Social Committee (ESC) and the Committee of the Regions play lesser roles in legislative affairs, while the Court of Auditors monitors expenditure. In addition, the EU system includes the European Investment Bank (EIB) and the European System of Central Banks (ESCB) and European Central Bank (ECB). There is also an array of secondary agencies and offices located throughout the territory of the member states that assist with policy implementation in particular areas such as health and safety, the environment, and law enforcement. These agencies are autonomous, having been established by Council decision rather than in the founding treaties.

Because the EU is a federation of member states that retain much of their sovereignty, policy-making responsibility (also known as competence) is shared between the member states and the Union, with the member states having more influence in some areas and the Union in others. The draft EU Constitution for the first time explicitly spelled out the division of competences for the various policy areas, as shown in table 3.1. The EU institutions inevitably are most active and visible in those areas in which the EU has exclusive competence and play lesser roles in areas where competence is shared between the Union and the member states.

Major Institutions

THE EUROPEAN COMMISSION

The Commission is the executive body of the EU. It enjoys an exclusive right to propose legislation (known as the right of initiative) in most policy areas and works with the member states to implement and enforce EU policy and law. It exercises much more limited powers in Common Foreign and Security Policy (CFSP), where the EU does not legislate and where responsibility for policy rests

Table 3.1   Competence of the EU and the Member States

Exclusive EU competence

> monetary policy (for member states that have adopted the euro)
> common commercial policy
> customs union
> conservation of marine biological resources under the common fisheries policy

Shared competence

> internal market
> area of freedom, security, and justice
> agriculture and fisheries, excluding the conservation of marine biological resources
> transport and trans-European networks
> energy
> social policy (for aspects defined in the constitutional treaty)
> environment
> consumer protection
> common safety concerns in public health matters
> research and technological development*
> space*
> development cooperation*
> humanitarian aid*
>
> > *Exercise of Union competence "may not result in Member States being prevented from exercising theirs"
> coordination of economic policy
> common foreign and security policy

Areas of supporting, coordinating, or complementary action

> industry
> protection and improvement of human health
> education, vocational training, youth, and sport
> culture
> civil protection

with the member states. Although they are nominated by the member states, the commissioners are not supposed to take instructions from national governments or to represent the countries of which they are citizens. They are to take an impartial view, based on what they believe are the interests of the Union as a whole and what is consistent with the letter and spirit of the founding treaties.

Often called the "guardian of the treaties," the Commission is charged with looking out for the interests of the Union as a whole and warning member states when they are violating, in the Commission's view, their obligations under the treaties. It is empowered to initiate legal action in the ECJ against member states perceived as failing to carry out their treaty obligations. The members of the Commission, and above all the Commission president, provide political leadership for the European integration process and are among the most visible symbols of the Union to the public. The Commission also represents the EU in international trade negotiations.

The European Coal and Steel Community (ECSC), Euratom, and the European Economic Community (EEC) originally each had separate commissions (the ECSC's was called the High Authority), but the three were merged in the Treaty Establishing a Single Commission of the European Communities (the Merger Treaty) that went into effect in July 1967. The Commission includes at least one national from each member state, which means that it has expanded with successive enlargements. From 1958 to 1972 it had just nine members—two each from France, Germany, and Italy and one each from Belgium, Luxembourg, and the Netherlands. Following the enlargement of 1995, it had twenty members—two from each of the five large states and one from each of the other ten member states—including a president and two vice presidents. From May 1, 2004, until the end of the year the size of the Commission temporarily rose to thirty, as commissioners from the new member states joined the twenty members of the Prodi Commission who were completing the 1999–2004 term, before falling to 25 in the new Commission in which the member states, under the terms of the Treaty of Nice, no longer had the right to nominate a second commissioner (table 3.2).

The term of a Commission and of the individual commissioners is five years, and coincides with the term of each European Parliament. Commissioners can be and often are reappointed, but the member states cannot dismiss the Commission or individual commissioners. The Parliament may vote to censure the Commission if it is dissatisfied with its performance. If a motion of censure on the activities of the Commission is introduced and receives a two-thirds majority of votes cast, the Commission as a body must resign and a new Commission must be formed to serve the remainder of the five-year term. The Parliament has never voted such a censure motion, although the likelihood that it would have done so led to the preemptive resignation of the Commission in March 1999.

The Commission takes decisions on a collegial basis, usually by consensus but sometimes by simple majority vote. Irrespective of the issue—antitrust, trade, the environment, agriculture—there is a unified Commission position approved by the body as a whole when legislation is proposed or other formal decisions taken. Although decisions are taken as a college, the individual commissioners have areas of responsibility which they exercise, chiefly by overseeing one or more of the twenty-three directorates-general responsible for particular policy areas (table 3.3). Most of the Commission staff of approximately 17,000 civil servants is employed in the directorates-general or in the twelve associated services of the Commission responsible for translation, legal affairs, statistics, and other support functions. Each commissioner also has a small personal staff, or *cabinet* (following the French bureaucratic model). Much of the work of the Commission is accomplished through behind-the-scenes coordination among the cabinets.

The Commission is closely identified with the Union, and its fortunes have tended to ebb and flow with changing levels of enthusiasm for a more integrated Europe. It reached the height of its powers in the late 1980s under Delors, when

Table 3.2   The Member States in the EU Institutions

	Commission-ers nominated	Votes in the Council of Ministers	Members of the European Parliament
Germany	1	29	99
France	1	29	78
Italy	1	29	78
United Kingdom	1	29	78
Poland	1	27	54
Spain	1	27	54
Netherlands	1	13	27
Belgium	1	12	24
Czech Republic	1	12	24
Greece	1	12	24
Hungary	1	12	24
Portugal	1	12	24
Sweden	1	10	19
Austria	1	10	18
Denmark	1	7	14
Finland	1	7	14
Slovakia	1	7	14
Ireland	1	7	13
Lithuania	1	7	13
Latvia	1	4	9
Slovenia	1	4	7
Cyprus	1	4	6
Estonia	1	4	6
Luxembourg	1	4	6
Malta	1	3	5
EU	25	321	732

it benefitted from enthusiasm for the single market project. In the late 1990s the Commission experienced considerable turmoil as popular enthusiasm for integration waned—making the Commission a lightning rod for broader concerns about integration and the transfer of powers to Brussels—and because the Commission itself made mistakes that alienated even strong supporters of European integration. The Commission was criticized by the press, member state politicians, and the European Parliament for failing to adequately control and monitor EU expenditure and, in the view of some, for concentrating too much on trying to expand its powers and not enough on effective implementation of policy. The Commission also had difficulty in adjusting to the growing range of EU involvement in new policy areas. Nationality rather than merit became an important factor in determining who got what job within the Commission bureaucracy, and there were many reports of corruption and mismanagement. These issues came to a head in March 1999, when the Commission headed by Jacques Santer, which was supposed to have served the five-year term from January 1995 to December 1999, was

Table 3.3   Directorates-General and Services of the Commission

Services under the Commission President
    Secretariat General
    Legal Service
    Press and Communication

Directorates-General
    Economic and Financial Affairs
    Enterprise
    Competition
    Employment and Social Affairs
    Agriculture
    Energy and Transport
    Environment
    Research
    Information Society
    Fisheries
    Internal Market
    Regional Policy
    Taxation and Customs Union
    Education and Culture
    Health and Consumer Protection
    Justice and Home Affairs
    External Relations
    Trade
    Development
    Enlargement
    Personnel and Administration
    Budget
    Financial Control

Other services
    Joint Research Center
    Common Service for External Relations
    Humanitarian Office—ECHO
    Eurostat
    Inspectorate-General
    European Anti-Fraud Office
    Joint Interpreting and Conference Service
    Translation Service
    Publications Office

forced to step down almost a year before completion of its term. The immediate issue that brought down the Commission was a confrontation with the European Parliament, which questioned the Commission's handling of the EU budget.[1]

Santer was succeeded by the former Italian prime minister Prodi, who was selected by the member states in March 1999 and who formed a new Commission that was approved by the Parliament in September 1999, but only after the customary parliamentary hearings with the individual nominees for Commission posts and after Prodi had announced plans for a wide-ranging reform of the Commission's methods of work and the Commission bureaucracy. By agreement with the Parliament and the member states, the Commission served the remaining four months of the 1995–1999 Commission as well as the five-year term slated to begin on January 1, 2000. Dissatisfaction with the functioning of the Commission and the broader need to prepare for enlargement led to an ongoing debate in the 1990s about reform of the Commission and to a series of changes in how it functions, some of which have been brought about by treaty revision and others by internal decisions by the Commission president, acting within the powers granted to him by the existing treaties.

Size has been the most controversial issue. With the enlargement of the Union to twenty-five and eventually thirty or more member states, the Commission threatened to become a large and unwieldy body that would lose its collegial character. All of the post-Maastricht Intergovernmental Conferences (IGCs) thus dealt with the question of a possible reduction in the size of the Commission. At Amsterdam, the five large member states that each had the right to nominate two commissioners agreed to give up their second commissioner provided votes were reweighted in their favor in the Council of Ministers. This adjustment was agreed in the Treaty of Nice, so that each member state would nominate only one national to serve in the 2005–2009 Commission. The treaty stipulated that the size of the Commission would be capped at twenty-seven, leaving room for the appointment of commissioners from Bulgaria and Romania, after which a rotation system would be instituted.

The European Convention reopened the issue of the ultimate size of the Commission. The smaller countries generally preferred an arrangement in which all countries at all times would have one of their nationals on the Commission. For countries that do not carry much weight in the Council of Ministers or the European Parliament, having at least one individual in the centers of power in Brussels who speaks, for example, the language of Finland, Malta, or Latvia and who can provide a perspective from those countries was regarded as essential to the legitimacy of the Commission and indeed the EU as a whole. For the larger member countries, in contrast, a twenty-seven-member Commission was regarded as likely to be weak and inefficient, with too many narrowly defined portfolios and a tendency to fragment into something like an assembly of nations, rather than become the efficient executive that the Union needed.

Under the chairmanship of Giscard, a former president of France, the large country perspective won out, at least in the European Convention. The draft constitutional treaty proposed new arrangements that are to take effect on November 1, 2009. The Commission will be comprised of fifteen members: its president, a vice president who also will be the EU foreign minister, and thirteen commissioners. The latter will be selected on a strict rotating basis, so that (in the clever language of the Constitution's drafters) "the difference between the total number of terms of office held by nationals of any given pair of Member States may never be more than one." The Commission president also will select nonvoting members from those countries not represented on a given Commission.

In addition to size and composition, the member states have grappled with the question of whether the Commission president should simply be first among equals in a college or have the power to form the Commission as a cabinet and to function in effect as an EU prime minister. In the original Treaty of Rome, the president had no formal powers over his fellow commissioners. This changed in the 1990s, as the member states approved treaty amendments that made the head of the Commission more like a national chief executive, able to choose his "ministers" and direct their work. The Maastricht treaty established a procedure whereby the nominee for president was to be consulted by the member states regarding the selection of the other commissioners. The Treaty of Amsterdam went a step further and gave the nominee for president a theoretical veto over the choices for the other commissioners put forward by the member states. It stipulated that in the last year of a Commission's term, the member states would nominate by common accord the person that they wished to see serve as Commission president. This nomination then had to be approved by the European Parliament. The nominee and the member state governments together then nominate the other members of the Commission. The nominees are subject to a vote by the Parliament and, once approved, are appointed by common accord of the member state governments. The treaty also stated that the Commission "shall work under the political guidance of its President."[2] The Treaty of Nice retained these provisions, but introduced one important change: from 2004 onward, the member states are to act by qualified majority voting (QMV) in selecting the Commission president and approving the Commission as a whole.

The draft Constitution does not fundamentally change the procedure established by the Nice treaty. It stipulates that after the elections to the European Parliament have taken place, the European Council is to elect by QMV a candidate for president of the Commission, who then is proposed to the Parliament. The candidate then must be "elected" by a majority of the members of the Parliament. The president-elect then selects the Commission vice president/foreign minister, the thirteen other commissioners, and the nonvoting commissioners from lists of candidates provided by the member-state governments. Each member state is to propose a list of three individuals representing both genders. Once the president has formed the Commission, it must be approved as a body by the European Parliament. The Commission president also will have the power to ask individual commissioners to resign, thereby ending the old pattern in which the Commission as a whole could be threatened by the malfeasance of a single member.

On paper, at least, the Constitution thus establishes a strong Commission and Commission president. Having the Commission president elected by the European Parliament was an attempt by the constitutional convention to respond to federalist demands that the Commission president be chosen by the European Parliament (much the way prime ministers are elected in national parliamentary systems) or even popularly elected by the voters, while recognizing the insistence by the member states that they keep firm control over the selection process. In fact, election by the European Parliament is a de facto confirmation of the individual chosen by the member states, and may not be seen by the Parliament or the voters as a major advance toward more democratic control.

THE COUNCIL OF MINISTERS

The Council of Ministers (also known as the Council of the European Union and often referred to simply as the Council) is where the member states are directly represented in EU decision making. It is, along with the European Parliament, the main legislative body of the Union. In areas such as Common Foreign and Security Policy (CFSP) where the EU generally does not legislate, the Council plays the leading role in taking such nonlegislative decisions as the adoption of common positions, joint actions, and common strategies on international issues and on deciding whether to enter negotiations with third countries on various issues.

The composition of the Council changes, depending upon the subject under discussion. The Legislative and General Affairs Council consists of the ministers of foreign affairs and is responsible for a broad range of EU-related issues. Another well-known and powerful Council configuration is the meeting of economics and finance ministers, traditionally known as ECOFIN. For other issue areas, there are councils of agriculture ministers, transport ministers, environment ministers, and so forth. EU legislation can be passed only by formal, ministerial-level votes in the Council.

Each year more than one hundred Council sessions take place. The frequency and importance of the different types of sessions vary depending upon the degree to which an issue area is subject to EU competence. Agriculture is an area in which the member states have transferred most policy-making responsibilities to the EU level. The agriculture ministers thus meet every month to decide such matters as commodity prices and subsidy levels. In contrast, education remains largely a member-state responsibility. Education ministers generally meet two or three times a year to discuss those aspects of education policy that may require EU-level action, for example, mutual recognition of diplomas or EU-wide student exchanges. Environment, transport, and other areas lie somewhere between these two extremes, and ministers responsible for these areas meet three or four times each year.

In June 2002, the member states decided to simplify and rationalize the organization of the Council by establishing nine configurations (table 3.4) that legislate on broad issue areas and that may bring together more than one minister. These Council formations are expected to have clearer identities than in the past. A Competitiveness Council, for example, has replaced the previously disparate meetings of internal market, industry, research, and tourism ministers.

The presidency of the Council rotates among the member states on a six-month basis. The presidency country is responsible for preparing the schedule of and chairing Council meetings, not only of the ministers themselves but of the many working groups of experts and civil servants from the member states that hammer out the technical details of legislation.[3] On contentious or deadlocked issues, the presidency country, often working with the Commission, will come up with compromise positions for presentation to the other member states. The presidency country also traditionally has had important external representation functions. Because CFSP is an intergovernmental rather than a supranational area of

Table 3.4   Formations of the Council of Ministers

General Affairs and External Relations
    (including CFSP and development cooperation)

Economic and Financial Affairs
    (including the budget)

Justice and Home Affairs
    (including civil protection)

Employment, Social Policy, Health, and Consumer Affairs

Competitiveness (Internal Market, Industry, and Research)
    (including tourism)

Transport, Telecommunications, and Energy

Agriculture and Fisheries

Environment

Education, Youth, and Culture
    (including audiovisual affairs)

responsibility, the prime minister or foreign minister of the presidency country has joined the Commission president in representing the EU at international meetings, for example, the regular summits with the United States or annual G-7/G-8 meetings.

The Council is assisted by a general-secretariat. With approximately 2,000 permanent staff members, including technical experts, translators, and specialists in EU law, this Brussels-based office provides continuity and institutional memory for the Council as the presidency rotates. It is headed by a general secretary, who is appointed unanimously by the Council. Another important body linked to the Council is the Committee of Permanent Representatives, or COREPER, which consists of the permanent representatives (ambassadors) of the member states to the EU in Brussels. There is also a second committee, consisting of deputy permanent representatives, that assumes part of the workload. These bodies (COREPER I and COREPER II) meet on a weekly basis and play a key role in working out policy issues before they reach the ministerial level. Many formal acts of legislation in the Council are in fact pro forma ratifications of positions that have been settled in COREPER. This prevents overloading of the agenda of the ministerial meetings and allows the ministers to concentrate on the more difficult issues where political decisions are required.

Unlike the Commission, which is a supranational body in which the member states as such are not represented, the Council combines elements of supranationality and intergovernmentalism. As in other international bodies, member states are represented on and through the Council. On most matters of EU legislation, however, the individual member states do not have a veto. Voting is by qualified majority in which each member state is assigned a number of votes, with a qualified majority made up (by tradition) of roughly 70 percent of the total votes.

QMV increases the efficiency of Council decision making. When a single state is able to block decisions, the Council can find it almost impossible to pass legislation or to take other decisions. There is almost always at least one member state with an objection to a given piece of legislation. Moreover, the knowledge that each state has a veto tends to encourage obstructionist behavior, as governments know they have to explain back home why they did not use the veto to block legislation that might adversely affect a national interest. Under QMV, one or two states are unable to block a law favored by the other members. National governments can claim that they were—or would have been—outvoted on a particular measure. QMV thus tends to discourage opposition, as member states which are skeptical about or opposed to a proposed law often are better served by joining the majority and working to modify what they see as its most objectionable parts rather than simply adopting a negative stance in which they are sure to be outvoted. At the same time, however, QMV balances the requirements of efficiency and supranationality with respect for the sovereignty and the distinctive economic and political circumstances of the member states. It represents a compromise between the kind of decision making by consensus that is used in many international organizations but that tends to block action on controversial issues and simple majority voting that may be appropriate for a fairly homogeneous federal state such as the United States but that could prove divisive in a body of diverse nation-states such as the EU.

In recent years debate in the EU about reform of the Council has focused on three areas: the weighting of national votes, the scope of QMV, and the system of rotating presidencies. As noted, the weighting of votes in the Council is based roughly on population size. In the original treaty of Rome, France, Italy, and West Germany each had four votes, Belgium and the Netherlands two, and Luxembourg one. Twelve of the seventeen votes were considered a qualified majority. Conversely, six votes were needed to block a decision. The way the votes were assigned and the setting of the threshold for a qualified majority meant that three big states could pass legislation but two alone could not; conversely, one large state and either Belgium or the Netherlands could block legislation, but the three smaller states acting in unison could not. This voting formula established several precedents that carried through to the enlargements of the next several decades. The three big member states (joined in 1973 by a fourth, the UK) all had equal numbers of votes, even though West Germany was somewhat larger in population than the others. Votes were allocated roughly in accordance with population, but the weighting of the votes did not fully compensate the large countries for their populations. The latter had four to six times the population of the Netherlands and Belgium, but only twice the number of votes.

Successive enlargements have required adjustments in the total number of votes and the thresholds needed either to pass or to block legislation. After the 1995 enlargement, there were eighty-seven total votes in the Council, as shown in table 3.5. Parity among the big four was preserved, even though Germany's popu-

Table 3.5   Evolution of Qualified Majority Voting in the EU

	1958	1973	1981	1986	1995	2004
Belgium	2	5	5	5	5	12
France	4	10	10	10	10	29
Germany	4	10	10	10	10	29
Italy	4	10	10	10	10	29
Luxembourg	1	2	2	2	2	4
The Netherlands	2	5	5	5	5	13
Denmark		3	3	3	3	7
Ireland		3	3	3	3	7
UK		10	10	10	10	29
Greece			5	5	5	12
Portugal				5	5	12
Spain				8	8	27
Austria					4	10
Finland					3	7
Sweden					4	10
Cyprus						4
Czech Republic						12
Estonia						4
Hungary						12
Latvia						4
Lithuania						7
Malta						3
Poland						27
Slovak Republic						7
Slovenia						4
Total	17	58	63	76	87	321
Qualified majority	12	41	45	54	62	232*

*from a majority of member states representing at least 62 percent of the total EU population

lation had increased by some 16 million people as a consequence of reunification. Sixty-two votes were required to form a qualified majority, which meant that twenty-six votes against a proposal constituted a blocking minority. Any three large member states thus could block a piece of legislation, but two alone could not. Even if they all joined together, the ten smaller states could not pass legislation over the objections of the larger members. Conversely, with only forty-eight total votes, the five largest member states had to win the support of at least three small states to pass a measure.

Enlargement inevitably would change all of these calculations. As the first post-Maastricht IGC approached, the larger member states led by France expressed concern that as a consequence of the admission since 1973 of many smaller member states and the systematic overweighting of their representation in the Council, the weight of the large member states had been diluted, relative both to their historic position and to their population as a percentage of the EU's total population. Enlargement to ten or more mostly smaller countries in central and eastern Europe and the Mediterranean would exacerbate this situation. Some experts even warned about a hypothetical situation in which member states representing a minority of the EU's population could pass legislation over the objections of states representing the majority of the population, a situation that was certain to exacerbate concerns about the democratic deficit.

As was seen in the previous chapter, this issue was addressed but not resolved in the IGC that resulted in the Treaty of Amsterdam. It could not be deferred beyond the next IGC, which was convened in 2000 in large part to set the terms under which the new member states would be admitted to the Union, and in particular the number of votes in the Council (as well as Members of the European Parliament [MEPs] and nominees to the Commission) they would receive upon accession.

France approached the IGC determined to increase its weight relative to the smaller member states but, somewhat illogically, insisting that the parity between France and Germany that had existed since 1958 had to be preserved. For its part, Germany demanded that because its population was, after reunification, more than 30 percent larger than that of the other members of the big four, it should receive more votes. Spain, which had less than half the population of Germany but only two fewer votes (eight as opposed to ten) in the Council, was arguing that as an erstwhile great power with a dynamic economy, it should not be treated on a strict one-person-one-vote basis but should have the same or almost the same number of votes as the other big countries in the Union. Even the Netherlands, which since 1958 had been satisfied to have the same number of votes as its smaller neighbor Belgium, was insisting that this parity had to be broken.

Against this background, the fifteen heads of state and government gathered in Nice in December 2000 to hammer out, in an atmosphere marked by bitter wrangling and national assertiveness that many thought had been overcome by a half century of integration, a compromise that would allow enlargement to proceed. In an important victory for the French, parity among the big four was preserved. The relative weight of the larger member states was increased. Spain did particularly well out of this adjustment, as it was awarded twenty-seven votes, only two fewer than the twenty-nine accorded each of the big four. With essentially the same population as Spain, Poland also was to receive twenty-seven votes upon accession. The Netherlands managed to break the traditional parity with Belgium by a largely symbolic single vote, and all other countries were assigned votes roughly in accordance with their populations, as shown in table 3.5. The qualified majority threshold was set at 321 votes—at 72.3 percent just slightly above the traditional 71 percent threshold. In addition, two new conditions were established for determining a qualified majority. For a QMV measure to pass, a majority of the member states (thirteen of twenty-five in an enlarged EU) had to be in favor, and the countries forming the majority had to account for at least 62 percent of the total population of the Union. These provisions were to go into effect on November 1, 2004.

The new triple majority system was in many ways an unsatisfactory compromise. It was hardly the simplification of voting procedures that advocates of reform saw as necessary to increase the efficiency and popular legitimacy of the EU institutions, and it actually increased the possibilities for forming blocking minorities to tie up legislation—precisely the opposite of what the reformers intended going into Nice. However, the compromise did have a certain logic that reflected the political realities surrounding this sensitive issue. The reweighting of votes responded to the concerns of large countries about underrepresentation. The requirement that a majority of member states must be part of a qualified majority in turn was a safeguard for the smaller countries, since it required that any combination of the big four or big six would have to garner support from a large number of smaller countries as well. Finally, establishing the 62-percent threshold was a politically face-saving gesture to Germany which, even though it had failed to have its number of votes increased relative to France, Italy, and the UK, would count more heavily in calculations based on population.

Not surprisingly, when the European Convention met in early 2002 to consider yet another reform of the institutions, the Nice triple majority system was high on the list of items singled out for possible change. In line with its mandate to draft a constitution that would be seen by the voters as coherent and legitimate and that could last for decades rather than having to be rewritten every few years as had been the case since Maastricht, the European Convention looked for a new and simplified approach to the QMV issue. The result was a rather ingenious proposal, contained in the draft European Constitution, to do away with the national weightings altogether and to define a qualified majority simply as a majority of the member states representing at least three-fifths, or 60 percent, of the population of the Union. As with the other institutional provisions of the draft Constitution, the new system would go into effect only on November 1, 2009, after the European Parliament elections for the 2009–2014 term had taken place, meaning that the Nice system would remain in effect for the 2004–2009 period.

The Convention proposal has certain obvious advantages. Assigning national voting weights by negotiation inevitably becomes a political process leading to distortions and awkward compromises. In the Nice weightings, Germany is underrepresented relative to France; Spain and Poland are overrepresented relative to the big four; the Netherlands is not fully compensated relative to Belgium for its larger size; and so forth. Moreover, any attempt to readjust the weights most likely would produce a different set of distortions, leaving one country or another unhappy and the public more confused than ever. In contrast, the proposed new system had the advantage of clarity and adherence to some basic principles that voters could understand. The requirement that a majority of the member states be part of a qualified majority means strict equality of the member states, with Malta counting as much as Germany. And the requirement that a qualified majority also be formed from states accounting for at least 60 percent of the EU population is consistent with the one-person, one-vote principle that underpins modern democracy.

In practice, Germany would be the big winner from such a system, since its population, at about 18 percent of the total population of a twenty-five-member Union, constitutes almost a third of the required majority and nearly half a blocking minority. It was for this reason that Poland and Spain joined forces to block adoption of the draft European Constitution in December 2003. The member states agreed to continue negotiations on this issue into 2004. Meanwhile, the Nice weightings will be used, as they would in any case until November 2009 even if the Constitution goes into effect.

The second controversial issue relating to reform of the Council concerns the question of where QMV is used, which is quite separate from the matter of how a qualified majority is formed. QMV was established in the 1957 Treaty of Rome and was to have been phased in during the 1960s in areas of limited political sensitivity. But, as has been seen, it ran into strong objections from France, with the result that under the Luxembourg Compromise the member states tacitly refrained from its use. In the early 1980s President Mitterrand ceased to insist on the Luxembourg Compromise. Since then, QMV has expanded into numerous areas of policy and law. In the Single European Act (SEA), it was instituted for single market legislation, and thus played a vital role in the completion of the 1992 single market program. In the Maastricht treaty, QMV was extended, generally in conjunction with an upgrading of the decision-making role of the European Parliament, to many other policy areas, including consumer protection, trans-European networks (TENs), and the environment.

Nonetheless, qualified majority voting has remained a subject of some political controversy in the EU. Those that support a strong, federal Europe, such as the Commission and some of the smaller states (e.g., the Benelux), tend to favor the extension of such voting to areas still subject to national veto. Other states, and especially the UK, have been much more cautious about extending majority voting to sensitive policy matters that are regarded as the prerogative of the nation state. In the IGCs that led to the conclusion of the treaties of Amsterdam and Nice, reformers led by the European Commission made a strong push for the almost universal application of QMV. In the Treaty of Amsterdam, the member states agreed to extend QMV to asylum, refugee, and some aspects of immigration policy, but only after a five-year phase-in period (which ended on April 30, 2004) in which unanimity still was to apply. QMV also was extended to measures relating to the implementation (although not yet the formulation) of common strategies under CFSP. In all, however, unanimity still applied in seventy-six first-pillar and in fifteen second- and third-pillar areas of EU policy making.[4]

At the 2000 IGC that resulted in the Treaty of Nice, reformers made another big push to extend QMV, arguing in particular that enlargement to another ten to twelve member states would increase dramatically the odds of a single member state tying up legislation by exercising the veto power. In the compromise reached at Nice, another thirty treaty articles were shifted from unanimity to QMV, but many had to do with the selection and approval procedures for various EU posts (for example, QMV can be used to nominate the president of the Commission and to adopt the list of commissioners to be approved by the European Parliament). On the key substantive issues such as the budget, taxation, CFSP, and many aspects of judicial cooperation, the member states dug in their heels and insisted on retaining their veto rights. On the Structural Funds and the Cohesion Fund (aid from the EU budget that is paid to poorer regions and countries in the Union to help level out income disparities) the member states agreed to shift to QMV, but only, at the insistence of Spain, in 2007 or after the budgetary allocations for 2007–2013 had been decided.

The European Convention again tackled the question of extending QMV, with the federalists arguing that the proposed Constitution was the place for the member states to give up, once and for all, their favorite reservations and to create a uniform legislative procedure that would cover all but purely constitutional issues such as treaty amendments and the admission of new member states. But these arguments did not carry the day, as the draft Constitution contained many articles that still require decision by unanimity using various procedures that may or may not involve the European Parliament (see table 3.6).

The third controversial issue relating to the reform of the Council is the presidency. Historically, the practice of rotating Council presidencies has worked quite well. Member states—particularly those newly admitted into the Union—have been socialized into the EU way of doing business as they have had to take partial responsibility for running the Union for a six-month period. Concerns that the small member countries would be unable to handle the workload or organizing and chairing so many meetings have proven overblown, as countries such as Finland and Denmark have managed highly successful presidencies in which they used their small size and relatively detached position to broker compromises on contentious issues. And different national presidencies have brought new ideas and energy to EU policy making by using their presidencies to focus on issues of special national interest—Spain by highlighting the Mediterranean, the UK job creation and economic deregulation, and Sweden the environment, for example.

Over time, however, many in the EU, particularly in the larger member states, have come to focus on the disadvantages of the rotating presidency system. External representation is a problem (only partly addressed by the establishment of the High Representative for CFSP in 1999), as foreign leaders must deal with a different prime minister or foreign minister every six months. With enlargement to twenty-five or more countries, each member state can expect to wait more than twelve years before its turn in the rotation comes, a circumstance that undercuts the socialization argument for the rotating system. And despite the relatively good performance of the small country presidencies in the past, many experts have expressed concern about how small and inexperienced countries, particularly those admitted in 2004, would cope with the sheer logistical challenges of a postenlargement presidency.

These considerations led to discussion of various reforms, ranging from team presidencies in which a group of countries (small and large) would share a presidency to doing away with the rotating system altogether. In the European Convention, representatives of some of the larger countries favored replacing the rotating presidency with an elected Council president who would serve for a period of several years. However, the smaller member states were adamantly opposed to the complete elimination of the rotating system, which would have deprived them of one of the main opportunities that they have to play a leading role in setting, if only on an infrequent basis, the agenda of the Union.

Table 3.6   Main Issues that Require Decision by Unanimity (Draft EU Constitution)

Subject	Procedure
Amending the Constitution	Ratification by all member states in accordance with their respective national constitutions
Admitting new member states	Unanimous vote in the Council after consulting with the Commission and approval by the EP; ratification by all member states in accordance with their respective national constitutions
Legal measures to combat discrimination based on sex, racial or ethnic origin, religion or belief, disability, age or sexual orientation	Unanimous vote in the Council after consulting the EP
Harmonization of member state laws affecting the internal market	Unanimous vote in the Council after consulting the EP
Negotiation of international agreements in the fields of trade in services involving the movement of persons and the commercial aspects of intellectual property	Unanimity in the Council (if such agreements touch upon matters for which unanimity is required for *internal* rule-making)
Measures of a fiscal nature; measures affecting town and country planning, water resources, and land use	Unanimous vote in the Council
Association agreements with third countries	Unanimous vote in the Council
Composition of the European Parliament, from 2009	European Council by unanimity
Establishment of the EU's revenue ("own resources")	Unanimous Council vote after consulting the EP
Location of the EU institutions	Common accord of the member state governments
Rules governing the selection and use of official languages	Unanimous decision by the Council
Decision to establish a common defense	Unanimous decision by the European Council
External action (CFSP)	Unanimous decision of the Council
Police cooperation	Unanimous vote in the Council after consulting the EP

In the compromise worked out in the final draft of the Constitution, meetings of the External Relations Council will be chaired by the proposed EU foreign minister. For all other Council formations, different member state representatives will exercise the presidency function for different formations, "on the basis of equal rotation for periods of at least a year." The European Council will decide which countries will chair which formations, adhering to the equality principle but also taking into account geographic balance and the mix of small and large countries. This arrangement thus preserves an element of the rotation system while making the presidency more manageable and lowering the burden on any particular country. The system should improve continuity, since presidents are to serve for at least a year. However, it may also damage policy coherence if different countries push different agendas in different Council formations with intersecting or overlapping policy responsibilities.

Of all the institutions of the Union, the Council is also the one that will be most affected by tendencies toward "variable geometry" in the EU, whether in the form of small groups of countries lagging behind or opting out of certain policies or in the form of small pioneer or vanguard groups that attempt to forge ahead. This issue already has arisen in connection with the euro, which in early 2004 had been adopted by twelve of the fifteen member states but not by the other three. With enlargement, another ten members states were outside the eurozone, at least temporarily, making for a 12:13 split.

The Maastricht treaty stipulated that for decisions directly related to the euro, only those countries participating in the single currency would have a say. But the treaty did not establish a formal Council structure of just the eurozone finance ministers. The UK in particular fought hard to prevent the establishment of separate Council structure and to uphold the primacy of ECOFIN with the full representation of all member states. As a practical matter, however, the eurozone finance ministers began meeting informally to concert policy relating to the euro. The proposed Constitution formalizes this process, by including a new article that provides for the adoption of "measures specific to those member states that are members of the eurozone."[5] The Constitution stops short of establishing a formal Eurozone Council, but a Protocol on the Euro Group attached to the Constitution formalizes the existence of a separate group and establishes procedures under which the eurozone countries, using QMV adjusted to take account of its modified membership, can adopt such measures.

THE EUROPEAN COUNCIL

At first glance the European Council seems very similar to the Council of Ministers, an institution with which it is sometimes confused. In fact, the two bodies are quite different. The European Council consists of the heads of state or government of the member states, along with the president of the Commission. Foreign ministers also are present at European Council meetings. The European Council was not one of the original institutions of the European Community (EC), but was established in 1974 when the European leaders agreed to hold regular summit meetings to discuss Community business and to provide political momentum to the integration process. Meetings are intended to be less structured and without the large staff of advisers that attend ministerial meetings. They provide the leaders a chance to work out compromises behind the scenes and to better understand the positions of their counterparts from the other member states.

Historically, the European Council has convened at least twice a year, and always in June and December near the end of each country presidency. The country that has the rotating presidency of the Council of Ministers also chairs the European Council and hosts the semiannual summit. The presidency country also may convene special sessions of the European Council to address problems or highlight particular issues, such as the April 1990 Dublin European Council that launched the IGC on political union, the March 1999 Berlin summit to work out the EU budget for 2000–2006, or the March 2000 Lisbon European Council that set in motion the Lisbon process of economic reform. Presidency countries have convened sessions of the European Council in their capitals or in other important national cities, thereby giving rise to such convenient shorthand as the "Copenhagen criteria," the "Helsinki headline goals," and the "Barcelona process." However, in 2000 the member states agreed to hold all future European Council sessions in Brussels, beginning in the second half of 2003.

The European Council was given treaty status in the Single European Act and further constitutional status and responsibilities in the Maastricht treaty, which stipulated that "the European Council shall provide the Union with the necessary impetus for its development and shall define the political guidelines thereof."[6] The European Council rarely takes a formal vote, and it tries not to get too involved in the details of legislation and policy making, which are left to the other institutions of the Union. It does set basic goals and ensures that the member states and the Commission are behind these goals. The European Council in fact has made the key decisions with respect to all of the major EU initiatives in recent decades: the single market program, economic and monetary union, political union, and enlargement. These decisions usually are codified in a single document called the presidency conclusions that is adopted at each summit and that usually includes requests or instructions to other EU institutions—the Council of Ministers and the Commission—to study certain matters or to come up with concrete policy proposals and legislative initiatives.

The European Council plays an especially important role in CFSP. It sets the general guidelines for EU external action, from which the Council of Ministers and the Commission take their lead. Its pronouncements on the Balkans, the Middle East, and other international issues reflect the consensus view of the member states and inevitably carry greater weight in international settings than would statements by individual governments and leaders. As noted, a common strategy adopted by the European Council—such as the strategies for Russia and Ukraine adopted in 1999—establishes a framework for action by the Council of Ministers and the Commission.

The establishment of the European Council and the codification of its role in the basic treaties have altered the institutional balance in the Union, marking a shift in the 1980s and 1990s to a more intergovernmental approach to decision making than was envisioned by Monnet and the founding fathers. The Commission's role as initiator of legislation to some extent was downgraded by default, as was the legislative oversight role of the Parliament. The European Parliament long struggled to increase its ability to oversee the activities of the European Commission and to share power with the Council of Ministers, only to see power accumulate in the hands of the European Council, over which it exercises no direct control. On the other hand, it was argued that the European Council was meeting a genuine need and that without it the EU would not be evolving along a federalist path but more likely would be stagnating from lack of political leadership and an inability to resolve complex problems. With fifteen and eventually twenty-five highly disparate members and a broad array of policy responsibilities in trade, monetary affairs, foreign policy, and other issues, experience suggested that the Union could only progress through the direct and sustained involvement of national leaders in taking key decisions and setting overall directions.

The draft European Constitution contains new provisions relating to the European Council that critics argue further shifts the EU in an intergovernmental direction. The European Council will elect by QMV a president who will replace the rotating six-month national presidencies. The president's term will be two-and-a-half years, renewable once. The president will chair the European Council, establish the agenda for meetings, and drive forward its work. The European Council will meet on a quarterly basis, convened by the president. The president also will be empowered to convene special sessions of the European Council.

The proposal to create a long-term European Council presidency was championed by the large member states, who saw a need to provide the EU with a single face who could represent the Union internationally and ensure more continuity from one European Council session to the next. It was strongly but in the end unsuccessfully opposed by the smaller member states, who feared that the further intergovernmental drift in the EU would mean a concentration of power in the hands of the big countries and who were reluctant to lose the chance to be the European Council presidency country, even though this would occur very infrequently in an enlarged Union. The proposal also was strongly opposed by the European Commission, which argued that a long-term European Council president could not but weaken the position of the European Commission president, who also serves as the external face of the Union. Having two presidents instead of one, the Commission argued, will hardly resolve the problem of coherence in EU policy making and external representation. Much will depend, of course, on the individual chosen by the member states to occupy this post. Most likely he or she will be a former prime minister, familiar with summitry and able to fulfill the daunting task of chairing meetings of twenty-five or more prime ministers and presidents as well as forging a good working relationship with the European Commission president and the proposed EU foreign minister.

THE EUROPEAN PARLIAMENT

The European Parliament is the only EU law- and policy-making body directly elected by the voters. The others all either represent or are appointed by the member states. Following the 2004 enlargement, the Parliament has 732 members (MEPs) who are elected to five year terms. Voting takes place within the same four-day period in all of the member states. Seats are allocated according to member-state population (table 3.2), but as with the Council the weighting does not fully compensate for differences in size. Germany has ninety-nine members

Table 3.7   Growth of the European Parliament

	1958	1973	1979	1981	1986	1993	1995	2004
Belgium	14	14	24	24	24	25	25	24
France	36	36	81	81	81	87	87	78
Germany	36	36	81	81	81	99	99	99
Italy	36	36	81	81	81	87	87	78
Luxembourg	6	6	6	6	6	6	6	6
The Netherlands	14	14	25	25	25	31	31	27
Denmark		10	16	16	16	16	16	14
Ireland		10	15	15	15	15	15	13
UK		36	81	81	81	87	87	78
Greece				24	24	25	25	24
Portugal					24	25	25	24
Spain					60	64	64	54
Austria							21	18
Finland							16	14
Sweden							22	19
Cyprus								6
Czech Republic								24
Estonia								6
Hungary								24
Latvia								9
Lithuania								13
Malta								5
Poland								54
Slovak Republic								14
Slovenia								7
Total	142	198	410	434	518	567	626	732

to represent its 81 million people (one MEP per 800,000), Luxembourg six members for a population of just over 400,000 (one per 60,000).

The Parliament began as the Common Assembly of the ECSC. Its members were appointed by the national parliaments and its role in making legislation was advisory and consultative. It was renamed the European Parliament in 1962, and direct election of members took place for the first time in 1979. The powers and responsibilities of the Parliament have increased with successive revisions of the founding treaties, both in response to pressures from the Parliament itself and as the member states have recognized a need to give the process of European integration greater democratic legitimacy based on accountability to the citizens.

While the Council of Ministers remains the primary legislative body, the EU has been evolving in recent decades toward a genuinely bicameral legislative system, with the Council in effect the upper and the European Parliament the lower chamber of the legislative branch. The legislative powers of the Parliament are uneven—strong in some areas and weak or nonexistent in others—the result of a process in which the member states have ceded powers to the Parliament only gradually, in some areas going quite far while in others holding back to preserve national control or else transferring powers to technocratic bodies such as the European Commission or the ECB. The Parliament also has almost no role in two of the most important areas of first-pillar policy-making, agriculture and foreign trade, and its powers generally do not extend to CFSP and to cooperation in police matters, where decisions must result from intergovernmental agreement among the member states.

Expansion of the Parliament's legislative powers has occurred in stages, with each of the major treaties and treaty revisions adding to its powers. Under the original 1957 Treaty of Rome, the parliament was a purely consultative body. The Council of Ministers was required to solicit its opinion regarding certain legislation, but it was free to ignore this opinion when passing directives and regulations. The Single European Act established a cooperation procedure under which the Parliament began to share genuine legislative responsibilities with the Council. Under this procedure, the Parliament could reject, by a vote of a majority of its members, a measure passed by the Council. The Council could still pass the measure, but only if it acted unanimously. Because the SEA also greatly expanded the use of qualified majority voting in Council decision making, the cooperation procedure constituted an important check on the legislative powers of the Council.

The Maastricht treaty introduced a third legislative procedure, co-decision. Under this procedure, the Council and the Parliament are obliged to agree on legislation for it to pass. If they do not agree, they are required to form a conciliation commission to work out their differences and approve a common legal text. If they cannot do so, the Parliament's opposition blocks passage, even if the Council acts unanimously. Legislation passed under the co-decision procedure is promulgated in the name of both the Parliament and the Council, as it is truly decided by both institutions wielding roughly equal powers. Another procedure, the assent procedure, involves a simple yes or no vote by the Parliament. It is used to approve decisions taken on a unanimous basis by the Council of Ministers in areas relating to international agreements and certain politically and constitutionally sensitive matters, such as the admission of new member states.

After the reforms introduced by the Amsterdam and Nice treaties, a simplified version of the co-decision procedure has become the general rule for the passage of EU legislation. The cooperation procedure has almost been abolished, and is still used only in certain matters relating to Economic and Monetary Union (EMU), where the Parliament has pressed for increased influence but in which the member states and the European central banking community are wary of greater political involvement. The assent procedure is used to approve the accession of new states, the conclusion of association and other international agreements with budgetary implications, certain specialized matters relating to regional aid and the functions of the ECB, and to approve sanctions against a member state regarded as in serious and persistent breach of fundamental rights. There is also a separate approval process for the EU budget.

In addition to its legislative role, the Parliament has come to exercise a growing influence over appointments to key EU posts. It also exercises controls over executive actions, often by uncovering and disseminating information. It can launch investigations, hold public hearings, set up temporary committees of inquiry, and pose oral and written questions to the Commission and the Council.

Originally, the Parliament had no say over appointments by the member states. Under the Maastricht treaty, it was to be consulted on the choice of the Commission president and on the Commission as a whole, as well as on appointments to the Court of Auditors and the key positions in the ECB. The Commission and the Commission president then were subject as a body to a vote of approval by the EP. Since the entry into effect of the Treaty of Amsterdam in 1999, the Parliament has been required to approve the member states' nominee for the president of the Commission, who then works with the member-state governments to select the other commissioners. The Commission is then subject as a body to a vote of approval by the Parliament. The Parliament first exercised its new rights under the Amsterdam treaty on May 5, 1999—four days after the new treaty went into effect—when it voted 392 to 72, with 41 abstentions, to approve Romano Prodi. It held hearings with the other Commission nominees in early September, and on September 15 approved the whole Commission by a vote of 414 to 142, with 35 abstentions.

The Parliament may dismiss the Commission if it passes a vote of censure against the body as a whole. (It may not dismiss individual commissioners.) There were four such votes of censure between 1979 and 1998, none of which was successful. However, the threat of censure is a powerful reserve weapon, and the likelihood that it would have been used successfully accounted in large part for the decision of the commissioners in March 1999 to step down voluntarily following the release of the independent experts' report documenting financial mismanagement and other failures by several commissioners.

The Parliament must approve and has certain powers to amend the preliminary draft budget submitted by the Commission and approved by the Council for the coming fiscal year. This gives it substantial influence over the budgetary process, which it has used to promote programs of special interest to MEPs, such as increased spending for research and development and certain forms of regional and foreign assistance. However, the Parliament's role in budgetary matters is circumscribed by two factors. First, the level of EU expenditures is largely set by the member states. The Parliament thus mainly can shift spending from one priority to another, but it cannot determine the overall size of the budget. Second, much EU spending is "compulsory," meaning it is dedicated to the Common Agricultural Policy (CAP) and the structural funds. In shifting spending priorities in the EU budget, the Parliament's powers apply chiefly to noncompulsory expenditures that are not already mandated by other EU policies.

In addition to approving the budget for the next fiscal year, the Parliament must "give a discharge" to the Commission for its implementation of the previous year's budget. In other words, it must check that in implementing the budget the Commission has spent the funds allocated in accordance with the categories and purposes established in the budget and without fraud or mismanagement. It bases its decision on the Commission's own financial report and reports by the Court of Auditors. The Parliament has used this power to bring pressure on the Commission to improve its management practices, most notably in December 1998 when it refused to approve the 1996 budget, precipitating the clash that led to the resignation of the Santer Commission early the following year.

In conducting its work, the European Parliament is organized much like a national parliament, although it confronts certain special problems owing to its multinational makeup and the complexity of its relations with other EU institutions.[7] The MEPs elect a president, traditionally from one of the two main political groupings, the Socialists and the Christian Democrats, for a two and one-half year period. The president and the fourteen vice presidents, elected for the same term, form the Bureau of the parliament, which is responsible for the overall direction of the Parliament's activities. As in national parliaments, the European Parliament conducts its work through committees and subcommittees. There are twenty standing committees, as shown in table 3.8.

In addition to serving on these committees, most MEPs are attached to political groups that correspond to the main European political parties. In the chamber of the parliament, members sit by political group, not by national delegations. The two largest groups by far are the Group of the Party of European Socialists and the Group of the European People's Party, or Christian Democrats (table 3.9). There are also Liberal, Green, radical left, and three other political groups. Each group must have a minimum of 29 members if they all come from one member state, 23 if they come from two member states, 18 if from three member states, and 14 if they come from four or more member states. A few MEPs are unattached, but in general members have an incentive to join or form political groups, since the groups work with the president in organizing the Parliament's work and drawing up its agenda.

Table 3.8   Standing Committees of the European Parliament

Foreign Affairs, Human Rights, Common Security, and Defense Policy
Budgets
Budgetary Control
Citizens' Freedoms and Rights, Justice and Home Affairs
Economic and Monetary Affairs
Legal Affairs and the Internal Market
Industry, External Trade, Research, and Energy
Employment and Social Affairs
Environment, Public Health, and Consumer Policy
Agriculture and Rural Development
Fisheries
Regional Policy, Transport, and Tourism
Culture, Youth, Education, the Media, and Sport
Development and Cooperation
Constitutional Affairs
Women's Rights and Equal Opportunities
Petitions

Table 3.9   Political Groupings in the European Parliament

Political group	Abbreviation	Number of seats (2003)
European People's Party (Christian Democrats) and European Democrats	EPP-ED	232
Party of European Socialists	PES	175
European Liberal, Democrat, and Reformist Party	ELDR	52
European United Left/Nordic Green Left	EUL/NGL	49
Greens/European Free Alliance	Greens/EFA	44
Union for Europe of the Nations	UEN	23
Europe of Democracies and Diversities	EDD	18
Non-attached	NA	31
Total		624

Despite the formidable array of powers that the Parliament wields, it suffers from several major weaknesses that have hindered its development into a co-legislative body with powers equal to those of the Council. The first area of weakness concerns the sheer complexity of the Parliament's legislative powers. This has tended to confuse the voters and to create the impression that the member states have carefully parceled out powers to the Parliament, always holding back in those areas about which national governments care most. Recent reforms have attempted to address this issue by evening out and simplifying the powers of the Parliament. The Treaty of Amsterdam effectively abolished the cooperation procedure, making most areas of legislation subject to the stronger co-decision procedure, which was itself simplified. The treaty also extended the power of the Parliament by moving certain matters previously handled in the third pillar, such as immigration and asylum, into the first pillar where they will be subject to parliamentary decision-making procedures. The Treaty of Nice extended co-decision to new policy areas, and the draft European Constitution establishes co-decision as the EU's "ordinary legislative procedure," with the implication that departures from this procedure should be few in number and based on valid reasons. Still, complexity remains a hallmark of the Parliament's role, reflecting as it does the underlying differences among and within the member states about the extent to which the Union should derive its powers directly from the voters as opposed to from the member states acting within the Council of Ministers.

The second area of weakness is practical, and concerns location, language, and parliamentary organization. The seat of the Parliament is Strasbourg, but it holds only some of its plenary sessions there. Committee meetings and some plenary sessions take place in Brussels, while most committee staff work in Luxembourg. MEPs and parliamentary staff spend an inordinate amount of time traveling between these cities as well as to their home constituencies, many of which are quite remote given the Union's enlargements to northern and eastern Europe and the Mediterranean. These arrangements in turn result in high costs for travel and duplicate facilities that increase public skepticism about the Parliament. While it is difficult to see how the Parliament can function as a truly equal branch in the EU's governing bodies without being located in the de facto capital city of Brussels, so far the member states have resisted such a move. France in particular argues that the Parliament is the only EU institution located on its territory and that a move to Brussels would be politically unacceptable.

Language presents another major challenge. To communicate with and represent their constituents, MEPs must speak in their national languages. But this makes open debate somewhat stilted and artificial as it must be conducted through simultaneous translation. With the addition of Finnish and Swedish as a consequence of the 1995 enlargement, the EU had eleven official languages. In 2004, this increased to twenty. This means that there are 190 possible language pairs (Estonian-French, Portuguese-Finnish, English-Polish, and so forth) that require simultaneous interpretation to facilitate debate in the Parliament. Finding enough skilled interpreters to cover all of these language pairs has proven so difficult and expensive that the Parliament has adopted a relay system of interpretation in which, for example, a Latvian MEP might be interpreted into English or French by a Latvian-English or Latvian-French interpreter (not difficult to find), and then further interpreted from English or French into Portuguese, Slovenian, Maltese, Dutch, and so forth. This system obviates the need for certain interpreting skills, but it undoubtedly will slow the work of the Parliament and hinder spontaneous debate.

Finally, sheer size is a problem. The Parliament began in 1958 with 142 members delegated by the national parliaments of the six member states. In 1973, it increased to 198 members with the accession of Denmark, Ireland, and the UK. In 1979, the size of the Parliament was increased to 410 members to create smaller electoral districts for the first direct elections of MEPs. By 1986 the Parliament's size had increased to 518 as a result of the accessions of Greece, Spain, and Portugal. There was a further increase to 567 members in 1994 to account for German unification, and to 626 members in 1995 with the accession of Austria, Finland, and Sweden.

Few national parliaments are this large, and the member state governments recognized that unchecked further growth would make the Parliament too unwieldy to serve as a forum for genuine democratic debate. The Treaty of Amsterdam thus included a provision stipulating that the total number of members of the Parliament would not exceed seven hundred. Adhering to this ceiling while bringing in ten to twelve new member states would have required a reapportionment of seats and some downward adjustment in the number of representatives from the existing member states—a step that European leaders were unwilling to take. Accordingly, the Treaty of Nice abolished the 700-seat limit and raised the size of the Parliament to 732 for a twenty-five-country Union as well as decided that Bulgaria and Romania will be represented by thirty-three and seventeen MEPs respectively once they are admitted, meaning that the size of the Parliament could reach 786 members.

The draft European Constitution stipulates that the "final" size will be 736 and that the apportionment of representatives among the member states will be established by unanimous decision of the European Council. This is to be done before the 2009 parliamentary elections, in accordance with a complex mathematical formula known as degressive proportionality that somewhat overweights the representation of the smaller states.

THE EUROPEAN COURT OF JUSTICE

The ECJ is the judicial authority that interprets EU law and ensures that it is applied uniformly throughout the member states. It is composed of one judge from each member state, all of whom are appointed by common accord of the member states. These individuals serve terms of six years, which may be renewed. The judges are assisted by eight advocates-general whose role is to impartially argue cases before the Court. Both judges and advocates-general must be independent and possess the qualifications required for appointment to the highest judicial office in their own countries. The Court is located in Luxembourg.

Attached to the ECJ is the Court of First Instance, which was established in 1989 to relieve the ECJ of part of its enormous workload. Its structure and composition is similar to that of the ECJ. It hears virtually all cases brought by individuals as well as competition policy cases and other cases of less than constitutional import, leaving the Court of Justice more time to concentrate on cases with broader implications. The ECJ must hear all cases brought by the Commission against a member state, by one member state against another, or between institutions of the EU. In addition, the Treaty of Nice inserted a new article into the EC Treaty that empowered the Council, acting upon a request from either the Commission or the ECJ, to create judicial panels to hear cases and make judgments regarding certain classes of actions. Such panels could be used, for example, to resolve personnel or intellectual property disputes as a way of not overloading the ECJ and the Court of First Instance so as not to divert them from cases of more general import for the Union.[8]

The Court sits in plenary session (with all judges present) when requested by a member state or an EU institution, or for very complex cases or those with important constitutional implications. Generally, however, the Court divides into chambers of three or five judges, allowing several cases to proceed in parallel. When a case is brought before the Court, it is assigned an advocate-general, who completes a preparatory inquiry into the case. Based on the views of the advocate-general, the Court then decides whether the case will be heard by the full Court or a chamber. This is followed by a public hearing for the judges and the advocate general. Within a period of weeks, the advocate general delivers his opinion on the case, which the judges then deliberate among themselves in private and modify as they see fit. The final verdict is decided by majority vote of the judges. All judges assigned to a case sign the decision, and no dissenting opinions are issued.

The Court mainly hears cases brought by the institutions of the Union and the EU member states or that are referred to it by national courts. It is not like the U.S. Supreme Court, in that it is not a forum in which the constitutionality of national or lower court rulings and legislative acts can be appealed. The ECJ can only rule on whether such decisions or acts are consistent with EU law. Since 1952, more than 9,000 cases have been brought before the Court, which has delivered more than 4,000 judgments. These cases can be divided into two general categories: direct actions and preliminary rulings. Direct actions apply to the parties in a given case. Preliminary rulings have no direct legal effect, but are delivered to courts or tribunals of the member states when they need advice on how points of national law relate to EU law, and especially on whether national legislation is in or may come into conflict with EU legislation.

In interpreting EU law, the Court often has taken an expansive view of its role, pronouncing not just on the appropriateness of measures in narrow, technical terms but interpreting these measures in terms of the broad objectives outlined in the founding treaties. In this way, it has developed a body of EU jurisprudence that underpins the integration process and that influences the work of the Commission as it formulates initiatives and drafts EU legislation. The development of EU law and the important role of the ECJ in deciding landmark cases on which this law is based are discussed later in this chapter.

The draft European Constitution introduces several innovations regarding the ECJ. The Court of First Instance is renamed the High Court to reflect its true status (the ECJ remains in effect the *highest* court, but its name is not changed). The draft Constitution further elaborates the legal basis upon which the third tier of the EU court system—the specialized judicial panels introduced by Nice—may be set up. In addition, the Constitution would change somewhat the procedure by which judges of the ECJ and the Court of First Instance/High Court and the advocates-general are selected. It provides for the establishment of a seven-member panel, comprised of former ECJ judges, members of national supreme courts, and qualified lawyers, that is to give opinions on the suitability of candidates for these posts. The panel will report to the member states, who will continue to appoint the judges and advocates-general by common accord. Establishment of the panel no doubt responds to concerns that some member states may have nominated or in the future could nominate unqualified judges, but that voting down nominees in the Council of Ministers is a rather blunt and unwieldy instrument for dealing with this problem.

Other EU Bodies

THE ECONOMIC AND SOCIAL COMMITTEE

The Economic and Social Committee (ESC) was set up under the Treaty of Rome at a time when the European Parliament still was very weak and played only a consultative role. It reflects a lingering corporatist tradition in Europe, which holds that different economic interests should have a direct role in economic and political decision making in addition to such representation that takes place through parliamentary bodies at the national and European levels.

The members of the committee are drawn from three constituencies: organizations of employers, of employees (mostly trade unions), and other representatives of civil society, "notably in the socio-economic, civic, professional and cultural areas."[9] Members serve on a part-time basis, and are appointed by the Council of Ministers for four-year terms (increased to five years in the European Constitution) from lists of nominees submitted by the member-state governments. Following the 1995 enlargement, the ESC had 222 members: 24 each from France, Germany, Italy and the UK, 21 from Spain, 12 each from Austria, Belgium, Greece, the Netherlands, Portugal and Sweden, 9 each from Denmark, Finland, and Ireland, and 6 from Luxembourg. With the 2004 enlargement, the ESC was expanded to include 21 representatives from Poland, 12 each from the Czech Republic and Hungary, 9 each from Lithuania and Slovakia, 7 each from Estonia, Latvia, and Slovenia, 6 from Cyprus, and 5 from Malta. Romania will have 15 members when it is admitted to the EU, Bulgaria will have 12.

The founding treaties stipulate that the ESC must be consulted before legislation can be adopted in various areas, for example, employment policy, social policy, and regional policy. The Committee also can offer opinions on subjects of its own choosing. Working through specialized subcommittees and in plenary sessions, it delivers about two hundred such opinions a year. The Committee's influence on legislation is quite limited, however. The Council of Ministers, Commission, and European Parliament are not required to accept its suggestions, and advice on legislation comes from many other sources including lobbyists working on behalf of particular interests that have direct access to the Commission, member-state governments, and the Parliament.

THE COMMITTEE OF THE REGIONS

The Committee of the Regions (CoR) was established in 1993 under the terms of the Maastricht treaty, largely at the urging of the Federal Republic of Germany (FRG). Germany has a federal system of government in which the states—Bavaria, Saxony, Hesse, and so forth—exercise important governmental responsibilities in such areas as education, culture, and regional development. Other EU member states in which subnational governments are especially important include Belgium, Spain, and the UK. Regional governments long had complained that they had no direct input into decisions taken in Brussels that affected areas for which they were responsible.

The establishment of the CoR was an attempt to remedy this situation by providing a vehicle through which subnational regions can influence EU decision making. The Committee has the same number of members as the Economic and Social Committee, distributed in the same way among the member states. These individuals are either elected officials from the regions, such as mayors, regional presidents, and chairpersons of county councils, or officials that are politically accountable to an elected assembly at the subnational level. They serve four-year terms (to be increased to five years under the European Constitution).

The Committee must be consulted on legislation relating to trans-European networks, public health, education, youth, culture, and economic and social cohesion. The Committee also can give opinions on other matters that affect regions and cities, such as agricultural and environmental policy. It is particularly active in the area of cross-border cooperation, for example, activities between adjacent regions in EU member states that are directed at solving transport, environmental, and other local problems or at promoting cross-border cultural cohesion. The Committee's role is purely consultative, however, and its ability to influence legislation is limited. Despite much talk of a Europe of the regions, the Committee of the Regions has not become an effective vehicle for direct subnational influence on EU policy making, in large part because national governments are unwilling to see their authority in EU decision making eroded by devolution to lower levels of government.

THE COURT OF AUDITORS

The Court of Auditors monitors the EU budget, both expenditures and the collection of revenues, and draws up an annual report of its findings. This report is an important part of the discharge procedure under which the European Parliament, acting upon a recommendation from the Council, releases the Commission, as the body responsible for implementing the EU budget, from further liability concerning the management of the previous year's budget. In evaluating the Commission's management of the budget, the Council and the Parliament rely heavily upon the report of the Court of Auditors. The Court also prepares special reports and delivers opinions at the request of other EU institutions.

Located in Luxembourg, the Court has one member from each EU state. Members of the Court are appointed by the Council after consultation with the Parliament. These individuals must have had experience in their national audit bodies or be otherwise especially qualified. They are supported by a staff of accountants, auditors, and other specialists. Members serve a six-year term, which may be renewed. The Court elects its own president who serves a three-year term, and individual members of the Court are assigned portfolios, for example, agriculture, external policy, the environment, and so forth.

The importance of the Court of Auditors and its work have been highlighted in recent years by the many cases of fraud and mismanagement in the handling of EU funds, for example, the irregularities that led to the resignation of the Commission in 1999 and the controversy that arose in 2003 over the Commission's accounting system and the use by Eurostat, the EU's statistical arm, of unofficial bank accounts into which millions of euros were channeled. While cases of fraud and mismanagement tend to place the Court in the headlines, it is not exclusively concerned with deliberate wrong-doing. It also evaluates the overall effectiveness of EU policies, in much the manner of the General Accounting Office in the

United States. Recent Court of Auditors reports have analyzed, for example, the effectiveness of European Regional Development Fund (ERDF) and European Social Fund aid in combating long-term unemployment, the success of EU efforts to combat BSE (mad cow disease), and the results of EU-funded environmental projects in the candidate countries of central and eastern Europe.[10]

THE EUROPEAN INVESTMENT BANK

The EIB was set up in 1958 to provide loans to public and private sector projects that advanced Community objectives, especially those that contributed to completing the common market. Headquartered in Luxembourg, the EIB is owned by the member states of the EU. Its excellent credit rating allows it to raise capital on global financial markets that it relends at favorable rates of interest, usually to cofinance projects with private sector and other governmental lenders and investors.

Most EIB lending goes to projects inside the EU, but a growing share of lending is to nonmember countries in support of the pre-accession process for candidate countries or to support EU foreign and development aid policies. In 2002, for example, the EIB signed contracts for loans totaling €39.6 billion, of which €33.4 billion was for projects inside the EU, €3.6 billion for candidate countries in central and eastern Europe (and Cyprus and Malta), and €2.5 billion for various other partner countries. The latter include the African, Caribbean and Pacific (ACP) countries with which the EU is associated (€298 million), the Balkans (€425 million), the countries of North Africa and the Middle East that participate in the Euro-Mediterranean Partnership launched by the EU in 1995 (€1.6 billion), and various other countries in Africa, Asia, and Latin America (€224 million).[11]

The EIB plays a key role in EU regional policy, where its loans to projects in depressed regions and to the poorer member states complement grant aid from the EU's structural funds. EIB loans also support EU environmental projects and trans-European networks, the large cross-border projects in transport, energy, and telecommunications promoted by the Union.

THE EUROPEAN CENTRAL BANK

The newest of the major EU institutions is the ECB, which was formally established in June 1998, taking over the responsibilities of a transitional body, the European Monetary Institute, that was set up under the Maastricht treaty to assist with preparations for the single currency. Located in Frankfurt, the ECB is the central institution of the ESCB, the network of national central banks established to conduct a single European monetary policy. The ECB is discussed in detail in chapter 6.

SPECIALIZED AGENCIES

In addition to the treaty-based institutions that make law and policy, the EU has established an array of specialized agencies that are responsible for monitoring and helping to implement policy in particular fields such as the environment, workplace health and safety, and testing and certification of technical standards. As the range of EU policies has widened and the body of legislation has grown, the need for such agencies has become more apparent. The Commission bureaucracy lacks the staff and expertise to involve itself in all of the technical and administrative aspects of policy implementation and must in any case focus on its key responsibilities of initiating legislative proposals, guarding against infringements of the treaties, and executing major policy initiatives. The member states have been wary of establishing agencies with real powers at the Union level, but they increasingly have recognized the need for bodies that can bring together the different national perspectives. For the most part they have limited the regulatory and inspection powers of these bodies and have stressed that their role is to gather information on policies and standards, many of which are made at the national level in accordance with EU directives.

These bodies are dispersed throughout the territory of the Union, as shown in table 3.10.

The oldest of these agencies are the European Foundation for the Improvement of Living and Working Conditions and the European Training Foundation (ETF), both established in 1975 to deal with aspects of social and economic policy. The European Foundation issues reports on living and working conditions in the EU, with the aim of providing authoritative guidance to policymakers on social policy. The ETF is responsible for coordinating and supporting all EU activities in the field of postcompulsory education and training, including those conducted under EU aid programs.

After a break of nearly two decades, in the mid-1990s the EU began a new and much more expansive phase of agency building that reflected the new responsibilities of the EU established under the SEA and the Maastricht treaty, as well as the desire of politicians to be seen as responding to complex problems by taking action at the European level. The European Environment Agency (EEA) began work in December 1993, and is responsible for coordinating environmental assessments from a network of institutes from throughout Europe and for disseminating the results of these assessments to the Parliament, the Commission, the member states, and the general public. The European Monitoring Centre for Drugs and Drug Addiction became operational in 1995, based on a Council regulation of February 1993. Its aim is to provide "objective, reliable and comparable information at European level concerning drugs, drug addiction, and their consequences."[12]

The European Agency for the Evaluation of Medicinal Products was established in January 1995, and is responsible for ensuring the uniform evaluation and labeling of products in the single market. The Office for Harmonization in the Internal Market began work in September 1994. It registers and administers EU

Table 3.10   EU Agencies and Bodies

Agency	Location	Date operational
European Center for the Development of Vocational Training	Thessaloniki	1975
European Foundation for the Improvement of Living and Working Conditions	Dublin	1975
European Environment Agency	Copenhagen	1994
European Training Foundation	Turin	1990
European Monitoring Center for Drugs and Drug Addiction	Lisbon	1995
European Agency for the Evaluation of Medicinal Products	London	1993
Office for Harmonization in the Internal Market (Trade Marks and Designs)	Alicante	1994
European Agency for Safety and Health at Work	Bilbao	1994
Community Plant Variety Office	Angers	1996
Translation Center for the Bodies of the European Union	Luxembourg	1994
European Monitoring Center on Racism and Xenophobia	Vienna	1998
European Agency for Reconstruction	Thessaloniki	2000
European Food Safety Authority	Parma	2002
European Maritime Safety Agency	Lisbon	2002
European Aviation Safety Agency	Cologne	2003
Justice and Home Affairs (JHA) bodies		
European Police Office (Europol)	The Hague	1998
Eurojust (European Body for the Enhancement of Judicial Cooperation)	The Hague	2002
CFSP bodies		
European Institute for Security Studies	Paris	2002
European Union Satellite Center	Torrejón	2002

trademarks and designs, an important function in the internal market for intellectual property. Other agencies are the Agency for Safety and Health at Work and the Community Plant Variety Office that administers intellectual property with regard to new plant varieties.

Europol (discussed in detail in chapter 7) is not technically an EU agency, since it deals with police and judicial cooperation, which falls under the intergovernmental (third-pillar) part of EU decision making. Whereas the other EU agencies were established by Council regulations on the basis of Commission proposals, Europol rests on a separate international convention concluded among the member states. Nonetheless, it functions very much as an EU agency in that it gathers information from the member states and seeks to assist in the coordination of policy. The same generalizations apply to Eurojust, which was set up in 2002 to facilitate coordination among national prosecutors, magistrates, and high police officials in prosecuting major cross-border crimes. So far, there are only a few relatively small agencies that operate under CFSP, and these were inherited from the Western European Union (WEU) when it effectively was absorbed by the EU in 2000. However, the European Armaments, Research and Military Capabilities

Agency that is to be set up by decision of the June 2003 Thessaloniki European Council and that is mandated in the draft European Constitution will be a major breakthrough in this area.

Responding to the need for more EU-level coordination and regulation in many areas, in recent years the Council of Ministers and the European Parliament have passed legislation establishing a range of new agencies. The European Food Safety Authority was set up in 2002 in response to crises involving "mad cow disease" and dioxin-tainted animal feed and in response to the ongoing controversy in Europe over the safety of genetically modified organisms. The European Maritime Safety Agency was established the same year after a series of damaging tanker accidents that spilled oil on Europe's beaches highlighted the need for stronger action in this area. The establishment of the European Aviation Safety Agency was a natural response to the continued deregulation of the European aviation industry and the creation of the "single European sky." Other agencies and offices that are planned but not yet fully operational include a European Railway Agency, a European Network and Information Security Agency, a European Center for Disease Prevention and Control, a European Chemicals Agency, and a European Agency for the Management of Operational Cooperation at the External Borders.

How the EU agencies develop and what powers they assume will be important indicators of the future of the Union. Two conflicting tendencies are at work in shaping the development of these bodies. On the one hand, the increasing complexity of technical issues involved in regulating the single market, the unevenness of national capabilities to regulate and inspect in certain areas, and the desire of the Commission and some member states to have strong European counterparts to such internationally influential U.S. agencies as the Food and Drug Administration, the Federal Aviation Administration, and the Environmental Protection Agency all argue in the direction of stronger central bodies and a certain federalization of regulation in the Union. Another factor encouraging the proliferation of such bodies in recent years has been enlargement and the desire of all member states—old and new—to have some EU institution located on their territory for the prestige and economic benefits that it brings. On the other hand, the member states and public opinion in general are wary of creating new centralized bureaucracies outside the control of national governments. This argues for a minimalist approach to institution building and explains why many of these agencies are small and relatively weak and why they mainly have coordinating and information-gathering responsibilities rather than strong powers to regulate directly. As these tendencies coexist and interact, the outcome is likely to be a dual system of monitoring and regulation in which powers are exercised at both the EU and member-state levels.

The Ongoing Role of the Member States

Before leaving the subject of the EU institutions and turning to EU law, it is important to recall the central role of the member states. The EU is unique among international bodies in the degree to which its members have pooled sovereignty and delegated powers to central institutions. At the same time, however, it is important not to underestimate the role of the member states or the ongoing relevance of national interest and domestic politics in the integration process. There are four reasons why the member states remain prime actors in the EU.

First, they are directly represented in two of the Union's key decision-making bodies, the Council of Ministers and the European Council, and they determine the membership of two other major decision-making bodies, the Commission and the ECJ. They also select the president and governing bodies of the ECB. The positions of the member states in the European Council and the Council of Ministers as well as efforts by national capitals to influence the Commission and the ECB are based on calculations of concrete national economic and political interest, rather than on commitment to the abstract ideal of European unity.

Second, in some EU policy areas, notably CFSP and some areas of justice and home affairs, decision making remains largely intergovernmental. The member states are committed by treaty to developing common positions and undertaking joint actions, but these are the positions and actions of sovereign states agreeing to work together, not a single position worked out by centralized institutions exercising their own powers. The difficulties that the EU has had in forging a CFSP or in tackling issues such as immigration at the European level underline the persistence of different national traditions and interests among the member states—differences that in some respects have grown wider with each enlargement.

Third, in other policy areas competence either remains entirely with the member states or is shared between the Union and the member states. Education, health, social welfare, and culture are largely matters of national responsibility, while competence for transport, regional development, the environment, and competition policy is shared between the EU institutions and the member states. From the early 1970s through the early 1990s there was a tendency for more and more issues to be transferred at least partially to the European level, but this trend was ended with the signing of the Maastricht treaty and the difficult ratification debate that followed. The subsidiarity concept now guides the member states and the central institutions (especially the Commission as the policy initiator) in determining which issues are to be handled at the Union level and which are better left to the member states. As noted, the draft European Constitution contains a catalog of competences that lists policy areas that are shared between the member states and the Union or in which the Union plays only a supporting role.

Fourth, the member states play a key role in implementing EU policies—even those that are subject to EU competence. Whereas in the United States the federal government has a nationwide bureaucracy, a huge budget, and a vast body of federal law on which to rely in implementing federal policy, this is not the case in the EU. It has only 20,000 or so employees in Brussels and Luxembourg and a number of modest-sized institutions spread elsewhere throughout the member states. The member states provide the administrative and legal apparatus to implement EU law and policy. Thus, for example, even when the EU adopts a Union-wide environmental protection measure, each member state usually must adopt or amend national legislation to ensure that the EU standard is reflected throughout the Union. National environmental protection agencies in turn are responsible for ensuring that individuals and industries comply with the legislation. As will be seen, much of the legal action that takes place in the ECJ arises from disputes over implementation of EU directives at the national level. Indeed, the importance of EU law is directly linked to the complexities inherent in a situation in which member states, having pooled or delegated their sovereignty in central institutions, still must use their sovereign powers to implement EU decisions.

EU Law

One of the most important features that distinguishes the EU from other international groupings is the existence of a body of law that constitutes, in the words of the ECJ, a "new legal order."[13] EU law is different from international law, in that it has direct effect on citizens and other legal persons, and that it must be obeyed by sovereign states that are members of the Union. At the same time, it has not replaced member state law, which coexists with and is supposed to be consistent with EU law. The EU legal system is sui generis—without ready parallels elsewhere in the world.

EU law can be divided into two main categories: primary and secondary. The founding treaties constitute the primary law of the Union. Such law is made by unanimous agreement among the member states, generally by means of an intergovernmental conference. Primary law requires ratification at the national level by national parliaments and in some cases national referenda. Treaties of accession, which are concluded between existing member states and new members when they join the EU, also constitute primary law, since they amend the existing treaties.

Secondary law consists of legislation passed by the institutions of the EU. It is used to translate the broadly stated objectives and intentions in the treaties into specific rules and policy measures. Although more detailed than national constitutions, the EU's founding treaties cannot possibly spell out all the details of the common policies in trade, transport, competition, and the many other areas covered in the treaties. This has to be done over time through subsequent action by the EU institutions. Legal measures adopted by and through these institutions constitute the secondary law of the Union.

REGULATIONS, DIRECTIVES, AND DECISIONS

The EC treaty specifies three main types of legislative measures (secondary law): regulations, directives, and decisions. Regulations are binding and are directly applicable throughout the Union. In this respect they are analogous to federal law in the United States, which applies directly to individuals and corporate entities. Regulations do not require legal action by the member states to take effect, although the states may need to take administrative steps to ensure implementation.

Regulations can be passed either by the Council of Ministers acting on a proposal from the Commission, by the Council and the Parliament (where the treaties provide for co-decision) acting on a Commission proposal, or by the Commission alone.

Council and Council-European Parliament regulations tend to be of a general nature, and deal with such matters as administration of the structural funds, rules under the common fisheries policy, or guidelines relating to actions by the EIB. Commission regulations are more narrow and technical, and are often of an administrative nature. Many are used to administer the CAP. Commission regulations are in many ways analogous to rules promulgated by federal agencies in the United States that are used to implement acts passed by the Congress but that do not in themselves require specific Congressional action. Regulations are used wherever there is a need for total uniformity throughout the Union on a particular matter of EU law.

Directives are binding, "as to the result to be achieved," upon the member states to which they are addressed (generally all of the member states), "but shall leave to the national authorities the choice of form and methods."[14] Directives specify, usually in considerable detail, an EU-wide result, but allow the member states to achieve this result in ways that reflect national legal and administrative traditions, the structure of local industry, and other factors. Examples of objectives pursued through directives include the introduction of competition in the market for voice telephony, reductions in urban air pollution, and policing money laundering and financial crime in the Union.

Directives are proposed by the Commission, based on its interpretation of what needs to be done to fulfill both the specific provisions and the broader purposes of the founding treaties. In accordance with the co-decision procedures introduced by the Maastricht and Amsterdam treaties, they are passed by the Council of Ministers and the Parliament, after consultation as required with the ESC, the Committee of the Regions, or both. Once directives are passed, it is up to the member states to ensure their implementation. The member states are not required to adopt identical implementing legislation, and laws continue to differ in accordance with national traditions and political preferences. But national legislation must accomplish the main objectives of the relevant EU directive. If a member state fails to transpose a directive into national legislation, the Commission can institute proceedings against that state in the Court of Justice.

Decisions are binding measures that are addressed to specific parties and that do not have general applicability. Examples of decisions include Commission actions in competition cases (blocking a merger between two firms or enjoining a national government from providing aid to a firm or industry), or actions taken with regard to specific TEN projects. Decisions can be addressed to all of the member states, often to assist them in clarifying the details regarding implementation of directives, in which case they function very much like regulations.

EU legislation in many sectors is a mixture of directives, regulations, and decisions. The member states generally have favored reliance on the directive with its greater latitude for national interpretation, and have resisted the use of regulations. Most legislation for the 1992 single market program, for example, took the form of directives. The extensive use of directives has both benefits and drawbacks. On the plus side, it moderates the intrusiveness of Brussels in national life and allows for adjustment to local conditions. On the negative side, it makes for a complicated legal order that imposes costs on firms operating across national borders and that is difficult to enforce. The Commission must check to see that national implementing legislation is adopted in each of the member states and that it conforms with the directives, and it must further check on an ongoing basis to ensure that such legislation is applied in practice.

KEY PRINCIPLES

EU law exists in a broader legal and political context—one that has developed over the years through the interaction of the ECJ and the national courts and that is based heavily on the case law of the ECJ. The two most salient principles of EU law are *direct effect* and the *primacy of EU over national law*. Neither principle is explicitly spelled out in the treaties; both developed over time as a result of court rulings.

In the van Gend and Loos case of 1963, a Dutch trucking firm of that name brought suit in a Dutch court against the Dutch state for imposing increased tariffs on a chemical product that it imported to the Netherlands from Germany. This was during the transition period in which all tariffs among the six were being phased out and in which the Treaty of Rome prohibited member states from introducing new tariffs or restrictions on trade. The action by the Dutch government thus appeared to contravene the spirit and letter of the treaty. The Dutch court referred the case to the ECJ, which ruled that the trucking firm enjoyed rights under the treaty. The Court further declared that the new national duties on chemicals that had harmed the business interests of the firm were a contravention of the treaty and were therefore void. The case established what is known as direct effect—the principle that European law has direct applicability to citizens and corporate bodies, conferring rights and imposing obligations.

In other important cases, the ECJ established that in situations in which European and national law were in conflict, EU law had primacy. In the Costa v. ENEL case of 1964, an Italian shareholder in an electricity company recently nationalized by the Italian government refused to pay his electricity bill on the grounds that the nationalization was illegal under Community (EEC) law. The Italian national court referred the case to the ECJ for a preliminary ruling. The ECJ used the case to develop the doctrine that Community law had supremacy over national law, arguing that in joining the Community the member states had irrevocably surrendered some of their sovereign powers. The court subsequently elaborated and strengthened its position on this matter, notably in the 1978 Simmenthal decision, in which it starkly concluded: "a national court which is called upon, within the limits of its jurisdiction, to apply provisions of Community law is under a duty to give full effect to those provisions, if necessary refusing of its own motion to apply any conflicting provisions of national legislation."[15]

The supremacy of EU law over national law is a remarkable development in the integration process. It in part explains the extreme care with which member countries—by reputation the UK and Denmark but *all* members to some extent— decide to add competence for sensitive policy matters to the EU's first pillar, and their decision at Maastricht to establish separate intergovernmental pillars, beyond the jurisdiction of the ECJ, for foreign and security policy and justice and home affairs.

Under the relevant provisions of the treaties, the Commission is obliged to take action to bring member states into compliance with their treaty obligations. These provisions were strengthened by the Maastricht treaty, which allowed for fines to be levied against member states that persistently failed to meet an obligation about which they have been warned. If the Commission believes that a member state has failed to fulfill an obligation under EU law, it issues a letter of formal notice to that state expressing concerns about the possible infringement. If it does not receive a favorable response about the matter, the Commission delivers a reasoned opinion on the alleged breach of compliance to the state and asks it to give its observations on the matter. If after a certain period of time the member state fails to comply with the Commission's opinion, the Commission may initiate proceedings against that state in the Court of Justice. If the Court finds that the member state has indeed failed to fulfill its obligations, it can order that state to take measures to bring itself into compliance. If the Commission considers that the state in question still has not taken the necessary measures to comply, it issues a second reasoned opinion specifying the points on which the member state has failed to comply with the judgment of the Court. If the member state still does not fulfill its obligations, the Commission returns to the Court, this time proposing a penalty that the Court can impose on that state for continued noncompliance.

Each year the Commission publishes an annual report on the application of EU law in the member states and across various sectors. In 2002, the Commission reported that it issued 995 letters of formal notice, 487 reasoned opinions, and made 180 referrals to the ECJ. The largest number of referrals to the Court concerned France, followed by Italy and then Spain. Of a total of 3,541 infringement cases open at all stages as of the end of 2002, the largest share concerned environmental legislation (38.9 percent), followed by internal market (21.1 percent), and health and consumer affairs (7.4 percent). The Commission had so-called Article 228 proceedings underway in 62 cases, meaning that it was preparing to ask the Court to approve penalty or lump-sum payments for noncompliance by member states.[16]

LAW AND THE EUROPEAN CONSTITUTION

The draft European Constitution contains a number of provisions that attempt to rationalize and clarify the status of EU secondary law. Some of these changes are terminological, and may add to confusion, but others are substantive. The Constitution lists six legal instruments that the Union will have at its disposal once the Constitution goes into effect: European laws, European framework laws, European regulations, European decisions, recommendations, and opinions.

European laws are to replace the current regulations. They will be binding in their entirety and directly applicable. *European framework laws* will replace the current directives. They are to be binding upon the member states as to the result to be achieved. *European regulations* (in the new sense of the term) and *European decisions* are nonlegislative legal acts, which means that they are binding upon those to whom they are addressed even though they are not passed as law by the European Parliament and Council of Ministers. Such regulations and decisions can be made by the various EU institutions in cases specifically provided for in the Constitution. Examples include the right of the Council, acting upon a proposal from the Commission, to provide financial assistance to a member state hit by natural disasters or other circumstances beyond its control; the responsibility of the Council, acting upon a proposal from the Commission, to establish specific research programs within the framework of the multi-annual programs established by European law; and the responsibility of the Commission to take decisions regarding the compatibility of state aids with EU internal market legislation.[17]

In addition to the European regulations and European decisions explicitly provided for in the Constitution, the Constitution establishes a new legal category, that of delegated regulations. The latter can be promulgated by the Commission, acting not under the direct authority of the Constitution but under the terms of individual European laws or European framework laws. For example, the Council and the Parliament might pass an environmental protection law setting forth certain standards, deadlines, and levels of protection, but delegate responsibility to the Commission to identify particular pollutants that might need to be banned or otherwise regulated in order to implement the regulation. This practice of allowing the legislative process to establish the essential policy elements and then delegating implementation to an executive agency is consistent with practice in most countries, including the United States, where rule-making authority is often delegated to federal agencies to implement laws passed by Congress. In the EU case, however, the proposed constitutional language stipulates that the laws and framework laws may contain provisions allowing the Parliament or the Council to revoke the delegation or, conversely, to allow a delegated regulation to enter into force only if no objection to it is expressed by the Parliament or the Council within a set period established by the law or framework law.

Recommendations and *opinions* are legal acts but they have no binding force. Examples include the broad economic policy guidelines drafted by the Commission and passed by the Council each year, opinions submitted to the EU institutions by the ECB on matters within its field of competence, and opinions by the Commission addressed to the member states on how they might coordinate social policy measures relating to employment, labor law and working conditions, and social security.[18] Member states and others to whom such recommendations and opinions are addressed are supposed to take them into account in their policies, but they cannot be brought before the ECJ for not following these recommendations and opinions.

The Budget

Apart from law, a second feature that distinguishes the EU from other international bodies and that reflects the depth of the integration process is its budget. Unlike international institutions that receive funding from their member states, the EU is financed exclusively by a system of "own resources." In the early years of the Community, the member states paid into the budget as in a traditional international organization. Under the budget treaties of 1970 and 1975, however, the EC gained an autonomous source of revenue. This consisted of three elements: the customs duties collected under the common external tariff, levies on imported agriculture products, and a proportion of the value-added tax (VAT) collected in each of the member states. In 1988 the EC added a fourth own resource, which consists of an automatic assessment of each of the member states based on their total and per capita gross national products (GNPs). The composition of the own resources has changed over time, as the relative share of revenue from agricultural and customs duties has declined. In 2004, 73.4 percent of the revenue of the EU budget was expected to come from national income assessments, 14.1 percent from VAT-based resources, 10.4 percent from customs duties, and 1.3 percent from agricultural duties.

The member states set the level of own resources—and by extension the overall spending level—by unanimous decision in the Council of Ministers. For much of the period that the own resource system has been in operation, the member states have been quite generous with the budget. It has grown more quickly than national budgets, allowing the EU to expand into new areas of activity such as regional policy, precompetitive industrial research, and extensive foreign aid programs for central and eastern Europe and the Mediterranean countries. In recent years, however, the member states have tried to rein in the growth of the EU budget, especially since their own national budgets have had to be trimmed to meet the Maastricht EMU convergence criteria and subsequently the strictures on government deficits contained in the Stability and Growth Pact (SGP).

Commitments in the 2003 EU budget totaled €99.812 billion, or some $125 billion.[19] This was the last budget for the EU of fifteen member states. Spending in 2004 was expected to increase by approximately 10 percent to account for the enlargement to ten new member states. In national terms, this is a modest figure, amounting to about 2.5 percent of combined public spending of the member states. By most other standards, it is a substantial sum that provides the means for the EU to pursue its internal and external policies. Approximately 45 percent of the EU budget goes to agriculture, down from nearly 70 percent in the mid-1980s. About a third of the budget goes to the structural funds to support economic development in the poorer regions of the Union. Approximately 7 percent of the budget is used to pay for EU internal policies, including research and development (by far the largest share of this category), the environment, transport, and trans-European networks. Almost 5 percent goes to external action, chiefly foreign aid but also actions undertaken under CFSP, not counting pre-accession aid for the candidate countries, which comprises another 3.5 percent of the budget. Administrative expenditure—staff, facilities, and other expenses associated with the EU's institutions—accounts for just over 5 percent of expenditure.

BUDGETARY PROCEDURE

Under the EU budgetary procedures, the Commission draws up a preliminary draft budget which it presents to the Council of Ministers. The Council may and usually does amend the Commission's draft. It then establishes, by qualified majority vote, the draft budget and sends it to the Parliament, which has the right to propose amendments before approving the final budget. In the event of differences between the Council and the Parliament, the Council makes the final decisions on compulsory spending, that is, spending essential to carrying out the obligations of the treaties, such as the CAP. The Parliament makes the final decisions regarding noncompulsory spending, but it is only allowed to increase such expenditure within a certain percentage that is determined each year on the basis of economic growth, inflation, and increases in government spending in the member states. The Parliament also can reject, by a two-thirds vote, the draft budget as a whole and ask that a new budget be submitted.

The budget frequently has been a matter of contention among the member states. In the early 1980s the Community went through a protracted crisis over Britain's contribution to the budget. Because support for farmers was the largest part of the budget and because Britain's agricultural sector was smaller in relative terms than those in other member countries, it paid far more into the Community budget than it received back, even though its per capita GDP trailed the Community average. Prime Minister Thatcher demanded a rebate to bring UK contributions more into line with payments. The other states were reluctant to meet this demand, which in their view would undermine the supranational basis of the Community and establish a principle that states must receive back the equivalent of what they pay into the budget (a principle known as *juste retour*, used in many cooperative European arms and industrial projects, but inimical to efficient decision making and incompatible with pursuit of such goals as redistribution among member states at different income levels). Nonetheless, after many acrimonious debates in the European Council, at the Fontainebleau summit of 1984 the other member states agreed to British demands for a rebate.

The accessions of Greece in 1981 and Spain and Portugal in 1986 also led to new budgetary challenges. Led by Spain, these countries and Ireland successfully pressed for transfers from the Community budget (structural funds) to help them cope with the economic and political challenges of joining with more advanced countries in the single market program and later EMU. More recently, the question of enlargement and excessive payments by Germany and the Netherlands into the budget have been points of contention.

DELORS I AND II

To introduce an element of predictability in the budget process, since the late 1980s the EU has adopted a series of multi-year budgetary packages that establish a framework for the annual budgets. This approach eliminates much of the political squabbling over money that used to dominate nearly every session of the European Council. It also began as part of a long-overdue effort to begin reining in agricultural spending. The first such multi-year package, known as Delors I, was concluded in February 1988 and covered the five budget years from 1988 to 1992. The package was a political compromise that contained something for everyone: increased aid for Ireland and the Mediterranean countries, the rebate for the UK, higher overall levels of spending for those committed to developing EC policies in new areas, and the beginnings of a reform of agricultural spending but on a gradual basis that would not bring hardship to farmers. Its basic elements included an increase in total funding up to a ceiling of 1.2 percent of Community GDP, the addition of a fourth own resource to cover the increased spending, a continuation of the British rebate, a doubling of the financial flows to the poorer regions of the Community, and a commitment to hold down the growth in agricultural spending to no more than 74 percent of the growth in EC GDP.

Delors I was followed by the seven-year 1993–1999 Delors II package, worked out by the member states at the December 1992 Edinburgh European Council.[20] The Edinburgh package followed the basic outlines of the previous budget agreement and even increased funding levels somewhat. The revenue ceiling was maintained at 1.2 percent of GNP for 1993 and 1994, but set to rise by increments to 1.27 percent of GNP by 1999. The 1988 guideline limiting increases in CAP expenditure to 74 percent of the rate of growth of EU GNP was retained, as was the British rebate. The member states agreed to another large increase in structural funds for the poorer parts of the Union, from European Currency Unit (ECU) 21.277 billion in 1993 to ECU 30.000 billion in 1999, or some 41 percent. The Cohesion Fund established by the Maastricht treaty to help countries with a per capita GNP of less than 90 percent of the EU average was funded at ECU 1.5 billion, rising to ECU 2.6 billion in 1999. Total spending on structural and cohesion funding was to reach 0.46 percent of EU GNP by the last year of the Delors II package. The other noteworthy aspect of the Edinburgh agreement was the rise in spending for external policies, from ECU 4.450 billion in 1993 to ECU 6.200 billion in 1999, undertaken largely in response to the upheavals underway in central and eastern Europe.

THE 2000–2006 BUDGET PACKAGE

The pending expiration of the Delors II package, the start of enlargement negotiations, and political change in the member states all converged at the end of the

1990s to produce a major debate about EU finances. This debate was driven by two factors: on the one hand the member states were concerned about their own financial positions. In the post-Maastricht period of skepticism about integration and EMU-driven austerity, those countries that paid most into the EU's coffers wanted to reduce their net contributions, while those that received net transfers from the budget were reluctant to give up this source of income. On the other hand, the EU was faced with potentially vast new demands on its budget as new members joined. As Belgian Prime Minister Jean-Luc Dehaene summed up the dilemma, "nobody wants to pay more, some want to pay less, nobody wants to get less and we have to spend more for enlargement."[21]

In *Agenda 2000* the Commission outlined what was in effect a "Delors III" proposal. It proposed retaining the budgetary ceiling at 1.27 per cent of EU GNP, holding increases in CAP at the existing limit of 74 percent of GNP growth, and keeping structural policies pegged at the level of 0.46 percent of total GNP.[22] It claimed that a budget along these lines would be adequate to finance enlargement, provided agricultural and cohesion policies were reformed to improve their efficiency.

Following the crucial December 1997 Luxembourg decisions regarding the start of accession negotiations with Cyprus and five central and east European countries, the June 1998 Cardiff European Council set March 1999 as the target date for the completion of the financial package—a timetable driven by the elections to the European Parliament scheduled for June 1999. The December 1998 Vienna summit reiterated the commitment to reaching an overall agreement on Agenda 2000 at a special session of the European Council set for March 24–25, 1999, in Berlin.

Despite the effort by the Commission to dampen controversy among the member states by maintaining continuity with past budget packages, the months preceding the Berlin summit were dominated by fierce debate and seemingly irreconcilable positions over financial issues. The analytical basis for this debate was a report issued by the Commission in October 1998, *Financing the European Union*, that offered a sophisticated and detailed analysis that covered revenues, expenditures, and the distributional effects of each of the four own resources and of the various categories of expenditure.[23] The report spelled out the net payment position of each of the member states in a way that was inevitably somewhat arbitrary and misleading, but that was difficult to ignore. Ireland received a whopping 5.1 percent of GNP per year in net payments, while Germany and Sweden each paid in 0.6 percent of GNP more than they received back. In absolute terms, Germany's net "loss" was €11.46 billion, or some $13 billion, while Spain was a net beneficiary of €5.54 billion, or some $7 billion.

In the early phases of the negotiations, member-state governments staked out widely divergent positions on the budget. Germany, Sweden, and the Netherlands wanted their net contributions cut. France wanted to rein in overall spending, but balked at reforms in the CAP that would fall disproportionately on France or French farmers. Britain was for austerity, but not for giving up its own rebate. Spain pressed for high levels of regional aid and no diversion of structural funds to the east.

The Berlin summit ultimately resulted in an agreement in the European Council on a seven-year budget framework, but only after twenty hours of continuous negotiation that saw many leaders back away from earlier positions and the EU as a whole retreat somewhat from its stated commitment to a sweeping financial reform. The framework once again established the own resources ceiling at 1.27 percent of EU GNP, thereby rejecting the position of those member states that would have preferred a freeze on the EU budget (assuming some real economic growth, the budget will grow as well) and left the agricultural guideline unchanged at 74 percent of GNP growth. It reined in growth in structural and cohesion funds for current member states, but stopped short of the freeze on growth in regional aid that some member states favored. It also retained the British rebate.

As shown in table 3.11, the financial framework assumed that the first enlargement would occur in 2002. Expenditures associated with pre-accession and post-accession costs for the new member states were "ring-fenced" from spending earmarked for the EU-15: "Expenditure reserved for EU-15 cannot at any time be used for pre-accession assistance and, conversely, expenditure reserved for pre-accession assistance cannot be used by EU-15."[24] The numbers subsequently were revised when enlargement was deferred to May 1, 2004, and extended to a larger group of countries than had been anticipated in Berlin, but the same basic principle held that there would be a guaranteed set of benefits for the existing member states that would not be reduced by enlargement.

THE 2007–2013 BUDGET PERSPECTIVE

Debate on the 2007–2013 financial perspective began early and was in full swing by the winter of 2003–2004. More than ever, questions of money were intertwined with issues of the balance of power among the member states and between the member states and the institutions of the Union. At the IGC of 2000, Spain had managed to secure a provision in the Treaty of Nice stipulating that qualified majority voting in decisions regarding Structural Funds and the Cohesion Fund would be instituted only after January 1, 2007, and the adoption of the next financial perspective.[25] It thus had a veto going into the budget discussions, which it made clear it would use to protect its longstanding claims on development funds.

But Spain, along with Poland, also was the country most opposed to certain provisions of the draft European Constitution. The question of finance thus inevitably was linked to institutional reform. As the 2003 IGC set to convene, German foreign minister Fischer explicitly drew the connection, noting that "a number of financially weak accession countries belong to the most enthusiastic advocates of changes in the draft Constitution."[26] The tight fiscal situation in most member states further heightened the stakes in the budget negotiations. In December 2003, the six leading net contributors to the budget—Germany, France, the UK, Sweden, Austria, and the Netherlands—sent a joint letter to Commission president Prodi calling upon him to produce a budget based on a ceiling of 1 percent of EU

Table 3.11   The EU Financial Framework (EU-21)

Millions of euros, 1999 prices

	2000	2001	2002	2003	2004	2005	2006
Agriculture	40920	42800	43900	43770	42760	41930	41660
CAP	36620	38480	39570	39430	38410	37570	37290
Rural development and accompanying measures	4300	4320	4330	4340	4350	4360	4370
Structural operations	32045	31455	30865	30285	29595	29595	29170
Structural funds	29430	28840	28250	27670	27080	27080	26660
Cohesion fund	2615	2615	2615	2615	2515	2515	2510
Internal policies	5900	5950	6000	6050	6100	6150	6200
External action	4550	4560	4570	4580	4590	4600	4610
Administration	4560	4600	4700	4800	4900	5000	5100
Reserves	900	900	650	400	400	400	400
Pre-accession aid	3120	3120	3120	3120	3120	3120	3120
Agriculture	520	520	520	520	520	520	520
Pre-accession structural instrument	1040	1040	1040	1040	1040	1040	1040
PHARE	1560	1560	1560	1560	1560	1560	1560
Enlargement			6450	9030	11610	14200	16780
Agriculture			1600	2030	2450	2930	3400
Structural operations			3750	5830	7920	10000	12080
Internal policies			730	760	790	820	850
Administration			370	410	450	450	450
Total appropriations for commitments	91995	93385	100255	102035	103075	104995	107040
Total appropriations for payments	89590	91070	98270	101450	100610	101350	103530
of which: enlargement			*4140*	*6710*	*8890*	*11440*	*14210*
Payments as % of GNP	1.13%	1.12%	1.14%	1.15%	1.11%	1.09%	1.09%
Own resources ceiling	1.27%	1.27%	1.27%	1.27%	1.27%	1.27%	1.27%

GDP for the 2007–2013 period. This was well below the ceiling of 1.27 percent agreed at Berlin, although in fact it might not mean a huge reduction in spending, since actual spending (as opposed to the budgetary ceiling) in recent years had averaged around 1.1 percent of Union GDP owing to lower than expected expenditures for agriculture, delays in disbursing regional aid, and certain other factors.

The Commission rejected this call, arguing that cutting spending at a time when the EU was integrating ten new member states and trying to upgrade its role in the world would be short-sighted. In February 2004, the Commission unveiled its draft financial perspective. It proposed that total appropriations for commitments start at €133.560 billion in 2007 and rise to €158.450 billion in 2013. In disregard of the recommendation in the letter of six, the own resources ceiling was set at 1.24 percent of gross national income. To better market the budget and convey a sense of the Union's political priorities, the Commission draft did not use the traditional budget categories (Agriculture, Structural Operations, Internal Policies, External Action), but grouped expenditures into four areas (plus a fifth for Administration): *Sustainable growth*, including both the structural funds and various expenditures to promote competitiveness, set to rise 28 percent over the framework period; *Preservation and management of natural resources*, a somewhat dubiously named category that included agricultural spending in which spending was held roughly constant; *Citizenship, freedom, security and justice*, covering third-pillar matters, set to increase 122 percent (albeit from a low base); and the *EU as a global partner*, essentially the old External Action account, in which proposed spending was to increase by 38 percent.[27]

The European Parliament, like the Commission a proponent of an expansive role for the EU within and outside Europe, generally welcomed the draft, but the member states were not amused. The stage thus was set for a major political battle—involving the fifteen, the ten new member states, and a newly elected European Parliament—before spending levels and priorities could be set for the 2007 budget and beyond.

Conclusions

The institutional, legal, and budgetary set up of the EU is complex and changing. The EU operates in accordance with two basic treaties: the Treaty establishing the European Community and the Treaty on European Union (TEU). The EC Treaty (TEC) initially was adopted as the Treaty of Rome in 1957, and later was amended by the Single European Act and parts of the Maastricht, Amsterdam, and Nice treaties. The TEU first was adopted at Maastricht, and amended by parts of the Amsterdam and Nice treaties. All of these revisions have brought about changes in the EU's institutions. In addition, these institutions have continued to evolve according to their own internal dynamics and in response to policy decisions that often do not require treaty change.

The draft European Constitution would repeal all of these treaties and replace them with a single legal text. However, as of early 2004 the member states had not yet agreed on all of the provisions of the future Constitution, much less secured the necessary ratifications in twenty-five member states for it to go into effect. The draft Constitution is in any case a phased document, with certain institutional provisions that are to apply until 2009, and others that go into effect only after that date.

Given the uncertainties surrounding the Constitution, much is unknown about the functioning and likely future evolution of the EU institutions. Efforts since Amsterdam to simplify and rationalize the treaties have had at best very mixed results. No EU politician can predict with certainty how the EU institutions will function in 2009. As for the general public, indications are that it is hopelessly confused, notwithstanding the repeated calls from reformers for a simple governance structure that the voters can understand and that they perceive as legitimate. That said, it would not be correct to conclude that the design and functioning of the EU's institutions have been failures. For all their flaws, these institutions, and the political leaders, officials, and judges working in and through them, have managed to push the integration process forward and to register a long list of achievements, from the introduction of the euro to the development of a fledgling foreign policy for the EU to enlargement to central and eastern Europe and the Mediterranean.

All of these achievements in some sense build upon the EU's first and arguably what is still its most important accomplishment: the creation of the single European market for goods, services, labor, and capital. The next chapter explores this aspect of the integration story.

Notes

1. Committee of Independent Experts, *First Report on Allegations Regarding Fraud, Mismanagement and Nepotism in the European Commission*, Brussels, March 15, 1999.

2. 1. Article 219 TOR, ex Article 163, amended.

3. *Rules of Procedure of the Council*, December 6, 1993, O.J. L31/14 (1995).

4. Wolfgang Wessels, "Nice Results: The Millennium IGC in the EU's Evolution," *Journal of Common Market Studies* 39, no. 2 (June 2001): 204–5.

5. Article III-85a, draft constitutional treaty.

6. Article 4 TEU, ex Article D.

7. *Rules of Procedure of the European Parliament*, December 7, 1995, O.J. L293/1 (1995).

8. Consolidated Version of the Treaty Establishing the European Community (2002), Article 225a.

9. *Draft Treaty establishing a Constitution for Europe*, Part I, Article 31.3.

10. O.J. C 334, November 11, 2001; O.J. C 324, November 20, 2001; and O.J. C 167, July 17, 2003.

11. EIB, *Annual Report, 2002*.

12. Council Regulation (EEC) No. 302/93, February 8, 1993 on the establishment of a European Monitoring Centre for Drugs and Drug Addiction, O.J. L 036, February 12, 1993.

13. Van Gend en Loos v. Nederlandse Administratie Belastingen, Case 26/62(1963) ECR 1, quoted in Karen Alter, "The Making of a Supranational Rule of Law: The Battle for Supremacy," in Ronald Tiersky, ed., *Europe Today: National Politics, European Integration, and European Security* (Lanham, Md.: Rowman & Littlefield, 1999), 305.

14. Article 249 TOR, ex Article 189.

15. Quoted in Alter, "The Making of a Supranational Rule of Law," in Tiersky, ed., *Europe Today*, 313.

16. European Commission, *20th Annual Report on Monitoring the Application of Community Law (2002)*, COM(2003) 669 final, November 21, 2003, Annex II, table 2.1.

17. *Draft Treaty*, III-69; III.144.4; III-54.

18. *Draft Treaty*, III-68; III-74; III-102.

19. European Commission, *General Budget of the European Union for the Financial Year 2003* (Brussels: CEC, 2003).

20. "Future Financing of the Community Delors II Package," *The European Councils, 1992–1994*, 63–67.

21. Quoted in Peter Norman, "Europe's Spoils Up for Grabs," *Financial Times*, December 14, 1998.

22. *Agenda 2000: For a Stronger and Wider Union*, in *Bulletin of the European Union*, Supplement 5/97, 61–69.

23. *Financing the European Union: Commission Report on the Operation of the Own Resources System*, Brussels, October 7, 1998; http://europa.eu.int/comm/budget/pdf/agenda2000/finue1998/en/en.pdf (accessed June 11, 2004).

24. *Presidency Conclusions: Berlin European Council, 24 and 25 March 1999*, Doc/99/1, 3.

25. Article 161 TEC, as amended by the Treaty of Nice (paragraph inserted).

26. "Fischer points to EU budget Ahead of Constitution Talks," EU Observer, www.euobserver.com, September 8, 2003.

27. *Building Our Common Future: Policy Challenges and Budgetary Means of the Enlarged Union 2007–2013*, COM(2004) 101 final, February 10, 2004, 29.

Suggestions for Further Reading

Borchardt, Klaus-Dieter. *The ABC of Community Law*. Luxembourg: Office for Official Publications of the European Communities, 1994.

Brown, L. Neville, and Francis G. Jacobs. *The Court of Justice of the European Communities*. London: Sweet & Maxwell, 1989.

Devuyst, Youri. *The European Union at the Crossroads: An Introduction to the EU's Institutional Evolution*. Brussels: P.I.E.—Peter Lang, 2002.

Dinan, Desmond. *An Ever Closer Union? An Introduction to the European Community*, 2nd ed. Boulder, Colo.: Lynne Rienner, 1999.

Duff, Andrew, John Pinder, and Roy Pryce. *Maastricht and Beyond: Building the European Union*. New York: Routledge (for the Federal Trust), 1995.

Nugent, Neill. *The Government and Politics of the European Union* (Fourth Edition). Durham, N.C.: Duke University Press, 1999.

CHAPTER 4

The Single Market
FROM CUSTOMS UNION
TO 1992 AND BEYOND

If institutions and law are the political heart of the European Union (EU), its economic core is the single market. With the enlargement of 2004, the EU market has grown to more than 450 million consumers and a yearly gross national product (GNP) of more than $8 trillion, an agglomeration of purchasing power rivaled in size only by the United States and the broader North American Free Trade Agreement (NAFTA) area. Admission of Bulgaria and Romania later in the decade will add another 30 million consumers. The European Economic Area (EEA) with Norway and Iceland, a special trade arrangement with Switzerland, the customs union with Turkey, and preferential trade arrangements with potential candidate countries in the Balkans expand the reach of the market. The development of this market goes back to the initial post–World War II trade liberalization in the Organization for European Economic Cooperation (OEEC) and to the founding in 1952 of the European Coal and Steel Community (ECSC), but it really only took off with the founding of the European Community (EC) in 1958 and the establishment by the Treaty of Rome of the customs union and the common external tariff.

The Customs Union

The Treaty of Rome provided for the creation of a customs union through the phasing out of all tariffs and quantitative restrictions on trade among the member states over a period of twelve years, from 1958 to 1970. Elimination of these barriers went so well that the member states agreed to speed up the process, and the customs union for goods was completed by July 1, 1968, eighteen months ahead of schedule.

The common market was an immediate success. The elimination of intra-EC barriers to trade helped to accelerate growth and to prolong into the 1960s Europe's postwar economic boom. Trade among the members of the Community increased by a factor of six over the transition period, and average gross domestic product (GDP) increased by 70 percent. Except in special circumstances such as southern Italy, unemployment all but disappeared, as industries in Germany, France, and the Benelux were forced to import workers from southern Italy and from outside the Community to keep up with the demand for labor. Europe's balance of payments problems, so troublesome in the early postwar period, were largely resolved as the European countries began to register surpluses in their trade and to accumulate reserves of gold and foreign currencies (mainly dollars). The Community's economic performance in these years was in part attributable to investments by U.S. multinational companies, which were quick to recognize the advantages of the common market and in many cases built large, efficient plants in one Community country to manufacture a particular product for the whole EC market.

Despite these impressive achievements, in many respects the Community remained segmented into national markets. The Treaty of Rome allowed member states to restrict imports and exports of goods on grounds of public policy or public security, health and safety, and for certain other reasons if such restrictions did not "constitute a means of arbitrary discrimination or a disguised restriction on trade."[1] When member states applied different health and safety standards to products sold within their borders, it had the effect—if not necessarily the intent—of limiting trade, since manufacturers that were forced to make different versions of a product to meet different standards often were deterred from or priced out of operating at the EC level. The treaty allowed the Council to pass legislation to harmonize health, safety, and other standards, but doing so proved to be extraordinarily difficult, both because of its sheer technical complexity and because member state governments often were reluctant to give up the hidden protection that national standards afforded. Government procurement was another area in which the common market for the most part did not operate. Governments and state-owned utilities were major purchasers of everything from paper clips to locomotives, which they generally bought from national suppliers.

The shortcomings of the common market were even more striking in the areas of free movement of services, capital, and people. The service sector was still largely divided along national lines, with little cross-border competition. Public services such as telecommunications and rail transport were regarded as natural monopolies with room only for one supplier that was either state-owned or subject to heavy regulation. In other areas, such as banking and medicine, governments imposed strict licensing requirements to protect the public. Competition based on market principles hardly applied in many service industries even in the national setting; to open these markets to competition from other European countries was even more difficult and was not seen as desirable by most governments.

Capital markets were segmented by country. Controls on cross-border financial transactions remained in place and served as important instruments of national economic policy. Indeed, the breakdown of the Bretton Woods system and the monetary turbulence of the 1970s led some EC countries to strengthen capital controls as a way of protecting their national currencies. There were also barriers to the free movement of persons. Citizens of one EC country still needed passports to enter other Community countries, and checks at border crossings and airports were a constant reminder that flows of people were controlled. The ability of Europeans to work or set up businesses in other Community countries was limited by rules on residency, work permits, and nationally oriented pension and insurance schemes.

During the boom years of the 1960s and early 1970s, there was little motivation to address these remaining barriers to trade. Workers, companies, and consumers enjoyed the benefits of rising incomes, higher productivity, and greater choice of products associated with the common market in goods, but there was no political impetus to take the complex and controversial decisions that would be required to realize free trade in services or the free movement of capital and persons. In the difficult economic conditions of the 1970s momentum toward establishment of a single market slowed still further, and there were even signs of backsliding in the common market for goods, as national governments sought to bolster struggling domestic industries by providing taxpayer subsidies or by imposing rules and regulations relating to health, safety, and consumer protection that kept out competing products from other EC countries. Only a prolonged period of economic difficulty and a series of crippling recessions caused a rethinking and a renewed push to complete the single market.

The Single Market Program

Economic growth in the EC averaged a robust 4.6 percent per year in 1961–1970, but fell to 2.8 percent in 1971–1975 and recovered only slightly to 3.0 percent per year in 1976–1980. The 1974–1975 recession, caused by the dramatic rise in the price of oil, marked the end of the long postwar economic boom that began with the Marshall Plan. By 1981 Western Europe was back in recession, with economic activity falling by 0.2 percent in that year before registering a weak 0.3 percent gain the following year.[2] Unemployment rates had risen from the very low levels during the postwar boom to 8.6 percent in France, 9.2 percent in West Germany, and 12.4 percent in the UK.[3] European political and business leaders were concerned that Europe was falling behind the United States and Japan, not only in macroeconomic performance but especially in the high technology industries of the future.

In explaining the causes of Europe's declining performance, many business leaders focused on the high costs of doing business across national borders in Europe and the barriers to trade and the flow of people and capital that still existed in the common market. A 1986 poll of 100 corporate executives revealed that the majority thought that the fragmented state of the European market was the major factor behind Europe's failure to compete with the United States and Japan in key industrial sectors. Forty-two percent of the respondents said that their firms incurred higher costs because of different specifications set by national laws; 25 percent cited the sheer cost of paperwork as a factor damaging competitiveness; and 20 percent identified extra warehousing and inventory costs due to different product standards as a source of higher business costs in Europe.[4] In 1983 the chief executives of seventeen of Europe's largest companies formed the European Roundtable of Industrialists (ERT) in order to generate ideas and mobilize governmental, parliamentary, and public support for creating a more favorable market climate in Europe. The stated goal of the ERT was to revitalize the EC by preparing a blueprint for completing the single market.

When Jacques Delors became president of the European Commission in January 1985, he chose to make completion of the single market a centerpiece of his presidency. Shortly after taking office, Delors announced, in his inaugural speech to the European Parliament, that the Commission would introduce a program to eliminate all barriers to the internal market by the end of 1992.[5] This concrete program of action with a firm date for completion (see box 4.1) was to capture the imagination and win the support of business, government, and ordinary citizens and workers. "1992" became the slogan of the late 1980s and early 1990s.

THE 1985 WHITE PAPER

Delors entrusted implementation of the program to Lord Cockfield, the British Commissioner responsible for the internal market. In the first six months of 1985 Cockfield and his staff produced a detailed plan that was presented to the European Council in the form of a White Paper outlining the basic program.[6] In an appendix to the report, the Commission listed some 300 measures that needed to be turned into Community law to complete the internal market. Each measure was assigned a target date, so that the whole program would be implemented by December 31, 1992.

The report identified three kinds of barriers to the operation of the internal market—physical, technical, and fiscal—all of which it proposed to dismantle. Physical barriers included customs posts and paperwork and inspections at borders. (It was indeed the elimination of these barriers that was to become the most visible manifestation of 1992 for the public.) Technical barriers included the vast array of national standards and regulations that did not always have the intent of impeding commerce among EC member states, but that in practice had this effect. They included rules on the content and labeling of foods, chemicals, and pharmaceuticals; car safety standards; different procedures for public procurement (including in important state-owned sectors such as water supply, the railroads, telecommunications, and electricity); different banking and insurance regulations; national rules on air, rail, road, and water transport; rules on copyright and trademark protection; and many other barriers to the free flow of goods, services, capital, and people. Fiscal barriers related both to types and levels of taxation, including value-added and excise taxes, both of which varied widely across Europe.

Box 4.1   The Commission Proposal

Unifying this market (of 320 million) presupposes that Member States will agree on the abolition of barriers of all kinds, harmonisation of rules, approximation of legislation and tax structures, strengthening of monetary cooperation and the necessary flanking measures to encourage European firms to work together. It is a goal that is well within our reach provided we draw the lessons of the past. The Commission will be asking the European Council to pledge itself to completion of a fully unified internal market by 1992 and to approve the necessary programme together with a realistic and binding timetable.

(*Source:* "Programme of the Commission for 1985.")

THE COMMISSION'S STRATEGY

Although the single market program generated enthusiasm throughout Europe, Delors and his team realized from the beginning that it would be difficult to implement. The Community had launched the Werner Plan for economic and monetary union in 1970 but had completely failed to meet its ambitious targets. European foreign policy cooperation, also launched in 1970, had been a disappointment as well. The Community had been through a long period of drift, and success was by no means assured.

Three factors in the way the Commission and the member states approached the single market program were vital to its eventual success. First, as discussed in chapter 2, the member states agreed, in the SEA, to revisions of the Treaty of Rome that made completion of the single market by the end of 1992 a binding commitment and that permitted the passage of single market legislation by qualified majority rather than unanimous voting. These changes made it easier to pass such legislation as was needed to complete the single market.

Second, the Community reduced the amount and complexity of the legislation that ultimately would be required by changing the way it addressed the problem of divergent national standards. Under the 1992 program, it relied to the maximum extent possible on mutual recognition of national standards rather than on the more difficult process of harmonization to a single Community standard, such as had been attempted in the 1960s and 1970s, and where possible it delegated harmonization and standard-setting tasks to nongovernmental, industry-based organizations.

Third, the Commission mounted a successful political and public relations campaign that helped to convince businesses and the general public of the merits of the program. It undertook several important studies that attempted to quantify the expected economic gains from the elimination of intra-EC barriers. The best known of these studies was the 1988 Cecchini report, officially known as *The Economics of 1992*. It tried to estimate, through detailed sectoral studies, "the costs of non-Europe," that is, the economic benefits that the EC would forgo by not completing the single market program. It estimated that compared to what would happen if the program were not implemented, completion of the single market would increase overall Community GDP by 4.5 percent, reduce prices by 6 percent, lower public sector deficits by 2.25 percent, result in a positive swing in the EC's balance of payments position amounting to 1 percent of GDP, and create 1,750,000 new jobs.[7]

Implementing 1992

GOODS

The creation of the customs union through the elimination of intra-Community tariffs and the establishment of the common customs tariff was, along with the

Common Agricultural Policy (CAP) and the addition of four new members, the EC's most important achievement during the first thirty years of its existence. In practice, however, free movement of goods as envisioned in the Treaty of Rome had never been fully achieved, and was to some extent threatened by the backsliding of the 1970s. While the member states did very well in removing tariffs and quantitative restrictions (quotas) on trade, they were less rigorous in eliminating what the treaty called measures having an "equivalent effect" as such restrictions. Such measures included rules and regulations that blocked or made more difficult intra-Community trade, divergent tax systems, and national preferences in public procurement, all of which needed to be addressed in the 1992 program.

To tackle regulatory barriers, the program relied on the principle of mutual recognition and the so-called new approach legislation. Mutual recognition went back to the landmark *Cassis de Dijon* case decided by the European Court of Justice in February 1979. The case involved the German importer of a French liqueur that the German authorities ruled could not be sold in Germany because it did not meet the minimum alcohol content requirements for this type of product specified in German law. The Court ruled that the German law contravened the common market provisions of the Treaty of Rome. National authorities could not block the import from another member state of a product that met the standards of that state, provided those standards offered equivalent levels of protection with regard to such objectives as health, safety, and public security. The Court did allow for continued differences among national standards, but it argued that any additional protection to the German consumer afforded by the German ban was disproportionate to the disruptive effects on the common market.[8] In the course of the 1980s, mutual recognition was firmly established as an underlying principle of the single market. It also came to play a major role in the service sector and in promoting the free movement of workers by, for example, helping to resolve the problem of different academic degrees and licensing standards for professionals in the member states.

For products for which regulatory standards among the member states were substantively different as well as for many service-sector issues and questions relating to the free flow of capital and people, the Community could not rely on mutual recognition alone to achieve the single market goals. For these areas, the Commission proposed in 1985 what it called the "new approach" to overcoming hindrances to trade resulting from different national regulation.[9] Endorsed by the Council in May 1985, the new approach entailed the adoption of legislative frameworks in the form of Community directives establishing standards for major industrial sectors. In drafting such directives, the Commission limited their scope to essential standards relating to health, safety, consumer protection, and the environment, thereby eliminating the need for much detailed regulation at the Community and the national levels.[10]

Once these directives were in place at the Community level, the member states would be required to adopt or amend national legislation to conform to these essential requirements. European standardization bodies, such as the European Standards Committee (CEN) and the European Committee for Electrotechnical

Standardization (CENELEC), were asked to draw up detailed technical specifications that reflected these essential requirements and that could serve as European standards. Member states then could issue certificates of conformity stating that products manufactured on their territory met these essential requirements. National authorities would be required to recognize that products manufactured in accordance with these standards met the essential requirements established at the Community level and could not be barred from import on grounds of health or safety. In 1990 the certification bodies of the member states also founded the European Organization for Testing and Certification to coordinate the mutual recognition of certificates of conformity.

For certain products where the nature of the risk to consumers required absolute uniformity of standards, the Community continued to rely on detailed product-by-product or even component-by-component harmonization. Sectors in which detailed harmonization continued to be used included pharmaceuticals, chemicals, motor vehicles, and foodstuffs. But passage of detailed harmonization directives was rendered easier by the introduction of qualified majority voting under the SEA. The single market program thus used an eclectic mix of mutual recognition, new approach legislation, and detailed harmonization—sometimes in combination for a single sector or product.[11]

Another major challenge was to address barriers to trade relating to taxation, notably value-added taxes (VAT) and excise taxes on alcohol, tobacco, luxury goods, fuel, and certain other products. Even after the common market had eliminated all intra-EC customs duties, member states maintained customs posts and checks on trucks and trains crossing their borders to insure that importers were paying these taxes in accordance with the relevant national laws. Requiring at the Community level that these laws be harmonized promised to be difficult, as the member states traditionally have protected their prerogatives in the area of taxation, which are politically sensitive and touch upon the ability of the states to fund generous social welfare programs. Nevertheless, the architects of the single market concluded that they could not ignore the effects of widely disparate levels and kinds of taxation on the functioning of the cross-border market.

The 1992 program did not attempt to fully harmonize member state tax policies, but it tried to do away with those discrepancies that most tended to distort the functioning of the single market. Commission and academic experts noted that U.S. states could levy different sales, gasoline, liquor, and other taxes without disrupting the functioning of the single American market. Some differences among jurisdictions were possible, provided they were not too large. The Council eventually agreed to set the standard VAT rate at 15 percent with a reduced rate of 5 percent for a limited list of goods and services.[12] The EC also instituted a new system for collecting VAT that eliminated the need for border controls by making exporters and importers responsible for reporting cross-border transactions to domestic authorities.

Another area of focus was public procurement. Purchases by governments and state-owned entities such as the postal service and state-owned telephone, airline, and railroad companies accounted for roughly 16 percent of all spending on goods and services in the EC.[13] Because government and state-owned companies were the most important buyers of high technology and high-priced capital goods such as aircraft, rolling stock, and telecommunications equipment, opening up public markets was vital to the success of the single market.

The 1992 program extended competition to four sectors previously exempt from the common market—water, energy, transport, and telecommunications—and tightened rules on the award of public contracts. In a series of directives dealing with public works, utilities, and public services, the member states were required to open up procurement by national, regional, and local governments as well as other public entities to competition from other Community countries. Contracts were to be announced for bidding in the official journal of the Community, and selection of suppliers was to be based on objective criteria such as price, quality, and qualifications without regard to nationality.

SERVICES

Before the 1992 program, liberalization of trade in services in the Community for the most part was confined to measures needed to facilitate the free flow of goods. Under the provisions of the Treaty of Rome calling for the establishment of a common transport policy, for example, the Community adopted a ban on discriminatory pricing or conditions of transport based on origin or destination. The transport sector itself was not opened to competition, however, and little progress was made toward achieving the Common Transport Policy mentioned in the Treaty of Rome.

Unlike the situation with regard to goods, creating the single market for services (and for capital and labor) required a much heavier reliance on passage of Community directives. Mutual recognition played some role in the service sector, but establishing a single market in such areas as transport, telecommunications, and banking required elaborate and detailed agreement on the rules of the game for competition and consideration at the European level of the same concerns that shaped national policy, for example, dealing with natural monopoly and ensuring the interoperability of complex technical systems.

In transport, the Council passed a series of directives gradually opening the major passenger and freight modes to competition. Frontier checks on road and inland water transport were eliminated, effective January 1, 1990.[14] All quantitative restrictions on trucking operations between member states were to be terminated by the end of 1992. Change in the trucking industry was controversial, however, and it was not until September 1993, nine months after the formal completion date of the 1992 program, that the Council passed a directive fully establishing, as of July 1, 1998, the right of a firm from one member state to carry freight between points in another EU country just as if it were a domestic firm (known as *cabotage*).

In rail transport, the Council passed a framework directive in 1988 requiring member states to begin operating national rail services according to commercial criteria. Management of the rail infrastructure, such as track and signals, was to be separated from management of the trains themselves, and competitors to the national railroad, including from other EC countries, were to be allowed limited access on a commercial basis to the infrastructure in order to operate rail services between member states. Market opening in the rail sector remained a very slow process, however, marked by resistance from national governments and foot-dragging by the powerful national rail authorities.

Civil aviation was one of the most politically sensitive areas of market liberalization. Governments had a long history of subsidizing national carriers for reasons of employment and prestige. High costs and chronic overcapacity in the sector meant that some national airlines might be forced to merge with rivals or go out of business if they were fully exposed to competition. In a first set of reforms agreed in 1987, the Council established that from January 1, 1993, carriers would be free to set prices on commercial grounds in order to compete with rivals. Previously, the fares between cities in different member states required approval by both sets of national authorities, a practice that tended to keep prices high as governments sought to protect small and inefficient carriers. Complete liberalization of the EU aviation market was set for April 1, 1997. Henceforth, any EU airline could operate between points in the Union, provided essential safety standards were met. Thus, for example, British Airways began competing on domestic routes in Germany. Such competition was still difficult, however, since new entrants to markets often had problems in gaining slots at major airports serving the most profitable markets. Elsewhere in the transport sector, there were market opening measures in inland waterway and maritime transport.

Telecommunications competition was introduced through a series of open network provision (ONP) directives.[15] As in the rail industry, ONP was based on the "unbundling" of the infrastructure needed to deliver a service, in this case the national and local telephone network, and the delivery of service through that network. The owners of the networks were the large national post, telephone, and telegraph authorities (PTTs) such as Deutsche Telekom and France Telecom. They were required to allow access to the network on a nondiscriminatory commercial basis to firms desiring to provide new services or to compete with the traditional monopoly supplier. ONP with regard to leased lines for businesses, various data services, 800-type numbers, and other services began on January 1, 1993, in line with the overall single market program. The big leap forward—competition in voice telephony—took longer to negotiate and was established after a long preparation period on February 1, 1998, with additional delays for several of the member states. Liberalization and market opening under the single market program contributed to and in turn was bolstered by the wave of privatizations to sweep the West European telecommunications sector. In the UK, the Thatcher government sold a majority share of British Telecom already in 1984. It took more than a decade for governments on the continent to follow suit, but by the end of the 1990s France Telecom, Deutsche Telekom, Telecom Italia, and the PTTs in most the other EU countries had been at least partially privatized or were scheduled be privatized in the near future.

In financial services, in 1989 the Council passed the Second Banking Directive, which established an EC-wide banking license effective January 1, 1993.[16] This enables any bank that is legally permitted to operate in one member state to open branches in or provide cross-border services to another member state. The banking authorities of the country where the bank is headquartered have the main responsibility for prudential supervision of the bank, while the regulatory authorities of the country in which the bank has branches can oversee their activities to protect consumers and ensure the soundness of the national banking system.

In professional services, the Council adopted a 1988 directive that deals with the cross-border provision of services requiring a license, such as law, medicine, nursing, and accounting. Following the mutual recognition principle, member states are required to accept as valid diplomas and certificates awarded in other member states. This directive applies to all diplomas requiring three or more years of study.

CAPITAL

Although the Treaty of Rome provided for the free movement of capital, the EC moved very slowly with regard to liberalization of capital movements. Convertibility of the European currencies into each other was restored with the establishment of the European Payments Union (EPU) in 1950, and in 1958 the European countries restored full convertibility into the dollar and other third currencies, thereby putting into effect the system of fixed exchange rates and full convertibility envisioned in the Bretton Woods agreements. But most European countries continued to use capital controls—restrictions on the movement of money into and out of the country by banks, other financial institutions, and private investors—to protect their currencies against rapid and destabilizing changes in value.

As in services, liberalization occurred mainly where it was needed to facilitate trade in goods, not in order to promote cross-border competition for its own sake. The Treaty of Rome required member states to eliminate all restrictions on the movement of capital "to the extent necessary to ensure the proper functioning of the common market."[17] In 1960 and 1962 the Community adopted directives on capital movement to facilitate payments for goods traded in the common market and the establishment of branches and subsidiaries in other EC member countries.

In May 1986 the Commission put forward a comprehensive plan to create a single Community-wide financial area in which all financial and currency flows would be free of national restrictions.[18] Under a decision taken in 1988, all intra-EC restrictions on the movement of capital were eliminated as of July 1990. This was important mainly for businesses, but it also had implications for individuals. It meant that member-state governments could not restrict their citizens from holding their bank accounts or other investments in other EC countries.

Free movement of capital was closely linked to liberalization in the market for financial services, and progress in these areas tended to reinforce each other. Banks, insurance companies, and stockbrokers could begin to operate efficiently across the member state markets only after capital controls were removed; conversely, the activities of banks and financial services wanting to operate at the European level helped to integrate the single market for capital in ways that government action alone could not have accomplished.

Together with the liberalization of the financial services sector, the removal of capital controls made the shift to a single currency later in the 1990s both more necessary and more feasible. Tommaso Padoa-Schioppa, an Italian economist and a member of the Delors committee on economic and monetary union, warned about the futility of trying to pursue an "inconsistent quartet" of objectives—free trade, full capital mobility, fixed exchange rates, and independent national monetary policies—since without controls speculative capital movements would overpower national attempts to hold stable the currency values. With the Community committed to pursuing the first two objectives in the single market program and the third within the European Monetary System (EMS), he argued that "in the long run the only solution to the inconsistency is to complement the internal market with a monetary union."[19]

PERSONS

Movement of persons was perhaps the most difficult of the four freedoms to implement and the one on which the least progress was made during the early years of the Community. In 1958 the EC put in place a system, taken over from the ECSC, to reduce the loss of social security benefits by migrant workers. In 1961 the Community adopted its first regulation to facilitate the movement of labor. But these were very preliminary steps and mainly had to do with working conditions and benefits of citizens of EC countries already employed in other member states. The treaty did not create a generalized right for European workers to move about the Community in search of employment and it conferred few if any rights on persons as individuals.

Free movement of labor was achieved, at least in a formal sense, by 1968, based on the principle of national treatment of workers from other EC countries. Such workers had to be granted the same rights and social benefits as those accorded to nationals.[20] As a practical matter, however, movement of labor was hindered by cumbersome administrative procedures relating to residence permits, different national standards with regard to vocational training qualifications, and restrictions on the right to establish businesses by the self-employed. In addition, EC legislation still tended to treat free movement of persons as an economic right, with limited application to those outside the labor force.

The single market program both improved mobility for the employed and extended the free movement of people to broader, noneconomic categories. With regard to the former, for example, it included directives on the mutual recognition of degrees and vocational training certificates and new legislation on the harmonization of income tax provisions for workers employed in another member state. With regard to the latter, in June 1990 the Council adopted three directives on the right of residence for students, retired people, and any other citizens who could show that they had sufficient means to live in another EU host country.[21]

With the introduction of EU citizenship in the Maastricht treaty, free movement of persons became less an economic right, guaranteed as a function of the single market and the roles of individuals as economic actors (workers, consumers), and more a human and political right, guaranteed to people as a function of their citizenship. The citizenship clause introduced by Maastricht states that "every citizen of the Union shall have the right to move and reside freely within the territory of the Member States, subject to the limitations and conditions laid down in the treaty and by the measures adopted to give it effect."[22] The "limitations" and "conditions" referred to are set by national governments, and relate to such issues as the portability of pensions and welfare payments, residence and labor permits, and other restrictions, many of which have been whittled away by successful challenges in the Court of Justice.

As a practical matter, however, the main barriers to the free movement of persons in the EU are not legal but cultural and linguistic. Some EU citizens take advantage of the free movement provisions of the treaties, but most are content to live and work in their native countries, where they speak the language, own property, and have social and family ties. An increasing number of EU citizens do move, however. They include workers at both ends of the income scale—for example, relatively poor migrants from Portugal who work in Luxembourg and France, and highly paid managers and professionals who move about in search of better jobs or who are transferred by multinational companies. Movement of retirees is also an important phenomenon in Europe, as can be seen, for example, in the large numbers of German, British, Dutch, and other pensioners who have settled on the Mediterranean coast of Spain.

OVERALL RESULTS

Implementing the single market program was a multi-stage process. In areas in which legislation was needed to overcome market barriers, the Commission had to propose EC-level directives. The Council of Ministers then had to adopt these directives as EC law, without watering down the essence of the proposal to secure the necessary qualified majority. Each member state then had to transpose these directives into national legislation. Finally, the member states had to be willing and able to enforce their national laws, without turning a blind eye to restrictive practices that favored domestic firms at the expense of outsiders. Only if all four of these stages were undertaken—the last on a continuous basis—would the single market truly operate. In addition, for areas in which mutual recognition was used to advance single market goals, it had to function as advertised: as a faster and more efficient but no less effective substitute for harmonization by directive.

The record of the EU and its member states in fulfilling these steps was good but by no means perfect. By the target date of December 31, 1992, the Community had completed most of the single market program. The number of single market proposals had been scaled back from 300 to 282, as the Commission backed away from certain controversial issues that were likely to fail in the Council of Ministers. By the end of 1992, 264 of 282 white paper actions had been passed at the EU level, leaving 18 still outstanding. Elements of the 1985 white paper that were not passed included the removal of border controls on persons at internal frontiers, certain tax harmonization measures, and the creation of a European system of company law.

Transposition of single market legislation into national law was also problematic, given the large volume of legislation, the slow pace of legislative action in the national parliaments, and the fact that even those countries that opposed passage of a directive at the European level but were outvoted in the Council of Ministers still had a legal obligation to transpose into national law. By the end of 1993—one year after completion of the EC legislative program—only a little over half of the single market directives passed by the Council had been transposed into national legislation in all twelve member states. Denmark and Britain (ironically both traditional Euroskeptics) had the best records with regard to transposition, while Greece had the worst. Areas in which the member states had the greatest difficulty in meeting their EU obligations were public procurement and veterinary controls.

Despite the obvious slippages in various stages of implementation, the single market program generally is regarded as one of the great successes in the history of European integration. The late 1980s was a period of dynamism and growing optimism in the EC. In 1986–1990 economic growth in the Community averaged 3.1 percent per year, a pace not seen since before the first oil crisis and more than double the 1.4 percent annual rate of 1980–1985. The Community-wide unemployment rate fell from 10 percent in 1985 to 7.5 percent in 1990, as millions of new jobs were created. Good economic performance was partly attributable to favorable trends worldwide, but the enthusiasm generated by the 1992 program also contributed. European and non-European firms increased their investments in the Community to prepare for increased competition as well as the expanded opportunities of the single market. The value of transborder mergers and acquisitions in the Community increased from $8 billion in 1984 to $167 billion in 1989.[23]

Politically, the 1992 program gave the EC and its member states the self-confidence to proceed with political and economic and monetary union in the Maastricht treaty. It rekindled enthusiasm for integration among the public and made the Community a far greater pole of attraction for potential new members. Austria, Cyprus, Finland, Malta, Norway, Sweden, and Switzerland all applied for membership in this period, in part because of changing political circumstances in Europe, but also because they did not want to be left out of the single market program. Perhaps most importantly, the perceived success of the single market project helped to strengthen the EC precisely at a time when West European unity and strength were needed to deal with the challenges and opportunities presented by the unexpected collapse of communism in central and eastern Europe in late 1989.

The single market clearly did not solve Western Europe's economic problems. EU unemployment began to climb in the early 1990s and economic growth slowed from the pace of late 1980s. But political leaders and economists argued that problems such as unemployment and slow growth would have been worse without the 1992 program and that full implementation of the single market program— including strict action against governments that failed to transpose single market directives or that distorted the market through new state subsidies to industry— was one of the keys to overcoming the recession of the early 1990s.[24]

In 1995 the EU attempted to quantify the benefits of the single market by commissioning thirty-eight detailed studies dealing with the effects of the 1992 program in six areas: manufacturing, services, dismantling of barriers, impact on trade and investment, impact on competition and scale effects, and aggregate and regional impact. Because so much else was happening as the Community worked to complete the 1992 program, it was hard to measure precisely those economic effects that were due to the single market; even sophisticated econometric models had difficulty in isolating the effects of the 1992 program from other factors such as global trade liberalization in the General Agreement on Tariffs and Trade (GATT), German reunification, and the opening of new markets in central and eastern Europe.[25] It was also too early to measure the long-term effects of the single market, many of which would be felt only over time as certain directives were phased in and implemented at the national level and as investment patterns in the Union shifted in response to the new realities of the single market.

Despite these methodological challenges, in October 1996 the Commission issued a summary report entitled *The Impact and Effectiveness of the Single Market* that drew together all the findings of the 1995–1996 studies.[26] It concluded that the single market had resulted in greater competition among companies in both manufacturing and services, an accelerated pace of industrial restructuring leading to improved global competitiveness of European firms, a wider range of goods and services available to consumers, especially in newly liberalized sectors such as transport and telecommunications, faster and cheaper transborder delivery of goods, and greater mobility of people between member states. In terms of overall economic effects, the study estimated that the single market program had resulted in the creation of 300,000–900,000 additional jobs, an extra increase in EU GNP of 1.1 to 1.5 percent over the 1987–1993 period, inflation rates of 1.0 to 1.5 percent lower than they would have been in the absence of the single market program, and further economic convergence between different EU regions.[27] These numbers were below the optimistic projections of the Cecchini report, but they nonetheless represented a substantial gain for the EU economy.

The Single Market after 1992

Since 1993 the Commission and, with varying degrees of enthusiasm, the member states have continued to plug away at the single market. This has included passing legislation that was not completed before the 1992 deadline, drafting and adopting new legislation in response to technological change and to fill gaps in the original legislative program, and, not least, seeking to improve compliance and implementation. As the guardian of the treaties, the Commission plays a special role in these efforts. One member of the Commission is exclusively responsible for internal market matters, and in that capacity oversees the Directorate-General for the Internal Market. Beginning in 1994, this directorate has prepared annual reports on the operation of the single market that highlight areas needing improvement.

ENFORCEMENT

Mutual recognition remained an ongoing challenge after 1992, affecting the core goal of free trade in goods along with many parts of the service sector. Although it was adopted with great fanfare in 1986 and was one of the key factors speeding completion of the single market program, it was not a panacea for trade barriers. In various reviews of the single market, the Commission and the internal market ministers of the member states identified standardization and mutual recognition as among the weakest areas of the single market. National and local authorities often refused to recognize as valid product standards set by regulatory bodies in other member states. According to a survey of 500 large companies undertaken by the Commission in 1997, continued failure to implement mutual recognition of national standards, testing and certification was the most important remaining obstacle to trade in goods in the single market.[28]

Another problem was failure by the member states to comply with single market legislation, and in particular to transpose single market directives into national law. The Commission initially was somewhat cautious about using its legal powers against member states in regard to single market matters, but it grew more aggressive in the last several years of the 1990s as EMU approached and Commission and independent economists became increasingly concerned about the dangers of launching the single currency in a still-uncompleted single market. In 1995 Internal Market Commissioner Mario Monti signed a total of 218 formal infringement letters regarding possible breaches of single market rules by member states. In 1996 this rose to 283 letters, of which 187 were letters of formal notice to member states about possible breaches of single market obligations, 76 were reasoned opinions on single market matters, 15 were first referrals to the Court of Justice, 4 were letters of formal notice to member states warning them that it was prepared to make a second referral to the Court, and 1 was a reasoned opinion prior to a second referral.[29]

Of the 283 actions taken by the Commission, about a third involved late transposition of legislation by the member states, a third arose from complaints by businesses and individuals to the Commission or to the European Parliament, and about a third came about because the Commission itself suspected market irregularities in a member state. The fact that the Commission issued many more letters of formal notice than reasoned opinions and more opinions than referrals to the Court reflected both the relative newness of much single market legislation and the readiness on the part of member states to correct or explain alleged violations of single market obligations once the Commission took note of a matter.

THE 1997 ACTION PLAN

In an effort to overcome the remaining problems in the single market in the run-up to the introduction of the single currency in January 1999, in early 1997 the Commission drew up an Action Plan for the Single Market that included stepped up enforcement measures and a more concerted effort to fill gaps in the existing body of legislation.[30] The plan was endorsed by the June 1997 Amsterdam European Council.

One of the instruments developed by the Commission to promote better implementation at the national level was the publication of a single market scoreboard showing the record of each member state in transposing legislation, broken down by category. The scoreboard first appeared in November 1997, and has been issued regularly twice each year ever since. At the time the 1997 plan was adopted, the "fragmentation factor"—the percentage of all single market directives that had not been implemented in national legislation in at least one member state—was a staggering 35 percent. This number fell to 26.7 percent in November 1997 and to 14.9 percent in November 1998, as the action plan drew to its close.[31] Finland had the best record in the Union, having failed to transpose only 0.9 percent of all directives, while Luxembourg had the worst, with 6.2 percent (see table 4.1, with updates to May 2003). The improvement over the period of the action plan was especially noteworthy for Austria, Belgium, and by far the largest national economy in the single market, Germany. Nonetheless, of 1,365 single market directives passed at the EU level, in October 1998, 203 still were not transposed in one or more member states.

As part of the action plan, the Commission also stepped up the pace of legal

Table 4.1   Member State Nonimplementation of Single Market Directives (percent)

	Nov '97	Nov '98	Nov '99	Nov '00	Nov '01	Nov '02	May '03
Aus	10.1	4.2	3.7	2.9	2.9	2.9	3.4
Bel	8.5	5.2	3.5	2.9	2.3	2.0	1.8
Dk	3.2	1.5	1.3	1.1	0.8	0.7	0.6
Fin	4.3	0.9	1.7	1.3	0.7	0.6	1.0
Fra	7.4	5.5	5.6	4.5	3.0	3.8	3.3
Ger	8.5	2.7	2.9	3.1	2.6	2.7	3.0
Gre	7.5	5.2	6.2	6.5	3.0	3.3	3.3
Irl	5.4	5.8	4.4	3.6	2.4	2.6	3.5
Ita	7.6	5.7	3.9	3.2	1.7	2.6	3.9
Lux	6.5	6.2	5.7	3.2	2.1	2.3	3.2
Neth	3.5	2.1	2.8	2.5	1.3	1.3	2.0
Por	5.9	5.6	4.9	4.4	2.5	3.1	3.7
Spa	4.7	2.7	2.2	1.6	1.3	1.6	1.2
Swe	6.2	1.5	2.1	1.2	0.9	0.4	1.0
UK	4.6	3.8	2.8	2.7	2.8	1.4	1.5

Source: European Commission, Internal Market Scoreboard, Nos. 1, 3, 5, 7, 9, 11, 12

action against member states that failed to implement or misapplied single market legislation. Difficulties in implementing the single market were apparent in just about every sector of the economy, with the greatest number of problems in the complex and politically sensitive areas of telecommunications, public procurement, and transport. In 1996 the Commission had sent a formal letter of notice to France about a local preference clause that ran counter to EU public procurement law in the call for bids to build the new stadium for the World Cup soccer championship, to be held in France in 1998. After failing to receive a satisfactory response from the French government, the Commission decided in June 1997 to refer the case to the Court of Justice. In March 1998 the French Minister for European Affairs formally recognized the existence of the infringement and agreed to improve future performance with regard to public procurement. The local preference clause was eliminated from the contracting document and the Commission dropped its case.[32]

In another case, the Commission singled out Finland for rules it had imposed subjecting imported used cars and trucks to higher safety and pollution standards than those that applied to the resale of domestic vehicles. The Finnish authorities amended these rules to eliminate the discrimination, and the Commission terminated its proceedings. Other infringement cases related to everything from the marketing of online databases (Belgium, Denmark, Greece, Ireland, Italy, Luxembourg, the Netherlands) to diplomas for psychologists (France) to the sale of nonalcoholic energy drinks (Italy).

In many cases, infringement of single market legislation occurred because local authorities were insufficiently aware of changes in national law made as a result of EU legislation. Many citizen complaints in fact arose out of encounters with police and local authorities. For example, an Irish citizen who entered Sweden as a student complained to the Commission that Swedish immigration authorities asked him about the purpose of his visit to Sweden and stamped his passport with an entry stamp. Since Ireland is a member of the EU, this action was contrary to EU legislation on free movement of persons. The Swedish authorities later issued instructions to their police and border agents to resolve this problem. Professional qualifications were another area in which local authorities or nongovernmental bodies sometimes frustrated the working of the single market, often without any overtly protectionist motives but simply because they are not used to recognizing foreign diplomas and qualifications as valid. Cases in which the Commission was asked to intervene on behalf of EU citizens involved a Danish architect in Germany, a British art conservator in Belgium, and German nurses in France.

In 1998 the Commission for the first time asked that financial penalties be levied against member states for persistent failure to correct shortcomings. In a case involving a 1985 directive on the approximation of laws concerning liability for defective products, the Court of Justice censured France in January 1993 for failing to transpose this directive into national law by the deadline of July 30, 1988. The directive provides that in all member states the manufacturer or importer of a defective product must pay damages and interest for harm caused by the product.

Following the initial judgment by the Court that France had failed to enact the necessary legislation, the Commission issued a second reasoned opinion on the case, which was followed by the decision to ask the Court to impose fines—in this case ECU 158,250 for each day the noncompliance continued—on France.[33] Similarly, the Commission asked the Court to impose financial penalties of ECU 39,975 per day on Greece for its failure to respect a 1996 Court ruling censuring Greece for not implementing in national law a 1992 directive on public procurement of services.

NEW ISSUES

In addition to stepped up enforcement and compliance measures, another major task was to extend the single market to areas that had been left uncompleted in the original 1992 program as well as to emerging economic sectors such as biotechnology and e-commerce. In the 1980s the Commission proposed single market directives that would require member states to enact legislation opening up gas and electricity transmission networks to competing firms. These directives were very much watered down by the member states, however, as major utilities such as Ruhrgas in Germany and Electricité de France opposed liberalization. In December 1996 the Council finally adopted an electricity directive that required all member states to enact legislation within two years (Belgium and Ireland were granted three and Greece four) that would open about a quarter of their national markets to competition in early 1999, followed by additional market opening in 2000 and 2003.[34] This was to be done by the establishment of common rules for the generation, transmission, and distribution of electricity that allow producers and consumers to contract supplies directly with each other after negotiating access to the transmission network with its operator. Similarly, in June 1998 the Council and the European Parliament adopted a natural gas directive that provided for the opening to competition by August 2000 of at least 20 percent of total gas consumption in each national market. This was scheduled to rise to 28 percent by 2003 and to 33 percent by 2008. These energy directives were expected to increase competition and lead to lower energy prices in Europe.

Financial services was another area in which integration of national markets had lagged, but in which the impending arrival of the euro seemed to offer new chances for cross-border integration that would enable the EU to establish a continental-scale financial services industry better able to compete with the United States. In response to a request from the June 1998 Cardiff European Council, in May 1999 the Commission presented a Financial Services Action Plan of forty-two measures to be adopted by the EU institutions and the member states in 1999–2002. The plan was built around three strategic objectives: creation of a single EU wholesale market that would enable, for example, corporate issuers to raise finance on competitive terms on an EU-wide basis; establishment of open and secure retail markets that, for example, would allow consumers to purchase banking, brokerage, insurance, and other financial services on an EU-wide basis;

and adoption of state-of-the-art prudential rules and supervision that would protect users of financial services at the wholesale and retail levels as well as strengthen Europe's role in setting financial standards at the global level.

New technologies and the development of whole new industries based on these technologies also posed challenges for the single market. National governments were quick to regulate these industries at the national level, in so doing threatening to fragment the single market in precisely those industries that will be most important in generating future employment and prosperity. To head off this danger, the EU moved to adopt European legislative frameworks in these industries. Examples of such legislation included a directive on the legal protection of biotechnological inventions (1998) and an electronic commerce directive and legal framework to guarantee the security of electronic signatures (2000).

The EU continued to make progress in most of these areas, but performance was uneven. According to the Commission's semiannual scoreboards, in the late 1990s most member states had succeeded in lowering their transposition deficits, but in a few member states the deficit actually had increased, with particular problems in directives related to transport, telecommunications, public procurement, and veterinary checks. In November 1999 more than 5 percent of internal market directives had not been transposed in France, Greece, and Luxembourg.[35] In France, where there was deep suspicion about the deregulation and privatization of public services, the national parliament failed to agree on implementing legislation to open the French electricity market to national and international competition as required by the 1996 electricity deregulation directive.[36] Germany complied with the terms of the EU directive, but how much real competition existed in the German market was open to question, particularly after the country's second and third largest electricity producers agreed to merge.[37] France, Germany, and Luxembourg also missed the August 2000 deadline to partially open their natural gas markets to competition.

In the transport sector, most member states had followed through on the decision to separate railroad operations from infrastructure, but little real competition involving other national, much less other EU-country, firms had developed. In the aviation sector, competition had increased, lowering fares significantly for consumers, but it was held back by traditional restrictions on the award of airport slots to new competitors. The Commission also complained about the conclusion by most member states of bilateral open skies agreements with the United States, which the Commission claimed had the effect of illegally segmenting the internal market. Other areas in which progress lagged included public procurement, financial services liberalization, and the elimination of remaining technical barriers to trade.

Food safety was another politically sensitive area in which the member states often were tempted to defy EU single market law. In December 1999 the Commission threatened to take France to the Court of Justice for failing to allow the import of beef from the UK—after the Commission lifted an earlier ban that had been imposed at the EU level to contain the possible spread of "mad cow disease" from Britain to other countries.[38] And several member states enacted blanket national bans on the sale of genetically modified organisms, in clear defiance of EU rules regarding the single market and the CAP.[39]

A final area of concern was competition policy, which arguably was relatively more important as collusive practices among firms and state aids from governments became among the few remaining means by which it was possible to escape the competitive discipline of the single market. Competition policy technically was not part of the single market program, but after 1992 the competition directorate of the Commission was especially attentive to corporate arrangements and government policies that would have the effect, if not necessarily the intent, of undoing progress made toward creating a single, integrated market in which competition would flourish across national borders. Issues of concern in this area included company mergers and acquisitions that promised to stifle rather than promote competition, illegal cartels among competing firms, and state aids given by national governments that threatened to distort the workings of the market. In 2000 the Commission blocked the merger of the truck divisions of Renault and Volvo on the grounds that such a concentration of market power would undercut competition in parts of Europe. With regard to cartels, the Commission was especially concerned about arrangements by which firms try to prevent cross-border competition. In 2001 the Commission fined eight companies a total of €855 million for being part of a cartel that involved secret market-sharing arrangements for vitamin products. Similarly, the Commission fined Volkswagen €90 million in 1998 and DaimlerChrysler €71 million in 2001 for failing to observe single market rules. Both companies were forcing authorized dealers in some member states to refuse to sell cars to buyers from other EU countries who wanted to benefit from lower prices (see also table 4.4).

ENLARGEMENT

In addition to the challenge of completing and sustaining the single market in the existing Union, in the 1990s the EU faced the daunting task of establishing the market in the formerly socialist, nonmarket countries of central and eastern Europe. When they first sought membership early in the decade, these countries had little in-depth understanding of the market. They thus had to engage in comprehensive efforts to remake their own domestic economies in its image. Doing so would have been difficult under any circumstances, but was made more so by the fact that the EU's single market was a moving target. The aspirant countries not only had to adopt the market rules in force in the EU at the time of their application, but they also had to transpose those directives that had since been put into or would be in place by the time of their accession, for example, those relating to the opening of the electricity and natural gas markets and the new steps to market opening in telecommunications.

To assist the candidate countries in preparing for accession, the December 1994 Essen European Council asked the Commission to prepare a detailed white paper that would explain the single market and identify all of the relevant EU legislation going back to the 1950s. The Commission delivered its paper in the spring of 1995, and it was quickly translated into all of the applicant country languages and distributed to the government bureaucracies and the offices of parliament.[40] The paper emphasized the demands that participation in the internal market places on the member states: "An internal market without frontiers relies on a high level of mutual confidence and on equivalence of regulatory approach. Any substantial failure to apply the common rule in any part of the internal market puts the rest of the system at risk and undermines its integrity."[41] It went on to note that "any systematic checks and controls that are necessary to ensure compliance with the rules take place within the market and not when national borders are crossed." It stressed that reliance on the mutual recognition principle placed a heavy premium on the establishment of adequate standards and effective regulatory and inspection bodies in the acceding countries, since any product that could be lawfully produced or imported in the new member states also would be available to everyone else in the Union.

The white paper contained a detailed appendix of some 438 pages that was intended to serve as a "user's guide" for candidate governments as they worked to align legislation and practice with EU norms. It was divided into twenty-three sections, dealing with topics ranging from movement of capital to transport to public procurement to taxation. In each of these sections, the Commission provided an overview of existing legislation, of conditions necessary to operate the legislation, and of key measures that needed to be implemented. Approximation to EU norms remained the responsibility of the applicant countries themselves who, consistent with practice in the Union itself, had a degree of latitude in drafting national legislation to implement EU directives. However, the EU offered help in the form of specialized technical assistance, assistance in estimating the costs and benefits of different sequences of approximation, and advice in strengthening or setting up monitoring or regulatory bodies. Much of this work was undertaken with financial support from the EU and involved partnerships and "twinning" arrangements with organizations and firms from EU member states.

The centrality assigned to the single market ultimately was reflected in the results of the 1998–2002 accession negotiations that settled the terms on which the accession countries entered the Union. The candidate countries were granted long phase-in periods for costly environmental regulations and certain social provisions, but full participation in the single market was made a requirement of admission virtually from day one of membership. There thus were remarkably few transitional arrangements in the negotiating chapters dealing with the internal market. The one major exception concerned the free movement of labor, which, owing to political sensitivities about unemployment and immigration, the existing member states insisted be restricted for a transitional period after accession.

The Lisbon Strategy and Beyond

Despite the completion of the single market program in 1992, the introduction of the euro in 1999, and the progress toward enlargement, by the end of the 1990s the EU in some respects appeared headed back to precisely where it had been almost two decades earlier: concerned that it was falling behind other parts of the world, failing to create enough new jobs, and not assuming leading positions in the industries of the future. This concern was fueled by rapid growth and productivity increases in the United States and the economic boom of the 1990s. Some aspects of the U.S. economic performance later proved to be illusory, as the U.S. economy soon experienced the bursting of the "dot.com bubble" and a series of damaging corporate scandals followed by the economic recession of 2000. Conversely, it was important to remember that Europe had made important strides in many areas, seizing world leadership of the cellular telephone industry, for example, and closing the gap with the United States in aircraft manufacturing.

Nonetheless, many European economists and business executives argued that there were reasons to worry. There had been a steady decline, decade after decade, in the average rate of growth of the EU economy. After making relative gains through most of the postwar period, per capita GDP in the EU had stagnated at about 70 percent of the U.S. level, without making further advances beyond the level reached in the early 1980s. In the second half of the 1990s, the gap in per capita and, even more so given higher U.S. population growth, overall economic growth again was beginning to widen.[42] The EU needed to address a growing list of competitiveness problems that the single market program and the euro had not managed to solve.

These concerns led to the convening of a special summit in Lisbon in March 2000, at which the European Council set the goal of making the EU by 2010 "the most competitive and dynamic knowledge-based economy in the world." It was impossible to say how much the continued failure to complete elements of the single market had contributed to Europe's lagging performance, but economists generally agreed that it played a part. The new Lisbon strategy thus called for "economic reforms for a complete and fully operational internal market."[43] The European Council asked the Commission to develop a strategy for the accelerated removal of barriers to trade in services and to speed up liberalization in the so-called network industries: gas, electricity, postal services, and transport. It also singled out for action public procurement (including better use of online purchasing), simplification of the regulatory environment, completion of the Financial Services Action Plan, and a further strengthening of EU competition policy to ensure that market liberalization was not undermined by cartels and state subsidies to industry.

The annual spring sessions of the European Council devoted to review of the Lisbon strategy have continued to stress the importance of the single market and to identify areas for priority action. At the Stockholm European Council in March 2001 the EU set the goal of reducing the EU-wide rate of nontransposition of internal market directives to 1.5 percent by the next such meeting in the spring of 2002. The European Council also reaffirmed its earlier support for accelerated aviation liberalization and the creation of a Single European Sky, and it reiterated the need to fully implement the Financial Services Action Plan, with particular emphasis on creating an integrated European securities market by the end of 2003. At Barcelona in March 2002 the European Council set a goal of "zero tolerance" for the nontransposition of internal market directives overdue more than two years.

In January 2003 the EU marked the ten-year anniversary of the completion of the 1992 program. On this occasion, the Commission issued a report documenting the gains from the program and the post-1992 follow-up efforts. The report concluded that EU GDP was 1.8 percentage points higher in 2002 than it would have been in the absence of the 1992 program, and that 2.5 million jobs in the EU had been created that would not have existed without the single market reforms. The report also documented direct benefits for consumers and businesses. Promotional airfares had fallen by 41 percent between 1992 and 2000, telephone charges were 40 to 50 percent lower, and some 15 million EU citizens had moved across borders for work or retirement.[44]

But this and other reports also pointed out that the single market faces major challenges that, if not resolved, will undercut Europe's ability to improve upon its unsatisfactory growth performance of recent years. Enforcement and implementation remain serious challenges. The Commission reported in September 2003 that the transposition deficit was rising again after a long period of decline, reaching 2.8 percent, up from the low of 1.8 percent in May 2002. This was almost double the 1.5 percent target set at Stockholm in 2001. Italy had moved into first place as the worst performer, but France and Germany, the two largest economies in the Union and the most enthusiastic proponents of a core Europe, also had deficits of three percent or above (table 4.1).

Table 4.2   Member State Performance in Meeting Single Market Targets (May 2003)

	Percentage of directives not transposed	Total number of outstanding directives	Outstanding more than 2 years	Total number of infringement cases	Infringement cases involving misapplication of law
Austria	3.4	52	3	79	27
Belgium	1.8	27	5	138	76
Denmark	0.6	9	0	36	64
Finland	1.0	16	0	47	26
France	3.3	50	9	220	95
Germany	3.0	46	4	136	64
Greece	3.3	51	4	144	96
Ireland	3.5	54	5	132	118
Italy	3.9	59	3	200	117
Luxembourg	3.2	49	6	34	17
Netherlands	2.0	31	1	68	41
Portugal	3.7	57	0	57	40
Spain	1.2	18	1	153	115
Sweden	1.0	16	1	32	17
UK	1.5	23	0	121	90
Total	2.4	558	42	1,597	1,003

Source: European Commission, Internal Market Scoreboard, No. 12.

Table 4.3   Differences in Prices of General Supermarket Goods

Brand	Highest prices		Lowest prices		Ratio: most/least expensive
Evian mineral water	Finland	189	France	44	4.3
Barilla spaghetti	Sweden	138	Italy	59	2.3
Heinz ketchup	Italy	138	Germany	66	2.1
Kellogg's cornflakes	Greece	152	UK	71	2.1
Mars bar	Denmark	143	Belgium	73	2.0
Coca-cola	Denmark	139	Germany	73	1.9
Fanta	Sweden	146	Netherlands	77	1.9
Nivea shaving cream	UK	142	France	81	1.8
Colgate toothpaste	UK	126	Portugal/Spain	76	1.7
Elvital shampoo	Ireland	126	Spain	76	1.7
Nescafé	Italy	133	Greece	77	1.7

Average price in the EU = 100.
Source: European Commission, *Internal Market Scoreboard*, Nos. 10, 20

Table 4.4   Index of Pre-Tax Differences in Prices for New Cars

	Ford Fiesta	VW Golf	Peugeot 307	Opel Vectra
Austria	119	121	120	114
Belgium	112	124	116	123
Denmark	102	102	89	122
Finland	111	100	109	107
France	107	121	119	114
Germany	126	132	123	114
Greece	104	103	100	105
Ireland	113	111	103	112
Italy	103	126	117	120
Luxembourg	112	132	116	123
Netherlands	103	123	112	110
Portugal	100	121	110	117
Spain	103	125	109	100
Sweden	114	122	105	119
UK	121	126	130	122

Lowest price available in the eurozone as of November 1, 2002 = 100
Source: European Commission, *Internal Market Scoreboard*, Nos. 12, 25

The member states also were ignoring the zero tolerance target set at Barcelona in 2002, as only four member states did not have directives unimplemented more than two years after their stipulated date for transposition (table 4.2). The total number of infringement cases relating to nonconformity or incorrect application of internal market law reached almost 1,600 in 2003 (up from fewer than 700 in 1992), reflecting both the continued failure to observe all of the increasingly complex internal market rules and the determination in Brussels to press on with better enforcement mechanisms.[45]

A further indication of the incomplete nature of the single market was the continued dispersion of prices in the EU. Economists noted that if the single market program had succeeded fully in establishing a single, continent-wide economy, the prices of standard products would converge, allowing for modest differences in local conditions. The euro was supposed to help with this process by facilitating price transparency. But this clearly had not yet been achieved, as can be seen in the wide dispersion of prices for standard products shown in tables 4.3 and 4.4.

Conclusion

Despite the difficulties encountered in recent years, the single market remains the core of the European integration process. It is a key factor in Europe's economic prosperity and its ability to compete in the global economy, as well as a point of leverage in the World Trade Organization (WTO) and other trade forums. It also underpins and in turn is strengthened by the EU's common policies, which are the subject of the next chapter.

Notes

1. Article 30 TOR, ex Article 36.
2. CIA, *Handbook of Economic Statistics, 1986* (Washington, D.C.: U.S. Government Printing Office, 1986), 39.
3. 1983 figures, in ibid., 60.
4. *Wall Street Journal* poll, March 6, 1986, cited in Carlo De Benedetti, "Europe's New Role in a Global Market," in Andrew J. Pierre, *A High Technology Gap? Europe, America and Japan* (New York: Council on Foreign Relations, 1987), 76.
5. "The Thrust of Commission Policy," Bull. EC Supplement 1/85.
6. European Commission, *Completing the Internal Market: White Paper from the Commission to the European Council* (Luxembourg: OOPEC, 1985).
7. "The Economics of 1992," *European Economy* 35 (March 1988).
8. *Rewe Zentral AG v. Bundesmonopolverwaltung für Branntwein*, Case 128/78 ECR 1979.
9. *Technical Harmonization and Standards: A New Approach*, COM(85) 19 final.
10. Bull. EC 5-1985, 11.
11. In a retrospective study of the 1992 program carried out in 1996, the Commission estimated that 76 percent of all intra-EU trade in goods was subject to some kind of techni-

cal regulation with the potential to hinder trade. Twenty-five percent of all such trade was covered by the mutual recognition principle, while another 21 percent was subject to mutual recognition agreements among the member states or some combination of mutual recognition and EU legislation. Fourteen percent of intra-EU trade in goods subject to technical barriers was covered by new approach legislation, while 25 percent was covered by detailed harmonized requirements. For 15 percent of intra-EU trade subject to technical regulation, barriers had not yet been eliminated by any of these methods. Commission, *The 1996 Single Market Review: Background Information for the Report to the Council and European Parliament*, Commission Staff Working Paper, Brussels, December 16, 1996, SEC (96) 2378, 20.

12. Council Directive 92/77/EEC, October 17, 1992, O.J. L316/92.

13. Loukas Tsoukalis, *The New European Economy Revisited* (New York: Oxford University Press, 1997), 65. With increased competition leading to lower costs and with privatizations, this share had dropped to 11.5 percent in 1994. European Commission, *Green Paper: Public Procurement in the European Union: Exploring the Way Forward*, Communication adopted by the Commission, Brussels, November 27, 1996.

14. Council Regulation (EEC) 4060/89, December 21, 1989, O.J. L390/89.

15. Commission of the EC, *Present Status and Future Approach for Open Access to Telecommunications Networks and Services (Open Network Provision): Communication from the Commission to the Council and the European Parliament*, COM(94) 513 final, Brussels, November 29, 1994.

16. Second Council Directive on the coordination of laws, regulations and administrative provisions relating to the taking-up and pursuit of the business of credit institutions and amending Directive 77/780 [the First Banking Directive], 89/646/EEC, O.J. L386/89.

17. Article 67 TOR (provision later abolished).

18. *Programme for the Liberalization of Capital Movements in the Community*, COM(86) 292 final; summary in Bull. EC 5-1986, 13-16.

19. "The European Monetary System: A Long-Term View," in Francesco G. Giavazzi, Stefano M. Micossi, and Marcus Miller, eds., *The European Monetary System* (Cambridge: Cambridge University Press, 1988), 376.

20. Tsoukalis, *The New European Economy Revisited*, 118.

21. Bull. EC 6-1990, 89-91.

22. Article 18, ex Article 8a.

23. Kalypso Nicolaidis and Raymond Vernon, "Competition Policy and Trade Policy in the European Union," in Edward M. Graham and J. David Richardson, eds., *Global Competition Policy* (Washington, D.C.: Institute for International Economics, 1997), 297.

24. See, for example, Leon Brittan, *Europe: The Europe We Need* (London: Hamish Hamilton, 1994), 84–87.

25. For a discussion of the methodological difficulties and the econometric models used, see Commission, *The 1996 Single Market Review: Background Information for the Report to the Council and European Parliament*, Commission Staff Working Paper, Brussels, December 16, 1996, SEC (96), 2378.

26. COM(96) 520 final.

27. European Commission, *The Impact and Effectiveness of the Single Market: Communication from the Commission to the European Parliament and Council*, October 30, 1996, at http://europa.eu.int/comm/dg15/en/update/impact.

28. *Single market: Business Survey Reveals Cautious Optimism*, November 1997, http://europa.eu.int/comm/internal_market/en/index.htm (accessed June 11, 2004).

29. *Single Market: Overview of Compliance Problems in 1996*, http://europa.eu.int/comm/internal_market/en/update/infr/362.htm (accessed June 11, 2004).

30. COM(97) 184.

31. European Commission, *Update on the Single Market: Single Market Scoreboard and Related Documents*, http://europa.eu.int/comm/internal_market/en/index.htm (accessed June 11, 2004).

32. This and the other cases cited in this section are documented on the home page of the Directorate-General for the Internal Market of the Commission, http://europa.eu.int/comm/internal_market/en/index/htm (accessed June 11, 2004).

33. "Liability for Defective Products: Commission Seeks Financial Penalties Against France," http://europa.eu.int/comm/dg15/en/goods/infr/311.htm.

34. Directive 96/92/EC concerning common rules for the internal market in electricity.

35. Economic Policy Committee, *Annual Report on Structural Reforms, 2000*, Brussels, March 13, 2000, p. 12.

36. "Opening Up Electricity Markets to Competition: Reasoned Opinions to France and Luxembourg," European Commission press release, IP/99/1034, Brussels, December 22, 1999.

37. "Commission Opens In-depth Investigation into Merger Between VEBA and VIAG," European Commission press release, IP/00/114, Brussels, February 4, 2000.

38. "Commission Opens Infringement Proceedings Against France for Refusal to Lift Embargo on British Beef," European Commission, Directorate-General for Agriculture, press release, November 16, 1999.

39. Simon Coss, "Commission Hints at GMO Rethink amid Calls for a Ban," *European Voice* 4, no. 37 (October 15–21, 1998): 1.

40. European Commission, *White Paper: Preparation of the Associated Countries of Central and Eastern Europe for Integration into the Internal Market of the Union*, COM(95) 163 final, May 3, 1995.

41. Ibid., 8–9.

42. André Sapir, et al., *An Agenda for a Growing Europe: Making the EU Economic System Deliver—Report of an Independent High-Level Study Group Established on the Initiative of the President of the European Commission* (Brussels: European Commission, July 2003).

43. *Presidency Conclusions: Lisbon European Council, 23 and 24 March 2000*, SN/100 00, 12.

44. European Commission, *The Internal Market—Ten Years without Frontiers*, SEC (2002), January 7, 2003.

45. European Commission, "Internal Market: Further Deterioration in Member States' Implementation of Rules," IP/03/1272, September 19, 2003.

Suggestions for Further Reading

Baldassari, Mario, and Francesco Busato. *Full Employment and High Growth in Europe*. London: Palgrave Macmillan, 2003.

Cockfield, Lord. *The European Union: Creating the Single Market*. London: Wiley Chancery Law, 1994.

Jacquemin, Alexis, and André Sapir, eds. *The European Internal Market: Trade and Competition*. Oxford: Oxford University Press, 1990.

Molle, Willem. *The Economics of European Integration*. Aldershot, UK: Dartmouth, 1990.

Tsoukalis, Loukas. *The New European Economy Revisited*. New York: Oxford University Press, 1997.

CHAPTER 5

Common Policies
A MIXED PICTURE

In addition to establishing the common market and common institutions, the Treaty of Rome provided for common policies in a number of areas. The treaty explicitly mentioned three such policies—the Common Agricultural Policy (CAP), the Common Commercial Policy, and the Common Transport Policy (CTP)—and indirectly suggested others by including provisions relating to competition, coordination of economic policy, approximation of national laws to facilitate the common market, and a few references to social policy and labor conditions. The treaty emphasized those areas in which policy integration was closely related to the functioning of the common market. The CAP was the foremost example of such integration.

Over time, policy integration expanded into new areas that were less directly linked to the market. In this way, the integration process to some extent continued to reflect the sectoral approach championed in the 1950s by proponents of the aborted European Defense Community (EDC) and Euratom. Legally, the expansion of the European Community's (EC) role into new policy areas often was based on Article 235 of the Treaty of Rome, which stipulated that "if action by the Community should prove necessary to attain, in the course of the operation of the common market, one of the objectives of the Community and this Treaty has not provided the necessary powers, the Council shall, acting unanimously on a proposal from the Commission and after consulting the European Parliament, take the appropriate measures."[1] This article provided a broad opening to advance new policy initiatives if doing so was seen as essential to the overriding goal of the treaty, the common market. On the basis of this catch-all article, the European Commission began developing Community environmental and regional policies in the early 1970s, long before they were identified as areas for Community action in the Single European Act, claiming that the proper functioning of the common market called for policies that would create a more even playing field among economic competitors and extend the market to all parts of the Community. The interaction between market integration and policy integration has been a constant theme in the development of the European Union (EU). Market integration focuses on tearing down barriers between and within the member states. It often is associated with a smaller role for government intervention, as it requires cutting back government rules and regulations that may favor particular firms and because it has led to the privatization of major state-owned industries. Policy integration, in contrast, means an ongoing role for governments at the national level as implementors of policy, as well as the transfer of powers to European institutions—chiefly the Commission.

While at first glance market integration and policy integration seem to be in tension with each other, under certain circumstances they can complement and reinforce each other. This certainly has been the case since the 1980s and the launch of the single market program. In complex industrial sectors such as transport and telecommunications as well as in more traditional sectors such as agriculture, market integration requires policy integration, while policy integration is economically and politically feasible only if it works in tandem with market forces. Thus in the 1960s and 1970s, the Community did rather badly in establishing a common transport policy, even though such a policy was mandated by the Treaty of Rome. In the 1980s, however, it made enormous strides toward unifying Europe's transport networks and industries, not by concentrating on transport for its own sake but by treating transport as an essential part of the single market.

In recent years EU policy in various areas has continued to evolve in response to internal and external challenges. One trend has been an effort by the EU to improve the coordination of policies in different but cross-cutting areas to achieve long-term, strategic objectives. A good example is the Lisbon process, launched at the March 2000 European Council, where the EU established the goal of becoming "the most competitive and dynamic knowledge-based economy in the world capable of sustainable economic growth with more and better jobs and greater social cohesion."[2] To achieve this goal, Lisbon mandated action in a wide variety of policy areas: research and development, education and training, investment in transportation and information infrastructure, reform of labor markets and social welfare systems, as well as continued efforts to complete the single market and to conduct a successful macroeconomic policy under Economic and Monetary Union (EMU).

Another factor forcing change in EU policies is enlargement. In principle, new member countries are charged with adopting EU policies on an as-is basis, with accepting what is known in EU parlance as the *acquis communautaire*, the sum total of treaty obligations, laws, regulations, and other commitments developed since the 1950s. In practice, European government recognized already in the early 1990s that EU policies had to be reformed before they could be extended to another ten countries with very different economic and social situations and relatively low per capita gross domestic products (GDPs). Agriculture and regional policies are most affected, but enlargement has implications for all areas of EU policy making, ranging from the need to integrate the fleets of Poland and the Baltic countries into the Common Fisheries Policy (CFP), to the challenge of adapting EU employment policy to the 20 percent unemployment rates still found in some accession countries, to the need to adjust EU environmental policy in response to the legacy of environmental degradation inherited from the communist era.

The Common Agricultural Policy
THE COMMUNITY AND THE CAP

The Community put in place its Common Agricultural Policy in 1958–1968, in parallel with the establishment of the common market for industrial goods. In the mid-1950s, about 20 percent of the working population of the six still was employed in agriculture. Average farm size was small (about 10 hectares), and many farmers were poor and economically vulnerable. The economic and social need for an agricultural policy thus was apparent. The member states of the new Community already operated extensive national systems of agricultural support and protection. To dismantle these systems to create a common market was politically unthinkable. The alternative was to establish a Community-level system that would be consistent with the goals of market integration but that still would provide the needed support for farmers. The CAP also was at the heart of the political compromises struck in the negotiations to establish the Community. In France there was deep skepticism about free trade in industrial goods and unfettered competition with German industry, but France had a large agricultural sector that needed new market outlets. France thus sought preferential access to the German market for its farm products and extensive agricultural support measures under the CAP as a trade-off for accepting the customs union.[3]

The treaty established five objectives for the CAP: (1) to increase agricultural productivity; (2) to ensure a fair standard of living for agricultural communities; (3) to stabilize markets; (4) to assure the availability of supplies; and (5) to ensure that supplies reach consumers at reasonable prices. These objectives have remained the basis for the CAP to the present, even though they are somewhat self-contradictory and help to explain many of the problems that the CAP has encountered in recent decades. Ensuring supplies to consumers at reasonable prices has tended to conflict with the goal of ensuring farmers' standard of living, which generally has required that they receive high prices for their products. The treaty did not spell out how these objectives were to be pursued. This was done in the first four years of the Community's existence through passage of legislation by the Council of Ministers, acting on proposals from the Commission.

In early 1958 the Commission and the member states formulated three basic operational principles for the design of the CAP: (1) unity of the market based on common prices; (2) Community preference; and (3) financial solidarity. Unity of the market meant that even though free market principles would not apply in the agricultural sphere, the Community would strive to operate a common market for agricultural goods just as it did for industrial products. Wheat would cost the same in France as it did in Germany (with some allowance for local conditions and transport costs), and governments would not be permitted to segment the Community market through tariffs, national export subsidies, or other devices prohibited under the Treaty of Rome. Community preference meant that member states would import first from each other and only secondarily go out on the world market for supplies. Financial solidarity meant that the costs of the CAP would be pooled and shared on a Community basis. These same goals and operational principles apply in today's EU. However, the Union is undertaking major reforms of the CAP designed to lower costs that many farmers claim are undermining the basis of the system as it has existed since the early 1960s.

The CAP was set up to operate through a complex system of prices and levies, determined not by markets but by the Commission and the member states in the

Council of Ministers. For commodities such as grain, beef, and milk, the EU sets a "target price"—the price that farmers are to receive for their products. This price is determined each year, and is set high enough to guarantee farmers a certain standard of living. Target prices generally are above world market prices, since European farms are on average smaller and less competitive than farms in other parts of the world. The EU also sets an "intervention price" for each commodity. This is the price at which intervention agencies are required to step into the market to buy commodities to ensure that prices on the market do not fall below the target price. The intervention agencies are designated by the member states, and receive their funding from the European Agricultural Guidance and Guarantee Fund (EAGGF), which was set up in April 1962 to fund the CAP. Finally, the EU sets an "entry price." This is the minimum price at which commodities from outside the Union can be imported. The entry price generally is near the target price, and is designed to keep lower-priced products from North America, Australia, and elsewhere from competing with European farmers. To maintain the entry price, the CAP imposes a levy that is calculated as the difference between the world market price and the entry price. The levy varies, depending upon the level of world market prices. Thus if world grain prices fall because of abundant harvests in major grain producing countries, the EU increases the levy on grain to ensure high entry prices, allowing EU farmers to maintain their share of the EU market at the same high target price.

With the EU deliberately choosing to maintain its internal farm prices above world market prices, it normally would not be expected to export agricultural products outside the Union. But the CAP also has a mechanism for exports that is in effect the reverse of the variable import levy—a variable export subsidy paid in the form of a refund to EU agricultural exporters. These subsidies enable Europe to sell on the world market products bought from farmers at the uncompetitive target price. To agricultural producers in other countries, this practice constitutes dumping and has been a major source of international trade tensions. Tensions over European export subsidies were particularly acute in the mid-1980s, when an undeclared price war caused by European subsidies and international (especially U.S.) retaliation came to dominate world grain markets. U.S. producers also complained about subsidized sales of cheese, wine, hams, and pasta on the North American market.[4]

The CAP accomplished the basic objective of extending the common market and the common external trade policy to agricultural products by application of the principles of unity of the market, Community preference, and financial solidarity. It did so, however, at a high economic and political price. Most of the financial burden of the CAP was borne by consumers, who were forced to pay higher prices for their food than they would have had they been able to purchase food at world market prices. The CAP also encouraged waste and overproduction. Since farmers were guaranteed a target price, they had no financial incentive to match production to demand. Farmers increased production for sale at the target price and used the higher revenues in part to improve productivity and raise output through investments in equipment, fertilizer, and land.

In the 1960s and 1970s many foreign suppliers gradually were squeezed out of the EC market as the variable levy neutralized the advantages they gained from lower prices. The CAP resulted in increased production and, under Community preference, substitution of intra-EC trade for imports from traditional overseas suppliers. The first major trade dispute between the United States and the EC, known as the "chicken war," arose in 1962 when American suppliers, who traditionally had sold large amounts of frozen poultry to West Germany, lost this market as German importers shifted their purchases to other EC member countries. As domestic production increased, the EC shifted from being a net importer to being a major exporter of food. The Community became the owner of "wine lakes" and "butter mountains" that became the object of political derision at home. The EC sought to dispose of these stocks by selling them on world markets at subsidized prices, cutting into sales by U.S. and other exporters and thereby increasing trade tensions. When the CAP was introduced in 1962, the EC produced about 80 percent of its food and imported the remainder. Today, the EU produces about 120 percent of the amount of food that it consumes, leaving a large surplus for export.

The CAP also became a major burden on the Community budget, accounting for over 70 percent of total expenditure by the early 1980s. This was especially problematic at a time when the Community was expanding its activities into industrial research and development, regional policies targeted at poor urban as well as rural areas, and other priority areas. However, the powerful farm lobby, represented both in Brussels and in the member states, strongly resisted changes in an agricultural system upon which farmers had become wholly dependent. France and Germany, each for somewhat different reasons, both resisted major reforms, and without the support of the Community's two leading powers little could be achieved.

Britain, in contrast, had long imported much of its food from its overseas empire and other countries such as Argentina, and it had a much smaller farming sector—measured either by share of agricultural production in GDP or by number of farmers relative to total employment—than the other Community countries. This meant that British consumers contributed to CAP financial solidarity by paying high prices for their food, while British farmers received far less back from the Community treasury than farmers in other countries. British governments generally favored reform but were unable to overcome resistance in other member states.

PRESSURE FOR REFORM

The problems of overproduction and the budgetary burden posed by the CAP led to growing pressures for change.[5] In 1979 the Community attempted to curb excess milk production by introducing a levy on dairy farmers that would be used to help pay for the storage and disposal costs of excess milk. When the levy system failed to cut overproduction, the Community introduced, in 1984, a system of national quotas on milk production that had some effect in holding down supplies.

The first major reform of the CAP came about in 1988 as part of the five-year Delors I budget package. At a special session of the European Council in Brussels in February 1988 the member states agreed that Community spending on agriculture could not increase at more than 74 percent of the rate of increase in Community GNP for the next five years. This meant that agricultural subsidies as a share of GNP and of the Community budget gradually would fall. To effect these savings, the Community put in place several measures to curb production, including a land set-aside scheme and a system of production quotas beyond which farmers would not receive full support payments for their products.

The 1988 reforms signaled a new readiness on the part of the political leadership to tackle the problems of the CAP, even if it meant conflict with the Community's farmers. They were too modest, however, to solve the problems of overproduction and ever-rising costs. The Community thus launched a second round of reforms in 1992.[6] Known as the MacSharry Plan after the Commissioner responsible for agriculture, Ray MacSharry of Ireland, these reforms were undertaken in response to both internal and external pressure. Agriculture had by this time become the main sticking point in the Uruguay Round of the General Agreement on Tariffs and Trade (GATT), and without changes in the CAP the successful conclusion of this negotiation would not have been possible. Internally, there were strong pressures to cut costs.

The distinctive element of the MacSharry plan was a move away from price supports for agricultural products to direct income support to farmers. Price supports were ruinously expensive, encouraged overproduction, benefited wealthy as well as poor farmers, and were at the heart of the international complaints about the CAP. In contrast, direct income payments did not encourage overproduction and did not disrupt global markets. Farmers had always resisted direct income support as the basis for the CAP, fearing that such payments would be seen as a form of welfare that was demeaning to farmers and potentially more vulnerable than other types of aid to future cost cutting, but they were unable to block the MacSharry proposals.

The reforms left in place the CAP's traditional basic price support mechanisms, but they called for steep cuts in the intervention prices for key commodities such as grain, beef, and dairy products. Grain prices were to be reduced by 29 percent over a three-year period in 1993–1994, beef prices by 15 percent, butter prices by 5 percent, and price supports for oilseeds eliminated altogether. To compensate for lower overall prices, the CAP instituted a system of compensatory payments to farmers based on the amount of land they had under cultivation and the historic yield level in their particular region of the Community—in other words on their capacity to produce. The CAP also instituted set-aside schemes under which farmers agreed to take land out of production or to reduce herd sizes in exchange for compensation payments. In addition to these core elements related to prices and incomes, the MacSharry reforms included measures to encourage more environmentally friendly farming and to promote the afforestation of land taken out of production.

These reforms were highly controversial among farmers, but in the end they were accepted by the member states and became the basis for the Blair House agreement between the EC and the United States in November 1992. The Community agreed to a 21 percent cut in export volumes over the six years 1993–1999, during which time the United States and the EC would observe a "peace clause" in agricultural trade disputes. These understandings became the basis for the breakthrough in the Uruguay Round GATT negotiations and the completion of the round in December 1993.

Whether the reforms would result in lower costs and reduced international trade tensions became key questions after 1992. For the most part these objectives were achieved. The ceiling of 74 percent of EU GNP in the growth of agricultural spending was renewed in the Delors II financial package for 1993–1999, which meant that the share of agriculture in the EU budget continued to decline even though the absolute level of spending still rose. Agriculture as a share of the EU budget fell to 42 percent in 1999, down from 50 percent in 1996 and 64 percent in 1988. In the course of the 1990s, the EU's vast commodity surpluses largely disappeared, lowering storage costs and reducing the incentive to dump on world markets. The EU remained a major agricultural exporter, but tensions with other agricultural nations were kept in check.

AGENDA 2000 AND THE BERLIN PACKAGE

By the end of the 1990s the CAP was facing new challenges and pressure for reform linked to enlargement. The Commission estimated that the ten candidate countries of central and eastern Europe had some 9.5 million agricultural workers and 60 million hectares of agricultural land—compared with 8.2 million agricultural workers and 140 million hectares in the EU of the fifteen. Over 22 percent of the total workforce in the candidate countries was employed in agriculture, compared with only 5 percent in the EU-15.[7] To extend the existing CAP to this many farmers would be ruinously expensive. *Agenda 2000* therefore called for continuing reform of the CAP in the context of a broader reform of EU finances. In its draft financial package for 2000–2006, the Commission proposed that increases in CAP spending be kept at the existing upper limit of 74 percent of GNP growth but acknowledged that holding agricultural spending at this level would necessitate further reform.

Building upon the proposals in *Agenda 2000*, in 1998 agricultural commissioner Franz Fischler proposed additional large cuts in the support prices for meat, cereals, and dairy products intended to reduce the costs of the CAP, to be replaced by direct payments to sustain income. Fischler proposed that the cereals intervention price be cut by 20 percent in 2000, beef prices by 30 percent between 2000 and 2002, and dairy prices by 15 percent by 2006. The Commission also suggested that the shift from price intervention to direct income support might make possible the transfer of responsibility for a portion of these direct payments (as much as 25 percent) to the member states.

For the next twenty months debate over CAP reform raged in the EU. Member state ministers of agriculture were nearly unanimous in denouncing the Commission's proposals as damaging to farmers but could agree on very little else. France was adamantly opposed to any "renationalization" of agricultural support payments, which in its view ran counter to the basic bargain embodied in the 1957 Treaty of Rome. Germany was equally firm that its large net payments to the EU budget had to be cut, and agriculture was the logical place to start. Final agreement was achieved only at the March 1999 Berlin session of the European Council, following a preliminary deal forged by the agricultural ministers the preceding month.

In the final deal negotiated at Berlin, cereals prices were to be cut 15 percent in two equal steps in 2000 and 2001. Ten percent of land devoted to cereals was to be taken out of production for each year to 2006. Beef prices were to fall 20 percent over three years, beginning in 2000. Dairy prices would be cut 15 percent but only in 2005–2006. Greece, Spain, Italy, Ireland, and the UK (Northern Ireland) were awarded increases in milk quotas beginning in 2000, equal to 0.9 percent of the EU total. Absolute levels of spending would continue to increase, as they had every year from 1962–1999. Berlin also called for a mid-term review of the CAP, to take place in 2002, to allow for further adjustments in response to progress in the enlargement negotiations and world market conditions.

ENLARGEMENT AND THE 2003 REFORM

Notwithstanding the progress made in Berlin, the CAP faced three long-term challenges that the Berlin agreements did not resolve. First, enlargement was certain to put enormous strains on the system. Prices would remain above world market levels, which would mean high costs for consumers and could encourage the production of large amounts of unneeded food in the countries of central and eastern Europe under subsidies from the EU budget.

Second, a new round of international trade talks, which the EU was committed to entering under World Trade Organization (WTO) auspices after the "peace clause" expired at the end of 1999, again promised to put EU agriculture in the world spotlight. The United States, Australia, and other agricultural exporters charged that the 1999 reforms did not go far enough in reducing export subsidies, which was certain to be one of the most contentious issues in these talks. The developing countries, backed by influential nongovernmental organizations in the developed world, were increasingly insistent that the EU and the United States both had to reduce drastically their farm subsidies in order to give farmers in poor countries a chance to compete in their home and global markets.

Third, the CAP faced a new set of environmental, food safety, and animal rights issues that had played almost no role when the CAP was established but that increasingly impinged on agricultural policy. Increases in agricultural production had been achieved by intensive use of fertilizers, herbicides, pesticides, and machinery, all of which contribute to environmental problems. Agriculture thus was becoming a priority area for EU environmental policy and the CAP itself placed increasing emphasis on environmentally friendly farming. New issues related to food safety and the ethical and scientific bases of modern farming also arose in the 1990s. The outbreak of bovine spongiform encephalopathy (BSE, commonly known as "mad cow disease") caused the Commission in 1995 to ban the sale of British beef to other EU and external markets, which in turn led to a political crisis between Britain and its partners before the ban was lifted. A similar ban was placed on exports of dioxin-contaminated products from Belgium in June 1999, again raising concern about EU food safety regulation. Consumer and environmentalist opposition to farming with genetically modified organisms (GMOs) had caused several member states to impose national bans on the sale of such crops, thereby undermining the unity of the market and exacerbating trade tensions with the United States. Animal rights issues also were thrust on the agenda. The Amsterdam treaty contained a new protocol on the protection and welfare of animals, in which the EU and its member states pledged to pay full regard to the welfare requirements of animals in formulating and implementing EU agriculture policy.

The need to adjust to these challenges led to further reforms of the CAP and related policy measures. In January 2002 the European Parliament and the Council of Ministers approved legislation to establish a European Food Safety Authority that was to provide independent, scientific advice on food safety issues.[8] Start-up of the agency was delayed, however, by a dispute over its location, with Finland and Italy putting forth competing claims. EU trading partners also were wary of the new agency, which was charged with operating under the controversial "precautionary principle" and which they feared might not prevent European political authorities from taking regulatory decisions to ban certain products (e.g., GMOs) without an adequate scientific basis.

The biggest challenge to the CAP, however, remained enlargement. Negotiations on the agricultural aspects of enlargement began in June 2000. The EU based its negotiating position on the 1999 Berlin framework agreement which, consistent with general EU practice, it asked the candidate countries to accept without major change. This proved difficult, however, as these countries had not participated in its adoption and found its provisions fundamentally unfair. In the Berlin agreement, CAP spending in the current member states in the first postenlargement year was set at €39.4 billion, while comparable spending for six new member states was set at a mere €1.6 billion. There was no provision for direct income support for farmers in the new member states, since incomes in these countries were historically low and such supports originally had been given to offset cuts in CAP price supports from which central and east European country farmers had never benefited. In view of the fact that there are more farmers in the candidate countries than in the EU-15, the highly uneven way in which the Berlin agreement proposed to allocate agricultural spending was politically problematic and, from the long-term perspective of integrating the new member states and raising their per capita incomes to western levels, economically questionable.

In their opening positions, all of the candidate countries requested that direct payments be granted to their farmers at the same level provided to farmers in current member states from day one of accession. There also were deep differences over national production quotas for major products. The Commission proposed that quotas be based on past performance levels during the 1995–1999 reference period. The candidate countries argued that in recent years their agricultural production had been hit by the collapse of communism, falling export markets, and adverse weather. They therefore generally opposed any agreement based on current output levels.

Reacting to the strong political response in Poland and other candidate countries to its position on direct payments, in early 2002 the Commission revised its initial approach and proposed that direct payments to farmers in the new member states be set at 25 percent of EU levels upon accession and rise to 100 percent over a ten-year period. The Commission proposal in some ways achieved the worst of all possible worlds. It was a departure from the fiscally conservative assumptions in the 1999 financial framework and thus had considerable potential to break the EU budget, but it still was seen as unfair from the candidate country perspective.

Acting under the Berlin mandate calling for a mid-term review of the CAP, in June 2002 Fischler circulated a new reform proposal that was to determine the shape of the CAP for years to come and serve as the basis for the EU's final offer to the candidate countries. Formally presented to the member states in early July, it called for cutting the link between EU subsidies and what farmers produced by replacing almost all market intervention with direct aid payments and increased aid for rural development. Payments to large farms would be capped at €300,000 per year. In addition, the CAP would place more emphasis on food quality and safety, animal welfare, and the environment.[9]

The Fischler proposals were so controversial that the member states agreed to postpone their consideration until October 2002, after the French and German elections. The Netherlands, Sweden, and the UK generally welcomed the proposals and urged that the reforms go even further, but France led a group of member states that criticized the proposed reforms as going too far and accused the Commission of exceeding the 1999 mid-term review mandate by introducing proposals for sweeping changes going beyond financial questions.

With German support, in the end the French view prevailed. On the basis of a bilateral Franco-German compromise that angered British prime minister Tony Blair, at the October 2002 Brussels European Council the fifteen agreed on a formula that effectively ruled out any drastic reform of farm subsidies before 2006 and ensured that agricultural outlays would continue to increase (at least in nominal terms) even for the period 2007–2013. This was a far cry from the deep cuts called for by Britain, the Netherlands, and Sweden and left unclear how the EU would square its agreement to maintain farm subsidies for at least another decade with the pressures in the WTO to phase out farm subsidies. It also seemed to leave open the question of whether the CAP had been sufficiently reformed so as to be able to accommodate enlargement.[10] The European Council proposal called for starting direct payments to new member-state farmers at the 25 percent level and raising them to full Union levels only by 2013. This was not essentially different from the deal on offer in the spring and was criticized by the Czech, Polish, and other candidate country governments as unfair and possibly endangering prospects for approval of the accession treaty in national referenda, particularly in Poland where Euroskeptics threatened to campaign for a rejection of membership if farm payments were not equal from the date of accession.[11]

However, the candidate countries were under enormous pressure to accept the October offer as the best deal possible, particularly given British and Dutch complaints that the Franco-German deal underlying the offer was *too* generous with regard to direct income support. In the compromise reached at the December 2002 Copenhagen summit, the EU stuck to its initial offer of direct payments to farmers in the accession countries at the 25 percent level, but the accession countries were granted the right to transfer rural development funds to direct payments. In addition, the accession countries won the right to spend more money from national budgets to support farmers so that subsidy payments could reach 55 percent of EU levels already in 2004, rising to 60 percent in 2005, and 65 percent in 2006. Production quotas also were adjusted upward in some cases.

With issues relating to enlargement basically settled, in June 2003 the Council finally approved a major reform of the CAP. The reform was based largely on Fischler's mid-term review proposals. Its timing was driven in part by the upcoming Cancun WTO ministerial, at which the EU was expecting to be attacked by the developing countries and the United States if it did not continue with its reforms. The essence of the 2003 reform was a further move away from production-linked subsidies to a single, flat-rate payment to farmers. The levels of these payments were to be determined by historical incomes, but the payments were to be made conditional upon farmers' performance in contributing to broader policy objectives, including maintaining high standards for the environment, food safety, animal and plant health, and animal welfare. In this way, the Commission could claim that "farmers will be rewarded for the service they provide to society instead of depending on public handouts."[12]

The reform also increased funding for rural development, which was to be financed by cutting subsidy payments to the largest farms. The CAP retained elements of the old system of price intervention, but the move toward lower prices more in line with world levels continued. The intervention price for butter, for example, was to be reduced by 25 percent over four years, and for skimmed milk powder 15 percent over three years. Export subsidies were retained, however, and remained a point of contention in international trade negotiations.

Beyond the continued bargaining over prices, tariffs, and quotas is a struggle about the future that is likely to continue for years. Despite the reforms of 1992, 1999, and 2003, the CAP was under attack from critics who argued that it was harmful to farmers in poor countries, a source of trade tensions, damaging to the environment, and a diversion of resources from other, more pressing tasks that Europe needs to address, such as upgrading its transport infrastructure, improving education and research and development, and meeting the pension costs of an ageing population. Defenders of the CAP countered with arguments old and new, citing traditional justifications such as food security and sustaining a traditional rural way of life in Europe, as well as the CAP's new focus on food safety, organic farming, the environment, and animal welfare. Out of this debate is likely to come a synthesis, or what might better be called a standoff. The CAP will have to change in response to the factors cited by its critics, but with its long tradition and powerful political backers, it almost certainly will find ways to defend a large and largely self-sufficient agricultural sector in Europe, even if this means high costs, clashes with trading partners, and continued resort to protections of one kind or another.

The Common Fisheries Policy

The legal basis for a fisheries policy was established in the articles in the Treaty of Rome dealing with the CAP, which defined agricultural products as "products of the soil, stockfarming, and of fisheries." However, the Community did not begin to develop common guidelines for commercial fishing until the 1970s, after the accession of Denmark, Ireland, and the UK, countries with long coastlines and substantial domestic fishing industries. The EC formally adopted its Common Fisheries Policy (CFP) in 1983, shortly before the accession of Portugal and Spain, also major fishing nations whose accession lent new urgency to the issue.

Commercial fishing accounts for less than 1 percent of GNP and employment in most EU countries, but it has become an important area of EU policy concern, for both internal and external reasons. European crews traditionally have fished in the waters off other European countries as well as on the high seas and off the coasts of Africa and North America. Overfishing is a serious worldwide environmental problem, and the member states look to EU action as a way of managing the industry in European coastal waters and of negotiating fishing rights with other countries around the world.

The CFP divides fishing grounds into three categories: coastal waters up to the twelve-mile limit, waters beyond twelve miles up to the 200-mile limit, and fishing grounds in international waters or under the jurisdiction of non-EU countries. Within twelve miles, access is reserved for fishermen from local ports who traditionally have fished in those waters. Small fishing boats from other EU countries with claims based on tradition also are allowed some access. EU legislation carefully sets out which boats from which countries and at what times of the year may fish in these waters. The twelve-mile preference is an exception to the EU's single market nondiscrimination principle. It was to have been phased out by the end of 2002, but in December of that year it was extended to the end of 2012 on the grounds that it helps to preserve local fishing communities and assists with conservation.[13]

Inside the 200-mile limit but beyond the twelve-mile coastal zone, freedom of access for boats from any EU country applies, irrespective of nationality. When Spain and Portugal joined the Community in 1986, the other member states insisted on a ten-year delay in putting this provision into practice for them. Nevertheless, it caused a stir in local communities when, in early 1996, Portuguese and Spanish trawlers appeared off the coasts of Ireland and the UK. Beyond the 200-mile limit, the EU negotiates bilateral agreements with other coastal nations to ensure access by its fishermen to those waters and participates in international regulatory bodies such as the North Atlantic Salmon Conservation Organization and the International Commission for the Conservation of Atlantic Tunas.

Since 1983, fisheries management in EU waters has been based on the concept of a total allowable catch (TAC) for each species in a given area. The EU's Scientific, Technical and Economic Committee for Fisheries (STECF), working with international scientific bodies, annually assesses stock levels with an eye toward conservation. On the basis of this scientific assessment, the Commission makes a recommendation to the Council, which in December of each year sets the TACs that are divided among the member states and their fleets. So far this approach has not solved the problem of overfishing in EU waters. Not all areas and species are covered by TACs, and member state governments in the Council too often have been tempted to avoid short-term political costs at the expense of long-term environmental damage by establishing quotas larger than those recommended by the experts. Overfishing by EU boats in international waters is also a problem, and has led to sharp disputes with other countries, notably in 1995 when Canada impounded Spanish trawlers for exceeding their allowable catches in waters off the Canadian coast.

In 1997 the Council adopted a new plan for the restructuring of the EU fisheries sector for the period 1997–2002, the main objective of which was to achieve a better balance between available stocks and the level of fishing. The financial framework for 2000–2006 allocated €1.1 billion to the EU's Financial Instrument for Fisheries Guidance, which supports improvements in the sector including help to the industry with processing and marketing. As in the agricultural sector, EU policy also aims to assist local communities that are heavily dependent on fishing to develop alternative sources of employment such as tourism.

Although useful up to a point, the 1997 plan failed to solve the problem of overfishing. Ministers voted to cut TACs but not to the extent recommended by the Commission based on the views of the scientific community. Poor enforcement and illegal fishing meant that actual catches were in any case above the TACs. At their December 1999 session, EU fishing ministers began to take drastic action by agreeing to large reductions in TACs for 2000. Cuts ranged from 62 percent for cod in the Irish Sea, 40 percent for haddock in the Atlantic west of France, and 20 to 25 percent for lobster in a range of areas. These cuts were bitterly protested by the fishing industry and resisted by some of the ministers, who succeeded in diluting Commission proposals for even more drastic cuts. Clearly the EU was caught in a vicious circle. Declining catches were causing economic hardship in fishing communities, which led governments to resist taking hard measures with regard to conversation, which in turn further depleted available stocks and led to still greater losses in the fishing communities. By late 2001 the Commission was warning, in its green paper on the future of the CFP, that stocks of cod, northern hake, and other species were close to collapse in European waters.[14]

Against this background, in the course of 2002 the Commission and the Council agreed on a basic reform of the CFP, to go into effect on January 1, 2003.[15] It called for a long-term approach of rebuilding fish stocks through lowered quotas, focus on multi-annual fishing quotas rather than exclusive reliance on TACs, new policies to cut the sizes of fishing fleets to match available stocks, and better enforcement and reporting to ensure that conservation measures actually were implemented. In 2003 the Commission began to produce an annual CFP compliance scoreboard designed to highlight the performance of the member states in observing quotas and stopping illegal fishing. As in the United States and other parts of the world, however, the long-term outlook is not good. At best, it will take many years of strict enforcement of rigid conservation policies to bring about the rebuilding of stocks off Europe's coasts.

The Common Transport Policy

Transport is important both as an economic sector in its own right, accounting for about 10 percent of EU GDP and employing more than 10 million people, and as an input to other sectors, notably manufacturing and agriculture.[16] The founders of the Community recognized that it would make little sense to eliminate tariffs and quotas if discrimination against imports in the cost of rail and other forms of transport persisted. The Treaty of Paris establishing the European Coal and Steel Community (ECSC) prohibited member states from using transport rates and policies to favor domestic suppliers of coal and steel at the expense of suppliers from other member states. The Treaty of Rome broadened the principle of nondiscrimination to trade in all goods by calling for the establishment of a common transport policy to support the overall objectives of the treaty. Under Article 80 of the treaty, the common transport policy was to apply automatically to road, rail, and inland waterway transport.[17] The Council of Ministers could extend the CTP to marine and aviation transport—sectors with a more important extra-European dimension—by unanimous vote, as eventually was done in 1974.

In contrast to what happened with respect to agriculture, however, the Community failed to develop a comprehensive transport policy until well into the 1980s. This failure was mainly the responsibility of the member states, which had different interests in the transport sector and could not agree among themselves on key aspects of the policy. The Benelux countries and, after the first enlargement, geographically peripheral states such as the UK and Denmark mainly were interested in free movement by their trucking and barge companies in and through the Community's core—Germany, France, and northern Italy—while the geographically central states wanted to open their domestic markets and transport infrastructures to foreign competition on a basis that would preserve certain advantages for domestic firms. The national railroad companies, state-owned and with proud traditions going back to the nineteenth century, also resisted opening to foreign competition.

In fulfillment of its responsibilities to propose legislation to implement the goals of the Treaty of Rome, in 1962 the Commission adopted an Action Plan for Transport.[18] It proposed three kinds of measures: (1) antidiscrimination measures to apply to goods shipped from other member states; (2) liberalization measures to allow carriers to supply services across national frontiers in the Community;

and (3) harmonization measures with regard to such matters as the size and weight of trucks, road taxes, and safety and working conditions in the transport sector. The Commission also proposed that the EC play a role in coordinating infrastructure investment, particularly with regard to trunk routes of Community importance. Very little of the action plan actually was adopted, however, and the transport sector remained highly fragmented along national lines. Truck transport, for example, was regulated by a series of bilateral agreements among the member states specifying how much freight firms from each country could carry to the other country in a given year. In the aviation sector, governments were mainly concerned with protecting the interests of their flag carriers, while in maritime shipping they continued to protect national fleets from international competition in the face of global overcapacity in the industry.

The Community finally began to develop a comprehensive transport policy in the 1980s. This was mainly the result of two factors. First, in 1983 the European Parliament brought an action in the Court of Justice against the Council of Ministers for failing to adopt a common transport policy as mandated in the Treaty of Rome. This was an excellent example of how the Court could be called upon to adjudicate disputes among the institutions of the Community, even if it meant challenging the positions of the member states (whose representatives, after all, made up the Council of Ministers). It also reflected the activist, prointegration stance of the European Parliament after the direct elections of 1979. In May 1985 the Court ruled in favor of the Parliament and called upon the Council to develop a plan to liberalize transport services within a reasonable time.[19] Second, as was seen in the previous chapter, transport liberalization became an important element in the single market program adopted under the 1986 Single European Act. Trucking, rail and inland waterway, shipping and air transport now are all at least partially open to competition under a body of EU legislation that aims to harmonize fiscal, technical, and social provisions in member states that affect competition in the transport sector.

In 1992 the Commission issued a white paper, *The Future Development of the Common Transport Policy*, that became the policy guideline for the remainder of the decade.[20] It specified three main goals: completing the single market in transport by the removal of remaining restrictions on competition; developing a comprehensive transport system able to serve the economic and social needs of the Union; and integrating environmental objectives into the common transport policy. Promoting transport safety was another important objective, added to the transport provisions of the Treaty of Rome by amendment in the Treaty of Maastricht.

Market liberalization continued throughout the decade, and included the opening of air transport in 1997 and continued steps toward open competition in road, rail, and other sectors. This was a slow and difficult process, however, technically complex and resisted by political forces in many of the member states. In road transport, for example, the member states had difficulty in harmonizing standards on maximum driving hours and other safety and employment provisions that affect competition in the industry. Similarly, the Commission and the transport ministers of the fifteen agreed on the need to revitalize rail transport in order to shift freight off Europe's congested roads, but the EU made only slow progress on the implementation of directives calling for the separation of infrastructure and transport operations and other measures to promote competition.

In 2001 the Commission issued a second white paper, *European Transport Policy for 2010: Time to Decide*, that called for policies that would build upon the market opening successes of the previous decades but that also would tackle problems that Union and national policies had failed to solve and that clearly were growing worse: the continued decline of the railroads, environmental problems, traffic congestion in urban areas, and lingering problems with transport safety.

Transport is, after the energy sector (electricity and refineries), the second largest source of greenhouse gas emissions in the EU and thus a major contributor to global warming. Carbon dioxide emissions from road transport in the Union increased by 18 percent from 1990 and 2000, offsetting emissions reductions in other areas and undermining the Union's efforts to meet its goal (mandated in the 1997 Kyoto Protocol) of cutting overall greenhouse gas emissions by 8 to 12 percent from 1990 levels by 2008–2012.[21] Reducing emissions in the transport sector will require shifting traffic to more environmentally friendly alternatives such as high speed and commuter rail, developing more fuel-efficient cars, land-use planning to cut the length of commutes, and other policy measures. Meeting this objective will be very difficult, however, particularly as people in the accession countries become more affluent and start to drive the same number of kilometers in the same-sized cars as people in Western Europe.

To address safety issues, the EU established a European Aviation Safety Agency in 2003 and a European Maritime Safety Agency in 2002. Aviation safety in Europe generally is at a very high level, but the air transport sector is burdened by a patchwork of different national air traffic control systems that limits capacity and contributes to congestion and flight delays. The new agency and a broader "single European sky" initiative are intended to tackle these deficiencies. Maritime safety is a far more problematic area, in part because European governments cannot directly regulate the safety standards of third-country tankers that ply the coasts of Europe and that have been responsible for damaging oil spills on the beaches of France, Spain, and elsewhere. The new agency is intended to tighten regulations and step up enforcement in this area. In both the aviation and the maritime sectors, EU efforts to create Union agencies also have a broader political purpose: the Commission and some member-state governments believe that EU-level agencies are needed to counterbalance globally influential U.S. agencies such as the Federal Aviation Administration and to place the EU on an equal footing with the United States in regulating these important industries.

Extending EU transport policy to the new member states entails a mix of infrastructure upgrading and the adoption of rules and regulations relating to safety, the environment, and labor conditions for workers in the transport sector. The accession countries have been required to adopt all EU-level transport legislation as part of the *acquis communautaire*. However, integration of the new member states and their transport firms (particularly in trucking and inland water transport) into the single market has been politically controversial, as firms in the older member countries fear that truckers and other transport operators from the new member countries will be able to compete unfairly in the EU market by compromising safety standards, working longer hours, and so forth. For this reason, full rights of cabotage for the accession countries in the EU-15 are being phased in over a period of years.

Most roads, railroads, and airports in the accession countries were built before or during the communist era and are totally inadequate to support the integration of the region into the single market or to attract the level of investment needed to raise these countries to West European standards of income. Ministerial-level conferences in 1994 and 1997 endorsed the building of ten pan-European corridors to complete the basic physical interconnection of the continent, but work has barely begun on translating the corridor concepts into actual projects. In 1998 the European Commission developed a Transport Infrastructure Needs Assessment for the overall central and east European network within the basic framework of the ten major corridors. This network comprises 18,030 kilometers of roads, 20,290 kilometers of railway line, 38 airports, 13 seaports, and 49 river ports. Completing this network is estimated to cost a total of €90 billion in the period to 2015.[22] EU aid funds and loans from the European Investment Bank (EIB) are underwriting a small part of the cost, but most of the investment has to come from the central and east European countries themselves.

Trans-European Networks

In addition to harmonizing standards and promoting competition, EU transport policy has placed a growing emphasis on the identification and completion of major transport projects known as trans-European networks (TENs). In its 1962 action plan the Commission had called for a Community role in coordinating infrastructure investment, but little was done to ensure that Europe's physical network of roads, track, and airports could accommodate the growing volume of cross-border freight and passenger traffic generated by the common market. The Maastricht treaty included new provisions that gave the Union powers and responsibilities to promote, through the TENs, the interconnection and interoperability of national networks in the context of the single European market. TENs are intended for transport, telecommunications, and energy infrastructure, but the bulk of spending and political attention has been on the transport sector. The EU does not finance the construction of these networks and it cannot compel national and regional governments or private investors to undertake specific projects, but it does promote the TENs by establishing guidelines and setting priorities for such projects, financing feasibility studies, providing loan guarantees and interest rate subsidies from the EU budget, providing loans from the EIB, and, for countries that are eligible, offering grant assistance from the Cohesion Fund.

In 1994 the Union selected fourteen major transport projects as priority TENs and called for construction of all of these projects to start by the end of 1996 (see table 5.1).[23] A heavy focus in these projects was on improved passenger and freight rail infrastructure aimed at improving the viability of Europe's railways and shifting traffic from the roads. A decade later, only three of these projects were complete. Two others had not yet been started. Of the remaining nine projects, large sections were in the planning stage or under construction, but only the high-profile Paris-Amsterdam/London high-speed train (HST) and the Betuwe dedicated freight line from Rotterdam to the German border were expected to be completed by 2007.[24] Lining up finance for many of these projects has been problematic, especially since banks and investors have lost heavily on previous mega-projects such as the Eurotunnel between France and Britain. Obtaining environ-

Table 5.1   Trans-European Networks—Priority Transport Projects

Project	Countries	Completion
HST/Combined Transport North-South Nuremberg–Erfurt–Halle/Leipzig–Berlin–Brenner axis (Verona–Munich)	Italy, Austria, Germany	After 2010
HST PBKAL Paris–Brussels–Cologne–Amsterdam–London	Belgium, Netherlands, France, Germany, UK	2007
HST South Madrid–Barcelona–Perpignan–Montpellier/Madrid–Vitoria–Dax	France, Spain	After 2010
HST East Paris–Metz–Strasbourg–Appenweier with junctions to Metz–Saarbrücken–Mannheim and Metz–Luxembourg	France, Germany, Luxembourg	After 2010
Betuwe Line Conventional Rail/Combined Transport Rotterdam–Dutch-German border	Netherlands, Germany	2007
HST/Combined Transport France-Italy Lyon–Turin/Turin–Milan–Venice–Trieste	France, Italy	After 2010
Greek Motorways	Greece	After 2010
Motorway Lisbon–Valladolid	Portugal, Spain	After 2010
Conventional Rail Link Cork–Dublin–Belfast–Larne–Stanraer	Ireland, UK	2001
Malpensa Airport Milan	Italy	2001
Oresund fixed link	Denmark, Sweden	2000
Nordic triangle multimodal corridor	Finland, Sweden	After 2010
Ireland/UK/Benelux road link	Ireland, UK	After 2010
West Coast Main Line (rail)	UK	2007

mental approvals also has been difficult and time-consuming, and member states often have differed over the design of particular transnational projects and the border points at which they should connect.

Against this background of rather limited success, the Commission has called for revising the guidelines for TENs to encourage greater private investment, increasing the EU's budgetary contribution to the completion of bottleneck sections, and updating the list of projects to include both new priorities in the old Union (e.g., better links across the Pyrenees) and new projects in the accession countries of central and eastern Europe. In October 2003 the Commission issued a new transport TENs proposal that included extension of already planned projects to the new member countries (e.g., extending the planned Lyon–Trieste rail line to Ljubljana, Budapest, and the Hungary-Ukraine border), and several new projects mainly or entirely in the accession countries, for example a new Gdansk–Warsaw–Bratislava–Vienna rail line and a Rail Baltica line linking Warsaw, Kaunas, Riga, and Tallinn.[25] The price tag for completing the Commission's list of old and new projects was a hefty €220 billion by 2020, however, and it was not clear that it would win the backing of the member states and private investors.

Competition Policy

The Treaty of Rome provided for the establishment of "a system ensuring that competition shall not be distorted in the Common Market."[26] The framers of the treaty recognized that with overt barriers to trade among the member countries no longer available, governments and firms might resort to other actions to frustrate cross-border competition. These concerns were especially valid in view of Europe's long history of industrial cartels and the weak-to-nonexistent role of antitrust legislation in most member states. Firms might get together to form cartels to set prices or control supplies in all or parts of the common market. Alternatively, governments might be tempted provide state aid (e.g., subsidies, low interest loans, excessively generous grants for training or R&D) to domestic firms that could disadvantage competitors from other Community states.

The ECSC Treaty gave the High Authority the power to block mergers in the coal and steel industries. This power was conceived as one of the ECSC's safeguards against a resurgence of German power, which it was feared might come about through mergers and acquisitions involving German firms. The power to block prospective mergers in these industries later passed to the European Commission by virtue of the Merger Treaty. However, the Treaty of Rome itself did not grant the Commission comparable powers in other industries. Rather, Article 85 banned as incompatible with the common market "agreements, concerted practices, and decisions between undertakings that have as their intention or effect the restriction or distortion of competition and that may affect trade between member states." Article 86 prohibited the abuse of a dominant position by firms that affected the functioning of the common market. Under Articles 87, the Council was required to pass within three years of the entering into force of the Treaty of Rome legislation giving effect to the general provisions of Article 85 and 86.[27] Thus in 1962 the Council passed Regulation 17, which gave the Commission powers to investigate anticompetitive practices and abuses of dominant position and to order a stop to any infringements.[28]

MERGERS

Under a new merger resolution adopted by the Council in 1989, from September 1990 onward the Commission was granted authority to control prospective mergers and takeovers that might restrict competition in the single market.[29] These powers applied only to large deals involving firms with business activities in two or more EU countries. For mergers that were smaller or that involved companies operating largely on a national scale, national legislation alone would continue to apply. In the first five years in which the new resolution was in effect, the Commission received approximately four hundred cases for review, but it blocked only one transaction, the proposed takeover of the Canadian commuter aircraft maker de Havilland by a joint venture of a French and an Italian firm engaged in the same business. However, in many cases in which the Commission did not block a merger, it established conditions—such as divestiture of particular business units—before granting approval.[30] Firms that failed to notify the Commission of intended mergers could be assessed large fines and forced to divest themselves of holdings or take other steps required by Brussels to restore competition in the marketplace.

Commission involvement in policing mergers and acquisitions has increased in recent years as companies have restructured and combined with each other in response to global economic trends and the anticipated introduction of the euro. In 1997 alone the Commission received 172 notifications of mergers and made 135 final decisions under the merger regulation.[31] By 2000 this had risen to 345 notifications and 345 decisions before dropping off somewhat in 2001 and 2002 as business conditions cooled.[32] The Commission approved most of the deals that it examined, but often only after the companies involved accepted conditions designed to ensure the continuation of effective competition after the proposed merger.

The Commission's authority under the Treaty of Rome and the merger regulation is not limited to companies that are based in the EU, but extends to many large mergers between European and U.S. firms and to third country firms that are active in the EU market. In 1997, for example, the Commission threatened to try to block the acquisition by the Boeing Company of the McDonnell Douglas Corporation. European involvement in a deal between two U.S. firms that had been cleared by U.S. antitrust authorities caused a certain amount of irritation in Washington, but it was justified in Brussels on the grounds that Boeing's dominant position in the worldwide commercial aviation market would be strengthened and could adversely affect European interests. In the end the Commission approved the acquisition, but only after Boeing gave assurances to open up to competition exclusive supply contracts that it had with U.S. airlines. In an even more contro-versial case, in 2001 the Commission blocked the takeover by U.S.-based General Electric of another U.S. firm, Honeywell, on the grounds that it would damage competition in European markets for some industrial products.

Although some U.S. officials and members of Congress raised questions about these decisions, for the most part the United States and the EU work together quite well in the antitrust area, as authorities on both sides of the Atlantic share an interest in protecting consumers from monopolistic practices. Tensions do arise, however, especially when one side suspects the other of using competition policy to advance the interests of its own firms. In the Boeing case, for example, it was widely believed that Commission concerns about competition were in reality a continuation in a different form of the longstanding European governmental sup-port for Airbus Industrie, the European competitor to Boeing in the civil aircraft market.

Notwithstanding the important role that antitrust policy has played in bol-stering the single market and raising the level of competition (and by implication economic efficiency) in the Union, since the mid-1990s there has been increasing controversy about a number of Commission antitrust decisions as well as ques-tions about the Union's overall approach to regulating mergers and the potential abuse of market positions. Companies and independent experts questioned some of the economic theories upon which the Commission based certain decisions, and the European Court of Justice (ECJ) in fact overturned several high-profile deci-sions by the Commission that were appealed by European firms. Companies also complained that the Commission serves in effect as prosecutor, judge, and jury in competition cases. Companies can appeal lost cases to the ECJ, but this is a long and complex process that usually offers a possible remedy to an erroneous deci-sion only long after a company's business plans have been disrupted and the deal in question has ceased to be relevant. Moreover, the Commission itself was con-cerned about its ability to keep up with the burgeoning workload associated with the growing volume and complexity of merger and takeover activity.

For these reasons, the Commission, with the backing of the member states, engineered a sweeping revision of EU merger control procedures that took effect in early 2003. The essence of the reform, as embodied in Regulation 01/2003, was to delegate responsibility for smaller, routine merger control decisions to the na-tional authorities, leaving the Commission free to concentrate on larger, more complex mergers with possible strategic implications for the EU market. The Commission would retain the right to intervene in lesser cases if it wanted to ques-tion the approach taken by a national regulator.

Although they were dissatisfied with aspects of the previous approach, many firms and outside experts expressed concern about the reform. In many of the member states, antitrust regulation is a relatively recent innovation, as competition authorities were established under EU influence only in the late 1980s and early 1990s. How well these authorities will perform and how to ensure consistency across national jurisdictions are major question marks over the new approach.[33] To ensure consistency, the reforms provide for an EU-wide network of national competition authorities that will exchange information and work to develop common approaches. The newly established competition authorities of the accession countries of central and eastern Europe will be part of this network, and their ability to implement complex EU and national legislation will be scrutinized closely in the early years of membership.

STATE AIDS

The provisions on state aid in the Treaty of Rome distinguish between permissible aid provided to foster social development in poor regions or for certain other legitimate purposes and aid, the intent or effect of which is to favor particular industries or firms in ways that distort trade among the member states. Aid that distorts or threatens to distort competition is banned. The treaty requires member states to notify the Commission of all state aids to industry or proposals for new aid. The Commission reviews all such notifications and in cases where it finds that such aid is incompatible with the functioning of the market orders the member state to cease the aid and recover from the beneficiary firm any funds already paid. The treaty recognizes the right of member states to operate public undertakings, that is, utilities or transport firms that enjoy a monopoly position or taxpayer subsidies, but prohibits these firms from interfering with the functioning of the market. In effect, state-owned or sanctioned monopolies are supposed to behave as much as possible as if they were private enterprises, in business to make profits and pay dividends rather than to carry out governmental objectives such as maintaining employment.

For much of the history of the EC, the record of the member states with regard to notification of state aids was weak, and the Commission often was reluctant to challenge governments seeking to support their national industries.[34] The prevailing wisdom of the day about the importance of developing national champions of adequate size and scope to compete in global markets tended to militate against strict enforcement. As with competition policy for firms, however, there was a sea change in the 1980s as the Commission became more convinced of the benefits of competition (including intra-European competition) and of the threat posed to the single market by state aids, and as the right-of-center governments of the period became more interested, for both ideological and financial reasons, in scaling back aid to industry.

Much of the initial focus in EU policy was on France and Italy, countries with large state-owned sectors and long records of subsidizing private and state-owned firms to save jobs and bolster international competitiveness. Subsequently, Germany, with its large subsidies to the sunset industries—coal, steel, textiles, and shipbuilding—became the target of many Commission actions. The Maastricht treaty inserted an amendment into Article 92 of the Treaty of Rome that expressly permitted aid to the former east Germany to overcome the economic legacy of division, but in some cases the Commission has questioned the size and appropriateness of such aid.

High-profile state aid cases in the first part of the 1990s involved French government support to Renault, the state-owned car company; aid by national governments to loss-making national airlines such as Air France, Olympic, and Iberia; German government aid to Volkswagen for the construction of new plants in the former East Germany; as well as UK government support to British Aerospace for the purchase of the car maker Rover.[35] More recent cases have involved the French engineering company Alstom and the French computer company Bull.

In cases where the Commission declines to approve an aid allocation, the government in question must recover the money from the company involved. In 2003, for example, the Commission ordered France to recover €450 million in aid that it provided to the loss-making Bull the previous year. If a member state refuses to comply with a Commission order regarding state aid, the Commission can take that state to the ECJ and, under the provisions introduced in the Maastricht treaty on enforcing EU law, may levy a fine against it for noncompliance.

In 1988 the Commission began to publish regular surveys of state aid to industry designed to highlight distortions in the single market. These reports were supplemented by a state aid scoreboard that was launched by the Commission in July 2001 and that provides online information about the overall state aid situation in the Union. According to the Spring 2003 scoreboard, in 2002 the Commission took 759 final state aid decisions, approving 706 of the aids notified by national governments and disapproving 53.[36] These figures understate the degree of Commission involvement, however, since many state aid packages are modified after informal consultations with the Commission before receiving approval. Total state aid in the EU in 2001 was €86 billion, down from €107 billion in 1997. This represented 0.99 percent of total EU GDP, with national shares ranging from a low of 0.66 percent of GDP in the UK to 1.58 percent in Finland, the highest in the Union.

As part of the overall Lisbon strategy of improving the EU's global economic competitiveness, the 2001 Stockholm European Council called on the member states to "demonstrate a downward trend in state aid in relation to GDP by 2003." Most member states managed to achieve this objective. As important if not more so than reducing the overall level of aid has been a parallel effort to shift its composition from aid devoted to particular sectors or firms within sectors (often to stave off bankruptcy and preserve jobs) to so-called horizontal measures—state aid devoted to research and development, environmental protection, energy saving, job training, and so forth. Such aid may benefit individual firms, but its intent is to upgrade the competitiveness of whole regions or national economies rather than to prop up ailing firms. The Stockholm European Council also called upon member states to redirect aid to such horizontal objectives.

As in other policy areas, the 2004 enlargement will create new challenges for EU state aid policy. On the one hand, the new member states are relatively poor and will be trying to reduce their budget deficits to comply with the requirements of EMU. This should make them reluctant to dole out aid to industry. On the other hand, these countries, having only recently emerged from communist central planning, have recent traditions of very heavy state interference in their economies.

In some cases, moreover, in the 1990s these countries offered foreign and domestic investors special incentives (e.g., Poland's special economic zones) that were seen as necessary to encourage postcommunist economic revival but that in the future could run counter to EU rules by distorting competition in the Union.

Environmental Policy
POLICY DEVELOPMENT

Environmental policy was not mentioned in the Treaty of Rome, an omission that reflected the relatively low importance accorded environmental issues in early postwar European politics. By the early 1970s, however, national governments and the general public were becoming increasingly aware of environmental degradation as a consequence of urbanization, industrial growth, and intensive farming. In 1972 the member-state governments asked the Commission to prepare the first EC Environmental Action Program for the period 1973–1976. Multiyear environmental action programs since have become the blueprint for policy at the European level.

Acting within the framework of these programs, the EU has adopted more than 200 pieces of legislation covering the pollution of air, water, and soil, waste management and recycling, chemical and biotechnology safeguards, product standards, environmental impact assessments, and protection of nature. Initially, the Commission proposed and the Council adopted these laws on the basis of the catch-all Article 235 of the Treaty of Rome, or by referring to the single market implications of environmental policy. The Single European Act (SEA) established for the first time a treaty basis for environmental policy, specifying three objectives: to preserve, protect, and improve the quality of the environment; to contribute toward improving human health; and to ensure a prudent and rational utilization of natural resources. The Maastricht treaty added a fourth objective: to promote "measures at international level to deal with regional or worldwide environmental problems."[37] The treaty also introduced environmental considerations into the overall framework of EU economic policy, specifying "sustainable and non-inflationary growth respecting the environment"[38] as one of the fundamental objectives of the Union.

There are two reasons why national governments often try to address environmental problems at an international level rather than simply within a national framework. First, many environmental problems such as long-range air pollution and the pollution of rivers that run through several countries cannot be dealt with effectively in a national context. Second, environmental regulations affect the competitiveness of firms and industries and thus can influence the working of the single market. If one country passes stringent national legislation compelling factories on its territory to dispose of industrial waste in an environmentally friendly manner while other countries do not, firms from the first country will be disadvantaged. Both of these rationales have played a role in the development of EU environmental policy.

Historically, the member states have differed markedly with respect to the importance of the environment in national politics. Germany, Denmark, and the Netherlands were known as traditionally "green" countries with strict national environmental legislation. (The new members of 1995—Austria, Finland, and Sweden—also fall into this category.) The Mediterranean countries, in contrast, had adopted very little environmental legislation before being compelled to do so by Community directives beginning in the 1970s. The pattern was for the green countries to adopt strict environmental legislation and then to try to "Europeanize" these laws, both in order to deal more effectively with environmental problems and to ensure that industry in all member states bears comparable environmental costs.[39] In recent years, however, even the Mediterranean countries have become increasingly green, as national movements and political parties rather than external pressures have become the driving force behind the adoption of stricter national regulations and support for more assertive stances on environmental issues at the EU level and in international forums.

The fifth environmental action program ran from 1993 to 2000. It focused on implementing the concept of sustainability throughout the Union. The sixth environmental action program was approved by the European Parliament and the Council in July 2002 for a ten-year period, with an interim review scheduled for not later than July 2006. It focuses on four areas: climate change, nature and biodiversity, environment and health and quality of life, and natural resources and reducing wastes. Specific objectives within these areas include, for example, meeting the EU's Kyoto Protocol commitments for greenhouse gas emission reductions (discussed below), halting biodiversity decline by 2010, and achieving a target of 22 percent of electricity production from renewable energies by 2010. To achieve these and many other ambitious objectives, the program calls for using an array of "strategic approaches," including new or amended EU-level legislation, more effective implementation and enforcement of existing legislation, better integration of environmental protection requirements into other EU policies (agriculture, regional development, transport, and so forth), and new collaborations and partnerships with the private sector.

Better implementation and enforcement are especially important. Approximately 40 percent of all infringement cases opened by the Commission against member states are in the environmental area, and involve the failure to transpose or properly implement EU legislation.[40] In some areas, the EU and its member states continue to pursue contradictory goals with different policies, for example, by subsidizing the coal industry while calling for a shift to renewable energy, or by using EU regional development funds to finance massive highway construction projects while promoting a shift to more sustainable transport modes such as rail and inland shipping. Recognizing these contradictions, the government of Sweden used its EU presidency in the first half of 2001 to add a third, environmental dimension (along with the economic and the social) to the Lisbon strategy. As agreed by the June 2001 Göteborg European Council, the European Council henceforth will issue policy guidance on promoting sustainable development in the Union at its annual spring meetings to review progress toward meeting the

Lisbon objectives. It was not clear, however, whether high-level monitoring and pronouncements in themselves would result in progress toward achieving ambitious objectives.

ENVIRONMENT AND ENLARGEMENT

The collapse of communism in 1989–1991 exposed a huge backlog of environmental and associated human health problems in the countries of central and eastern Europe and the former Soviet Union. The environmental ministers of all the European countries met for the first time in 1991 at Dobris Castle near Prague in what was then Czechoslovakia, where they commissioned the Dobris Assessment, the first comprehensive, pan-European inventory of environmental problems.[41] The assessment highlighted severe problems with regard to air, water, and soil pollution; toxic waste dumps; and aging and unsafe nuclear power plants. Environmental remediation and nuclear safety subsequently became important elements of the EU's technical assistance programs for the transition countries.

EU-level environmental laws and regulations are part of the *acquis communautaire*, and environment was one of the thirty-one chapters negotiated between the Union and the candidate countries to prepare for accession. As in other policy areas, the candidate countries were in principle supposed to adopt and be prepared to implement the environmental *acquis* from the start of membership, with a minimum of transitional arrangements or permanent derogations. However, the World Bank and the European Commission estimated that achieving compliance with the environmental *acquis* in the ten central and east European countries would cost €80 billion–120 billion in investment—money that the candidate countries did not have and that the EU was not prepared to provide in the form of aid.[42] The EU thus faced a choice between delaying accession until well beyond 2010 or watering down or otherwise delaying the application of the environmental *acquis* in the candidate countries.

To resolve this problem, the EU effectively split the environmental *acquis* into those policy measures that have direct implications for the internal market and those that are not market-related. The former included legislation on such issues as the marketing, labeling, and control of chemicals, vehicle emissions, and product-related noise; the latter included policies on such matters as nature protection in the candidate countries or the local discharge of air and water pollutants. In the negotiations, the candidate countries generally were required to comply with the first set of rules from date of accession. In the second category, where effects on the single market are limited and in which long-term investment, much of it in the public sector, will be required to meet EU standards, the candidate countries were granted transition periods of differing lengths. Various air pollution directives in effect in the EU thus will be phased in by the new member states only in 2006–2007, and provisions on recovery and recycling of packaging waste will take effect generally only by 2007. The Czech Republic and Estonia do not have to comply fully with EU directives on the treatment of urban waste water until 2010; Cyprus until 2012; and Latvia, Hungary, Poland, Slovakia, and Slovenia until 2015.

As these dates suggest, the new member states are facing a long period of effort and investment to bring their environmental norms up to EU levels—to comply with the terms of the accession treaty but also because this is likely to be expected by their increasingly affluent and Europe-oriented populations. A small portion of the needed funds will come from EU regional aid funds dedicated to environmental projects. Other funds could come from long-term EIB or World Bank loans. Most of the funding, however, will have to come from domestic sources in the accession countries and will need to be spread over a period of years if not decades.

KYOTO AND GLOBAL WARMING

The addition of a new environmental policy objective to the Maastricht treaty—promoting measures at the international level to deal with regional or worldwide environmental problems—reflected the growing awareness in the 1990s of environmental problems outside the EU and a readiness on its part to try to play a leadership role in global environmental issues. The EU's most high-profile stance in international environmental diplomacy has been in regard to global warming and the 1997 Kyoto Protocol, which the United States rejects. EU activism in this area began in October 1990 when a joint Council of energy and environment ministers adopted a target of stabilizing carbon dioxide emissions by 2000 at their 1990 level. To implement this ambitious goal, the Commission began working on a package of measures that was to include support for renewable energy resources, a climate tax to discourage the burning of fossil fuels, and programs to promote energy efficiency. The package was intended to give Europe a world leadership role at the June 1992 Rio Earth summit. As this meeting approached, however, several of the member-state governments, lobbied intensively by business interests concerned about Europe's global competitiveness, grew increasingly nervous about approving a unilateral tax on energy in the absence of similar action by the United States and Japan. In the end the Council approved the package of global warming measures, but it made actual implementation of a carbon tax conditional upon acceptance of similar taxes by other Organization for Economic Cooperation and Development (OECD) countries.[43]

The UN Framework Convention on Climate Change (UNFCCC) was signed at Rio by 160 parties, including the EU and its member states and the United States. It requires all parties to cooperate in controlling, reducing, or preventing anthropogenic emissions of greenhouse gases. Industrialized country parties are further required to take specific actions to limit emissions, with the aim of returning to their 1990 levels by 2000. The agreement provides for periodic review conferences to assess the adequacy of national responses to the long-term threat of global warming and to negotiate new measures as needed.

The apparent failure of the voluntary emissions controls adopted at the UNFCCC (along with accumulating evidence about the reality of climate change) led to the first Conference of the Parties, COP 1, in Berlin in 1996, at which the EU made a strong push for binding targets. Negotiations eventually led to the conclusion in December 1997 of the Kyoto Protocol, which established legally binding limits on greenhouse gas emissions for industrialized countries. For the EU and its member countries, the target for the specified commitment period, 2008–2012, was set at 92 percent of the base year of 1990, or an 8 percent reduction. For the United States, the corresponding target was 93 percent, or a 7 percent reduction; for Japan, 94 percent, or an ambitious 6 percent reduction. Targets for Russia and Ukraine were set at 0 percent.

One of the most controversial issues in the Kyoto negotiations was the insistence by the EU that so-called Regional Economic Integration Organizations (REIO) be allowed to adopt differentiated targets among their member states provided an overall commitment was met. Other industrial countries strongly opposed this provision, but eventually yielded to the principle of what became known as the EU "bubble." Under the burden-sharing agreement, the EU's 8 percent target could apply to the Union as a whole, with some member states being allowed to increase their emissions above 1990 levels provided others decreased by more than 8 percent to make up the difference. In June 1998 the Union finalized arrangements for sharing reductions under the EU bubble. Germany was assigned a target of − 21 percent, reflecting the shutdown of industry in the eastern *Länder* and the shift away from coal in the Ruhr. Luxembourg (− 28 percent) and the UK (− 12.5 percent) also were given above-average targets (meetable by coal-to-gas conversion), while the Mediterranean countries were allowed whopping increases (Spain, + 15 percent, Portugal, + 27 percent).[44]

Although the EU bolstered its leadership credentials by accepting the largest percentage cuts of the developed countries (8 percent), several factors promised to ease the difficulty of compliance. The first was the above-mentioned bubble. Second was the selection of 1990 as a base year, which allowed Germany to credit the shutdown of East German industry against its Kyoto targets. The third was the "dash for gas" underway in Europe—the replacement of coal-generated electricity plants with new gas-fired units supplied by sources in Norway and Russia.[45]

The EU now is struggling to meet its Kyoto targets (see table 5.2). The 2000 goal more or less was met, but largely because emissions dropped precipitously in 1990–1994, owing to restructuring in the former East Germany, slow overall economic growth, and other factors. Since 1994 emissions again have been rising, and are projected, in the absence of new policy measures, to increase by some 6 percent in 2010 over 1990 levels, meaning that the EU will miss its reduction target by 14 percent.[46] The Commission and the Council thus are considering new measures to curb emissions, including various taxes. The experience of the 1990s demonstrated, however, that the member states are not prepared to accept a uniform carbon or energy tax with a high degree of harmonization across the EU. Instead, they are looking at a more politically feasible approach that will allow the individual member states more flexibility in deciding how to use energy taxes and other measures to meet the Kyoto targets. The EU also is preparing to implement an intra-EU system of emissions trading, under which companies and countries that

Table 5.2   The Kyoto Targets (all greenhouse gases)

Country	Protocol target	EU "burden-sharing" target	Actual change, 1990–1999
Austria	−8	−13	+2.6
Belgium	−8	−7.5	+2.8
Denmark	−8	−21	+4.0
Finland	−8	0	−1.1
France	−8	0	−0.2
Germany	−8	−21	−18.7
Greece	−8	+25	+16.9
Ireland	−8	+13	+22.1
Italy	−8	−6.5	+4.4
Luxembourg	−8	−28	−43.3
Netherlands	−8	−6	+6.1
Portugal	−8	+27	+22.4
Spain	−8	+15	+23.2
Sweden	−8	+4	+1.5
United Kingdom	−8	−12.5	−14.0
EU-15	−8	−8	−4.0
United States	−7		+11.0

Source: Third Communication from the European Community under the UN Framework Convention on Climate Change, November 30, 2001

exceed emissions reduction targets will be allowed to sell their rights to emit to companies and countries unable to meet their targets.

Research and Development

Community involvement in this area began in the late 1970s, prompted by concern about Western Europe's failure to keep pace with leading U.S. and Japanese firms in information technology, medical and biotechnology, robotics, and other research-intensive industries of the future. In 1979 Internal Market and Industrial Affairs Commissioner Etienne Davignon launched a dialogue with the heads of Europe's leading information technology companies about what could be done collaboratively to accelerate technological progress. This led to the launching, in 1982, of the European Strategic Program for Research and Development in Information Technology (ESPRIT), under which the Commission made available a pool of ECU (European Currency Unit) 11.5 million to fund precompetitive collaborative projects involving partners from several member states. By late 1983 an initial thirty-eight projects involving 600 companies and institutes were under way.[47] Based on its initial success in launching real projects, ESPRIT was funded at the more substantial level of ECU 1.5 billion for the ten-year period 1984–1993. It became the model for an array of programs, usually designated by a catchy French or English acronym, designed to promote collaboration in different technical fields, for example RACE (Advanced Communications Technologies for Europe), COMETT (Community Action Program in Education and Training for Technology), and SPRINT (Strategic Program for Innovation and Technology Transfer).

The SEA for the first time provided an explicit treaty basis for a Community-level R&D policy. The main instrument for this policy has been a series of multi-year framework programs, beginning with the 1984–1987 First Framework Program that incorporated ESPRIT and other sectoral initiatives. The Fourth Framework Program for 1994–1998 was funded at ECU 13.1 billion, consisting of an initial allocation of ECU 12.3 billion in 1994 and a supplementary allocation in 1996 of ECU .8 billion to make room for Austria, Finland, and Sweden. It focused on four main themes: research, technological, and demonstration projects; cooperation with third countries and international organizations; dissemination of results; and training and mobilization of scientific and technical personnel. The Fifth Framework Program for the period 1998–2002 was approved by the Council and the European Parliament in 1998 and began soliciting its first proposals in early 1999. Funded at a level of €14.96 billion over the five-year life of the program, it was intended to engage private industry and academic researchers in the key issues facing the EU in the early twenty-first century: jobs, the environment, and the social implications of new technologies.

The EU's budget for research is only a small proportion of all such spending by national governments and private industry, but the framework programs are an important catalyst for promoting cross-border cooperation among European firms, universities, and research institutes. More than 10,000 organizations have been involved in EU-funded research programs. These programs usually require organizations from three or more member countries to work together. In writing their proposals, researchers must focus on substance and scientific merit, but they often are careful to achieve a politically attractive mix of partners from large and small, northern and southern member countries. In addition to running the framework programs, the EU has four of its own joint research centers located in Italy, Belgium, the Netherlands, and Germany that work on energy and industrial projects.

Support for research also figures prominently in the Lisbon strategy adopted in March 2000. At Lisbon, the European Council endorsed a Commission plan to create a European Area of Research and Innovation as part of the effort to improve Europe's competitiveness. In May 2001 the Commission put forward its proposals for the Sixth Framework Program, which was aimed at supporting the creation of the research area. This was also the first framework program to integrate fully researchers from central and eastern Europe into EU programs. Scheduled to run from 2002 to 2006 and to be funded at the €17.5 billion level, the program emphasized strengthening networks of excellence throughout Europe and singled out seven priority research areas: genomics and biotechnology for health; information society technologies; nanotechnologies, intelligent materials and new production processes; aeronautics and space; food safety and health risks; sustainable development and global change; and citizens and governance in the European knowledge-based society.[48]

Continuing the trend toward the use of benchmarks and scoreboards already applied with regard to the single market and other policy areas, the European Council called for identifying methods to assess the performance of national R&D policies in different fields and mandated the introduction by June 2001 of a European innovation scoreboard. The intent was to shift the focus from quantitative levels of support to actual results, scientific and especially commercial. Other research-related measures endorsed in Lisbon included the establishment by the end of 2001 of a high-speed European electronic network linking universities and research institutes, further steps to promote the mobility of researchers, and the establishment of an EU-wide patent by the end of 2001.

Recognizing the limited role that direct funding from Brussels can play, at its March 2002 session in Barcelona the European Council set the goal of increasing the EU-wide level of investment in research from 1.9 percent of GDP to 3 percent of GDP by 2010, of which two-thirds should be funded by the private sector. This was another example of the EU moving beyond its own centrally funded and administered program to try to play a broader role in cajoling the member states and even private firms to work together to pursue Union objectives. In another positive development, in March 2003 the Council finally reached agreement on an EU patent, to be granted by the European Patent Office. Companies no longer would need to file for patent protection in all of the member states but could obtain a single European patent—a move that was expected to spur innovation by lowering costs and increasing profits.

It remains to be seen, however, whether the ambitious Lisbon and Barcelona goals for research can be met. Reaching the Barcelona target of 3 percent of GDP dedicated to R&D will require a 6 percent annual growth rate in public investment (member state– and EU-funded) and a 9 percent annual growth rate in private investment in research for the remainder of the decade.[49] Beyond the problem of budgetary stringency at a time of slow economic growth, there is also the question of broader public attitudes to science and technology. Many European companies increasingly are concentrating their research efforts outside Europe (e.g., in the United States) in response to what they see as a hostile public attitude and regulatory climate in regard to biotechnology, difficulty in recruiting scientists and engineers, and continued "brain drain" of European scientists to the United States and elsewhere.

Regional Policy
POLICY DEVELOPMENT

After agriculture, the largest share of EU expenditure (34 percent of the 2004 budget) is accounted for by programs that Brussels funds to help raise disadvantaged countries and regions to EU levels of per capita GDP. Funding is divided into two main categories, the Structural Funds, which are allocated to relatively poor regions and to economic restructuring in areas and sectors of high unemployment, and the Cohesion Fund, which is paid directly to member states with per capita GDPs of less than 90 percent of the EU average. The EU has three structural funds—the European Social Fund, the European Regional Development Fund, and the European Agricultural Guidance Guarantee Fund of the CAP. Structural Funds are spent on projects developed in conjunction with regional governments and have a matching requirement. Cohesion Funds do not have matching requirements and are intended to be spent on transport and environmental infrastructure projects. Project-based lending from the EIB is also an important component of EU regional policy.

The economies of the six original EC member states all were roughly at the same level of economic development, with the exception of southern Italy. The EIB, the provisions in the Treaty of Rome allowing free movement of labor, and the CAP all provided assistance to southern Italy, as did national programs under which the Italian government transferred massive amounts of money from the north and center to the south of the country. The six did not, however, develop an explicit regional policy for this special, albeit important, situation. The development of a full-fledged Community regional policy began in 1972 when, at the Paris summit, the leaders of the six agreed to establish a Community regional policy, to be overseen by a Commissioner responsible for regional affairs and supported by a new European Regional Development Fund (ERDF). The enlargement of the Community in the 1970s and 1980s, as well as a realization that market integration was leaving behind depressed regions even within the wealthier countries, led to a growing emphasis on regional policy. Ireland, Greece, Portugal, and Spain were the countries whose per capita incomes lagged the Community average by a substantial margin. In the late 1980s and early 1990s these countries argued, for the most part successfully, that ambitious initiatives like the single market and later EMU would be politically and economically sustainable only if these disparities were narrowed. Building upon the decisions of the 1972 Paris summit and the establishment of the ERDF, the SEA included new articles on cohesion (another term for regional policy) which henceforth became a treaty-based objective of the EC, to be both pursued through a separate cohesion policy and considered as a factor in the making of other Community policies such as trade, transport, and the environment.

Making regional policy for the most part has involved a process of bargaining between the poorer and the wealthier member countries in which the former have been able to win concessions by dragging their feet on other issues valued by the wealthier countries, such as the 1992 program and EMU. The poorer countries also have benefitted from a relatively sympathetic attitude in Brussels (both the Commission and the Parliament stand to gain power by exercising control over a large regional aid budget) and from the willingness of Germany essentially to foot the bill for cohesion policy by paying much more into the budget than it receives back.

After becoming a member of the Community in January 1986, Spain emerged as the leader of a group of four states that consistently demanded larger cohesion payments from the Community budget. In February 1988 the twelve agreed to double the size of the structural funds. This decision was the result of a bargain between the poorer member states, led by Spain and its prime minister, Felipé Gonzalez, and the wealthier north led by Germany and Helmut Kohl. In essence, the poorer countries agreed to go along with implementing the Community's single market program, but only in exchange for larger amounts of aid. This deal was seen as politically necessary, since the adverse effects of heightened competition in the single market were expected to fall disproportionately on countries such as Spain and Portugal, whose industries would be exposed to new competition from the north.

At the 1990–1991 Intergovernmental Conference (IGC) Spain and the other cohesion countries again made the argument that more aid from the north was needed if the economically weaker states were to meet the convergence criteria for EMU. Some of Spain's demands were excessive, but in the end Kohl and Gonzalez struck a bargain, subsequently endorsed by their counterparts in the other member states, to create in effect a fourth structural fund, the Cohesion Fund that was formally set up in May 1994. Countries eligible to access the fund were those with a per capita GNP less then 90 percent of the EU average, that is, the four traditional recipients, provided they were making progress on meeting the convergence criteria that were stipulated in the Maastricht treaty.

The relatively favorable political climate for cohesion policy largely evaporated in the course of the 1990s. With reunification, Germany acquired five new states in which economic and social conditions lagged the EU average. As the federal government began providing large amounts of aid to the former East Germany, it became less willing to bankroll EU solidarity. Governments in the south became increasingly concerned about competition with the east for regional funds and threatened to veto EU enlargement if it meant the loss of support from the structural funds. The stage thus was set for a major debate over the size, composition, and ultimate beneficiaries of regional aid.

THE 2000–2006 PACKAGE

In designing its cohesion policies, the EU has had to manage a tension between concentrating aid in a few regions to maximize effectiveness and dispersing aid over a wider area in a way that dilutes the effect of the aid but that generates broader political support. In the 1990s, the structural funds were targeted at seven objectives: Objective 1 to assist those regions whose per capita GDP was less than 75 percent of the EU average, Objective 2 to facilitate redevelopment in regions seriously affected by industrial decline, Objective 3 to combat long-term unemployment and improve youth employment opportunities, Objective 4 to assist the adaptation of workforces to industrial change, Objective 5a to assist with modernization of agricultural and fishing industries, Objective 5b to help with development and economic diversification of vulnerable rural areas, and Objective 6, created in 1995 to benefit Finland and Sweden, to help sparsely populated Arctic regions. In addition, the Cohesion Fund supported environmental, energy, and transport projects in the four eligible countries.

Although the bulk of the structural funds went to poor regions in poor countries, the Commission's eligibility criteria also channeled aid to many disadvantaged urban and rural regions in the more affluent countries of the Union. The share of the EU population covered by Objectives 1 and 2 in the late 1990s was in fact 51 percent. Regions that received aid included the five eastern states of Germany; rust belt regions of France and Belgium; a sparsely populated part of the Netherlands north of Amsterdam; Scotland and northern England; and of course southern Italy. Additional aid to backward or disadvantaged regions came from funds set aside under the CAP and the Common Fisheries Policy.

In *Agenda 2000*, the Commission tried to move in the direction of more concentration and greater effectiveness. It proposed that the seven objectives be reduced to just three and that their management be simplified and decentralized. This would reduce the share of the EU's population covered by Objectives 1 and 2 to 35–40 percent. Objective 1 would become the most important component of EU regional policy, but the per capita GDP threshold would be strictly enforced to ensure that regions graduate as their standard of living rises. A new Objective 2 would tackle economic and social restructuring in areas outside Objective 1 regions where unemployment is above the EU average and where help with economic redevelopment is needed. Pockets of urban poverty in otherwise affluent regions could be covered by Objective 2. Objective 3 would be a new program covering human resources and training EU-wide. The Commission also proposed that the Cohesion Fund be retained, but that a review of the 90-percent threshold take place at the halfway point of the 2000–2006 budget period.

The Commission's proposals implied a gradual shift in regional aid from the south to the east and were bound to be politically controversial. In late 1998 the Commission issued a report predicting that under its plan eleven regions could lose Objective 1 aid: the whole of Ireland; two regions each in France and the UK; and one region each in Germany, Spain, Italy, Portugal, Belgium, and the Netherlands. Each of these countries could sustain the loss of one or two regions, but Spain (with eleven Objective 1 regions) and the other cohesion countries were particularly concerned about the impending enlargement to central and eastern Europe, when the addition of 100 million people and a very small GDP would lower the EU average that determines the 75 percent threshold.

The Berlin European Council ultimately adopted the main outlines of the Commission's approach but only after very hard bargaining involving Spain, Germany, and other member states. The 2000–2006 financial framework set aside a total of €213 billion for regional policies for existing member states, of which €195 billion was for the structural funds, and €18 billion for the Cohesion Fund. Allocation of the structural funds under the Berlin agreement is as shown in table 5.3. The Cohesion Fund was to be divided along strictly national lines. Spain was pledged 62 percent of the total, Greece 16–18 percent, Ireland 2–6 percent, and Portugal 16–18 percent.

Table 5.3   Structural Funds—2000–2006

	Criteria	Funding (billion euros)	Share
Objective 1	Regions with per capita GDP less than 75% of EU average	135.9	69.7%
	Most remote regions (Azores, Madeira, French Overseas departments)		
	Subarctic regions of Finland and Sweden		
Objective 2	Industrial (10%), urban (2%), rural (5%), and fisheries-dependent (1%) areas undergoing economic adjustment	22.5	11.5%
Objective 3	EU-wide "horizontal" programs to promote employment	24.05	12.3%
Other	Cross-border actions, innovative programs	12.6	6.5%

In addition to the €213 billion allocated to the existing member states, the Berlin framework called for some €39.6 billion in regional aid for the new member states on the assumption (subsequently revised by events) that a small number of member states would join the Union already in 2002. This money was to be used to continue pre-accession aid programs funded by the EU, including investment in environmental upgrades and road, rail, and other infrastructure projects, and for tackling the same problems of unemployment and rural and urban poverty that persist in the EU of the fifteen.

ENLARGEMENT

Considering the scale of the pending enlargement and the relative backwardness of the candidate countries, the envisioned aid for the new members was less generous than the applicants might have hoped and would not reach the per capita levels that Ireland, Greece, and the Iberian countries received in the 1980s and 1990s. The Berlin framework did plan for a peaking of structural funds for the EU-15 in 2000 and a gradual tapering off, as countries and regions in the existing EU raise their level of income and graduate from assistance, freeing resources for the east. The shift is gradual, however, owing to strong resistance from current member-state recipients such as Spain and to concerns about the ability of the new member states to absorb large amounts of cash from Brussels on productive projects. In 2006 aid for regions in the current EU-15 was still set at €26.660 billion, while assistance for new members will be less than half that level. Given the scale of the economic and social needs in the east, this distribution would appear to make little sense. It reflected, however, the power of incumbency and the ability of the current member states to use their positions in the European Council and the Council of Ministers to head off a more radical redistribution, as manifested in the insistence by Spain and the other cohesion countries that aid for existing member states be "ring-fenced" from aid for new member countries.

Even with these efforts to limit the shift in aid from old to new member states, substantial changes are expected to occur in EU cohesion policy as a result of enlargement. Under the Objective 1 element of the Structural Funds, all regions with less than 75 percent of EU per capita GDP are eligible for aid. With the accession of ten relatively poor countries in 2004, the overall per capita GDP of the Union was set to fall by 13 percent. On this basis, the Commission estimated that post-enlargement Objective 1 regions would have a total population of some 115 million people, 60 percent of whom would be in the accession countries, and only 40 percent in the poorer regions of the old member states. Regions comprising approximately 25 million people in the existing EU would lose their eligibility for aid because of the change in the statistical cut-off rather than because of any appreciable change in their objective welfare.[50] The shift will become even more pronounced if Bulgaria and Romania are admitted to the Union as planned in 2007. Per capita income in the Union will fall by 18 percent with enlargement to twenty-seven member states, which will have the effect of bumping many more regions in the current fifteen-member states from the list of those eligible for structural funds and of displacing even some of the more prosperous regions in the first ten accession countries.[51]

The actual amount of regional aid allotted to the accession countries was worked out in the final negotiations to the accession treaty that took place in late 2002. In the final deal agreed at the December 2002 Copenhagen summit, structural and cohesion funding for the new member states in 2004–2006 was set at €23.847 billion, with additional funds allocated for transitional measures relating to nuclear safety, institution building, and the Schengen system of external border controls.[52] Aid would be capped at 4 percent of GDP, considerably below the levels received by Portugal and Ireland in the 1990s, but in the Commission's view the maximum that these countries could absorb and use effectively. EU aid per capita in the new member countries would reach €137 in 2006, compared with €231 in the four EU-15 member-state cohesion countries.[53]

A key question was what would happen to EU cohesion policy when the 2000–2006 financial framework reform expired and a new financial perspective had to be negotiated in a Union of 25. As was seen in chapter 3, in the Nice treaty negotiations Spain insisted that qualified majority voting be applied to decisions regarding Structural Funds and the Cohesion Fund only after January 1, 2007.[54] This would allow Spain to wield a veto over the financial framework for the next budgetary period of 2007–2013. The stage thus was set for a major political battle in which the south would try to preserve its traditional position, the east would argue for more aid on the basis of need, and the north—the affluent countries that pay most into the funds—would seek to limit the costs to themselves.

EFFECTIVENESS

The effectiveness of EU regional policy long has been a matter of debate. Critics have noted the large amount of waste and fraud in some EU programs and have questioned whether structural and cohesion funds have been spent wisely or should even be spent at all. Other critics argue that the effect of closer European integration is to marginalize the economic periphery, as capital and other resources are attracted from the periphery to the dynamic core of the Union—often defined as the area inside the London-Paris-Milan triangle that includes the affluent and high technology regions of the largest EU countries. They claim that regional aid and regional policy in general have not done enough to counter the effects of concentration.

The Commission argues that regional policy has been effective in achieving its main goal of evening out economic disparities in the Union. Table 5.4 shows that in 1988–2001, the four cohesion countries made gains relative to the EU average. In the 1990s alone, per capita GNP for the cohesion countries rose from 68 percent to 78 percent of the EU average. Progress has been most spectacular in Ireland, which now surpasses the EU average in per capita income, and least impressive in Greece, which was overtaken by Portugal to become the poorest country in the Union and which even lags the per capita income level of some of the most advanced accession countries such as Slovenia and the Czech Republic. Progress in leveling disparities among regions within countries has been more mixed. In some cases regional aid may even exacerbate disparities within countries, as it has helped cities such as Dublin and Lisbon rapidly raise their incomes, leaving behind the rural areas and smaller cities.

It also is difficult to determine how much effect regional policy as such has had in closing income disparities and how much importance should be ascribed to other factors such as market integration and foreign direct investment. In successful cases, these factors all work together. In Ireland, for example, accession to the EC made the country a popular investment location for foreign companies such

Table 5.4   GDP per Capita, Percentage of EU-15 Average (purchasing power parity basis)

	1988	1989	1990	1991	1992	1993	1994
Gre	58.3	59.1	57.4	60.1	61.9	64.2	65.2
Irl	63.8	66.3	71.1	74.7	78.4	82.5	90.7
Por	59.2	59.4	58.5	63.8	64.8	67.7	69.5
Spa	72.5	73.1	74.1	78.7	77.0	78.1	78.1

	1995	1996	1997	1998	1999	2000	2001
Gre	65.9	66.6	65.9	66.9	68.2	67.7	64.7
Irl	93.3	93.5	103.7	106.1	112.2	115.2	117.9
Por	69.7	70.0	73.3	72.2	71.9	68.0	69.0
Spa	78.2	79.3	79.9	79.2	82.1	82.2	84.1

as U.S. electronics firms seeking a base from which to manufacture and sell to the broader European market. Regional funds helped to build the roads and other infrastructure needed to accommodate this investment.

The key questions for the future are how effective aid will be in tackling some of the remaining transition problems in central and eastern Europe (e.g., inadequate transport and environmental infrastructure) and whether the east-south/new-old division of aid is politically durable. The former will depend heavily on how successful the accession countries have been in setting up the regional levels of government and the administrative structures needed to use aid effectively and on their ability to leverage limited grant aid with loans and private-sector investment. The latter is clearly linked to the broader political evolution of the Union.

Social Policy

Ever since its founding in the 1950s, the EC was vulnerable to criticisms by trade unions, political parties, and various other groups that European integration unduly favored big business to the detriment of workers, small businesses, and ordinary citizens. Critics also argued that integration tended to concentrate wealth in those parts of the Community that were already prosperous, leaving peripheral regions less well off, at least in relative terms. While political opponents of integration tended to exaggerate these negative side effects, even supporters recognized that integration *has* distributional consequences—that it produces gainers and losers—and that social and regional policies designed to offset the negative effects of integration were needed to maintain political support for the Community. Another argument for a Community role in social and regional policy was that highly disparate national approaches to such questions as labor standards or aid to industry in depressed regions can distort competition and disrupt the functioning of the single market.

The Treaty of Rome established a European Social Fund to finance retraining and relocation programs for displaced workers. It also took a strong stand against sex discrimination in the workplace by guaranteeing equal pay for equal work for women and men.[55] This provision was included at the insistence of France and is a good example of the interaction between social conditions and market competition. The French negotiators were motivated less by concern for the plight of women in other European countries than by a fear that France, which already had strong national equal pay provisions in place, would suffer in competition with other countries whose industries might employ female workers at substandard wages. In addition to these specific provisions, the member states agreed on the need to promote improved working conditions and standards of living for workers. For the most part, however, social welfare, employment policy, and health and safety matters remained national responsibilities, with only a limited role for the Community through the 1960s.

The completion of the common market, the impending first enlargement, and the expectation of monetary union by the end of the decade led to renewed interest in social policy in the early 1970s. European political leaders believed that such policies were needed to defuse the social tensions that were apparent in the strikes and youth revolts of the late 1960s and that were bound to grow worse, it was thought, as economic competition intensified in an enlarging Community. At the 1972 Paris summit the leaders of the six instructed the Commission to draw up a Social Action Plan aimed at promoting full and better employment; improved living and working conditions; better dialogue among employers, unions, and government; and workers' participation in enterprise management. This burst of activism in the early 1970s resulted in some Community-level social legislation, for example directives mandating firms to consult with their employees before undertaking large layoffs. For the most part, however, the ambitious objectives formulated in 1972 fell victim to the difficult economic conditions of the 1970s. Pressed by inflation, rising unemployment, and other economic and social problems, member states focused on immediate actions at the national level rather than on building a European social order.[56]

The relaunch of the Community in the 1980s under Jacques Delors led to new developments in social policy but also to new debates about the proper distribution of European and national responsibilities. Delors was a French Socialist who genuinely believed in the values of social solidarity and in promoting a European model of capitalism different from that in the United States. He strongly believed that the launch of the single market program called for the Community to develop a stronger social dimension. To maintain political support for the largely business-driven program of deregulation and market opening, the trade unions and ordinary workers needed to be convinced that European integration offered benefits for them as well as for business.[57] In addition, intensified competition in the single market could be expected to produce a degree of unemployment and worker dislocation. Employment, welfare, and job training policies mainly had to be implemented at the national level, but Delors saw an important role for Europe as well. The Single European Act contained a number of new provisions that strengthened the Community's social policy role, including articles committing the EC to upgrade and harmonize national health and safety standards, to strengthen "economic and social cohesion" through use of the European Social Fund and other Community funds, and to promote dialogue at the European level between business and labor.

At the December 1989 Strasbourg summit, the European Council adopted a non-treaty document, the Community Charter of the Fundamental Social Rights of Workers, that covered such general topics as freedom of movement, living and working conditions, freedom of association and collective bargaining, and equal rights for men and women (see box 5.1). EC involvement in most of these areas was new, and the significance of the agreement was largely symbolic—a political gesture in the face of continued high unemployment and concern by the trade unions that workers receive a share of the benefits of the economic growth being generated by the single market program. Known as the Social Charter, the agreement was purely declaratory, and had to be followed by Community and national legislation to be translated into binding commitments. The British government of

Margaret Thatcher opposed the creeping involvement of the Community in employment and social policies, and declined to endorse the Social Charter. As part of her effort to revitalize the British economy, Thatcher was committed to rolling back the welfare state and the power of the trade unions in the UK. She did not want to achieve this at the national level only to see the same "socialist" policies reimposed from Brussels.

The Social Charter became the basis for the Social Protocol to the Maastricht treaty. Prime Minister John Major, who succeeded Thatcher in November 1990, refused to accept inclusion in the treaty of a social chapter that would expand the scope of EU legislative authority in this area. With the other member states (especially France, Italy, and Belgium) committed to the chapter, this became one of the most hard-fought issues of the Maastricht negotiations. In a last-minute compromise that averted a breakdown of the conference, the member states agreed to an arrangement under which eleven of the member states signed a separate protocol that was appended to the treaty. The protocol allowed the eleven to apply Community decision-making procedures to issues covered by it, but without Britain's participation and without its being bound by the legislation passed. The substantive provisions of the protocol were the same as those covered in the Social Charter, but instead of being purely declaratory they allowed the EU (minus Britain) to adopt directives setting minimum requirements for implementation of standards with regard to workers' health and safety, working conditions, information and consultation of workers, equality between men and women in the labor force, and "the integration of persons excluded from the workforce."[58] The agreement also charged the Commission with promoting dialogue between management and labor at the EU level.

This unorthodox arrangement undermined the constitutional coherence of the EU and set a bad precedent for future à la carte arrangements. It was contro-

---

Box 5.1   The Twelve Principles of the Social Charter

1. The right to work in the EU country of one's choice
2. The freedom to choose an occupation and the right to a fair wage
3. The right to improved living and working conditions
4. The right to social protection under prevailing national systems
5. The right to freedom of association and collective bargaining
6. The right to vocational training
7. The right of men and women to equal treatment
8. The right of workers to information, consultation and participation
9. The right to health protection and safety at work
10. The protection of children and adolescents
11. A decent standard of living for older people
12. Improved social and professional integration for disabled people

(*Source:* European Commission, *How Is the European Union Meeting Social and Regional Needs?* Brussels, OOPEC, 1996, 7.)

versial on the continent, where politicians accused Britain of "social dumping"—competing unfairly for investments and jobs by applying lower labor and social standards—and in the UK itself, where the Labour party attacked Major for failing to go along with a European consensus on basic issues of worker rights. The anomalous situation of having eleven members observing the Social Protocol and using it as a framework to pass directives and one not (fourteen and one, after the 1995 accession of Austria, Finland, and Sweden) was ended by a political shift in Britain and the electoral victory of Labour in the spring of 1997. Prime Minister Tony Blair's first weeks in office coincided with the final stages of the negotiation of the Treaty of Amsterdam. Reversing Major's position, Blair announced that the UK would sign the Social Protocol. The protocol thus could be integrated into the amended Treaty of Rome as originally intended by the eleven before Maastricht and made binding on the EU as a whole. Blair also agreed that the UK would accept all of the directives that had been passed by the other member states under the interim arrangement and transpose those directives into national law as required.

By the late 1990s, the debate in Europe over social policy had shifted to the question of how Europe's generous welfare state and social protections could be adapted to the more competitive demands of globalization, the knowledge-based economy, and such challenges as the aging of Europe's population. Following the British lead, many politicians and business leaders argued for structural reforms that would make Europe more dynamic by, for example, giving firms more latitude to hire and fire workers, cutting down on business regulation, and lowering health care and pension costs tacked onto the basic wage. The trade unions and traditional leftists resisted these reforms, while politicians such as Blair argued for a "third way" that would combine American-style economic dynamism with European social protections.

A consensus of sorts on these issues emerged from the March 2000 Lisbon Council which, as noted, established the strategic goal of making the EU the world's most dynamic economy but also declared that this could and should be done while preserving a distinctive European approach to social policy. The European Council called for modernizing the European social model "by investing in people and building an active welfare state." To some extent this was the result of political compromise, as those member states, notably France, that were somewhat skeptical of trends in global capitalism insisted upon an emphasis on social protection and the continued role of the state to counterbalance more economic liberalization. Apart from the need for political compromise, however, the Lisbon document reflected a genuinely held view that European systems of social protection must be preserved. While they acknowledge the U.S. record in achieving high economic growth and low unemployment, many European leaders argue that these achievements have had costs in terms of greater income inequality, less social protection, financial volatility, and massive trade and payments deficits linked to low savings and excessive consumption.[59]

Beyond defending the intrinsic merits of the European economic and social model, the Lisbon European Council proclaimed that the key features of this model, far from being incompatible with a dynamic economy, could provide the basis for superior European competitive performance in the coming years. It claimed that a stepped-up commitment to overcoming social exclusion through increased education and training, along with the continued pursuit of targeted employment policies, could raise employment and increase the market for and the EU's ability to deliver innovative information technology products.

To follow through on these ambitious social policy goals, Lisbon called upon the Commission and the Council of Ministers to prepare a European Social Agenda for adoption at the Nice European Council in December 2000. The agenda called for action in six areas: more and better jobs; creating a more flexible work environment through reform of labor laws; fighting poverty, and what the EU calls social exclusion; modernizing social protection (i.e., welfare) policies; promoting gender equality; and strengthening the social policy aspects of enlargement and the EU's external relations.

The member states and the Commission have begun to implement this agenda, relying upon a mix of legislative measures introduced by the Commission and dialogue among the member states aimed at comparing experiences and identifying best practices. Beyond the generalities contained in the social agenda, however, there often is sharp disagreement within and among member states and between the Commission and the member states about how to translate broad objectives into actual policy and about the extent to which the pursuit of social goals can be allowed to impose economic and commercial costs. These differences became especially apparent in 2003, for example, when the social affairs commissioner Anna Diamantopolou, claiming a mandate under the Treaty of Amsterdam, introduced sweeping new anti–gender-discrimination legislation that would have outlawed sex discrimination in television programming, advertising, insurance premiums, taxation, newspaper content, and education. The proposals immediately ran into a storm of criticism from industry associations and others who argued that proposals—which subsequently were deferred—would have outlawed much existing advertising in EU countries and intruded deeply into the workplace.[60]

Employment Policy

The limited social policy provisions of the original Treaty of Rome focused on the rights of workers, with some attention to the migration of labor in the common market and the retraining of displaced workers in what was essentially a full-employment economy. Unemployment as such was not a Community concern. By the 1990s, however, unemployment had become the EU's most intractable economic problem, and the policy focus shifted to helping those excluded from the workforce. The social chapter of the Maastricht treaty proposed greater "development of human resources to achieve lasting employment," and the treaty empowered the EU to legislate by qualified majority voting (QMV) on issues dealing with the integration of excluded groups into the labor force. Overall, however, the treaty emphasized EMU and combating inflation and deficits, with far less attention paid to employment.

At the June 1993 Copenhagen summit Delors delivered a special report on the growing problem of unemployment in Europe, claiming that lack of competitiveness with Japan and the United States was a fundamental cause of Europe's failure to generate jobs. Under a mandate from the European Council, the Commission subsequently produced a white paper that proposed to create 15 million new jobs and to reduce the unemployment rate by 50 percent by 2000. The Delors plan called for extensive investment in infrastructure and TENs, training, R&D, and, perhaps most importantly, for efforts to hold down growth in the cost of labor to below increases in worker productivity.[61]

The Treaty of Amsterdam inserted into the Treaty of Rome a new Employment Chapter that called for EU involvement in this crucial issue, stipulating that member states "shall regard promoting employment as a matter of common concern and shall coordinate their action in this respect within the Council."[62] Arguing that a new policy in itself would not create jobs—a task that had to be accomplished by a growing private sector—many member states initially were opposed to the employment chapter. But governments increasingly came round to accepting Sweden's position that positive action to generate jobs was necessary to counterbalance the overwhelming emphasis on economic austerity in the run-up to EMU.

The key element in EU employment policy after Amsterdam is a member-state peer review process. The Council and the Commission are charged with producing a joint annual report on employment in the Union. The European Council then is required to draw conclusions from the report and to establish guidelines for the employment policies of the member states. Each member state in turn is required to provide the Council and the Commission with an annual report detailing its actions and policies taken to comply with the guidelines. This process is intended to keep pressure on national governments to make employment a priority policy area and to encourage the sharing of best practices among the member states.

Following the signing of the Amsterdam treaty, the EU began a series of high-level political dialogues focused on employment, beginning with the first-ever jobs summit, which took place in Luxembourg in November 1997. Convened at the initiative of French Prime Minister Lionel Jospin, the Luxembourg Jobs Summit was used to begin formulating among the member states the employment guidelines called for in the Amsterdam treaty. It focused on four pillars of employment policy: employability, entrepreneurship, adaptability, and equal opportunity. At the Cardiff summit in June 1998 marking the conclusion of the British presidency, the EU adopted further proposals for reform of national labor markets to promote employment. The Cologne summit in June 1999 approved a nonbinding European Employment Pact designed to bring together all of the disparate elements of the EU's new employment policy. Cologne called for closer coordination of member-state economic policy and called upon the EIB to release additional funds, such as for TENs, that would generate jobs. As has been seen, the EU's reformed regional policy also had a new emphasis on employment, rather than simply on the elimination of income disparities.

Unemployment began a slow fall in the second half of the 1990s, as labor market reforms and other job-creating policies took hold in some countries and as economic growth accelerated, increasing the demand for labor. Between 1995 and 2001, some 12 million new jobs were created in the Union. The overall unemployment rate fell from 10.1 percent in 1995 to 7.3 percent in 2001 before inching back up to 7.6 percent in 2002 as economic growth deteriorated. Most heartening from the perspective of employment policy was the fact that the "employment intensity" of growth in Europe was increasing. In the early 1990s, growth in GDP was accompanied by little growth in employment, as companies improved productivity and substituted capital for labor to achieve the same output with fewer workers. In the late 1990s, this situation reversed—a sign that EU and national policies to price workers back into the labor market were having some effect. However, the overall improvements reflected in the aggregate statistics continued to mask huge disparities within and between countries in the incidence of unemployment. National rates of employment ranged from 10.6 percent in Spain to 3.8 percent in Ireland and 2.0 percent in Luxembourg. Unemployment also remained high in the accession countries ranging from 19.4 percent of the labor force in Slovakia, 18.4 percent in Poland, to 5.7 percent in Hungary and Slovenia and just 4.0 percent in Cyprus.[63]

The March 2000 Lisbon summit marked an important change of direction in EU employment policy. For years national governments had focused on the politically sensitive unemployment rate. Certain policies were designed to encourage workers to take early retirement to free up jobs for younger workers. By the late 1990s, however, it was apparent to economists and government officials that Europe was facing a looming pensions crisis, as relatively fewer younger workers would be available to support an aging population dependent on pay-as-you-go pension systems. Economists also estimated that a large part of the gap between the EU and the United States in GDP growth was attributable to higher labor force participation in the United States where a larger percentage of women worked, men and women retired later, there were fewer part-time workers, and unemployment rates were lower.

The Lisbon European Council therefore set goals for increasing the overall employment rate in the EU from 61 percent of the population in 2000 to 70 percent by 2010 and to increase the number of women in employment from the 51 percent average to more than 60 percent by the same date. Achieving these goals required labor market reforms at the national level, many of which were politically controversial. The March 2002 Barcelona European Council called for a progressive increase of about five years in the age at which people retired in the EU. Other measures put into effect included improving child care to encourage mothers to return to work and the reform of tax and benefit systems to remove disincentives to work.

These reforms, which to a large extent amounted to an EU-level endorsement of measures that fiscally pressed national governments knew they had to undertake in any case, were unpopular and difficult to pass. In Italy, for example, the country's three main trade union confederations organized a general strike in October 2003 to protest government proposals to raise the age at which workers could receive full pension benefits from 57 to 65 for men and 60 for women. Similarly, in Germany the government of Chancellor Gerhard Schroeder came under harsh criticism after a government-appointed commission recommended, in April 2003, a gradual rise in the retirement age from 65 to 67. In general, however, the trend, albeit politically costly to the governments in power, was toward less generous retirement systems aimed at establishing a better balance between the growing number of retirees that would have to be supported by the contributions of a relatively smaller working age population.

Other Policy Areas

In addition to the major policies discussed in this chapter, the EU plays a secondary policy role in many other areas, generally by adding a European dimension to what remain essentially national responsibilities. These areas include public health, culture, education, vocational training and youth, consumer protection, energy, civil protection, and tourism. In health, for example, the Treaty of Rome provides for close coordination among member states and assigns certain special responsibilities to the EU level, for example, setting high standards for the protection of the blood supply and fostering international cooperation with third countries and international organizations. Delivery of health services and medical care to individuals remains, however, a national responsibility. In consumer protection, the Treaty of Rome merely states that consumer protection requirements shall be taken into account in defining other EU policies and activities. In education and vocational training and youth, the EU promotes cooperation among the member states and seeks to develop the European dimension in education, for example, through language teaching and exchanges. EU-funded and -administered programs such as TEMPUS (Trans-European Mobility Scheme for University Students) play an important role in encouraging students and academics to study and conduct research in other EU countries. As in the health area, however, European action is complementary to that of the member states, which retain full responsibility for organizing and financing their educational systems at the primary, secondary, and higher levels.

Perhaps most importantly, the member states retain responsibility for pensions, health care, and unemployment insurance. These are the big-ticket items that account for the bulk of spending in the modern welfare state and that will loom even larger as populations age and the cost of health care continues to rise. Retention of these responsibilities at the national level sets limits to the share of spending and taxation that takes place at the European level and ensures that national politics will continue to be a primary focus for citizens concerned about their personal interests and welfare.

Conclusions

The expansion of EU policy responsibilities has been an uneven and politically controversial process. In some cases, the Commission has pressed to acquire new policy responsibilities at the European level. In other cases, member states have shifted policy responsibilities—or at least the appearance of such responsibilities—to the European level, sometimes in the face of skepticism in Brussels. They have done so for a variety of reasons: to show domestic interest groups that the national government is pursuing their concerns in Brussels, to open the door to harmonization at the EU level, or to secure funds from the EU budget for programs of national concern.

The all-pervasiveness of the single market has tended to increase EU involvement in new policy areas. While it is true that the EU has very limited explicit policy-making authority in such areas as health and education, the reality of the single market and the growing role of competition policy mean that the member states are no longer completely free to make policy and set rules in these areas. National governments are responsible for their national health and education systems, for example, but under the free movement of services and people legislation of the single market they must accept the credentials of students, academics, and health-care professionals trained in other EU countries. Similarly, the explicit consumer protection provisions of the Treaty of Rome are sketchy, and there is no mandate to establish the EU equivalent of the U.S. Consumer Protection Agency. Nonetheless, there is a large body of single market legislation and ECJ case law that has the effect of protecting consumers across national frontiers in the Union, if only because doing so is an essential underpinning of the single market. In these areas as in many others, the indirect working of negative integration—of removing barriers to trade in the single market—has had the paradoxical effect of achieving at least a part of what has been sought by the advocates of positive integration, namely, common or harmonized standards at the EU level.[64]

Notes

1. Article 308 in the renumbered TOR.

2. *Presidency Conclusions: Lisbon European Council, 23 and 24 March 2000*, SN 100/00, March 24, 2000, 4.

3. Andrew Moravcsik, *The Choice for Europe: Social Purpose and State Power from Messina to Maastricht* (Ithaca, N.Y.: Cornell University Press, 1998), stresses the centrality of agriculture in French thinking about the EC.

4. Timothy E. Josling, "Agriculture in a Transatlantic Economic Area," in Bruce Stokes, ed., *Open for Business: Creating a Transatlantic Marketplace* (New York: Council on Foreign Relations, 1996), 61.

5. "EC Agricultural Policy for the 21st Century (Report of an Expert Group)," *European Economy: Reports and Studies* 4 (1994): 1–147.

6. European Commission, "Reform of the CAP and Its Implementation," *CAP Working Note 1993*, VI/2024/93-EN.

7. European Commission, *Agenda 2000*, 113.

8. European Commission, *White Paper on Food Safety*, COM (1999) 719 Final, Brussels, January 12, 2000; and Regulation 178/2002, OJ L 31/1, February 1, 2002.

9. European Commission, *Communication from the Commission to the Council and*

the European Parliament: Mid-Term Review of the Common Agricultural Policy, Brussels, COM(2002) 394 final, July 7, 2002.

10. The European Council reaffirmed an earlier decision—itself a departure from the assumptions in *Agenda 2000* and the Berlin budgetary framework—to phase in direct payments to farmers in the new member states, beginning at the 25 percent level in 2004 and reaching the full EU level by 2013. "Presidency Conclusions: Brussels European Council, 24 and 25 October 2002," SN 300/02.

11. "Stir over EU Farming Subsidies," *Poland, Belarus, and Ukraine Report* 4, no. 7 (February 19, 2002): 1.

12. Council of the EU, "CAP Reform—Presidency Compromise," 10961/03, Brussels, June 30, 2003, p. 2.

13. European Commission, Directorate-General for Fisheries, *The New Common Fisheries Policy* (Luxembourg: OOPEC, 1994), 11–12.

14. European Commission, *Green Paper on the Future of the Common Fisheries Policy*, COM(2001) 135 final, March 20, 2001.

15. Council Regulation (EC) No. 2371/2002 of 20 December 2002, O.J. L 358, December 31, 2002, 59–81.

16. European Commission, *White Paper: European Transport Policy for 2010: Time to Decide* (Luxembourg: OOPEC, 2001), 10.

17. Ex Article 84 TOR.

18. "Community Transport Policy: Action Programme," Bull. EC 7-1962, 14–16; and "Memorandum Showing the Lines On Which the Common Transport Policy Should Be Based," Bull. EC 7/8-1961, 38–44.

19. *European Parliament v. Council of the European Communities: Common Transport Policy—Obligations of the Council*, Case 13/83, ECJ, Report of Cases before the Court, 1985-4, 1513–1603.

20. Bull. EC, Supplement 3/93.

21. Bernd Gugele et al., *Greenhouse Gas Emission Trends and Projections in Europe* (Copenhagen: EEA, 2002), 24–26.

22. Press Release, European Commission, Directorate-General for Transport, June 24, 1998.

23. *Trans-European Networks: Interim Report of the Chairman of the Group of Personal Representatives of the Heads of State or Government to the Corfu European Council* (Christophersen group).

24. *Report of the High Level Group on the Trans-European Transport Network*, June 27, 2003.

25. *Enlargement of the Trans-European Transport Network: Commission Proposes New Projects and New Funds to Dynamise Europe*, IP/03/1322, Brussels, October 1, 2003.

26. Article 3, ex Article 3, with "internal" substituted for "common" in the amended version.

27. Articles 85, 86, and 87 became Articles 81, 82, and 83 with the Amsterdam renumbering.

28. "Council Regulation No. 17: First Regulation Implementing Article 85 and 86 of the Treaty," in George A. Bermann et al., eds., *European Community Law Selected Documents* (St. Paul: West Group, 1997), 492–502.

29. "Council Regulation 4064/89: On the Control of Concentrations between Undertakings," ibid., 558–578.

30. Nicolaidis and Vernon, "Competition Policy and Trade Policy in the European Union," in Graham and Richardson, eds. *Global Competition Policy*, 302.

31. *General Report on the Activities of the European Union, 1997*, 231.

32. *European Merger Control—Council Regulation 4064/89—Statistics*, at http://europa.eu.int/comm/competition/mergers/cases/stats.html (accessed June 11, 2004).

33. See Sapir et al., *An Agenda for a Growing Europe*, 87–88.

34. Mitchell P. Smith, "Autonomy by the Rules: The European Commission and the Development of State Aid Policy," *Journal of Common Market Studies* 36, no. 1 (March 1998): 55–78.

35. *Aid to British Aerospace for its Purchase of Rover Group Holdings—United Kingdom*, O.J. 1993, L143/349; *Aid to the Renault Group*, O.J. 1991, C11/c/11/03; *Aid Granted to the Volkswagen Group for Investments in the New German Länder*, O.J. 1994, L385/1068.

36. European Commission, *State Aid Scoreboard: Spring 2003 Update*, COM(2003)225 final, April 30, 2003.

37. Article 174 TOR, ex Article 130r.

38. Article 2 TOR; subsequently amended by the Treaty of Amsterdam, Article 2.

39. Alberta Sbragia, "Environmental Policy," in Helen Wallace and William Wallace, eds., *Policy-Making in the European Union*, 4th ed. (Oxford: Oxford University Press, 2000), 237–41.

40. European Commission, *Nineteenth Annual Report on Monitoring the Application of Community Law (2001)*, COM(2002) 324 final, June 28, 2002, 39–52.

41. David Stanners and Philippe Bourdeau, *Europe's Environment: The Dobris Assessment* (Copenhagen: European Environment Agency, 1995).

42. See European Commission, *The Challenge of Environmental Financing in the Candidate Countries*, COM(2001) 304 final, Brussels, June 8, 2001.

43. Jon Birger Skjærseth. "The Climate Policy of the EC: Too Hot to Handle?" *Journal of Common Market Studies* 32, no. 1 (March 1994).

44. Green Paper, COM(98) 353.

45. See European Commission, *For a European Union Energy Policy: Green Paper*, Com (94) 659 final, January 11, 1995, pp. 49–51.

46. *Commission Communication to the Council and the Parliament: Preparing for Implementation of the Kyoto Protocol*, COM(1999) 230, May 19, 1999.

47. Peter Stubbs and Paolo Saviotti, "Science and Technology Policy," in Mike Artis and Norman Lee, eds., *The Economics of the European Union* (Oxford, N.Y.: Oxford University Press, 1997), 154.

48. Sixth Framework Programme, 2002–2006.

49. *Communication from the Commission: Investing in Research: An Action Plan for Europe*, COM(2003) 226 final, June 4, 2003, p. 3.

50. Data and calculations from European Commission, *Commission Communication: First Progress Report on Economic and Social Cohesion*, COM(2002) 46 final, Brussels, January 30, 2002, esp. 15–16.

51. European Commission, *First Progress Report on Economic and Social Cohesion*, 2.

52. "Presidency Conclusions: Copenhagen European Council, 12 and 13 December 2002: Annex 1: Budgetary and Financial Issues," SN 400/02.

53. European Commission, *Communication from the Commission: Information Note—Common Financial Framework 2004–2006 for the Accession Negotiations*, Brussels, SEC(2002) 102 final, January 30, 2002.

54. Article 161 TEC, as amended by the Treaty of Nice (paragraph inserted).

55. Article 141, ex Article 119.

56. David Purdy and Pat Devine, "Social Policy," in Artis and Lee, eds., *The Economics of the European Union*, 287–89.

57. Grant, *Delors*, 83–87.

58. Article 137, ex Article 2 of the "Protocol on Social Policy."

59. Gerard Baker, "Europe's Illusion about Americas Weakness," *Financial Times*, March 28, 2000.

60. Lizette Alvarez, "A Push to Make la Différence Verboten in the New Europe," *New York Times*, July 27, 2003.

61. European Commission, *Growth, Competitiveness, Employment* (Luxembourg: OOPEC, 1994).

62. Article 126 TOR.

63. *Towards the Enlarged Union*, 97.

64. Stephan Leibfried and Paul Pierson, "Social Policy," in Wallace and Wallace, *Policy-Making in the European Union*, 200–202.

Suggestions for Further Reading

Grant, W. *The Common Agricultural Policy*. London: Macmillan, 1997.

Majone, Giandomenico. *Regulating Europe*. London: Routledge, 1996.

Mortenson, Jorgen. *Improving Economic and Social Cohesion in the EC*. New York: St. Martin's Press, 1994.

Wallace, Helen, and William Wallace, eds. *Policy-Making in the European Union*. 4th ed. Oxford: Oxford University Press, 2000.

CHAPTER 6

Economic and Monetary Union
THE EURO AND THE EUROSYSTEM

Few developments in the history of European integration have so directly affected the average citizen or have been as politically controversial as Economic and Monetary Union (EMU), the culmination of which was reached on January 1, 2002, with the entry into circulation of euro notes and coins in twelve participating member states. The euro is now the only money used in these countries, having replaced national currencies such as the mark, franc, lira, and peseta that had been in use in one form or another for centuries.

Establishing the euro was the European Union's (EU's) number one policy goal of the 1990s, just as completing the single market was the priority of the previous decade. The proponents of the single currency put forward three main arguments in its favor. First, it would complete the single market by eliminating the last remaining major barrier to the free circulation of goods, capital, and services: different national currencies, the values of which could change, introducing price distortions, and imposing the transactions cost of converting from one currency to another. Second, it would compel a tremendous leap toward political union, as governments and central banks would be forced to adopt common policies and to create stronger central institutions in order to make the single currency work and as individual citizens came to feel more "European" by having European money in their pockets. Third, the euro would strengthen Europe's position in the global economic and political system by challenging the dominant role played by the dollar since the 1940s. Critics of the euro were skeptical about whether these objectives could or should be achieved, and pointed to the enormous political and technical problems likely to arise from the attempt to use a single currency in a region that included such economically disparate countries as Finland and Portugal. Skepticism about EMU was so strong in Denmark, Sweden, and the UK that these countries chose not to abandon their national currencies when the electronic euro was introduced in 1999.

Although EMU was an economic project, it was fundamentally about politics. It was carried out by a group of European political leaders, led by Kohl and Mitterrand, who were convinced of the need to keep Europe moving ahead on its path toward "ever closer union"—a position that in their view complemented rather than undercut the pursuit of national economic and political interests. Apart from the original 1957 decision to establish the common market and the customs union, EMU was the most far-reaching act of deepening in the history of European integration. By turning responsibility for money over to supranational bodies in

Frankfurt and Brussels, European governments believed they were entering a qualitatively new stage in the integration process—one that would be visible to every citizen in the form of euro notes and coins. The fact that they attempted to do this at a time when, despite the optimism caused by the success of the single market and the collapse of communism, much of the initial political impetus behind the integration process was fading made the achievement of EMU all the more remarkable. It also helps to explain the dogged resolve with which European governments pursued EMU in the 1990s. The single currency was the gamble on which they staked the future of the integration process—a gamble that they were afraid to lose.

By successfully launching the euro in 1999, European political leaders "won" this gamble, at least in the short run. Over the longer term, however, the issue of whether EMU was worth the huge political investment made in the 1990s and that continues to be made as the euro countries strive to make the single currency work will depend on the answers to two questions. First, will EMU prove to be economically sustainable or, better yet, deliver the economic benefits its backers promised? Second, will EMU deliver the political pay-offs envisioned in the late 1980s and 1990s in the form of a deepening of the political integration process and a change in citizen attitudes? Will it mean greater popular identification with European integration as a political project or, as one commentator has suggested, will it simply mean the depoliticization of money, without a decisive shift in loyalties from the national to the European level?[1] These questions are crucial to the future of both EMU and the EU as a whole. They can only be answered in the context of the long road that the EU has traveled on the path to monetary union.

Background

At its founding in 1958, the European Community (EC) played no role in monetary affairs. These were handled at the national level, by national central banks and ministries of finance, and at the global level through the IMF in Washington. Europe did not have a distinctive monetary identity. There was no need to create such an identity; currencies were stable against each other and against the dollar. This situation began to change in the 1960s, as the U.S. balance of payments deteriorated and as the leading European countries came under pressure from Washington to help to shore up the dollar and to preserve the par value system backed by the convertibility of the dollar into gold. In January 1962 the United States, Canada, Japan, and seven European countries concluded a General Arrangements to Borrow agreement under which they pledged to lend supplemental funds to the IMF in the event of a major financial crisis, most likely involving the dollar, that strained the IMF's own resources. The Group of Ten (G-10) subsequently became the major forum for the discussion of international monetary issues involving the developed countries. The Organization for Economic Cooperation and Development (OECD) and several of its committees also became important for monetary and financial discussions among member countries.

The EC as such played very little role in monetary matters, as the member states took rather different approaches to the question of the dollar and international monetary stability. West Germany, the chief European military ally of the United States, helped to support the dollar by refraining from purchasing gold, buying large amounts of military equipment from the United States, and by other measures. France, in contrast, followed a diametrically opposite policy, accumulating gold and seeking to reduce the role of the dollar, which de Gaulle saw as an instrument of American hegemony.[2]

The movement toward monetary union was born in the late 1960s, as European leaders saw an increasing need to develop a Community monetary profile in a world in which the dollar was no longer stable and the United States was increasingly preoccupied with the war in Vietnam (itself a major contributor to U.S. balance of payments deficits and domestic inflation, both of which weakened the dollar) and social and political problems at home. Currency stability in Europe also was threatened by internal developments, notably the strikes and student uprisings that rocked France in May 1968, resulting in the weakening of the French economy and enormous pressure on the franc as investors and speculators shifted money into Germany and the German mark. After more than a year of economic and political uncertainty, in August and September 1969 France devalued the franc by 11.1 percent while Germany revalued its currency by 9.3 percent. The outbreak of currency turmoil in Europe threatened to undermine the common market just as it had come into being with the removal of the last intra-EC tariffs on July 1, 1968. It also ruled out progress toward the free movement of capital, even though this was one of the four freedoms proclaimed in the Treaty of Rome.

These developments led to the first ambitious effort to develop an EC economic and monetary union. At the Hague summit in December 1969, the leaders of the six EC countries agreed in principle to the gradual formation of an economic and monetary union and appointed Pierre Werner, prime minister of Luxembourg, to chair a committee of experts to develop a plan. This was the same meeting at which the leaders of the six agreed to launch their foreign policy cooperation and to undertake the Community's first enlargement. As in the 1990s, economic and monetary union was seen as a political step toward deepening the Community that needed to be taken in advance of a projected widening that, while valuable in its own right, had the potential to dilute the Community's identity and undermine its effectiveness.

The Werner committee report called for the completion of monetary union in three stages by 1980.[3] During the first three or so years of the transition, governments would work to coordinate monetary and fiscal policies. In the second stage, exchange rate fluctuations would be narrowed and the Community would set up a monetary cooperation fund to provide balance of payments credits to member states to support their currencies against devaluation. Toward the end of the transition period, the EC countries would fix irreversibly the values of their currencies against each other, abolish all capital controls, and set up a system of European central banks that would take over monetary policy for the Community. The report also called for much stronger fiscal coordination among the member states, including decisions at the EC level regarding the size and financing of national budgets. Many of the ideas contained in the Werner report later were to appear in the Maastricht treaty provisions relating to EMU—although not the recommendation to determine the size of national budgets at the European level.

The deliberations over the Werner report revealed a gap concerning monetary union between two schools of thought that became known as the "economists" and the "monetarists."[4] The economists, represented chiefly by the hard currency, low-inflation countries of West Germany and the Netherlands, argued that monetary union would be feasible only if the participants managed to achieve convergence in their economic policies and, better still, in their actual economic performance. Since Germany had no intention of allowing its rate of inflation to increase, this meant that France, Italy, and the other Community countries had to reduce inflation and bring their main economic indicators into line with those of Germany. The monetarists, in contrast, argued that the Community should take an essentially political decision to proceed with monetary union. The existence of a common currency then would force policy coordination and convergence in the performance of the real economies. The result would be the same—greater uniformity of economic policy and performance—but the order would be reversed. The debate between the economists and the monetarists was never really resolved in the 1970s, and it was to come back in the late 1980s in the next debate over EMU.

The economic convergence that a successful economic and monetary union required became more difficult after the breakdown of the Bretton Woods system of fixed exchange rates. In December 1971 the United States and its key monetary partners in Europe and Japan announced a realignment of currencies, including a devaluation of the dollar, designed to bolster the U.S. balance of payments. The G-10 countries participating in the Smithsonian Agreement (so-named because the talks took place in the historic castle building of the Smithsonian Institution in Washington) pledged to allow their currencies to fluctuate against each other by no more than 4.5 percent. This attempt to preserve the old par value system was unsuccessful, however. Continued turmoil in the currency markets and economic imbalances among the leading industrial countries led to abandonment of the 4.5 percent band and adoption of a generalized system of floating exchange rates in March 1973.

The EC countries still were officially committed to monetary union by 1980, and they took some steps to advance this goal and to buffer themselves against the broader international trends. In March 1972 the six agreed to limit swings in their currencies to no more than 2.25 percent. This became known as the "snake in the tunnel" system, with the 2.25 percent band the snake and the global 4.5 percent band the tunnel. As long as the tunnel existed, keeping the snake within its narrower band was not all that difficult. Once the tunnel disappeared, however, as occurred with the global move to floating in March 1973, the snake became all but impossible to maintain, as some EC currencies moved up against the dollar while others moved down.

Germany, the Benelux countries, and Denmark (as well as several non-Community countries, i.e., Austria, Norway, and Sweden) managed to keep their currencies within the narrow 2.25 percent band, but the other major EC countries—Britain, France, and Italy—all left the snake and allowed their currencies to float freely against each other and against the mark. What survived of European monetary integration was a de facto Deutsche mark zone in northwestern Europe. The German Bundesbank set monetary policies for Germany, while the central banks of the smaller countries shadowed German policy to make sure that their currencies did not fall out of the 2.25 percent band. If Germany raised its interest rates, they did likewise; if Germany cut rates, they followed suit—in either case usually within days if not hours.

The Deutsche mark zone had no institutional connection with the EC and it was a far cry from fulfillment of the ambitions of the Werner report to create a Community monetary union. While it tightened the economic linkages between Germany and its smaller neighbors, it both reflected and tended to perpetuate a situation of economic divergence among the major Community member states. In 1974–1979, for example, Germany's inflation rate averaged 4.7 percent per year, while the rate in France averaged 10.7 percent, Italy 16.1 percent, and the UK 15.6 percent per year. Comparable rates for the same period were 9.9 percent in Japan and 8.5 percent in the United States.[5] The inflation rates of the European countries thus were diverging more relative to each other than they were against the U.S. and Japanese rates. Since higher inflation generally leads to a falling currency on world markets (since more of the same currency is needed to buy actual goods and services), the dollar could be expected to weaken against the mark but strengthen vis-à-vis the franc, lira, and pound sterling. Europe thus was headed for increasing monetary disunion, a situation that threatened the core achievement of the common market and that ran counter to the plans to use monetary union to relaunch the Community in tandem with the first enlargement.

The European Monetary System
EUROPE RESPONDS TO THE DOLLAR

By the end of the 1970s the EC countries began to look anew at the problem of restoring monetary coherence in the Community. The first major proposal for a new approach to monetary integration came in an October 1977 speech by Commission president Roy Jenkins, who was looking for ways to lift the Community out of the doldrums of the 1970s and who, as a former British finance minister, was acutely aware of the economic and political problems associated with currency instability. With strong support from French president Giscard and German chancellor Schmidt, both also former finance ministers, this led to the founding, in March 1979, of the European Monetary System (EMS).

In the EMS, each national currency had a fixed rate against the European Currency Unit (ECU), an artificial currency whose value was set by a weighted basket of EC member-country currencies (see table 6.1). Central rates in ECUs then were used to establish a grid of bilateral exchange rates. Authorities in member countries were responsible for ensuring that these rates fluctuated by no more than 2.25

Table 6.1   Composition of the ECU (percentage)

Currency	March 1979	September 1984	September 1989
Deutsche mark	33.00	32.00	30.53
French franc	19.80	19.00	20.79
Pound sterling	13.60	15.00	11.17
Netherlands guilder	10.50	10.10	10.21
Belgian and Luxembourg franc	9.50	8.50	8.91
Italian lira	9.50	8.50	8.91
Danish krone	3.00	2.70	2.71
Irish punt	1.10	1.20	1.08
Greek drachma	—	1.30	0.49
Spanish peseta	—	—	4.24
Portuguese escudo	—	—	0.71

Source: Eurostat

percent (6 percent in the case of Italy) against each other currency in the grid. This system for regulating the EMS currencies within established bands was called the Exchange Rate Mechanism (ERM). The central rates were not intended to be set for all time, but they could only be changed with the consent of the other members of the EMS. The EMS operated within the framework of the Community, but participation in the ERM was not mandatory for the member states. The UK chose not to participate. Greece, Portugal, and Spain, all relatively poor countries that had their hands full in coping with the demands of the common market, also chose to stay out of the ERM when they became EC members in the 1980s.

The initial ECU basket was established in March 1979. The weights of the member-state currencies in the ECU were adjusted every five years to reflect changes in the relative economic performance of the member states. The enlargements of 1981 and 1986 also necessitated changes in the composition of the ECU, since all member-state currencies were represented in the basket. The value of the ECU fluctuated on world markets as the national currencies in the ECU basket floated against the dollar, generally in the area of $1.15 per ECU. The general approach of using a weighted basket of member-state currencies later was adopted to create the euro, with the crucial difference that from January 1, 1999, onward the member-state currencies were "irrevocably fixed" against each other and against the euro, thus ruling out the controlled realignments allowed in the EMS.

The EMS worked surprisingly well throughout the 1980s, providing a high degree of at least intra-European monetary stability at a time when the dollar went through several wild gyrations, rising to astronomical heights in the early years of the Reagan administration before falling back after 1985. The relative success of the EMS thus paved the way for the revival, at the end of the decade, of plans to achieve EMU. But EMS most likely would not have survived had it not been for the strong political support that it enjoyed in the key member states, above all France and Germany. This support was reflected not only in the rhetoric of these governments, but more importantly in their willingness to make adjustments in their *domestic* economic policies in order to preserve the EMS and reap its promised benefits.

One of the major turning points on the road to monetary union occurred in early 1983, and involved a key decision by the socialist government of François Mitterrand in effect to subordinate the pursuit of certain deeply cherished domestic economic and political goals to the external disciplines of the EMS. After taking power in 1981, the socialists nationalized many French companies and pursued a policy of Keynesian reflation through high government spending and a permissive attitude toward wage increases. These policies, designed to combat unemployment and appeal to Mitterrand's left-wing political base, led to high inflation and two devaluations of the franc. By 1983 the French currency was under severe pressure from the markets, and the government faced a stark choice between leaving the EMS and pursuing a distinctly French economic path or staying in the system but adjusting France's economic policies to bring them more into line with those of Germany. Without a change in policy, it was unlikely that the franc could stay within the EMS bands without large and repeated devaluations.[6]

At the urging of the minister of finance at the time, future Commission president Delors, Mitterrand chose the latter course. Henceforth, France increasingly gravitated to the so-called *franc fort* (strong franc) policy by keeping its currency closely aligned with the mark in the EMS, even if it meant abandoning politically driven domestic economic priorities, such as the campaign against unemployment or the socialist program to bring much of French industry under state ownership. France's 1983 policy choice prevented the EMS from contracting into another politically marginal D-mark zone as had happened in the 1970s, and kept France and Germany, the two main drivers of European integration, on the path toward an EC-wide economic and monetary union. It also began a new era in the interaction between the external monetary environment and domestic economic reform in France and the other EC countries.

TOWARD A FIXED REGIME

The EMS began as an attempt to achieve at the European level the benefits of the par value, adjustable peg system that were provided at the global level by the Bretton Woods system until its breakdown in 1973. Those benefits are a combination of rigidity and limited flexibility—of externally imposed discipline combined with the possibility to make adjustments as needed. After 1983, however, the elements of rigidity began to dominate the system, with both positive and negative effects for the European economies.

The bugbear of the interwar system had been competitive devaluation. Faced with low internal demand and high unemployment, countries sometimes sharply reduced the values of their currencies relative to the currencies of their trading partners in order to make their exports cheaper and imports more expensive in their home markets. In this way, currency manipulation could have the same beggar-thy-neighbor effects as tariffs, quotas, and other barriers to trade. The postwar Bretton Woods monetary system was designed to rule out competitive devaluations by making changes in par value subject to international rules. At the same time, however, the designers of the system recognized that too much currency rigidity was also undesirable. If a country had higher inflation or lower productivity growth than its main trading partners, it would find that its exports would decline and imports increase as its own goods became more expensive and were priced out of the international and eventually even its domestic market. The result would be large trade deficits and rising unemployment. Along with steps to restore competitiveness (for example, by reining in inflation), the main remedy for such a situation was to devalue the currency so as to make imports more expensive and exports cheaper and thus more competitive on world markets.

After World War II, the European countries for the most part managed to avoid competitive devaluations, but there were several hefty currency realignments designed to restore the competitiveness of lagging national industries. France devalued the franc by 16.7 percent in August 1957 and again by 14.8 percent in December 1958. These devaluations were regarded by some experts as excessive, but they helped to ensure the price competitiveness of French exports during the formative period of the common market.[7] The same pattern of behavior persisted into the 1960s, and was seen even in the early stages of the EMS, when frequent and substantial realignments of the franc, lira, and other currencies against the mark were used to offset the effects on trade and growth of different rates of inflation among the countries of the system. Governments tended to avoid currency devaluations if possible, but when they did choose to devalue they made sure that the devaluation was large enough to give a boost to their domestic industries.

The Mitterrand decisions of 1983 marked a turnabout in intra-European policies with regard to currency adjustments. In the currency realignments of 1979–1983, devaluations generally were larger than inflation differentials. France realigned its currency four times vis-à-vis the mark in this period, each time an average of 7.1 percent to offset a rise in French prices relative to those of Germany of an average of 6.7 percent between devaluations. In other words, all else being equal, France was using currency realignment in the EMS to gain modestly in competitiveness relative to Germany. In the period after 1983, however, France and the other traditional soft currency countries took much smaller currency devaluations. France had only two devaluations against the mark between 1984 and 1989, averaging 4.5 percent each, while in the same time frame prices rose an average of 8.3 percent more in France than in Germany in the periods between devaluations. Currency devaluation was offsetting only 54.5 percent of France's loss of competitiveness (because of higher prices) relative to Germany in this period, compared with 105.4 percent in the earlier period.[8]

The reason for this change in approach was a rethinking in France and elsewhere about the nature of comparative advantage in the integrating European economy. Governments could not fail to notice that no matter how many times they devalued their currencies relative to the mark, Germany always seemed to have a large trade surplus. In highly integrated economies, devaluation did not necessarily result in a long-term gain in competitive advantage. Firms in countries with weak currencies had to pay more for imported energy and components. Higher prices for imports quickly translated into higher inflation, which in turn resulted in higher wage demands from trade unions and a further loss of cost advantage. (In countries such as Italy, where wages were indexed to inflation, higher import prices automatically led to wage increases.) A weak currency also made foreign direct investment more expensive, precisely at a time when moves toward completing the single market created new opportunities for firms to strengthen their competitive positions by buying or establishing subsidiaries in other European countries. For these reasons, the French and others concluded that their long-term economic interests would be served by breaking the inflation-devaluation cycle and instead following policies to preserve the strength of their national currencies relative to the mark. With France committed to monetary stability and all of the Community countries focused on combating inflation, the EMS began to evolve into a system of nearly fixed exchange rates. During the first four years of EMS, from 1979 to 1983, there were twenty-seven currency realignments in the system, compared with only twelve parity changes in 1983–1989. The changes in the later period also were smaller, averaging 3.8 percent per adjustment compared with 5.3 percent for the earlier period.[9]

Gradually, inflation differentials in Europe converged, as workers and consumers in France and the other traditional high inflation countries were convinced of their governments' commitment to fighting inflation. In effect, other countries "imported" the inflation fighting credibility of the Bundesbank by their commitment to monetary stability. French and Italian firms were forced to try to maintain their competitiveness by holding down costs at the microeconomic level, rather than depending upon macroeconomic action in the form of a currency devaluation. Much of the work of convergence that had been called for in the Werner report but that had not been accomplished in the 1970s thus took place in the late 1980s through the mechanism of the EMS.

One indication of the relative success of EMS was the increase in its membership. Spain joined the ERM in June 1989, although the peseta was allowed to fluctuate within the wider 6 percent band used by Italy. In Britain, there was a bitter debate about the EMS that pitted Prime Minister Thatcher against many of her advisors. Ever the Euroskeptic, Thatcher was against joining. She was opposed by members of her cabinet who were concerned about being left out of the accelerating integration process. Britain finally entered the ERM in October 1990, also at the 6 percent fluctuation margin. Portugal joined in April 1992. Greece, which was still struggling to bring down its stubbornly high rate of inflation, was the only member country not inside the ERM.

In the end, however, the increasing rigidity of the EMS almost proved to be its undoing, as the narrow currency bands turned out to be unsustainable. France and Italy lost competitiveness relative to Germany in the late 1980s, as inflation in these countries remained higher than in Germany and as currency devaluations were used more sparingly than in the past to compensate for inflation differentials. In the changing economic conditions of the early 1990s, this trend ultimately led to financial crisis.

Toward EMU

DELORS LEADS THE WAY

Along with the successes of the single market program, the EMS and the economic convergence that it helped to promote created a favorable economic and political climate for the revival of plans to move beyond a mere system of monetary coordination to the establishment of a full-fledged monetary union. Taking this next step was largely the achievement of Commission president Delors, a firm believer in both the political and the economic benefits of monetary union.[10] Already in the fall of 1984, as he prepared the assume the presidency, he contemplated making a push for EMU, but in view of the lack of political support from the British and others instead decided to focus on the single European market. The most that could be achieved with regard to EMU was a reference in the preamble to the Single European Act (SEA) recalling the Community's 1969 commitment to the "progressive realization of economic and monetary union" and a short chapter in the treaty entitled "Cooperation in Economic and Monetary Policy." However, the SEA also stipulated that any move toward EMU would require another intergovernmental conference—an eventuality that in early 1986 seemed rather remote.

By 1988 talk of EMU again was becoming fashionable in the Community, despite Thatcher's distaste for the idea and the skepticism of many others, including in the powerful central banking community. By this time, the EMS had been operating for nearly a decade and had been quite successful in its original goal of insulating intra-European trade from turbulence in global currency markets and from the wild swings in the value of the dollar that marked the Reagan years. As the EMS evolved toward a de facto fixed rate regime, a growing number of economists and political leaders argued that Europe should take the next logical step and move to full EMU. The single market program also strengthened the case for EMU. Proponents of monetary union argued that there was an inconsistency between the creation of a single internal market and the maintenance of separate currencies, since changes in the value of these currencies affected the prices of goods and services traded in the internal market and thus constituted a barrier to trade. National currencies also imposed transactions costs on businesses and consumers. The idea that the 1992 program virtually required EMU was later captured in a Commission report entitled *One Market, One Money*.[11]

A further factor strengthening the case for EMU was the elimination of national controls on capital. Free movement of capital had been enshrined in the Treaty of Rome, but it was never put into effect, as national governments relied on controls to influence the exchange rates. However, in 1988 the twelve agreed, as part of the single market program, to remove all such controls by 1990. Economists warned that it would be very difficult to sustain the EMS—a system that retained different national currencies but that sought to limit variations in the value of these currencies relative to each other—in circumstances in which investors had complete freedom to move money across borders to seek the highest rate of return.

Responding to the growing interest in EMU, at the June 1988 Hanover summit the European Council agreed to establish, under the chairmanship of Delors, a committee to propose concrete steps leading to economic and monetary union. Composed mainly of the central bank heads from the member states, the Delors Committee developed a detailed three-stage plan for the establishment of EMU. It did not explicitly call for the creation of a single currency, but it proposed that in Stage 3 exchange rate parities be "irrevocably fixed" and full authority for determining economic and monetary policy be transferred to EC institutions. The report stressed that with the expected completion of the single market and the establishment of competition and regional policies, the Community had already accomplished much of the work toward EMU.

The June 1989 Madrid European Council approved the Delors Committee's three-stage approach and declared that Stage 1 of EMU should begin on July 1, 1990.[12] The key elements of Stage 1 were closer coordination of member-state economic policies and completion of plans to free the movement of capital. Stage 1 thus was in part an extension of the single market program. The member states pledged to place all of their currencies within the narrow band of the ERM. They also agreed that another Intergovernmental Conference (IGC) would be held to consider moving to Stages 2 and 3, although they did not yet set a date for convening such a meeting.

There was still considerable skepticism in Europe about the Delors plan. The Bundesbank was at best lukewarm about EMU, and the British were outright opposed to what they rightly believed would be another major loss of sovereign powers to Community institutions. On the other hand, Kohl and Mitterrand both were strong backers of EMU, even though they had differences over its precise form and how it was to be achieved. Their support was crucial, and ultimately assured that EMU became a reality.

ECONOMIC PROS AND CONS

While the Thatcher government questioned the political desirability of EMU, many economists raised doubts about its economic feasibility. Concerns about whether a single currency could work tended to focus on two considerations: the fact that the EC was not an optimum currency area, and the absence of fiscal federalism in the Community. An optimum currency area is one in which the existence of a single currency does not impose real costs on the economy, particularly as it adjusts to external economic shocks that differently affect different regions of that economy. The optimum currency area is a theoretical construct, developed by economists in the 1960s, and no country or trading bloc fully conforms to the ideal.[13] But economies like the United States that have high internal mobility of capital and labor come much closer to the ideal than does Western Europe, with its still uncompleted single market and its administrative, cultural, and linguistic barriers to internal movement, especially of labor.

In a currency area such as the United States, the economy responds to asymmetric external shocks through the internal redeployment of resources rather than through currency realignments. If, for example, as happened in the 1970s, the world price of oil increases dramatically, it inevitably will have different effects on Texas than on the Midwest. All else being equal, as world oil prices rise economic activity will fall and unemployment will rise in the energy-poor Midwest. In oil-producing Texas, in contrast, employment and economic activity will tend to rise as companies increase energy production and as higher wages and profits diffuse through the economy. In an open, flexible economy such as the United States, workers from the Midwest will head for Texas in search of employment, while capital will flow from other parts of the country into Texas to finance construction and investment. After a time, a new equilibrium will be established. Unemployment rates in the two regions will tend to converge, as labor costs fall in the Midwest and rise in Texas (at least in relative terms), as capital and labor shift from one region to the other, and as industries in the Midwest increase their "exports" to Texas and other booming parts of the country. That, at any rate, is the theory.

In Europe, where mobility of capital and especially labor are lower than in the United States, currency devaluations rather than movement of factors of production traditionally have played the major role in bringing about adjustments to external shocks. If, for example, Portugal faced a trade deficit and rising levels of unemployment because its domestic manufacturing industry was suddenly exposed to a new low-cost competitor from the developing world while Germany encountered no such increased competitive threat, Portugal might have devalued its currency to restore the competitiveness of its products and thereby bolster employment. As has been seen, France, Italy, and the other traditionally high inflation countries in Europe effected numerous devaluations over the years to assist their domestic industries. Monetary policy and shifts in the external value of the currency in effect were used as a substitute for the kinds of internal adjustments that occurred in the United States, such as the downward adjustment of wages and the movement of workers from one state or region to another. Because French workers always would be unwilling to move to Germany and vice versa, critics argued, Europe could never become an optimum currency area. Countries suffering low growth and high unemployment would be deprived of one of their main means of adjustment, currency devaluation, with the result being further economic problems and ultimately a political backlash against EMU and economic integration as a whole.

Whatever the technical merits of the optimum currency argument, ultimately the question boiled down to one of politics. Proponents of the single currency acknowledged that the EC was not yet an optimum currency area, but that it surely had to become one. In their view, the transition period preceding the introduction of the single currency had to be used to introduce greater wage flexibility and freer movement of labor and capital into the European economy. Increased flexibility and mobility of capital were worth pursuing in their own right, and they were prerequisites to a successful EMU. While the relative success of the single market program argued for EMU, making EMU work in turn called for renewed efforts at completing the single market and the efficiency improvements that it entailed.

The argument about fiscal federalism also drew upon empirical evidence from the United States and from other federal systems using a single currency, such as Switzerland and the Federal Republic of Germany (FRG).[14] In the United States, the existence of a unified federal budget acts as an automatic economic stabilizer that counters recessions in lagging regions and somewhat dampens economic activity in boom regions, thereby smoothing out economic imbalances among these regions. If New England falls into recession, for example, income and other taxes paid by workers and firms from that region to the federal treasury automatically decline, while payments from Washington for unemployment insurance and welfare increase. If California is enjoying an economic boom at the same time, tax payments to the federal treasury will rise and receipts from Washington for certain programs will fall. If California is in recession and New England is enjoying strong growth, the same processes will occur but in reverse. In either case, the federal budget will act to dampen disparities between regions of the United States. In studies prepared partly in anticipation of EMU, economists calculated that the countercyclical effects of the federal budget offset somewhere between 20 and 40 percent of differences in economic performance among regions.[15] Other federal systems use different mechanisms (in Germany, the states transfer money directly to each other and less adjustment is left to the automatic workings of individual income taxes and benefit programs), but all such systems are based on an assumption that a unified fiscal system must exist alongside a single currency and a centrally operated monetary policy.

In the EC of the 1980s, however, fiscal responsibilities were highly decentralized and likely to remain so. Even with the increases in the structural funds since the late 1970s, the Community budget still only amounted to a few percentage points of gross domestic product (GDP). The Werner plan had called for closer fiscal coordination among the member states, but these ideas were quietly abandoned as politically impractical and did not reappear when EMU was revived in the late 1980s. Even though European governments tax and spend a much higher proportion of GDP than in the United States (as well as tend to be more overtly redistributional in their fiscal policies), they did so mainly in a national context. EMU skeptics thus argued that the EC was adopting a centralized monetary system and policy, without an accompanying degree of centralization in the fiscal realm. As with regard to the optimum currency area, economists were concerned that governments would be giving up a traditional tool—currency devaluation—for countering recession and unemployment, without gaining any new instruments for dealing with these problems. Ultimately, however, the arguments for EMU were political, and concerns about fiscal federalism were set aside, much as were those relating to the optimum currency area.

THE MAASTRICHT NEGOTIATIONS

EMU most likely would have gone ahead in any case, but developments in eastern and central Europe lent new urgency to the project. As German unification became all but inevitable following the November 1989 opening of the Berlin Wall, Mitterrand saw a single currency as the key to a deeper process of European integration and deeper integration as the key to anchoring a larger and more powerful Germany in a European framework. Kohl was aware of the economic arguments against EMU and the skepticism that prevailed in Germany about giving up the mark, but he shared Mitterrand's political concerns. With the leaders of France and Germany strongly committed to moving ahead with EMU and most of the other European leaders supportive as well, the December 1989 Strasbourg European Council agreed to convene an IGC on EMU by the end of 1990.

The IGC on economic and monetary union formally began in Rome in December 1990 and ran concurrently with the IGC on political union. In a year of intense negotiations carried out mainly by finance ministry officials from national capitals, the twelve member states thrashed out the design for EMU. The final compromise, as embodied in the provisions of the Maastricht treaty amending the Treaty of Rome, reflected French preferences with regard to timing and German preferences regarding conditions. The French obtained an ironclad, treaty-based commitment that the final stage of EMU would begin no later than January 1, 1999. In return for agreeing that EMU was a sure thing—no longer a question of whether but of when—Germany gained agreement to a long transition period before the phasing out of the mark and was able to determine the structure of and mandate for the future European central bank.

Stage 2 of EMU would begin on January 1, 1994, and would last as little as three but no longer than five years. In this period, all member states would work to align fiscal and monetary policies. Participation in the single currency was to be limited to member states that successfully used Stage 2 to converge with each other in having lower inflation and reduced budget deficits and levels of national debt. In effect, Germany had reasserted the old "economist" position with regard to convergence and had managed to incorporate its tenets into the Maastricht treaty. In Stage 2, the member states also were obliged to ban central bank financing of government debt and to enact legislation to ensure the independence of their national central bank. Shortly after the start of Stage 2, the European Monetary Institute (EMI) would be established to undertake the technical preparations for the introduction of the single currency and to help monitor member-state performance with regard to the convergence criteria.

Stage 3 would begin no later than January 1, 1999. Its key feature would be the launch of the new currency, provisionally referred to in the treaty as the ECU but later named the euro by decision of the European Council. The new currency was to be managed by a European Central Bank (ECB), which in turn would be part of a European System of Central Banks (ESCB) consisting of the ECB and the national central banks of the countries adopting the euro. In this respect, the European national central banks would become analogous to the regional federal reserve banks in the United States. Modeled on the German system, the ECB and the ESCB were to pursue the primary policy objective of price stability.

The treaty specified that the ECB was to be led by a six-member Executive Board, composed of a president, vice president, and four other members who are

appointed by consensus of the member states and serve for eight-year nonrenew-
able terms, and a Governing Council comprised of the members of the Executive
Board and the governors of the national central banks of those countries participating in the single currency. The members of the Executive Board were to be
fully independent in the performance of their duties and not to take instructions
from national governments or other EU institutions. The relatively long term in
office was intended as a further safeguard against political interference. The ECB
would not be established until shortly before the start of Stage 3 and the launch
of the single currency.

The UK remained skeptical about the whole enterprise but, as with the social
protocol, it chose not to alienate its partners by blocking EMU—as it might well
have done given the unanimity required to amend the founding treaties. Instead,
it negotiated an opt-out protocol from those sections of the treaty dealing with
the single currency. Britain was not required to move to the third stage of EMU,
although it had the option to do so if it chose. Traditionally Euroskeptic Denmark
negotiated a similar opt-out protocol.

The Mediterranean countries were not opposed to the single currency, but
many observers doubted whether they would be able to meet the strict conditions
for Stage 3 included in the treaty. Not falling behind the northern members and
thereby creating a two-tier union became an important concern for the Mediterranean states. This was especially so for Italy, which carefully guards its status as a
founder member of the EC. Spain, ever the champion of redistribution of wealth
from the more to the less developed member states, managed to secure, in the form
of the Cohesion Fund, additional aid to the poorer member states to help them
meet the Stage 3 convergence criteria. The Maastricht provisions on EMU thus
were a compromise, similar to many other such deals negotiated in the history of
the EC, but with the German imprint dominant and the Franco-German tradeoffs
on timing and conditions clearly the essence of the deal.

Before the Maastricht design could be put into effect, however, Europe was to
face one final bout of currency instability that for a time called into question many
of the assumptions about EMU and seemed to confirm the arguments of those
who said that Western Europe was too economically disparate to make a currency
union work.

THE CRISIS OF 1992–1993

While German reunification provided a strong if indirect political boost for EMU,
the way in which the Kohl government managed the absorption of the five new
German states created new and unforeseen challenges for currency stability in Europe. This, combined with the political uncertainties surrounding the Maastricht
treaty ratification process and the accumulating competitiveness problems associated with the *franc fort* policy (and its analogues in Italy and the other traditionally soft-currency countries), very nearly derailed the whole plan for EMU in the
late summer and early fall of 1992.[16]

In June 1992 the Danish voters rejected the Maastricht treaty by a narrow vote of 50.7 percent for and 49.3 percent against. A similar vote was scheduled for France in September, and polls suggested that the treaty might be rejected there as well. Although there was no direct connection between Maastricht and the ERM, the difficulties of the former put growing pressure on the latter. Without Maastricht there would be no EMU, and without the prospect of EMU governments would have far less incentive to maintain their links with the German mark in the ERM at a time when doing so was causing real pain to their domestic economies.

Attempting to control inflation amidst the heavy borrowing and spending associated with German reunification, the Bundesbank had raised interest rates in July 1992 to 8.75 percent. With free movement of capital, banks and other investors were able to move their money out of Italy, the UK, and other EMS countries to reap the benefits of high real German interest rates. This put downward pressure on the currencies of these countries, forcing them to raise interest rates in order to compete with the German currency. Alignment with the policies of the Bundesbank had been the pillar of the ERM and the EMS system, but the markets began to suspect that countries such as Italy that were suffering high unemployment eventually would be forced to devalue rather than continue to raise interest rates in a way that further dampened domestic economic activity. Speculators began to sell the franc, lira, and pound in anticipation of devaluation.

In the face of massive selling in the markets, Italy and Britain were unable to maintain the value of their currencies, and both countries left the ERM in mid-September. Turbulence in the currency markets persisted into 1993, with attacks on the Spanish peseta, the Portuguese escudo, and the Irish and Swedish currencies. In August 1993 the EU effectively put an end to the speculation by widening the currency bands for all of the ERM currencies to $+/-$ 15 percent (an exception was the Dutch guilder and the mark, which remained within their narrow band). It appeared as if Europe was moving further away from EMU, rather than continuing the quasi-automatic progression from the single market and EMS to monetary union that Delors and other proponents had pictured and had used so effectively to promote EMU.

Ratification of the Maastricht treaty finally was secured in the fall of 1993, and the twelve, notwithstanding the bitter lessons of the last year, proceeded to implement their now treaty-based commitment to begin Stage 2 of EMU. This was the real hard part of the transition to monetary union—the convergence phase in which states were required to cut their deficits and lower inflation in order to qualify for Stage 3—and there were reasons to suspect that once again the European countries might fail in their quest for monetary union.

Stage 2 and Convergence

Stage 2 of EMU began on January 1, 1994. The ban on financing government debt by national central banks took effect, as did the excess deficit provisions of the treaty. The member states began working in earnest to meet the convergence criteria that would determine whether they would be eligible to adopt the euro in 1999. They also began to implement a common economic policy, with a stress on eliminating government deficits.

Member states began to enact or amend central bank legislation to ensure the political independence of the national central banks that were to become members of the ESCB. The precursor to the ECB, the EMI, was formally established in Frankfurt and charged with strengthening cooperation among national central banks and beginning the detailed technical preparations for the switch-over to the single currency. These preparations included the development of new electronic payment systems, arrangements for improved statistical reporting in the euro area, and the design of euro coins and notes. (The timetable for transition to full economic and monetary union is shown in box 6.1.)

THE MAASTRICHT CRITERIA

By far the most difficult task in Stage 2—and the one that became identified in the public's mind with EMU—was meeting the convergence criteria specified in the Maastricht treaty to qualify for participation in the currency union. The treaty stipulated four such criteria: the achievement of a high degree of price stability,

---

Box 6.1   Steps to the Euro

July 1, 1990	Stage 1 of EMU begins. Capital movements among member states fully liberalized.
Nov. 1, 1993	Maastricht treaty comes into effect.
Jan. 1, 1994	Stage 2 of EMU begins. EMI is set up in Frankfurt. Procedures for economic policy coordination are improved. Member states strive to achieve economic convergence and avoid excess deficits.
May 3, 1998	European Council decides on countries eligible to adopt the euro; appoints leadership of the ECB.
June 1, 1998	ECB established in Frankfurt, replacing the EMI.
Jan. 1, 1999	Stage 3 of EMU begins. Euro becomes a currency in its own right. Member states issue new public debt only in euros. ESCB begins to frame and implement a single monetary policy and to conduct foreign exchange operations in euros.
Jan. 1, 2002	ESCB puts euro notes into circulation and withdraws national banknotes. Member states put euro coins into circulation and withdraw national coins.
July 1, 2002	Changeover to the euro complete in all participating member states.

the sustainability of the government financial position, exchange rate stability, and the durability of the convergence as reflected in long-term interest rates. To meet the criterion for price stability, inflation had to be not more than 1.5 percent above that of the three best performing member states in terms of price stability. The standards for government finances were the same as those used in the excess deficit provisions of the section of the treaty on economic policy: gross debt of 60 percent or less of GDP and a budget deficit 3 percent or less of GDP. Exchange-rate stability was defined as managing to keep the national currency within the normal fluctuation margins of the exchange-rate mechanism of the EMS for at least two years without devaluation. The durability criterion was defined as having an average nominal long-term interest rate that did not exceed by more than 2 percentage points that of the three best performing member states in terms of price stability.

Many economists were skeptical that the member states could meet these criteria. At the beginning of Stage 2, Germany, Ireland, and Luxembourg were the only member states with budget deficits below the 3 percent threshold. Inflation had been on a downward trend in the EU for over a decade, but rates in 1994 still ranged from over 10 percent in Greece to just 1 percent in Finland (a member from January 1, 1995). Long-term interest rates also diverged significantly, as lenders to countries such as Greece, Italy, and Portugal demanded higher nominal rates of return to compensate for higher inflation and greater risk of currency depreciation. The gross debt position of most EU countries was either beyond or dangerously close to the 60 percent limit in the treaty. Given the disparities in economic performance, there was much talk at this time about a likely inner core EMU of five or six countries that would be ready to adopt the single currency, and even some speculation about possible postponement of the whole project, especially if France, whose participation was a political necessity, was unable to meet the convergence criteria.

Over the course of the next several years, however, the member states did remarkably better than expected in converging toward each other and toward the objective standards for deficits set in the treaty. By 1997—the key year on which the European Council was to base its decisions regarding participation in Stage 3—every member except Greece had met the deficit criterion. In France, for example, the budget deficit was reduced from 6.0 percent of GDP in 1994 to 3.0 percent in 1997, while in Italy the improvement was even more dramatic, from 9.0 percent to 2.7 percent over the same period. In a sign that investors believed in the durability of convergence and the growing likelihood of a successful launch of the single currency, long-term interest rates had converged toward the German rate of 5.6 percent. Lowering the huge stock of government debt as a ratio of GDP was proceeding very slowly, but most member states were moving in the right direction, as lower annual deficits added less each year to the stock of government borrowings and as some debt was redenominated in bonds at lower rates of interest.

There was some grumbling among central bankers and finance ministers about the durability of the shift to fiscal austerity and suspicions about the use of "creative accounting" to embellish especially the debt and deficit figures. Italy levied a Eurotax that it claimed was temporary and would be paid back to taxpayers after the start of EMU, several countries sold gold or other state-owned assets to pay down debt, and France used the pension funds of state-owned France Telecom to strengthen its government accounts. For the most part, however, the Commission, the EMI, and the statistical arm of the EU, Eurostat, kept a sharp eye on such practices and sought to gain assurances that convergence was real.

THE STABILITY AND GROWTH PACT

Convergence in the 1990s undoubtedly was real; whether it was permanent was another question. Germany in particular was concerned that some EU states might be making a one-time effort to reduce their deficits in order to qualify for the euro, after which they might revert to high levels of borrowing that could reignite inflation and endanger the stability of the new currency. To guard against such a possibility, Germany demanded the conclusion of a supplemental "stability pact" that would not be a part of but that would strengthen the deficit provisions of the Maastricht treaty.

The European Council adopted such an agreement at its June 1997 Amsterdam meeting, but only after it was renamed the Stability and Growth Pact (SGP) in deference to France, Sweden, and other governments worried that the intense focus on fighting inflation might lead to overlooking the issues of growth and employment.[17] The pact clarified how fiscal deficits were to be handled after the launch of the euro. Germany was especially concerned that countries suffering an economic slowdown and rising unemployment might fail to observe the strictures in the excessive deficit procedure. The pact thus specified how fiscal policy can and cannot respond to economic shocks.

A country that experiences a fall of 2 percent of GDP in one year or that is hit by an unusual event outside its control (for example, a major natural disaster) may run an excess deficit (over 3 percent of GDP) without penalty. A country that experiences a drop of 0.75 percent or less of GDP must adhere to the excess deficit procedure. For cases in between—recessions that entail a fall in output of between 0.75 and 2.0 percent of GDP—the finance ministers of the euro countries may decide whether or not to impose a penalty. The latter takes the form of a mandatory interest-free deposit with the ECB by the offending state totaling from 0.2 to 0.5 percent of GDP, depending on the size of the deficit. If the excessive deficit is corrected within two years, the deposit is returned to the member state, although without interest. If the deficit persists for more than two years, the deposit becomes a fine. As will be seen, however, these harsh, self-imposed limitations proved to be politically unrealistic, and ultimately were brushed aside in late 2003 when the Council decided to suspend the penalty provisions of the pact after major countries, notably France and Germany, had failed to live up to its provisions.

THE BIRTH OF THE EURO

The year 1998 was the final year of Stage 2 in which the European Council made its crucial decisions about the leadership of the ECB, the list of countries that qualified to adopt the euro and, very importantly, the rates at which the national currencies of the participating states would be "irrevocably locked" to make up the euro. The EMI was abolished and the ECB formally established on June 1, 1998, thereby allowing a seven-month shakedown period before the actual start of Stage 3.

The run-up to the May 1998 session of the European Council that was slated to make the key decisions regarding the launch of the euro was marred by an unseemly battle over the selection of the ECB's first president that for a while boded poorly for the future of the whole enterprise. Germany favored for the post Wim Duisenberg, at the time president of the EMI and former head of the central bank of the Netherlands. With the ECB located in Frankfurt, there was no chance that a German would be selected as the first ECB president. But as the successful guardian of the link over the years between the Dutch guilder and the mark, Duisenberg was, from the German perspective, a satisfactory alternative. He also had strong support from his own government, which had vivid memories of how former prime minister Ruud Lubbers had lost in his 1994 bid for the European Commission presidency and believed that it was high time for a Dutchman to occupy a top EU post.

While the other ECB members were ready to fall in behind the German-Dutch position in favor of Duisenberg, France chose to go against the tide. In December 1997 President Jacques Chirac announced that he was proposing Bank of France Governor Jean-Claude Trichet to be the first ECB president. The other member states were dismayed that France was attaching such importance to the nationality of the ECB president, which seemed to run counter to the principle that he was to be completely independent of national government controls. But Chirac seemed intent on using the presidency issue to underline the French view that the ECB, while independent in the day-to-day conduct of monetary policy, ultimately had to be subject to political control by Europe's elected leaders.

With consensus required, a deadlock ensued between France on the one hand and Germany and the Netherlands on the other. After months of speculation about the possible withdrawal of both Duisenberg and Trichet in favor of possible third candidates, at a special session on May 2–3 the European Council broke the impasse with a compromise. Duisenberg was awarded the post, but only after volunteering that he did not intend to serve for much more than four years of his term.[18] Germany and the Netherlands were unwilling to abandon Duisenberg in a way that they believed would cripple EMU from the outset, not least by raising public concerns about political manipulation of the currency that was to replace the mark and the guilder. For his part, Chirac needed to emerge from the dispute with something to show for his efforts, but he was also wary of further alienating Kohl and inflicting damage on the Franco-German relationship.

Although there was no formal deal, the implication that the member states had engineered a politically based split term seemed to run counter to the spirit of the Maastricht treaty provisions stressing the independence of the ECB and the deliberate choice of an eight-year term as a safeguard against governmental lobbying. The European Council chose Christian Noyer, a French civil servant with long experience in economic matters, as vice president. The other members named to the Executive Board were a German economist and member of the Bundesbank directorate, the chairwoman of the Bank of Finland, a Spanish professor of economics who was also a member of the executive committee of the Bank of Spain, and an Italian economist with many years of experience with the Bank of Italy. Because the members of the Executive Board are supposed to be independent, nationality in theory should not matter a great deal. But as with the European Commission, when it came to filling these posts member state governments argued strongly for their own candidates.

At the same special summit, the European Council selected the countries that in its view had met the convergence criteria and thus qualified to adopt the single currency. The selections were based on detailed reports by the Commission and the EMI on the progress made by each of the member states in meeting the convergence criteria and in adapting national legislation, including that governing the national central bank, along the lines stipulated in the Maastricht treaty. The choice of eleven countries was a remarkable achievement that ran against nearly all expectations of the early 1990s when it was thought that only a few countries would qualify or that the project itself might be abandoned.

After continued technical preparations for the remainder of 1998, the actual launch of the euro went surprisingly smoothly. On December 31, 1998 (a Thursday), the finance ministers of those countries scheduled to adopt the euro met in Brussels to set the irrevocable conversion rates between the euro and the national currencies of the eleven participating states (table 6.2). This translated into a rate of approximately $1.18 per euro at the opening of trading on January 4, 1999.

With New Year's Day falling on a Friday, thousands of employees at banks, stock brokerages, and government agencies worked over the long holiday weekend to be ready to conduct national and international business in the euro on Monday morning. Major tasks included redenominating all outstanding public debt in euros, converting bank balances into euros, redenominating stocks and bonds in euros, and activating euro accounts for customers. They also had to make the final tests of and activate the new computer systems developed to handle the euro, in-

Table 6.2   Irrevocable Conversion Rates, December 31, 1998

One euro equals:
1.95583 German marks
6.55957 French francs
1936.27 Italian lire
166.386 Spanish pesetas
2.20371 Dutch guilders
40.3399 Belgian francs
13.7603 Austrian schillings
200.482 Portuguese escudos
5.94573 Finnish markka
0.787564 Irish pounds
40.3399 Luxembourg francs

cluding the TARGET (Trans-European Automated Real-time Gross settlement Express Transfer) system operated by the ECB to make cross-border euro payments among banks in the euro zone. All of the hard work, investment, and testing of the previous months and years paid off, however, as euro trading began on the first business day of the new year with only a handful of technical glitches in the leading financial centers of Europe. The euro was still only an electronic currency, however, used in credit card and checking accounts, for major transactions by companies, and for trading in stocks, bonds, and government debt. For everyday cash purchases, consumers continued to use their national notes and coins, while retail shops used a dual pricing system—euros and national currencies—throughout the transitional period.

With the euro successfully launched, one of the few unresolved questions for EMU concerned relations between the euro and the currencies of the four EU countries that had not adopted the single currency. To help ensure monetary stability in the EU as a whole as well as to facilitate eventual adoption of the euro by these countries, the EU established a new exchange rate mechanism designed for the euro and the national currencies of non-euro EU member states. Called ERM II, the new mechanism became operational on January 1, 1999. Greece and Denmark chose to participate, thereby linking their national currencies to the euro. The Danish krone would fluctuate against the euro at the pre-1993 band of $+/-$ 2.25 percent, the Greek drachma at the $+/-$ 15 percent rate established after the 1992–1993 crisis. Sweden and the UK came under pressure from the ECB to join ERM II but, still smarting from the devaluations of the early 1990s, at least initially declined to participate.

Greece continued to make progress in meeting the convergence criteria, especially in lowering its rate of inflation. On the basis of a favorable assessment by the European Council, on January 2, 2001, Greece became the twelfth EU member state to adopt the euro. In Denmark, however, the traditionally Euroskeptic electorate rejected adoption of the euro in a September 2000 referendum. Sweden also held a referendum on joining the euro, in September 2003. Despite strong support from the government and the business community, voters decisively rejected joining the single currency, again underlining the Euroskeptic strain in the Scandinavian electorate. In Britain, Prime Minister Blair was committed to bringing his country into the euro zone, but he faced a skeptical public and diehard resistance in the opposition Conservative party. He pledged that the UK would adopt the euro only if doing so was approved in a national referendum, but his government postponed scheduling the referendum out of concern that the euro would be rejected by the voters for economic and political reasons.

The final and most visible stage of EMU began on January 1, 2002, with the introduction of euro notes in coins in the twelve participating states. To lower the costs for banks and retail establishments of simultaneously working with two currencies and to minimize public confusion, the European Council shortened the period for the phasing in of the euro from the six months allowed in the Maastricht treaty to just two months. By February 28, 2002, all national currencies were withdrawn from circulation. Replacing a dozen national currencies virtually overnight with a new currency was an enormous logistical task, but one that went remark-ably smoothly. Steps taken to prepare the changeover included the design and pro-duction of millions of new notes and coins, distribution of the new currency to banks and shops, putting in place special measures to guard against counterfeiting, training staff and educating consumers and the general public through publicity campaigns, retooling ATMs and vending machines, and withdrawing and dispos-ing of old national notes and coins. About the only serious problem encountered in the whole process were the widespread complaints from the public, some valid and some no doubt exaggerated, that merchants were using the switch-over to round prices up in a way that was unfair to consumers and that risked stoking inflation.

EMU in Operation

There are two parts to EMU, the economic and the monetary. Responsibility for economic policy is shared between the member states and the Union, where the Commission, the Council of Ministers, and the European Council all play impor-tant roles. Monetary policy for eurozone countries is the responsibility of the ECB and the ESCB.

ECONOMIC POLICY

Economic policy coordination was seen by the drafters of the Maastricht treaty as an essential part of the preparations for monetary union (the old "economist" position), but also as valuable in its own right, to be continued after the launch of the euro and to embrace even those countries that were EU members but that did not adopt the single currency. The treaty required all member states to begin to coordinate their economic policies within the Council of Ministers at the start of Stage 2. The treaty defined the overall objectives of EU economic policies as a "harmonious and balanced development of economic activities, sustainable and non-inflationary growth respecting the environment, a high level of employment and social protection, the raising of the standard of living and quality of life, and economic and social cohesion and solidarity among Member States."[19] These ob-jectives remain in effect.

Under the economic policy provisions of the treaty, each year the Council of Ministers (in the composition of Council of Ministers [Economics and Finance Ministers] [ECOFIN] must adopt broad guidelines for the economic policies of the EU and its member states. The Commission provides the first draft of these guidelines, which then are examined by ECOFIN and approved by the heads of state and government in the European Council in a way that gives them added political weight. The Commission is charged with monitoring member-state eco-nomic policies and performance to ensure that the guidelines are implemented. The guidelines include, in addition to general recommendations that apply to the

EU as a whole, country-specific guidelines that address particular problems or policy failures in member states.

In 2003 the EU began adopting its economic guidelines for a three-year, rolling period to allow better medium-term planning. The guidelines also are coordinated with the Employment Guidelines adopted under the Treaty of Amsterdam and with the Lisbon strategy. The *Broad Economic Policy Guidelines for 2003–2005* call for further reform of restrictive labor market rules that hinder the creation of jobs, the reform of pension and health care systems to make them more affordable and, as ever, redoubled efforts to complete the internal market. In addition to these recommendations addressed to the EU as a whole, the policy document contains specific recommendations addressed to each of the member states. For 2003–2005, for example, the Commission and the Council recommend that Belgium take steps to enhance competition in network industries (utilities, postal, communications), Germany improve its education system, Italy reform its public pension system, and the UK take steps to improve basic skills in its workforce.[20]

The real crux of economic policy making in the EU is not, however, these long lists of microeconomic measures, desirable though they might be. The key is macroeconomic stability, as defined in the Maastricht treaty and reiterated in the SGP. The treaty assigns a special priority to coordinated action against excessive government deficits defined, as in the original convergence criteria of 1994–1998, as a deficit of 3 percent or more of total GDP. The SGP reinforces the treaty, requiring eurozone member states to adopt stability programs, to be updated annually, that indicate what they are doing to keep their fiscal deficits in check.

If a eurozone country appears to be exceeding the reference value of 3 percent, it can be designated as having an "excess deficit" and compelled to take remedial action. The Commission prepares a report on the situation in the country, taking into account such factors as whether the deficit is rising or falling, whether it is the result of structural or cyclical economic factors, and whether it is being used to finance current consumption or government investment (e.g., public goods such as roads and schools). The Commission sends its report to the Council of Ministers, which by qualified majority vote may determine that an excessive deficit exists and issue recommendations to the member state for its elimination. If a member state persists in having an excess deficit, the Council of Ministers, again by qualified majority vote, may take concrete measures against that state. These measures include requiring the state to publish additional information before issuing bonds and securities, limiting access to European Investment Bank (EIB) credits, requiring the member state to make a non–interest-bearing deposit with the EU institutions until the deficit has been corrected, or imposing fines of an appropriate size.

In the first three years of EMU, the eurozone countries continued on the virtuous path of reducing deficits and thus did not test the punitive provisions of the treaty and the SGP. However, with the economic downturn of 2001, some countries began to run into trouble. Portugal was the first to breach the 3 percent ceiling, as its deficit hit 4.2 percent of GDP in 2001. Far more problematic for the credibility of the stability pact was the performance of France and Germany, both of which breached the ceiling for three years running, in 2002, 2003, and 2004.

This situation set up a sharp confrontation between the Commission and these countries, especially France, and between some of the smaller member states and the French. Throughout 2003 the Commission demanded that France cut spending or raise taxes to come into line with the stability pact. The French government took the position that the 3 percent stricture was arbitrary and bureaucratic and insisted that it could not take steps that in its view would worsen unemployment and deepen a protracted economic slowdown. Germany was less openly defiant than France, but the continued stagnation of the German economy nonetheless made it impossible for Berlin to meet the 3 percent target.

Many economists and government officials agreed that the 3 percent rule was arbitrary and failed to take account of real economic and political circumstances. Even Commission president Prodi, in one of the verbal missteps for which he was known, at one point called the EMU rules "stupid," thereby undermining the position of his colleagues on the Commission trying to enforce the SGP. For the smaller member states, however, the issue was one of adherence to law. Most of them had continued to make painful budget cuts to meet the terms of the stability pact, and they could not accept that the larger countries could openly flaunt the same rules. The Netherlands even threatened to take France to the European Court of Justice (ECJ) for its willful breach of the treaty. There also was the question of the long-term credibility of the euro. While the 3 percent rule may have been arbitrary, there was general agreement that the euro would work only if its participating states lived by some set of common rules.

This issue came to a head in late 2003 when the Commission, concerned that falling growth and tax revenues would increase Germany's deficit, demanded that Berlin make an additional €6 billion in spending cuts for 2004. Finance Minister Hans Eichel refused, thereby setting up a tense confrontation at the November 25 session of the eurozone ministers. Rather than accept the humiliation of having its budget effectively dictated by Brussels, Germany argued that the penalty provisions of the stability pact should be suspended. After four hours of tense debate, Germany, backed by France, Italy, and most of the smaller eurozone countries, prevailed in a vote to suspend the pact. The Netherlands, Austria, Finland, and Spain stood with the Commission in arguing that the pact should be upheld, but they did not have the qualified majority needed to win on this issue. With some support from the Dutch, the Commission threatened to take the decision to the ECJ, arguing that a mere Council decision was not enough to suspend the provisions of what had been intended to be a treaty-like agreement among the eurozone countries. After an internal debate in which several of the commissioners argued against a politically provocative court case, in January 2004 the Commission decided to go ahead with a referral to the ECJ.[21]

Whatever the outcome of a court case, the suspension of the penalty provisions of the SGP soured political relations among the member states, contributing to the failure of the IGC to adopt the draft Constitution less than a month later. The smaller countries and the Commission complained bitterly that the actions by the large countries undermined the very premises upon which the entire EMU project had been based: that decisions relating to the euro had to be insulated from

domestic politics, that uniform measures had to be applied and enforced throughout the eurozone, and that measures had to be taken to ensure that countries did
not exploit the euro to export inflation and budgetary problems to other parts of
the Union. Critics replied that these arguments were politically naive and ignored
the fact that Europe's number one economic problem was not, as it once had been,
inflation, but rather slow economic growth. Most observers expected that once
tempers cooled, the eurozone countries would try to negotiate some kind of revised pact, one that would preserve the principle that the eurozone needed common rules on debt and deficits, but the provisions of which would make greater
allowance for cyclical fluctuations in economic growth. States might be enjoined
to bring their budget deficits to 2 percent or less of GDP during years of good
economic growth, but be allowed to run deficits above 3 percent in recession
years, thereby achieving a balance over a longer time period.

MONETARY POLICY

As noted, the institutional setup of EMU in the Maastricht treaty was modeled on
the postwar German system, which in turn had many points of similarity with the
U.S. Federal Reserve System. Before EMU, each of the national central banks was
responsible for conducting monetary policy on a national basis. This meant determining the money supply, setting the discount rate (the rate of interest at which
the central bank lends to commercial banks), and managing official foreign reserves. For countries adopting the euro, these responsibilities were transferred on
January 1, 1999, to the ESCB and its core institution, the ECB, which together
were dubbed the "Eurosystem" in the EU's official terminology.[22] The key actors
in setting monetary policy for the euro area were the president of the ECB, the
Executive Board of the ECB, and the Governing Council of the ESCB. With
eleven countries adopting the euro, the latter body began with seventeen members
in all (increased to eighteen two years later when Greece joined the system).

Under the guidelines established by Maastricht, the ESCB defines and implements monetary policy in the euro area. The ECB establishes the basic short-term
interest rate in the euro area, just as the Federal Reserve sets interest rates in the
United States. It also imposes reserve requirements on banks and credit institutions. It conducts open market operations to manage the money supply and influence the trend of market interest rates. It operates a European payments system,
and has the exclusive right to authorize the issue of banknotes in the euro area,
which may be done by the national banks with ECB authorization.

Operating a successful monetary policy in the euro zone promised to be both
technically and politically difficult, especially during the early years of monetary
union in which the ECB had to establish its credibility and deal with problems of
transition. Measuring and regulating the money supply in the euro area was an
especially complex assignment, given the parallel existence until the end of 2001
of euros and national currencies and the amount of euro-induced financial restructuring underway. The birth of the euro also was marked by political controversy

over the old question of the relative importance of fighting inflation versus the pursuit of higher growth and employment.

Even before the euro was launched, the ECB came under a barrage of criticism from political leaders who argued that Europe desperately needed lower interest rates in order to promote growth and combat unemployment. Germany, which under conservative finance minister Theo Waigel had been the strongest proponent of a "hard" euro and the need to combat inflation through fiscal and monetary restraint, ironically became a strong backer of pro-growth policies following the election of the Social Democratic Party (SPD)–Green coalition in the fall of 1998. Waigel's SPD successor, Oskar Lafontaine, repeatedly called for the ECB to lower interest rates. Duisenberg brushed aside these calls as flawed on their merits and inconsistent with the independence of the ECB. Relations between the ECB and Germany settled into a calmer pattern after Lafontaine resigned his post in March 1999, but the early squabbling between governments and central bankers took a toll. The euro fell from $1.18 to $1.08 in the first ten weeks of its existence, surprising many experts who had predicted a rapid appreciation of the new currency.

Freed from the visible public lobbying of the German finance ministry, in April 1999 the ECB cut its bank refinancing rate by 0.5 percentage points, to 2.5 percent. This decision was taken by the ECB's Governing Council, and was intended to head off the threat of deflation and recession. As in the United States, where the press and financial markets closely follow meetings of the Federal Reserve's Board of Governors for hints about interest rate trends, European and world markets began scrutinizing statements by ECB officials and press reports from meetings of the Governing Council for indications of where eurozone rates were headed. In November 1999 the Governing Council decided to raise the ECB's financing rate back to 3 percent. By this time, economic growth in the euro zone had accelerated and the ECB was more concerned about inflationary pressures than recession.

The euro continued to show a pattern of relative weakness against the dollar. By the summer of 1999 it was approaching parity with the dollar at $1.02. European governments and central bankers insisted that this fall reflected generally weak economic conditions in Europe, contrasted with the continued economic boom in the United States, and not something fundamentally flawed in the EMU project. The currency rallied for a while, but closed the year at near-parity with the dollar, a 15 percent drop from the rate established at the end of 1998. In late January 2000 it broke through the symbolically important one dollar level, closing below $0.99 in New York on January 27. By late October 2000, the euro had fallen to $0.83, a decline of about 30 percent since the new currency's launch some 22 months earlier.

The puzzling spectacle of the euro's almost continuous fall against the dollar surprised most economists, causing concern in the ECB and focusing attention once again on underlying problems in basic economic performance. The euro area was running a large trade surplus with the rest of the world that should have bolstered the new currency's value. But statistics showed that companies were diverting investment away from the euro area, thereby depressing demand for the currency. This in turn provoked new questions about the competitive situation of the EU in the global economy and led back to the debate about reform. EMU could hold out great economic benefits for Europe but only, as the ECB and others repeatedly warned, if the Union and the member states continue with the structural reforms and other changes needed to meet the challenges of globalization, an aging population, unemployment, and other policy issues.

The ECB raised interest rates four times in the course of 2000, from 3.0 percent to a high of 4.75 percent in October 2000—as it sought to contain inflationary pressures linked to rising oil prices, improved economic growth in Europe, and the fall of the euro relative to the dollar, which pushed up the price of many imported goods. A key challenge throughout this period was to meet the ECB's target for growth in the money supply, which had been set in 1998 at 4.5 percent per annum but was sometimes exceeded, with potentially inflationary implications. As economic growth decelerated in 2001, the ECB cut rates four times, from the 2000 high of 4.75 percent to 3.25 percent in November. Nonetheless, some in Europe criticized the ECB for not doing enough to stimulate the eurozone economy and contrasted its rather cautious approach with the very accommodative monetary policy and extremely low interest rates engineered by the Federal Reserve to revive U.S. economic growth, especially after the September 11, 2001, terrorist attacks.

The euro stabilized in the $0.85–$0.90 range in late 2000 and throughout 2001, and then began a steady rise against the dollar that wiped out all previous declines. By mid-2002 it was back to parity with the dollar, and by May 2003 it had risen to its launch level of $1.18. Just as the fall of the euro in 1999–2000 reflected the relative strength of the U.S. economy and was caused by the flow of funds into U.S. stocks, bonds, and foreign direct investment, its subsequent rise was attributed by many economists to economic weakness in the United States. With the bursting of the dot-com bubble, the fall of the U.S. stock market, and corporate scandals over Enron, WorldCom, and other companies, European and other investors stopped pouring money into the United States and thereby depressing the value of the euro relative to the dollar. By year's end it had reached nearly $1.30.

Much of the rise reflected the dollar's weakness, as investors continued to avoid U.S. assets and to worry about the long-term effects of the massive U.S. trade and fiscal deficits. It was exacerbated by the practice of China and other Asian countries artificially holding down the price of their currencies against the dollar to fuel export growth to the United States, which meant that the euro had to absorb the bulk of the dollar's fall. And it was driven by differentials in interest rates across the Atlantic. While the U.S. Federal Reserve continued to leave interest rates at the very low level of 1 percent, the ECB left its key rate unchanged at 2 percent, giving investors an incentive to profit from higher yields by putting their money into euros. Critics blamed the ECB for excessive conservatism with regard to interest rates, which they saw as choking off economic revival in Europe, to which the ECB tended to reply with its familiar argument that Europe needed structural economic reforms in product and labor markets, and that until such reforms were made cuts in interest rates would lead only to higher inflation rather than sustainable real economic growth. On November 1, 2003, Jean-Claude Trichet became the new head of the ECB, replacing Duisenberg who, carrying out the understanding reached in May 1998, stepped down from the post. Trichet pledged continuity with the policies of his predecessors, but critics of the ECB hoped for change.

As the experience of 1999–2004 suggested, the euro is likely to fluctuate against the dollar and other currencies, going through "strong" and "weak" periods in response to trends in Europe and the rest of the world. While these variations both reflect and in turn contribute to global economic developments, their effects within Europe are limited. Indeed, the whole point of the creation of the euro was to insulate the European economy from the currency fluctuations that were so problematic in the 1970s and 1980s. In this regard, the euro clearly has been a success. Whether it is up or down against the dollar on world markets, its very existence ensures that prices between France and Germany, Italy and Greece, or Finland and Portugal will not vary because of currency shifts, much the way prices between different parts of the United States are largely unaffected by what happens to the dollar on world markets.

The Euro and the Future of European Integration

Turning to the two questions posed at the beginning of this chapter—is the euro economically sustainable and able to deliver the economic benefits promised, and will EMU propel the EU forward toward political union—it is possible to draw some initial conclusions. The answer to the first question would seem to be a tentative and preliminary "yes." Many of the anticipated benefits of the single currency were apparent during its first three years. Economic growth in the eurozone was 2.8 percent in 1999 and 3.5 percent in 2000 before falling back to 1.6 percent in 2001. Inflation remained in check, although it inched up from 1.1 percent in 1999 to 2.1 percent in 2000 and 2.4 percent in 2001. As discussed in the previous chapter, unemployment rates fell from 1999 to 2001 before creeping slightly upward amid the economic downturn of 2002.[23] The eurozone also continued to enjoy healthy surpluses in its trade and payments balances with the rest of the world, in contrast to the United States with its huge and growing deficits.

Although it is difficult to judge what effects are attributable to EMU and what to other factors, the euro clearly played some role. The major economic benefits of EMU were expected to include greater price transparency leading to a larger and more competitive single market, deeper and more liquid stock and bond markets that will lower the costs of capital for businesses and promote the restructuring of European industry on a continental scale, and more cross-border mergers and acquisitions among European firms leading to stronger global competitors.

As was seen in chapter 4, the existence of the common market since the 1960s and the single market since the end of 1992 notwithstanding, many product and service markets in the EU are still fragmented along national lines. Manufacturers and retailers often charge higher prices in some countries than in others by retaining control of the distribution channels that set prices or simply by taking advantage of different local expectations as to what constitutes a fair price. Prices for the same car, for example, can vary by as much as 25 percent among the member states while those for everyday items such as toys and clothing can vary by 50 percent or more. EU competition policy aims to break down such segmentation, but the single currency may provide an even more powerful impetus to the evening out of prices across markets. With euro pricing, consumers and business purchasers are able to recognize instantly the kinds of disparities in pricing that hitherto have characterized the single market. Those companies that respond effectively to the new and more competitive environment will become stronger global players, while those that have survived in the single market by the implicit protection offered by national currencies will be forced to adapt or go out of business. The growth of electronic commerce via the Internet will accelerate this trend.

As in the market for products and services, the euro facilitates comparisons across national stock markets and should lead to a single European market for stock similar to the one in the United States. With the shares of companies all denominated and paying dividends in euros, closer comparison of profitability and other performance measures is inevitable and will lead to greater Europeanization of ownership and new pressures on companies to create shareholder value. Small and medium-sized companies will enjoy lower capital costs as they benefit from lower interest rates and have better chances to issue stock in the broader euro-market for new equities. Since 1999, the euro has encouraged the restructuring of financial markets, as companies (including U.S. companies operating in Europe) have issued a huge volume of euro-denominated stocks and bonds at uniform rates across the eurozone, thereby lowering the cost of capital and promoting business investment.

The euro also may help Europe to deal with its looming pension crisis, caused by an aging population that will have to be supported in retirement by a relatively smaller workforce. Insurance companies and pension funds that formerly had to match investments and liabilities, that is, promised payments to pensioners, in the same currency and country now can operate on a broader European scale.

The euro also will have important implications for the international monetary system and Europe's role in maintaining international economic stability. These implications are examined in chapter 8, which deals with the EU as an international economic actor.

But if EMU has started to deliver some of its promised benefits, the single currency is by no means a panacea for Europe's economic problems. It has not solved what is clearly the continent's number one economic challenge: inadequate growth. In the late 1990s, increases in GDP were relatively healthy by European standards, but they lagged the even better performance in the United States. In 2001 the United States went into recession, giving Europe a chance to close the growth gap and to become the "engine" of global economic expansion—a prospect welcomed by the United States. But this did not happen, as the euro failed to insulate Europe from the effects of recession in the United States and as the U.S. economy emerged from the slowdown sooner and with faster growth than the eurozone.

Unless it finds a way to accelerate its rates of growth over both the medium and the longer term, both absolutely and relative to the United States (not to mention still more rapidly growing economies such as China), the EU will miss its Lisbon goal of becoming the world's most dynamic economy. More importantly, slow growth will make it harder to meet many of the other policy objectives that the EU and its member states have set themselves for the coming years: coping with the effects of an aging population, renewing the European social model, successfully integrating the accession countries of central and eastern Europe, and playing a more influential role on the international stage through continued high levels of foreign aid, increased defense spending, and by playing a key role in finding solutions to global health and environmental problems.

With regard to the second question, the jury is still out. Definitive conclusions about the political implications of the euro will not be possible until after European citizens have used the euro for a while and after its positive secondary effects—for example increased price transparency and integration of financial markets—have been realized. At least initially, however, there does not seem to be much evidence that EMU in itself constitutes a decisive step toward political integration. It is an important step, but one that must be seen in the context of the continued primacy of national politics, intergovernmental decision making in the Union, and other projects in the EU that also are intended to propel the integration process forward. Indeed, the renewed emphasis on several of these projects (notably a stronger Common Foreign and Security Policy [CFSP] and closer cooperation in justice and home affairs) in the new century was perhaps the clearest if still tacit admission that EMU alone cannot transform the Union. One of the most important of these new projects, the development of what the EU calls "a new area of freedom, justice and security," is the subject of the next chapter.

Notes

1. Pierre Jacquet, "European Integration at a Crossroads," *Survival* 38, no. 4 (Winter 1996-97), 91.

2. Accounts of monetary diplomacy in the 1960s by participants include Robert Solomon, *The International Monetary System 1945–1981* (New York: Harper & Row, 1986); and Paul Volcker and Toyoo Gyohten, *Changing Fortunes: The World's Money and the Threat to American Leadership* (New York: Times Books, 1992).

3. *Interim Report on the Establishment by Stages of Economic and Monetary Union: "Werner Report,"* Supplement to Bull. EC 7-1970.

4. Tsoukalis, *The New European Economy Revisited*, 138–42.

5. Tsoukalis, *The New European Economy Revisited*, 18, citing OECD.

6. Patrick McCarthy, "France Fears Reality: Rigeur and the Germans," in David P. Calleo and Claudia Morgenstern, eds., *Recasting Europe's Economies: National Strategies in the 1980s* (Lanham, Md.: University Press of America), 25–78.

7. Solomon, *The International Monetary System, 1945–1981*, 25; 384–85.

8. Robin Bladen-Howell, "The European Monetary System," in Mike Artis and Norman Lee, eds., *The Economics of the European Union: Policy and Analysis* (Oxford: Oxford University Press, 1997), 332–36, based on European Commission, "One Market, One Money: An Evaluation of the Potential Benefits and Costs of Forming an Economic and Monetary Union," *European Economy* 44 (1990), table 2.4.

9. Ibid., 334.

10. Moravcsik, *The Choice for Europe*, takes an alternative view, and argues that Delors had much less to do with EMU than Kohl and Mitterrand. It seems fair to say that all three men agreed on the principle (if not the details) of EMU and can claim a share in the credit.

11. Michael Emerson, et al., *One Market, One Money: An Evaluation of the Potential Benefits and Costs of Forming an Economic and Monetary Union* (Oxford: Oxford University Press, 1992).

12. Bull. EC 6-1989, 11.

13. Robert Mundell, "A Theory of Optimum Currency Areas," *American Economic Review* 51 (September 1961): 657–65.

14. Cliff Walsh, Horst Reichenbach, and Roderick Meiklejohn, "Fiscal Federalism and Its Implications for the European Community," *European Economy* 5 (1993): 3–20.

15. Peter Kenen, *Economic and Monetary Union in Europe: Moving Beyond Maastricht* (New York: Cambridge University Press, 1995), 88–89.

16. Barry Eichengreen and Charles Wyplosz, "The Unstable EMS," *Brookings Papers on Economic Activity* 1 (1993): 51–124.

17. "Resolution of the European Council on the Stability and Growth Pact," Bull. EU, 6-1997, 17–18; and IMF, *World Economic Outlook*, October 1997, 58–59.

18. "Appointment of the Members of the Executive Board of the European Central Bank," and "Oral Statement by Mr. Duisenberg, President of the European Monetary Institute," *Council of the European Union, Meeting in the Composition of Heads of State or Government*, C/98/124.

19. Article 2.

20. European Commission, *Commission Recommendation on the Broad Guidelines of Economic Policies of the Member States and the Community (for the 2003–2005 Period)*, COM(2003) 170 final. Brussels, April 8, 2003.

21. George Parker and Bertrand Benoit, "Brussels Insists on Mounting Stability Pact Legal Challenge," *Financial Times*, January 14, 2004.

22. ECB, *Monthly Bulletin* (January 1999): 7.

23. European Commission, *Economic Forecasts: Autumn 2003*, October 29, 2003, Statistical Annex.

Suggestions for Further Reading

De Grauwe, Paul. *The Economics of Monetary Integration*. Oxford: Oxford University Press, 1994.

Dyson, Kenneth, ed. *European States and the Euro: Europeanization, Variation, and Convergence*. Oxford: Oxford University Press, 2002.

Gros, Daniel, and Niels Thygesen. *European Monetary Integration: From the European Monetary System to European Monetary Union*, 2nd ed. London: Longman, 1997.

Jones, Erik. *The Politics of Economic and Monetary Union*. Lanham, Md.: Rowman & Littlefield, 2000.

Kenen, Peter B. *Economic and Monetary Union in Europe: Moving Beyond Maastricht*. New York: Cambridge University Press, 1995.

Solomon, Robert. *Money on the Move: The Revolution in International Finance Since 1980*. Princeton, N.J.: Princeton University Press, 1999.

Ungerer, Horst. *A Concise History of European Monetary Integration: From EPU to EMU*. Westport, Conn.: Quorum Books, 1997.

CHAPTER 7

The Citizen's Europe
AN AREA OF FREEDOM, SECURITY, AND JUSTICE

Western Europe emerged from World War II committed not only to restoring peace and economic prosperity, but to safeguarding civil and political rights and the rule of law—values that had been trampled upon by the Nazi and fascist dictatorships in the 1930s and that again were being denied by the communist authorities in central and eastern Europe after 1945. These values were enshrined at the national level in the new postwar constitutions of France and Italy and in the Basic Law of the Federal Republic of Germany, adopted when that state was founded in 1949. At the European level, they were reflected in the statute of the Council of Europe, also signed in 1949 as an outgrowth of the Hague conference of European federalists.

Unlike the European Coal and Steel Community (ECSC) that was founded several years later, the Council of Europe was not endowed with supranational powers and strong central institutions. It worked and continues to work on the basis of conventions adopted by its member states, the earliest and most important of which was the November 1950 European Convention for the Protection of Human Rights and Fundamental Freedoms.[1] The convention set certain basic standards that all members of the Council of Europe were pledged to observe. Along with several follow-on agreements, it also established mechanisms for addressing human rights abuses: a European Commission of Human Rights to investigate alleged breaches of the convention submitted to it by states and individuals and a European Court of Human Rights (established in 1959) to adjudicate cases sent to it by the human rights commission.

In contrast, the ECSC, the European Community (EC), and Euratom were set up as essentially economic organizations, albeit ones that reflected the long-term political aspirations of the founding fathers. As such, they did not directly concern themselves with civil and political rights. The Treaty of Rome guaranteed free movement of "workers," but it did not confer a general right upon the citizens of one member state to reside or seek employment elsewhere in the Community. The treaty had a modest social dimension, but it was narrowly focused on economics and the functioning of the single market. It dealt with persons as economic actors rather than as citizens. This meant, for example, that it contained rather strong language about equal pay for equal work for men and women, but it had nothing to say about combating discrimination unrelated to the workplace. This remained a national responsibility, enshrined in different ways in the constitutions and national laws of the member states.

As the EC developed, however, it began to involve itself in matters that touch upon the rights and responsibilities of individuals as citizens: police and judicial cooperation, immigration, asylum and refugee matters, and eventually the citizenship rights granted by the new European Union (EU). Three factors contributed to the growing importance of citizenship and other people-related issues in the integration process: (1) the need to address the potentially negative consequences of the lowering of intra-European borders, especially as it related to the free movement of people; (2) the growth in the Union's social dimension and the links between the economic and social rights of EU citizens and their civil and political rights; and (3) the need to address the "democratic deficit" in the Union and the link between political rights and citizenship.

EU involvement in citizenship and related issues has developed in stages. In the 1970s the EC member states began to cooperate among each other on an intergovernmental basis, initially mainly to deal with the transnational problem of terrorism. In the 1980s, largely under the impetus of the single market program, they started to negotiate formal agreements among each other making cooperation on justice and home affairs matters mandatory, albeit still on an intergovernmental basis outside the formal structures of the Community. In 1992 they concluded the Maastricht treaty, which established an EU citizenship and the EU's third pillar, thereby formally bringing citizens' rights and certain aspects of justice and home affairs under the purview of the Union. In 1997, the EU member states agreed in the Treaty of Amsterdam to an extensive transfer of responsibility for matters relating to justice and home affairs to the first pillar of the EU, thus giving the Union's supranational institutions a major role in shaping and executing policy in these areas. A new section in the treaty entitled "Freedom, Security and Justice" reiterated provisions on fundamental rights and nondiscrimination contained in other EU documents and called for the progressive establishment of an EU-wide area of freedom, security, and justice.

The 1970s

THE TREVI GROUP

Cooperation among the EC member states on police and judicial matters began in 1975 with the agreement to establish, under the auspices of European Political Cooperation (EPC), the Trevi Group (named after the fountain in Rome near where the group held its first meeting) of senior officials from justice and home affairs ministries.[2] The mid-1970s were marked by mounting international terrorism emanating both from the Middle East and from home-grown groups such as Italy's Red Brigades and West Germany's Baader-Meinhof gang. The Trevi Group was to serve as a forum for the exchange of information and the discussion of steps to combat terrorism in Europe. As was the case with EPC, the policy issues dealt with by the group were outside the competence of the Community. Coordination took place on an intergovernmental basis, with no role for the European Commission and other central institutions and no basis in the treaties or EC law.

Like the Council of Ministers, the Trevi Group operated on several levels. The ministers met every six months. A group of senior officials met as needed to prepare the agenda for ministerial meetings and to monitor the progress of the working groups, which dealt with cooperation among national authorities to combat terrorism, for example by sharing information about known terrorist organizations. Cooperation at these three levels helped to lay the basis for future cooperation among the member states on other matters with judicial implications, including combating narcotics trafficking and illegal immigration.

As the member-state governments increased their cooperation on police and judicial matters, often through working-level links that attracted little public attention, more public moves were afoot to add a citizenship dimension to European integration. The December 1975 Rome European Council, the same meeting that called for the first direct elections to the European Parliament, reached agreement in principle on creating a uniform passport for citizens of all EC member states. In the same month, Belgian Prime Minister Leo Tindemans presented his report to the European Council arguing the need to make Europe more relevant to the everyday needs of citizens and outlining a series of proposals concerning citizenship.[3] Little was accomplished along these lines, however, until the relaunch of the 1980s.

The 1980s and the Single European Act

CITIZENSHIP ISSUES

The 1980s saw continued slow progress toward a de facto Community citizenship. In June 1981 the member-state governments reached agreement on the introduction of an EC passport. On January 1, 1985, the first such passports were issued in most member states. At the June 1984 Fontainebleau summit, the European Council set up a committee chaired by Italian politician Pietro Adonnino to develop ideas for a "people's Europe." The Adonnino committee presented its report to the European Council the following year. Entitled *Citizen's Europe*, it recommended a list of measures that would have immediate practical benefit for citizens including simpler border controls, mutual recognition of diplomas and qualifying examinations, and measures to allow citizens of one member state to live and work in other member states. The Adonnino report was largely forgotten, but some of its recommendations were subsumed under the 1992 program.

Under Delors, the Commission began to promote a sense of European patriotism and identity.[4] In May 1986 the Commission raised the new European flag—the familiar ring of yellow stars on a blue background—to the strains of Beethoven's famous "Ode to Joy," which had been proclaimed the European anthem. For the most part, however, the big story of the 1980s was not citizenship but borders: the progressive dismantling of the internal borders of the Community, various attempts to strengthen its external borders, and the political and institutional implications of these attempts.

SCHENGEN AND THE SINGLE MARKET

The renewed interest in the 1980s in completing the single market—for labor, capital, and services as well as for goods—had important implications for cooperation in justice and home affairs. On the one hand, it stimulated efforts by the member states, in bilateral and multilateral forums, within the Community and outside of it, to accelerate the removal of border checks and other frontier-related measures that still impeded the functioning of the internal market. On the other hand, it led to new efforts among governments to cope with the anticipated negative side effects of the elimination of border controls through closer cooperation. To some extent there was a tension between these two responses to the single market program, as the search for controls at the European level on occasion complicated implementation of the free market provisions of the Single European Act (SEA) that they ostensibly were intended to advance.

In July 1984 France and Germany concluded an agreement on the gradual elimination of border checks between the two countries. The Franco-German agreement was an important precursor to both the Schengen Agreement and the SEA. In June 1985, Belgium, France, the Federal Republic of Germany, Luxembourg, and the Netherlands concluded the Schengen Agreement on the elimination of border controls among these five countries.[5] Named for the town in Luxembourg where it was negotiated, the agreement was to enter into force on January 1, 1990. It was concluded as an intergovernmental accord outside the framework of the EC, but its intent was to give effect, in a part of the Community, to the provisions on free movement that were in the Treaty of Rome and that were expected to be included in the single market program then under discussion. In addition to eliminating border controls among the signatory states, it called for establishing common rules in the Schengen area for visa and asylum policies and comprehensive cooperation among the national authorities on such matters as combating trafficking in drugs and weapons, combating terrorism and illegal immigration, and hot pursuit by police across national borders. A key element of the implementation plan was to be the development of a Schengen Information System (SIS), a database established and maintained by the Schengen country governments to help police track aliens, individuals wanted for extradition, suspected terrorists, and certain other categories of persons whose movement across borders was of interest to the authorities.

Schengen was followed by the signature, in January 1986, of the SEA, which provided for an area in which the free movement of persons was to be ensured. As an annex to the treaty, the member states adopted a "Political Declaration by the Governments of the Member States on the Free Movement of Persons," in which they agreed to cooperate on immigration matters and the combating of terrorism, crime, and traffic in drugs and illicit trading in works of art and antiques. As with other aspects of the single market program, however, the lowering of barriers to cross-border movement did not flow automatically from the language of the treaty. Member states had to adopt implementing directives at the Community level and to transpose these directives into national legislation. This they did with great difficulty. Britain, Ireland, and Denmark took the position that the free movement provisions of the SEA should apply only to citizens of Community countries, and not to third-country nationals. The other nine member countries (all actual or prospective signatories of the Schengen Agreement) took the view that any individual having legitimately entered the Community had the same right of movement throughout the Community as nationals of the member state. (Thus under the majority position, for example, an Indian citizen living in Germany on a student visa should be free to travel to Belgium, Italy, or any other EC country, much as if he were a German; under the minority position, the student would have to obtain a visa to travel to another EC country, much as if he were coming directly from India.) This issue was important not only—or even primarily—for the third-country individuals concerned, but because the British position implied the maintenance of intra-EC border controls that would affect EC citizens as well, as continued checks of everyone crossing the national border was the only way to police the movement of third-country nationals.

These agreements to open the EC's internal borders were paralleled by moves to strengthen controls at the Community's external frontiers through expanded cooperation in the Trevi process. In 1985 Trevi set up a working group to coordinate action against international drug trafficking and other forms of serious international crime. This was followed, in 1986, by establishment of an Ad Hoc Group on Immigration to work on migration-related issues associated with the lifting of border controls.

The Ad Hoc Group on Immigration was instrumental in negotiating two intergovernmental conventions that addressed issues relating to migration from outside the Community. The Dublin Convention on Asylum, concluded by the twelve EC member states in June 1990, established common rules for dealing with asylum seekers. It set criteria by which to determine which country was responsible for examining an asylum seeker's application and, if warranted, for granting that individual's request under the terms of the 1950 European Convention for the Protection of Human Rights and Fundamental Freedoms and the 1951 Convention Relating to the Status of Refugees. If a country decided to admit an individual, this decision would be accepted by all other member states. A second agreement, the July 1991 Convention on the Crossing of EC External Borders (also known as the External Frontiers Convention) was modeled on the Schengen Agreement but was intended to apply to all member states. It provided for drawing up a common list of countries whose nationals would or would not require visas for entry into the Community. Neither the Dublin Convention nor the External Frontiers Convention proved easy to implement, however, as the national governments dragged their feet on putting these agreements into effect. The External Frontiers Convention was not signed, owing to Britain's refusal to remove its intra-EC border controls. The Dublin Convention ran into opposition from Ireland and the UK, which were concerned about its security implications.

IMMIGRATION AS A POLICY PROBLEM

The Dublin and External Frontiers Conventions and the provisions of the Schengen Agreement dealing with visa and asylum policies were all responses to the rising saliency of immigration as a policy problem. The European countries traditionally saw themselves as countries of *emigration*, not *immigration*. During the economic boom years lasting from the late 1950s to the early 1970s, industry in West Germany, France, and the Benelux countries suffered shortages of labor that it alleviated by importing "guest workers" from abroad. Many of these workers came from southern Italy and thus were citizens of a Community country covered by the free movement provisions of the Treaty of Rome. Others came from Yugoslavia, Spain and Portugal (still not members of the EC), Turkey, and North Africa. When the economic recession of 1974–1975 occurred, many of the West European countries hoped that these migrants would return to their home countries. By this time, however, many of these people had put down roots in their adopted countries and had no wish to return to where they or in many cases their parents had originated. With the Turks and North Africans especially, Western Europe was confronted with large numbers of people who were not fully integrated into European society but who also had little prospect of return to their countries of origin. This resulted in educational, crime, and other social problems with alienated immigrant youth, particularly in large cities, and in a racist and xenophobic backlash in a part of the local population.

The late 1980s and early 1990s again became a time of rapidly expanding legal and illegal immigration into the Community as migrants from the developing world were attracted to Western Europe by strong economic and employment growth, political and economic turmoil in many parts of the developing world, and as borders in eastern Europe began to break down. Once inside one member country, an illegal immigrant could make his or her way to other countries in the Community. Requests for political asylum also exploded, initially as a result of political and ethnic upheavals in the developing world and later as a consequence of the civil war in the former Yugoslavia.

By the early 1990s it was estimated that there were some 14.1 million resident aliens living in the twelve member states of the Community. Some 4.9 million of these people were citizens of one EC country living in other member states, but more than 9 million were nationals of third countries, for example Turkey, Yugoslavia, and many African, Asian, and Latin American countries.[6] In 1991 alone, Eurostat reported the immigration of 1.24 million non-EC nationals into the member states. Emigration of non-EC nationals was just over 500,000, leaving a net inflow of more than 700,000 people, more than half of whom settled in Germany.[7] Apart from the numbers of people involved, there was, as is shown in table 7.1, a confusing array of different legal categories of migrants, all of which were covered by different national laws and in some cases international treaties.

PROBLEMS WITH IMPLEMENTATION

The upsurge of immigration in the late 1980s coupled with the dismantling of internal borders in connection with the 1992 program led to intensified efforts within the Community to strengthen external borders and to upgrade police and

Table 7.1   Categories of Cross-Border Movements

Category	Applicable laws and treaties
Citizens	Different national laws on citizenship apply
	Being native born does not necessarily confer citizenship
	Different naturalization procedures
	All citizens of a member state also EU citizens (TEU)
Citizens of EU countries resident in another EU country	Right to move and reside throughout the territory of the Union as EU citizens (TEU)
	Can vote in municipal and EP elections
Non-EU country nationals on temporary stays	EU to draw up common visa list, set standard visa procedures (TOR, as amended by Amsterdam)
Legal immigrants from non-EU countries	EU to draw up common immigration policies, set standard visa procedures (TOR, as amended by Amsterdam); exceptions for UK and Ireland
Illegal immigrants	EU to draw up common immigration policies, set standard visa procedures (TOR, as amended by Amsterdam); exceptions for UK and Ireland
Asylum seekers	Dublin Convention; Common European Asylum System (in progress)
Refugees and displaced persons	Convention Relating to the Status of Refugees; Common European Asylum System

judicial cooperation both in the Trevi process and among the subset of countries that had signed the Schengen Agreement. As the member states moved closer toward true cross-border mobility of persons and capital, governments became increasingly concerned that organized crime would be among the main beneficiaries of the single market. Member states were dismantling their national controls, but they had not put in place at the Community level common policies on the control of external borders or procedures for sharing information about organized crime, illegal immigration, and other cross-border matters. Within Trevi, permanent and ad hoc groups were set up to deal with the policing implications of the reduction in border controls (Trevi '92), the possible establishment of a European Criminal Police Office, and judicial cooperation on such matters as extradition, legislation against fraud, and the mutual recognition of court decisions.

But the slow pace of progress in Trevi and more importantly problems with implementing Schengen soon revealed how politically difficult it was for governments to dismantle their external borders and to entrust key aspects of internal security to untested European mechanisms. Many governments were looking to preserve or even strengthen their national border controls. This was especially the case for Ireland and the UK, island countries that still found it relatively easy to control the entry of foreigners, but it was true even for some of the continental countries committed to Schengen. As the January 1990 deadline approached, the Schengen signatory states began backpedaling on implementing the agreement, citing a number of issues including unresolved matters relating to the movement of migrant workers from third countries, technical deficiencies in the SIS, as well as certain matters completely unrelated to immigration such as differences between the Netherlands and Luxembourg over bank secrecy laws and their implications for the fight against tax and fiscal fraud.

In an attempt to resolve these differences, the five countries reopened negotiations in early 1990. In June of that year they finally concluded the Schengen Implementing Convention that spelled out detailed arrangements for the free movement of persons, particularly with regard to asylum policy, visa regime harmonization, hot pursuit by police across borders, and the SIS.[8] Italy acceded to the Schengen Agreement and the implementing convention in 1990, Portugal and Spain in 1991, Greece in 1992, and Austria in 1995. However, differences among member states and continuing problems with the Schengen database led to further postponements in actually putting the agreement into effect, and it was not until April 1, 1995, that six countries—Belgium, Luxembourg, Germany, the Netherlands, Portugal, and Spain—declared the complete elimination of border controls in what the press quickly dubbed "Schengenland." The other signatory states, including France, were not yet ready to put the agreement into effect on their territories. France claimed to be upset with the liberal drug policies in the Netherlands and was unwilling to open its borders until the Dutch cracked down on practices that made soft drugs freely available for possible transport to other European countries. In reality, the French government was caught off guard by a strong domestic political backlash against the opening of borders, and seemed to be using the drugs issue as a way to defer fulfillment of its Schengen obligations.

Full implementation of Schengen, the most ambitious of the 1980s initiatives in justice and home affairs, thus was pushed off until well into the 1990s. The Dublin and External Frontiers Conventions encountered a similar fate. The Dublin Convention finally was ratified by all member states and went into effect on September 1, 1997. The External Frontiers Convention still had not been ratified at the time of the Amsterdam Intergovernmental Conference (IGC), owing to a dispute between Spain and the UK over Gibraltar.

The Maastricht Treaty

The Maastricht treaty was significant in bringing into a single structure—the new European Union—many of the mechanisms for cooperation on citizenship and justice and home affairs that had developed in past decades on an ad hoc basis, mostly outside the formal structures of the EC. Germany was the strongest proponent of expanding immigration and police cooperation, both because it faced the most immediate problems in these areas caused by the collapse of communism and the rise of instability in central and eastern Europe and because it preferred to "Europeanize" certain issues that, given Germany's past, were politically difficult to handle in a purely domestic context. Dissatisfaction with the pace of development in Trevi and with implementation of the Schengen Agreement were important considerations in German thinking.

The treaty introduced three major changes. First, it introduced human rights and fundamental freedoms into the treaty structure, albeit mainly by linking the EU to agreements concluded earlier under Council of Europe auspices. The treaty stipulated that "the Union shall respect fundamental rights, as guaranteed by the Convention for the Protection of Human Rights and Fundamental Freedoms . . . and as they result from the constitutional traditions common to the member states, as general principles of Community law."[9] Second, it established EU citizenship. Third, it established cooperation in justice and home affairs as the Union's third pillar. As with the second pillar (Common Foreign and Security Policy [CFSP]), the establishment of a separate pillar was a compromise between two competing sentiments: on the one hand, the desire of the member states for closer and more effective cooperation on matters that increasingly defied national treatment, especially with the elimination of border controls under the SEA, and, on the other, the requirement of the member states, and especially Britain, to retain sovereignty in these areas. As with CFSP, the intergovernmental pillar was a means to reconcile increased cooperation at the EU level with the continued maintenance of the national veto.

EU CITIZENSHIP

Citizenship issues had become increasingly prominent in the Community in the 1980s, after the first direct elections to the European Parliament in 1979 and in response to concerns about a "democratic deficit" in an EC that seemed to be acquiring ever more influence over the everyday lives of European citizens. The Maastricht treaty established citizenship as an aspect of the political union. All persons who are citizens of a member state also are citizens of the Union. EU citizenship supplements but does not replace national citizenship. The establishment of an EU citizenship removed a lingering ambiguity about whether free movement of persons in the Union is an economic right, linked to the functioning of the single market, or a civil right rooted in the very essence of citizenship. The treaty takes the latter interpretation, specifying that "every citizen of the Union shall have the right the move and reside freely within the territory of the member states."[10] However, as was seen in chapter 4, it makes the exercise of this right subject to limitations and conditions set by the member states.

As a practical matter, EU citizenship conferred very few real new rights upon individuals, who for the most part seemed satisfied with the rights they enjoyed as citizens of EU member states. Nationals of one member state residing elsewhere in the Union have a right to vote or be a candidate in elections for the European Parliament and for municipal offices. They have the right to diplomatic and consular assistance from the representatives of other EU member states when traveling or living in a third country where their own country has no embassy or consular offices. They have the right to correspond with the institutions of the Union in any of its official languages, and they may petition the European Parliament and the Ombudsman according to certain procedures. The latter position, established in the Maastricht treaty, was set up to hear citizen complaints about maladministration by EU institutions and offices.

THE THIRD PILLAR

The third-pillar provisions of the Maastricht treaty defined nine areas to be of common interest among the member states of the newly established Union: (1) asylum policy; (2) rules governing the crossing of external borders; (3) immigration policy, including conditions of entry, conditions of residence, and combating unauthorized immigration, residence, and work by nationals of third countries on the territory of EU member states; (4) combating drug addiction; (5) combating fraud on an international scale; (6) judicial cooperation in civil matters; (7) judicial cooperation in criminal matters; (8) customs cooperation; and (9) police cooperation for the purposes of preventing and combating terrorism, unlawful drug trafficking, and other serious forms of international crime. The list did not extend to ordinary crime, which remained the responsibility of national and local authorities.

In addition to these nine areas, the Maastricht treaty specified one policy area—visas—that was to be handled as a first-pillar matter and made subject to decision making by the EU's supranational institutions. A new article inserted into the Treaty of Rome called upon the Commission to draw up proposed lists of countries whose nationals required a visa to cross the external borders of the Union for approval by the Council of Ministers. Beginning in 1996, the Council was empowered to act by qualified majority voting with regard to visa policy. This provision was important not only because it helped to establish a unified EU visa policy, but also because it established a precedent for handling other matters relating to justice and home affairs in the first pillar.

To facilitate cooperation in the nine areas listed in third pillar, the Maastricht treaty established an intergovernmental decision-making process that more or less corresponded to the one set up for the second pillar. The Trevi Group was abolished, and its responsibilities turned over to the new K.4 committee (named after the relevant treaty article), whose job was to prepare the work of the Council of Ministers in the nine areas of common interest. Apart from day-to-day cooperation at working levels between the appropriate national ministries and departments (justice and home affairs, customs services, tax authorities, and so forth), the treaty specified three ways in which the member states were to work together in the third pillar: (1) by adopting joint positions; (2) by adopting joint actions; and (3) by drawing up conventions among all or some of the member states for specific purposes. In this way, agreements already negotiated, such as the Dublin Convention and the External Frontiers Convention, could serve as building blocks for cooperation under the third pillar.

Conventions, long used in the Council of Europe, establish a certain kind of law of general or partial application in the Union. In the first pillar, laws passed by the Council or by the Council and the Parliament either apply directly or they must be transposed into national law in all of the member states. The European Court of Justice (ECJ) has jurisdiction over such laws and can levy fines against member states for failing to transpose or enforce Community law. Conventions, in contrast, are adopted voluntarily by the member states, albeit under the umbrella of the third pillar. The Maastricht treaty further stipulated that implementing measures for such conventions could be adopted by the Council of Ministers by a two-thirds vote of the signatory states and that the signatories could stipulate in these conventions that the ECJ had jurisdiction over their interpretation. In this way, the method of harmonization long used in the intergovernmental Council of Europe was incorporated into the largely intergovernmental third pillar of the new EU. It was a looser form of cooperation than that used on economic and related matters in the first pillar, but it represented an important interim step toward creating an EU-wide area for justice and home affairs.

EUROPOL

Police cooperation had been developing since the 1970s under the auspices of the Trevi Group, but it received a strong new impetus from Germany in the early 1990s. At the June 1991 Luxembourg summit, Chancellor Kohl called for the establishment of a new European central criminal investigation office. What the Germans had in mind was something like a full-fledged European Federal Bureau of Investigation (FBI), which could investigate serious crimes and help to enforce law at the European level. In August 1991 an Ad Hoc Working Group on Europol was set up within the Trevi process. Building upon the work of Trevi, the Maastricht treaty identified as an area of common interest police cooperation for the purpose of preventing and combating terrorism, unlawful drug trafficking, and other serious forms of international crime. It called for organizing a Union-wide system of exchanging information within a European Police Office—otherwise known as Europol—but left establishment of this body to further negotiation and the conclusion of a separate convention among the member states.

Consistent with the mandate in the Maastricht treaty, the member states began drafting a Europol convention. Progress was slow, however, owing to differences over the organization's powers and activities and over whether the Court of Justice should be granted jurisdiction over Europol actions. Germany, with its long borders and heavy exposure to crime and instability in central and eastern Europe, was the strongest proponent of EU-level police cooperation, while France and the UK, traditionally jealous of their national prerogatives, were skeptical about the need for a strong Europol. As an interim step, in June 1993 the member states agreed to establish a European Drugs Unit as a precursor to Europol. Located in The Hague, it became operational in 1994. Its initial tasks were to collect and analyze information from national police forces about drug trafficking. However, it did not have the power to conduct criminal investigations or to maintain files on individuals.

The fifteen reached agreement on and signed the Europol Convention in July 1995, but only after a long delay caused by a dispute about the role of the ECJ that pitted Britain against the other fourteen member states.[11] The latter supported an article in the draft Europol Convention stipulating that the ECJ would be given the responsibility to resolve any dispute among the member states concerning the interpretation or implementation of the convention that the Council was unable to solve in a six-month period. The Netherlands, concerned about the power of the large states and about upholding the rule of law, insisted on such a provision; the UK, determined to maintain the strictly intergovernmental role of Europol and to preserve the autonomy of the British courts, refused to accept the article. The impasse finally was broken through an "opting in" provision reminiscent of the Social Protocol to the Maastricht treaty. All member states except the UK stated in an appended declaration that they would refer cases concerning the interpretation or implementation of the Europol convention to the ECJ, which is not explicitly referred to in the convention.

By June 1998 all fifteen member states had ratified the Europol Convention, and Europol formally became operational on October 1, 1998, absorbing the activities of the European Drugs Unit and acquiring new responsibilities to combat illicit trafficking in nuclear and radioactive substances, human beings, and vehicles as well as drugs, and money laundering related to these activities. It began with a staff of 155, including 41 European Liaison Officers representing different law enforcement agencies from all fifteen member states, that was projected to grow to 350 by 2003. It served primarily as a coordinating mechanism for the sharing of data and experience, including through the Europol Computer System. It was not given jurisdiction to conduct criminal investigations or to bring prosecutions on its own authority, but was charged with working through the national authorities.

THE EXTERNAL DIMENSION

Police cooperation in the EU also has an important foreign policy dimension. The most immediate threat to the security of the EU member countries no longer comes from conventional or nuclear attack, as was the case when the Warsaw Pact existed and the Soviet Union stationed hundreds of thousands of troops in the heart of Europe. External threats now come in the form of terrorism, illegal smuggling of people, weapons, and drugs, and the spread of nuclear, biological, and chemical materials that could be used to develop weapons of mass destruction.

Rampant corruption, organized crime, and the breakdown of order in neighboring states make dealing with these problems especially difficult. As is discussed in chapter 9, Italy and several other EU member states organized an intervention force for Albania in 1997 following the collapse of law and order that was precipitated by a political crisis and near–civil war linked to massive fraud in the financial sector. Elsewhere in the Balkans, one of the most pressing challenges following the end of the wars in Bosnia and in Kosovo was to establish strong, effective, and noncorrupt local police forces that could replace NATO peacekeeping forces and provide security against ethnic killing as well as combat the corruption that stifles economic revival.

In response to these threats, EU external policy in the 1990s placed a strong emphasis on police and judicial cooperation. The Europe Agreements used to help the candidate countries prepare for membership provided for expanded cooperation and technical assistance in these areas. Similarly, the common strategies toward Russia and Ukraine adopted by the European Council in 1999 called for expanded cooperation between the law enforcement authorities of these countries, Europol, and national police forces in the EU member states. Police and judicial cooperation also had increasing importance in relations between the United States and the EU, as both sides began to work together to address money laundering, cyber-crime, drug trafficking, and other crimes with a strong international character.

The Amsterdam Reforms

The justice and home affairs provisions of the Maastricht treaty did not work very well. In the first eighteen months in which the third-pillar provisions were in effect, the Council did not adopt a single common position. It adopted joint actions in only two cases, one dealing with Europol and one on a decidedly secondary issue—travel facilities for school pupils from nonmember countries resident in a member state. It also had adopted the text of a convention on simplified extradition procedures, but one that dealt only with cases in which the subject of the extradition agreed with the procedure. This convention was in any case not yet ratified and put into effect by the member states.[12]

The dismal performance of the EU with regard to third-pillar cooperation led to calls for reform. In its review of the treaty prepared for the reflection group that began work on the Amsterdam treaty, the Commission noted the second and third pillars used essentially the same intergovernmental decision-making procedures, but that "the two fields are utterly different. Foreign policy mainly has to deal with fluid situations, whereas justice and home affairs frequently involve legislative action which, because it directly affects individual rights, requires legal clarity."[13] The approaching enlargement to central and eastern Europe provided additional arguments to strengthen cooperation in justice and human home affairs, as the EU faced the prospect of incorporating new member states with weak traditions and administrative and judicial infrastructures in criminal and civil law, and of managing long and possibly unstable borders with Russia, Ukraine, and the Balkans.

The Amsterdam treaty instituted two major reforms, both essentially procedural: It incorporated the Schengen Agreement into the structure of the EU, making it part of the *acquis*, and it effectively "communitized" the areas of asylum and immigration, judicial cooperation in civil matters, and police and judicial cooperation in criminal matters by moving them out of the intergovernmental third pillar and introducing into the Treaty of Rome, by way of amendment, a new title called "Visas, Asylum, Immigration and Other Policies Related to the Free Movement of Persons." Much of what had been the EU's third pillar was moved to the first pillar, becoming subject to stronger and more uniform decision-making processes and to the binding jurisdiction of the ECJ.

With the entry into force of the Treaty of Amsterdam, the Schengen Agreement became the Schengen Protocol to the treaty.[14] Decisions about the control of external borders henceforth were to be made within the EU's institutional framework and involve the Commission and the Council rather than in a separate structure outside the Union. There still were many anomalies, however, reflecting the slow and uneven development of EU competence in this area. Ireland and the UK remained exempt from the Schengen Protocol, and there were special arrangements for Denmark, while Iceland and Norway, countries that long have had free movement arrangements with fellow Nordic countries Sweden, Denmark, and Finland, remained part of the Schengen area and participated in the Schengen Information System even though they were not members of the Union.

The "communitarization" of formerly third-pillar matters was accomplished in a cautious manner that reflected the lingering reluctance by member-state governments to surrender national powers in an area of political sensitivity. The new provisions (amendments to the Treaty of Rome introduced by the Treaty of Amsterdam) included derogations, long phase-in periods, and complex decision-making procedures that weakened the effect of the reforms. As with Schengen, Ireland and the UK secured the right to opt out of the provisions on asylum and immigration policy. In addition, the treaty divided implementation of the provisions on immigration, asylum, and police and juridical cooperation into two periods. During a transitional phase lasting five years from the entering into effect of the treaty (i.e., from May 1, 1999, to April 30, 2004) the Commission and the member states both had the right to submit legislative proposals, the European Parliament's role was limited to consultation and, most importantly, member states had to agree unanimously on all decisions. After this period, decision making was to revert to the procedures used in the economic area: the Commission would have the exclusive right to introduce legislation, the European Parliament the right of co-decision with the Council, and the Council could adopt decisions by qualified majority voting.

In addition to these important procedural reforms, the Amsterdam revisions included several changes intended to strengthen the rule of law and to bolster the rights of citizens. A new article inserted into the Treaty of Rome stipulated that the Council, acting unanimously on a proposal by the Commission and after consulting the European Parliament, "may take appropriate action to combat discrimination based on sex, racial or ethnic origin, religion or belief, disability, age or sexual orientation."[15] Although this sweeping, high-profile language signaled a new determination on the part of the member states to combat discrimination, it too was essentially procedural; it did not in itself guarantee rights or combat discrimination in any way. This still had to be accomplished through secondary legislation, generally in the form of directives that have to be transposed into national law. The unanimity requirement set a high barrier for passage of such legislation.

The Amsterdam treaty also adopted a new procedure for dealing with a serious and persistent breach by a member state of the principles of freedom and the rule of law. At the 1996–1997 IGC some member states floated the idea of a mechanism for expelling human rights violators from the Union. This was rejected as too severe and possibly helping to establish a legal basis for secession from the Union. Instead, the treaty stipulated that a member state may lose certain rights, including voting rights in the Council, if the other member states unanimously condemn its human rights practices. Under the procedure, the Commission or one third of the member states may propose a measure condemning a member state. The measure must be approved by a two-thirds vote in the Parliament, and then unanimously by the Council, meeting in the composition of heads of state and government. The country being singled out in the proposal does not vote. If the Council decides that the breach exists it may, acting by qualified majority, suspend certain rights under the treaties.[16] These provisions apply to all member states, but they clearly were adopted by the fifteen at Amsterdam with an eye toward enlargement to the former communist countries. The controversy in early 2000 over the formation in Austria of a coalition government including the far-right Freedom Party of Jörg Haider led to calls in the European Convention for a review and possible strengthening of sanctions on member states perceived as not meeting the standards set in the treaties.

Racism and Xenophobia

The new antidiscrimination provisions of the Treaty of Amsterdam reflected a growing sensitivity in the EU to issues of tolerance and equality in an increasingly multicultural Europe. With the upsurge of immigration in the early 1990s, Western Europe saw a growing number of racially and religiously motivated attacks on foreigners and immigrants. Anti-foreigner sentiment also was rampant in the applicant countries of central and eastern Europe, where it was fueled by high unemployment. While seeking to stem the flow of new migrants, member-state governments and the institutions of the Union also felt compelled to take action to combat anti-immigrant and other forms of violence and discrimination.

In 1995 the Commission presented a communication on racism, xenophobia, and anti-Semitism that was intended to initiate discussion in this area. This was followed by a decision in principle by the European Council, at the June 1996

Florence summit, to establish a European Monitoring Center on Racism and Xenophobia. The EU also designated 1997 as the European Year Against Racism, and in March 1998 the Commission issued an Action Plan Against Racism that contained concrete proposals aimed at changing public attitudes through education and other programs.[17] The action plan also was intended to start a debate on legislative action, which the Commission would be empowered to propose once the Treaty of Amsterdam went into effect.

The European Monitoring Center on Racism and Xenophobia was formally established in June 1997.[18] By decision of the Council, it was based in Vienna—an ironic and perhaps unfortunate choice given the rise of the Austrian Freedom Party with its pronounced anti-foreigner and anti-immigration program. The center's mandate is to provide objective, reliable, and comparable information on racism and xenophobia and to engage in research and documentation that will assist in formulating policies in these areas. It pursues these efforts in part through its own activities in Vienna, but also through a European Racism and Xenophobia Network linking universities and research centers in the member states.

The Tampere Summit

Implementing the provisions of the Treaty of Amsterdam to create a genuine "area of freedom, security, and justice" promised to take time and be fraught with controversy over many legal and practical details. Looking to the pending entry into force of the Amsterdam treaty, in 1998 the Council and the Commission drew up an action plan of concrete steps to realize this area. The European Council endorsed the plan and scheduled a special session, to be held in October 1999 in Tampere under the Finnish presidency, to evaluate progress in justice and home affairs cooperation.

At the Cologne summit in June 1999 the European Council had agreed to work toward adoption of a Charter of Fundamental Rights of the European Union by the end of 2000.[19] This proposal, pushed heavily by Germany, was designed to repair what was seen as a missing piece of the Maastricht and Amsterdam treaties, which affirmed human rights and freedoms already codified in national law and in Council of Europe conventions but that did not codify any rights specific to the citizens of the Union. The Tampere European Council established an ad hoc body responsible for drafting the EU Charter of Fundamental Rights. Composed of fifteen representatives of the member-state governments, one representative of the Commission president, sixteen members of the EP, and thirty members of national parliaments (two from each national parliament), this body became the model for a similar group that later drafted the European Constitution.[20]

The Tampere summit emphasized the importance of security and justice for citizens as a counterpart to the economic achievements of the Union as well as made some progress on implementation of the Amsterdam commitments. The most concrete achievement was an agreement to establish a Common European

Asylum System, the elements of which were to include a shared understanding of the method for determining the member state responsible for examining an asylum application, common standards for a fair and efficient asylum procedure, common minimum conditions of reception for asylum seekers, and the approximation of rules on the recognition and content of refugee status. The leaders also agreed to look into the question of providing financial compensation from EU sources to member states affected by sudden and unexpected influxes of refugees. Countries such as Germany and Austria that were likely to be affected by refugee surges generally favored compensation, while the UK was opposed.

Tampere made some progress on the issue of third-country nationals resident on the territory of the EU member states. The European Council endorsed efforts to approximate national laws on this matter and endorsed the principle that "long-term legally resident third country nationals be offered the opportunity to obtain the nationality of the member state in which they are resident."[21] Recognizing that third-country nationals (many from Africa, Asia, the Middle East, and the Caribbean) are often targets of discrimination, the European leaders again called for stepping up the fight against racism and xenophobia, based on the Commission's 1998 action plan.

The summit achieved more modest results with regard to the establishment of "a genuine European area of justice," a relatively new sphere for concentrated EU action. The Commission and some member states were in favor of approximation of laws covering serious crimes, but this met with stiff resistance from the UK and other member states. The European Council endorsed mutual recognition of judicial decisions as the cornerstone of judicial cooperation on civil and criminal matters, with approximation of laws to be pursued where necessary. In civil matters, for example, the European Council endorsed as a first step automatic recognition in other EU member states of national or local court decisions regarding small claims and family litigation (e.g., child support, visiting rights for parents). In the criminal sphere, they called for mutual recognition of court orders concerning search and seizure and measures to ensure that evidence lawfully gathered in one member state would be admissible in the courts of other member states.

Tampere also gave new impetus to longstanding efforts to improve cooperation in the fight against organized and transnational crime. The European Council called for measures to strengthen Europol and to broaden its areas of responsibility, as well as agreed to the establishment of a EUROJUST network composed of national prosecutors, magistrates, and high police officials that would help to coordinate the work of national investigators and prosecutors in actions against organized crime. Like most of the other measures agreed at Tampere, establishing EUROJUST required further legislative action by the Council of Ministers.

Enlargement

One of the criteria for accession adopted by the European Council in 1993 specifies that "membership requires that the candidate country has achieved stability of institutions guaranteeing democracy, the rule of law, human rights and respect for and protection of minorities."[22] In its July 1997 opinions on the level of preparation of the candidate countries for accession, the Commission concluded that all but one of the candidate countries met this criterion. The sole exception, Slovakia, subsequently improved its performance in this area following the elections of September 1998 that resulted in a more democratic government. The European Council recognized Turkey as a candidate for membership at the December 1999 Helsinki summit, but it was not asked to begin negotiations alongside the other twelve candidate countries, precisely because it did not meet the political and human rights criteria.

While the twelve countries that began negotiations in 1998 and 2000 were judged to have met the basic standard set by the Copenhagen criteria, they were being pressed to make further progress in this area during the pre-accession period. Traditions of rule of law in many of these countries are less developed than in Western Europe and were disregarded under communist rule. There were also shortages of trained judges, lawyers, and officials able to administer and enforce the law. In its reports on the progress of the candidate countries toward accession, the Commission singled out these factors as well as continued discrimination against the Roma (Gypsy) minority in many countries, protection of minority language rights (for example, of Russians in Estonia and Latvia), and safeguards against governmental interference in radio and television.

During the 1990s membership in the Council of Europe played a role in helping the candidate countries to prepare their legal structures for EU membership. The EU's PHARE (Pologne et Hongrie: Actions pour la Reconversion Économique) program of assistance for the candidate countries made justice and home affairs one of four priority areas for pre-accession work in central and eastern Europe. PHARE-funded projects included strengthening border police and customs administration through training and provision of equipment; help in preparing for Schengen implementation, including establishment of the requisite information systems, training for judges and administrators in dealing with asylum and migration issues in accordance with EU norms; and projects to strengthen the capacity of justice ministries and other institutions to combat corruption and organized crime. Most of these projects involved twinning arrangements with border guards, police forces, court systems, and other counterpart institutions in EU member states.[23]

Beyond the need to anchor democracy and the rule of law in the candidate countries themselves, the pre-accession process sought to prepare these countries to deal with immigration, international crime, and related problems in Russia, Ukraine, and other Newly Independent States (NIS) countries which, with enlargement, were to become the eastern neighbors of the Union. The current members of the EU insisted that the candidate countries tighten their own borders with non-EU countries as a condition of membership. The candidate countries were required to adopt the Schengen rules and become part of the Schengen Information System (SIS) as well as to adopt the EU's uniform visa policy. This meant that countries such as Poland that had allowed visa-free travel from Ukraine and Russia following the collapse of communism would have to begin to require visas for visitors from these countries.

Critics of the enlargement process argued that extending the justice and home affairs provisions of the EU treaties to the new member countries threatened to draw new lines in Europe and contribute to the isolation of countries such as Russia and the other NIS that were unlikely ever to join the Union. Proponents answered that secure external borders are a necessary concomitant to the single market and the free movement of peoples in the Union, and that new member states could expect to reap the gains of the latter only by accepting the former. In the end the candidate countries had no choice but to go along with the Justice and Home Affairs (JHA) *acquis* and to bring their policies into line with those in effect in the Union. To assist with this process, the EU offered at the December 2002 Copenhagen summit that settled the final terms of the enlargement additional financial aid to help the new member states underwrite the costs of training additional border guards, erecting guard posts, purchasing airplanes and helicopters, and upgrading their computer systems to facilitate integration into the SIS.

September 11 and the EU Constitution

In the period since the entering into force of the Treaty of Amsterdam and the Tampere European Council, two developments have shaped the evolution of EU justice and home affairs policy: the September 11, 2001, terrorist attacks on New York and Washington and the convening of the European Convention in early 2002 and the decision by the member states to adopt an EU constitution.

Whatever differences later emerged over the U.S.-led war on terrorism and the war in Iraq, Europeans initially reacted to the September 11 attacks with horror and warm expressions of sympathy for the American people. This sentiment was captured in the headline, "We are all Americans" that appeared in France's frequently anti-American newspaper *Le Monde* on September 12.[24] It was given concrete expression in statements by the EU and in NATO's decision, backed by its European members, to invoke Article 5, the defense and mutual assistance clause of the 1949 Washington treaty, in response to the attacks. In addition to expressing support for the United States, the Europeans pledged to work with each other and with the U.S. administration to reduce societal vulnerabilities and to combat the terrorist threat. This meant an acceleration or in some cases redirection of plans underway since Tampere to further develop JHA as an area of EU action.

The European Council held an extraordinary meeting on September 21, 2001, at which it approved a plan of action to combat terrorism.[25] The plan included measures to enhance police and judicial cooperation, for example, by replacing the cumbersome extradition procedures in use within the Union with a common arrest warrant, stepping up cooperation among member states to identify presumed terrorists and organizations that supported them in order to develop a common list subject to EU countermeasures, and setting up a special antiterrorist team within Europol. The European Council also called for new and more effective measures to cut off sources of funding for terrorists in Europe and around the world. To implement these measures, in September 2001 the Commission presented a Framework Decision on Combating Terrorism that the Council of Ministers adopted in June 2002.[26]

The heightened sense of the terrorist threat also gave new impetus to discussions of an expanded EU role in controlling external borders. The Tampere European Council endorsed closer cooperation and mutual technical assistance between member-state border services, particularly in the maritime area, and called for continued assistance with border control capabilities to the applicant countries in central and eastern Europe. Those countries most exposed to external migration long had pressed for Europeanizing responsibility for policing external borders, either through the establishment of a full-fledged European border authority or, at a minimum, some form of burden sharing. Other member states were skeptical of this idea.

September 11 tipped the balance of political momentum toward the Commission and those member states interested in some form of Europeanization of border control. The Laeken European Council of December 2001 asked the Council and the Commission to "work out arrangements for cooperation between services responsible for external border control and to examine the conditions in which a mechanism or common services to control external borders could be created."[27] In May 2002 the Commission presented a communication, *Towards Integrated Management of the External Borders of the Member States of the European Union*.[28] The main elements of the Commission plan were the establishment of a "common unit" of senior border control officials to oversee implementation of a common border control policy, procedures to exchange information among various sources, and the establishment of a Common European Border Corps with powers to check visas and passports and to apprehend individuals for the appropriate enforcement or preventive measures. The June 2002 Seville European Council endorsed the plan and initiated various pilot projects to develop joint capabilities, and the June 2003 Thessaloniki European Council asked the Commission to consider the establishment of a permanent EU institution dedicated to border control policy.[29]

In November 2003 the Commission put forward draft legislation to establish a European Agency for the Management of Operational Co-operation at the External Borders.[30] Scheduled to become operational under the Commission proposal in January 2005, the new agency would be small (i.e., with an initial staff of twenty-seven people) and would be charged with coordinating cooperation among member states in border control matters to ensure that national authorities apply and enforce the common EU policy to the same standards. The new agency also would assist with training of border guards, carrying out common risk assessments (i.e., of those categories of people seeking to enter EU territory that were most likely to become illegal immigrants), and conduct research and development relating to border surveillance. It would have neither the manpower nor the legal authority to police borders directly, although this was not ruled out as a long-term possibility.

In addition to stepping up efforts to control borders, the EU continues to work on implementing a European asylum policy, based on a common list of countries that pose human rights risks to their citizens. It has set up Eurodac, a database of fingerprints of asylum seekers that is intended to stop asylum seekers from "shopping" their requests around to the various member states and make it possible to determine which country first admitted an asylum seeker and thus has responsibility for granting or denying asylum. Other post–September 11 steps in JHA cooperation have included the formal initiation of EUROJUST, which became operational in December 2002 and was located in The Hague with Europol, the start of development work on a new Schengen Information System, SIS II, that will have upgraded investigative capabilities and be designed to work in an enlarged Union, and an initial decision to begin work on a Visa Information System (VIS) that will allow authorities in member states to exchange information on the issuing of visas to third-country nationals.

While progressing on these operational matters, the Union and its member states also were involved in the politically more exalted task of drawing up an EU constitution, an exercise certain to have implications for JHA policy making, given the inherently constitutional nature of issues relating to citizenship and the relationship between the state and the individual. As noted, the Tampere European Council established a body to draft an EU Charter of Fundamental Rights. In an exercise that engaged the interest of representatives from the EU institutions and the member states, including the national parliaments, this group produced a consensus document for presentation to the December 2000 Nice European Council. The content of the charter was largely based on existing documents such as the European Convention on Human Rights (ECHR) and the Social Charter, and thus was not in itself very controversial. It reaffirmed the ban in Europe on the death penalty, guaranteed freedom of thought, conscience, and religion, freedom of expression, freedom of assembly, and other basic freedoms, as well as prohibited "discrimination based on any ground such as sex, race, colour, ethnic or social origin, genetic features, language, religion or belief, political or any other opinion, membership of a national minority, property, birth, disability, age or sexual orientation."[31] In addition to these fundamental civil and political rights, the charter guaranteed a long list of social and economic rights, for example workers' rights to information and consultation within their places of employment, fair and just working conditions, consumer and environmental protection, and even a right to "good administration." Some critics suggested that guaranteeing such a long catalog of rights that were inherently difficult to define and that depended heavily on the performance of the European economies might tend to trivialize truly fundamental rights such as those contained in the Bill of Rights to the U.S. Constitution. In general, however, comprehensiveness of this kind had long been a feature of EU law and aroused little debate.

More controversial than content was the question of what form the charter would take and hence its legal status. Some in Europe favored the adoption of a binding European charter of rights that would become part of the founding treaties and thus be enforceable by action of the ECJ. Others were skeptical of this approach, which seemed like a huge encroachment on the traditional constitutional prerogatives of the member states and believed that the charter should remain a political declaration, with moral but not binding legal force. At Nice, the heads of the European Parliament, the Council of Ministers, and the Commission "solemnly proclaimed" the charter, but left the question of its ultimate legal status to the next IGC. This issue effectively was resolved by the European Convention, however, which decided to incorporate the entire charter, virtually unchanged, as Part II of the proposed draft constitution. This move aroused remarkably little controversy in the member states, where political leaders across the spectrum generally recognized that any constitution worthy of its name had to include explicit provisions relating to fundamental rights.

Conclusions

Europe continues to make progress on building the "area of freedom, security and justice" that was announced in 1997. Meeting in Brussels in December 2003, the European Council endorsed plans to have the European border agency up and running by January 1, 2005. It also welcomed progress on including biometric identifiers (fingerprints) in visas, residence permits, and eventually passports. It noted steps toward the development of the VIS and progress in Europol on measures to fight terrorism and narcotics trafficking. The European arrest warrant went into effect on January 1, 2004, albeit only in the eight member states that had managed to transpose the directive on time. Early in the same year, the Council of Ministers approved a €30 million fund to assist member states in dealing with the return of asylum seekers. The government of the Netherlands announced that it would make completion of the Tampere agenda an emphasis of its presidency in the second half of 2004.

These and many related developments were signs that the Union was making progress toward the goals established in Amsterdam and reaffirmed in Tampere. Looking at the bigger picture, however, it was less clear that the EU really was succeeding in creating an area of freedom, security, and justice, or at least one imbued with the positive content that was intended when European federalists, weary of continued debates over financial and economic rules, called for creating a "citizens' Europe" in addition to the euro and the single market. The mood in many ways had turned inward and negative, wary of enthusiastic calls for such a Europe and focused more on the dangers and drawbacks of freer movement across borders than on the opportunities. UN Secretary General Kofi Annan used a January 2004 speech to the European Parliament to chide Europe for not being more welcoming to immigrants, warning that "a closed Europe would be a meaner, poorer, weaker, older Europe."[32] In its own diplomacy, the EU seemed obsessed with negotiating re-admission agreements—arrangements under which illegal immigrants could be returned to countries from which they had come or that had allowed them to transit their territory. Jewish organizations complained about an anti-Semitic wave, a charge that may have been exaggerated but that nonetheless gained a credence from the worrisome number of attacks on Jews and Jewish institutions in some European countries. In France, the government moved to ban head scarves in schools, prompting debate throughout Europe about what was the proper way to respond to rising Islamic militancy, by reaffirming France's secular traditions or by making exceptions to those traditions in the name of religious tolerance. The March 2004 terrorist bombings in Madrid lent new urgency to the debate on these issues.

These issues all suggested that to create an area of freedom, justice, and security—one that would be recognized as such by the voters and that would command their allegiance—would have to be more than a bureaucratic process of drawing up regulations and passing laws. It would have to deal with deep questions relating to Europe's values and identity.

Notes

1. Text in Mark Janis, Richard Kay, and Anthony Bradley, *European Human Rights Law: Text and Materials* (Oxford: Clarendon Press, 1995), 468–82.

2. John Benyon, "Policing the European Union: The Changing Basis of Cooperation on Law Enforcement," *International Affairs* 70, no. 3 (1994): 507–9.

3. *Tindemans Report on European Union to the European Council*, EC Bull. Supplement 1/1976.

4. "A People's Europe: Final Report of the *Ad Hoc* Committee," Bull. EC 6-1985, 21–23.

5. *Agreement between the Governments of the States of the Benelux Economic Union, the Federal Republic of Germany and the French Republic on the Gradual Abolition of Controls at the Common Frontiers*, June 14, 1985.

6. Rey Koslowski, "Intra-EU Migration, Citizenship and Political Union," *Journal of Common Market Studies* 32, no. 3 (September 1994): 369.

7. European Commission, *Communication from the Commission to the Council and the European Parliament: On Immigration and Asylum Policies*, COM (94) 23, February 23, 1994, tables 1B and 1D.

8. *Convention Implementing the Schengen Agreement of June 14, 1985 between the Governments of the States of the Benelux Economic Union, the Federal Republic of Germany and the French Republic on the Gradual Removal of Controls at Common Frontiers*, 1990, *EEUL*, v. 2, 11-0016-11-0078.

9. Article 6 TEU, ex Article F.2.

10. Article 18 TOR, ex Article 8a.

11. *Convention Based on Article K.3 of the Treaty on European Union, on the Establishment of a European Police Office (Europol Convention)*, Brussels, July 26, 1995, O.J. C316/2.

12. European Commission, *Intergovernmental Conference 1996: Commission Report for the Reflection Group*, 51.

13. Ibid.

14. "Protocol Integrating the Schengen *Acquis* into the Framework of the European Union," *Treaty of Amsterdam*, 93–96.

15. Article 13, TOR.

16. Article 7 TEU; Article 309 TOR.

17. European Commission, *Communication from the Commission: An Action Plan Against Racism*, COM(1998) 183 final, Brussels, March 25, 1998.

18. Council Regulation (EC) no. 1035/97, June 2, 1997, O.J. L 151, June 6, 1997.

19. "European Council Decision on the Drawing Up of a Charter of Fundamental Rights of the European Union," Annex IV, *Presidency Conclusions: Cologne European Council, 3 and 4 June 1999*, SN 150/99 CAB, 43.

20. Presidency Conclusions, Tampere European Council, October 15 and 16, 1999, SN 200/99, Brussels, October 16, 1999.

21. Ibid.

22. *The European Councils, 1992–1994*, 86.

23. "Annex 3—Twinning Projects 1988–1999," in European Commission, *Regular Report from the Commission on Progress towards Accession by Each of the Candidate Countries: Composite Paper, 1999*, IP/99/751, October 13, 1999. This and other reports on the progress toward enlargement are available on http://europa.eu.int/comm/enlargement (accessed June 11, 2004).

24. Jean-Marie Colombani, "Nous sommes tous Américains," *Le Monde*, September 12, 2001.

25. Conclusions and Plan of Action of the Extraordinary European Council Meeting on 21 September 2001, SN 140/01.

26. Commission, Proposal for a Council Framework Decision on combating terrorism, COM(2001) 521 final, September 19, 2001.

27. Laeken Presidency Conclusions, paragraph 42.

28. COM(2002) 233 final, May 7, 2002.

29. Thessaloniki Presidency Conclusions, paragraph 14.

30. Proposal for a Council Regulation establishing a European Agency for the Management of Operational Co-operation at the External Borders, COM (2003), November 2003.

31. Article 21.

32. Kofi Annan, "Migrants Can Help to Rejuvenate an Ageing Europe," *Financial Times*, January 29, 2004.

Suggestions for Further Reading

Anderson, Malcolm, et al., eds. *Policing the European Union*. Oxford: Clarendon Press, 1995.

Meehan, E. *Citizenship and the European Community*. Newbury Park, Calif.: Sage, 1993.

Occhipinti, John D. *The Politics of EU Police Cooperation*. Boulder, Colo.: Lynne Rienner, 2003.

Robertson, A. H., and J. G. Merrills, eds. *Human Rights in Europe: A Study of the European Convention on Human Rights*. Manchester: Manchester University Press, 1994.

Springer, Beverly. *The European Union and Its Citizens: The Social Agenda*. Westport, Conn.: Greenwood Press, 1994.

CHAPTER 8

Europe as a Global Actor
TRADE AND FINANCE

The European Union (EU) accounts for about 20 percent of all world trade in goods, not counting trade within the Union, which no longer can be considered truly international (table 8.1). It is the world's largest exporter of goods, and ranks second to the United States in total imports. Unlike the United States, with its large and chronic trade deficits, the EU in recent years has had substantial trade surpluses with the outside world. Along with the United States, it is also the world's leading exporter and importer of commercial services. The size of the EU market has grown as successive enlargements have transformed once-important external trading partners into member states. The 2004 enlargement added another 80 million consumers to the EU market, and future enlargements to Bulgaria, Romania, and the Balkans for all practical purposes will mean the consolidation of the entire European continent—excluding most of the former Soviet Union—into a single trading entity.

The key instrument that makes the EU an international trading power is the common external tariff. Established by the Treaty of Rome and fully put in place by July 1, 1968, the tariff helped to consolidate the common internal market by eliminating the need (although not entirely, as was seen in chapter 4) for internal border checks to ensure that imported goods were not transshipped from low- to high-tariff countries within the European Community (EC). The common external

Table 8.1 Leading Exporters and Importers, World Merchandise Trade, 2002

(billions of dollars)

Exporters	Value	Share (%)	Importers	Value	Share (%)
European Union	939.0	19.1	United States	1202.5	23.2
United States	693.5	14.1	European Union	931.3	18.0
Japan	416.0	8.5	Japan	336.4	6.5
China	325.6	6.6	China	295.2	5.7
Canada	252.5	5.1	Canada	227.6	4.4
Hong Kong	200.6	4.1	Hong Kong	208.6	4.0
South Korea	162.5	3.3	Mexico	176.5	3.4
Mexico	160.8	3.3	South Korea	152.1	2.9
Taiwan	130.3	2.6	Singapore	116.2	2.2
Singapore	125.6	1.2	Taiwan	112.6	2.2

Source: World Trade Organization

tariff also increased the EC's bargaining power in international trade negotiations, since six countries began to negotiate as a unit. The member states remained members of the General Agreement on Tariffs and Trade (GATT), but the European Commission, as the executive arm of the Community, took over international trade negotiations for the six, both with individual countries and in the periodic multilateral trade talks carried out under the auspices of the GATT. With each enlargement, new member countries have had to give up their old tariff schedules to adopt the common external tariff. They also have had to adopt the Common Agricultural Policy (CAP), which has important implications for international trade. These enlargements have increased still further the relative weight of the EU in the GATT system and its international power to bargain.

The 1961–1962 Dillon Round of the GATT and the 1964–1967 Kennedy Round took place as the Community was establishing the common external tariff and were particularly important for setting the pattern of the Community's trade relations with the outside world. Customs unions can cause both trade creation and trade diversion, and the United States and other trade partners of the Community were concerned that establishment of the customs union and the common external tariff proceed in tandem with external liberalization to minimize its trade-diverting effects. By playing a positive role in these negotiations, the Community laid to rest the worst fears in Washington and other capitals about trade diversion. In the Dillon Round, the EC agreed to lower the planned external tariff by 20 percent. The Kennedy Round was even more ambitious, and reduced tariffs worldwide an average of 35 percent, with tariffs on some industrial goods reduced by as much as 50 percent.

Nevertheless, in its formative years the Community still had many difficulties in its trade relations with the rest of the world. The most problematic issue tended to be agriculture. Other countries regarded the CAP as highly protectionist and a major source of international trade tensions. The Community insisted that agriculture be kept off the table at the Kennedy Round, and it was not until the completion of the Uruguay Round in late 1993 that the EU reached an uneasy accommodation with its main trading partners over the issue of its agricultural subsidies and protection. Agriculture remains a bone of contention between the EU and its trading partners, however, as can be seen in the ongoing disputes with the United States and Canada over hormone-treated beef and genetically modified organisms and with the developing countries over farm subsidies.

Other countries also were concerned about the EC's widespread use of preferential trade and cooperation agreements that were concluded outside the framework of the GATT and that ran against the spirit, if not always the letter, of the most-favored nation (MFN) principle. The Treaty of Rome provided for "the association of overseas countries and territories with the Community with a view to increasing trade and pursuing jointly their effort towards economic and social development."[1] This provision was included at the insistence of France, which in the mid-1950s still had a large African empire in which it hoped to preserve a special role. When most of the overseas colonies became independent in early 1960s, the Community revamped its association relationships with these countries, concluding the 1963 Yaoundé Convention with eighteen independent African countries, all but one of which were former French, Italian, or Belgian colonies. The convention provided these countries with preferential trade access to the Community market as well as access to grants and loans. In recent years the EU has tried to tone down its use of preferential agreements, but reliance on them remains a source of international trade tension and was at the heart, for example, of the long-running U.S.-E.U. dispute over banana imports.

In the 1970s the EC also began to make heavy use of subsidies and non-tariff barriers (NTBs). By that time successive rounds of GATT negotiations had lowered tariffs worldwide, but they failed to arrest the growth of such barriers, including quotas, voluntary export restraints (VERs), and aggressive use of anti-dumping measures. The industrial countries increasingly resorted to these measures as the level of tariff protection fell and domestic industries were exposed to the full brunt of import competition. Many of these measures were directed against low-cost imports from the newly industrializing countries, especially in Asia.

The most significant NTB agreement was the Multi-Fibre Arrangement (MFA) that the EC, the United States, and the developing countries concluded in 1974. It limited textile imports to the industrial countries by a rigid system of bilaterally negotiated quotas. The MFA originally was justified as a temporary measure to assist threatened industries while they adjusted to competition, but it was repeatedly renewed in the 1970s and 1980s and expanded to include more categories of textiles as well as clothing, thus becoming a semipermanent feature of the international trading system. The EC was a strong proponent of the MFA system, and adopted a tough line in negotiations with such leading textile and clothing exporters as Hong Kong, South Korea, and Taiwan.

Cars are another area in which the EC adopted a high degree of nontariff protection, mainly against Japan. Italy had a national quota of only 2,500 cars that could be imported from Japan. France set a limit of 3 percent of its national market for direct imports from Japan. Spain and the UK also set national limits on market share—the UK a relatively generous 11 percent of the total market, Spain a derisory 1,000 units per year. These national limits—along with an EC-wide tariff on cars that was negotiated in the GATT—were allowed to persist in the common market until 1993, when they were abolished as incompatible with the single market. They were replaced by a voluntary export restraint agreement concluded by Japan and the EC in July 1991 under which the Japanese agreed to an overall annual quota of 1.23 million cars and light trucks by 1999, after which the quotas were to be abolished.

As will be seen, many of these EC trade practices were regarded as incompatible with the GATT, and they have been the subject of hard negotiations in the successive GATT rounds and the focus of disputes in the new World Trade Organization (WTO) that was established to supersede the GATT in 1995.

GATT and the Uruguay Round

Because of the sheer magnitude of its exports and imports, the EU has been, along with the United States, the major protagonist in the shaping of the international trading system in recent decades. The basic outlines of that system were established in 1947 by the GATT. There have been eight rounds of tariff reduction and trade promotion talks within the GATT, four of which took place in the late 1940s and 1950s before the EC was established. The first six GATT rounds dealt mainly with reductions in tariffs, which at the time were perceived as the main barriers to trade in goods. The last two rounds of trade talks—the 1973–1979 Tokyo Round and the 1986–1993 Uruguay Round—were concerned with tariffs as well, but they also began to deal with NTBs and, at Uruguay, new subjects such as services and investment. At Doha in 2001 the WTO launched a ninth round of trade talks, aiming at a new agreement by the target date of 2005.

The Tokyo Round took place in the mid- and late-1970s, a time of global economic crisis and rising protectionism linked to concerns in many countries about unemployment and recession. Its main proponent was the United States, which saw a new set of talks as a way to head off a worldwide drift to protectionism. Washington also wanted to repair the damage to its interests caused by the exclusion of agriculture from the Kennedy Round, and it entered the negotiations prepared to press the EC hard on this issue. The results of the round were mixed, however. The members of the GATT negotiated another 33 percent reduction in tariffs on industrial goods. By the end of the round, the tariffs of GATT-member industrialized countries had fallen to 4.5 percent, down from an average of 40 percent in the early 1950s.[2] The Community's tariff on some 9,500 items was a weighted average of 6.5 percent. In the end, however, the EC again refused to yield on agriculture, even though many other countries sided with the United States on this issue.

The Tokyo Round also produced nine nontariff codes on such issues as standards and technical barriers to trade, subsidies and antidumping measures, public procurement, import licenses, and civil aircraft exports in connection with government subsidies to industry. These codes were largely toothless and did not fundamentally alter the nature of the international trading system. However, they pointed to a growing recognition on the part of the GATT members that further tariff reductions in themselves were not enough to sustain world trade. In this respect, the Tokyo negotiations foreshadowed the Uruguay Round, which were to focus on establishing means to ensure that trade was free in fact as well as on paper.

Taking its name from the resort city of Punta del Este where the talks were launched in September 1986, the Uruguay Round lasted more than seven years before concluding, in December 1993, with some 26,000 pages of agreements, including a 550-page Final Act that was signed at a special ceremony in Marrakesh, Morocco, in April 1994. The Uruguay Round agreements went into force on January 1, 1995. The round completed the work begun at Tokyo and resulted in a major revamping of the international trading system. Its most politically visible result was the establishment of a new institution, the WTO, to replace the GATT. The new organization ties together the various trade agreements negotiated over the years under GATT auspices, including the Tokyo Round codes and the agreements negotiated in the Uruguay Round itself: the 1994 GATT agreement on trade in goods, a new General Agreement on Trade in Services (GATS), the Agreement on Trade-Related Aspects of Intellectual Property Rights (TRIPs), various agreements relating to dispute resolution and regular review of national trade policies, and four plurilateral agreements (operating under WTO auspices but not accepted by all WTO members) dealing with civil aircraft, government procurement, and trade in meat and dairy products. A separate agreement covers Trade-Related Investment Measures (TRIMS).[3] These agreements provide the framework in which the EU conducts its international trade policy.

The Uruguay Round covered four major areas affecting trade: (1) trade liberalization and market access; (2) trade rules; (3) new issues; and (4) institutional issues and dispute settlement.[4]

TRADE LIBERALIZATION AND MARKET ACCESS

Like previous GATT rounds, the Uruguay agreement improved market access for industrial goods by lowering tariffs. The EU reduced its external tariff an average of 37 percent for all goods from GATT member states and obtained roughly comparable tariff concessions from its main trading partners. For all products, developed country tariffs after the completion of the round fell to an average of just 3.9 percent. For some sectors—construction equipment, agricultural equipment, medical equipment, steel, beer, distilled spirits, pharmaceuticals, paper, toys, and furniture—the industrialized countries agreed to eliminate tariffs altogether. Under the 1994 agreement, the EU's average tariff on manufactures was to fall to 3.7 percent by 2000.[5]

Unlike previous GATT rounds, the Uruguay negotiations dealt with agriculture. The United States, scarred by its experience in the Tokyo Round and backed by a coalition of developing and developed country agricultural exporters, insisted that the negotiations address this sector and that they result in real changes in how CAP affected world markets. This was a very difficult issue for Europe, and one on which the Commission negotiators were on the defensive almost to the very end of the round. In the Blair House agreement of November 1992 the United States and the EU reached a bilateral deal that became the basis for the overall agreement accepted by all partners in the GATT. The EU was able to make concessions only because it was already committed to the MacSharry reforms aimed at drastically lowering the level of EU farm subsidies and at shifting from market intervention to direct income support.

The Uruguay agreement called for the phasing out of nontariff import charges—such as the CAP's long-established system of variable levies—with fixed import tariffs similar to those on industrial goods. For the "tariffed" items, the EU introduced duties based on the differences between internal and external prices in the base period 1986–1988. The actual tariff levels were still so high that they resulted in little actual trade liberalization, but with "tariffication" the EU could claim that its farm policies for the first time were fully compliant with its external obligations under the GATT and WTO agreements. Along with the United States and the other developed country signatories of the WTO Agreement on Agriculture, the EU was further committed to a 36 percent reduction in average agricultural tariffs by July 1, 2001. The EU also agreed to cut the level of its export subsidies over six years by 36 percent and to reduce the volume of subsidized exports by 21 percent over the same period.

The Uruguay negotiations also agreed finally to do away with the MFA for textiles and clothing. This was another awkward issue for Europe, albeit one that tended to unite it with the United States against the negotiators from the developing world. The developing countries entered the round insisting on ending a system that subjected their exports to strict country-specific quotas. They made clear that without satisfaction on this issue they would not respond to industrial country pressures for market opening in the industrial and service sectors. The developing countries eventually prevailed on this issue, as the round concluded with agreement to phase out all quotas and to dismantle the MFA system over a ten-year period ending in 2005. Even though many of the most restrictive quotas were to remain in place until the very end of the phase-out period, this measure proved controversial and pitted member states such as Portugal that were still dependent on textile and apparel production themselves against more advanced EU countries such as Germany. Apart from the obvious benefits for European consumers, the textile provisions of the Uruguay agreement were also helpful to EU exporters of textiles and apparel (mostly high-priced goods made in countries such as Italy and Germany) by opening markets to their products.

In addition to the main areas of tariffs, agriculture, and phasing out of the MFA, the Uruguay Round promoted trade liberalization in the area of government procurement. The WTO Agreement on Government Procurement strengthened the provisions of a previous GATT undertaking on government purchases, requiring its signatories (which included the United States, the EU, and Japan, but not most major developing countries) to make market access commitments for goods, services, and construction contracts by central governments, subcentral governments (e.g., states, provinces, and cities), and public utilities.

TRADE RULES

Building upon a start made in the Tokyo Round, the Uruguay agreements addressed trade rules and the circumstances under which countries are permitted to block imports for domestic economic reasons or to protect themselves from unfair practices in other countries. These rules cover antidumping, subsidies and countervailing measures, and safeguards.

The GATT allows countries to restrict imports that are dumped on their home market, that is, priced at "less than their normal value," when such imports cause harm to domestic industry. This is done by imposing a temporary antidumping duty that raises the final price of the imported good, usually by the margin of dumping. All countries agree in principle on the need for antidumping rules, but they vary widely in their views on what constitutes dumping and how these rules should be applied. Newly industrializing countries seeking to establish industries see nothing wrong with aggressive pricing aimed at establishing a market presence, while the EU, the United States, and other developed countries increasingly have resorted to antidumping measures, especially against imports from Asia, to protect domestic industries that claim to be the victims of unfair pricing.

In response to developing country complaints that antidumping cases were being used as a disguised form of protectionism, the Uruguay Round tightened the rules for applying antidumping duties, set new requirements for how authorities calculate dumping margins, and introduced a sunset clause requiring that anti-dumping measures be reviewed periodically and that they expire automatically after five years to prevent temporary relief for domestic industry from evolving into a permanent form of protection.

The Uruguay Round also tightened existing GATT rules on the use of subsid-ies to gain unfair trade advantages. It provided a precise definition of what consti-tutes a subsidy and banned all nonagricultural subsidies explicitly linked to the promotion of exports. As in the antidumping provisions, the Uruguay agreement allows countries adversely affected by subsidized exports, either in their home or third-country markets, to take countervailing measures, such as the imposition of duties, to neutralize the effect of the subsidy. The Uruguay agreement also was noteworthy for specifying precisely which government subsidies are permitted under international trading rules. These include support for research and develop-ment that does not contribute directly to the development of products traded on national and world markets, general aid to regions suffering high unemployment or where per capita income is less than 85 percent of the national average, and subsidies to help existing plants meet stricter environmental requirements. These exemptions are all important for the EU in that they permit EU research, regional assistance, and environmental policies to go forward without leading to problems on the international trade front.

The original GATT agreement of 1947 included various safeguard provisions allowing member countries to take temporary action against imports that cause "serious injury" to domestic industry or that result in general balance of payments problems. These provisions were much abused over the years, both by developed and developing countries. In the 1970s and 1980s the EU and the United States resorted to so-called "voluntary export restraint" agreements under which ex-porters in particularly sensitive industries "voluntarily" agree to hold down the level of their sales to another country to provide relief to its domestic industry. The Uruguay Round banned such voluntary agreements, which meant that the EU had to phase out its VER agreement with Japan relating to automobiles within a four-year period, or by the end of 1999. The agreement also tightened the defini-tion of "serious injury" and provided for the phasing out of safeguards after eight years, thereby preventing such measures from turning into permanent instruments of protection.

NEW SUBJECTS

The Uruguay Round tackled a long list of new subjects that had only been touched upon in the supplemental codes negotiated in the Tokyo Round. Like other developed economies, the EU derives an increasing share of gross domestic product (GDP), employment, and trade from services, a sector that was almost completely unregulated in the international trading order before 1994. Along with the United States, the EU pressed for and achieved, largely in exchange for concessions to the developing countries on textiles and other matters, the conclusion of a GATS as a natural complement to the GATT for goods. In theory, the GATS extends the MFN principle to trade in all commercial services. In practice, the GATS includes many exemptions, exceptions, and long phase-in periods. Many issues, including basic telecommunications, maritime transport services, and financial services were left to subsequent negotiations to be carried out after the completion of the round. Nonetheless, the agreement was an important breakthrough into a whole new area of market opening that resulted in specific commitments by the signatory states to open up markets in professional services (accounting, auditing, management consulting, and computer services), value-added telecommunications (e.g., electronic mail, voice mail, database retrieval), and tourism.

Besides services, the Uruguay Round opened up two other areas—foreign direct investment and intellectual property—for negotiation. A separate agreement on TRIMs limited the ability of states to enact national laws relating to investment that restrict or distort trade. Requirements that investors include a certain percentage of locally produced components in their manufactures or that they export a certain percentage of their production were banned. However, as in many other areas of the Uruguay package, the TRIMs accord was only a first step that included a large number of exemptions, long phase-in periods for the developing countries (five and seven years, depending on level of national income), and no mechanism for follow-on negotiations or sanctions against violations of the agreement.

Intellectual property rights are an important issue for the EU, as for the United States. Such property includes patents for pharmaceutical and chemical products, integrated circuit designs, sound recordings, films, books, and computer programs. Claiming that they lost hundreds of millions of dollars each year from pirated and counterfeited goods produced mainly—although by no means exclusively—in the developing countries, EU businesses pressed for action in this area. The Uruguay Round resulted in the conclusion of a separate agreement on TRIPs that strengthens protection for patents, copyrights, and industrial designs and that obliges countries to crack down on piracy and counterfeiting.

DISPUTE SETTLEMENT AND FOLLOW-ON NEGOTIATIONS

As trade agreements have become more comprehensive, uneven enforcement of domestic and international trade rules and the lack of redress with countries perceived as violating their international obligations have become pressing problems for many trading powers, including the EU and the United States. Partly at the urging of the EU, the Uruguay Round addressed these concerns by establishing new dispute settlement procedures within the context of the WTO. Under the Uruguay agreements, a government involved in a trade dispute is not permitted to resort to unilateral retaliatory action but is required to take the dispute to the WTO for resolution. The WTO establishes impartial panels of governmental and nongovernmental experts to rule expeditiously on particular disputes. There is also an appellate body that can review and overturn panel findings. If a country is found to be violating its trade obligations, the WTO can ask it to comply with those obligations or ask that it compensate those countries that are damaged by its noncompliance. If the country fails to act in this way, an injured country can request and receive permission for trade retaliation. After some initial hesitation based on a concern that they would benefit mainly the United States, the EU became a strong proponent of these more rigorous dispute settlement procedures, both because it shared with the United States a desire to crack down on rampant disregard of trade obligations in many developing countries and because it wanted additional leverage over the United States, which from the EU perspective has had a tendency to resort to unilateralist responses to trade disputes.

Since 1995, the mandatory dispute resolution provisions in the WTO agreements have been the most visible and politically controversial results of the Uruguay Round. In the late 1990s, the EU lost a number of high-profile trade disputes to the United States and then had great difficulty in amending its internal legislation to come into compliance with WTO rulings. At the same time, however, the EU has been an aggressive user of the WTO dispute resolution mechanism, particularly against the United States, and it has won a number of high-profile cases with which Washington, especially given congressional reluctance to amend laws in response to non-U.S. judicial rulings, also has had difficulty in complying.

In addition to setting up a permanent mechanism for adjudicating trade disputes, the Uruguay agreements contained commitments to launch new negotiations. This was mostly in areas where the parties had been unable to agree on major breakthroughs, or where the Uruguay Round's achievements were largely procedural—setting up new rules and institutions, with actual trade liberalization to follow in successive negotiations. Talks on government procurement of services, for example, were to start by July 1, 1997. More importantly, the parties were committed to new negotiations on services and agriculture. Under the terms of the GATS, the WTO member states were committed to entering successive rounds of negotiations, "with a view to achieving a progressively higher level of liberalization," beginning no later than five years after the entry into force of the GATS, or by January 1, 2000, at the latest. Similarly, under the terms of the Agreement on Agriculture, they were committed to launching a new round of talks on agricultural trade by the same date.

EXTERNAL TRADE AND THE INTERNAL MARKET

A recurrent question in the history of European integration has been whether the elimination of barriers within Europe would lead to higher barriers with the outside world. Would trade creation in Europe mean trade diversion from elsewhere, or would the development of an open European market contribute to broader trade liberalization that would benefit the United States, Japan, and the developing countries? In the late 1940s and early 1950s the United States actually *encouraged* the European countries to discriminate in favor of each other's products and against imports from the United States as a way of promoting economic revival. This was a temporary measure, however, designed to cope with the postwar economic crisis. By the early 1960s, the United States and other countries were concerned about the trade diverting potential of the common market, to which they responded by convening the Dillon and Kennedy Rounds of the GATT. The single market program of the 1980s also led to widespread concerns in the United States about a "Fortress Europe" that would be liberal internally but closed to non-EC exporters and investors.

As in the 1960s, these fears proved to be overstated, as completion of the single market program proceeded almost in parallel with the Uruguay Round and dealt with many of the same sectors and issues. For the most part, internal and external trade liberalization tended to complement and reinforce each other. As European countries dismantled barriers to trade and investment with other EU countries, they found it easier to take the same steps with regard to non-EU members. Conversely, the requirements of global trade liberalization pressed on the EU by the international community in the Uruguay Round helped to break down longstanding intra-EU barriers to the single market. The single market program made it easier for the EU to negotiate away the MFA in the Uruguay Round, since implementing the MFA entailed assigning national quotas within the EU market and maintaining border checks to ensure that textiles and clothing imported under one country's national quota were not shipped to and sold in another member state—all of which was incompatible with the internal market provisions of the Single European Act. French, Italian, and Spanish quotas on the import of cars from Japan also had to be abolished as incompatible with the single market, thereby making it easier for the EU to accept the ban on VERs in the Uruguay Round. Similarly, the EU was able to agree to the liberalization of services such as banking and telecommunications within the Uruguay Round largely because its member states had achieved a certain degree of liberalization within the EU itself. In this case, regional liberalization proved to be a precursor to global liberalization.

Nevertheless, there have been cases in which the lowering or elimination of barriers to intra-European trade has been accompanied by the raising of new or higher barriers to trade with the rest of the world. The well-known banana dispute between the United States and the EU in part grew out of such a case. Prior to 1993, bananas from Latin America (produced and sold by U.S. companies) entered Germany tariff free. To comply with an EU decision establishing a uniform regime for bananas, Germany subsequently imposed tariffs on so-called dollar bananas and joined its EU partners in giving preference—tariff free import—to higher cost, lower quality fruit from Europe's former colonies. In other cases the EU has tried to develop a European market by discriminating against products from outside. The EU's television directive, *Television without Frontiers*, was put into effect in

October 1991, ostensibly to ensure equal access throughout the EU market for EU productions. The most controversial element of the directive was a provision stipulating that member states "shall ensure where practicable and by appropriate means, that broadcasters reserve for European works . . . a majority proportion of their transmission time."[6] Clearly directed at limiting imports of American television programs and giving a boost to the EU's own industry, this provision resulted in EU-U.S. friction over audiovisual trade.

Looking to the future, the same conflicting tendencies—toward a more open Europe and toward a Europe that selectively closes itself off from global competition—are likely to contend in shaping EU policy. On the one hand, as globalization of the European economy proceeds, and especially as the largest and most successful EU multinationals come to rely increasingly on their exports to and investments in the world outside Europe, a Fortress Europe approach is becoming even less politically feasible and economically attractive than in the past. On the other hand, the sheer size of the EU market, the capacity of the EU to use this market to favor domestic suppliers or firms in countries that have preferential arrangements with the EU, and the political backlash in some quarters against globalization may increase the temptation toward some kind of economic regionalism on the part of the EU. Trade in agriculture already fits this pattern, and armaments are becoming an area in which pressure to buy European is growing. The Commission also has shown interest in developing EU technical standards as a way of challenging U.S. influence in the standard-setting process and perhaps of giving European firms advantages in home and global markets. Which of these tendencies prevails will depend in part on the future of the global trading system and the success of the post-Uruguay negotiations.

The Doha Round

THE BATTLE IN SEATTLE

As noted, under the Uruguay agreements the WTO member states were committed to beginning new negotiations on trade in services and agriculture no later than January 1, 2000. In addition to these built-in agenda items, many WTO members were keen on launching a new round of talks that, like the Uruguay Round, would cover the entire range of trade issues. The trade ministers of the WTO member states convened in Seattle on November 30, 1999, to decide the mandate and modalities for the new round of negotiations.

While the United States was lukewarm about a comprehensive new round (after a skeptical Congress refused to grant the Clinton administration "fast track" negotiating authority), the EU was one of its strongest proponents—in part because the Commission was eager to seize a leadership position on international trade issues, but also for tactical reasons. With the EU once again on the defensive for its agricultural protectionism, it preferred a forum in which agriculture would blend into a broader setting with other issues rather than be singled out in a separate negotiation. This would allow tradeoffs among other issues, enabling Brussels in effect to win acceptance of some agricultural protectionism by making concessions in other areas. It also could facilitate EU concessions on agriculture by creating a domestic political constituency for a broader agreement covering manufactured goods, services, market access, and new trade rules for investment and competition policy. Critics of EU negotiating tactics took a more skeptical view, suspecting Brussels of planning to thwart any real liberalization of agriculture by tying up the WTO in endless negotiations on issues such as competition policy that would be almost impossible to resolve in the 135-country forum.[7]

As the Seattle meeting approached, the Council of Ministers struggled to settle on a negotiating mandate for the Commission. Member states agreed on the desirability of pressing for a broad agenda and a comprehensive round but were divided on two important issues, the so-called cultural exception and labor rights. France wanted to sustain the position, extracted from the United States in a last-minute compromise that saved the Uruguay Round, that audiovisual trade be exempted from discussion in the new round. Other member states were sympathetic to the French view, but thought that pressing for such a blatant exclusion would undermine the EU's position in favor of a comprehensive round. On labor rights, Germany, with some support from other member countries, took a strong line on the need to establish a WTO working group on labor rights, a position vigorously opposed by the developing countries, which believed that discussion of such issues in the WTO context would be the opening wedge of a drive by the developed countries to use charges of "social dumping" to block imports from poor countries with lower wages and labor standards, thereby blunting the developing world's main advantage in the global economy. On agriculture, the fifteen had little trouble uniting behind a position declaring agriculture a "multifunctional" activity that fulfills social and environmental as well as economic roles. The EU wanted to see "multifunctionality" written into the Seattle ministerial statement that would set the agenda for a new round, a position that was opposed by the United States and the Cairns group of agricultural exporters, which saw this as providing a thinly disguised justification for continued high levels of protection.

After months of wrangling, the Council finally adopted a mandate that the Commission could take to Seattle and to preparatory bilateral talks in the United States. On labor rights, the EU ministers agreed to call for a "joint standing working forum" on globalization and worker rights, to be set up by the International Labor Organization (ILO) and the WTO. It was hoped that this position would be acceptable to the developing countries. On culture, the fifteen declared that the EU would "maintain the possibility to preserve and develop their capacity to define and implement their cultural and audiovisual policies for the purposes of preserving their cultural diversity."[8] This stopped short of the complete exception demanded by France, but left the Commission with limited room for negotiation.

The difficulties in agreeing to the Commission's mandate were just a foretaste of the problems that would be encountered in Seattle. Once the meeting got underway, thousands of protestors disrupted the proceedings, preventing delegates from reaching the official sessions and causing millions of dollars in damage to the downtown business district. The positions voiced by the protestors were confused and self-contradictory, but they reflected the degree to which nongovernmental organizations representing environmental, labor, human rights, and other concerns had made the WTO the focal point of protest against the perceived evils of globalization. On the one hand, the protestors accused the WTO of being like a secretive world government, behind closed doors reaching deals that affected the lives and livelihoods of ordinary citizens. On the other hand, the same protestors seemed to be castigating the WTO for *not* acting more like a world government—for not imposing stronger labor and environmental standards, especially on the developing countries. WTO Secretary General Mike Moore and others sought to counter the protestors with the argument that the ministers in Seattle were from democratically chosen governments and that the nongovernmental organizations in the streets could not arrogate to themselves the right to represent the public. President Clinton took a more sympathetic line, stating that the WTO process should be opened up "to all those that are demonstrating on the outside."[9] In what was widely seen as a move to placate organized labor on the eve of an election year, Clinton infuriated the developing countries by stating that he might support sanctions in the WTO framework for countries that abused labor standards. Inside the conference center, developing country ministers complained about their inability to influence the proceedings, which were dominated by the major trading powers, above all the EU and the United States. For their part, Brussels and Washington failed to make significant progress on the issues that divided them. In the end the meeting broke down, and the ministers headed home having failed to adopt a mandate to launch what many had come to call the Millennium Round.

THE ANTI-GLOBALIZATION MOVEMENT

The demonstrations in Seattle marked the most dramatic if not the first appearance on the international political stage of the mass anti-globalization movement. The basic message of the protestors was that globalization was driven by large corporations interested only in profit and that it was bad for people—in the developed world, where workers lost jobs as production shifted overseas, and in poor countries, where production was said to depend on low wages, substandard working conditions, and child labor. They also claimed that globalization was harmful to the environment, which in many places was being destroyed by rapid exploitation of the rain forests and the building of roads and dams to promote industrialization.

The response of European leaders to the wave of anti-globalization protests was complex. On the one hand, they argued that while the protestors had some valid points, they were not correct in their basic contention that globalization was bad—or at least necessarily bad—for people and the environment. Taking advantage of new developments in transportation and communications, poor countries could raise their standards of living and lift millions out of poverty by producing for the developed markets of the West. Workers in the developed world did indeed lose jobs as production shifted overseas, but as long as the overall rate of unemployment was low, they would find new and in many cases better jobs. Industrial development could damage the environment, but in general high environmental standards such as existed in Europe and the United States correlated with high standards of living rather than with poverty.

On the other hand, European leaders tried to associate themselves with the anti-globalization wave by arguing that globalization needed to be tamed through more and better governance at the local and global levels and that this in fact was what the EU was all about. In its *Strategic Objectives 2000–2005*, drafted in the shadow of Seattle, the Commission called for the EU to seize the initiative in the globalization debate and work to shape the globalization process in ways that will minimize its negative effects on culture, labor, and the environment:

> Globalisation opens up new prospects for trade, investment and technological development. But it does have certain negative side-effects. The process has turned out to be exclusive rather than inclusive and has widened the inequalities between countries and between social categories and regions within them. Moreover, the emergence of global actors with global strategies can have the effect of marginalising democratic mechanisms and jeopardising policies for sustainable development.
>
> Europe's objective must be to make globalisation compatible with the common interest of society. . . . The Union must work to secure greater coherence in the management of the world economy, gradual integration of the developing countries, sustainable development and the definition of new "ground rules," which are essential if the fruits of globalisation are to be divided fairly and benefit the largest number of people possible. Minimum levels should be established for competition, social and environmental standards and investment.[10]

Particular EU policies followed from or drew intellectual support from the emerging EU line on globalization. As had been the case in Seattle, the EU continued to press for international recognition of the multifunctional character of agriculture, purportedly to defend small and environmentally friendly farms against the interests of global agribusiness. Similarly, the EU continued its longstanding efforts to have the precautionary principle enshrined in international trade and environmental agreements, in its view to defend the environment and food safety against the dangers posed by unregulated flows of genetically modified crops and other potentially unsafe products. These arguments may have helped to dampen anti-globalization sentiment in Europe by deflecting hostility away from the EU, but governments in the developing world—the purported beneficiary of the EU's governance agenda—remained deeply suspicious of European motives. The Commission line on globalization also had a vaguely anti-American thrust, since its message seemed to be that only American-led globalization had harmful effects, while a more powerful EU that could check the excessive U.S. devotion to the market and to profit was in the interests of the peoples of Europe and indeed of humanity as a whole.

THE DOHA MINISTERIAL

The November 2001 WTO ministerial in Doha, Qatar, was the first major attempt by the WTO member states to pick up where Seattle had left off and to see whether a consensus could be reached on starting a new round of trade talks. The September 11, 2001, terrorist attacks of less than two months earlier lent a certain urgency to the meeting as they increased the incentives for governments to deliver results that could bolster business and investor confidence that had been badly shaken by the attacks and as they related at least indirectly to the problem of poverty in the Middle East (and the developing world more generally) and the need for the international economic system to begin addressing this problem. In formal terms, Doha was a success, in that it resulted in a negotiating mandate for a new round of talks among the WTO members, aiming at a new set of agreements by January 2005. Officially dubbed the Doha Development Round, the talks were to aim at a balance between further market opening measures of interest to the industrialized countries and commitments to a better deal for the developing countries, who generally thought that they had gotten too little out of the Uruguay Round.

The EU approached Doha hoping both to assert greater trade leadership in the international community and to achieve specific objectives with regard to agriculture, the environment, labor standards, and other issues. On agriculture, EU objectives were to fend off further pressures from other countries for the complete dismantling of the trade-distorting effects of the CAP and to secure recognition of the multifunctionality of agriculture—both for its own sake and as a line of defense for agricultural protection. Other WTO members were adamant that multifunctionality (like precaution) was EU jargon that should not appear in the mandate. On the environment, the EU's goals were to secure more explicit recognition of the relationship between multilateral environment agreements (MEAs) and WTO rules, gain endorsement of precaution in the negotiating mandate, and secure positive clarification of WTO rules to ensure the legitimacy of "eco-labeling."[11] The Union also needed to counter an overall perception on the part of other countries that its environmental agenda was, as the Commission itself summed up the prevailing external view, "driven by protectionist intent."[12]

As might have been predicted from the outcome in Seattle, the Doha negotiations were intense and hard fought. On agriculture, the EU was on the defensive throughout the talks. Apart from the EU, the WTO membership was nearly unanimous in holding that all agricultural export subsidies eventually should be phased out. France, tacitly backed by a few other EU member states, insisted that an advance commitment to phasing out subsidies was unbalanced and was blocking agreement on a mandate over this issue at the time the conference was scheduled to adjourn.[13] Talks were extended beyond the deadline, however, and in the end the EU agreed to accept negotiations aimed at "reductions of, with a view toward phasing out, all forms of export subsidies." The French were mollified by language stipulating that the outcome of negotiations on agriculture would not be "pre-judged," giving future EU negotiators leverage to condition acceptance of the elimination of subsidies on agreement on other elements of the agriculture package of interest to the Union. The Doha mandate did not endorse multifunctionality, but the ministerial declaration did contain the following concession to the Union: "We take note of the non-trade concerns reflected in the negotiating proposals submitted by Members and confirm that non-trade concerns will be taken into account in the negotiations as provided for in the Agreement on Agriculture."[14]

With regard to the environment, the ministers agreed to negotiations on the relationship between WTO rules and any trade obligations contained in MEAs, but the scope of the negotiations was carefully circumscribed. The Doha mandate stated that such negotiations "shall be limited in scope to the applicability of such existing WTO rules as among parties to the MEA in question" and that "the negotiations shall not prejudice the WTO rights of any Member that is not a party to the MEA in question." The parties agreed that there would be more dialogue between trade and environmental negotiating forums, but on the whole Doha did not sanction so-called "green protectionism," the use of trade barriers against countries perceived by their trading partners as having inadequate environmental standards. On precaution, EU negotiators failed to achieve explicit endorsement of this politically provocative term, even though in post-Doha assessments they emphasized that the negotiations had confirmed that precautionary regulation was consistent with WTO agreements.

On investment and competition policy, the EU entered the talks with ambitious objectives to launch new negotiations on these contentious issues. Widely regarded as protectionist by much of the rest of the world, these proposals were largely deferred. The ministers agreed that the WTO Working Group on the Relationship Between Trade and Investment and the WTO Working Group on the Relationship Between Trade and Competition would begin discussions in their respective areas of competence with a view toward possibly launching formal negotiations after the fifth WTO ministerial meeting in 2003. The EU and the United States both backed off from pressing the link between trade and labor standards in the way that they had in Seattle. The United States had ceased to favor such a linkage under the Bush administration (although support remained high in the Congress). The EU continued to argue that trade negotiations should encompass "a broad and regular dialogue on Trade and Social Development, which should include—but not be limited to—the issue of core labor standards," but in the end Doha resulted in nothing more than a perfunctory reaffirmation of the commitment to core labor standards and to cooperation between the ILO and the WTO, both of which had been agreed to at the first WTO ministerial meeting in Singapore in 1996.[15]

CANCUN

The next big test for the international trading system was the WTO ministerial in Cancun, Mexico, in September 2003. In the nearly two years since Doha, the working level negotiations in Geneva had produced few results, and the ministers gathered in Mexico with the task of giving new political impetus to the talks.

In the run-up to the round, international attention focused heavily on EU and U.S. agricultural subsidies. Whatever other differences they may have had, developing country governments and the anti-globalization movement based mainly in the developed world could agree that agricultural subsidies in the wealthy North depressed world food prices and resulted in agricultural surpluses being dumped on African and Latin American markets, making it impossible for farmers in poor countries to earn a living. Coming fresh from the sweeping reforms of the CAP agreed in July 2003, the EU claimed that it was no longer a serious offender in this area. While this argument was rejected by critics of the CAP, EU officials could take some comfort from the fact that the debate in Cancun was not being cast as one of the developed country agricultural exporters (United States, Canada, Australia, and so forth) *and* the developing world against the EU, but rather of the developing world against the EU and the United States, which was also being severely criticized for raising its agricultural subsidies in recent years.

However, the matter over which Cancun ultimately broke down was not agriculture but the so-called Singapore issues, named after the 1996 WTO ministerial where they were first raised. After downplaying and agreeing to defer these issues in Doha, the EU came to Cancun determined to make progress in four areas: investment rules, competition policy, transparency in government procurement, and trade facilitation. After five days of tough wrangling, the Mexican foreign minister chairing the talks declared that there was no basis for agreement and suspended the meeting. Led by a newly assertive G-20 grouping that included Brazil, India, and South Africa, the developing countries declared that none of the four issues of interest to the EU was negotiable. While negotiations were expected to resume in December as ministers attempted to pick up the pieces, the outcome in Cancun signaled a shift in the global order and the rise of new actors such as Brazil and China. For the EU, the outcome called into question the claims made in Europe, above all by the Commission, that the EU was the natural ally of the developing world and that there was a convergence between the latter's interest in a fairer trade deal and the Union's global governance agenda. Moreover, the anti-globalization protestors, who for the most part had been unable to make their presence felt at the remote Doha venue in 2001, were back in force at Cancun, protesting U.S. but also EU policies and world capitalism in general, and celebrating enthusiastically when the failure of the talks was announced.

INSTITUTIONAL ISSUES IN THE EU

The complexity of the Uruguay Round and that of the follow-on negotiations launched at Doha have focused attention on the process by which the EU negotiates and implements trade agreements. The EU's authority to negotiate trade agreements goes back to Article 113 (Article 133 in the Amsterdam renumbering) of the Treaty of Rome. Under the procedure established by this article, the European Commission is responsible for developing recommendations for the EC's negotiating policies for submission to the Council of Ministers. Once the Council approves the Commission's negotiating mandate (which is done by qualified majority voting [QMV]), the Commission is empowered to conduct negotiations directly with third powers. The individual member states refrain from direct participation in international trade negotiations that might give the appearance that they are conducting a national trade policy in contravention of EC law. G-7/8 consultations with the United States, Canada, and Japan on trade matters, for example, take place in a G-4, or "Quad," in which the European members of the G-7—Germany, France, Italy, and the UK—are replaced by the commissioner responsible for trade. Article 133 also provides for the establishment of a special committee appointed by the Council that oversees the work of the Commission as negotiations proceed. Consisting of senior officials from trade ministries of the member states, the 133 Committee has played an active but behind-the-scenes role in all trade negotiations, ensuring that any agreement negotiated by the Commission on behalf of the Union is acceptable to the member states.

These procedures for negotiating trade agreements can be cumbersome and have provoked complaints from both within and outside the Union. Prominent EU trade negotiators have argued that the Union has been unable to take a leadership role in world trade negotiations and unable to respond swiftly enough in bargaining situations because of its slow-moving decision-making process.[16] Countries that have negotiated with the EU often complain about a rigidity in its negotiating positions that results from the need to seek agreement among the member states. The position presented by the Commission in international forums such as the WTO inevitably is the result of hard-fought compromises among the member states in the 133 Committee. The Commission finds it difficult to change its position in the course of a fast-moving international negotiation, especially since any change in the international negotiating position may alter the balance of gains and losses accruing to the member states from any particular agreement.

The Uruguay Round's push into new areas of negotiation raised further questions about the relationship between the Union and the member states in the trade area. Because so many new subjects—services, intellectual property, investment—were included in the Final Act, the member states claimed that it was a mixed agreement, subject to both EU and member-state competence. The Commission argued that the Treaty of Rome made it the sole external negotiator on trade issues, and that these topics were covered under the Commission's trade mandate. In April 1994, just before the scheduled signing of the Marrakesh document, the Commission requested an opinion from the European Court of Justice (ECJ) on the subject of competence as it related to the new issues. Although in the past the Court had frequently strengthened the central powers of the Union by its decisions, it did not uphold the Commission's view. In its opinion, delivered in November 1994, the Court held that the exclusive right of the Commission to negotiate agreements on trade in goods did not extend to the full range of subjects covered in the Uruguay Round.[17] Authority over certain key aspects of trade policy—including many that are of growing importance in the services- and investment-driven global economy—were, in the Court's view, to be shared between Brussels and the member states.

In the 1996–1997 intergovernmental conference (IGC) on institutional reform the Commission urged an amendment of Article 133 of the Treaty of Rome to extend its authority over these issues, arguing that the EU's international negotiating position was undercut by this situation of dual competence. The member states were unwilling, however, to surrender permanently their negotiating authority in these areas. Instead, they added a paragraph to Article 133 stating that the Council, acting unanimously on a Commission proposal, could extend Commission competence to international negotiations and agreements on services and intellectual property. In the Treaty of Nice the member states finally agreed to extend QMV to trade in services, although France stubbornly and in the end successfully held out for retaining the national veto in trade in cultural and audiovisual services.

The negotiation of international agreements in the field of transport has been another area in which the EU has been struggling to sort out the respective roles of the Union and the member states. Since the 1980s, the United States has concluded bilateral "open skies" agreements with most of the member states of the Union. These agreements give U.S. air carriers the right to pick up passengers in one European country for subsequent transport to other destinations, in exchange for giving European carriers similar rights in the United States. The Commission has claimed that such agreements adversely affect the EU's internal market for aviation by distorting competition between airlines and airports in the Union. It has argued that the EU would have greater bargaining power with the United States if it were to negotiate as a unit, with the Commission conducting the talks with the aim of achieving a single U.S.-EU open skies agreement. After issuing repeated complaints against these agreements, in March 1998 the Commission initiated legal action against eight member states for their bilateral aviation treaties with the United States, sending a reasoned opinion to these countries stating the Commission's case that they were in breach of EU law.

In November 2002 the ECJ ruled on this matter, and largely sided with the Commission. The Court found that certain aspects of the bilateral agreements with the United States were in conflict with EU law in that they discriminated against non-national carriers from other EU member states trying to serve the U.S. market. The U.S.-German agreement, for example, discriminated in favor of German and against French carriers in the German market, while the U.S.-France agreement did the reverse in the French market. In both cases, these agreements undermined competition in the EU single market. However, the Court did *not* rule that the Commission had the authority to negotiate a U.S.-EU agreement, which required explicit authorization from the Council. The implication was clear, however. The member states would be forced to abrogate or renegotiate their bilateral agreements with the United States, and the best way to do this would be to replace all of these agreements with a single U.S.-EU accord that would create equal conditions for all EU-based carriers. Thus in June 2003 the Council voted to give the Commission a mandate to negotiate such an agreement, and the United States and the EU subsequently announced that they would begin talks on establishing a comprehensive "Open Aviation Area" between the EU and the United States.

Assuming that the EU over time can work out solutions to the competing claims of the Commission and the member states in the negotiation of international trade agreements in services and other non-goods trade-related areas, the most pressing institutional issues for the EU with regard to international trade will be those relating to implementation and enforcement. The EU is a strong supporter of a rules-based international trading system, which it sees as vital to restraining tendencies toward protectionism and economic unilateralism in the United States and the widespread tendency to flaunt international rules in the developing world. The EU and the United States both agree that strengthening the rule of international trade law will be essential if rising economic giants such as China and India are to be accommodated in the global economic system. But like other trading powers, the EU often finds it easier to launch legal action against real or suspected infringements of international trade rules by others than to comply with rulings against itself.

Adjusting domestic laws to comply with unfavorable trade rulings has been difficult in all countries, including the United States (where the Congress has been asked to amend several non–WTO-compliant trade, tax, and antitrust laws), but seems especially difficult in the EU, where the complex institutional and decision-making structure has hindered efforts to change laws and policies in response to WTO rulings that they are illegal. WTO panels ruled that the EU's banana import regime and its ban on the import of hormone-treated beef were illegal, but the EU was unable to comply with either ruling in a timely manner, as the member states, reflecting domestic economic interests and public opinion, blocked action in the Council of Ministers. To some extent the EU's problems in complying with global trade laws can be seen as an extension of the Union's own internal difficulties in applying its own single market legislation, as discussed in chapter 4. The ad hoc and uncoordinated bans on GMOs that member states have put in place are a probable violation of EU internal market and agricultural policy rules as well as a violation, in the U.S. view, of WTO rules that require health and safety regulations to be based on valid scientific findings.

Regional Trade Agreements

In addition to participating in the global trading system, the EU has developed special relations with important economic and political partners, including countries on the southern and eastern periphery of the EU, the former European colonies known as the African, Caribbean, and Pacific (ACP) countries, and regional groupings such as Mercosur. Within Europe, such relationships often have been a stepping stone to full membership in the Union. Outside Europe, these relationships have been based on a mix of historical and cultural ties, strategic interest, and economic motives.

THE EU's NEAR ABROAD

The European Economic Area (EEA). With the 1995 enlargement of the Union to Austria, Finland, and Sweden, only a handful of countries in what traditionally has been called Western Europe remained outside the EU: Norway, Switzerland, Iceland, and tiny Liechtenstein. This of course had not always been the case. The original EC of the six constituted a substantial portion of European economic output, but it did not include such important industrial countries as Britain or the Nordic and Iberian countries. Most of these countries were members of an alternative and much looser trade organization, the European Free Trade Association (EFTA), that included Austria, Denmark, Norway, Portugal, Sweden, Switzerland, and later Finland, Iceland, and Liechtenstein. Over time, the EC emerged as by far the stronger of the two organizations. Britain, along with Denmark and Ireland, joined the EC in 1973, largely to gain a seat at the table of the organization that increasingly set the economic rules and standards on the continent. EFTA continued to exist without its founder and largest member, but its remaining members had strong incentives to develop closer ties with Brussels.

In 1972–1973 the EC concluded separate free-trade agreements with all of the EFTA countries, under which by January 1, 1984, all customs duties and quantitative restrictions affecting bilateral trade were to be removed. In April 1984 the EC and EFTA issued a joint declaration calling for closer economic cooperation and the further elimination of barriers to trade through harmonization of standards, simplification of border procedures, and other measures leading to the creation of what was called a European Economic Space.[18] This agreement notwithstanding, the EFTA countries were in a weak bargaining position vis-à-vis the Community, and became concerned about possible exclusion from the Community's single market program. The EC had less to fear from EFTA, but it had important trade relations with its member countries and a keen interest in the issue of road and rail transit across the Alpine passes in Austria and Switzerland.

These interests came together in the conclusion, in May 1992, of an agreement to establish an EEA on January 1, 1994. The EEA essentially extended the four freedoms of the Treaty of Rome to the EFTA countries, in exchange for which the latter were compelled to adopt EU legislation on standards, competition policy, public procurement, and other matters. The EEA was never satisfactory from the EFTA-country perspective, however, given its highly asymmetrical character. The EFTA countries were obliged to accept decisions (including future decisions) taken in Brussels but had very little voice in making those decisions.

Voters in Switzerland rejected the EEA agreement in a December 1992 referendum. Austria, Finland, Norway, and Sweden entered the EEA, but decided to press ahead with applications for full EU membership. Voters in Norway rejected EU accession, but the other three countries completed the accession process and became full members of the EU in 1995. The EEA thus operated in its originally envisioned form for only one year—1994. The EEA continues to exist, but only as a relatively minor arrangement that integrates three EFTA countries—Iceland, Norway, and Liechtenstein—into the EU's single market.

Roughly three quarters of Norway's exports go to the EU, while two thirds of Norway's imports originate in the Union. Norway is especially important as a supplier of natural gas to the EU.[19] As an EEA member it has full access to the

Table 8.2 Extra-EU Trade in Goods by Main Trading Partner (billions ECU/EURO)

Exports To	1991	1995	1996	1997	1998	1999	2000	2001	2002
U.S.	76.8	103.3	114.9	141.4	161.6	183.0	232.5	239.9	242.1
Candidate countries	51.5**	70.7	86.0	105.0	116.8	118.5	151.3	152.8	164.0
DAEs***	35.3	65.6	70.2	77.7	60.1	62.0	81.6	81.9	78.2
Switzerland	43.6	51.0	51.5	53.0	57.2	62.6	70.8	74.8	70.7
OPEC	41.0	39.0	41.9	51.1	47.1	43.9	54.0	63.9	66.8
Japan	23.9	32.9	35.8	36.1	31.6	35.4	44.9	44.9	42.7
ACP	22.6	26.5	27.5	30.2	32.7	31.5	38.4	40.2	40.2
China	6.3	14.7	14.8	16.5	17.4	19.4	25.5	30.1	34.2
Russia	7.1*	16.1	19.1	25.5	21.2	14.7	19.9	28.0	30.5
Norway	14.2	17.5	19.8	23.4	25.1	23.2	25.6	26.2	26.6
Total Extra-EU-15	403.4	573.3	626.3	721.1	733.4	760.2	942.0	985.3	997.2

Imports From	1991	1995	1996	1997	1998	1999	2000	2001	2002
U.S.	97.0	103.7	113.1	137.9	152.0	160.6	199.0	195.6	175.5
Candidate countries	36.6**	55.5	58.8	69.9	82.7	92.8	117.8	134.1	143.0
DAEs***	43.2	54.4	57.9	68.1	77.9	85.2	109.4	98.1	91.9
Switzerland	37.3	43.2	42.8	45.1	49.5	52.9	60.0	60.8	58.7
OPEC	46.9	38.4	44.0	51.3	40.5	48.4	86.2	77.0	67.6
Japan	56.9	54.3	52.6	59.9	66.0	71.9	87.1	76.3	68.5
ACP	28.5	27.7	30.3	32.1	31.2	32.6	43.3	47.6	81.9
China	16.0	26.3	30.0	37.5	42.0	49.7	70.3	75.9	47.7
Russia	10.9*	21.5	23.4	27.0	23.2	26.0	45.7	47.7	46.5
Norway	21.4	25.5	27.9	33.7	28.1	29.6	45.8	45.1	44.8
Total Extra-EU-15	471.6	545.3	581.0	672.6	710.5	779.8	1033.4	1028.0	989.3

Source: Eurostat

* = 1992; ** = 1993; *** Dynamic Asian Economies (Hong Kong, South Korea, Malaysia, Singapore, Taiwan, Thailand)

Union market for goods, services, capital, and people, and grants reciprocal access to its own market. Free movement of people between Norway and the EU is further underpinned by its adherence to the Schengen agreement.

With the 1992 vote against the EEA, Switzerland indefinitely postponed its application for membership. Instead, it sought to develop a bilateral relationship that would preserve access to the EU market and gain participation in EU research and technology programs. In an arduous process of negotiation that began in December 1994 and took four years to complete, the EU and Switzerland concluded a package of seven bilateral agreements in the areas of free movement of persons, overland transport, air transport, agriculture, research, technical barriers to trade, and public procurement. Switzerland retained its access to the EU market and its right to participate in many EU programs, but it had to give way on EU demands that it lift a ban on 40-ton trucks from EU countries transiting Switzerland. The Swiss parliament approved these agreements in the fall of 1999, and the agreements came into force on June 1, 2002. Switzerland does not participate in Schengen, and in recent years it has had more differences than Norway with the EU over certain policy matters, for example, bank secrecy and Switzerland's subsidies to its national airline. But Switzerland is also highly integrated with the EU, which accounts for just over 60 percent of Swiss exports and nearly 80 percent of imports.

Given the high degree of integration that already exists, Norway and Switzerland both could at some point revive their applications for EU membership. In Norway, this would only happen if the government were confident that popular attitudes had changed sufficiently to ensure that there was little risk of a third rejection. At present, Euroskepticism remains high in Norway where it has been fueled by the intra-EU splits over the war in Iraq and the Stability and Growth Pact and bolstered by the rejection of the euro in neighboring Sweden and Denmark. In Switzerland, business and government elites are worried about isolation in Europe and for the most part favor membership. The EU remains unpopular with many voters, however, particularly in the German-speaking cantons, and a future referendum on accession might not succeed.

Other European Countries. Because of its size, wealth, and level of economic development, the EU came to dominate trade relations with the formerly communist countries to the east and southeast of the Union following the collapse of the planned economic systems in 1989–1991. These countries divide into three groups: those in central and eastern Europe that have become or soon will become members of the EU, the countries of the western Balkans, and Russia, Ukraine, and the other New Independent States (NIS) of the former Soviet Union.

Starting from a very low level during the communist period, trade between central and eastern Europe and the EU increased rapidly during the 1990s as these countries prepared for membership and were progressively integrated into the EU market. As shown in table 8.2, already by the mid-1990s the candidate countries as a group had become the EU's second largest export market, trailing only the United States. Economic relations were regulated by the so-called Europe Agreements, which were negotiated in the early 1990s and that established bilateral free-trade areas between the EU and each of the candidate countries as well as provided for the harmonization of health and safety standards, business regulations, and antitrust and other policies. With accession to the Union on May 1, 2004, the Europe Agreements between the EU and eight of these countries were terminated. Bilateral trade ceased to be external as these countries became part of the EU internal market. Bulgaria and Romania were not yet ready for membership in 2004, and their Europe Agreements with the Union will remain in effect until 2007 when they are expected to be admitted to the Union.

The countries of the western Balkans—Albania, Bosnia-Herzegovina, Croatia, Macedonia, and the federation of Serbia and Montenegro—are small and generally quite poor, and their integration into the EU market in some form as they recover from the wars of the 1990s is virtually a foregone conclusion. In June 1999, following the conclusion of the war between NATO and Serbia over Kosovo, the EU launched the regional Stability Pact for Southeastern Europe and offered to negotiate bilateral Stabilization and Association Agreements with each of the southeast European countries that participated in the pact. The latter agreements are very similar to the Europe Agreements in that they provide for the establishment of free-trade areas with the EU as well as cooperation across a wide range of policy areas.

Macedonia signed such an agreement with the EU in April 2001 and Croatia in October of the same year. At the Feira European Council in June 2000 the EU leaders declared the countries of the western Balkans "potential" future members of the Union, and Croatia in fact presented its application for membership in February 2003. As in the case of the Europe Agreement countries, the prospect of membership will accelerate the process of economic integration between these countries and the EU, although this naturally will take longer in the more economically backward and politically troubled parts of the region.

Unlike the Balkans, Russia, Ukraine, and the other NIS generally are not considered potential candidates for EU membership, at least in the medium term. However, they are becoming extensively integrated with the EU market and could at some point become part of a broader European trade area. The EU has concluded Partnership and Cooperation Agreements (PCAs) with these countries that, although they are not intended to lead to membership, are similar to the Europe Agreements in that they stress regulatory convergence with the EU. PCAs were signed with Russia and Ukraine in June 1994, Moldova in November 1994, Belarus and Kazakhstan in early 1995, and all but two of the remaining non-Baltic Soviet successor states by the end of 1996. The EU-Russia and EU-Ukraine PCAs both provide for the eventual establishment of free-trade areas, but negotiations toward such arrangements have not begun and are unlikely to do so until these countries are admitted to the WTO.

Along with the United States, the EU has been the main player in Russia's WTO accession negotiations, which hold the key to a full normalization of bilateral EU-Russia trade relations and to progress on the eventual establishment of the free-trade area called for in the PCA. The EU has been insisting on improved market access commitments in such areas as banking, financial services, and telecommunications and an end to the dual pricing of energy products that gives Russian industry an unfair subsidy that contravenes WTO norms. For their part, the Russians complain about restrictions on their access to the EU market for nonenergy products which have been constrained by sectoral agreements in steel and textiles and by Commission antidumping and antisubsidy actions.

Notwithstanding the differences over these issues, trade between Russia and the EU has grown rapidly in recent years, fueled by the dramatic rebound of the Russian economy from the crisis of 1997–1998. In 2001 Russia ranked as the EU's sixth largest national external market, accounting for €28.0 billion in exports and €47.7 billion in imports. The large surplus in Russia's favor reflects extensive Russian oil and gas exports, which comprise about half of all EU imports from Russia. Trade will expand even further with EU enlargement as countries such as Poland and the Czech Republic that traditionally were important trading partners for Russia are counted in the EU statistics and covered under EU-Russia trade agreements.

The Mediterranean. The countries on the southern and eastern littoral of the Mediterranean are in Africa and Asia, and their populations (with the noteworthy exception of Israel) are mainly Muslim. However, these countries are linked to Europe by geography, history, and economic interests, and they are considered by the EU as part of the "wider Europe" that for both economic and strategic reasons should be integrated more closely with the Union. Special economic ties with these countries go back many decades, and build upon relationships established during the colonial period when Algeria, Morocco, and Tunisia were controlled by France and Libya by Italy.

The island states of Malta and Cyprus are even more tightly bound to Europe by historic and religious ties. The EC concluded association agreements with Malta in 1970 and Cyprus in 1972. These agreements facilitated the growth of trade with these countries, both of which applied for full EU membership in 1990. Both were admitted to the Union on May 1, 2004, thereby becoming part of the EU's internal market.

Turkey and the EC signed an association agreement in September 1963, similar to the 1962 agreement between the Community and Greece that helped to pave the way to eventual membership of that country. The 1963 agreement referred to "the accession of Turkey to the Community at a later date."[20] It was followed in 1970 by the conclusion of an additional protocol to the 1963 agreement that came into effect in January 1973 and that stipulated that the two sides were to establish a customs union within a twenty-two-year period, or no later than the end of 1995. Despite deteriorating political relations between the two sides over human rights and other issues, Turkey and the EU finally concluded a customs union in March 1995, along with an accompanying package of ECU 375 million in financial aid for Turkey. The European Parliament threatened to disapprove ratification of the agreement over Turkey's human rights record, but under heavy prodding from the Commission and member-state governments finally approved it in December 1995, allowing the customs union to begin on January 1 of the following year.[21] The customs union does not extend to trade in services or agricultural goods, the latter an area in which Turkey is well placed to compete in EU markets.

Apart from its economic shortcomings, Turkey and the EU have differed over the long-term political significance of the customs union. Many in Western Europe saw the 1995 agreement as a substitute for EU membership, which Turkey applied for in 1987. Turkey, in contrast, regarded the customs union as a step toward EU membership, which remained a key Turkish objective. These differences were at least partially resolved in December 1999, when the European Council affirmed that Turkey was a candidate for EU membership. This is at best a long-term prospect, however, which means that the customs union agreement will govern Turkish-EU trade relations for the foreseeable future.

The other southern and eastern Mediterranean countries generally are not considered possible candidates for EU membership, although Morocco at one point did apply and EU membership for Israel sometimes is discussed and has been endorsed by a few politicians, notably Italian Prime Minister Silvio Berlusconi. The EC began to forge special trade and cooperation links with most of these countries in the 1970s, concluding cooperation agreements with Israel in 1975, Algeria, Morocco, and Tunisia in 1976, and Egypt, Jordan, and Syria in 1977. In 1978 the Community began to provide direct financial assistance to the Mediterranean countries in the form of grants from the Community budget and loans from the European Investment Bank (EIB).

With the coming into effect of the Maastricht treaty and the start of the Common Foreign and Security Policy (CFSP), the EU began to revitalize its policies toward this region by launching, at a special summit in Barcelona in November 1995, a new Euro-Mediterranean Partnership. Twelve countries of North Africa and the Middle East signed the partnership agreement. In the economic sphere, it called for the progressive establishment by 2010 of a free-trade area and for other measures to promote economic growth in the Mediterranean region, including financial aid and EIB loans. To implement the partnership, the EU has negotiated bilateral Euro-Mediterranean Association Agreements that supersede the earlier cooperation agreements and that are intended to liberalize trade between the EU and these countries and that encourage these countries to liberalize trade among themselves. By the end of 2003 the EU had concluded such agreements with Tunisia, Israel, Morocco, Jordan, the Palestinian Authority, Lebanon, Egypt, and Syria, although not all of these agreements had been ratified and put into effect. Other mechanisms designed to promote trade and investment in the Mediterranean include the EU's MEDA program of technical assistance and ministerial and subministerial working groups on regional integration, industrial cooperation, and other economic issues. The EU also has established a special EIB lending facility for the Mediterranean that began its activities in September 2002.[22]

Notwithstanding this impressive network of agreements and the other institutional mechanisms that underpin the Barcelona Process, many of the non-EU Mediterranean countries are not satisfied with EU trade practices, which from their perspective concentrate on opening markets for EU manufactured goods while restricting access for the agricultural products, cut flowers, fish, and textiles that these countries have to sell. To address these problems, Brussels has been negotiating supplemental protocols on trade and fisheries with several of the Mediterranean partners. In addition to lowering trade barriers, it is widely recognized that the success of cross-Mediterranean integration will depend heavily on investment and on the number and kind of European (and other) companies that set up operations in the region to serve local markets and to export to EU and third markets, thereby creating much-needed jobs for the region's burgeoning population.

THE ACP COUNTRIES

The ACP—African, Caribbean, and Pacific—countries are a group of seventy-seven former European colonies that have had preferential trade and economic relations with the EU going back to its foundations. The early years of European integration coincided with the great wave of post–World War II decolonization. To some extent these processes were linked, as European countries that previously had focused their political and economic energies on their empires redirected their attention to Europe. Even as they granted or were forced to grant independence to their colonies, the European powers sought to retain a degree of political and cultural influence in these countries, as well as preferential access to their markets. This was especially the case with France, which established the French Community of French-speaking countries in Africa. The Treaty of Rome provided for the association of the French, Belgian, and Dutch overseas colonies and territories with the original Community. An annex to the treaty established a European Development Fund (EDF) financed by member-state contributions to assist with economic and social development.

As the largest and most important colonies became independent countries, their relations with the EC were revamped in the 1963 Yaoundé convention, which provided preferential access to the European common market and continued access to aid from the EDF. With the accession of Britain to the Community in 1973, many former British colonies were made eligible for the same basic arrangement. In February 1975 the EC and forty-six ACP countries signed the first Lomé Convention. Named after the capital of Togo where the agreement was signed, the convention provided for a mix of trade concessions, development aid, and institutional association with the Community, including an ACP-EC council and a joint parliamentary assembly that meets once each year. Under the leadership of the largest ACP member, Nigeria, the ACP countries organized themselves into a loose grouping to negotiate collectively with the Community.

The first Lomé Convention ran for five years (1976–1980), and was followed by Lomé II (1980–1984), Lomé III (1985–1989), and the ten-year Lomé IV (1990–1999).[23] The number of ACP countries increased from the original forty-six to more than seventy. The EDF grew from ECU 581 million ($726 million) in its first five-year period to ECU 14.625 billion ($18.3 billion) for the 1996–2000 funding cycle.[24] This, along with bilateral assistance from the member states and other assistance provided from the EU budget (e.g., disaster relief and help in combating AIDS), made the Union and its member states by far the largest source of aid for the African and other ACP states, as well as their leading trade partner.

Despite this commitment of resources and the institutional continuity of the Lomé process, the Lomé conventions were criticized in the EU and the ACP countries on a number of grounds. Other countries criticized the Community for the preferential aspect of the Lomé agreements, which could divert trade from other partners. (The preferences are incompatible with the MFN provisions of the GATT/WTO, and have required a waiver that is granted by a vote of the GATT/WTO signatories.) The EU has defended these preferences as justifiable for development reasons, but critics point out that the ACP countries have been less successful than the East Asian and Latin American countries in industrializing and exporting manufactured products. In any case, the EU-ACP relationship has become relatively less preferential as the EU has developed special relations with its own periphery and as global trade barriers have come down.

When the European Commission sat down with the ACP countries in September 1998 to negotiate "Lomé V," the EU hoped to achieve radical changes in the next agreement. It proposed splitting Lomé into six regional agreements and favored a gradual phasing out of ACP trade preferences. The EU also wanted to include provisions in the new agreements relating to human rights, political freedom, and "good governance," issues that in the 1990s came to figure prominently in the EU's relations with its Mediterranean and European peripheries but that were not originally an element of its relations with the ACP countries. The ACP countries, many still among the poorest in the world, resisted these proposals. They were afraid that they would lose negotiating leverage in a regional approach, concerned about a perceived decline in their importance relative to central and eastern Europe and the Mediterranean, and wary of attempts to introduce political and human rights conditionality into longstanding trade and aid arrangements.

After nearly eighteen months of negotiation, in February 2000 the EU and the ACP countries reached a new twenty-year trade, development, and political package that reflected a compromise between these positions. Signed in Cotonou, Benin, on June 23, 2000, the new agreement extended the major provisions of the Lomé IV agreement for another eight years. It also stipulated that the EU and the ACP countries will negotiate, by 2008 at the latest, a set of regional trade agreements phasing out all barriers to trade. These agreements may include 12–15 year transition periods in which the ACP countries will retain their preferences. The regional agreements will encompass thirty-three of the largest and most economically advanced ACP countries. The thirty-eight poorest members of the group will not participate in these agreements, but will gain market access to the EU for "substantially all" of their products by 2005. The Cotonou Convention, as the new agreement was called, also contained a new aid package of €13.5 billion for the first five years of the agreement. The EU also managed to secure language on human rights and good governance, the latter a code phrase for efforts to combat corruption.[25]

Preferential trade relations and aid thus can be expected to remain a factor in EU-ACP relations, but their relative importance for both sides will decrease. For both economic and political reasons, the EU is looking to its own periphery and to larger markets in Asia and Latin America. For their part, the ACP countries understand that over the long run they must rely more on their own resources and look to new markets, including the United States, and to international organizations such as the International Monetary Fund (IMF), World Bank, and WTO to speed economic development.

For countries that are not members of the ACP, the EU participates in the UN-sponsored Generalized System of Preferences, under which developed countries grant tariff concessions to developing countries on a nonreciprocal basis. The EU has been unwilling, for commercial reasons, to extend participation in the Lomé agreements to certain large countries that are former European colonies, including India, Pakistan, and, more recently, South Africa after the establishment of black majority rule. It has been open to separate, less preferential agreements with these countries.

The 1995–2000 negotiations with South Africa toward such an agreement illustrate the difficulties the EU has had in reconciling its complex internal decision-making processes with its attempts to use trade agreements to serve broader economic and political objectives. Negotiations on a bilateral free-trade agreement began in 1995, after EU leaders promised President Nelson Mandela expanded cooperation in support of the post-*apartheid* transition, but they quickly bogged down. While pressing for expanded access to the South African market for European manufactured goods and for a dismantling of South Africa's extensive system of state aid for industry, the EU was willing to allow only 62 percent of South African agricultural exports to enter the Union duty-free after a ten-year phase-in period—up substantially from the 18 percent at the start of the talks, but short of what the South African negotiators were demanding in exchange for concessions in other areas.[26] As with other trading partners, the EU also took a very tough line on South Africa's use, in exports to Europe and in third markets, of product names originating in Europe for wines and spirits, demanding that it stop using such names.

The talks were not completed until October 1999, when the two sides concluded an agreement that even then several EU member states threatened to veto. Product labels remained a sticking point to the very end. South Africa provisionally agreed to phase out the use of the terms "port" and "sherry" on any of its products, but it balked at EU attempts to claim exclusive use of more than 150 "traditional expressions," including such terms as "ouzo," "grappa," "tawny," and "vin de pays."[27] For their part, the five major EU wine-producing countries—France, Greece, Italy, Portugal, and Spain—threatened to block the agreement if Pretoria did not yield. In the end, the difficult and protracted negotiating process left many in the South African government embittered against the EU and its tactics, thereby calling into question the very purpose of an agreement that was intended originally by the EU as a gesture of support for the new black majority government.

On a more positive note, in 2001 Brussels launched its "Everything But Arms" initiative, under which the EU grants duty-free access to imports of all products from the least developed countries without any quantitative restrictions, except for arms and munitions. The only exceptions were bananas, rice, and sugar, for which tariffs were to be reduced gradually so that they would be eliminated for bananas by 2006 and rice and sugar by 2009. This initiative applied to forty-nine countries, mostly small and all very poor. The EU also played a positive role in brokering an August 2003 WTO deal under which the poorest developing countries can receive at reduced cost access to pharmaceuticals needed in the fight against AIDS and other diseases.[28]

ASIA

East Asia is the world's most economically dynamic region and among the fastest growing potential markets for European exports. Trade between the EU and the dynamic Asian economies grew in the early 1990s, stalled later in the decade as these countries were hit by financial crises that severely depressed their economies, and then resumed rapid growth in 2000. Like their U.S. counterparts, European firms engage in much low-cost manufacturing of products in these countries to serve both third markets and the EU home market.

In 1993 the Pacific rim countries, including the United States, Canada, Chile, and the most important Asian countries, established a new forum, Asia Pacific Economic Cooperation (APEC), that met for the first time in Seattle. The EU was not invited to participate. At the time, APEC was widely seen as part of a U.S. strategy to prod the EU into taking a more positive stance in the then-stalled Uruguay Round. Determined not to lose economic opportunities and political influence, the EU stepped up its own economic diplomacy toward East Asia. The first Euro-Asian summit took place in Thailand in early 1996 and brought together the fifteen EU member states and the European Commission with the leaders of China, Japan, South Korea, and the Association of Southeast Asian Nations (ASEAN) countries to address an agenda that included trade, energy, and security. These meetings then were institutionalized on a biannual basis, with Euro-Asian summits taking place in London in 1998, Seoul in 2000, and Copenhagen in 2002. The EU also intensified its bilateral diplomacy with China and India and continued its series of annual summit meetings with Japan in accordance with a joint declaration signed in 1991. Much of the emphasis in EU policy and that of the member states in Asia has been on the expansion of trade and investment through such initiatives as the Asia-Europe Investment Promotion Action Plan, the Asia Europe Business Forum, and the Asia-Europe Environment Technology Center, all of which were agreed at the Bangkok meeting.

While in the 1980s and early 1990s European political and business leaders focused on the smaller dynamic Asian economies, in recent years attention increasingly has shifted to China and its seemingly inexorable rise to the status of an economic superpower. Along with the United States, the EU played the key role in determining the timing and conditions of China's accession to the WTO in December 2001. In 2002, China surpassed Japan as the EU's second largest trading partner outside Europe (after the United States), with a total trade volume of €115 billion. China enjoyed a €47 billion trade surplus with the EU, however, which Brussels would like to reduce by promoting European exports and ensuring that

China fully abides by its WTO commitments to open its markets. European firms are also major investors in China, accounting for 7.6 percent of aggregate foreign direct investment (FDI) in China at the end of 2000, compared with 8.9 percent for the United States and 8.1 percent for Japan.[29]

LATIN AMERICA

Latin America is an important market for the EU, and a region that is culturally linked to Europe through Spain and Portugal, the former imperial powers. European leaders have been concerned that the EU could lose out in trade with this region as the United States and Canada go forward with initiatives such as the North American Free Trade Agreement (NAFTA) (which includes Mexico) and the Free Trade of the Americas Agreement (FTAA) while the EU concentrates on its near abroad. The EU thus has stepped up its trade diplomacy with the region, in many cases building upon patterns of cooperation that were established decades ago.

The EC concluded cooperation agreements with Mexico in 1975 and with the Andean Pact (Bolivia, Colombia, Ecuador, Peru, and Venezuela) in 1983. It launched the San José process with the Central American countries in 1984 and it has since had regular meetings with the five members of the Central American Common Market and Panama to discuss trade and other issues. In late 1995 the EU concluded a Framework Agreement on Trade and Cooperation with Mercosur, the Latin American trade grouping of Argentina, Brazil, Paraguay, and Uruguay that to some extent is modeled on the original EC.

In November 1998 the EU and Mexico began negotiating a free-trade agreement. The two sides reached a tentative accord a year later, under which all tariffs on bilateral trade are to disappear by 2007. Mexico will grant EU suppliers improved chances to compete for public procurement contracts, better investment opportunities in financial services and telecommunications, and stronger protections for intellectual property. At the instigation of the EU, the first-ever summit of EU heads of state and government and their counterparts from Latin America and the Caribbean countries took place in Rio de Janeiro in June 1999. One of its results was an agreement between the EU and Mercosur to begin negotiations on tariff negotiations in July 2001, leading to a possible bilateral free-trade agreement. Progress on concluding such an agreement has been disappointingly slow, however, and has been hampered by continued differences over access by Latin American agricultural exporters to the EU market, public procurement, and other issues.

MULTILATERALISM VERSUS REGIONALISM

As European integration proceeds and interacts with other developments in the global trading system, notably the rise of East Asia and the retreat of the United States from undisputed leadership of the international economic system, some experts have expressed concern about what they see as a trend toward economic regionalism, possibly culminating in the creation of three huge trading blocs, one in Europe centered on the EU, one in the Americas that would be built around the U.S. economy, and one in East Asia that centered around China, Japan, or the ASEAN countries.

While participating in the GATT/WTO system, the EU always has been the main user of preferential regional trading schemes. As has been seen, it long has had such arrangements with countries on its eastern and southern peripheries, the ACP, and other regional trade groupings. In contrast, the United States and Japan traditionally shunned such arrangements, the former because it saw itself as the post-1945 champion of an open, multilateral system, the latter because it was relatively isolated by geography and culture and feared that economic regionalism would lead to Japan's exclusion from key non-Asian markets.

In recent years, however, the positions of the major economic powers with regard to regionalism have converged. The United States is now busily pursuing bilateral and regional free-trade agreements with many countries around the world, which it sees as catching up with the EU's long record of pursuing preferential agreements. The shift in U.S. policy began in the early 1990s with NAFTA and later continued with the negotiation, largely for political reasons, of relatively minor free-trade agreements with Israel and Jordan. But the Clinton and George W. Bush administrations both have pursued potentially more substantial arrangements, such as the proposed FTAA and the free-trade agreement reached with Australia in early 2004. Similarly, China is promoting the ASEAN + 1 proposal, under which Beijing and the ten ASEAN countries would create a free-trade area by 2010, while Japan concluded its first ever bilateral trade agreement in 2002, with Singapore, and the following year announced the start of bilateral trade talks with Malaysia, Thailand, and the Philippines. The EU, meanwhile, has been positioning itself as the leading champion of the global multilateral system without, however, abandoning any of its preferential agreements.

Balancing the merits of global multilateral versus regional approaches to trade will be a challenge for EU leaders in the coming years. Some experts and political leaders in Europe have expressed interest in creating an extended regional bloc that in their view would afford Europe greater protection against the vicissitudes of globalization as well as serve as a powerful platform from which the EU could promote its own ideas about governance of the global economic system. Following the launch of the EU Common Strategy for Russia in 1999, Brussels proposed the creation of a "common European economic space" embracing Russia and the EU. This concept was endorsed bilaterally at the May 2001 EU-Russia summit, and at their October 2001 Brussels summit Russia and the Union agreed to establish a high-level group charged with elaborating a concept for closer economic relations between the two sides and specifically with defining "the core elements which will need to be put in place in order to create a Common European Economic Area." Development of this common economic area also could be extended southward to the Mediterranean region, creating a vast co-prosperity space that in the view of a leading French research institution would enable Europe to hold its own in the year 2050 with North America and what it calls Greater China.[30]

But how such schemes would work in practice is unclear. Any sharp turn to regionalization of this kind is likely to be opposed by the major European multinational firms which, while they might derive some benefit from the protections that a regional bloc would offer, would lose far more from any trends that threatened these companies' access on an equal basis to the markets and investment opportunities of the other major economic regions, that is, North America and East Asia. Thus on balance the EU's position is likely to be one of continued commitment to an open multilateral system, albeit with a strong dose of economic regionalism and a willingness to use its position as a regional bloc at the core of other regional groupings in the ongoing competition with the United States, Japan, China, and other economic actors for markets, jobs, and profits.

The International Implications of the Euro
THE EURO AND THE DOLLAR

The launch of the euro on January 1, 1999, added a new dimension to the EU's role as a global economic actor. With the Economic and Monetary Union (EMU), many experts predicted that the world monetary system would evolve into an effective duopoly, with the dollar and the euro rivaling each other as the leading currencies and the European Central Bank (ECB) becoming a player in international monetary affairs at or nearly at the level of the U.S. Federal Reserve.

The argument for the euro rested heavily on an analogy with trade. As has been seen, the United States and the EU are the dominant players in the WTO, as they were in the previous GATT system. Without agreement between Washington and Brussels on key trade issues, global agreement is not possible. The situation in the world financial system has been quite different. Although as economic actors the United States and the EU are roughly comparable in size (table 8.3), the share of the dollar in international transactions has been far greater than that of the EU currencies, and larger than would be predicted based on U.S. shares of real economic activity. The dollar is the dominant currency held by central banks and ministries of finance in their official foreign exchange reserves, in international lending, and in the conduct of international trade (table 8.4). It is common for

Table 8.3   Basic Economic Indicators (2002)

	United States	EU	Euro-12
Population (millions)	282 (2002)	378 (2001)	300 (2001)
GDP (share of world, %)	21.1	19.7	15.7
Economic growth (annual average %, 1993–2002)	3.3	2.1	1.8
Share of world merchandise exports, %	14.1	19.1	—
Share of world merchandise imports, %	23.2	18.0	—

Source: European Commission; IMF

countries and firms that have no direct connection with the United States to use the dollar in private or governmental transactions—for example, when a Swiss bank lends money to an Asian country or when a Mexican firm exports a product to Africa. A key question is whether in the future more of these transactions will be carried out in euros, and what implications this might have for the EU, the United States, and the international system.

The effects of the euro most likely will be seen first in international trade. World trade in some commodities, for example oil and commercial aircraft, generally is priced in dollars. Traders may begin to use euros for some of these transactions, particularly in countries or regions that conduct a high proportion of their trade with the EU. This will eliminate the currency risk that European firms now face and put them on a par with U.S. competitors. The EU has been pressing Russia to begin pricing exports of oil and natural gas to Europe in euros, a move that would dramatically bolster the international status of the currency.

Over a longer time frame, public and private portfolio rebalancing is expected to occur. As can be seen in table 8.4, dollars account for nearly two-thirds of all official foreign exchange reserves held by central banks and finance ministries. The euro is likely to develop as an official reserve currency, as countries diversify their holdings from dollars to euros. One expert predicts that eventually the dollar and the euro each may account for about 40 percent of reserves, while the yen and other currencies account for the remainder.[31] Developing country governments that now tend to issue their debt in dollars may begin to borrow in euros.

What effects these shifts will have on the EU and U.S. economies are as yet unclear. European financial centers and companies may reap some benefits from the euro at the expense of New York- and other U.S.-based firms. European and other borrowers who earn the money to repay their debts mainly in euros will be better protected against rapid appreciation of the dollar that can increase their dollar debts (in real terms) overnight. Conversely, exporters of commodities that are priced in euros will be protected from real declines in the prices of their products caused by dollar depreciation.

Table 8.4 Currency Shares in Global Finance (percent)

	$ U.S.	All EU currencies	Japanese yen
Official foreign exchange reserves (1996)	64.1	21.2	7.5
Denomination of world exports (1992)	47.6	33.5	4.8
International private assets	37.9	33.5	12.4
International note and bond markets (1997)	50.0	28.0	12.0
International bank lending (1997)	45.0	17.0	4.0

Source: C. Fred Bergsten, *Weak Dollar, Strong Euro? The International Impact of EMU* (London: Centre for Economic Reform, 1988), 14

Officially, the U.S. government and Federal Reserve have welcomed the creation of the euro, which they note could help to make Europe a more dynamic and rapidly growing economy with better opportunities for U.S. exporters and investors. Nonetheless, loss of dollar hegemony could have some negative implications for the United States. A relative decline in the dollar's role might even make it more costly for the United States to borrow internationally. As a result of its chronic balance of payments deficits, the United States is the world's largest debtor country. Most of the money lent by foreigners to U.S. public and private entities is denominated in the United States' own currency, the dollar. But as international lenders have more opportunities to lend in euros, the rates at which the United States can borrow may increase.

INSTITUTIONAL ISSUES

Institutionally, the euro is transforming how Europe relates to the international financial system. Ever since the 1970s, the finance ministers and heads of central banks of France, Germany, Italy, and the UK have been represented in the G-7. With a single currency and monetary policy, it would be logical to expect the emergence of a G-3 comprised of the United States, the EU, and Japan. For the moment this is not happening, however, since fiscal and other economic policies (not to mention the many political issues dealt with by the G-7) are still partly or entirely decided at the national level. Assuming that something like a G-3 eventually does emerge, a key question will be whether this will hinder or facilitate EU-U.S. harmony and promote better, less crisis-prone management of the international financial system. On the surface it would seem that a directorate of three would be more workable than a larger grouping of more disparate powers. In practice, however, it is unclear how effective G-3 coordination would be compared with the pre-1999 system. With its cumbersome decision-making processes, the ECB could have difficulty in reacting to a worldwide financial crisis that required immediate attention.

The Maastricht treaty also contained certain ambiguities relating to international monetary policy that could hinder decision making. The treaty stipulated that the EU can conclude formal agreements on an international exchange rate system in which the euro participates only with the unanimous agreement of the member states in the Council, acting on a recommendation from the ECB or the Commission. In the event that the international community wanted to overhaul fundamentally the post–Bretton Woods monetary system, the treaty set a very high hurdle to EU participation. Such a case is unlikely, given the technical and political difficulties associated with moving back to anything like a system of fixed exchange rates, but over the long term it cannot be dismissed altogether. None of the post-Maastricht treaties—Amsterdam, Nice, or the proposed Constitutional treaty—fundamentally altered these provisions.

More relevant to current and medium-term policy were the Maastricht treaty's provisions on exchange-rate policy in the existing system and on the negotiation of ad hoc or informal currency arrangements, such as the Plaza and Louvre accords negotiated by the G-7 in the 1980s to bring down the value of the dollar. The treaty stipulated that the Council—in this case ECOFIN—will formulate "general guidelines" for exchange-rate policy based on recommendations from the Commission or the ECB, and always after consultation with the ECB. The Council may act by QMV. This allows for conflict between the political leaders of the EU and the ECB over exchange rate policy, such as was seen in late 1998 and early 1999 when the left-wing governments of France and Germany pressed the ECB to adopt more accommodative policies to stimulate growth.

The treaty was especially vague on the question of how the EU can negotiate informal or ad hoc monetary agreements. It left the question of who is to negotiate on behalf of the EU to a future decision by the Council, acting by QMV on a Commission recommendation after consultation with the ECB. The treaty merely specified that "these arrangements shall ensure that the Community expresses a single position."[32] This provision could come into play if, for example, the political leaders of the EU wanted to establish "target zones" for the euro in relation to the dollar and the yen. This idea was floated by the French and German finance ministers in late 1998, but resisted by the ECB and in any case rejected by the United States, which would have to agree to such a scheme.

The treaty also was not definitive on the question of representation of the ECB and the Eurosystem in international forums. It states only that the Council should decide this question by QMV. As the start of the euro approached, the EU not surprisingly sought to avoid tough choices by proposing additional seats in international forums for the institutions of EMU, rather than the consolidation of national positions into a single EU representation. In November 1998 the Commission proposed that the single currency be represented in the G-7 meetings of finance ministers and central bank governments by a triad of the Commission, the ECB, and the finance minister of the country holding the rotating presidency of the eurozone (if this was not France, Germany, or Italy), in addition to the existing national representations (finance ministers and central bank governors) of these three countries. (The UK, a non-euro country but still an EU member, also would be represented on the G-7.) This approach threatened to worsen what is already an absurdly overrepresented position for Western Europe in the G-7, and was rejected by the United States. Under a compromise worked out in early 1999, the national central bank governors of the euro countries do not attend the first half of G-7 finance meetings, when purely monetary issues are addressed. They do join the second part of the meeting, however, when the agenda is broader.[33]

The proposed EU Constitution stresses the importance of ensuring that the euro is adequately represented in the international system and that the eurozone countries speak with one voice on monetary and related issues, but it does not contain any radical institutional innovations. The Constitution stipulates that the members of the eurozone shall "coordinate their action among themselves and with the Commission with a view to adopting common positions within the competent international institutions and conferences" and allows for the possibility of establishing a "unified representation" in such institutions and conferences, which can be done, presumably on a case-by-case basis, by decision of the Council, acting on a proposal from the Commission.[34] What the Constitution does *not* do, however, is establish anything like an EU or eurozone finance ministry that would represent the EU internationally. Such a step, which could be done supranationally by assigning more powers to the Commission or intergovernmentally by creating something like a Mr./Ms. Euro along the lines of the Mr. CFSP (the High Representative for CFSP) established by the Treaty of Amsterdam, has remained a bridge too far for member states interested in retaining their status as players in international monetary affairs.

EMU AND THE GLOBAL ECONOMY

While institutional issues as they relate to global economic affairs are important, it could be argued that the more important question for the international system is internal to the EU: How and for what purpose will it pursue a unified economic and monetary policy? In particular, how will the ECB manage the possible trade-offs between price stability and the pursuit of other economic objectives such as higher growth and lower unemployment. As a newcomer to the international financial system, the ECB clearly saw a need to establish its credibility as a successor to the Bundesbank by fulfilling its Maastricht treaty commitment to maintaining price stability. As ECB president Duisenberg told a Washington audience in September 1999, "the most important task and challenge of the Eurosystem is to build up a track record of actual price stability in the euro area. Action speaks louder than words. Showing in practice that we are capable of providing stable prices is what really counts. We have to ensure that European citizens are confident that the euro is a currency which can sustain its value over time, and that the ECB is an institution which they can trust. The ECB should be perceived as an institution that says what it does and does what it says."[35]

But whether this continued very heavy emphasis on price stability is warranted has become a matter of debate, both in Europe and internationally. During Stage II of EMU, Europe experienced relatively slow economic growth, in part because governments were forced to rein in spending in order to meet the Maastricht criteria and as central bankers kept interest rates relatively high to combat lingering inflation in the system. With the euro launched, the trade unions and some left-wing political leaders expressed a desire see the ECB and the Eurosystem take measures to stimulate economic growth. Even in Washington there was concern that the ECB might have a tendency to pursue tight-money, slow-growth policies that could impart a deflationary impulse to the world economy. U.S. officials expressed a hope that economic growth in Europe would accelerate so that it could absorb more imports from the crisis-ridden developing countries. As the euro moved toward and ultimately fell below parity with the dollar in early 2000, U.S. Secretary of the Treasury Lawrence Summers spoke out against what he called the "complacency of diminished expectations" in Europe and Japan that resulted in acceptance of continuing slow rates of economic growth and of growth based largely on exports rather than increased domestic demand.[36]

This pattern continued into the early 2000s, despite the persistence of slow economic growth and the dramatic rise of the euro. Economic growth in the EU hit 1.6 percent in 2001, compared with only 0.3 percent in the United States, but in 2002 U.S. growth was 2.5 percent compared with 1.1 percent in the EU, a pattern that was repeated in 2003 and 2004 (see table 8.5). Throughout this period, the ECB continued to hold interest rates higher than in the United States, arguing that the European economies needed further structural reform before they could profit from lower rates. Although many in Europe were skeptical about the underpinnings of U.S. economic performance, which they saw as based on an unsound combination of huge federal budget deficits, an unsustainable trade deficit, and high levels of household borrowing, others expressed concern about the persistent gap in rates of growth, and called for renewed efforts under the Lisbon process to increase Europe's long-term growth potential. The euro was certain to play a key role in these efforts, but it was not in itself a cure-all for the economic challenges of the twenty-first century.

Table 8.5   Relative Performance of the EU and Euro Area

	EU-15	*Euro area*	*United States*	*Japan*
Real GDP growth (%)				
1991–2000	2.1	2.1	3.2	1.4
2001	1.6	1.5	0.3	0.4
2002	1.1	0.9	2.5	0.3
2003	0.7	0.5	2.9	2.7
2004 (est.)	1.9	1.6	4.7	3.0
Inflation (%)				
1991–2000	2.7	2.6	2.1	0.1
2001	2.4	2.4	2.4	−1.6
2002	2.5	2.4	1.1	−1.6
2003	2.1	1.9	1.6	−2.5
2004 (est.)	1.8	1.7	1.7	−1.8
Current account balance (% of GDP)				
1991–2000	0.1	0.3	−1.7	2.4
2001	0.2	0.9	−3.8	2.1
2002	0.7	1.0	−4.7	2.8
2003	0.1	0.4	−5.0	2.9
2004 (est.)	0.1	0.5	−4.7	3.8

Source: Eurostat; OECD

Notes

1. Article 3.

2. Hugo Paemen and Alexandra Bensch, *From the GATT to the WTO: The European Community in the Uruguay Round* (Leuven [Louvain, Belgium]: Leuven University Press, 1995), 27.

3. The texts of all of these agreements can be found on the website of the WTO, at www.wto.int/english/docs_e/legal_e.htm (accessed June 11, 2004).

4. These categories and much of the analysis that follows is based on Jeffrey J. Schott, *The Uruguay Round: An Assessment* (Washington: Institute for International Economics, 1994); and European Commission, *The Uruguay Round*, Background Brief 20, Brussels, March 14, 1994.

5. World Trade Organization, Trade Policy Review Body, *The European Union: Report by the Secretariat—Summary Observations*, July 1995, on www.wto.int/english/tratop_e/tpr_e/tpr_e.htm (accessed June 11, 2004).

6. Philip R. Schlesinger, "Europe's Contradictory Communicative Space," in *Daedalus* 123, no. 2 (1994) *(Europe through a Glass Darkly)*, 31.

7. Michael Smith et al., "Anything but Agriculture," *Financial Times*, November 19, 1999.

8. Neil Buckley, "EU Agrees Position for Trade Talks," *Financial Times*, October 25, 1999.

9. Francis Williams, "Clinton Is Sympathetic to Concerns," *Financial Times*, December 1, 1999.

10. European Commission, *Strategic Objectives 2000–2005*, 8.

11. "Trade and Environment: What Europe Really Wants and Why," Commission Memorandum, Doha, November 11, 2001.

12. "Proposals For a New Round," EC discussion paper, October 2000.

13. Guy de Jonquières and Frances Williams, "Trade Talks Falter as France Blocks Farm Subsidy Deal," *Financial Times*, November 14, 2001.

14. WTO, "Ministerial Declaration: Ministerial Conference, Fourth Session, Doha, 9–14 November 2001," WT/MIN(01)/DEC/W/1, November 14, 2001.

15. "Prospects For a New Round," EC discussion paper, October 2000. See Rorden Wilkinson, "The WTO in Crisis: Exploring the Dimensions of Institutional Inertia," *Journal of World Trade* 35, no. 3 (2001): 397–419, esp. 411.

16. Paemen and Bensch, *From the GATT to the WTO*, 93.

17. Opinion 1/94, *Competence of the Community to Conclude International Agreements Concerning Services and the Protection of International Property*, ECR I-5267-I-5422 (1994-11/12).

18. Bull. EC 4-1984, 9-10.

19. Economist Intelligence Unit, *Norway: Country Profile 2003* (London: EUI, 2003), 44.

20. *Agreement Establishing an Association between the European Economic Community and Turkey*, Ankara, September 12, 1963, O.J. 3687 (1964).

21. *Decision I/95 (96/142/EC) of the E.C.-Turkey Association Council on Implementing the Final Phase of the Customs Union*, O.J. L35/1 (1996).

22. *Euro-Mediterranean Conference of Ministers of Foreign Affairs, Naples, 2-3 December 2003: Presidency Conclusions*, in *Euromed Report*, Issue no. 71, December 5, 2003.

23. *Fourth ACP-EEC Convention*, Lomé, December 15, 1989, O.J. L229/3 (1991).

24. Christopher Piening, *Global Europe* (Boulder, Colo.: Lynne Rienner, 1997), 184.

25. European Commission, EU-ACP Negotiation, Information Memo no. 10, "Conclusions of the Brussels Ministerial Conference Held on 2 and 3 February," Brussels, February 4, 2000.

26. Caroline Southey, "Compromise Sought as Talks Break Down," *Financial Times*, October 21, 1998.

27. Victor Mallet, "Pretoria Condemns EU Wine Policy," *Financial Times*, November 5, 1999.

28. "EU Strongly Welcomes WTO Deal on Generic Medicines," EC press release, August 30, 2003.

29. European Commission, *A Maturing Partnership: Shared Interests and Challenges in EU-China Relations*, COM(2003) 533 final, September 10, 2003.

30. Institut français des relations internationales (IFRI), *Le commerce mondial au XXIe siècle* (Paris: IFRI, 2002).

31. C. Fred Bergsten, *Weak Dollar, Strong Euro? The International Impact of EMU* (London: Centre for European Reform, 1999), 15.

32. Article 111(3) TOR, ex Article 109(3).

33. I wish to thank C. Randall Henning for clarifying this point.

34. Article III-85b, draft Constitutional Treaty.

35. "The Past and Future of European Integration: A Central Banker's Perspective," 1999 Per Jacobsson Lecture, Washington, D.C., September 26, 1999.

36. Stephen Fidler and Gillian Tett, "Summers Urges More Structural Reforms," *Financial Times*, January 22–23, 2000.

Suggestions for Further Reading

Hayes, J. P. *Making Trade Policy in the European Community*. New York: St. Martin's Press, 1993.

Henning, C. Randall. *Cooperating with Europe's Monetary Union*. Washington: Institute for International Economics, May 1997.

Messerlin, Patrick A. *Measuring the Costs of Protection in Europe: European Commercial Policy in the 2000s*. Washington: Institute for International Economics, 2001.

Paemen, Hugo, and Alexandra Bensch. *From the GATT to the WTO: The European Community in the Uruguay Round*. Leuven (Louvain, Belgium): Leuven University Press, 1995.

Piening, Christopher. *Global Europe*. Boulder, Colo.: Lynne Rienner, 1997.

CHAPTER 9

Europe as a Global Actor
FOREIGN POLICY AND DEFENSE

The European Union's (EU) emergence as a global economic power inevitably raised questions about its potential as a political and military power, able to defend its political and security interests with the same level of commitment and unity that it brings to the economic sphere. In the heady days after the collapse of communism, there was great optimism that following decades of security dependence on the United States, Europe again could be the master of its strategic destiny. The Maastricht treaty established the Common Foreign and Security Policy (CFSP) as the second pillar of the EU and called for the creation of a European Security and Defense Identity (ESDI).

For the most part, however, progress in the second pillar has been a disappointment to advocates of a stronger and more integrated Europe. The EU failed to resolve the crisis in the former Yugoslavia in the early 1990s and ended the decade still mired in Balkan conflicts. It was unable to arrest the economic crises in Russia and Ukraine, and it still plays only a limited role in the Middle East and other world regions. Recognition of the failures of CFSP led to reforms in the Amsterdam treaty and to the development of new political and military structures intended to give the EU an autonomous capacity for military action. Little was done to upgrade Europe's military capabilities, however, and the Iraq war of 2003 exposed deep rifts among the EU member states in how they viewed the international situation and approached relations with the United States. In late 2003 the troika of Britain, France, and Germany began working together to reassert an EU role in global affairs, for example by negotiating with Iran regarding its nuclear weapons program and by stepping up defense cooperation. The problem of a European political and defense identity was likely to persist, however, as it reflected the different historical traditions and attitudes of the EU member states.

The Cold War Legacy

One of the reasons why the EU has had such difficulty in developing a strong CFSP is the legacy of the Cold War and the long period of security dependence on the United States. Acceptance of this dependence was not foreordained. As was seen in chapter 1, after World War II the West European countries took a number of steps toward political and security integration that did not involve the United States. In March 1947 Britain and France concluded the Treaty of Dunkirk in which they pledged to come to each other's defense if either was attacked by Germany. In March 1948 Britain, France, and the three Benelux countries signed the Treaty of Brussels that also contained a mutual defense clause and that provided for a standing consultative council of foreign ministers. In September of that year the five formed a Western Union Defense Organization to coordinate military planning. One objective of the Brussels treaty was to create a collective European framework that would encourage the United States to take a more active role in European security (much the way the Organization for European Economic Co-operation [OEEC] facilitated American economic involvement in early postwar Western Europe), but it also served as a possible fallback against American disengagement.

At the time it was unclear whether the West European countries would be forced to fend for their own security or whether they would succeed in forming an alliance with the United States. The United States had withdrawn most of its troops from Europe after World War II and initially had no plans to depart from its long tradition of "no entangling alliances" by concluding a peacetime military alliance with its wartime allies. As the Cold War deepened, however, views in Washington shifted. In April 1949 the United States, Canada, and nine European countries signed the Treaty of Washington establishing the North Atlantic alliance. The key provision of the treaty, Article 5, stated that an attack on one or more signatory states "shall be considered an attack against them all" and that in the event of such an attack the members would take actions deemed necessary, including the use of armed force. The treaty also provided for establishment of a council of member states and for regular consultations on issues of common concern.[1]

Communist North Korea's attack on the South took place in June 1950—a month after then-French foreign minister Robert Schuman made his bold proposal for what became the European Coal and Steel Community (ECSC)—and led to three further developments that shaped the security order in Europe. First, fearing that war in Europe was imminent, the United States decided to rearm West Germany and to include it in the Western alliance. Second, the alliance established the permanent peacetime command structure that became known as the integrated NATO military command and that took over the responsibilities of the Western Union Defense Organization. Third, in order to deter against a possible Soviet attack, the United States dramatically increased its military presence in Western Europe. General Dwight D. Eisenhower was appointed the first allied supreme commander and by 1952 the United States had raised its troop strength in Europe to 346,000 from a postwar low of 145,000.[2]

With the United States committed to the defense of Europe and to the rearming of West Germany, a key question became how to integrate a reviving German power in the Western alliance system. Initially, there was some hope that the structures of the ECSC could be extended and adapted to the defense realm. Had this hope been realized, Western Europe would have had a defense component from the very beginning of its integration process in the early 1950s. But Europe was unable to realize the plans for a European defense community at this time. As a result, NATO became the dominant security organization for the remainder of the Cold War era. It was not until the Maastricht treaty of the early 1990s that the European states again tackled the question of adding a security dimension to European integration.

Although the Korean War led many in the West to conclude that West German manpower was needed if there was to be a chance of stopping a Soviet attack in Europe, there was still great reluctance, especially in France, to see Germany rearm so soon after World War II. As in the case of the ECSC, French leaders saw integration as a way of tapping into German resources while ensuring that Germany would not emerge as an independent threat in the heart of Europe. In October 1950 French prime minister René Pleven proposed the establishment of a European army whose forces would be drawn from the six ECSC states. The Pleven Plan as such was not adopted, but it led to a follow-on proposal for a European Defense Community (EDC) with the same membership as the ECSC. Like the ECSC, the EDC was to be a supranational organization with its own common institutions and budget. A council of member states would oversee a supranational executive. The EDC and the ECSC would share the same parliamentary assembly. National military units would be retained up to the division level, but they would be commanded by an integrated general staff. The EDC would develop common equipment and infrastructures. The proposed European army would constitute the military contribution of the six powers to NATO and would operate within the NATO framework.

In May 1952 the six ECSC countries signed a treaty establishing the EDC and a European army. It soon became apparent, however, that the EDC was too ambitious for the Europe of the 1950s. Misgivings about the plan arose in all of the signatory states, but were strongest in France, where the Gaullists on the right and the communists on the left opposed submerging their national army in a supranational organization. In August 1954 the French National Assembly voted not to ratify the EDC treaty, effectively killing the project.

The collapse of the EDC project caused consternation in Bonn, Washington, and other Western capitals and led to a frantic search for an alternative security arrangement that would satisfy U.S. interest in German rearmament, French concerns about a revival of German power, and West Germany's own insistence on rough equality of status in the Western alliance. Adopting a proposal by British Prime Minister Anthony Eden, the West European governments agreed to a new arrangement under which West Germany and Italy acceded to the 1948 Brussels Treaty, making both countries members of a modified Western European Union (WEU). Under the terms of their accession to the WEU, both countries agreed to accept limits on their production of certain sophisticated conventional weapons and to forswear the development and possession of nuclear, chemical, or biological weapons. West Germany also became a member of NATO, and pledged to place its armed forces entirely under the NATO integrated command.

The WEU thus served as a legal mechanism for integrating West Germany into Western security structures. However, the WEU lost its original operational significance. The West European powers effectively abandoned their efforts to create a distinctly European military organization with a European military force. Military integration went ahead under NATO rather than European auspices, with the dominant role played by the United States. Security integration in Europe thus developed on a separate track from the intensive economic integration that had been launched by the six in the ECSC and that was soon followed by the European Community (EC) and Euratom.

The Quest for a European Pillar

The failure of the six founding members of the ECSC to establish a European defense organization led back to a focus on economics and thus indirectly to the founding of the second and the third European Communities, the EC and Euratom. Scarred by their experience with the EDC, the founding members steered clear of foreign and defense matters in the treaties of 1957. Indeed, Article 223 of the Treaty of Rome specifically exempted production and trade in arms, munitions and war materiel from the strictures of the common market.[3]

To be sure, elements of a Community foreign policy were implicit in the Treaty of Rome. The treaty established a European Development Fund (EDF) and provided for the conclusion of association agreements between the Community and third countries. Over time, the Community became involved in a wide range of activities with international implications, including trade and development assistance, humanitarian aid, international environmental matters, international transport and telecommunications policies and, in Euratom, the implementation of safeguards against the spread of nuclear technologies to non-nuclear states. But these were all examples of what political scientists call "low politics"—spillovers from the Community's involvement in day-to-day economic life. Fundamental issues of war and peace, or "high politics," remained the province of the member states rather than the Community.

The member states pursued rather different foreign policies, especially after de Gaulle's return to power in 1958. France became critical of American policy toward Europe and the global economy, and eventually withdrew from the NATO integrated command in 1966. West Germany and the other member states continued to align their foreign policies more closely with that of the United States. The Community and its member states thus faced what many saw as an increasingly anomalous situation: in some international forums, for example, the General Agreement on Tariffs and Trade (GATT), the EC spoke with one voice, whereas in others the member countries went in different policy directions. While each member state preserved its diplomatic freedom of action, the EC as a whole lacked influence on the global stage because of its failure to develop a common foreign policy.

EUROPEAN POLITICAL COOPERATION

Prospects for foreign policy cooperation brightened in the late 1960s after de Gaulle's departure from politics and as the Community looked toward its first enlargement. At the Hague summit in December 1969 the leaders of the six asked the Community foreign ministers to prepare a report on progress toward "political unification." The foreign ministers concluded that "efforts ought first to concentrate specifically on the co-ordination of foreign policies in order to show the whole world that Europe has a political mission."[4] To that end, they recommended the launch of what became known as European Political Cooperation (EPC). They agreed to "consult on all questions of foreign policy" and where possible to undertake "common actions" on international problems. They further agreed that the Community foreign ministers would meet at least every six months and that a committee of political directors (the highest-ranking civil servants in each foreign ministry) would meet at least four times each year to prepare the ministerial meetings.

EPC took place outside the structures and institutions of the Community. The member states agreed as sovereign states to consult and if possible to arrive at common positions. They did not agree to pool sovereignty or to delegate decision-making authority to supranational institutions. The Commission and the Court of Justice thus did not have competence in foreign policy matters, making EPC a much weaker form of cooperation than that established in the economic sphere by the Treaty of Rome. It also did not extend to the security sphere. Countries such as West Germany, the Netherlands, and, after its accession in 1973, the United Kingdom were staunchly Atlanticist and wary lest any assertion of a European security identity be misconstrued in Washington and lead to a weakening of NATO. In addition, Ireland, which also joined the EC in 1973, was a neutral country certain to resist any move by the Community into the security sphere.

Externally, the member country holding the rotating presidency of the Council of Ministers became the official representative for EPC. To ensure continuity and to bolster the status of EPC when smaller member countries held the presidency, the EC developed the troika system, under which three countries jointly represented the Community: the presidency country and the countries that had previously held and that were next in line for the presidency. This meant, for example, that when the Community decided under EPC to deliver a protest over human rights or some other issue to a foreign government, the ambassadors from the three member states in the troika would go as a group to that country's foreign ministry to deliver the protest.

EPC led to some practical results in the 1970s. The governments of the six and later the nine member states issued joint statements on Cyprus, southern Africa, the Middle East, and other international problems and crises, thereby establishing a higher international political profile for Europe. EPC was used to coordinate member-state policies in the thirty-five-nation Conference on Security and Cooperation in Europe (CSCE) that convened in 1973. It also was used to launch a Euro-Arab dialogue with the twenty member countries of the Arab League. Perhaps most important, EPC led to the development of a "European reflex" in national decision making. Confronted by an international crisis or a new policy issue, member-state foreign ministries learned to look to the other member states to share information and to ascertain how they intended to react.

Nonetheless, the results of EPC were in many ways disappointing. Most EPC actions were purely verbal—statements deploring or praising international developments—but without the economic, political, and military follow-up that is essential to translate words into foreign policy results. The troika system was useful in ensuring continuity in a system without a central decision-making body, but it tended to confuse foreign governments unable to deal with a single EPC representative. Moreover, major international crises tended to confirm that Europe remained divided over foreign policy matters. In the Arab-Israeli war of October 1973 and the ensuing Arab oil embargo, for example, the European states could not agree on a common policy, as each country scrambled to protect its own interests and its access to oil. The 1979 Soviet invasion of Afghanistan had similar results as, for example, West Germany followed the U.S. lead in boycotting the 1980 Moscow Olympics, while the other member states chose to participate.

REFORM IN THE 1980s

Dissatisfaction with the results of EPC led to efforts in the 1980s to strengthen foreign policy coordination. In a report adopted at their meeting in London in October 1981, the EC foreign ministers called for EPC to become more anticipatory in its approach—to work toward shaping the international environment in desired directions rather than to react to crises after they occurred. They also agreed to extend the subject of EPC to "certain important foreign policy questions bearing on the political aspects of security."[5] This very cautious step into what traditionally had been the exclusive domain of NATO reflected a growing sense on the part of the member states that Europe needed to take greater responsibility for its own security.

The conclusion, in 1986, of the Single European Act marked a further step forward. Although best known as the agreement that launched the single market program, the act introduced important institutional reforms into the Community, one of which was the establishment of the EPC on a treaty basis. With its entering into force, the member states were bound by legal agreement rather than just a political commitment to consult together in the foreign policy sphere and to seek to develop common actions. The act did not, however, change the essentially inter-governmental nature of EPC. Responsibility for foreign policy remained with the member states, and there was no transfer of decision-making powers to the central institutions of the Community.

The other major development of the 1980s was the partial revival of the WEU. As has been seen, the WEU played an important role in the 1940s in establishing security cooperation among the West European democracies and in the mid-1950s in integrating West Germany into NATO. However, once the United States became the dominant player in West European security affairs the WEU lost its original rationale. The Brussels treaty remained in effect, but the WEU as an organization was virtually moribund by the 1970s. In October 1984 the seven members of the WEU, all of them also members of the Community and participants in EPC, decided to activate the WEU as a forum for discussion of security issues. They agreed to hold meetings of foreign and defense ministers every six months and to work to harmonize member-state views on defense questions, arms control, East-West and transatlantic relations, and European armaments cooperation. An important advantage of the WEU, as seen by those countries most interested in developing a European defense identity, was that it did not include Denmark, Greece, and Ireland, EC member countries that had been most resistant to adding a security dimension to EPC. In October 1987 the WEU adopted the Hague Platform on European Security Interests. In 1987–1988 the WEU coordinated European participation in mine-sweeping operations in the Persian Gulf associated with the Iran-Iraq War. Portugal and Spain became members of the organization in 1988, strengthening its Mediterranean dimension and making WEU and EC membership nearly coterminous. In late 1990 and early 1991 the WEU helped to coordinate the enforcement by European naval units of UN sanctions in the Gulf following Iraq's seizure of Kuwait, and again continued with the clean-up of mines after the end of the Gulf War. After Greece announced its decision to join in 1992, Denmark (where WEU membership was complicated by the country's complex relations with Germany) and neutral Ireland were the only EU members that were not also members of the WEU.

CFSP

Despite the developments in EPC and the WEU, most of the member states remained dissatisfied with the level of cooperation Western Europe had managed to achieve in the realm of foreign and security policy. The Community's weaknesses in this area left it particularly badly positioned to try to shape the changes that were sweeping the communist world at the end of the 1980s. Foreign policy cooperation thus was high on the agenda of the 1991 Intergovernmental Conference (IGC) on political union.

France favored radical reforms that would allow the proposed Union to act independently of the United States if it chose to do so. Britain was satisfied with the level of foreign policy cooperation mandated in the SEA and was opposed to any "Europeanizing" of security that might offend the United States and damage NATO. As a neutral country, Ireland also was wary of introducing security into the European integration process. Germany tended to lean toward the French position, although like Britain it was cautious about damaging NATO and offending the United States.

The conference eventually hammered out a set of compromises among these different views. The Maastricht treaty abolished EPC and replaced it with the CFSP, which became the second pillar of the new European Union. CFSP in turn was linked to the ESDI and a new and formal relationship between the EU and the WEU. The treaty specified five very general objectives for the CFSP: safeguarding the common values and interests of the Union; strengthening its security; preserving peace and strengthening international security in accordance with the principles of the UN Charter; promoting international cooperation; and developing and consolidating democracy and the rule of law and respect for human rights and fundamental freedoms.

Decision making in the second pillar was to be largely intergovernmental, but the treaty broke new ground in giving the central institutions of the Union a role in foreign policy. The Commission was given the right to suggest actions under CFSP, although not a sole right of initiative as in the first pillar. The member states were given a co-equal right to make proposals under CFSP. CFSP decisions were not made subject to the jurisdiction of the Court of Justice. The treaty also stipulated that the EC budget could be used to underwrite CFSP actions by the Union. The European Council was charged with formulating general guidelines for the CFSP. On the basis of the guidelines, the Council of Ministers was expected to take decisions on concrete actions, generally by consensus. Externally, the presidency country was charged with representing the Union, and the troika system was retained. The Maastricht treaty thus built upon the provisions of EPC in the Single European Act (SEA), but it created a stronger legal commitment on the part of the member states to develop a common foreign policy. The member states were to consult with each other on matters of mutual interest and to ensure that national policies were in conformity with common positions of the Union. Following the practice already begun in EPC, they were to coordinate their positions in the UN and other international forums.

In what was potentially its most far-reaching change, the Maastricht treaty stipulated that the CFSP "shall include all questions related to the security of the Union, including the eventual framing of a common defence policy, which might in time lead to a common defense."[6] This cautious and somewhat vague wording reflected a compromise among the member states. It left open the question of how long the "eventual" framing of a defense policy would take and whether this policy "in time" would be followed by a real common defense. The treaty further stated: "The Union requests the Western European Union (WEU), which is an integral part of the development of the Union, to elaborate and implement decisions and actions of the Union which have defence implications."[7] In a separate "Declaration on the Western European Union," the WEU member states identified specific ways in which the WEU would work with the EU (and with NATO) and outlined concrete steps that the WEU would take to upgrade its operational capabilities.[8] These included the establishment of a WEU planning cell, work toward the creation of a European armaments agency, establishment or designation of military units answerable to the WEU, and possible establishment of a European Security and Defense Academy.

The WEU Council of Ministers met again in Petersberg, Germany, in June 1992 and issued a three-part declaration further clarifying the role of the WEU in European security. The ministers reaffirmed the WEU's role as the defense component of the EU and as the strengthened European pillar of the Atlantic Alliance; called for further practical steps to improve coordination among the WEU, EU, and NATO; and declared that the WEU would be prepared to make forces available for conflict prevention or crisis management, such as peacekeeping activities of the UN or the CSCE.[9] Military measures short of collective defense against an external attack, including peacekeeping, rescue, and humanitarian relief missions, subsequently became known as the "Petersberg tasks," and were designated an area in which Europe should be prepared to take full responsibility, if necessary without assistance from the United States.

These changes took place just as the EU was preparing to start enlargement talks with four European Free Trade Association (EFTA) countries, three of which—Austria, Finland, and Sweden—were neutral countries that were not members of NATO or the WEU. This raised concern on the part of some EU member states about an increased diversity of security outlooks in an enlarged Union and about these countries' neutrality becoming perhaps a permanent obstacle to the further development of the CFSP. These concerns were put to rest, at least for the time being, in November 1993 when the Belgian presidency, acting on behalf of the twelve, negotiated with the applicant countries a joint declaration on CFSP that was later annexed to their accession treaties. It stated that "the acceding states will from the time of their accession be ready and able to participate fully and actively in the CFSP" and that they accepted without reservation the provisions of the Maastricht treaty establishing the second pillar.[10]

In January 1993 the seat of the WEU Council and Secretariat was transferred from London to Brussels to facilitate cooperation with the EU and NATO. A WEU Planning Cell staffed by about forty personnel headed by a general officer became operational in April 1993, following a formal decision by the WEU ministers in October 1992. A Center for the Interpretation of Satellite Data began operations at Torrejon, Spain, in April 1993, following a decision by the WEU Council at the June 1991 ministerial meeting.[11] Little by little the EU was acquiring, through the WEU, its own defense identity and structures.

THE AMSTERDAM REFORMS

Already at Maastricht the member-state governments recognized that many of the awkward compromises contained in the second pillar would have to be reevaluated and possibly renegotiated in the next intergovernmental conference (IGC). For this reason, the Maastricht treaty contained specific language requiring the Council to review, in a report to be presented by the end of 1996, the security provisions of the treaty. Maastricht also specified the security-related aspects of CFSP as an item to be addressed in the next IGC. The weaknesses of the CFSP and above all the failure of the EU to deal with the crisis in the Balkans led to increasing pressures for reform as the post-Maastricht IGC approached. The European Council declared that one of the key themes of the conference had to be "a strengthened capacity for external action of the Union."[12]

The IGC convened in March 1996, shortly after the conclusion of the Dayton agreement ending the war in Bosnia. Much of the discussion focused on ways to strengthen the operational capabilities of the Union, an area in which CFSP had proven to be especially inadequate. France, Germany, and most of the other member states favored the complete merger of the EU and the WEU, but this was opposed by Britain and those EU countries that were not members of the WEU. The discussion also focused on the slow and cumbersome decision-making processes in CFSP and on the absence of a single individual who could represent EU policy to the outside world.

In response to these weaknesses, the Treaty of Amsterdam introduced several organizational reforms. In addition to the principles and general guidelines already mentioned in the Maastricht treaty, the treaty added a clause giving the European Council the responsibility to decide on common strategies for the Union in areas where the member states have important interests in common. It did not bring about the merger of the EU and the WEU, but it strengthened the links between the two organizations and reemphasized the latter's role as the operational arm of the Union in CFSP. The treaty sharpened the language on the circumstances under and procedures by which the member states might adopt a common defense. In place of the vague and open-ended wording in the Maastricht treaty, it stated that the European Council was empowered to decide upon the "progressive framing" of a common defense policy, in which case the member states would have to adopt "such a decision in accordance with their respective constitutional requirements."[13] The European Council was formally given the right to establish policy guidelines for the WEU. All member states agreed to participate as necessary in EU and WEU military actions relating to humanitarian and rescue tasks, peacekeeping, and crisis management or peacemaking operations. This was particularly significant for Austria, Finland, and Sweden, relatively new member states that as neutrals were not members of the WEU or NATO but that had a long history of involvement in UN peacekeeping and humanitarian missions.

Another reform was the introduction of a new article on decision making that was intended to stop the near paralysis on some foreign and security policy issues by providing a mechanism for enhanced cooperation by which "coalitions of the willing" could take action under the EU umbrella using EU and WEU resources, but not necessarily involving all of the EU states. The treaty revisions still formally respected the unanimity procedures of the Council of Ministers in the CFSP, but member states were allowed to abstain, and abstentions could not prevent a measure from being carried. A state that abstains can declare that it is not required to apply the decision—which might entail, for example, supplying troops or equipment to a particular military mission—but it must recognize the Union's commitment to the decision and is obliged, "in a spirit of mutual solidarity," to refrain from steps that conflict with or impede action by the Union. To address the problem of weak and disparate voices articulating the CFSP, the Amsterdam treaty established a new post, High Representative for the CFSP, to be exercised by the secretary general of the Council. The treaty also abolished the old troika system and replaced it with a new troika consisting of the High Representative, the Council presidency (assisted by the country next in line), and the Commission. In June 1999, a month after the Amsterdam treaty went into effect, the member-state governments selected Javier Solana, the then Secretary General of NATO, to become the first CFSP High Representative.

The Amsterdam reforms had some positive effects in raising the foreign policy profile of the EU. Solana became an effective spokesman for the Union, for example, by meeting frequently with the U.S. secretary of state and other foreign ministers, developing a dialogue with the new NATO secretary general, and representing the EU in the U.S.-EU-Russia-UN quartet that sponsored the Middle East peace process. In many respects, however, the Amsterdam reforms fell short. The provisions on enhanced cooperation were never invoked, as member states seemed to prefer least-common-denominator decision making among themselves to decisive action by smaller groups. In addition, external representation continued to be divided among several individuals. Establishment of the post of CFSP High Representative was an important step forward, but external representation still was shared with the foreign minister of the rotating presidency country and the EU commissioner for external policy.

Defense in Europe

A EUROPEAN FORCE

At the time of Maastricht, the key EU member states had agreed "on the need to develop a genuine European security and defense identity and a greater European responsibility for defense matters."[14] Progress toward a security identity was painfully slow, however, chiefly as a result of three factors: lingering differences among the member states about the role of NATO and cooperation with the United States and about how far Europe should go in asserting an identity separate from the United States; differences among the member states about the use of force in international politics—in effect different views about the fundamental rationale for a defense identity; and limited financial and material resources to give substance to this identity. In the period since Maastricht, the first two obstacles to a European defense role have diminished, but the third remains a significant problem.

As has been seen, Britain long opposed defense cooperation in Europe that took place outside the NATO framework and that might alienate Washington. France pursued the opposite policy, consciously seeking to build a European defense identity as a way of diminishing NATO's role and U.S. influence on the continent. The other EU countries were ranged between the British and French positions. These differences narrowed in the course of the 1990s, as France moderated its stance under the pressure of events in the former Yugoslavia and as the United States itself came to embrace a stronger and more autonomous European defense identity. Most importantly, the British government under Prime Minister Tony Blair modified its previous position on ESDI, coming to accept a strong European defense component as important for British national interests and compatible with a strong NATO.

At the time of Maastricht, the European countries also had very different views regarding the use of force in international relations. France and Britain were former great powers with long military traditions and residual global territories and interests. They were not averse to using force overseas to protect those interests, as Britain showed in the 1982 Falkland Islands war and France had demonstrated over the years by its repeated interventions in Africa. But most of the other European countries faced stronger domestic constraints on their ability to use force as an instrument of foreign policy. In Germany, several of the major political parties long took the view that the Federal Republic's constitution, adopted after World War II to ensure a peaceful Germany, banned the deployment of German troops outside the country. But just as the crisis in the former Yugoslavia helped to unify the key EU states on the need to develop a stronger European defense identity, it contributed toward a certain convergence of views on the use of force for political ends by propelling Germany into an active military role. In December 1996 the German parliament finally broke the taboo on Bundeswehr participation in out-of-area operations by voting overwhelmingly to contribute 3,000 German troops to the NATO-led stabilization force in Bosnia. A little more than two years later, Germany was a major contributor to the 1999 NATO war against Yugoslavia, as German Tornado aircraft joined those of the United States, France, the UK, Italy, and the Netherlands in attacking targets in Serbia.

There was less progress on overcoming the third major obstacle to a stronger European defense component, inadequate military resources. The crisis in the former Yugoslavia highlighted Western Europe's military weaknesses and demonstrated that without U.S. help the EU could not mount large-scale military operations even in its own backyard, much less in more distant regions such as the Persian Gulf. EU countries spent too little on defense, and much of what they did spend contributed little to the capabilities needed to make a European defense identity a reality. The EU member states had over 2.4 million personnel in their armed forces compared with some 1.45 million in the United States. Collectively they allocated some $173 billion each year on defense, or about 60 percent of the U.S. total.[15] But too large a share of this spending was for manpower and not enough for purchasing new equipment or for effective research and development. The defense industry was fragmented, resulting in wasteful duplication of effort across defense establishments. A large share of French and UK defense spending went to maintaining national nuclear weapons capabilities.

The Kosovo crisis, the new British attitude toward European defense under Tony Blair, and the entering into effect of the Treaty of Amsterdam with its strengthened security provisions all combined to produce new momentum toward a strengthened CFSP with a real security component. Britain signaled its long-awaited shift on CFSP at the informal European Council meeting in Pörtschach in late October 1998, at which Blair called for "fresh thinking" on European defense cooperation and mentioned different institutional options, including possible full merger of the WEU into the EU, a step previously opposed by the UK. In early December Blair and French President Chirac issued their pathbreaking "Declaration on European Defense" at their meeting in Saint-Malo. It stated that the EU "must have the capacity for autonomous action, backed up by credible military forces, the means to decide to use them and a readiness to do so in order to respond to international crises."[16] It stressed "full and rapid implementation of the

Amsterdam provisions on CFSP," including "the responsibility of the European Council to decide on the progressive framing of a common defense policy in the framework of CFSP." The first-ever meeting of EU defense ministers occurred in November 1998 during the Austrian presidency. It was followed in early December by the first-ever meeting between an EU Council president, in this case Austrian Foreign Minister Wolfgang Schüssel, and the NATO Secretary General. At its Vienna session in December, the European Council welcomed the Saint-Malo developments and called upon the Council to develop specific proposals for operationalizing the provisions in the Treaty of Amsterdam regarding closer EU-WEU cooperation, to be examined at the Cologne summit in June 1999.

The Kosovo crisis subsequently added a sense of urgency to the preparations for the Cologne decisions. At their Bremen meeting in May 1999 the WEU defense ministers set an informal eighteen-month deadline for concrete progress toward a European defense identity, meaning that key decisions could be taken under the French presidency at the end of 2000. Incoming Commission president Romano Prodi told interviewers that a "logical next step" for CFSP would be the creation of an EU army, and suggested that the alternative would be "to be marginalised in the new world history."[17] Meeting in Brussels at the end of the month, the EU foreign ministers finalized many of the details concerning the eventual absorption of the WEU by the EU.

The Cologne European Council adopted the report prepared by the foreign ministers endorsing the general goal of abolishing the WEU by the end of 2000 and transferring its capabilities to the EU.[18] Under plans to be worked out by the member-state governments and incorporated in subsequent agreements, the EU was set to establish a permanent, Brussels-based political and security committee and an EU military committee consisting of military representatives that would make recommendations to the political and security committee. It also would convene regular and ad hoc meetings of defense ministers and would take over the WEU planning cell, situation center, and satellite center. The WEU treaty containing mutual security obligations among the signatory states would remain in effect, but the WEU itself would cease to exist as an organization.

At the December 1999 Helsinki summit the European Council adopted a report by the Finnish presidency calling for the establishment of a 50,000–60,000–person military force that would be able, by 2003, to deploy within sixty days and be sustained for at least one year, capable of carrying out the full range of Petersberg tasks.[19] To ensure the necessary political guidance and strategic direction for EU-led operations, the summit called for the establishment, as envisioned in the Cologne decisions, of new political and military bodies that would operate within the framework of the Council of Ministers. They included a standing Political and Security Committee (PSC) in Brussels, a Military Committee, and a Military Staff. These bodies were established on an interim basis in February 2000, and the PSC was given formal legal status in the Treaty of Nice concluded in December of the same year.[20]

At Helsinki and in subsequent declarations, the EU and its member states emphasized that an EU defense role was not a threat to NATO—that EU-led military operations in response to international crises would be launched only when NATO as a whole was not engaged, that unnecessary duplication of forces would be avoided, and that modalities would be developed for full consultation and cooperation between the EU and NATO. How such cooperation would be organized and how the countries involved would avoid creating security structures that at best would be wasteful and duplicative, at worst would be rivals, became key questions that would preoccupy diplomats on both sides of the Atlantic throughout the 1990s and into the next decade.

THE EU-NATO NEXUS

When communism collapsed in 1989–1991, eleven of twelve EU member states were also members of NATO. The debate about a future security identity for the EU thus could not be separated from a parallel debate about the future of NATO that arose as the alliance's Cold War rationale disappeared. As has been seen, one of the major points of contention at Maastricht was how far the EU should go in creating a defense identity that might be seen as an alternative to NATO. This debate soon was followed by another discussion about whether NATO should enlarge—and if so to which countries—and how the enlargement of NATO should relate to that of the EU. France preferred to see a drastic downgrading of NATO's role relative to the EU and the WEU, while Britain resisted this view. For its part, the United States was determined to preserve NATO through reform, adaptation, and ultimately expansion. As the 1990s unfolded, the failure of the EU to cope with the Yugoslav crisis on its own and the desire of the central and east European states to join NATO as insurance against a possible resurgence of Russian power helped to preserve the political centrality of NATO.

Reform of NATO began at the June 1990 London summit, when the leaders of the alliance declared that NATO was prepared to turn to the countries of central and eastern Europe and "extend to them the hand of friendship." At the November 1991 Rome summit the members of the alliance agreed to a new strategy document that eliminated all references to a specific enemy in the east and identified instability as the new danger confronting the alliance. These changes were part of the diplomatic maneuvering that preceded the unification of Germany, and were designed to make the membership of a united Germany in NATO (and the concomitant loss of the German Democratic Republic (GDR) from the Soviet security sphere) more palatable to Soviet leader Gorbachev and his domestic critics.

While NATO undertook these initial reforms, U.S. officials kept a wary eye on the security discussions in the 1991 IGC on political union. At one point in the negotiations, the U.S. Department of State sent a demarche to the eleven NATO members of the EC in which it indicated that the United States supported a stronger European foreign and security policy but that it opposed the formation of a European caucus within NATO that would present the United States with a unified European position. From the European perspective, the U.S. intervention was heavy-handed and self-contradictory, since it was difficult to see how a European pillar could be formed within NATO without the Europeans being able to concert their policy outside the NATO forum. In the end, the United States professed to be satisfied with the Maastricht arrangements, and the CFSP provisions of the treaty contained a passage stating that EU policy would respect "the obligations of certain Member States under the North Atlantic Treaty and be compatible with the common security and defence policy established within that framework."[21]

Nonetheless, tensions between the EU and the United States, and especially between Paris and Washington, ran high in the early 1990s as both sides seemed to pursue different and incompatible visions of Europe's future security order. In the end, what helped to save the alliance and to defuse these tensions was the crisis in the former Yugoslavia. The prolonged and bloody impasse with Serbian president Slobodan Milosevic convinced the European powers that they needed more rather than less U.S. involvement in the security affairs of the continent, while it helped to convince the United States of the advantages of a stronger European security organization that could take responsibility for crises in Europe in which the United States might not want to become involved. The humanitarian and peacekeeping operations in the former Yugoslavia also gave NATO, the EU, WEU, Organization for Security and Cooperation in Europe (OSCE, as the Cold War CSCE was renamed in 1994), and national bureaucracies concrete tasks that helped to divert attention from and defuse abstract debate over the relative importance of European versus transatlantic security institutions.

The other major development that bolstered the relevance of NATO in the late 1990s was enlargement. The central and east European democracies began pressing for NATO membership soon after the collapse of Soviet power. Along with admission to the EU, they saw alliance membership as a way of bolstering their own internal reforms and of gaining insurance against a possible resurgence of Russian power. The United States and its allies initially were reluctant to expand the alliance, which was seen as unnecessarily provocative to the Russians and in any case irrelevant to the primarily economic and political problems of transition facing these countries. In 1994 the United States proposed—and NATO quickly adopted—a Partnership for Peace (PfP) program under which non-NATO member countries could cooperate with the alliance on military activities ranging from joint training exercises, exchanges of personnel, and various other forms of cooperation. At least initially, PfP was seen by many as a way for NATO to reach out to the central and east European countries without offering membership.

But under pressure from domestic lobbies and leaders such as Czech President Václav Havel and President Lech Walesa of Poland, the United States as the leading power in the alliance gradually moved toward embracing full membership for at least a subset of the former Warsaw Pact countries.[22] This decision provoked controversy in Europe and the United States, as politicians and experts debated the timing and sequencing of EU and NATO enlargement and the relationship between these two processes. At the 1997 Madrid summit the sixteen NATO members invited three countries—Poland, Hungary, and the Czech Republic—to negotiate treaties of accession to the alliance. These countries formally acceded to the

Washington treaty in March 1999, just in time for the NATO fiftieth anniversary celebrations in Washington the following month. NATO also developed agreements and instruments, including special charters with Russia and Ukraine and a continuation of the PfP program, to facilitate cooperation between the alliance and those former communist countries that were not yet—and might never be— members of the alliance, even as it reaffirmed its commitment to further enlargement involving new candidate countries.[23]

BERLIN AND "BERLIN PLUS"

By the mid-1990s, the EU and its key member states had affirmed on numerous occasions that CFSP and the European defense identity were not intended to challenge NATO. For its part, the United States as the leading power in NATO was signaling that it welcomed a stronger European defense capability and that it did not regard European efforts toward defense unity as a threat to NATO and the U.S. role in Europe. But these mutual protestations of loyalty, while politically useful, masked an important dilemma facing both the EU and NATO.

On the one hand, the United States was wary of any trend in Europe that threatened to duplicate NATO's role and capabilities, both because this was seen as a waste of scarce defense resources and, more importantly, because it could lead to the EU becoming a rival to NATO that ultimately would undermine U.S. influence in the security affairs of the continent. On the other hand, many Europeans were determined to develop an autonomous capability of their own and an ability to act in the event that the United States and NATO decided not to get involved, as in fact had been the case early in the Yugoslav crisis. Some way therefore was needed to square this circle: to give Europe the means to act autonomously if the need arose, but to do so in a way that did not become a self-fulfilling route to a transatlantic defense divorce.

The way to square this circle was to ensure that European national armies could operate either under NATO or WEU/EU command, and to establish access arrangements under which the EU would be able to call upon NATO assets under certain predefined circumstances and thus would not be impelled to develop them on its own. Particularly important in this regard was the planning capability that since the 1950s had resided in the alliance military staff at Supreme Headquarters Allied Powers Europe (SHAPE) in Mons, Belgium. Initial steps in this direction began after the WEU's June 1992 Petersberg Declaration, as the leading West European powers began reconfiguring their military forces so that they could operate under either WEU or NATO command (or both). In January 1994 NATO agreed to the concept of the Combined Joint Task Force (CJTF), under which NATO equipment and infrastructure could be used for certain non-NATO missions.[24] In June 1996 the allies took a further step toward resolving transatlantic defense tensions by agreeing, in the Berlin communiqué, that NATO might in the future facilitate WEU military operations by making NATO assets available for approved WEU operations.[25]

The Berlin arrangements were never tested in practice, however, before they needed to be revised to take account of the further development on the European Security and Defence Policy (ESDP), and in particular the decision by the EU to abolish the WEU and transfer of its Petersberg task responsibilities directly to the Union. NATO thus had to begin to define itself directly in relation to the EU, rather than to rely on the WEU as a "bridge" between NATO and the EU. NATO's revised strategy document issued at the April 1999 Washington summit thus declared the alliance's readiness "to define and adopt the necessary arrangements for ready access by the European Union to the collective assets and capabilities of the Alliance, for operations in which the Alliance as a whole is not engaged militarily as an Alliance."[26] In the summit communiqué, the heads of state and government pledged to work in four areas that would enable the EU to have access to NATO capabilities for operations in which NATO itself was not engaged. Known as "Berlin plus" because they built upon the understandings reached in Berlin in 1996, these arrangements included assured EU access to NATO planning capabilities able to contribute to military planning for EU-led operations, the presumption that pre-identified NATO capabilities and assets would be available for use in EU-led operations, and the identification and elaboration of command options for EU-led operations.

Almost three more years of often very difficult negotiations were required to work out definitive arrangements for future NATO-EU cooperation. The reason for the delay was that the shift in responsibilities from the WEU to the EU was not just a technical and administrative matter; it also involved certain political sensitivities. Turkey was an associate member of the WEU, but it was not a member of the EU. It therefore was concerned about a potential loss of influence and in particular a situation in which Greece might be able to call upon the EU's rapid reaction force, which in turn would be able to call upon NATO assets for use in a conflict with Turkey in the Aegean. At one point the UK worked out a compromise that satisfied Turkey by guaranteeing consultations before military measures were undertaken, but this went too far for Greece, which threatened to veto the NATO-EU agreement.

These issues finally were resolved in December 2002 in the run-up to the Copenhagen summit that not coincidentally advanced Turkey's bid for EU membership. The two organizations adopted the EU-NATO Declaration on ESDP, their first formal framework for cooperation. The document acknowledged the importance of both organizations and the need for partnership between them. It reaffirmed that NATO "remains the foundation of the collective defense of its members," but it also welcomed ESDP, "whose purpose is to add to the range of instruments already at the European Union's disposal for crisis management and conflict prevention in support of the Common Foreign and Security Policy, the capacity to conduct EU-led crisis management operations where NATO as a whole is not engaged."[27] With regard to mutual consultations and the sharing of assets, NATO reaffirmed its Washington summit decisions, and in particular its pledge of assured access to NATO planning capabilities, while the EU, in order to assuage the concerns of Turkey, pledged to ensure "the fullest possible involvement of non-EU European members of NATO within ESDP."

Conclusion of the long-awaited NATO-EU understanding had almost immediate operational consequences in that it allowed the EU to take over, on April 1, 2003, the NATO mission in Macedonia but to do so by drawing upon NATO assets essential for the completion of the mission. Discussion also began of the EU eventually taking over the much larger NATO operation in Bosnia, again something that would be possible only if the EU borrowed certain NATO assets.

As a consequence of the NATO-EU agreement and other developments in the defense sphere, the European countries now have the potential to choose among a wide and somewhat confusing array of political and organizational flags for conducting military operations. As shown in table 9.1, these include operations that are NATO only, those that are EU only, those that are led by the EU but that draw upon NATO assets, and finally operations that formally involve neither the EU nor NATO but that entail cooperation between individual European countries and the United States in ad hoc "coalitions of the willing."

DEFENSE INDUSTRY

The issue of a European security and defense identity cannot be separated from the fate of defense industry in Europe. European leaders have argued that by consolidating defense industry on a European scale to make it more efficient and cost effective, Europe may be able to achieve economies of scale that will result in greater defense capabilities at current or only modestly increased levels of funding. They also have made the case that if Europe is to develop its own autonomous defense capability, it must be able to produce the full range of defense equipment, without undue dependence upon the United States.

Throughout the Cold War, European countries cooperated with each other on some weapons projects, but they also were free to pursue purely national solutions to armament needs or to buy U.S. weapons. Efforts at defense industrial collaboration were marked by high overhead costs, inefficiency, and delays caused by differences among the collaborating countries about the specifications of particular weapons systems. There were a few notable successes, such as the Tornado combat aircraft built by Germany, Italy, and the UK, but they came at high financial cost. One of the main sources of inefficiency in European defense projects was the strict application of *juste retour*—the principle that shares of development and production work on a particular aircraft or ship or missile must be apportioned to the various national industries according to how much of the project is paid for by each partner. This meant loss of time in haggling over which company was responsible for what subsystems and components and often resulted in firms being chosen to develop and produce subsystems or components not because they were the best qualified, but as the result of political maneuvering. It also tended to stifle competition, as national firms were guaranteed a share of work on collaborative projects regardless of their price or technical competitiveness.

The CFSP provisions of the Amsterdam treaty called for stronger cooperation in the field of armaments production. The treaty did not, however, repeal Article

Table 9.1   Command Arrangements for Recent Military Operations

Operation	Mission	Command arrangements	Main countries involved
IFOR/SFOR Bosnia (December 1995–)	Under UN mandate, deter renewal of interethnic violence in Bosnia; provide security	NATO	NATO member states and third countries
KFOR Kosovo (June 1999–)	Under UN mandate, deter renewal of interethnic violence in Kosovo; provide security	NATO	NATO member states and third countries
Concordia FYROM (March 2003–)	Under UN mandate, prevent conflict between ethnic Slavs and Albanians	EU (with assistance of NATO assets; France as "framework nation")	25 EU member states; Canada, Iceland
Artemis Democratic Republic of Congo (June 2003– September 2003)	Under UN mandate, contribute to the stabilization of security conditions and improve the humanitarian situation in Bunia	EU (no NATO assistance; France as "framework nation")	5 EU contributors (France, UK, Sweden, Germany, Belgium); 3 non-EU contributors (Canada, South Africa, Brazil)
Enduring Freedom Afghanistan (September 2001–)	Under UN mandate, defeat the Taliban and al Qaeda following the September 11, 2001, terrorist attacks	U.S. national command	U.S., Canada, Denmark, France, Germany, Norway, Poland, Australia (with smaller contributions from other countries)
ISAF 4 Afghanistan (August 2003–)	Under UN mandate, assist the Afghan Transitional Authority to maintain security around Kabul	NATO (previously commanded by lead nations: UK ISAF 1, Turkey ISAF 2, Germany-Netherlands ISAF 3)	Most NATO member countries (but *not* the United States); other European countries; New Zealand
Iraqi Freedom Iraq (March 2003–)	Enforce UN sanctions against Iraq, defeat the regime of Saddam Hussein; search for WMD. No explicit UN mandate	U.S. national command	U.S., UK, Australia, Poland (combat phase), Denmark, Netherlands, Italy, Spain, Japan, South Korea, other countries (noncombat phase)

Sources: NATO; EU; U.S. Central Command

223 of the Treaty of Rome exempting defense production from the provisions of the treaty, such as the European Commission had proposed. Had the Commission's campaign for repeal of this article been successful, it would have brought defense production under EU trade, competition, research and development, and single market provisions and would have created one path, at least, toward a stronger European defense industry. But this was unacceptable to the larger member states, which were unwilling to surrender so much control over defense industry to Brussels. Instead, the leading military powers in the EU followed the more cautious path of intergovernmental cooperation. In November 1996 France, Germany, Italy, and the UK established a new Joint Armaments Cooperation Agency (also known by its French acronym, OCCAR) to coordinate development and production of major weapons systems.

Cross-border consolidation at the company level also got underway. In December 1997 the defense ministers of France, Germany, and the UK jointly instructed their leading defense and aerospace companies—British Aerospace, Daimler-Benz Aerospace (Dasa) of Germany, and France's Aerospatiale—to draw up plans to form a unified European defense industry giant. These companies (along with Casa of Spain) were the partners in the Airbus Industrie consortium that manufactures civilian aircraft and thus already had much experience in working together on high-technology projects. The privately owned British and German groups were reluctant to cooperate with the state-owned Aerospatiale, but this obstacle to pan-European cooperation was partly removed when the French government announced plans to sell the majority of its holdings in the company to private investors. Aerospatiale subsequently merged with a non–state-owned French missile and defense company, Matra, to form Aerospatiale Matra. Leading companies in Italy, Spain, and Sweden also announced that they hoped to become part of a new, Europe-wide aerospace and defense company.

British Aerospace subsequently opted out of the pan-European merger by purchasing the defense division of another British company to become BAe Systems, an all-British company with strong subsidiaries in the United States. But in October 1999 Aerospatiale Matra and Dasa (by that time DaimlerChrysler Aerospace, following the merger of Chrysler and Daimler-Benz) merged to form a new company, the European Aeronautics, Defense and Space Company (EADS). In December of the same year, Germany, France, and Spain signed an agreement under which Casa also was merged into EADS. The political and commercial motivation for forming this new defense giant was to create a firm that could compete as well as partner with the leading U.S. defense companies.

Industrial consolidation was followed by further discussion of improved coordination at the governmental level. After considerable debate in the Commission, among member states, and in the think tank community, in June 2003 the Thessaloniki European Council approved the establishment, in the course of 2004, of an intergovernmental agency for defense capabilities development, research, and armament acquisitions.[28] The purpose of the agency will be to help to identify member-state military capability objectives and evaluate efforts to achieve them, promote harmonization of operational needs and more effective and compatible procurement methods, propose multi-member-state equipment projects, support defense technology R&D, and contribute to identifying ways to strengthen the industrial and technological base of the defense sector. The overall objective of the agency will be to increase EU defense capabilities under circumstances in which prospects for large spending increases in military budgets are remote. The draft EU Constitution also contains a provision that gives constitutional status to the European Armaments, Research and Military Capabilities Agency.

CFSP in Action

The discussion so far has focused on the debate among the European powers over the need for a common foreign policy, the modest progress they have made in achieving such a policy, and the parallel debate on security and defense and the even more limited progress they have made in that area. Critics of the EU have grown weary of the seemingly endless discussion of institutions and have asked fundamental questions about the purpose of EU policy. What must or should the EU try to accomplish internationally that requires it to have a foreign policy? What, in other words, should be the substance rather than the institutional form of CFSP?

The Maastricht treaty established four objectives for the CFSP that were repeated, in slightly modified form, in the Treaty of Amsterdam. These objectives were very general, however, and did not offer guidelines for specific foreign policy actions. European political leaders recognized this already at the time of the 1991 Maastricht summit, where they asked the Council of Ministers to prepare, for the June 1992 Lisbon session of the European Council, a report identifying regional priorities for the CFSP.

The Lisbon report singled out two groups of countries as priority regions for EU foreign policy: the formerly communist countries of central and eastern Europe and the Maghreb and the Middle East.[29] In other words, it recommended that the emphasis in CFSP be on the arc of instability to the east and south of the EU. It suggested that the EU become more active and anticipatory toward these regions—that it work to head off political and economic crises with potential implications for EU security by dealing with such underlying problems as poverty and unemployment, intraregional ethnic and religious tensions, environmental decay, and the absence of democratic institutions and guarantees of civil and political rights. Following the June 1993 Copenhagen decisions on enlargement, policy toward those countries of central and eastern Europe that were eligible for EU membership increasingly was subsumed under the pre-accession strategy aimed at preparing them for membership—a subject that is discussed in the next chapter. CFSP as such thus came to focus on three other regions—the Balkans, the Newly Independent States (NIS) of the former Soviet Union, and the Mediterranean countries of North Africa and the Middle East.

Stabilization of the periphery has remained a priority focus for CFSP, reiterated in the European Security Strategy adopted by the European Council in December 2003 and even given a special status in the proposed European Constitution. It has not remained, however, the sole focus of CFSP, which increasingly has had to turn to challenges further afield, for example East Timor, Afghanistan, and Iraq as well as global issues such as terrorism and the proliferation of weapons of mass destruction.

STABILIZING THE PERIPHERY

The Balkans: Conflict and Negotiation. Policy toward the former Yugoslavia was the first major test for the CFSP—and one that most European political leaders acknowledge failed. The crisis in this region erupted in June 1991 when two of the six Yugoslav republics, Slovenia and Croatia, declared independence from the Serbian-dominated federation. The Yugoslav army moved into Slovenia, provoking clashes between federal forces and the Slovenians. There also were clashes involving federal and Croatian forces and ethnic Serbs living in Croatia and the newly formed Croatian army.

At the time, the governments of the twelve EC member states were preoccupied with negotiating the Maastricht treaty and still digesting the implications of German unity, as well as concerned about developments in the USSR where Gorbachev was losing his grip on power and ethnically based tensions were mounting. Nevertheless, this was a time of great optimism for Western Europe. The soon-to-be formed European Union appeared set to play a new role on the world stage and perhaps the decisive role in European affairs. In June 1991 Luxembourg foreign minister Jacques Poos, representing the Council of Ministers, made his famous statement, "This is the hour of Europe, not the hour of the United States."[30] The Community seized the initiative, jointly convening with the UN the Hague conference on Yugoslavia to discuss a negotiated cease-fire and a compromise peace plan for an association of sovereign Yugoslav republics. The twelve sent observers to the region and pressured the Serbs to accept the EC peace plan or to face economic sanctions. At the request of the European Council, the WEU began drawing up plans for a possible peacekeeping operation involving European troops.

Over the course of the next several years the EU was much chastened by events on the ground, as it failed to impose a peace settlement and at times was unable to maintain its own unity in the face of the escalating conflict. The first major disagreement among the member states was over whether to recognize Croatia and Slovenia following their unilateral declarations of independence. Germany, which had close historic ties with Croatia and a large Croatian minority living inside its borders, pressed for immediate recognition. France and Britain traditionally had had closer ties with Serbia and were concerned that recognition of the post-Yugoslav states would inflame rather than dampen the conflict. At the December 1991 meeting of the Council of Ministers, the Community foreign ministers collectively decided to establish diplomatic relations with the two new states, but this was largely in response to German pressure and because they knew that Germany, CFSP commitments notwithstanding, was prepared to act unilaterally.[31]

Meanwhile, fighting intensified as Serbian forces besieged the Croatian cities of Zadar, Dubrovnik, and Vukovar and bombed the capital Zagreb—actions that were widely seen on European television and demonstrated to the public both the brutality of the conflict and the apparent failure of Europe's diplomatic efforts. As tensions mounted, the international community agreed to establish the UN Protection Force (UNPROFOR) to help maintain peace and later to provide security for the relief efforts directed at the growing number of refugees and displaced persons. The EU countries provided half of UNPROFOR's 25,000 soldiers, with the largest contingents supplied by France and Britain.

As stability returned to Croatia and Slovenia in the course of 1992, the focus of the conflict shifted to Bosnia-Herzegovina, the most ethnically and religiously diverse of the six former Yugoslav republics. After Bosnia declared independence from Yugoslavia in March 1992, the Serb minority in the country declared its independence from Bosnia and formed its own mini-state, closely allied with Serbia proper, and an army that was heavily supported by the Yugoslav federal (i.e., Serbian) army. The Bosnian Serbs then began a program of "ethnic cleansing" in which non-Serbian citizens were killed or driven out of their villages. By the end of 1992 the self-styled Republic of Srpska, covertly assisted by the Yugoslav army, had seized 70 percent of the territory of Bosnia and had established a blockade of the capital of Sarajevo. More than a million Bosnians fled their homes to avoid the fighting. Most found refuge in camps located elsewhere in Bosnia or in other parts of the former Yugoslavia, but many made their way to Western Europe. Germany alone took in more than 200,000 Bosnian refugees and displaced persons in the course of the conflict.

The EU countries (along with the United States) recognized Bosnia in April 1992, even as they continued to press for a diplomatic solution to the conflict among the Serbs, Croats, and Muslims living in Bosnia. In August 1992 the EU and the UN convened another peace conference, this time in London under the UK presidency, aimed at finding a negotiated solution to the Bosnian crisis. Following detailed discussions among the warring parties throughout the fall of 1992, in January 1993 the EU and UN mediators, David Owen and Cyrus Vance, put forward a peace plan based on a confederal solution. Bosnia would be divided into three autonomous regions—Muslim, Serb, and Croat—that would be loosely united in a single state. All three parties rejected this solution, however, and the war continued, punctuated by televised atrocities, usually although not exclusively linked to the Serbs, that increased worldwide revulsion about the conflict. As the war dragged on, UNPROFOR was increasingly discredited.[32]

Prompted by the continued fighting and convinced that only decisive U.S. action would end the conflict, the United States, acting through NATO, finally became more directly involved in the conflict. In May 1995 NATO aircraft, acting under a UN Security Council mandate, struck Bosnian Serb targets in an attempt to halt an offensive. This initial NATO involvement had limited effect, however, as the Bosnian Serbs took UN soldiers hostage and chained them to likely military targets as a defense against further air strikes. In July 1995 Bosnian Serb forces captured the town of Srebrenica, supposedly a safe area under UN protection, and committed numerous atrocities against the civilian population seeking refuge in the town. The following month, a Bosnian Serb–fired mortar shell fell into a marketplace in Sarajevo, killing thirty-seven civilians.

These atrocities finally galvanized the West into belated action. During a two-week period from August 30 to September 17, NATO planes flew some 800 combat missions against Bosnian Serb targets. In parallel with the military intervention, the United States became more directly involved in efforts to find a diplomatic solution. A U.S. team led by Assistant Secretary of State for Europe Richard Holbrooke used shuttle diplomacy to broker a ceasefire that took effect in October. In November, the United States invited all of the parties involved to continue the negotiations at Wright-Patterson Air Force Base near Dayton, Ohio. After three weeks of intense discussions, Holbrooke managed to broker a settlement that was signed by the presidents of Serbia, Croatia, and Bosnia in a ceremony in Paris the following month. All parties recognized that Bosnia would remain a unified state, but it was to be composed of two distinct entities, the Bosnian-Croat Federation and the Republika Srpska, the former with 51 percent, the latter with 49 percent, of the country's territory.[33]

UNPROFOR forces were withdrawn and replaced by a new Implementation Force (IFOR) under NATO command that was charged with enforcing the peace agreement. IFOR's 60,000 troops included units from the United States, EU member states, central and eastern Europe, Russia, and Ukraine. Pending the reestablishment of Bosnian democratic institutions capable of standing up to pressures from the country's ethnic groupings, all of which remain highly suspicious of each other, civilian administration in Bosnia was assigned to an Office of the High Representative, which could call on NATO forces to deal with potential threats to the peace and to assist with postwar reconstruction.

Elsewhere in the Balkans, Macedonia, Albania, and Kosovo were additional flashpoints. EU policy toward Macedonia, the smallest and the poorest of the ex-Yugoslav republics seeking independence after 1991, initially was paralyzed by a dispute with Greece over the country's name. As long as Macedonia was a constituent republic of the Yugoslav federation, Greece had no objection to its name. But Macedonia is also the name of Greece's northernmost province, redolent with history going back to Alexander the Great. The Greeks claimed that the use of the name by an independent state reflected a latent desire to seize Greek territory. Athens managed to block recognition by the other EU member states of the new republic, and in the summer of 1992 it imposed a blockade of petroleum deliveries to Macedonia in an effort to pressure the government to change the country's name. The issue was defused somewhat when Greece agreed, in February 1993, to accept recognition of the country under a name to be decided by international arbitration. The arbitrators proposed that, pending a final settlement of the issue, the country be called the Former Yugoslav Republic of Macedonia (FYROM), and it was under this slightly absurd name that this small, impoverished, and landlocked country was admitted to the UN in April 1993.

In Albania, the collapse of the communist regime in early 1991 led to rising economic and political disorder in the country, causing ethnic Greeks to flee southward and an exodus by boat of more than 20,000 Albanians to Italy. The Italian authorities clamped down on illegal migration in August 1991 and began to repatriate many of the refugees, but only after Western Europe had been given a vivid example of how instability on its doorstep could quickly spill over onto its own territory. Albania made some economic and political progress in the early 1990s, but fraudulent elections in 1996 followed by a financial crisis in early 1997 led to a breakdown of law and order and civil war between the government of President Sali Berisha and rebel forces seeking his overthrow. Concerned about another massive influx of refugees, Italy took the lead in organizing a multinational force of peacekeeping troops that supervised food distribution and other humanitarian tasks and managed to restore order in the country. Italy contributed 2,500 troops to the 5,915-member Multinational Protection Force, France 1,000, and smaller contingents came from Greece, Spain, Romania, Austria, and Denmark.

The difficulties in Albania soon were overshadowed by even greater problems in Kosovo, formally still a province of Serbia but with a 90 percent ethnically Albanian population that had long suffered at the hands of Milosevic. In March 1989 the Serbian parliament voted to suspend the autonomy that the province had enjoyed for much of its history as part of the Yugoslav state. The older generation of leaders in Kosovo counseled nonviolence and looked to the international community for support. As Serb oppression continued, however, and after the international community failed to address the issue of Kosovo in the Dayton accords, the underground Kosovo Liberation Army (KLA) emerged as the province's leading political force. Smuggling weapons into Kosovo from neighboring Albania, the KLA established military control over large parts of the country and became more assertive in pressing its demand for a completely independent state. The international community did not support the demands of the KLA, but it also warned the Serbs about overreacting to the KLA threat and continued to call for a peaceful solution to the tensions based on a restoration of the province's autonomy, perhaps as a third republic in a Yugoslav federation along with Serbia and Montenegro.

Ignoring Western warnings, in early 1998 military and police units operating from Serbia struck the province hard, destroying villages and driving out their populations in what Belgrade said was a legitimate campaign against KLA terrorists. Once again, European and American audiences could see on television the violence and the streams of refugees on Western Europe's Balkan doorstep. Using the threat of NATO air strikes as leverage, in October 1998 the United States managed to broker a cease-fire between the Serb authorities and the Kosovo separatists, to be followed by talks on a political settlement and the return of refugees. Serbian leader Milosevic agreed to the dispatch of 1,500 OSCE observers to monitor the cease-fire, and NATO deployed an "extraction force" of troops in Macedonia to be prepared to come to the rescue of the unarmed observers should they come under attack from either side.

The October 1998 agreement failed to resolve the crisis, however, and a continuing deterioration of conditions in the province led to open war between Serbia and NATO in the spring of 1999.[34] In an effort to halt the escalating violence in the province, in February 1999 the Western powers convened a peace conference in Rambouillet, France, at which they essentially presented the Yugoslav government with an ultimatum, demanding that it withdraw its forces from Kosovo and allow NATO peacekeeping forces to enter the province or face allied air strikes. Belgrade refused, and on March 24 NATO began attacks against Serb targets in Kosovo and Serbia proper. This accelerated the campaign of ethnic cleansing by the Serbs, as almost the entire Kosovar population fled their homes to escape Serb military and police forces engaged in widespread killing and burning of whole villages. Some 800,000 people crossed the borders into Macedonia and Albania, threatening the economic and political stability of these countries, while many more were displaced inside Kosovo.

Despite doubts among critics about the wisdom of NATO strategy and the skill with which the United States and its allies had conducted the prewar diplomacy, NATO was able to maintain support for its bombing campaign for seventy-eight days, causing widespread destruction to Yugoslav forces, industry, and infrastructure. Milosevic finally accepted a UN- and Russian-brokered peace agreement that met the essence of NATO's demands: that Serb forces withdraw from the province and that Kosovo be occupied by a NATO-led peace force that would allow the refugees to return home in relative safety. Known as KFOR, this force of 40,000 troops deployed to Kosovo in June, with the EU countries providing most of the manpower and equipment. The question of final status for Kosovo was deferred, partly in deference to Russian sensibilities. Technically the province remained part of Serbia, but there was no expectation in the international community that the people of Kosovo would be placed again under rule from Belgrade.

The Balkans: Reconstruction and Integration. The Kosovo conflict was the last of the Balkan wars of the 1990s. The EU was given a prominent and formally recognized role in postwar reconstruction. UN Security Council Resolution 1244 established the United Nations Interim Administration in Kosovo (UNMIK), which in turn was divided into four "pillars" with different functional responsibilities for Kosovo. The Humanitarian Assistance pillar was led by the UN High Commissioner for Refugees; the Civil Administration pillar by the UN itself; the Democracy and Institution pillar by the OSCE; and the Reconstruction and Economic Development pillar by the EU. The EU quickly responded to the cessation of the NATO bombing campaign with a large package of aid intended to assist with the return of refugees and cope with the looming hardships of the coming Balkan winter.

The Kosovo war also gave new impetus to a broader EU regional policy toward the western Balkans and to the beginnings of a new discussion of eventual membership for these countries. Hit by the economic costs of the war and the huge refugee flows from Kosovo, Albania and the FYROM sought an accelerated timetable for EU (and NATO) membership. The EU turned aside this request as unreasonable (given the low level of economic and political development in these countries), but it did respond by holding out the prospect of more rapid and comprehensive integration with the Union. In June 1999 the EU launched the Stability Pact for Southeastern Europe and offered to negotiate Stabilization and Association Agreements (SAAs) with all of the southeast European countries in the context of the pact. A kind of pre–pre-accession arrangement, the SAAs were to emphasize regional cooperation, democratization, capacity building, and trade liberalization, both with the EU and intra-regionally. The EU concluded an SAA with FYROM in April 2001, Croatia in October 2001, and began negotiations with Albania in late 2002.

In December 2000, the Council established the Community Assistance for Reconstruction, Development, and Stabilisation (CARDS) program as the primary means to implement the objectives of the Stabilisation and Association Process (SAP). For the 2000–2006 period, CARDS was slated to provide €4,650 million in grant aid for investment, institution building, and other measures aimed at achieving four objectives: reconstruction, democratic stabilization, and the return of refugees; institutional and legislative development, including harmonization with EU norms and approaches; structural reform and sustainable economic and social development; and promotion of closer regional cooperation among the SAP countries and between them and the current and other prospective members of the EU. The Union also granted preferential access to its internal market for the SAP countries beginning in late 2001.

As EU presence and influence in the region have grown, attention has shifted to forward-looking policies aimed at heading off crises rather than responding after the fact, as happened in the 1990s. A case in point was the successful effort by CFSP High Representative Solana in August 2001 in brokering the Ohrid Framework Agreement to defuse escalating interethnic conflict in FYROM. The EU used the offer of assistance under the Stability Pact and a long-term membership perspective to pressure and cajole all sides into accepting internal constitutional and political compromises. Solana also worked to head off a unilateral declaration of independence from Yugoslavia by Montenegro and to reconstitute a loose Serbian-Montenegrin federation in which Montenegrin demands for autonomy and Belgrade's claims of sovereignty could be balanced, at least temporarily. The Ohrid agreement initially was monitored by a force of NATO peacekeepers but, as has been seen, in April 2003 the EU assumed responsibility for this operation, the Union's first out-of-area military operation and the first-ever use of the Berlin plus arrangements.

With the emphasis on crisis management and prevention, the western Balkans has become the key laboratory and testing ground for the ESDP component of CFSP. In 2002, EU member states were providing some 36,000 troops (or 80 percent of the total) of peacekeeping forces in the region, along with the largest number of civilian police, most under NATO command. In addition to the operation in Macedonia, the EU signaled its willingness to assume responsibility for Bosnia. On January 15, 2003, the European Union Police Mission (EUPM) in Bosnia-Herzegovina was officially inaugurated, becoming the first civilian crisis management operation under the CFSP. Comprising 500 police officers and 300 international and local civilian staff, EUPM is charged with helping Bosnia-Herzegovina to develop its own police force to European standards. Taking responsibility for all peacekeeping in Bosnia, a far more ambitious task, was next on the list. In February 2003 the EU foreign ministers endorsed a UK-French position paper outlining a "seamless transition" from NATO's Stabilization Force (SFOR) to an EU peacekeeping force by early 2004.

The EU faces daunting long-term challenges in the Balkans. The potential for instability in the region was highlighted by the assassination, in March 2003, of the reform-minded prime minister of Serbia, Zoran Djinjic. Bosnia remains an international protectorate, making slow progress on such challenges as economic development, refugee return, and making its complex political and constitutional system function. In Kosovo, another protectorate, the question of final status (whether Kosovo becomes an independent state or is linked in some way with Serbia) cannot be deferred indefinitely. Independence for Montenegro also will return to the agenda as the interim agreement nears its term. Meanwhile, Croatia formally submitted its application to join the EU in February 2003, thereby signaling its desire, underpinned by its better economic performance and more central location, to separate itself from the rest of the region. Member states noted, however, that Croatia's economic performance was not matched by adequate cooperation with the Hague International Criminal Tribunal for the former Yugoslavia (ICTY) in handing over suspected war criminals for trial.

While unenthusiastic about the timing of the Croatian application, the EU has become increasingly clear in offering a longer-term membership perspective to all of the countries of the western Balkans. At the European Council session in Thessaloniki in June 2003, the fifteen adopted the *Thessaloniki Agenda for the Western Balkans: Moving towards European Integration* that reaffirmed the membership perspective for these countries and outlined steps needed to move them from their current pre-candidate status to the formal start of preparations for membership. With enlargement to most of the countries of central and eastern Europe complete, many of the financial and human resources that the EU has devoted over the last decade to helping to prepare these countries for membership will be freed up for assistance in the Balkans. In addition, the accession countries themselves will be well positioned to share their own recent experiences in preparing for EU membership with the countries of the western Balkans. Although much could yet go wrong, the track record of enlargement suggests that over the long term the EU has a good chance of bringing these countries into the Union in a way that would help to ensure their stability and prosperity and put an end once and for all to the crises that have plagued this region since the early 1990s.

The Newly Independent States. With the accession of Finland in 1995, the EU acquired its first common border with the former Soviet Union, a 1,000-kilometer stretch where Finland's relative prosperity confronts the poverty and environmental degradation of Russia's northwestern provinces. With enlargement to central and eastern Europe in 2004, the EU gained even longer borders with Russia (including with the Russian province of Kaliningrad, which is entirely surrounded on land by EU member-state territory), as well as with Belarus and Ukraine. What happens in these countries thus is of increasing interest for the EU.

EU policy toward the NIS has roots in the late Soviet era, when Mikhail Gorbachev, abandoning the earlier Soviet policy of shunning the EC and seeking to undermine West European integration, turned to Brussels for support with his reforms. In November 1989 the USSR and the EC concluded their first trade and cooperation agreement.[35] With the breakup of the Soviet Union at the end of 1991, the terms of the EC-USSR agreement were transferred to Russia and the other successor states. The 1989 agreement did not, however, provide an adequate basis for cooperation with these states as they began moving, some more rapidly than others, to create market economies and multiparty political systems. The EU thus offered to conclude Partnership and Cooperation Agreements (PCAs) with the NIS that would establish a framework for more comprehensive relations based on trade, financial aid, regular political dialogue, closer cultural ties, and efforts to work together to harmonize legislation in important areas such as antitrust.

The EU also established a Technical Assistance to the CIS (TACIS) program as a counterpart to the PHARE program of aid for central and eastern Europe. Beginning with ECU 396 million in committed funding for 1991 and rising to ECU 536 million in 1996, TACIS funded nuclear reactor safety projects, the development of private enterprise, food production and distribution, and transport and telecommunications infrastructure. Russia and Ukraine received the lion's share of the aid, but smaller amounts were apportioned to all of the NIS, including the Caucasus and Central Asia. In December 1999 the Council renewed TACIS for another seven years, with funding set at €3.138 billion for 2000–2006.[36] The EU coordinates its overall assistance toward the NIS with the other leading Western states in the G-7 as well as working through multilateral institutions such as the World Bank, the IMF, and the European Bank for Reconstruction and Development (EBRD).

Throughout the 1990s Russia made progress toward creating a market economy and a political democracy by, for example, privatizing most of its economy, holding relatively free and fair elections at the national, regional, and local levels, and developing a vigorous and independent press. But Russia continued to be plagued by political instability and frequent changes of government under President Boris Yeltsin, pervasive corruption, and poverty and low incomes in much of the population. A short-lived economic boom came to a crashing end in August 1998, when a financial crisis forced the Russian government to devalue the ruble and to postpone repayment of some public and private debt. Some foreign investors abandoned the Russian market, and the small Russian middle and entrepreneurial class was in danger of being thrust into poverty.

The December 1998 Vienna European Council decided on the preparation of a common strategy for Russia, to be ready by the end of the German presidency in the first half of 1999. Adopted at the Cologne summit, the common strategy reaffirmed the goal of a "stable, democratic and prosperous Russia, firmly anchored in a united Europe free of new dividing lines."[37] The EU set four goals for its Russia strategy: consolidation of democracy, the rule of law and public institutions, integration of Russia into a common European economic and social area, cooperation to strengthen stability and security in Europe and beyond, and meeting common challenges on the European continent (e.g., energy and nuclear safety, environment, the fight against organized crime and drugs). It also outlined a long list of instruments and mechanisms for pursuing these objectives and stressed that the key to implementation of the common strategy was effective coordination of exchange and assistance programs run by the EU itself and the member states.

Despite the development of an impressive institutional architecture for bilateral cooperation, EU-Russia relations have remained troubled in many areas, with lingering differences over trade, managing the effects of enlargement, human rights, and the war in Chechnya. Vladimir Putin took over from Yeltsin in early 2000 and soon enjoyed a measure of success in stabilizing the Russian economy and winning the popular support of the Russian people. Putin himself developed close personal relations with European leaders such as Schroeder, Blair, Chirac, and Berlusconi, but his relations with the EU, which he tended to regard as rigid and bureaucratic, were often tense.[38]

Beyond the specific differences in bilateral relations, the broad question of Russia's ultimate relationship with the EU is unresolved and a potential source of misunderstanding. EU policy toward Russia, as reflected in the PCA and the common strategy, has been one of integration without membership. Since the fall of communism, Russia has been pressured and cajoled to adopt EU norms and standards and to follow the EU lead on key international questions (e.g., the Kyoto Protocol), but at the same time it was told that it was too large and too different from the EU to be considered for membership. Meanwhile, the EU and NATO both were expanded up to Russia's western borders, raising the prospect of an integrated European order that would include all countries except Russia.

For its part, Russia wanted the benefits of integration with Europe, but as its economy revived and as Putin helped to restore and in turn capitalized on a new Russian sense of national pride, it increasingly chafed at the idea of being little more than a junior partner in an EU-dominated Europe. Increasingly Russia was making clear that it regarded itself as a great power in its own right, not on the scale and certainly not with the threatening posture of the old Soviet Union, but a force that Brussels (and for that matter, Washington) had to listen to and treat with respect rather than regard as a mere object of the aid and integration policies that were being used to stabilize central and eastern Europe and the Balkans. The EU-Russia relationship thus is likely to have elements of both cooperation and tension, as the two sides work together, particularly on economic matters, but have somewhat different views on internal and external political questions.

With a population the size of France and territorially the second largest country in Europe after Russia, Ukraine is an important factor in the future stability of Europe and a key country for EU interests. Relations between the EU and Ukraine have been complicated, however, by corruption and the slow pace of economic reform in Ukraine, the dispute over the shutdown of the Chernobyl nuclear power plant, and differences over trade and development. The Ukrainians long have complained about what they see as an ongoing neglect of their interests by the Union and a refusal by Brussels and the member states to accelerate the integration of Ukraine into Europe. For its part, the EU has stressed the effect that corruption and political deadlock in Ukraine have had in deterring foreign investment and the development of trading links. Officials in Brussels have argued that the EU can do only so much to help a country that did not do more to help itself.

EU policy toward Ukraine is pursued within the framework of the EU-Ukraine PCA that was signed in June 1994 and that went into effect on March 1, 1998, with additional guidance provided by the Common Strategy for Ukraine, adopted in December 1999. After Russia, Ukraine is also the largest recipient of EU aid in the NIS, with some $1.072 billion allocated over the ten-year period to 2002, mainly within TACIS. The actual level of EU-Ukrainian integration remains uneven, however, with numerous barriers to further cooperation both sides. Annual summits began in 1998, after the entry into force of the PCA, along with regular meetings of the ministerial-level Cooperation Council. At the June 2001 meeting of the Cooperation Council, the EU and Ukraine designated six areas as priorities for bilateral cooperation: approximation of Ukraine's legislation to that of the EU; energy; trade; justice and home affairs; environmental protection; and transport and science and technology. A seventh area, investment and cross-border cooperation, was added at the 2002 session of the Cooperation Council.

Like Ukraine, Moldova has expressed its aspirations to join the EU and has been frustrated by not being accorded candidate status. The EU and Moldova signed a PCA in 1994, which went into effect on June 1, 1998. Moldova became a member of the World Trade Organization (WTO) in July 2001, but EU-Moldova trade relations remained troubled in a number of areas. Moldova benefits from certain EU preferences, but its chief exports—wine, fruit, and other agricultural products—are politically sensitive and subject to strict EU quotas and tariffs. Less than a quarter of Moldovan exports are directed to the EU, a figure indicating that it has not made the fundamental redirection of trade toward the West that the accession countries experienced in the 1990s.

Transnistria, a separatist region that declared independence from Moldova when the latter became an independent country in 1991, is a major concern in EU policy toward Moldova. Brussels has continued to press Moscow to fulfill the commitments that it made at the 1999 OSCE summit in Istanbul to withdraw all of its forces from the region. As the Russian presence has receded, however, the separatist authorities in Transnistria increasingly have turned for survival to criminal activities, including smuggling of arms, people, and narcotics, that have very negative implications for Romania, the western Balkans, and the EU itself. In a sign of how seriously these threats are taken, in early 2003 the EU and its member states joined with the United States in imposing a complete travel ban on officials from the breakaway republic.

Belarus remains the odd country out in the western NIS, in that it has reverted to authoritarianism and has made almost no progress toward a market economy. The EU and Belarus signed a PCA in 1994, but the agreement was never put into effect, owing to displeasure on the EU side with the turn toward authoritarianism in Minsk and in particular the undemocratic outcome of the 1996 referendum on the amendment to the constitution that was staged by President Alexander Lukashenko. EU-Belarus bilateral relations at the ministerial level were suspended, and EU technical assistance under TACIS frozen, except for humanitarian aid, regional programs in which Belarus participates, and programs aimed at promoting democracy.

With bilateral relations in a deep freeze, the EU has been forced to work primarily through the OSCE and the Council of Europe, both of which have had programs in Belarus to monitor elections and promote human rights. The EU also provides limited TACIS funding to support nongovernmental organizations and the development of civil society. Policymakers in Brussels and the national capitals are well aware, however, that improved relations and expanded cooperation with Belarus are likely to be of increasing importance for the EU, particularly in the context of enlargement, even if a fundamental shift in relations will have to await Lukashenko's departure from the political scene.

The Mediterranean. The third and perhaps most difficult target of the EU's stabilization policy is the Mediterranean, long a focus of European economic and foreign policy but one in which progress can be difficult to detect. The enlargements of the 1980s brought the Community more directly into contact with this region and created new incentives for policies that would help to narrow the wide economic and cultural differences between Europe and its southern neighbors. Per capita gross national product (GNP) in the countries of the Middle East and North Africa is only around $1,800 per year compared with more than ten times that level in the affluent countries of Western Europe. The countries on the southern littoral of the Mediterranean are expected to increase their populations by some 85 million between 1995 and 2015, which could result in higher levels of legal and illegal immigration into Europe as young entrants to the labor force are unable to find jobs in their own countries.[39] Europeans also are concerned about the rise of Islamic radicalism in countries such as Egypt and Algeria, which is fueled by difficult economic conditions and could spill over into Europe itself, where substantial numbers of immigrants from these countries already live and work. The situation is further complicated by the fact that Europe obtains much of its oil and gas from this region, by tanker and by gas pipelines that cross the Mediterranean from Algeria to Italy and from Algeria to Spain via Morocco.

The EU's overall strategy toward the region was launched with the 1995 Barcelona Euro-Mediterranean Partnership. The driving force on the European side behind the partnership was the Mediterranean countries of the Union, especially France and Spain. With the fall of communism and the new focus on enlargement and the stabilization of Russia, they were concerned about an eastward tilt in EU foreign and development policy that in their view was inspired mainly by Germany and that most served German interests. They argued that while stabilization of the EU's eastern borders was important, dealing with instability to the south deserved equal attention.

The Barcelona partnership was based on expanded cooperation in three spheres: economic; political; and social, human and cultural. As was seen in chapter 8, in the economic area it called for the progressive establishment by 2010 of a free-trade area and for other measures to promote economic growth in the Mediterranean region, including financial aid and EIB loans. In the political sphere, the Barcelona agreement called for respect for human rights and the rule of law, joint efforts to prevent the spread of chemical, nuclear, and biological weapons, and other measures aimed at building confidence in the region. In the social and cultural area, the agreement provided for the development of direct contacts between nongovernmental organizations, educational and cultural institutions, and local and regional authorities on both sides of the Mediterranean.

The partnership was underwritten from the EU side by a major financial commitment. At the Cannes summit in June 1995 the European Council reached agreement on the division of grant aid between the countries of central and eastern Europe (both the NIS under TACIS and the accession candidates under PHARE) and the Mediterranean countries for the period 1995–1999. €4.685 billion was allocated to the Mediterranean, less than the €6.693 billion earmarked for the former communist countries, but a substantial sum nonetheless. Most of this money—€3.435 billion—was earmarked for the MEDA program to fund bilateral and regional economic, social, and cultural projects. The EIB also was asked to increase its lending to the non-EU Mediterranean countries.

In June 2000 the European Council approved a common strategy for the Mediterranean, the EU's third such document since the entering into effect of the Treaty of Amsterdam.[40] Funding for MEDA was increased to €5.35 billion in the 2000–2006 budget perspective. Along with the long-term plan to create an EU-Mediterranean free trade area, EU policy has focused on initiatives intended to bridge cultural gaps between the two sides of the Mediterranean and to head off a damaging "clash of civilizations." Much of the emphasis in the common strategy is on strengthening civil society in the partner countries by fostering direct links with civil society in Europe. Initiatives undertaken along these lines have included the establishment of a Euro-Mediterranean Parliamentary Assembly, establishment of a Euro-Mediterranean Foundation for the Dialogue of Cultures, and numerous MEDA-funded projects to build networks of nongovernmental institutions and organizations across the Mediterranean.

New Neighborhood Policy. As has been seen, the EU responded to the collapse of communism in 1989–1991 by fashioning policies aimed at stabilizing all of the ex-communist countries and supporting their transitions to democracy and free market economies. However, the Union drew a sharp distinction between those countries in central and eastern Europe that were considered candidates for membership and that were offered Europe Agreements, and those countries of the former Soviet Union (the Baltic states excepted) that were not considered as future member states and that were offered PCAs. There was some ambiguity about the Balkans, but by 2000 the facts of geography had begun to assert themselves as it became apparent that these countries had to join their immediate neighbors as members of the EU, albeit after what promised to be a long transition.

As the 2004 enlargement approached, however, it was clear that the EU's early 1990s vision for its eastern and southern periphery needed some adjustment. If accession to the EU for eight and soon ten countries of central and eastern Europe marked a spectacular success for the policy laid out more than a decade earlier, the Union's performance with regard to countries that were not regarded as candidates was far more mixed. Russia was reviving, but EU assistance probably played a very minor role in this process which in any case entailed a certain distancing of Russia from Europe. The record with regard to the other NIS was even less favorable, as both democracy and economic revival seemed stalled in many of these countries. This was a particular problem with regard to the western NIS—Ukraine, Moldova, and Belarus—future neighbors of an expanded Union. Progress with North Africa and the Mediterranean region, also destined to be brought closer to the EU's doorstep by the pending enlargement to Cyprus and Malta, likewise was at best mixed, even as the issue of relations between Europe and the Islamic world became more pressing as a consequence of the September 2001 terror attacks and the subsequent wars in Afghanistan and Iraq.

Against this background, EU experts and officials began to discuss the development of a new policy, variously referred to as "proximity" or "neighborhood" policy, that would try to stabilize the EU's immediate periphery by creating something of a middle ground between exclusion and membership. Some experts even began to refer to the EU as a sort of "benign empire" that was duty-bound to spread its stabilizing influence to the east and south.[41] Responding to these various currents in the debate, in April 2002 the Council asked the Commission and CFSP High Representative Solana to develop a New Neighbors Initiative for relations with these countries, with the goal of improving relations with them and narrowing the gap in stability and prosperity between them and the Union.

At their November 2002 session, the EU foreign ministers reiterated the "need for the EU to formulate an ambitious, long-term and integrated approach towards each of these countries with the objective of promoting democratic and economic reforms, sustainable development and trade, thus helping to ensure greater stability and prosperity at and beyond the new borders of the Union."[42] In March 2003 the Commission issued its *Wider Europe—Neighbourhood: A New Framework for Relations with our Eastern and Southern Neighbours. Communication from the Commission to the Council and the European Parliament*, which proposed that the EU "should aim to develop a zone of prosperity and a friendly neighbourhood—a 'ring of friends'—with whom the EU enjoys close, peaceful and co-operative relations."[43] The European Convention further proposed the constitutionalization of the new policy in Article 42 of the draft constitution, which states: "The Union shall develop a special relationship with its neighbouring states, aiming to establish an area of prosperity and good neighbourliness characterised by close and peaceful relations based on cooperation."

The key factor driving the search for a more effective policy toward the western NIS was enlargement, which focused attention on the challenges for the EU of a "wider Europe" in which the new member states would have a direct stake in expanded relations with their eastern neighbors. But exactly how the New Neighbours Initiative would go beyond the limits of the existing pattern of relations with these countries was unclear, as these relations already were highly institutionalized along lines established in the 1990s. The March 2003 Commission document was in fact greeted rather skeptically in Ukraine and Moldova, both because it did not come with offers of increased aid or trade benefits and, more importantly, because it seemed to place these countries in the same category as fellow "neighbors" in North Africa and thus to deny their European aspirations.

For their part, the foreign ministers of the Mediterranean partner countries "took note" of the EU Wider Europe—New Neighborhood Policy at their regular meeting with their EU counterparts in Naples in December 2003. But what being lumped with countries as different and as distant as Belarus and Moldova meant for partners such as Morocco and Algeria was unclear, as was what effect the new neighborhood policy would have on the Barcelona process and the EU's common strategy for the Mediterranean, both of which remained in effect. However well-intentioned, the new policy was EU-centric and bureaucratic, adding another layer of verbal complexity in an area already thickly settled with acronyms, initiatives, action plans, working groups, and so forth. How effective these mechanisms would be in addressing very real problems of both regions— unemployment, poverty, environmental degradation, trade barriers, corruption, illegal immigration, and terrorism—remained a question mark at best.

OTHER REGIONS AND GLOBAL ISSUES

While the focus of CFSP is on regional issues and efforts to shape events on the eastern and southern peripheries of the EU, in recent years the EU has come to see itself increasingly as a global actor, with worldwide interests and responsibilities. As was seen in chapter 8, the EU has launched regular processes of dialogue with Asia and Latin America. The focus of these dialogues has been on trade and the promotion of EU exports and investment, but they also have a political dimension, which has been reflected in such actions as EU support for democracy and human rights in Burma, involvement in the East Timor dispute in Indonesia, and financial backing for efforts to encourage North Korea to abandon its nuclear weapons program by developing alternative sources of energy. The EU is the world's largest provider of humanitarian aid, which it administers through the European Community Humanitarian Office (ECHO) to regions as diverse as Kosovo, Central America, and southern Africa. The EU member states concert with each other on issues at the UN and other international organizations and vote together over 95 percent of the time, a circumstance that tends to multiply the EU's clout by making it one of the larger ready-made blocs at the UN.

Much of the emphasis in EU policy beyond the European periphery is on conflict prevention, alone or in concert with other international actors such as the United States and the UN. In February 2001 the Council adopted a regulation establishing the EU Rapid Reaction Mechanism (RRM) designed to allow the Union to respond quickly and flexibly, outside regular programs such as TACIS and MEDA, to crisis situations with financial and material assistance.⁴⁴ Activities undertaken by the RRM since have included immediate assistance to Afghanistan in early 2002 following the defeat of the Taliban, support for peace negotiations and UN missions in Somalia, Ethiopia/Eritrea, and Sudan, and support for the June 2003 Round Table Conference on Liberia aimed at finding a solution to the country's internal conflict. Growing out of the colonial heritage of several of its member states, the EU remains heavily involved in sub-Saharan Africa. Individual member states such as France, the UK, and Belgium long have been involved in the political and security affairs of their former colonies, but in 2003 the EU as such mounted its first Union-level intervention in Africa, the Artemis operation in the Democratic Republic of the Congo.

In addition to greater involvement in regions beyond the EU periphery, the Union has begun to emerge as a leader in the search for solutions to global problems that cut across regions, for example, tackling climate change and other international environmental challenges; the fight against international crime, terrorism, and trafficking in drugs; international migration; proliferation of weapons of mass destruction; and sudden outbreaks of deadly contagious diseases such as the Ebola virus. The EU member states (with the noteworthy exception of Finland, which remains concerned about the security of its long border with Russia) are signatories of the 1997 Ottawa treaty banning land mines, and the Union has backed efforts against mines with an EU Mine Action Strategy and funding for de-mining efforts in post–conflict situations around the world. The Union has been a strong backer of the International Criminal Court (ICC) established under the Rome Statute of 1998, and took a hard line with the accession countries when some of them were tempted to conclude bilateral agreements with the United States (which does not support the ICC) that the EU saw as undermining the authority of the court. And the EU has been the main international sponsor of the Kyoto Protocol on curbing greenhouse gas emissions, which Brussels regards as not only important for the environment but as a test of the EU's diplomatic clout in the world and whether it can get countries such as Canada, Japan, and crucially Russia to ratify the agreement despite the nonparticipation of the United States.

The progress that the EU has made in forging a common external policy is of course no guarantee that the member states will see eye-to-eye on all international questions. This point was driven home in early 2003, when the member states were sharply divided over the impending war in Iraq, with France, Germany, and Belgium strongly opposed and the governments of the UK, Spain, and Italy more supportive of U.S. policy. Perhaps the worst part about these divisions from an EU perspective was that they had less to do with Iraq as such than with deep, unresolved differences over the distribution of power in Europe. In September 2002, Chancellor Schroeder successfully capitalized on antiwar and anti-American sentiment in Germany to win his re-election campaign. Chirac then rallied to Schroeder's side, forming an implacable coalition in the UN Security Council (of which France is a permanent, and Germany at the time a rotating, member) against the war. Many observers concluded that Chirac was using the prospect of war and the public opposition it aroused to bolster the Franco-German partnership, draw

Germany away from the United States, and thereby cement French leadership of the EU. Blair even came to believe that Chirac was out to force his resignation, the better to bolster Chirac's own role in Europe. These moves in turn provoked an intense counter-reaction in the other member states and candidate member states, not only in Britain, but also in Spain, Poland, and Italy, by leaders who resented what they saw as a Franco-German bid to hijack the Union.

One effect of the crisis was to accelerate talk once again of a two-speed Europe. At the initiative of Belgian Prime Minister Guy Verhofstadt, Belgium, France, Germany, and Luxembourg held the so-called "chocolate summit" in April 2003 at which they discussed plans to establish a European Security and Defense Identity separate from NATO with a separate military headquarters. Other EU member states, especially Britain, and the United States were suspicious of this initiative, which they saw as an attempt to put the Union—or at least a part of it—on a path of long-term confrontation with the United States.

The EU as a Global Actor in the Twenty-first Century

If the divisions over the war in Iraq were alarmingly wide, one positive effect of the crisis was a renewed effort within the Union to develop a consensus on the nature of the international environment, the security threats to Europe, and the strategies that the EU would follow in attempting to counter these threats. This effort took the form of a draft strategy document that was prepared by CFSP High Representative Solana and presented to the European Council in Thessaloniki in June 2003. Entitled *A Secure Europe in a Better World*, the paper was intended to serve as the basis for a new European Security Strategy to be adopted by the European Council in December 2003.

The paper characterized the international security environment as marked by three new threats—terrorism, proliferation of weapons of mass destruction, and failed states and organized crime—each of which has the potential to combine and interact with the other. In responding to the new threat environment, Solana proposed three strategic objectives for the EU. First, building upon the recent Wider Europe—New Neighborhood initiative and longstanding EU policies toward the periphery, the document called for extending the zone of security around Europe.

Second, the paper endorsed strengthening the international order, repeating the familiar European emphasis on multilateralism and respect for international law and mentioning the UN, the WTO, the international financial institutions, the transatlantic relationship, and important regional organizations such as the Association of Southeast Asian Nations (ASEAN), Mercosur, and the African Union as valuable multilateral instruments. Conversely, the paper noted the existence of certain countries that had "placed themselves outside the bounds of international society" and recommended that these countries be forced to pay a price for their internal and external behavior in their relations with the EU.

Finally, the strategy paper called for actions to counter the new threats. In language that cautiously echoed parts of the controversial U.S. national security strategy document of September 2002, it declared that, unlike in the Cold War, certain threats are so dangerous and dynamic that they require reaction even before crises arise. The emphasis in the paper was on crisis prevention—taking political and economic steps to ensure that the need for military action will not arise—but the way the threat was characterized seemed to open the door somewhat to possible preventive/preemptive military action.

To meet these objectives, Solana called for an EU foreign policy that is more active, more coherent, more capable, and that works with partners. To be active, the paper argued that the Union must develop a "strategic culture that favors early, rapid, and when necessary, robust intervention" to try to head off or defuse crises. To be coherent, EU policy needs to do a better job in getting the various Union-level policies (trade, aid, political dialogue, and so forth) and those of the member states to work together more effectively. The section on capabilities identified four areas for improvement: defense assets (more spending and less duplication), civilian crisis management assets, diplomatic capabilities (including getting the member-state diplomatic services to work together), and intelligence (improved sharing among member states contributing to common threat assessments). The paper also stressed the importance of working with major partners to solve international problems. It termed the transatlantic relationship "irreplaceable" and called for strengthened U.S.-EU ties, but it also singled out five other countries as key partners: Russia, Japan, China, Canada, and India.

As expected, the Solana paper was approved by the European Council at the December Brussels summit, thereby officially becoming the European Security Strategy. Largely in deference to concerns (especially in Germany) that the EU might be gravitating toward approval of preemptive war, language in the first draft regarding "pre-emptive engagement" was stricken and replaced by a weaker endorsement of actions to avert conflicts and threats. Otherwise the text remained largely intact.

Along with the adoption of a document that supposedly defined the substance of CFSP, the member states continued to wrestle with institutional questions. Amsterdam had resulted in the establishment of the post of High Representative for CFSP, but most of the delegates at the 2002–2003 European Convention were convinced that the new Constitution should go further in creating a stronger, single voice that could raise the EU's external profile and pull together its large but disparate foreign policy resources to pursue strategic objectives. Accordingly, the draft EU Constitution contained a number of reforms of the CFSP decision-making structures, the most radical of which was the establishment of the post of an EU foreign minister. The latter individual would be responsible both to the Council of Ministers, serving in effect as the CFSP High Representative, and be a member of the Commission with full voting rights. In the former capacity, the EU foreign minister will chair the regular meetings of the Council of Ministers in its external affairs composition. In the latter capacity, the EU foreign minister will have all of the responsibilities exercised by the EU external affairs commissioner, notably control of the EU external affairs budget and the Commission's network of delegations (in effect embassies) around the world.

How this arrangement will work in practice of course remains to be seen. The elected European Council president, also to be established under the Constitution, also may be a foreign policy voice, as will be the Commission president. Nor is it likely that the foreign ministers of the member states will defer to the EU foreign minister. This is likely to be especially the case with the larger member states, and above all France and the UK, which retain their seats as permanent members of the UN Security Council. Nor does the proposed Constitution replace the current system of consensus decision making for CFSP matters with qualified majority voting (QMV), as many of the more integration-minded Convention delegates favored. The problem of discordant voices thus is likely to remain an issue for the EU in the foreign policy realm, impervious to ultimate solution by further institutional reform and adjustment, but rather an inevitable result of the fact that the member states still have not agreed to unite the substance of their foreign policies or to give up the attractions of independent external representation on key issues. That said, the creation of a foreign minister clearly marks a further step forward toward the creation of a more visible and coherent EU external policy.

The other institutional issue that arose in late 2003 concerned the oft-revisited question of command responsibilities for military operations and the division of labor between NATO and the EU. As noted, at the end of 2002 NATO and the EU finally reached the Berlin plus agreement on assured EU access to NATO assets in crisis situations. But this agreement threatened to become unhinged by the Iraq crisis and the continued push by France, Germany, and Belgium, seemingly in disregard of the 2002 agreement, of an independent EU military planning capability. The impasse over this issue persisted through much of 2003, with the UK strongly opposed to the four-power initiative. Shortly before the December 2003 summit, however, France, Germany, and the UK reached a compromise that subsequently was endorsed by all of the EU member states as well as by NATO. The fifteen agreed that they would establish a separate EU military planning cell, to be located in Brussels. However, the cell would not have the full range of capabilities available to NATO at SHAPE and would be used only as a last resort. In the first instance, the EU member states pledged to consider using NATO assets to plan a crisis operation. If for some reason this was not feasible, they would turn to individual EU member countries, whose national military establishments could be multilateralized to provide a planning capability. Only as a very last resort would the EU rely upon its own planning cell in Brussels. As a further safeguard against the planning cell leading to a NATO-EU divorce, it was agreed that NATO would have a permanent liaison office at the EU headquarters, while the EU would establish a presence at SHAPE.

Notes

1. www.nato.int/docu/basictxt/treaty.htm (accessed June 11, 2004).
2. Richard L. Kugler, *Commitment to Purpose: How Alliance Partnership Won the Cold War* (RAND: Santa Monica, 1993), 54.

3. This provision remains in effect as Article 296 of the renumbered treaty.

4. "First Report of the Foreign Ministers to the Heads of State and Government of the Member States of the European Community (Luxembourg Report)," in *European Political Co-operation (EPC)*, 4th ed. (Bonn: Press and Information Office of the Federal Government, 1984), 30.

5. Bull. EC 10-1981, 55–56.

6. Article J.4. This language is found in amended form in Article 17(1) of the amended TEU.

7. Ibid.

8. *EU: Selected Instruments Taken From the Treaties*, Book I, 1, 80–85.

9. WEU Council of Ministers, "Petersberg Declaration," June 19, 1992.

10. "Joint Declaration on the CFSP Annexed to the Accession Treaties," quoted in Fraser Cameron, *The Foreign and Security Policy of the European Union* (Sheffield: Sheffield Academic Press, 1999), 104.

11. *Western European Union: History, Structures, Prospects* (Brussels: WEU Press and Information Service, June 1995).

12. "Presidency Conclusions: Turin European Council, 29 March 1996," in *The European Councils: Conclusions of the Presidency 1996* (Luxembourg: OOPEC, 1997), 7.

13. Article 17.

14. "Declaration on the Western European Union," *European Union: Selected Instruments*, 80.

15. IISS, *The Military Balance 1998/1999* (London: Oxford University Press, 1999), 295–300.

16. "Declaration on European Defense," UK-French summit, Saint-Malo, December 3–4, 1998, www.fco.gov.uk (accessed June 14, 2004).

17. Peter Norman and Andrew Parker, "Common EU Army the 'Logical Next Step,'" *Financial Times*, May 10, 1999.

18. "Presidency Report on Strengthening of the Common European Policy on Security and Defence," *Presidency Conclusions (Cologne)*, Annex III, 36–42.

19. "Presidency Progress Report to the Helsinki European Council on Strengthening the Common European Policy on Security and Defence," *Presidency Conclusions (Helsinki)*, Annex IV.

20. Article 25 TEU.

21. Article J.4.4.

22. James M. Goldgeier, *Not Whether But When: The U.S. Decision to Enlarge NATO* (Washington, D.C.: Brookings Institution Press, 1999), 77–107.

23. "Charter on a Distinctive Partnership between NATO and Ukraine" and "Founding Act on Mutual Relations, Cooperation and Security between NATO and the Russian Federation," *NATO Review*, no. 4, 1997.

24. *NATO Press Communiqué* M-1(94)3, Declaration of the Heads of State and Government, Ministerial Meeting of the North Atlantic Council, Brussels, January 11, 1994; Jeffrey Simon and Sean Kay, "The New NATO," in Ronald Tiersky, ed., *Europe Today* (Lanham, Md.: Rowman & Littlefield, 1999), 369–99.

25. *Final Communique*, NAC-1(96)63, Ministerial Meeting of the North Atlantic Council, Berlin, June 3, 1996.

26. "An Alliance for the 21st Century," Washington Summit Communiqué, www.nato.int/docu/pr/1999/p99-064e.htm (accessed June 11, 2004).

27. "EU-NATO Declaration on ESDP," NATO Press Release (2002) 142, December 16, 2002.

28. "Presidency Conclusions: Thessaloniki European Council, 19 and 20 June 2003," paragraph 65.

29. "Report to the European Council in Lisbon on the Likely Development of the Common Foreign and Security Policy (CFSP) with a View to Identifying Areas Open to Joint Action Vis-à-vis Particular Countries or Groups of Countries," *The European Councils, 1992–1994*, 16–20.

30. Quoted in Grant, *Delors*, 192.

31. Hanns W. Maull, "Germany in the Yugoslav Crisis," *Survival* 37, no. 4 (Winter 1995–96): 99–130.

32. See David Owen, *Balkan Odyssey* (New York: Harcourt, Brace, 1995).

33. Richard Holbrooke, *To End a War* (New York: Random House, 1998).

34. Tim Judah, "Kosovo's Road to War," *Survival* 41, no. 2 (Summer 1999): 5–18.

35. John Van Oudenaren, *Détente in Europe: The Soviet Union and the West Since 1953* (Durham: Duke University Press, 1991), 275–82.

36. "New TACIS Regulation Enters into Force," IP/00/66, Brussels, January 21, 2000. For historical data in funding, see the External Affairs website at http://europa.eu.int/comm/dg1a/tacis.

37. *Common Strategy of the European Union on Russia of 4 June 1999*, Annex II, *Presidency Conclusions: Cologne*, 14–32.

38. See John Van Oudenaren, "Russia's Elusive Place in Europe," in Simon Serfaty, ed., *The European Finality Debate and Its National Dimensions* (Washington: CSIS, 2003), 232–57.

39. Russell King, "Labour, Employment and Migration in Southern Europe," in John Van Oudenaren, ed., *Employment, Economic Development and Migration in Southern Europe and the Maghreb* (Santa Monica: RAND, 1996).

40. O.J. L 183, July 22, 2000, 5–10.

41. See Michael Emerson, *The Wider Europe as the European Union's Friendly Monroe Doctrine*, CEPS Policy Brief no. 27, October 2002.

42. General Affairs Council, 2463rd Council meeting, Brussels, November 18, 2002, 14183/02.

43. European Commission, COM(2003) 104 final, March 11, 2003, 4.

44. Council Regulation (EC) no. 381/2001, O.J. L 57, February 27, 2001, 5–7.

Suggestions for Further Reading

Asmus, Ronald D. *Opening NATO's Door*. New York: Columbia University Press, 2002.

Batt, Judy et al. *Partners and Neighbours: A CFSP for a Wider Europe*. Paris: EU Institute for Security Studies, 2003.

Buchan, David. *Europe: The Strange Superpower*. Aldershot: Dartmouth, 1993.

Cameron, Fraser. *The Foreign and Security Policy of the European Union*. Sheffield: Sheffield Academic Press, 1999.

Gasteyger, Curt. *An Ambiguous Power: The European Union in a Changing World*. Gütersloh: Bertelsmann, 1996.

Nuttall, S. *European Political Cooperation*. Oxford: Clarendon Press, 1992.

Regelsberger, Elfriede, et al., eds. *Foreign Policy of the European Union: From EPC to CFSP and Beyond*. Boulder, Colo.: Lynne Rienner, 1996.

CHAPTER 10

Enlargement

At the time of the third enlargement in January 1986, few politicians in the European Community (EC) countries would have predicted that within six years they would be debating membership for ten candidate countries from central and eastern Europe, three of which were then still part of the Soviet Union. It was assumed that with the accession of Portugal and Spain, the Community more or less had reached the limits of its expansion in Western Europe and that the challenge of the future was to deepen rather than widen to new members. By mid-1993, however, the then twelve member states had taken a decision in principle to admit those countries just emerging from the shadow of more than forty-five years of communism. As the European Union (EU) concentrated during the remainder of the 1990s on implementing the Maastricht treaty and especially its provisions on Economic and Monetary Union (EMU), the candidate countries embarked on an arduous pre-accession process designed to prepare them for membership early in the twenty-first century. This process culminated in the accession, on May 1, 2004, of ten new member states to the Union. Bulgaria and Romania were judged not quite ready for membership, which was deferred to the target date of 2007. The other candidate country, Turkey, had not yet begun accession negotiations, and whether it would ever overcome the internal problems and external reservations standing in the way of its membership remained a subject of lively debate in Europe.

The Collapse of Communism

The initial groundwork for enlargement was laid in the late 1980s, after Soviet leader Gorbachev abandoned the previous Soviet policy of trying to undermine the EC by refusing to deal with it and the Community began to develop its relations with central and eastern Europe. In June 1988 the EC and the Soviet-led Council for Mutual Economic Assistance (CMEA) signed an agreement according each other diplomatic recognition and pledging to cooperate in such areas as the environment, harmonization of standards, and science and technology. This was followed by the conclusion of bilateral trade and cooperation agreements between the EC and the CMEA member countries, beginning with a ten-year trade and cooperation agreement with Hungary signed in June 1988. Until this time there had not been any formal political or trade relations between the Community and its eastern neighbors.

These first generation agreements soon were rendered obsolete, however, by the accelerating pace of change in the communist world. In June 1989 partially free elections took place in Poland, resulting in a resounding victory for the opposition Solidarity movement. In the same month, roundtable talks between government and opposition began in Hungary aimed at fundamental change in the political system. By mid-1989 there was reason to hope that at least these two countries were on a path that would lead to the establishment of market economies and pluralist political systems. Western governments sought to respond to these changes and support them with external aid. At the July 1989 Paris summit, the G-7 issued a declaration of support for economic and political reform in eastern Europe and called for an international conference to coordinate Western aid to Poland and Hungary. In December 1989 the Council of Ministers approved PHARE (*Pologne et Hongrie: Actions pour la Reconversion Économique*), a Community-funded program of technical assistance to encourage the development of private enterprise and the building of market-oriented economies.[1]

Once again, however, within a short time the West European governments found themselves playing catch-up with rapid change. In September 1989 Hungary opened its border with Austria, allowing thousands of East German citizens to travel to West Germany. After months of mass demonstrations in Leipzig, Dresden, and other cities, on November 9 the Berlin Wall was thrown open by an East German government that could no longer control its borders. In November and December opposition rallies led to the ouster of the communist regime in Czechoslovakia. In December, roundtable talks between government and opposition began in Bulgaria. For the most part these revolutions were peaceful, but they culminated in late December with bloody fighting in Romania between opposition and security forces and the execution, on Christmas Day, of former dictator Nicolae Ceausescu and his wife Elena. By 1990, the communist regimes in central and eastern Europe all had been swept away.

The most immediate political challenge facing Western governments as a result of these upheavals was German unification. Chancellor Kohl quickly seized the initiative on this issue, putting forward, in November 1989, a ten-point plan for creation of a German confederation. The United States supported unification, but Britain and France were skeptical. The Soviet Union had taken a hands-off attitude toward the changes in eastern Europe, but it declared itself opposed to unification. The Soviet Union still had several hundred thousand troops in the German Democratic Republic (GDR), and as a World War II victor power it had certain legal rights in Germany. In the GDR itself it was initially unclear whether the voters would opt for rapid absorption by West Germany or whether they would seek to maintain some kind of separate identity within a German confederation. By the fall of 1990 these uncertainties were resolved. In July, Kohl and Gorbachev met at a Soviet retreat in the Caucasus and reached agreement on the external aspects of German unity. Germany would remain in NATO, Soviet troops would be withdrawn, and a special bilateral treaty of friendship and cooperation between Germany and the Soviet Union would be signed. On August 31 the two German states signed a treaty on unification, and on September 12 the four victor powers concluded a treaty on the "final settlement with regard to Germany." On October 3, less than a year after the breaching of the Wall, Germany was united. The five states of the former GDR automatically became part of the Community, and immediately qualified for aid from the structural funds.

Europe's Initial Response

PHARE, THE EBRD, AND EARLY DISCUSSION OF ENLARGEMENT

While focusing on the immediate question of Germany, the Community and its member states took up the broader challenge of stabilization in central and eastern Europe as a whole. At an extraordinary session of the European Council in November 1989, French President Mitterrand proposed the establishment of a special bank to help finance economic transition in the central and east European countries. The other member states embraced Mitterrand's idea, which led to the founding of the European Bank for Reconstruction and Development (EBRD) the following year. The EBRD is not an EU institution, but the EU and its member states are its largest shareholders (the United States, Canada, Japan, and other countries also own shares in the bank).

In July 1990 the Community extended its PHARE program to Bulgaria, Czechoslovakia, Yugoslavia, and East Germany. Assistance to Romania was temporarily delayed, owing to the post–Ceausescu government's suppression of student demonstrations in the spring of 1990, but in 1991 Bucharest became eligible for PHARE grants. Following the breakup of the Soviet Union, PHARE was extended to Estonia, Latvia, and Lithuania, an early indication that the EU was determined to treat the three Baltic countries as part of central and eastern Europe rather than lump them with Russia and the Commonwealth of Independent States.[2]

Almost immediately after assuming power, the post-communist leaders of central and eastern Europe began to suggest that their countries should be admitted to what soon was to become the EU, as well as NATO. These suggestions evoked an ambivalent response in Western Europe. On the one hand, political leaders were concerned about instability emanating from the region and its potential implications for the EU: the spread of ethnic conflict such as had erupted in the former Yugoslavia, surges of refugees and migrants, environmental disasters, and political extremism. Membership in a strengthened EU was probably the only way to ensure, over the long term, that instability and reversion to dictatorship were banished from the continent. In addition, many in Western Europe felt a strong sense of obligation to the peoples of central and eastern Europe and especially to those who had led the fight against communism. Welcoming these people into the European family was clearly the right thing to do.

On the other hand, the costs and complications of enlargement promised to be enormous and could well derail the ambitious plans of the early 1990s to deepen—to create a Union with a single currency, a common foreign and security policy, and increased powers for the Union's central institutions. There was also the difficult question of where to draw the line: Even if the decision in principle to admit former communist countries was taken, it was still necessary to decide which countries, how many, and according to what criteria. It was not too difficult to envision Germany's eastern neighbors, Poland and the Czech Republic, becoming members, but what about the countries in the unstable Balkans? The question of membership became even more acute when, at the end of 1991, the Soviet Union dissolved into fifteen constituent states, raising the prospect that the Baltic countries or Ukraine or even Russia might apply.

Initially, there was some discussion about alternative arrangements to membership, such as the proposal for a European confederation advanced by Mitterrand in his 1989 New Year's speech, or in the various proposals for a Europe of "concentric circles" in which the EU would form an inner core, the European Economic Area (EEA), perhaps expanded to include the more advanced countries of central and eastern Europe, would form a second circle, and Russia and the other countries of the former Soviet Union would form the outermost circle. None of these schemes had enduring appeal, however, especially to the countries of eastern and central Europe, which continued to press for nothing less than full EU membership.

THE EUROPE AGREEMENTS

In addition to PHARE, the most important element in the EU's response to the changes in central and eastern Europe was the Europe Agreements, so named to distinguish them from the association agreements that the Community had concluded with many countries in other parts of the world. These agreements established a legal framework for the expanding economic, commercial, and human contacts between the Union and countries that were rapidly emerging from communism. They also were an interim response to the requests from the countries of the region for rapid admission to the Union. By establishing a form of association that would help to prepare these countries for membership as well as provide concrete and symbolically important links to the Union, the EU hoped to put off the question of membership. The preambles to the Europe Agreements noted the aspirations of the signatories to join the Union, but they stopped short of guaranteeing that membership was assured.

In August 1990 the European Commission proposed the conclusion of Europe Agreements between the Community and Hungary, Poland, and Czechoslovakia. The key economic provision of the Europe Agreements was the establishment, within a ten-year period, of free-trade arrangements between the Community and the signatory countries (also known as associated countries). Expanded market access was controversial in some of the Community member states, where protectionist lobbies sought to maintain tight quotas on the import of iron and steel, textiles, and agricultural goods—the very items these countries had to sell. At one point Hungary and Poland threatened to suspend the negotiations unless they received a better offer from the Community negotiators. The offer was improved, and in December 1991 these two countries and Czechoslovakia concluded the first of the Europe Agreements. (The agreement with Czechoslovakia later was replaced, following the breakup of that country in 1993, by separate agreements with the Czech Republic and Slovakia.) Europe Agreements subsequently were concluded with Romania (February 1993), Bulgaria (March 1993), Estonia, Latvia, and Lithuania (June 1995), and Slovenia (June 1996).

Because the Europe Agreements dealt both with economic matters that are the responsibility of the EU as a unit and with political and cultural matters that are the shared or exclusive responsibility of the individual member states, they were mixed agreements, concluded by the European Communities (EC, ECSC [European Coal and Steel Community], and Euratom) and the member states. They thus required a lengthy ratification process involving the European Parliament, each of the EU member-state national parliaments, and the parliament of the associated country. In order to facilitate trade and investment during the ratification process, the Commission put into effect Interim Agreements with each associated country covering just those areas—trade and commerce—reserved for Community competence. All of the associated countries thus were able to benefit from expanding trade and investment with the EU even before the Europe Agreements went into effect.

The agreements were asymmetrical in that they provided for faster dismantlement of trade barriers on the Community than on the associated countryside. With the exception of textiles and clothing and iron and steel products, all quantitative restrictions on the import of industrial goods to the Community were eliminated from the date of entry into force of the trade provisions of the agreements.[3] Market access for agricultural products was enhanced, although quantitative restrictions remained in place. The agreements also called for the progressive approximation of legislation in the central and east European countries to Community norms and adoption of Community competition rules. Under the liberalizing effect of the agreements and in response to broader changes in the region, trade in central and eastern Europe was rapidly redirected toward the EU market. By 1996, the region accounted for 10.2 percent of EU exports and 8.1 percent of imports, and Poland alone had surpassed Norway as the fourth-ranking export market for EU goods.[4]

Through approximation of legislation and other means, the Europe Agreements went a long way toward extending the four freedoms of the single market to the candidate countries well in advance of actual membership. The one major exception was the free movement of people. Reflecting the concern in Western Europe about possible surges of immigrants from the economically distressed central and east European countries, the agreements were very cautious with regard to the movement of workers. Their main contribution was to improve the lot of workers already in EU countries rather than to facilitate new flows of people. In addition to their trade and economic provisions, the Europe Agreements provided for expanded political dialogue and cultural cooperation. They called for regular meetings of foreign ministers and other high officials to discuss topics of common interest with the aim of achieving convergence in the foreign policy positions. In the cultural sphere, the central and east European countries became eligible to participate in many EU and member-state cultural and educational programs. To monitor implementation, each Europe Agreement provided for the establishment of an Association Council consisting of representatives of the EU (i.e., the Commission), the member states, and the associated state. These councils were to meet at the ministerial level at least once each year to review progress and to take decisions regarding further action.

While attempting to slow the momentum toward EU membership, the West European countries, supported by the United States, encouraged the gradual integration of the former communist countries into other Western economic and political institutions, notably the Council of Europe and the Organization for Economic Cooperation and Development (OECD). Hungary joined the Council of Europe already in 1990; Poland in 1991; Bulgaria in 1992; and the Czech Republic, Estonia, Lithuania, Romania, Slovakia, and Slovenia in 1993. In 1990 the OECD established a Center for Cooperation with European Economies in Transition. The following year the Czech and Slovak Federal Republic, Hungary, and Poland became special OECD Partners in Transition. The Czech Republic became a full member of the OECD in 1995, followed by Hungary and Poland in 1996. As discussed in chapter 9, these countries also became candidates for NATO membership, and Poland, Hungary, and the Czech Republic secured admission already in 1999.

The Copenhagen Decisions

The debate on enlargement simmered throughout the early 1990s. British Prime Minister Thatcher and her successor, John Major, were among the most enthusiastic proponents of enlargement. They tended to favor the earliest and broadest possible expansion. As Thatcher later wrote, "having democratic states with market economies, which were just as 'European' as those of the existing Community, lining up as potential EC members made my vision of a looser, more open Community seem timely rather than backward."[5] At the other end of the spectrum were federalists such as Delors who, while they recognized that something had to be done for central and eastern Europe, were concerned that a broader and more diverse membership would undermine progress toward a more cohesive Union. Delors was skeptical about the admission of even the European Free Trade Association (EFTA) countries and warned that it would take fifteen to twenty years before the ex-communist countries were ready for membership.[6]

In the end the most decisive voice in the debate was that of Kohl, who favored enlargement to central and eastern Europe—including the three Baltic states—but ruled out membership for Russia, Ukraine, and other states of the former Soviet Union. Kohl's position was somewhere between that of the British, who were accused by many of favoring indiscriminate and hasty enlargement, and that of Delors and many in the southern European countries, who sometimes were suspected of wanting to postpone enlargement indefinitely. The German view therefore tended to emerge as the consensus position.

Enlargement became a matter of "not whether but when" at the June 1993 Copenhagen European Council. This was the first occasion on which the EU member states formally declared enlargement as an explicit goal of the Union. Although they did not set a timetable, the EU leaders stated that accession would "take place as soon as an associated country is able to assume the obligations of membership by satisfying the economic and political conditions required."[7] (The associated countries were those countries with which the Union had concluded or planned to conclude Europe Agreements.)

The European Council further specified four criteria for determining whether an associated country was ready for membership: (1) stability of institutions guaranteeing democracy, the rule of law, human rights, and respect for and protection of minorities; (2) the existence of a functioning market economy; (3) capacity to cope with competitive pressures and market forces within the Union; and (4) the ability to take on the obligations of membership, including adherence to the aims of political, economic and monetary union, that is, the *acquis communautaire*. These conditions subsequently became known as the Copenhagen criteria by which the readiness of the candidate countries to begin accession negotiations and later their suitability for membership were judged.

In addition to these criteria that applied to the applicants, the European Council established one condition for the EU itself to meet, stipulating that "the Union's capacity to absorb new members, while maintaining the momentum of European integration, is also an important consideration in the general interest of both the Union and the candidate countries." This statement reflected an awareness in the EU that despite the progress made in the Treaty of Maastricht, the EU needed to undertake further institutional and policy reforms in order to be ready to accept such a large group of new members. It later was interpreted to mean that negotiations regarding the admission of additional candidates would not begin until at least six months after the completion of the post-Maastricht Intergovernmental Conference (IGC) that was scheduled to convene in 1996. The EU ultimately stuck to this timetable, taking the decision to begin negotiations with five central and east European countries and with Cyprus in December 1997, exactly six months after the signing in the Treaty of Amsterdam negotiated at the IGC.

Meeting the Criteria
PRE-ACCESSION STRATEGY

With the Copenhagen decision, the EU had committed itself to admitting ten countries with a combined population of 105 million. Measured at purchasing power standards, per capita gross domestic product (GDP) in the region was less than one-third of the EU average. In addition to its relative poverty, the central and east European region is highly diverse, with different languages, religions, and historical traditions. The magnitude of the enlargement challenge thus called for an effective pre-accession strategy to prepare the candidates for membership.

The main instruments used to help the candidate countries get ready for membership were the Europe Agreements and PHARE. Proposed at first in part to deflect demands for membership, the Europe Agreements soon became the key means to advance the pre-accession process. In addition to helping to redirect trade from what had been the CMEA to the EU market, the agreements provided a framework for the alignment of candidate country laws and regulations with EU norms and a mechanism, through the Association Councils, for regular bilateral dialogue. Initially established in 1989 to promote the transition from communism, PHARE was expanded and adapted to serve the needs of a longer term pre-accession process. PHARE provided technical and financial assistance to help align legislation with EU norms, address environmental and nuclear safety problems, and develop the telecommunications and transport infrastructure needed to bring about integration into the European and world markets. PHARE was allocated ECU 4.2 billion for the period 1990–1994, an amount that was increased to ECU 6.693 billion for 1995–1999. The candidate countries also benefited from U.S. aid under the Support for East European Democracy (SEED) Act, technical assistance programs mounted by the OECD, and loans from the EBRD and World Bank. U.S. aid tapered off over time, however, as it became clear that the integration of these countries into the West was primarily the responsibility of the EU.

THE ESSEN DECISIONS

Although the European Council took the decision in principle to enlarge in June 1993, at first there was little real momentum behind the enlargement effort. There were delays in putting into effect the Europe Agreements. The unexpectedly difficult Maastricht ratification process preoccupied the twelve through much of 1993, and was followed by the complex task of finalizing the accession agreements with Austria, Finland, and Sweden. The EU was widely criticized in the United States and in the candidate countries for a perceived lack of seriousness about the accession process. This in turn helped to strengthen the rationale for the NATO enlargement that was discussed in the previous chapter.

The stage finally was set for more rapid progress at the June 1994 Corfu European summit, at which the Greek presidency prepared to turn its responsibilities over to Germany, which had announced that it intended to make enlargement a priority of its presidency in the second half of 1994. The European Council invited the Commission to make specific proposals for the further implementation of the Europe Agreements and the Copenhagen decisions. On the basis of this request, the Commission produced several documents that became the basis for the pre-accession strategy adopted by the European Council at Essen in December 1994.

The Essen European Council reviewed all of the areas in which progress was needed to prepare the candidate states for membership and singled out several issues that were expected to be especially difficult and that had the potential to derail the admission of the candidates. These issues included the internal market, agricultural policy, and the structural funds. As discussed in chapter 4, the European Council instructed the Commission to prepare a detailed white paper on the internal market that was to serve as a guide for the candidate countries to the EU-level legislation that they needed to transpose into national law and be prepared to implement and enforce. The European Council also called for the Commission to prepare a paper on agriculture policy as it related to enlargement and that could serve as the basis for tackling this sensitive area.[8]

The most noteworthy institutional innovation at Essen was the establishment of the Structured Dialogue. Unlike the Association Councils, which brought each associated country together with the Council in a 1 + 15 format, the Structured Dialogue would bring together all of the Europe Agreement states and all of the EU member states, in effect prefiguring future Council sessions in an enlarged Union. Under the Structured Dialogue, foreign ministers, economics ministers, and ministers of transport, health, the environment, and other specific areas began to meet with their EU counterparts to conduct a dialogue on policy convergence and other forms of cooperation.

The Accession Process

THE LEGAL BASE

The formal procedures governing accession are set forth in Article 49 of the Treaty of European Union, as revised by the Treaty of Amsterdam (see box 10.1). It stipulates that any European state that respects democratic principles and the rule of law may apply to become a member of the Union. References to political rights and political freedoms were not included in the earlier article governing enlargement, Article O of the Maastricht treaty. Their incorporation by the 1996–1997

Box 10.1   The Treaty Basis for Enlargement

Article 49, Treaty on European Union

Any European State which respects the principles set out in Article 6(1) may apply to become a member of the Union. It shall address its application to the Council, which shall act unanimously after consulting the Commission and after receiving the assent of the European Parliament, which shall act by an absolute majority of its component members.

The conditions of admission and the adjustments to the Treaties on which the Union is founded which such admission entails shall be the subject of an agreement between the Member States and the applicant state. This agreement shall be submitted for ratification by all the contracting States in accordance with their respective constitutional requirements.

Article 6(1)

The Union is founded on the principles of liberty, democracy, respect for human rights and fundamental freedoms, and the rule of law, principles which are common to the Member States.

IGC reflected heightened concern about the political situation in formerly communist countries and in Turkey.

The first step in the process is a formal application to the Council of Ministers, which is done by submission of a letter and accompanying documentation to the government of the country occupying the rotating presidency of the Council. After it receives an application, the Council asks the Commission to offer an opinion on the candidate's suitability for membership. Based on these opinions, but exercising its ultimate political authority to override the Commission's opinion, the Council then must take a unanimous decision whether or not to begin accession negotiations with the candidate country.

The member states then conduct what are in effect separate IGCs with each candidate country aimed at concluding treaties of accession. While the member states are the formal parties to these negotiations, in practice the Commission, along with the EU presidency country and the Council secretariat, undertake much of the work. The draft treaty of accession then must be approved by the European Parliament by an absolute majority and by the Council unanimously. Following formal signature, the treaty must be ratified by all fifteen member-state parliaments and by the parliament of the applicant country. Once this is accomplished, the accession process is complete and the candidate country can take its place as a full member.

Since the 1993 Copenhagen decisions, the EU has gone step-by-step in accordance with the procedure outlined in Article 49. Beginning with Hungary in March 1994 and concluding with Slovenia in June 1996, all ten associated countries formally applied for membership. (Turkey had already applied in 1987; Cyprus and Malta in 1990.) Having in principle already decided at Copenhagen to proceed with enlargement, the Council of Ministers instructed the Commission to begin work on opinions for each of the ten candidate countries shortly after receiving their applications. The prospective members were asked by the Commission to complete detailed questionnaires to determine how much convergence with EU norms and legislation had been achieved and to identify remaining problem areas. Because accession negotiations could not begin until after completion of the 1996–1997 IGC, the Commission decided to withhold the formal issuing of any opinions until after the signature of the Amsterdam treaty.

AGENDA 2000

At its December 1995 Madrid session the European Council asked the Commission to prepare a composite paper that would include opinions on all ten candidate countries as well as a review of the Cyprus candidacy, noting that "this procedure will ensure that the applicant countries are treated on an equal basis."[9] In addition to asking the Commission to look at all of the applicants at the same time and in the same general framework, the Madrid European Council directed the Commission to examine the likely effects of enlargement on the Union, particularly with regard to agricultural and structural policies, but also in relation to the long-term budgetary outlook. The budgetary question was particularly important, given the fact that new members were expected to be, at least initially, a substantial drain on the EU budget and that the EU itself needed to adopt a new seven-year budget plan in 1999.

The Madrid request was the basis for *Agenda 2000: For a Stronger and Wider Union*, which the Commission delivered in July 1997, a little less than a month after the Amsterdam summit closing the IGC. Running to some 1,300 pages, the report consisted of three parts: an analysis of EU policies and the expected effect of enlargement on the EU, the detailed assessment of each of the eleven candidate countries requested by the Council and required under the enlargement provisions of Article 49, and the new financial framework proposals that were discussed in chapter 3. In judging the preparedness of the candidate countries for enlargement, the Commission referred explicitly to the political and economic criteria established by the European Council at Copenhagen.

As measured against these criteria, the Commission recommended that five countries were ready to begin accession negotiations: the Czech Republic, Estonia, Hungary, Poland, and Slovenia. In addition, it reiterated an earlier opinion that Cyprus was ready to start accession talks. It rejected one applicant—Slovakia—for political reasons, namely, the lack of democracy and respect for human rights under Prime Minister Vladimir Meciar. It concluded that four other countries—Bulgaria, Latvia, Lithuania, and Romania—needed to make greater progress with economic transformation before accession negotiations could begin. (The twelfth candidate country, Malta, had temporarily suspended its application, for reasons that are discussed below.)

The Commission opinions were controversial with the five countries being left behind in the next step of the enlargement process and with some member-state governments. Latvia and Lithuania complained that Estonia had been singled out for special treatment in the Baltic region and appealed to their traditional backers, the Nordic countries, for inclusion in the first round of talks. Slovakia argued that its political situation had been misunderstood by the Commission, while Bulgaria and Romania warned that instability might arise if they were excluded both from NATO and the EU.

THE LUXEMBOURG DECISIONS

Agenda 2000 triggered a broad debate among EU experts and political leaders about how to manage enlargement. There were very real concerns about timing and sequencing. Bringing some countries in ahead of others might, it was feared, divert investment from or contribute to political demoralization in those countries that were left behind, possibly encouraging them to drift back into the Russian sphere of influence. There were also practical considerations. Bringing the Czech Republic into the Union ahead of Slovakia would be difficult to reconcile with the existing Czech-Slovak customs union, while admitting Hungary but not Romania could create hardships for ethnic Hungarians living in Romania and used to traveling freely across the border. On the other hand, maintaining the credibility of the enlargement process and keeping the pressure on laggard countries to improve their performance required some degree of differentiation. Economic performance in Romania and Estonia was so widely disparate that it was difficult to justify treating both in the same group.

The question of Turkey also arose to complicate the enlargement discussion. Privately, many European politicians argued that Turkey was too culturally and economically different from Europe ever to become a member of the Union. Even those in Europe who believed that Turkey some day might join had concluded that it was by no means ready for accession negotiations—or even a serious pre-accession strategy. For its part, the Turkish government accused the EU member states of an anti-Islamic bias and was especially incensed that the Commission had recommended that the EU begin accession negotiations with Cyprus—meaning in effect the Greek Cypriot government in Nicosia that was boycotted by the Turkish minority on the island.

The various currents in the enlargement debate confronted the EU governments as they gathered in Luxembourg in December 1997 to take their decision on a first wave of accession negotiations. In the main, the EU heads of government endorsed the Commission's recommendation in favor of Cyprus and five central and east European countries, but they also put in place certain mechanisms intended to minimize any sense of exclusion on the part of the other five transition candidates. They announced that the accession process would begin on March 30, 1998, at a twenty-six-member meeting in London. The participants in the meeting would be the fifteen EU member states, the ten associated states, and Cyprus. This meeting would set the overall framework for accession talks with the candidates and symbolically underline that all eleven had the same status and the same theoretical chance to achieve membership. Within this framework, the EU proposed to establish an "enhanced pre-accession strategy" based on a new mechanism, the "accession partnership," and to begin the first accession negotiations. The EU stressed that those countries not asked to begin negotiations in 1998 were not necessarily being left permanently behind: They could catch up by improving their economic and, in the case of Slovakia, political performance. The Commission was asked to make annual reports to the Council of Ministers and to recommend when additional countries were ready to begin accession negotiations.[10]

In addition to these mechanisms involving the candidate countries, the European Council proposed the convening of an annual European Conference consisting of the fifteen EU member states, the eleven candidates, and Turkey. The conference was described as "a multilateral forum for political consultation, intended to address questions of general concern to the participants and to broaden and deepen their cooperation on foreign and security policy, justice and home affairs, and other areas of common concern, particularly economic matters and regional cooperation."[11] In reality, the conference was little more than a consolation prize for Turkey: a forum in which it could participate with the current and prospective EU member states, but one that was not in itself a part of the enlargement process. The Turkish government denounced this arrangement as confirming Turkey's "third-class" status in EU eyes, and chose not to participate in the conference when it took place in London the following March.

As decided by the Luxembourg meeting, the negotiations with the first six candidate countries were to begin in parallel with the implementation of an enhanced pre-accession strategy for all eleven of the applicant countries. This strategy was based on existing mechanisms—the Europe Agreements, PHARE, and the Structured Dialogue—along with the new instrument, the accession partnerships that were to be negotiated bilaterally between the Union and each of the candidate countries. Each partnership was to consist of a detailed program aimed at helping the candidate country adopt as much of the Union *acquis* as possible in the run-up to accession. PHARE aid was to be conditioned on how well the candidate countries did in implementing their accession partnership programs. The EU also pledged to increase the overall level of its pre-accession aid and opened certain programs (e.g., in education and training and research) to the applicant countries even before they became members. This was intended to give the candidates experience in EU working methods and to provide opportunities for students, teachers, business people, and academics from the candidate countries to cooperate on joint projects with counterparts from EU member states.

Opening the Negotiations
THE FIRST WAVE

Negotiations with the first six candidate countries began in March 1998. Based on the four previous enlargements and the situation in the candidate countries, most experts predicted that the first enlargement negotiations and the ensuing ratification process would take three to five years. Many in central and eastern Europe questioned why the negotiations should take so long.

In principle, a country joining the EU is asked to accept the *acquis communautaire*. There thus would not seem to be all that much to settle in the accession negotiations. In practice, however, candidate countries often try to negotiate transition periods for the phasing in of Union rules and policies on their territory, or even to secure permanent derogations from certain EU policies or legal provisions. In such negotiations, the current EU member states and the Commission generally try to minimize all such derogations and to keep transition phases relatively short, so as to preserve the unity and coherence of the Union and especially its single market. The acceding countries, on the other hand, may have incentives to delay the adoption of certain costly standards or to seek other exceptions to the *acquis* in response to particular domestic economic or political circumstances. The negotiations also deal with budgetary, policy, and institutional questions: how much each new member state will pay into and receive back from the EU budget, production quotas and subsidy levels under the Common Agricultural Policy (CAP), and how many seats it will receive in the European Parliament, votes in the Council of Ministers, and so forth.

The first stage of the accession negotiations was an elaborate screening process carried out for thirty-one chapter headings. As shown in table 10.1, the process covered both first-pillar matters and Common Foreign and Security Policy (CFSP) and Justice and Home Affairs (JHA) issues. Screening began with relatively straightforward and uncontentious areas, such as small and medium-sized enterprises, science, education, and external relations, and then only later proceeded to the more difficult areas, such as agriculture, competition policy, and free movement of persons.

Following a series of multilateral meetings at which experts from the Commission presented their understanding of the *acquis* for each of these areas, the Commission undertook bilateral meetings with each of the six applicants to determine how far they had come in accepting the *acquis* for each chapter. The candidate countries were asked whether they were prepared to accept all of the EU legislation and regulation for a given chapter and if so whether they had adopted the necessary domestic laws and established the requisite administrative structures to

Table 10.1   Chapter Headings of the Screening Exercise

1. Free movement of goods
2. Freedom of movement for persons
3. Freedom to provide services
4. Free movement of capital
5. Company law
6. Competition policy
7. Agriculture
8. Fisheries
9. Transport policy
10. Taxation
11. Economic and monetary union
12. Statistics
13. Social policy and employment
14. Energy
15. Industrial policy
16. Small and medium-sized enterprises
17. Science and research
18. Education and training
19. Telecommunications and information technologies
20. Culture and audiovisual policy
21. Regional policy and coordination of structural instruments
22. Environment
23. Consumers and health protection
24. Cooperation in the fields of justice and home affairs
25. Customs union
26. External relations
27. Common foreign and security policy
28. Financial control
29. Financial and budgetary provisions
30. Institutions
31. Other

Source: European Commission

implement those laws and regulations. This was also the stage at which the candidate countries declared whether they intended to request transitional arrangements for some chapters. For some countries and some areas, acceptance of the *acquis* presented relatively little problem. For others, the transition periods requested were so long as to render almost meaningless the concept of an *acquis*. In the environmental area, for example, several applicant countries suggested that they would be ready to comply with EU drinking water directives only by 2017. Screening of some chapters was complete by the fall of 1998, and was followed by the start of actual negotiations for those chapters. The screening process as a whole for the first-wave candidates was completed by the summer of 1999.

PROGRESS REPORTS AND THE SECOND WAVE

In November 1998 the Commission issued the first of the reports detailing how well the candidates were preparing themselves for enlargement. As mandated by the Luxembourg European Council, the reports covered both the six countries already engaged in accession talks and the others that had been placed on hold. For the former, the reports drew heavily on the initial results of the screening process.

The overall assessments were blunt and somewhat surprising. Of the six leading countries already involved in negotiations, Estonia and Hungary were given high marks for continuing to make progress on accepting the *acquis*, while Poland was given a more mixed report for its delays in addressing standards, state aids, the environment, agriculture, and administrative capacity. The Czech Republic and Slovenia, two front-runners at the top of the per capita income scale in the region, were castigated for making almost no progress since the Commission opinions of July 1997. On the other hand, several of the countries in the second tier were praised for real progress on reform. Latvia in particular was singled out as nearing the point where it might be ready to join the first tier and begin the actual negotiation process.[12] The report thus was mixed, suggesting that in some leading countries the pre-accession process was bogging down, but that the overall EU strategy of trying to narrow the gap between the first and second tiers was working, at least in part.

The Commission issued its second regular report on the progress of the candidate countries in October 1999, after the six leading countries had completed the screening process and after the six other candidate countries had had the benefit of nearly two years of intensified pre-accession assistance. The Commission again was upbeat about the economic performance of Hungary, Latvia, and Bulgaria and about the turn to democracy in Slovakia. It noted that in Poland delays in transposing EU directives into national law were accumulating, and was again critical of the Czech Republic. It expressed continuing concern about the disastrous economic situation in Romania, where reform still lagged.

The 1999 report also tackled the question of transition periods that had come up in the screening process and that was emerging as an important issue in the negotiations. Some of the candidate countries were asking for post-accession transition periods of a decade or more for EU urban waste water directives, the drinking water directive, and various other environmental laws, arguing that they did not have the resources to bring their performance up to EU standards except over the very long term. The EU had begun the negotiations with the position that transition periods be limited to no more than five years, but gradually showed a greater willingness to grant the candidate countries more time and latitude in nonmarket areas of the *acquis*—while still driving a hard bargain on the internal market.

Despite the somewhat mixed assessment in the 1999 report, the Commission recommended that the Council authorize the start of accession negotiations with all of the candidate countries left out in 1997 and that it elevate Turkey's status to that of a formal candidate. This gave rise to some concern among the member states that the Commission was rushing the enlargement process, but at the Helsinki summit in December 1999 they endorsed the recommendations in the October 1999 progress report. In February 2000 negotiations got underway with six additional countries: Bulgaria, Latvia, Lithuania, Malta, Romania, and Slovakia.

Cyprus and Malta

Although most of the focus in the 2004 enlargement was on central and eastern Europe, Cyprus and Malta, two small Mediterranean island countries with historic ties to Europe, were also part of this process and presented some special difficulties. The population of Cyprus—about 770,000—is approximately 80 percent ethnically Greek, with the remainder Turkish Cypriot. Under the 1960 constitution, power was apportioned between the Greek and Turkish communities. However, Cyprus has been partitioned since the 1974 invasion of the island by Turkey. The northern part of the island declared itself to be an independent state, which the international community does not recognize. The Turkish Cypriots do not participate in the legally recognized government in Nicosia, which is effectively in the hands of the Greek majority.

Prompted by Greece's admission to the EC in 1981 and Cyprus's own economic interests, in July 1990 the Cypriot government applied for membership. In June 1993 the Commission issued a favorable opinion on the application, noting the relative strength of the Cypriot economy and the progress that Cyprus had made in using its association agreement with the EU to align itself with many EU laws and practices.[13] Both sides began preparing for accession negotiations, but it was not until the June 1994 European Council in Corfu that the member states confirmed that the next phase of the enlargement process would include Cyprus (and Malta), a decision that was taken under pressure from Greece. It meant that the European Council was pledged not to proceed with any eastward enlargement without also taking up the Cypriot application, either simultaneously or beforehand. The Cyprus candidacy thus was at least tacitly linked with those of the central and east European countries.

In response to these developments, Turkey argued that any move to incorporate Cyprus into the EU would run counter to the 1960 Treaty of Guarantee that was signed by Greece, Turkey, and Britain and that bars Cyprus from joining any international organization of which Greece and Turkey are not both members. The Turkish government further warned that if the Greek Cypriot government joined the EU against its wishes, it would incorporate the northern part of the island into Turkey. The EU rejected this interpretation of the 1960 treaty and argued as a matter of principle that Turkey could not wield a veto over the actions of the legally recognized government in Nicosia. As a practical matter, however, the EU was concerned about the implications of proceeding with enlargement in the face of Turkish opposition and bringing a still-partitioned island into the Union. Incorporation of the northern zone into Turkey would be particularly problematic, as it would mean the occupation of a part of EU territory by a non-EU power.

The EU hoped to avoid this situation by achieving a political settlement to the division of the island prior to enlargement. In the optimistic scenario, the prospect of EU membership would soften the differences between the Greek and Turkish communities, much the way EU membership for Ireland and the UK helped to defuse conflict over the status of Northern Ireland, contributing to the April 1998 Belfast agreement. Per capita income in the Turkish sector of Cyprus was only one-third the level of that in the south, and the Turkish minority stood to benefit enormously from the structural aid and market access that would come with enlargement. By the time the EU began accession talks with Cyprus in March 1998, however, there was still little sign that this approach was working. The Turkish community turned down an invitation to participate in the talks and repeated its threats to accept an offer to merge with Turkey. Although it did not attempt to block a start of talks, France vowed to block actual accession if the negotiations concluded before a solution to the partition of the island was achieved. For its part, Greece threatened to block any enlargement to central and eastern Europe if Cyprus was not accorded membership as well. The elevation of Turkey to candidate status in December 1999 helped to ameliorate the tension over the island, but did not in itself provide an answer to the question of whether a divided Cyprus could be admitted to the Union.

The candidacy of Malta, a relatively prosperous country with a population of just over 360,000, did not present major difficulties for the EU, but the Maltese themselves were somewhat ambivalent about joining the Union. After achieving independence from Britain in 1964, Malta was for many years governed by the neutralist Labor Party, which opposed closer ties with Western Europe. The Nationalist Party took power in 1987 and adopted a pro-integration position. Following the lead of Cyprus, in July 1990 the Nationalist government applied for EC membership. In June 1993 the Commission issued a favorable opinion on Malta's candidacy and in June 1994 the European Council pledged that Malta could participate with Cyprus in the next wave of enlargement negotiations.[14] However, after the October 1996 elections the Labor party returned to power and promptly suspended Malta's application. Malta thus was left out of the key decisions about enlargement that were made at the 1997 Luxembourg European Council.

The Nationalist Party returned to power in the elections of 1998 and quickly sought to reactivate Malta's bid for membership. The December 1998 Vienna European Council welcomed this decision and asked the Commission to undertake an update of its 1993 opinion. Malta was included in the list of countries approved for the start of accession negotiations by the December 1999 Helsinki European Council, and negotiations began in February 2000.

Turkey

As noted above, Turkey was accorded the status of formal candidate for EU membership at the December 1999 Helsinki European Council. This was only the latest step in a long and complex relationship between Turkey and Western Europe. A country of 70 million people, most of whom are Muslim, Turkey was a recipient of Marshall Plan aid and thus a founding member of the OEEC/OECD. It has been a member of the Council of Europe since 1949 and of NATO since 1952. Since Kemal Attaturk's reforms of the 1920s, it has been a secular republic in which people are free to practice their religion but in which Islam is given no special political status. Turkey thus considers itself a European power that should be welcome in all European bodies, including the EU.

But Turkey also faces economic, political, and security problems that distinguish it from the rest of Europe. Its economy suffers from high inflation and budget deficits in the 10 percent of GDP range. Economic growth has been strong, but from a low base. Per capita GDP is only one-third the EU average. Turkey's population is young and growing and according to current projections will surpass even that of Germany by 2015, which would make Turkey the largest country in the Union were it to become a member.

Internally, Turkey faces a severe political challenge from its Kurdish minority in the southeastern part of the country. The struggle with the Kurdish independence movement has resulted in thousands of deaths and harsh criticism in Western Europe about violations of human rights by the Turkish government and armed forces. Turkey also faces a complex international security situation. It historically has had tense relations with its southern and eastern neighbors, Syria, Iraq, and Iran, as well as disputes with Greece over Cyprus, oil rights under the Aegean Sea, and the ownership of a small island off the Turkish coast. The 2003 war in Iraq, in which Turkey was at the heart of disputes over whether it should support the U.S.-UK effort to oust Saddam Hussein or join with France and Germany in trying to block the war, only served to highlight the complexities of Turkey's international situation.

As noted in chapter 8, in 1963 Turkey and the EC concluded an association agreement that pointed to eventual full membership. But relations between Turkey and the Community deteriorated in the 1970s, at first over Cyprus and later because of internal developments in Turkey. In order to forestall the annexation of Cyprus by Greece, in July 1974 Turkey invaded the island, occupying its northern part. Some 200,000 Greek Cypriots fled south to escape Turkish rule. The United Nations adopted resolutions calling for the removal of foreign troops and the return of refugees, but over the years the division of the island hardened and became a permanent irritant in Greek-Turkish and EC-Turkish relations. In 1983 authorities in the Turkish sector unilaterally proclaimed the establishment of the Turkish Republic of Northern Cyprus.

These developments were accompanied by a deterioration of economic and political conditions in Turkey. In September 1980 a group of Turkish military officers seized power, dissolved the parliament, and suspended the constitution. In January 1982 the European Parliament responded by voting to suspend the Turkey-EC association agreement. The accession of Greece to the Community in 1981 cast a further shadow on the EC-Turkish relationship, as it meant that henceforth there was one member state with strongly anti-Turkish feelings that was able to block all important initiatives toward Turkey under the unanimity provisions of the founding treaties.

Between 1983 and 1987 civilian rule gradually was restored. In April 1987 Turkey formally applied for EC membership, and in September 1988 the suspension of the EC-Turkey association agreement was lifted, resulting in a renewal of economic aid to Ankara. As required by the provisions in the Treaty of Rome governing accession of new members, the European Commission delivered an opinion on Turkey's candidacy for membership in December 1989. It concluded that the Community was not ready to accept any new members until completion of the single market program. It also identified problems specific to Turkey that would have ruled out enlargement negotiations in any case: Turkey's relatively poor record on democracy and human rights, its disputes with Greece, and the failure to find a solution to the Cyprus problem. In the absence of real progress toward membership, the keystone of the EU-Turkey relationship became the 1996 customs union that was discussed in chapter 8.

Throughout the 1990s, the fact that Western Europe seemed to be backing away from earlier pledges regarding membership contributed to a sense of betrayal in Turkey. Relations with the EU were badly strained as the pre-accession process with the central and east European countries and with Cyprus gathered momentum, leaving Turkey in its wake and suggesting that the West European countries were more ready to accept the formerly communist countries of central and eastern Europe than a country that had been a loyal ally throughout the Cold War and in the 1990–1991 Persian Gulf war against Iraq. These tensions came to a head in 1997 with the approach of the crucial Luxembourg decisions about the start of enlargement talks.

As has been seen, at Luxembourg the European Council declined to affirm Turkey's candidacy by treating it in the same way as the other twelve candidate countries, but it did propose the ill-fated European Conference, as well as instructed the Commission to draw up a new strategy to prepare Turkey for accession "by bringing it closer to the European Union in every field." The Turks were not impressed with these measures, and instituted a deep freeze in relations with the Union. The Turks were well aware of how far they needed to go to be ready for membership. But they also had come to believe that the real reasons for rejection by the EU had less to do with their own economic and political problems than with the fact that Turkey is an Islamic country and as such was fundamentally unwelcome in Europe. In the Turkish view, the EU was relegating Turkey to a third-tier status, not only behind the leading candidates such as Poland but also behind relative laggards such as Romania and Bulgaria—countries that in some cases had barely begun the market reforms called for by the end of communism.

Relations finally took a dramatic turn for the better in December 1999 when the European Council, endorsing the recommendation in the Commission's October 1999 progress report, formally upgraded the status of Turkey to candidate member. The heads of state and government declared that "Turkey is a candidate state destined to join the Union on the basis of the same criteria as applied to the other candidate states." To lend substance to this claim, the EU agreed to develop a pre-accession strategy for Turkey and to conclude an accession partnership agreement on the same basis as those negotiated with the other candidate countries. Turkey also was granted the right to participate in certain EU programs and in multilateral meetings among the EU member states and the candidates for membership.

Given the plethora of internal and external problems that Turkey faces, many experts and political leaders in Europe argue, privately if not in public, that the EU would be extremely foolish to accept Turkey as a member. To do so would be to internalize these problems, dramatically increase the numbers of poor in the Union, and give it extended borders with several unstable Middle Eastern countries. Others in Europe, supported by the United States, stressed that the door must be kept open for Turkey and that EU membership holds the best prospect for overcoming many of these problems. With the December 1999 decision, the EU seems to have embraced the latter position, stressing that Turkey *is* welcome in Europe and placing the onus on Turkey to meet the same Copenhagen criteria that apply to central and eastern Europe. Actual membership is likely to be at best a long-term prospect, however, and one that will provoke renewed political controversy in the Union.

From Copenhagen to Copenhagen: Finalizing the Deal

Following the Helsinki decisions, by early 2000 the EU was conducting parallel negotiations with twelve countries, all of which were struggling to bring their domestic legislation into line with EU norms and to improve their competitiveness before becoming part of the single market. Progress varied among the candidates, with small and relatively advanced countries such as Estonia and Cyprus (leaving aside the political question of the division of the island) in the lead, and large and poorer countries such as Bulgaria and Romania lagging behind. In general, the "Helsinki six" were managing to close the gap with the Luxembourg group that had started negotiations two years earlier, as the former made rapid progress on the less complex and contentious chapters while the pace of progress with the latter slowed as the negotiations turned toward the difficult questions of agriculture, regional funds, free movement of labor, and competition policy and state subsidies to industry.

Although at times difficult, the negotiations proceeded relatively smoothly. Beginning with the easiest and least controversial areas, the negotiators "closed" successive chapters with the candidate countries, as the latter continued to make progress in adopting their economic and political systems to EU norms. In the crucial area of the single market, the Commission largely prevailed in its insistence on acceptance of an undiluted *acquis*. With the important exception of free movement of labor, remarkably few transitional arrangements were granted in the three most relevant chapters. The free movement of goods chapter was closed with the ten leading candidate countries with a mere six transitional arrangements, all relatively short in duration and dealing with marketing authorizations for pharmaceuticals and in one case medical devices. Similarly, there were only a few transitional arrangements in the freedom to provide services chapter, all having to do with the financial sector and such issues as the status of credit unions in various accession countries. In the free movement of capital chapter there were eleven agreed transitional arrangements, but they dealt with the politically sensitive issues of the purchases of secondary residences and farm and forest land in the accession countries rather than the movement of capital for general business purposes.

The one area in which the single market *acquis* was affected by transition arrangements was the free movement of labor, which was done largely at the insistence of the existing member states. Under the terms of the free movement of persons provisions included in the accession treaties, for two years following accession each of the member states in the existing Union may apply national measures to limit access to their labor markets from the new member states. Following this period, there will be reviews of new member state labor market access to the old member states. The old member states may keep transition arrangements in place for another three years. The transition period should end after five years, but member states in the old Union retained the right to prolong transition arrangements for another two years if there are serious disturbances of the labor market or the threat of such disturbances. These provisions were in large part a political gesture aimed at assuaging concerns in countries such as Austria and Germany about unemployment and competition for jobs from workers in the new member states. Most experts predicted that immigration pressures after enlargement would be modest, as workers in the accession countries will be encouraged to stay where they are (or even return from Western Europe) by the rising incomes and increased job opportunities in their own countries after enlargement (much as happened in Portugal and Spain when they joined the EC in 1986).

In view of the steady progress being made in the accession negotiations, at the European Council meeting in Göteborg in June 2001 the fifteen set the end of 2002 as the target date for concluding accession treaties with those countries judged ready for membership, a timetable that would allow these countries to join the Union in 2004 and to take part as members in the elections to the European Parliament set for June of that year.[15] At the Laeken European Council in December

2001, the fifteen confirmed this timetable and named the ten countries that they regarded as on track for membership in 2004: the Czech Republic, Cyprus, Estonia, Hungary, Latvia, Lithuania, Malta, Poland, Slovakia, and Slovenia.[16] The stage thus was set for a "big bang" enlargement that among the negotiating candidate countries would leave out only Bulgaria and Romania, whose economic performance and progress in adopting the *acquis* still lagged that of the other candidate countries.

However, as 2002 began there still were many unresolved issues relating to agricultural payments and production levels, the EU budget, and certain rules and regulations for which various candidate countries sought exceptions or transitional arrangements. Because the negotiations with the candidate countries on agriculture were linked to the EU's own internal discussions on the reform of the CAP, finalization of this issue was deferred from the initial target date of the spring of 2002 to the fall of that year, after the scheduled national elections in France and Germany. The stage thus was set for an intense round of negotiations during the Danish presidency in the second half of 2002, aiming at a finalization of the accession terms at a December summit in Copenhagen.

In October 2002 the European Commission delivered its long-awaited recommendations on which countries were ready to finalize accession negotiations by the end of the year. It reaffirmed the choice of the "Laeken 10" and stated that Bulgaria and Romania were not ready for membership, but that they could join the main group by 2007.[17] Meeting in Brussels in late October, the heads of state and government of the fifteen made the final decisions about the financial terms to be offered to the new member states upon accession, tackling the contentious issue of direct payments to farmers in the accession countries. In the compromise final offer on agriculture, the fifteen agreed to start such payments at the 25 percent level and raise them to full Union levels only by 2013, a stance that was criticized by candidate country governments as unfair and possibly endangering prospects for approval of the accession treaty in national referenda. The October European Council also settled on the amount of aid under the structural and cohesion funds to be given to the new member states in 2004–2006, cutting assistance from the €25.567 billion level agreed at Berlin to €23 billion, in part in order to find the funds for the direct payments, which had not been included in the Berlin agreement.

These decisions paved the way to an intense final round of negotiations with the ten lead candidate countries, aiming toward conclusion at the December Copenhagen summit. Acting on its own initiative, in late November the Danish presidency put forward a supplementary package intended to win final accession country acceptance of the deal. It called for additional spending of €2.45 billion beyond the levels agreed by the European Council in October, to be devoted to agriculture, improving border security, and for Slovakia and Lithuania, nuclear dismantling. Following continued hard bargaining in the days leading up to the Copenhagen summit, the Danish package became the basis for the final accession deal. It was agreed that some €40.4 billion would be paid by the Union to the accession countries in 2004–2006, half of it to Poland. This was a gross figure, not counting payments into the EU coffers from the accession countries. Net of such payments, total transfers to the new members in the remainder of the budget period were projected to be about €12 billion. The EU stuck to its original position that direct payments to farmers in the new member states would be set at 25 percent of EU levels, but the accession countries won the right to transfer money from long-term EU aid funds and their own national budgets to direct payments, with the effect that such payments could reach 60 percent of EU levels already by 2004. These terms ultimately were accepted by all ten of the candidate countries in the days leading up to the summit, resulting in a triumphant outcome in Copenhagen.

Apart from the terms of the accession deal, one of the most noteworthy aspects of the enlargement endgame was the set of final premembership checks that the EU put in place to ensure that the candidate countries would follow through on implementation before May 1, 2004, the target date set by the EU Council of Ministers for formal entry following the completion of all ratification procedures.[18] At the insistence of member-state governments that were skeptical of the degree of real convergence with EU norms in the candidate countries or worried about their own domestic public opinion, the accession process included final checks in the period between signature of the accession treaties and the official entry into the Union following ratification. If one or more candidate countries failed to complete agreed pre-accession tasks, formal admission to the Union could be delayed. The accession treaties also contained safeguard clauses that could be invoked by the existing member states after accession that would allow for the temporary suspension of full market access in the event of economic crisis.

CYPRUS AND TURKEY

The most suspenseful issue in the enlargement endgame concerned the question of Cyprus. At the December 1999 Helsinki European Council, the fifteen expressed support for a comprehensive political settlement on the island, to be negotiated under UN auspices, that would allow a united Cyprus to enter the Union. However, they also stipulated that if no settlement was reached by the completion of the accession negotiations, the European Council would decide on accession without a settlement being made a precondition. The Helsinki decision subsequently became the standard EU formulation on this issue, the last word in effect to which the Turkish community and Turkey were expected to respond.

Eleventh-hour hopes that a settlement could be reached that would enable a united Cyprus to enter the Union were concentrated heavily on the initiative put forward by UN Secretary General Kofi Annan in the fall of 2002. It called for the establishment of a loose confederation that then would enter the Union. Accepted by the Greek Cypriote government but rejected by Turkish Cypriote leader Denktash, the UN offer remained the basis for negotiations that were to extend beyond the December 2002 Copenhagen decisions into the period before Cyprus accedes in May 2004 and possibly into the membership period itself. Absent an agreement, however, the EU was determined to admit a divided Cyprus into the Union, a prospect that was certain to heighten tensions with Turkey and create certain practical problems with regard to trade and the free movement of people.

What to do about Turkey itself was a key question for the fifteen as they approached the final decisions on enlargement. Turkey had been elevated to formal candidate status in December 1999, and the Turks had used the ensuing three years to make progress on economic and political reforms in line with the accession criteria. The government and public opinion in Turkey generally believed that Turkey was ready to start negotiations for membership and that the Copenhagen summit should set a definite date for when this process could begin. This in turn provoked demands in EU member states that Turkey should make major concessions—for example, by pressing the Turkish Cypriots to accept a pre-accession settlement on the island—in return for settling a date. The old issue of Turkey's European identity also resurfaced, most dramatically in November 2002 when European Convention president Giscard d'Estaing, in a move that was seen as aimed at heading off setting a date for the start of accession talks with Ankara, spoke out against membership for Turkey, telling *Le Monde* that it had "a different culture, a different approach, a different way of life." "Its capital is not in Europe, 95 percent of its population live outside Europe, it is not a European country." In his view, Turkey's entry into the EU would lead to demands to admit other Middle Eastern and North African states, starting with Morocco. Ultimately it would mean "the end of the European Union."[19]

Giscard's foray clearly backfired, however, and the reaction to it was a factor in the turn of events that led to decisions at the Copenhagen summit that, while they fell short of Turkey's maximal demands, advanced its prospects for membership. The European Council declared that it would take a decision on negotiations in December 2004 (following the Commission's regular report on the progress of the candidate countries), and that if it was satisfied that Turkey met the Copenhagen political criteria, the EU would open accession negotiations "without delay." The failure to secure a guaranteed date was a setback for pro-EU sentiment within Turkey and raised the prospect that Cyprus, which would participate in the December 2004 decision as an EU member, could block its candidacy. However, the fairly mild response of the Turkish government seemed to confirm a widely held view than an informal guarantee had been extended and that if Turkey continued on its existing trajectory, negotiations indeed would begin in 2005. The depth of political support for admitting Turkey remained questionable, however, especially as the war in Iraq in early 2003 and the ensuing rash of terrorist attacks in Istanbul linked to Islamic extremist groups further heightened concern about Turkey's exposed geopolitical position.

Meanwhile, a divided Cyprus entered the EU on May 1, 2004, although not under circumstances that EU negotiators had envisioned. In April 2004 the *Greek* Cypriote community surprised and disappointed the EU by rejecting the UN plan in a referendum. The Turkish community approved the plan, however, prompting the EU to lift longstanding sanctions on the northern part of the island. Prospects for reunification of the country seemed especially bleak, and some officials in Turkey went so far as to claim that the division was now permanent.

AN ENLARGED UNION AND A WIDER EUROPE

The conclusion of the accession negotiations at the December 2002 Copenhagen summit took place amid deepening intra-European and transatlantic tensions over the post–September 11 international situation and in particular over the U.S.-UK project to drive Iraqi dictator Saddam Hussein from power on the grounds that his possession of weapons of mass destruction posed a grave threat to regional and global security. France and Germany led the opposition to U.S. policy, backed by Belgium and several other smaller European countries and the overwhelming majority of European public opinion, while Britain, Spain, and Italy were more supportive of U.S. policy. The divisions among the EU member states and across the Atlantic placed the candidate countries in an awkward position, forcing them to choose between solidarity with the United States or with key European countries.

The crisis came to a head in January 2003, as France took the lead in opposing the United States in the UN Security Council. Asked to comment on the growing opposition to U.S. policy in Europe, U.S. Secretary of Defense Donald Rumsfeld provoked a storm of controversy by claiming that the opposition was centered in "old Europe" and that the "center of gravity is moving east." A week later, the leaders of Spain, Portugal, Italy, the UK, Denmark, and three accession countries—Hungary, Poland, and the Czech Republic—published an open letter in the European edition of the *Wall Street Journal* in which they declared their commitment to solidarity with the United States. The "Letter of Eight," as it became known, was followed by a declaration by the Vilnius 10—the central and east European accession countries, as well as Bulgaria, Romania, Albania, and Croatia—declaring their support for Washington. Both letters had been drafted and approved by a series of ad hoc consultations among the governments concerned, without involving the EU machinery in Brussels or Greece as the EU presidency country. French president Jacques Chirac was furious at these apparent breaches of intra-European solidarity and claimed that the accession countries had "missed a good opportunity to keep quiet." This remark in turn caused deep offense in the accession countries and raised questions about whether "old" member states such as France in fact were prepared to welcome the new member states as equals.

Although these developments severely strained political relations in Europe, they did not derail the enlargement process, which went ahead as planned. Under the auspices of the Greek presidency, the leaders of the ten accession countries met in Athens on April 16, 2003, with their member-state counterparts to sign the accession treaty. Moreover, despite the earlier controversies over agriculture and finance, voters in the acceding countries overwhelmingly approved the accession treaty: 84 percent for and 16 percent against in Hungary, 93–6 in Slovakia, 77–23 in Poland, 77–23 in the Czech Republic, 54–46 in traditionally Euroskeptic Malta, 90–10 in Slovenia, and 91–9 in Lithuania. In most of these countries, the only shadow over the referenda was low turnout: only 46 percent of eligible voters cast their ballots in Hungary, and 52 percent in Slovakia, numbers that suggested more indifference and ignorance than outright opposition. Parliaments in the existing member states also approved the treaty, and in no country was opposition to enlargement strong enough to provoke calls for a national referendum on the issue.

With ratification assured, the key question for the EU was what kind of Europe would emerge in the future. The EU and the accession countries still face years of hard work and difficult economic, political, and institutional adaptation to fully overcome the division of Europe. Income levels in the accession countries still only range from 33 percent (Latvia) to 80 percent (Cyprus) of the EU per capita average, and convergence to EU levels may take decades. While the accession countries have adopted nearly all of the *acquis* in the accession negotiations and transposed it into national law, developing all of the ingrained habits of trust and cooperation that have grown over decades in the western part of Europe still will take time.

The EU also will face some important challenges relating to the "leftovers" and "left outs"—countries that are slated to become members of the Union but are not yet ready, as well as countries that are unlikely ever to become members of the Union but that nonetheless are still part of Europe and will need to find ways to relate to an expanded EU. Bulgaria and Romania are expected to join the EU in 2007, but only if they use the intervening period to make up the deficiencies that prevented them from joining with the other ten candidate countries in 2004. The fate of Turkey also remains a question mark for the Union. Whether it can make the reforms needed to launch accession negotiations in 2005 and whether the EU itself can hold true to its—in many places politically unpopular—promise to make Turkey a member will be key issues for the future.

The western Balkans—Albania, Bosnia-Herzegovina, Croatia, Macedonia, and Serbia and Montenegro (the loose federation that replaced Yugoslavia in 2003, and that technically includes the province of Kosovo)—also are likely to become members of the EU at some point, as these countries are virtually surrounded by present and future EU member states. The task of actually preparing these poor, war-torn, and crime-ridden countries to rejoin Europe is likely to be long and difficult, however, and will require large amounts of political and financial capital from the international community and above all from the EU itself. To the east, there is the question of the Newly Independent States (NIS). Given its size, diversity, and great power traditions, Russia is unlikely ever to become a member of the EU, but building a solid and cooperative Russia-EU relationship, probably in the form of a free-trade agreement, is in the interests of both sides. As was seen in the previous chapter, Ukraine, Belarus, and Molodova are the focus of the EU's New Neighborhood policy. But these countries are not likely to be satisfied forever with association status. They will continue to press for candidate status or, if permanently frustrated in their quest to join Europe, possibly could drift back into closer association with Russia. Either way, their ultimate path will be of huge significance for the EU and the wider international community.

Conclusion

Perhaps the biggest question looming on the horizon is how the EU itself will change as a consequence of enlargement and of the important institutional changes that are being driven by the enlargement process. The accession countries have rejoined Europe only to find "Europe" itself engaged in a vast debate about how Europe should be defined, where its ultimate borders lie, and how it can be made to work efficiently with an expanded and more diverse set of members—all issues that were addressed in the European Convention and the ensuing Intergovernmental Conference. These questions ultimately lead back to the fundamental issue of a European identity and its meaning for the citizen, which are discussed in the final chapter.

Notes

1. Council Regulation (EEC) 3906/89 on economic aid to the Republic of Hungary and the Polish People's Republic, December 18, 1989.

2. Council Regulation (EEC) 2698/90, September 17, 1990; Council Regulation (EEC) 3800/91, December 23, 1991.

3. Bartlomiej Kaminski, "The Significance of the 'Europe Agreements' for Central European Industrial Exports," *Policy Research Working Paper* (1314), The World Bank, June 1994.

4. European Commission, "EU Trade Facts and Figures," November 1998.

5. Margaret Thatcher, *The Downing Street Years* (New York: HarperCollins, 1993), 769.

6. Charles Grant, *Delors: Inside the House That Jacques Built* (London: N. Brealey Pub., 1994), 143.

7. *The European Councils, 1992–1994*, 86.

8. "Report from the Council to the Essen European Council on a Strategy to Prepare for the Accession of the Associated CCEE," *Presidency Conclusions, 1992–1994*, 155–62.

9. *The European Councils, 1995*, 48.

10. *Luxembourg European Council, 12 and 13 December 1997: Presidency Conclusions*, Brussels, SN 400/97.

11. Ibid.

12. "The New Bogeymen," *Business Central Europe*, December 1998/January 1999, 46–47.

13. *The Challenge of Enlargement: Commission Opinion on the Application by the Republic of Cyprus for Membership*, Bull. EC Supplement 5/93.

14. *The Challenge of Enlargement: Commission Opinion on Malta's Application for Membership*, Bull. EC Supplement 4/93.

15. "Presidency Conclusions: Göteborg European Council, 15 and 16 June 2001," SN 200/1/01.

16. "Presidency Conclusions: European Council Meeting in Laeken, 14 and 15 December 2001," SN 300/1/01.

17. European Commission, *Towards the Enlarged Union: Strategy Paper and Report of*

the European Commission on the Progress towards Accession by Each of the Candidate Countries, Brussels, COM (2002) 700 final, October 9, 2002.

18. "Presidency Conclusions: Copenhagen European Council, 12 and 13 December 2002," SN 400/02.

19. "Pour ou contre l'adhésion de la Turquie à l'Union européenne," Le Monde, November 8, 2002.

Suggestions for Further Reading

Much information is available on the website of the European Union, http://europa.eu.int, and in particular the home page of the Directorate-General for Enlargement of the European Commission, http://europa.eu.int/comm/enlargement/index_en.html (accessed June 11, 2004).

Avery, Graham, and Fraser Cameron. *The Enlargement of the European Union*. Sheffield: Sheffield Academic Press, 1998.

Baun, Michael. *A Wider Europe: The Process and Politics of European Union Enlargement*. Lanham, Md.: Rowman & Littlefield, 2000.

Cameron, Fraser, ed. *The Future of Europe—Integration and Enlargement*. London: Routledge, 2004.

European Commission. *Towards the Enlarged Union: Strategy Paper and Report of the European Commission on the progress towards accession by each of the candidate countries*, Brussels, COM(2002) 700 final, October 2002 (available at http://europa.eu.int).

———. *Agenda 2000: For a stronger and wider Union. Bulletin of the European Union*, Supplement 5/97.

CHAPTER 11

The United States and the EU
PARTNERS OR RIVALS?

It is difficult to overestimate the importance that the United States and the European Union (EU) have for each other and the role that Washington has played in shaping the history of European integration. The United States helped to launch this process through the Marshall Plan and continued to lend it political support from the 1950s onward. By some measures, the United States and the EU remain each other's primary economic partners, notwithstanding the rise of Asia and the relative shift in global trade to the Pacific. The United States also remains engaged, through NATO, in the security affairs of Europe. Washington at times also has played a *negative* role in inspiring moves toward increased European unity. Economic and Monetary Union (EMU), for example, resulted in part from efforts by the European countries to free themselves from dependence on an unstable dollar, while progress in recent years toward a stronger EU defense and foreign policy reflects European resistance to U.S. approaches to some foreign policy questions.

Nonetheless, the importance of the United States for the EU appears to be diminishing and is likely to continue to do so over time. Most of what happens in Europe, including progress toward further integration, has little to do with the United States, as Europeans proceed with their own projects for their own reasons. This trend is in part a result of the end of the Cold War, as Europeans no longer need the United States to protect them from the Soviet military threat or, as was the case in central and eastern Europe, look to the United States as a beacon of freedom. The diminished U.S. role is also an effect of the European integration process itself—its very complexity and its character as a work in progress. Policy-makers, academics, think-tank researchers, and editorial writers in Europe increasingly operate in an intellectual climate in which they debate in conferences, meetings, and study groups such issues as how to establish a qualified majority in the Council of Ministers, how to organize EU military operations, and whether a UK-France-Germany troika is good for the Union. Collectively, these questions are crucial to the future of Europe, but the time and intellectual resources devoted to them divert attention from the rest of the world and contribute to an inward focus that attaches less importance to developments in other parts of the world.

Assessing the EU-U.S. relationship—its character, importance, and future direction—is thus an inherently tricky exercise, one in which it is possible to underestimate the role that the United States has played in shaping the development of Europe, but also where it is easy to make the opposite error and to attribute U.S. causes to purely European effects. This chapter attempts to strike a balance by examining three aspects of this relationship: the institutional, the economic, and the political and security.

Institutions

Although the United States strongly supported European integration since the 1950s, the institutional side of U.S.-EC/EU relations long remained curiously underdeveloped. The EC as such had no competence for political and security issues, and Washington in any case preferred to deal with Europe on these issues in NATO and through its bilateral relations with such key allies as Britain and West Germany. Trade was the focal point of the U.S.-EC relationship, but it was dealt with mainly in the multilateral General Agreement on Tariffs and Trade (GATT) forum. Highly institutionalized U.S.-EU relations began only in the 1990s, as the EU assumed broader policy responsibilities under the Maastricht treaty and the United States recognized that the end of the Soviet threat would mean a shift in relative importance from NATO to the EU.

The impetus for a new relationship initially came from Washington. In a speech in Berlin in December 1989, a month after the opening of the Berlin Wall, Secretary of State James Baker acknowledged the need to develop stronger ties between the United States and the EC in the political as well as the economic spheres and proposed that the two sides "work together to achieve, whether in treaty or some other form, a significantly strengthened set of institutional and consultative links."[1] This proposal was greeted warily in some European capitals (notably Paris), where the United States was suspected of wanting to gain a "seat at the table" in internal European deliberations. But these concerns were overcome, and in November 1990 the United States and the Community signed their first general agreement, the Transatlantic Declaration.[2] It called for improved cooperation and consultations in both the political and the economic spheres, the latter in the context of joint efforts to strengthen the multilateral trading system, and for institutionalizing U.S.-EC consultations at the summit, ministerial, and working levels. The agreement also singled out combating terrorism, fighting narcotics trafficking and international crime, and preventing the spread of nuclear, chemical, and biological weapons as areas for increased cooperation.

The 1990 agreement was a symbolic breakthrough, but in itself it did not lead to better U.S.-EU relations. The early 1990s was a period of heightened transatlantic tensions over the war in the former Yugoslavia, trade issues, and the future of NATO. These strains arose during the presidency of George H. W. Bush and continued into the Clinton administration, some of whose officials declared that they saw U.S. interests shifting toward Asia and away from Europe. Relations began to improve only in the mid-1990s with the completion of the Uruguay Round and the new and vastly more positive transatlantic cooperation with regard to the former Yugoslavia.

In December 1995 the United States and the EU signed a more comprehensive agreement, the New Transatlantic Agenda (NTA), that expanded the range of U.S.-

EU dialogue and cooperation. Many observers on both sides of the Atlantic were concerned that in the absence of a unifying threat, Europe and America were beginning to drift apart. Some political leaders were calling for a grand gesture to breathe new life into the transatlantic relationship. One of the most frequently heard proposals was for the creation of a Transatlantic Free Trade Agreement (TAFTA) on the model of the 1993 North American Free Trade Agreement (NAFTA).[3] While governments agreed that action of some kind was necessary, they rejected the TAFTA proposals as premature and unrealistic. Both sides were suffering from trade liberalization fatigue following the stormy conclusion of the Uruguay Round and feared that a new set of negotiations might do more harm than good by stirring up controversies over such unresolved issues as audiovisual products and agriculture.

Instead, the NTA called for progress on an economic agenda that was more modest but more concrete and achievable over the short run. The two sides agreed to carry out a joint study of ways to facilitate trade in goods and services and to further reduce or eliminate tariff and nontariff barriers. In addition to its trade and economic provisions, the NTA called for expanded cooperation in three other areas: promoting peace, stability, democracy, and development worldwide; responding to global challenges; and building bridges across the Atlantic. Appended to the NTA was a Joint EU-U.S. Action Plan in which the two sides committed themselves to 150 specific actions that were intended to give substance to the four fields of cooperation covered in the NTA.

Unlike the 1990 agreement, which was negotiated during a period of tension between the United States and France over the future of NATO and thus contained only a perfunctory affirmation of the Atlantic alliance, the NTA contained a strong and more explicit affirmation of NATO as the "centerpiece of transatlantic security" as well as of the emerging European security and defense identity as an element strengthening the European pillar of the alliance.[4] It thus reflected a certain convergence of views on security issues, with the United States coming to embrace a stronger European security identity while the Europeans, including France, explicitly recognized the enduring role of NATO. The sides pledged to work to implement the peace in the former Yugoslavia, strengthen democratic and market institutions in central and eastern Europe, build a European framework including Russia, Ukraine, and the other newly independent states (NIS), promote Turkey's further integration into the transatlantic community, and work toward a resolution of the Cyprus question. Beyond Europe, they affirmed the global nature of their partnership and pledged "to act jointly to resolve conflicts in troubled areas, to engage in preventive diplomacy together, to coordinate our assistance efforts, to deal with humanitarian needs and to help build in developing nations the capacity for economic growth and self-sufficiency."[5]

With regard to global issues, the agreement called for cooperation in combating the proliferation of weapons of mass destruction and common efforts in the area of international disarmament. It also expanded upon the commitments made in the 1990 declaration for mutual cooperation in responding to global challenges covered by the EU's third pillar: the fight against organized crime, terrorism and drug trafficking, and immigration and asylum matters.

The section of the NTA on building bridges across the Atlantic called for stronger people-to-people links among educational institutions, sister cities, and other groups in civil society, including by means of the emerging medium of the Internet. Transatlantic links in these areas were already very extensive (albeit organized mainly along U.S.-individual country rather than U.S.-EU lines) and it was not readily apparent what a new agreement could do to expand these links. But the NTA did lead to some concrete results, for example a U.S.-EU Science and Technology Agreement that went into effect in 1998 and a U.S.-EU Agreement on Higher Education and Vocational Training. Another innovation was the Transatlantic Business Dialogue (TABD), a regular conference of U.S. and European business leaders that was launched in Seville, Spain, in November 1995 as a lobby for business interests favoring further U.S.-EU trade liberalization. The TABD played an important role in facilitating conclusion, in June 1997, of the first EU-U.S. Mutual Recognition Agreement (MRA), a framework document covering technical and safety standards for certain electrical and electronic equipment, pharmaceutical products and certain medical devices, and the safety of recreational boats. The TABD was followed by the establishment of other sectoral dialogues—the Transatlantic Environment Dialogue and the Transatlantic Consumers' Dialogue—that promoted transatlantic discussion between nongovernmental organizations (NGOs) in these areas.

Under the 1990 and 1995 agreements, the EU and the United States instituted a pattern of regular bilateral summits. These meetings were to occur every six months, at the end of each EU presidency in June and December. The EU is represented by the Commission president, the prime minister of the EU presidency country and, since 1999, the CFSP High Representative. The NTA also instituted regular working-level consultations on global, regional, and bilateral issues and a Senior Level Group of diplomats from both sides that prepares a report on progress in the runup to each summit. These meetings resulted in commitments to joint actions and positions in many areas, for example, the Joint Statement on Ukraine (December 1997), the Declaration on Non-proliferation (May 1998), the Declaration on the Middle East Peace Process (December 1999), the EU-U.S. Summit Statement on Chechnya (December 1999), and the EU-U.S. Statement of Common Principles on Small Arms and Light Weapons (December 1999).

In 2001, following the inauguration of the Bush administration and the adoption by the Commission of a communication analyzing five years of experience with the NTA, the two sides agreed to hold fewer summits—yearly rather than semi-annual meetings—but to ensure that these meetings were better prepared, focused on a few key themes, and that they delivered tangible results.[6] Thus in June 2001 President George W. Bush traveled to Göteborg, Sweden, for what was his first European trip as president. U.S.-EU summits in 2002 and 2003 took place in Washington, and in June 2004 Bush traveled to Dublin for the summit hosted by the Irish presidency.

Following the September 11, 2001, attacks on New York and Washington, cooperation in the fight against terrorism assumed a new prominence in the EU-U.S. relationship. At a ministerial meeting on September 20 that was organized at the initiative of the Belgian presidency, the two sides announced a broad agreement to cooperate to combat international terrorism and to reduce societal vulnerabilities on both sides of the Atlantic.[7] This agreement was followed by expanded cooperation between the FBI and the Department of Homeland Security and Europol and Eurojust. At the regular U.S.-EU summit in June 2003, the EU and the United States signed extradition and legal assistance agreements designed to help in the fight against terrorism and other forms of serious transnational crime.[8] They also issued a Joint Statement on the Proliferation of Weapons of Mass Destruction in which they pledged renewed cooperation to improve the global nonproliferation system as well as to deal with the particular cases of Iran and North Korea.

While the focus in the U.S.-EU relationship is on solving concrete problems and working together to address particular global and regional issues, some political leaders on both sides continue to advocate a "big idea" that in their view is needed to revitalize transatlantic economic and political relations. In early 2004, for example, Prime Minister Aznar of Spain proposed that the United States and the EU set up a high-level bilateral economic committee that would work to create a transatlantic free trade zone by 2014.[9] Other European officials believe that in the long run, after the EU has completed its institutional development and put in place an effective foreign policy, the United States and the EU should conclude a bilateral treaty that would supplement or replace the existing patchwork of transatlantic economic and political agreements.

Economic Relations

TRADE AND INVESTMENT

U.S.-EU trade in 2002 totaled over $500 billion worth of goods and services, making this the world's largest bilateral trade relationship.[10] In the early 1990s, U.S.-EU trade was relatively balanced, but in recent years the United States has run very large deficits with the EU—some $82.4 billion in 2002, up from $61.3 billion in 2001. Economists attribute this change to the strength of the dollar relative to the euro and to higher rates of economic growth in the United States than in Europe. Nonetheless, both sides have continued to increase both exports and imports. The drop in the dollar relative to the euro since 2002 along with a pickup in European economic activity should help to reduce these trade imbalances. Enlargement to central and eastern Europe also will present new opportunities to U.S. exporters, as the accession countries adopt the generally favorable EU common external tariff on imports from the United States.

In purely quantitative terms, U.S.-EU investment ties dwarf the trade relationship. The U.S. stock of foreign direct investment (FDI) in the EU in 2001 was $640.8 billion. Many U.S. companies derive a large share of their profits from their operations in Europe. In 2000, the total sales of U.S. foreign affiliates in Europe was some $1.4 trillion.[11] These numbers partly reflect historic trends, as U.S. multinational corporations have been operating in Europe for over a century, but much of this investment is quite recent. Indeed, investment flows increased dramatically in the 1990s and reached a peak in the 2000 transatlantic merger and acquisitions boom.

Moreover, whereas for much of the postwar period the United States invested more in Europe than it received in return, in recent years this pattern has been reversed. For the 1998–2001 period, U.S. investment in the EU averaged €72.04 billion per year, compared with annual flows of €162.66 billion from the EU to the United States. EU company investments in the United States include both mergers and acquisitions (for example Daimler's 1998 takeover of Chrysler to create DaimlerChrysler) and "greenfield" investments such as the car factories built by BMW in South Carolina and Mercedes in Alabama.

The scale of transatlantic flows reflects the fact that in recent decades the United States and the EU have dismantled many of the barriers to trade and investment that once existed. Much of this work has been accomplished in the multilateral GATT and World Trade Organization (WTO) frameworks. However, following upon the economic provisions of the NTA, Washington and Brussels also have undertaken specific bilateral initiatives to tackle remaining barriers, many of which involve regulation rather than the traditional tariffs and quotas. In May 1998 they launched a new framework, the Transatlantic Economic Partnership (TEP), that included three elements: measures to improve near-term market access for goods, services, and agricultural products; promotion of multilateral and bilateral trade liberalization in the WTO and other forums; and deepening transatlantic dialogue between representatives of nongovernmental, parliamentary, and governmental organizations on trade and investment issues. This was followed in late 1998 by adoption of an EU-U.S. action plan for the TEP that outlined a program of bilateral and multilateral negotiations with specified target dates for completion in nineteen areas, including dispute settlement, tariffs, intellectual property, investment, government procurement, trade and environment, and core labor standards.[12] Concrete results achieved under the TEP included the entry into force on December 1, 1998, of the first EU-U.S. mutual recognition agreement, and agreement at the June 1999 U.S.-EU summit in Bonn on a set of early warning principles intended to identify problems before they erupted into trade disputes.

Continuing in the tradition of the TEP, at the May 2002 U.S.-EU summit Presidents Bush and Prodi launched a new initiative, the Positive Economic Agenda (PEA), under which the two sides agreed to identify sectors for near-term negotiation of the removal of barriers to trade. In December 2002 the two sides agreed to a roadmap listing eight priority areas for action under the PEA, including implementation of the EU-U.S. Guidelines for Regulatory Cooperation and Transparency, resolving plant and animal safety concerns that had hindered exports of Spanish clementines to the United States and of U.S. poultry to Europe, a financial markets dialogue, and several other issues. Another area of intense interaction has been the negotiations toward a possible transatlantic open aviation agreement that were agreed in June 2003.

TRADE DISPUTES

Despite the generally positive economic relations, trade disputes long have been a disturbing element in transatlantic ties. Moreover, these disputes seem to have grown more severe since the establishment in 1995 of the WTO and its Dispute Settlement Body (DSB). In the late 1990s the United States won landmark suits on two issues—bananas and hormone-treated beef—over which the two sides long had clashed but in which the United States had been unable to compel Brussels and the member states to come into compliance with GATT trade rules. The banana dispute went back to 1993 when the EU, acting to create a uniform import regime consistent with the single market, eliminated tariff-free access for Latin American–produced bananas to the German market and extended the preferences given to former European colonies to the whole of the single market. The United States and four Latin American countries complained to the GATT. Two GATT panels found that EU import restrictions were in violation of GATT rules, but under the old dispute resolution procedures the EU was able to block adoption of the panel report by the GATT Council.[13]

The United States and its Latin American partners brought another case against the EU in 1996, after the Uruguay agreements had gone into effect and the WTO, with its much tougher dispute resolution provisions, had been established. In May 1997 a WTO panel found against the EU regime. The EU appealed the finding, but it was upheld by the DSB in September 1997. A WTO arbitrator gave the EU until January 1, 1999, to make significant changes in its banana import regime, but the EU continued to make only cosmetic changes that did not address the underlying complaint. In December 1998 the United States announced that it was planning to take retaliatory action against the EU for failing to implement the WTO decision and issued a list of EU export products totaling some $500 million on which it would impose punitive import duties on EU suppliers.

Although much derided in the press, the banana dispute was a crucial test of the WTO and its powers of enforcement. For the United States, it was essential to establish that the EU and other trade partners could not string out indefinitely the WTO compliance process with delays, appeals, technical changes in the policy followed by more appeals, thereby frustrating the original WTO design for binding dispute resolution provisions and effective action against protectionist practices. The EU, in contrast, claimed that the readiness of the United States to impose unilateral sanctions was itself a violation of WTO rules. In April 1999 the WTO formally authorized the United States to impose sanctions on EU imports as compensation for the latter's failure to comply with the ruling on bananas, although only on $191.4 million of imports rather than the $500 million originally claimed. The United States hailed the decision as a victory for the WTO and its enforcement mechanisms. The EU announced that it would not appeal the ruling, and began work on a new banana import scheme that would still give preferences to the African, Caribbean, and Pacific (ACP) countries but that would be consistent with WTO agreements. The issue finally was resolved in April 2001, when the EU announced that it would institute a new banana import licensing scheme that would expand access for fruit of Latin American origin, prompting the United States to suspend its sanctions, effective July 1, 2001.

The beef hormone dispute had similarities with the banana case, in that it dealt with enforcement of WTO rules. In 1989, the EU banned the import of beef raised using growth-promoting hormones, a widespread practice in the United States and Canada. WTO rules allow signatories to block imports for reasons of health and safety, but only if there is valid scientific evidence showing that health and safety concerns are legitimately grounded and not an excuse for protection. The WTO ruled against the Union on this issue, arguing that there was no valid scientific basis for the ban. However, the EU was unable to comply with the rulings, both because hormone-treated beef was politically unpopular and because European producers benefited from the ban. The EU instead commissioned numerous lengthy scientific studies, none of which was able to substantiate harm to human health.

The WTO granted the EU a "reasonable period"—defined as by May 13, 1999—to bring its regulations on beef hormones into conformity with the WTO Sanitary and Phytosanitary Agreement. The EU stated that it could not comply with this deadline, and ultimately chose to resolve the dispute by paying compensation through trade concessions. The WTO ruled that the United States and Canada could impose €120 million of sanctions on the Union in compensation for the trade benefits denied them by virtue of the unilateral hormone ban. This long-running dispute entered a new stage in October 2003 when the EU declared that it had come into full compliance with WTO rules, not by lifting the ban, but by producing a new study that it claimed finally proved that the hormones were unsafe. U.S. officials contended that the study was not based on a genuine risk assessment as required by WTO rules and announced that the sanctions would stay in place.

The U.S.-EU dispute over genetically modified organisms (GMO) is similar to the beef hormone case, in that it concerns EU bans on biotechnology products that are widely used in North American agriculture and that are not seen by the scientific community as posing a risk to human health and the environment. In October 1998, the EU instituted a moratorium on approving any new GMO products for planting or import. Previously, the EU had approved nine such products. In addition, six member states put in place bans on GMO crops already approved by the EU regulatory process. These bans almost certainly were in violation of the Union's own agricultural and single market legislation, but the Commission, fearing a political backlash, chose not to challenge them. These decisions at the EU and member-state level resulted in a growing share of U.S. agricultural products being excluded from the EU market.

Washington held off on filing a WTO action on the basis of assurances from the Commission that the Union would lift the moratorium and establish, as required by WTO rules, a genuinely scientific basis for evaluating the safety of GMO products. The controversy over this issue grew increasingly bitter in 2002, as the United States began supplying large amounts of food aid to drought-stricken countries in southern Africa. Several African countries turned down the aid in response to what critics claimed were pressures emanating from the EU's worldwide campaign to discredit biotechnology.[14] Development experts generally agree that genetically modified plant varieties are especially needed in poor countries where they can reduce soil erosion and cut down on harmful and expensive pesticide and herbicide use. Against this background, in May 2003 the United States, Canada, and Argentina requested that a WTO dispute resolution panel take up the legality of the EU moratorium.[15]

In addition to these major cases, the United States has filed or considered filing actions against the EU on a number of other issues. The latter include European subsidies to its aviation industry, national-level tax subsidies that the United States claims mirror U.S. tax provisions about which the EU has complained, and rules on the protection of geographic indications for food (e.g., Parmesan cheese and Florida orange juice) that the United States claims the EU applies in a discriminatory fashion. The EU would like to ban the use by U.S. winemakers of all semi-generic names (e.g., burgundy, champagne, chablis), a step that U.S. producers see as unwarranted and potentially damaging to U.S. industry and consumers.

Even as it has been placed on the defensive by these actions brought by the United States against its trade practices, the EU has initiated and won its own share of WTO cases against Washington. Unlike U.S. complaints against the EU, which tend to revolve around the actual closure of particular markets to specific products, EU complaints against Washington generally involve systemic issues in which the EU challenges some aspect of U.S. trade, antitrust, or tax law that is inconsistent with international trade law and that may confer an indirect advantage on U.S. firms to the detriment of EU competitors. For example, in 1997 the EU initiated a case against the U.S. Anti-Dumping Act of 1916, claiming that a provision that allowed for private lawsuits for treble damages and criminal penalties against imports of products sold at below market value contravened international trade agreements. The United States argued that the law was susceptible to interpretation that would permit compliance with WTO obligations. The WTO panel rejected these arguments, and the EU, which claimed that threats of adverse decisions under the act cast a cloud over the business plans of European steel exporters, prevailed in the case.

In what so far is the most significant dispute with the United States, in 1998 the EU launched a case against the U.S. Foreign Sales Corporation (FSC) system, which it claimed constituted a violation of the WTO subsidy agreement by providing tax breaks for export-derived income of U.S. corporations. The United States argued that the EU's action in filing the suit contravened a 1981 understanding that permitted FSCs as a way of counterbalancing the favorable tax treatment granted to EU exporters by member states. But the EU prevailed in the WTO panel and appeals process, forcing the Clinton administration and the Congress to reform the FSC system to eliminate its discriminatory features.

In November 2000 President Clinton signed legislation amending the FSC system. However, the EU subsequently launched a second case, claiming that the new law did not remove the underlying export subsidy. In January 2002 the WTO again ruled in favor of the EU. This prompted the Bush administration and Congress to work on a more fundamental overhaul of the U.S. legislation that would be certain to respond to the points in the WTO ruling. Meanwhile, the EU asked for and obtained WTO authorization to impose sanctions on $4.043 billion of U.S. exports if the FSC system remained in place. Both the Congress and the administration were committed to complying with the WTO ruling, but moving the legislation through both houses of Congress proved to be very slow. In late 2003 the Commission decided, with the approval of the member states, to begin imposing countermeasures on a list of U.S. products as of March 1, 2004, if the dispute was not settled. These countermeasures were imposed, as scheduled, but on a graduated basis designed to increase the pressure on the Congress to amend the offending law. Brussels placed an additional duty of 5 percent on a range of U.S. imports, to be increased by 1 percent each month up to a ceiling of 17 percent by March 1, 2005. Meanwhile, Congress began debating overhaul of the FSC regime with a somewhat greater sense of urgency, although it was not clear whether the EU strategy of graduated increases in pressure would lead to faster compliance or a lingering backlash against the Union in the Congress.

Another highly emotional case was that of steel safeguard tariffs which, unlike most EU complaints about the United States in the WTO, was not system-related but involved the de facto exclusion of a European product from the U.S. market. In March 2002 the Bush administration imposed tariffs of up to 30 percent on steel imports from the EU, Japan, and other countries, claiming that these tariffs were legal under the safeguard provisions of GATT/WTO agreements that allowed countries to take emergency actions to provide temporary relief to industries threatened by surges of imports. The EU immediately adopted its own safeguard measures to protect against what it feared could be a flood of cheap steel diverted from the U.S. market and, joined by other affected countries, filed a case in the WTO. A WTO panel and the Appellate Body ultimately held that the tariffs did violate international trade agreements, and in December 2003 the United States lifted the offending tariffs in what could be seen as a victory for prompt compliance with a WTO ruling.

In addition to these cases, the EU has filed and won suits regarding how the United States sets countervailing duties on exports of steel by privatized European companies that previously benefited from government subsidies, a provision of the U.S. Copyright Act that allows certain retail establishments to play recorded music without paying royalties to songwriters and publishers, and the so-called Byrd amendment, a notorious U.S. law that funnels the proceeds from U.S. anti-dumping and countervailing duty actions, mainly in the steel sector, to the companies responsible for bringing these cases. These U.S. infringements do not apply to large amounts of trade, and they have had little effect on the EU's $80 billion plus annual trade surplus with the United States. However, they do constitute infractions of the international legal order, and both the Clinton and Bush administrations have urged the Congress to amend the offending laws to bring them into line with WTO rules and to satisfy EU concerns.

Apart from these suits that are largely commercial in character, the EU and the United States have clashed on the issue of trade sanctions on so-called rogue states that support international terrorism or that flaunt global regimes to control the spread of nuclear, chemical, and biological weapons. In 1996 the Congress passed legislation—the Cuban Liberty and Democracy Solidarity Act and the Iran Libya Sanctions Act or ILSA (known respectively as the Helms-Burton and the D'Amato acts after their main Congressional sponsors)—that seeks to punish non-U.S. companies that trade with or invest in these countries. One of the key factors underlying Helms-Burton was the expropriation, by the Castro regime in the 1960s, of property owned by U.S. firms and citizens. The law threatened to cripple European and Canadian investment in Cuba by giving U.S. nationals the right to file suit against foreign companies with assets in Cuba and to impose U.S. entry restrictions on executives and shareholders of third-country firms "trafficking" in Cuba. The EU protested these acts, arguing that their extraterritorial reach was illegal under WTO treaties and contrary to general principles of international law. In October 1996 it filed a case in the WTO against the Helms-Burton Act.

In April 1997 the EU temporarily suspended its complaint in the WTO in exchange for concessions by the United States on both Helms-Burton and ILSA. Both laws remained on the books, but the Clinton administration promised to waive the right for its nationals to file suit against foreign companies under provisions of the Helms-Burton Act. For its part, the EU agreed to address the expropriation issue, pledging to work with the United States on the development of disciplines that would inhibit investment in countries that had illegally expropriated assets. The United States and the EU extended and reinforced their understanding at the May 1998 London summit. Trade sanctions remain an unresolved issue in EU-U.S. relations, however, with the EU continuing to deplore the U.S. use of extraterritorial and unilateral measures, while the United States, and in particular the Congress, is determined to reserve its right to use broad economic sanctions for political and security objectives.

The scope and intensity of EU-U.S. trade disputes have led to discussions in academic and policy-making circles regarding the underlying causes of transatlantic trade conflicts. Officially, the EU and the United States explain the number of disputes by invoking the "traffic" analogy—the argument that the sheer volume of transatlantic trade means that some accidents are bound to happen, much the way that collisions happen on crowded highways rather than on empty back streets. Economists reject this view, however, and note that the number of disputes is higher than what a gravity model of relative trade flows would predict.[16] The methods used by governments to calculate the share of U.S.-EU trade said to be affected by disputes—variously given as 2–4 percent—are in any case questionable. Many of these cases revolve around systemic issues—antitrust, antidumping, taxation, perceptions of risk in regulatory affairs, and the role of preferences in international trade—that theoretically affect a much larger share of trade than those transactions directly subject to WTO litigation. Expressed differently, the EU and the United States differ over important aspects of how they manage their domestic economies, and the WTO to some extent has become an arena in which these differences are battled out.

The simplest explanation for the large number of transatlantic trade disputes may be that the United States and the EU both aspire to lead in setting rules for global trade and investment, including environmental and safety rules that impinge on trade. In the United States, the sense that U.S. rules should prevail grows out of the historically dominant role of the U.S. economy, arguably reinforced during the technology-driven economic boom of the 1990s. The fact that the United States serves as the market of last resort for the entire world economy—absorbing the trade surpluses of the EU, China, Japan, and other countries—also leads to a certain impatience with foreign complaints about U.S. trade laws, even when such laws are not technically WTO-compliant. In Europe, aspirations to lead reflect a desire (most visible in the Commission and a few member states) to challenge U.S. positions worldwide in all areas and a conviction that the timely setting of European standards can lead to commercial success. Challenging the United States on trade issues also helps to bolster the Commission's role vis-à-vis the member states and to burnish its image as the protector of EU economic interests and a leading defender of rules-based multilateralism and global governance.

Political and Security Issues

The basis for U.S.-EU political partnership goes back to the 1990 Transatlantic Declaration, in which the two sides agreed to pursue common goals and pledged, in order to achieve those goals, to "inform and consult each other on important matters of common interest, both political and economic, with a view to bringing their positions as close as possible." Proponents of such a partnership on both sides of the Atlantic argue that preserving a strong transatlantic link is important in the post–Cold War era and that NATO is too narrowly focused on defense and security issues to serve as an appropriate forum for cooperation on an agenda that includes economic development, transnational crime, migration and refugee flows, the environment, and diseases such as AIDS. On the European side, a special EU-U.S. partnership is attractive in that it implies a certain coming of age on the part of the EU and its rise to co-equal status with the United States as an influential force in global affairs. On the U.S. side, officials and commentators have argued that even in the supposedly unipolar world that emerged from the collapse of the Soviet Union, the United States does not have the human, financial, and political capability to tackle the world's problems. It needs a partner, which, by virtue of size, wealth, and shared values, can only be the EU.

AREAS OF COOPERATION

Such, at any rate, is the theory. In practice, giving substance to a U.S.-EU political partnership dedicated to solving regional and global problems has not been easy. Sometimes it is difficult to separate fierce commercial rivalry from the promotion of shared political interests. The two sides also have somewhat different approaches to international problems. The Europeans see themselves as the world's most generous providers of foreign aid and often criticize the United States for what they see as its excessive reliance on military solutions to international problems. American critics, in turn, point to the wasteful and ineffective record of many international aid programs, including those of the EU, and often see the Europeans as unwilling to contemplate tough choices, including the possible use of military force, when confronted with issues such as terrorism and the proliferation of weapons of mass destruction.

Brussels and Washington have had the least difficulty in agreeing on a strategy for Europe. The United States has strongly supported the enlargement of the EU, including to Turkey, as a major contribution to regional stability. It has encouraged the EU to take the lead in helping to stabilize the Balkans, and the two sides have coordinated policy regarding transition issues and crisis situations in the NIS. For example, the EU and the United States worked successfully to encourage Ukraine to shut down its aging nuclear reactors at Chernobyl and they have adopted joint statements and measures aimed at pressuring the authoritarian government of Belarus to respect human rights and at finding a solution to the conflict in Moldova where the separatist region of Transdniestria refuses to recognize the authority of the central government.

Further afield, cooperation is less developed. The two sides could do more to work together in Africa, but cooperation has been hindered by commercial and political rivalries and disputes over seemingly secondary matters such as the presence of genetically modified crops in food aid to the continent. In the Middle East, European officials long have complained that Washington has excluded them from a major role in the Middle East peace process. U.S. officials have countered by pointing to what many see as the pro-Arab bias in European policies and the lack of trust on the part of the Israelis as to whether Europe could play an honest broker role in attempting to facilitate peace between Israel and the Palestinians. Many Europeans, in turn, see the United States as too pro-Israel and argue that Washington has not done enough to pressure Israel to come to a peace settlement based on a withdrawal from occupied territory in the West Bank and Gaza.

However, in recent years the United States and the EU have begun to work together more closely in the region. In early 2002, the Bush administration joined with the EU, Russia, and the UN to establish the Quartet, an informal grouping responsible for promoting an Arab-Israeli peace settlement. In 2003, when the administration launched its Greater Middle East initiative to promote democracy and economic development in the region, the EU emphasized that it already had in place the Barcelona Process, and the two sides undertook discussions on how their approaches could be made to complement each other. On Iran, the two sides have longstanding differences, with the United States following a policy of sanctions and isolation on the grounds that Iran supports international terrorism and is undercutting the Middle East peace process, while Europe has preferred a policy of engagement—of building economic and cultural ties—in the hope of strengthening reformist forces in the country. Nonetheless, in 2003–2004 the two sides downplayed these differences and worked together in seeking to pressure and cajole Iran to cooperate with the International Atomic Energy Agency in disclosing and if possible dismantling its secret programs to build nuclear weapons.

THE UNILATERALISM DEBATE

One of the most contentious issues in the U.S.-EU relationship and, by extension, one of the major impediments to closer bilateral political cooperation, has revolved around the roles of unilateralism and multilateralism in the international system. Even though the 1995 NTA contained a long and inspiring list of global and regional problems on which the United States and the EU pledged to work together, within a few years the two sides were bitterly divided over precisely these issues, as the Europeans complained about what they saw as U.S. unilateralism and the failure of the United States to work cooperatively with friends and allies. While some Americans, particularly after the inauguration of President George W. Bush in 2001, echoed the European complaint, others took a more nuanced view, noting that there were two sides to this issue, and that much of the blame for tensions in these areas could be ascribed to Europe. Some EU countries were using multilateralism less as a means to work *with* the United States in solving international problems than as a means to impose constraints *on* U.S. power that they found difficult to match by their own exertions.[17]

An early manifestation of trouble in this area came in connection with the 1996–1997 negotiations convened by Canada and Norway to achieve a ban on antipersonnel land mines. The United States was very active in supporting de-mining activities around the world and would have signed the Ottawa treaty banning land mines had it been allowed a temporary exception for the Demilitarized Zone between North and South Korea, where it maintains 37,000 troops facing a much larger North Korean army. But the backers of the treaty refused any compromise on this issue and the United States (along with many other important military powers) decided not to sign the treaty.

Similarly, an EU-led "like-minded group" pushed through the creation of the International Criminal Court (ICC) at the 1998 Rome conference. The Clinton administration supported the idea of an ICC, but it wanted the court to be subject to the authority of the UN Security Council and was concerned about provisions in the Rome Statute that extended the jurisdiction of the court to nationals of non-party states. Proponents of the court brushed aside these objections and declined to continue negotiations toward a consensus position that the United States was prepared to support.[18] As a consequence, the ICC came into being, but it was not supported by the three largest countries in the world (China, India, and the United States) and did not include among its members three of the five members of the UN Security Council (China, Russia, and the United States).

Another major point of contention was the Kyoto Protocol. Since the early 1990s, the EU had taken the lead in the fight against global warming, but it also used its leadership to secure for itself some highly advantageous provisions in the Kyoto agreement, for example, the selection of 1990 as a base year from which to count EU reductions in greenhouse gas emissions (thus allowing it to count emissions reductions attributable to the shut-down of East German industry against its targets) and recognition of the EU "bubble" that allowed emissions increases in one EU member state to be offset by reductions elsewhere. The Clinton administration reluctantly went along with Kyoto, even though it saw little near-term prospect of securing the ratification of the treaty, given the 97–0 vote against it in the U.S. Senate. At the November 2000 Hague Conference of Parties, the EU refused to compromise with the United States on agreeing to implementing rules for Kyoto that the administration believed were necessary to secure possible ratification down the road.

EU-U.S. differences over multilateral agreements thus were well entrenched by the end of the Clinton administration. They grew even more pronounced in 2001 as the Bush administration took office. The new administration announced that it considered Kyoto fatally flawed and would not even try to bring the treaty into effect. It also denounced the ICC as an attempt by the signatories of the Rome Statute to extend its provisions to nonsignatory states, in disregard of the fundamental principle of international law that states only are bound by treaties that they have signed and ratified. The U.S.-EU dispute over the ICC grew especially bitter as the United States undertook a campaign to conclude agreements with other countries ensuring that U.S. military forces would not be handed over to the jurisdiction of the court. Other issues over which EU officials complained about unilateralism included the U.S. decision to abrogate as obsolete and irrelevant to post–Cold War conditions the U.S.-Russia Anti-Ballistic Missile treaty, U.S. treatment of prisoners at Guantanamo Bay, Cuba, following the 2001 war in Afghanistan, and certain trade issues (notably the 2002–2003 steel tariffs).

The debates over unilateralism came to a head in late 2002 and early 2003 as the United States prepared for war in Iraq. The EU as such was not a major player in the Iraq dispute, as its members were sharply divided over policy toward Iraq. However, European public opinion generally was opposed to the war, and France and Germany held very strongly to the position that only the UN Security Council could authorize action against Saddam Hussein. Supported by the British, the Bush administration argued that Iraq's violations of existing UN Security Council resolutions justified military action. As a practical matter, deferring to the UN Security Council was tantamount to giving France a veto over U.S. policy, which the United States rejected as a matter of principle.

PARTNERSHIP VERSUS RIVALRY

The bitter debates over unilateralism are symptomatic of a broader debate, both across the Atlantic and within Europe, about whether the United States and the EU will operate as partners or as rivals in the twenty-first century. On one side of this debate are those, most prominently but by no means exclusively in France, who follow the traditional Gaullist line and believe that Europe must build itself up as a counterweight to American power. This position was expressed already in the late 1990s by French president Jacques Chirac when he proclaimed that the EU had to become a major pole in an emerging multipolar world. Working with other poles such as China, Russia, India, and regional groupings such as Mercosur and the African Union, Europe would help to check what he saw as the excessive power of the United States and contribute to a better global balance.[19] Although not shared by the governments of all the member states, this logic also pervades the thinking of the European Commission, which has been active in promoting "strategic partnerships" with other powers, for example, India and Russia, implicitly aimed at countering U.S. power. Many of the Commission's favorite projects—the Galileo satellite navigation system, the Kyoto Protocol, and the International Criminal Court—are attractive at least in part because they present political and diplomatic challenges to the United States. Although the Commission insists that its real goal is to make Europe stronger so that eventually it can serve as a full-fledged partner to the United States, it is not clear how and when, following years of transatlantic strain over issue after issue, the EU will declare that it is "strong enough" to de-emphasize challenging the United States and shift to the more cooperative mode that partnership entails.

On the other side of the debate are those in Europe, of whom Tony Blair has been the leading spokesperson, who argue that multipolarity is a dangerous notion that can only divide the West. In April 2003, at the height of the intra-alliance crisis over Iraq, Blair told an interviewer that Chirac's vision of the United States and Europe as separate power centers was dangerous and destabilizing and would lead to the kinds of rivalries seen in the nineteenth and twentieth centuries with such disastrous results for world peace. In his view, it was better to consider the West as a single pole, working together to confront international problems.[20]

If Chirac and Blair represent the opposite ends of this debate, many other countries and political leaders are ranged somewhere between them. They reject the French view that the EU must become a full-fledged counterweight to the United States, but some of them are more assertive than Blair in stressing a strong and independent role for Europe, including in the defense sphere. This debate thus may well persist for some time without a definite resolution. Indeed, looking to the future it is difficult to see a U.S.-EU relationship in which elements of partnership and rivalry would *not* coexist to some degree.

Conclusions

The United States and the EU cooperate in a wide range of areas, to the benefit of both sides. Much of this cooperation is routine and hardly makes the headlines. However, in recent years strains have grown in the relationship, prompting talk of a transatlantic "divorce" or a collapse of the Atlantic alliance. While these strains reflect different economic and political interests as well as differences in values, they are also about power. Having succeeded in uniting a large and disparate group of countries into an increasingly cohesive economic and political union, many Europeans believe that Europe ought to have more influence in the world than it does at present, particularly vis-à-vis the United States. Indeed, some EU officials come close to suggesting that building a solid EU-U.S. relationship is largely a matter of psychology—of getting a powerful America and its leaders to adjust to the necessity of ceding power to what they see as a rising Europe. These feelings are shared to a degree by the European public, which by wide margins believes that the EU should become a power on an equal level with the United States.[21]

How governments on both sides of the Atlantic respond to this European desire for more influence is likely to hold the key to the future EU-U.S. relationship. In areas where the EU effectively wields power, the United States has been ready to acknowledge its role and to deal with it on an equal basis. This clearly is the case with regard to trade, but it is also increasingly so with regard to many political issues, for example, the Balkans, where Washington has welcomed the EU's desire to assume the leading role in providing security to and eventually integrating this region.

But how far any administration in Washington can go in simply ceding to the EU the influence that many European officials believe is their due is unclear. In many respects Europe is already a rather privileged region of the world, highly overrepresented in international economic and political forums. In 2004, fully one third of the members of the UN Security Council—two permanent and three rotating—were EU member states. Four European countries plus the European Commission are represented in the G7/G8. In the UN General Assembly and other international forums, the EU member states, the closely allied members of the European Economic Area, the candidate countries, and the European microstates (Andorra, Liechtenstein, Monaco, San Marino) constitute a bloc of forty countries that lends an instant "multilateral" appeal to any proposal that the EU supports, whether or not it has significant backing in other parts of the world.

Europeans occupy eight of the twenty-four executive director seats of the International Monetary Fund (IMF), compared to one for the United States and two for the forty-seven countries of sub-Saharan Africa. The aggregate voting power of the EU members in the IMF is 32.8 percent, compared with 17.2 percent for the United States and 18.0 percent for the whole of Asia.[22] It is not obvious how European influence in these and international bodies can be augmented without aggravating what is already a systemic underrepresentation for other parts of the world. To the degree that the EU proclaims itself or is seen as a rival to the United States, Washington will be even less willing to yield to Europe still greater influence in such international forums.

Beyond the largely formal but nonetheless politically symbolic question of Europe's weight in international forums, there is the issue of its economic, demographic, and cultural dynamism. Integration undoubtedly has succeeded, over a period of more than fifty years, in bringing peace and prosperity to core Europe, expanding these benefits to a wider periphery to the south and east, and completing a series of projects ranging from the single market to the euro. These could not have been realized had Europe remained a loose agglomeration of nation states. But Europe has been less successful in maintaining its place in the world with regard to other dimensions along which power can be measured. Europe and the United States each have a declining share of world population, but Europe's share is falling more rapidly than that of the United States, owing to lower birth rates and lower immigration. Both the EU and the United States can be expected to account for a smaller share of world gross domestic product (GDP) in the future, as giants such as China, India, and Brazil continue to develop. However, in recent years the United States has done a better job than the EU in holding its own, so to speak, in the global economic competition. Indeed, according to one study prepared for the European Commission, in 1995–2001 the U.S. economy accounted for over 60 percent of the cumulative expansion of world GDP, while the EU accounted for less than 10 percent.[23] Similarly, European efforts to increase military capabilities, R&D potential, and other elements of material power are having at best mixed results.

These factors suggest what may be an ongoing source of frustration in Europe for years to come that could lead to further EU-U.S. political tensions. The EU may have to adjust to a form of partnership with the United States in which it accepts that in some areas at least it is unlikely to match U.S. power. Rhetorical restraint and skillful diplomacy on Washington's part could encourage such an adjustment. Alternatively, the EU and its key member states could persist in efforts to forge the EU into a "pole" capable of challenging the United States in the international arena. Given the EU's power deficiencies in some areas, such efforts are likely to rest heavily on the strengths that Europe brings to such a competition: activism and a high level of representation in international bodies and the ability to promote rules in the name of "governance" that constrain U.S. power. This in turn could lead to a certain level of ongoing tension between the two sides as the United States resists efforts to have its hands tied by a weaker power that it may see as less interested in solving international problems than in bolstering its own global role. Which of these alternatives predominates in the coming years will shape and in turn be shaped by the question of how Europe and the European citizenry define their roles in the world, a key question that is addressed in the concluding chapter.

Notes

1. Text in *New York Times*, December 13, 1989.

2. European Commission, *Transatlantic Declaration on EC-US Relations*, Brussels, November 23, 1990.

3. Bruce Stokes, ed., *Open for Business: Creating a Transatlantic Marketplace* (New York: Council on Foreign Relations, 1996).

4. "The New Transatlantic Agenda," *Presidency Conclusions (Madrid)*, Annex X, in *The European Councils, 1995*, 77.

5. "Joint EU-US Action Plan," Madrid, December 16, 1995.

6. European Commission, *Communication from the Commission to the Council: Reinforcing the Transatlantic Relationship: Focusing on Strategy and Delivering Results*, COM(2001) 154 final, March 20, 2001.

7. U.S.-EU Ministerial Statement on Combating Terrorism, September 20, 2001.

8. Texts in O.J. L 181, July 19, 2003, 27–42.

9. "Brussels Mulls Transatlantic Trade Body," *EU Observer*, February 3, 2004.

10. USTR, *Foreign Trade Barriers Report, 2003*, p. 107.

11. Joseph P. Quinlan, *Drifting Apart or Growing Together? The Primacy of the Transatlantic Economy* (Washington: Center for Transatlantic Relations, 2003), 5–6.

12. "Transatlantic Economic Partnership Action Plan," November 9, 1998, http://europa.eu.int/comm/trade/bilateral/usa/1109tep.htm (accessed June 11, 2004).

13. Christopher Stevens, "EU Policy for the Banana Market: The External Impact of Internal Policies," in Helen Wallace and William Wallace, eds., *Policy-Making in the European Union*, 4th ed. (Oxford: Oxford University Press, 2000), 325–51.

14. See, for example, Sebastian Mallaby, "Phony Fears Fan a Famine," *Washington Post*, September 2, 2002.

15. "United States Requests Dispute Panel in WTO Challenge to EU Biotech Moratorium," USDA-USTR Press Release, August 7, 2003.

16. Gary Hufbauer, "US-EU Trade Disputes: Why So Many?" Paper presented at the Department of State conference, "EU Trade Policy," October 15, 2001.

17. For a more detailed treatment of the multilateralism issue, see John Van Oudenaren, "What Is Multilateral?" *Policy Review*, no. 117, February–March 2003 (also available at www.policyreview.org, accessed June 11, 2004).

18. David C. Scheffer, "The United States and the International Criminal Court," *American Journal of International Law* 93, no. 1 (January 1999): 12–22.

19. "La France dans un monde multipolaire," *Politique Étrangère*, no. 4, 1999.

20. *Financial Times*, April 28, 2003.

21. In a poll commissioned by the German Marshall Fund in 2002, only 14 percent of Europeans agreed that the United States should remain the only superpower, while 65 percent of Europeans agreed with the statement that "the European Union should become a superpower like the U.S." Another 17 percent of Europeans believed that *no* country should be a superpower. Thus some 82 percent of Europeans could be classed as broadly opposed to the existing "unipolar" system and would welcome a shift in relative power from the United States in favor of the EU Chicago Council on Foreign Relations-German Marshall Fund, *Worldviews 2002*, 19 (Question 12).

22. Leo Van Houten, *Governance of the IMF: Decision Making, Institutional Oversight, Transparency, and Accountability*, IMF Pamphlet no. 53 (Washington: IMF, 2002).

23. Sapir et al., *An Agenda for a Growing Europe*, 123.

Suggestions for Further Reading

Gompert, David C., and F. Stephen Larrabee, eds. *America and Europe: A Partnership for a New Era*. Cambridge: Cambridge University Press, 1997.

Lindstrom, Gustav, ed. *Shift or Rift: Assessing US-EU Relations after Iraq*. Paris: EU Institute for Security Studies, 2003.

Peterson, John, and Mark A. Pollack, eds. *Europe, America, Bush: Transatlantic Relations in the Twenty-first Century*. New York: Routledge, 2003.

CHAPTER 12

Conclusion

THE EU, THE CITIZEN, AND EUROPE'S PLACE IN THE WORLD

The failure of the December 2003 European Council to adopt the final text of the proposed Constitutional Treaty was a sharp albeit temporary setback to the process of building a more effective Union in advance of enlargement. Coming at the end of a year that had seen bitter divergences among the actual and prospective member states over the war in Iraq and policy toward the United States, the breakdown of the meeting raised doubts about whether the European Union (EU) could get its internal act together at a time of daunting external political and economic challenges. The squabbling over the Constitution continued into 2004. Poland and Spain rejected charges that they had caused the breakdown of the constitutional process, arguing that there was no reason why they should give up the favorable positions they had won at Nice. The leaders of France and Germany, in contrast, complained about the narrow national perspectives of the two holdouts and issued vague threats about forming a pioneer group of core Europe.

When the deadlock over the Constitution was broken, it was largely in response to the tragedy of the March 11 terrorist bombings in Madrid that killed 190 people and wounded over a thousand more. Coming four days before scheduled elections, the bombings led to the end of the rule of the right-of-center Popular party, as Spanish voters reacted to what they saw as the Aznar government's mishandling of the crisis and its initial attempts to blame Basque separatists even as evidence mounted that the attacks were the work of Islamic extremists. The new government of Socialist José Luis Rodríguez Zapatero pledged to withdraw Spanish troops from Iraq (absent a new UN mandate) and to move Spain closer to France and Germany on European and international issues. This shift left Poland untenably isolated in defending the Nice voting arrangements and, combined with signs of a new willingness to compromise on the part of the other member states, revived hopes for a deal on the Constitution. Also contributing to the improved outlook for the Constitution was a general change of mood in European leadership circles. As one EU diplomat noted, "to a certain extent, what happened in Madrid has caused people to sober up," reminding political leaders of the need to work together at a time of mounting internal and external challenges.[1]

Thus at its previously scheduled March 25–26 meeting, the European Council decided, on the basis of behind-the-scenes diplomatic efforts by the Irish presidency, to restart the negotiations on the Constitution with the aim of reaching an agreement by June. In what could be seen as a positive omen for the future, this was also the first meeting of the European Council in which the accession countries of central and eastern Europe participated as full member states.

Formally, the March 2004 session of the European Council was the annual spring session for reviewing progress toward the Lisbon goals, the fourth such event since 2001 and the last before a major midterm review of the Lisbon strategy set for 2005. In looking at the Union's economic performance, the leaders put the best face on the situation, calling progress since 2000 "mixed." Business and labor groups, academic economists, and the Commission's own reports were far less complimentary. They noted that according to key measures of economic performance, the EU was continuing to fall even further behind the United States, notwithstanding the fact that U.S. economic performance in the early 2000s had been far weaker than in the boom years of the 1990s. The European Council once again exhorted the member states to implement commitments and to step up the pace of reform at the national level. It endorsed a Quick Start Program of transport, energy, telecommunications, and R&D projects agreed to at the December 2003 summit; called for increased research spending by the private sector; and reaffirmed EU objectives with regard to employment generation, reform of pension and welfare systems, and protection of the environment.[2]

The European Council also reviewed the Union's antiterrorism strategy in the wake of the Madrid bombings. Here as well, progress was mixed, with a wide gap between commitments to action and actual implementation. The European leaders issued a "Declaration on Combating Terrorism" in which they urged the member states to enact, no later than June 2004, national implementing legislation to give effect to EU-level decisions and framework decisions relating to the European arrest warrant, joint investigative teams, money laundering, Eurojust, and new measures for police and judicial cooperation to combat terrorism. To facilitate implementation of this ambitious agenda, the European Council established a new post of Counter-Terrorism Coordinator within the office of Council Secretary General/CFSP High Representative Solana and agreed on the choice of a former deputy interior minister of the Netherlands, Gijs de Vries, for this post.

The Madrid bombings also served to intensify what was already a simmering debate in Europe about relations with the Islamic world and the challenges of integrating Europe's large and in many places alienated population of young Muslims. In the first round of the 2002 presidential elections in France, National Front leader Jean-Marie Le Pen scored a surprise second place finish with his anti-immigrant message. The French decisively rejected Le Pen in the second round of voting, but a re-elected President Chirac went on to enact a controversial headscarf ban in French schools in response to rising Islamist militance that cut against the country's deep-seated tradition of secularism in public life. Even more surprising was the turn of events in the Netherlands, where in the March 2002 Rotterdam city council elections the populist Pim Fortuyn took first place under the slogan "Liveable Rotterdam." Campaigning in a city whose population was some 40 percent foreign born, Fortuyn argued that Holland was "full" and that immigrant groups from Islamic countries were undermining the rights of women, homosexuals, and others in a country traditionally known for its tolerance. (Fortuyn subsequently was assassinated by an animal rights activist, cutting short what most likely would have been a political career at the national level).

The fact that the Madrid bombings were planned and carried out by Moroccan immigrants living in Spain and other EU countries was bound to heighten tensions in Europe over these issues. Attitudes toward the Muslim world also played a huge role in the emerging debate over eventual membership for Turkey. Opponents argued that admitting Turkey would dilute the European character of the Union, open the doors to a wave of immigrants, and extend the Union's borders to unstable Iran, Iraq, and Syria. Others argued that turmoil in the Islamic world was precisely the reason why the EU had to embrace Turkey and to turn it into a prosperous and democratic example for and bridge to the rest of the Islamic world. Beyond these practical questions, Europe's relations with Islam raised broader questions of identity: Was Europe mainly a community of civil and political values, as its most ardent backers generally claimed, or did it have a common cultural and religious core, as some argued?

With the governments set to agree on the European Constitution by June 2004, ratification in all twenty-five member states emerged as the next big political issue—one that was certain to interact with parallel debates over the selection of a new European Commission president and a new Commission, the election of a new European Parliament, the establishment of the new budgetary framework, and, not least, the question of membership for Turkey. Denmark, Ireland, Luxembourg, the Netherlands, Portugal, Spain, and the UK all declared that they would hold referenda on the Constitution, a step that most of the new member states as well as France also were contemplating.

No one could be certain about the results of these referenda. Based on polls taken in the fall of 2003, the Eurobarometer survey reported that support for EU membership had fallen to 48 percent of the public EU-wide, down from over 70 percent in the early 1990s. Outright hostility was limited—only 15 percent of citizens saw the EU as a "bad thing" for their country—but lack of enthusiasm was widespread. Thirty-one percent of citizens were more or less indifferent, seeing the EU as neither good nor bad for their country. Support for membership was highest in Luxembourg and Ireland (77 and 73 percent respectively) and lowest in the UK and Austria (28 and 35 percent).[3] This indifference also was reflected in turnout for the elections to the European Parliament, which fell to 49 percent in 1999 and which some observers feared could go still lower in the 2004 elections.

On a more positive note, large numbers of EU citizens identified themselves in some way with Europe. Only 10 percent of citizens saw themselves as solely European (3 percent) or as Europeans first and citizens of their own countries second (7 percent), but 47 percent felt that they were first citizens of their own countries as well as citizens of Europe. Thus some 57 percent of EU citizens saw themselves as European to some degree, with the sentiment strongest in Italy and weakest in the UK.[4]

Asked what the EU meant to them personally, the largest number of respondents mentioned freedom to travel, study, and work anywhere in the EU (49 percent) and the euro (48 percent), a clear indication that citizens did connect with concrete achievements for which the EU was responsible.[5] On the other hand, respondents mentioned unemployment (42 percent) and crime (28 percent) as the most important issues facing their country and generally did not give the EU high marks for tackling these issues.[6]

Other surveys and much anecdotal evidence suggest that many Europeans, especially younger ones, simply take for granted many of the hard-won benefits of integration. They travel around the continent on inexpensive rail passes, participate in student exchanges or enroll in universities in other countries, and buy and use products aimed at European rather than national markets.[7] In this sense, a European identity is emerging, but what this means is unclear. How far this identity can be stretched (whether it includes Turkey, for example), what it means for the integration of foreigners from *outside* Europe, and whether it will lead to stronger support for ambitious political projects, for example, EU-level taxation or a European army, is not known. This European identity also coexists with national identities that it is unlikely to supplant. And it does not mean the emergence of a European nationalism or European patriotism of the kind traditionally associated, for better or for worse, with the nation-state.

Opinion polls do reveal growing popular support for CFSP and a stronger European voice in world affairs—positions that coincide with generally negative views of the United States. In the fall of 2003, 64 percent of those polled supported CFSP, down somewhat from 67 percent in the spring of that year, at the height of the Iraq crisis. Fifty-three percent of EU citizens considered it a priority for the Union to assert its political and diplomatic importance in the world.[8] In a separate survey conducted by the Pew Global Attitudes Project, 90 percent of respondents in France, 70 percent in Germany, and 50 percent in Britain agreed that it would be a good thing if the EU became as powerful as the United States. A majority of those taking this view also said that they would continue to hold it even if it meant that Europe would have to pay to become a more influential international actor.[9] This relatively high level of support for a stronger EU external role combined with the rather lackluster support for many of the Union's domestic activities raises the question of whether a stronger European identity might be built from the outside in—in opposition to external challenges such as globalization, the Islamic threat or, to name the most obvious candidate, excessive American power.

As shown in table 12.1, European respondents generally see the EU as playing a positive role in the world in contrast to a more negative image of the United States as an international actor. (This is true even in regard to the growth of the world economy, where most objective analysts would compare U.S. performance quite favorably with that of the EU.) That European citizens see the United States and the EU in these terms reflects a number of factors, including the unpopularity of certain U.S. policies, the failures of U.S. public diplomacy, and the quite natural bias of Europeans toward things associated with Europe. These findings also suggest, however, that integration-minded elites in Europe have been at least somewhat successful in convincing the general public that the EU leads in bringing peace and prosperity not only to its own citizens but to much of the rest of the world.

Table 12.1   Perceptions of the U.S. and EU Role in the World

Issue	The role of the United States in the world			The role of the EU in the world		
	Negative	Neither negative nor positive	Positive	Negative	Neither negative nor positive	Positive
The fight against terrorism	37	15	43	11	25	54
Growth of the world economy	36	20	34	16	31	40
Peace in the world	53	16	27	9	23	60
The fight against poverty in the world	52	22	17	19	33	40
Protection of the environment	58	18	14	16	26	46

Source: Eurobarometer 60, 78–79

In extreme form, this sentiment is reflected in the views of certain European intellectuals and political figures who argue that Europe has a mission to save the world from poverty, war, environmental degradation, and other ills, and to do so in opposition to the United States. As the British journalist Will Hutton argued in his 2002 book *The World We're In*, "The building of Europe has become the precondition for securing prosperity, peace and justice not only in Europe, but across the globe. We must succeed."[10] In Hutton's view:

> The US is hostile to all forms of international co-operation and multilateralist endeavour. It is wedded to the exercise of autonomous power guaranteed by its military superiority; and its world view is supported and entrenched by the vigorous conservative ideology that dominates its politics and economics. As a result it is not only actively dismantling the complex web of international treaties that underpin Western security and economic interests; it is obstructing any creative development of those that it cannot attack. Without a countervailing power of sufficient strength prepared to provide finance and political muscle, the development of multilateral institutions and processes by which a rampant globalisation may be governed will cease. Only the EU has the weight in the world to assume this role.[11]

Along similar lines, in May 2003, at the height of the transatlantic crisis over Iraq, the German philosopher Jürgen Habermas and his French counterpart Jacques Derrida published an article in which they claimed that the mass antiwar demonstrations of February 15 marked the beginning of the "rebirth of Europe." They called on a core group of EU member states to form a common foreign policy that would be built around opposition to the United States. In their view, "Europe must, within the framework of the United Nations, throw its weight in the scale in order to counterbalance the hegemonic unilateralism of the United States."[12] Breaking ranks with the youthful antiglobalization protestors, some of whom have drawn inspiration from the "post-modern" Derrida in their attacks on the International Monetary Fund (IMF), World Bank, and the World Trade Organization (WTO), the two philosophers called for strengthening these organizations and other global governance mechanisms, all in the cause of constraining U.S. power.

Perhaps more interesting than the standard call for a stronger and more independent European foreign policy was the authors' analysis of the differences between U.S. and European societies. They argued that in the second half of the twentieth century Europe managed to find solutions to two basic problems: developing a form of rule "beyond the nation state" and creating a European welfare system that rejected wide social inequalities and that held out the promise of taming the excesses of capitalism and globalization. Having solved these two fundamental problems, Europe, the authors suggested, was well placed to promote something like a "global domestic policy" that would spread these values beyond Europe. Habermas and Derrida also contrasted Europe's secularism with the greater religiosity of the United States, remarking of President Bush, "in our latitudes, it would be hard to imagine a president who begins his daily official duties with a public prayer and links his important political decisions to a divine mission."[13]

These excessively self-congratulatory views are not embraced by European political leaders. They also would be rejected as preposterous by many analysts who could point to EU's failure in the Balkans in the 1990s, its agricultural subsidies and fishing practices that damage developing countries, its inability to meet its own environmental targets, and many other shortcomings. Nonetheless, the sense that Europe embodies a morally superior alternative to the United States and that it has a mission that transcends the mere pursuit of economic and political advantage increasingly pervades what might be called the "ideology" of European integration and is reflected in the statements and speeches of such figures as Romano Prodi, Jacques Chirac, Chris Patten, and others.

According to Prodi, for example, "other societies, where inequality tends to be regarded as the natural outcome of individual ability and commitment and the necessary driving force behind growth, may consider social marginalization unavoidable. Other societies may tolerate a situation where a large portion of their citizens are in reality excluded from democratic life. Europe has other traditions, other values, other ambitions."[14] Needless to say, the "other society" that Prodi has most in mind, as numerous references elsewhere in the same statement make clear, is the United States. In yet another echo of the Habermas-Derrida critique, CFSP High Representative Solana has endorsed the view that the greater importance of religion in American life is one of the main sources of foreign policy dissonance across the Atlantic. According to Solana, the U.S. approach to fighting terrorism after September 11, 2001, can be attributed to the "moral certainty of religious America." Whereas a religious society such as the United States perceives evil "in terms of moral choice and free will," a secular society seeks causes of evil in "political or psychological terms."[15]

Much along the lines of Hutton, Habermas, Derrida, and other critics, many European political leaders also suggest, albeit in milder tones, that one of the most important arguments for building Europe is to develop and preserve a civilization built on principles and norms different from those said to prevail in the United States. While few would question (and indeed even many Americans welcome) the desire of Europe to preserve a distinct identity, those who make this argument sometimes tend to invert cause and effect. The argument that "the American model is flawed, therefore we must build Europe" easily slides into "we must build Europe, even if it requires emphasizing everything that is bad or flawed about America while constantly trumpeting Europe's own virtues."

Apart from the damage it does to transatlantic relations, this way of thinking tends to lower the quality of policy debate in Europe itself. Americans can be nationalistic, insensitive to external points of view, and unaware of developments in other parts of the world. But the nature of the U.S. political system does ensure vigorous debate on most issues. If a Republican administration is seen as neglecting the problem of climate change, the Democrats are certain to challenge it. If neither party pays attention to policy failure, the media or the NGO community most likely will do so. This same dynamic between government and opposition plays out in democratic Europe, but the existence of the European project creates a temptation to deflect blame for policy failures with ritual calls for "more Europe." While in some cases a more unified European approach or stronger European institutions *is* the proper response to an issue, calling for such remedies also can be a substitute for analyzing past performance or for debating real trade-offs—between economic growth and environmental protection, for example, or between privacy protections and measures to combat terrorism.

Whether a European identity can or will be forged in opposition to the United States remains to be seen. Most European political leaders vehemently deny that there is anything anti-American in the drive to integrate. Indeed, they argue that much of what Europe is attempting is designed to ensure that Europe can serve as a "partner" of the United States at some point in the future. Certainly it would be preferable, for the United States but also for Europe itself, if the EU could focus on the positive elements in the integration process and rely on policy performance to bolster both its domestic legitimacy and international standing. This would require coping with the many challenges highlighted in the Lisbon process, at the European Convention, and in the soul-searching that followed the Iraq war and the Madrid bombings: making a success of enlargement, raising Europe's rate of economic growth and boosting employment, rekindling a culture of excellence in universities and research institutes, successfully integrating Europe's minorities, and coping with the challenges of an enlarged periphery. If the EU performs well in these areas, it is likely both to win the loyalty of the citizens and position Europe to be a stronger player—a "pole," to use Chirac's favored term—on the world scene. If it cannot meet these challenges, however, it is unlikely that the mere contrasting of Europe with the United States, however favorable in some areas, will be able to sustain the progress of building a European identity and a united Europe.

Notes

1. George Parker, "Talks on EU Constitution Face Point of No Return," *Financial Times*, March 24, 2004.
2. Presidency Conclusions: Brussels European Council, 25–26 March 2004.
3. European Commission, *Eurobarometer 60*, February 2004, 36–37.
4. *Eurobarometer 60*, 27.
5. Ibid., 33.
6. Ibid., 9.
7. See A. S. Byatt, "What Is a European," *New York Times Magazine*, October 12, 2002.
8. *Eurobarometer 60*, 82.
9. Pew Global Attitudes Project, *A Year after Iraq War: A Nine-Country Survey*, 9.
10. Will Hutton, *The World We're In* (London: Little Brown, 2002), 370.
11. Ibid., 365.
12. The article was published in the *Frankfurter Allgemeine Zeitung* and *Liberation* on May 31, 2003; for a full English text, see J. Habermas and J. Derrida, "February 15, or What Binds Europeans Together: A Plea for a Common Foreign Policy, Beginning in the Core of Europe," *Constellations* 10, no. 3 (September 2003), 291–97.
13. Ibid.
14. Romano Prodi, "Europe: The Dream and the Choices"[Translation of Romano Prodi's contribution to the debate on the future of Europe, published in Italy on 12 November 2003], on http://europa.eu.int/comm/commissioners/prodi/pdf/europedream_en.pdf (accessed June 11, 2004).
15. Judy Dempsey, "Solana Laments Rift between Europe and 'Religious' US," *Financial Times*, January 8, 2003.

Suggestions for Further Reading

Balis, Christina V., and Simon Serfaty, eds. *Visions of America and Europe: September 11, Iraq, and Transatlantic Relations*. Washington: CSIS Press, 2004.

Revel, Jean François. *Anti-Americanism*, translated by Diarmid Cammell. San Francisco: Encounter Books, 2003.

Index

About the Author

John Van Oudenaren is chief of the European Division at the Library of Congress and adjunct professor at the BMW Center for German and European Studies, Edmund A. Walsh School of Foreign Service, Georgetown University. Prior to joining the Library of Congress, he was a senior researcher at the RAND Corporation. From 1991 to 1995 he was director of RAND's European office in Delft, the Netherlands. He has served on the Policy Planning Staff of the U.S. Department of State and has been a research associate at the Kennan Institute for Advanced Russian Studies, Woodrow Wilson International Center for Scholars, Washington, and at the International Institute for Strategic Studies in London. He received his Ph.D. in political science from the Massachusetts Institute of Technology and his A.B. in Germanic languages and literature from Princeton University. His publications include *Détente in Europe* (1991) and numerous reports, articles, and chapters on international relations and European and Russian politics.